OMNIBUS 11

I AM
A HERO

Art and story
KENGO HANAZAWA
花沢健吾

This Dark Horse Manga omnibus
collects *I Am a Hero* chapters 239
to 264, first appearing in Japan as
I Am a Hero Volumes 21 and 22.

Translation
KUMAR SIVASUBRAMANIAN

English Adaptation
PHILIP R. SIMON

Lettering
STEVE DUTRO

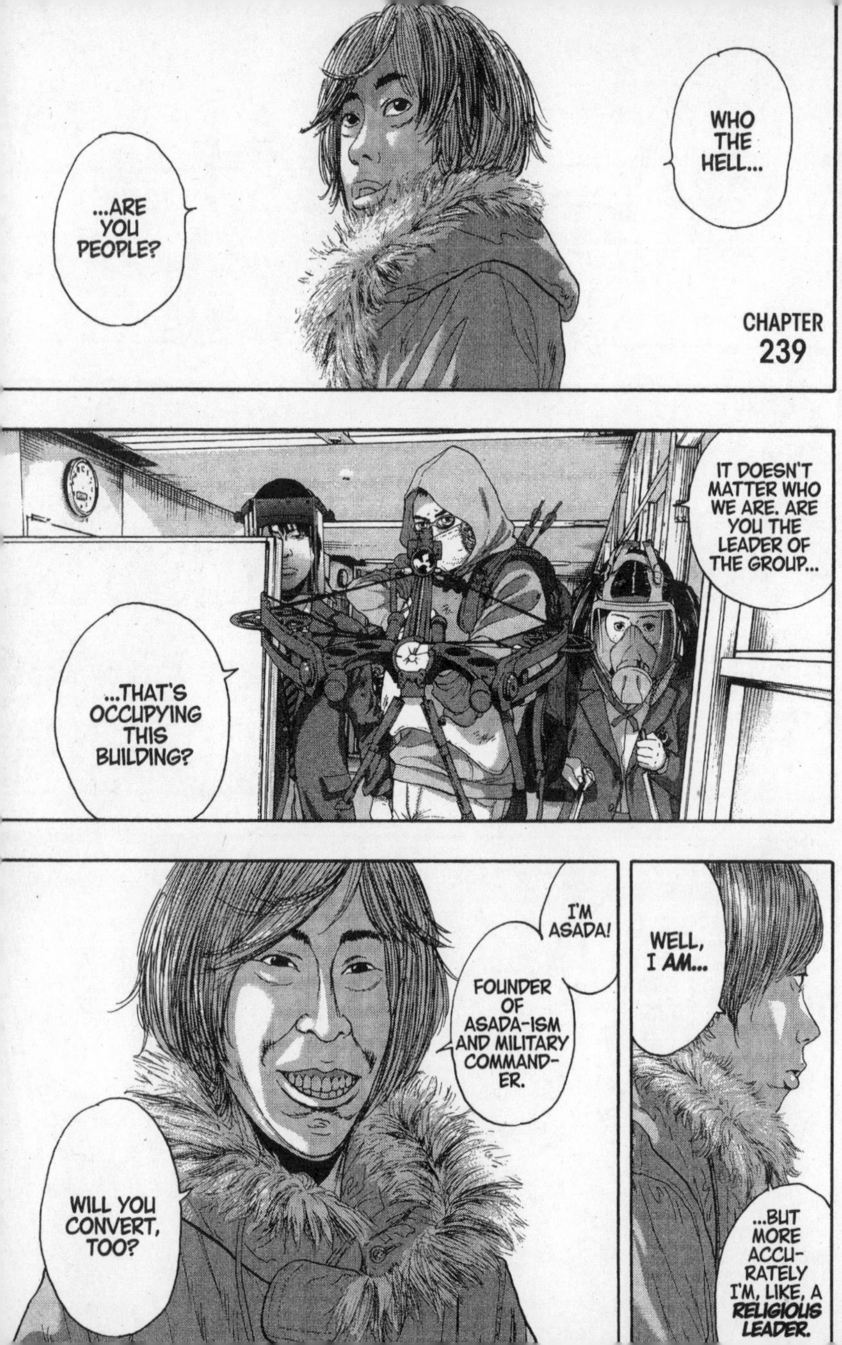
WHO THE HELL...
...ARE YOU PEOPLE?
CHAPTER 239
IT DOESN'T MATTER WHO WE ARE. ARE YOU THE LEADER OF THE GROUP...
...THAT'S OCCUPYING THIS BUILDING?
WELL, I AM...
...BUT MORE ACCU-RATELY I'M, LIKE, A **RELIGIOUS LEADER.**
I'M ASADA!
FOUNDER OF ASADA-ISM AND MILITARY COMMAND-ER.
WILL YOU CONVERT, TOO?

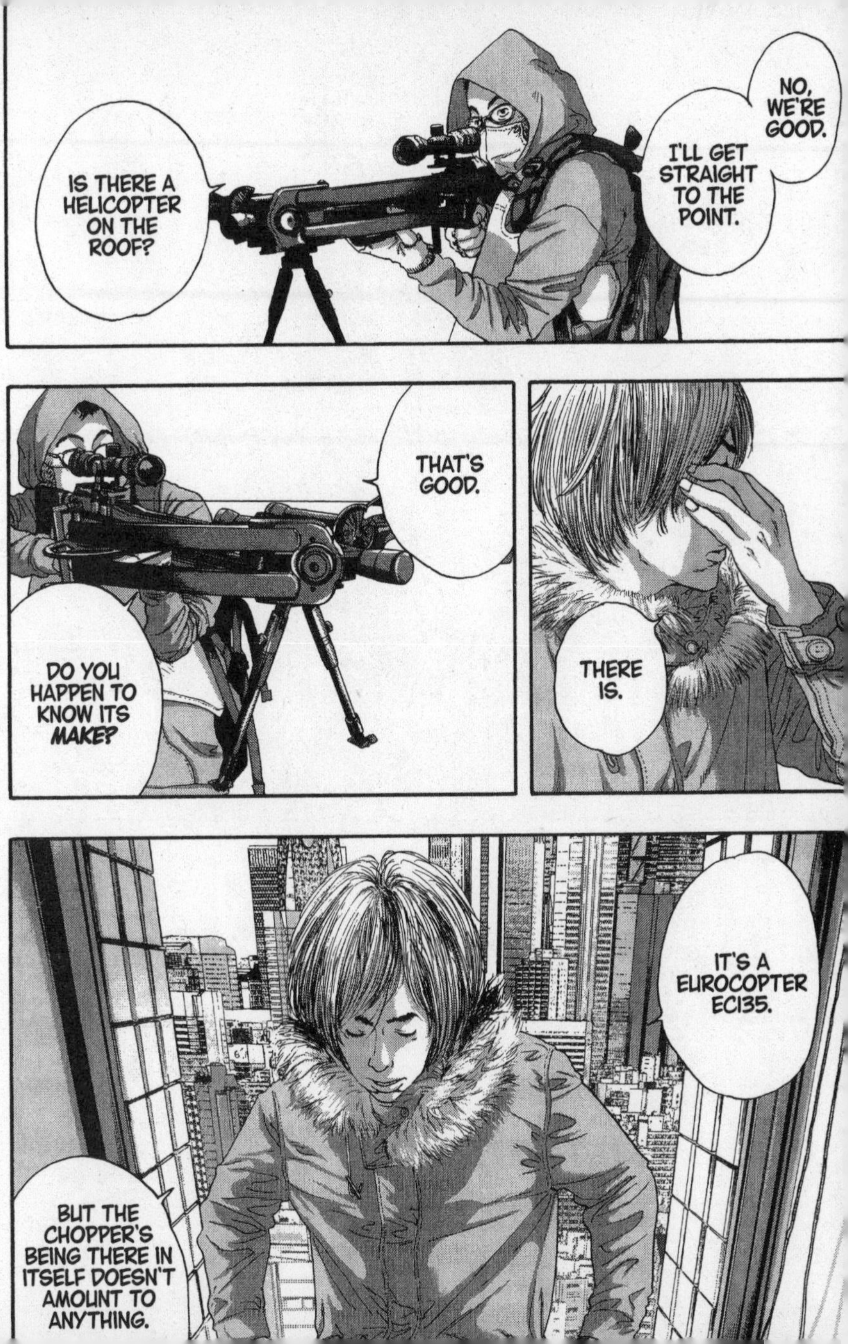
NO, WE'RE GOOD.
I'LL GET STRAIGHT TO THE POINT.
IS THERE A HELICOPTER ON THE ROOF?
THERE IS.
THAT'S GOOD.
DO YOU HAPPEN TO KNOW ITS *MAKE?*
IT'S A EUROCOPTER EC135.
BUT THE CHOPPER'S BEING THERE IN ITSELF DOESN'T AMOUNT TO ANYTHING.

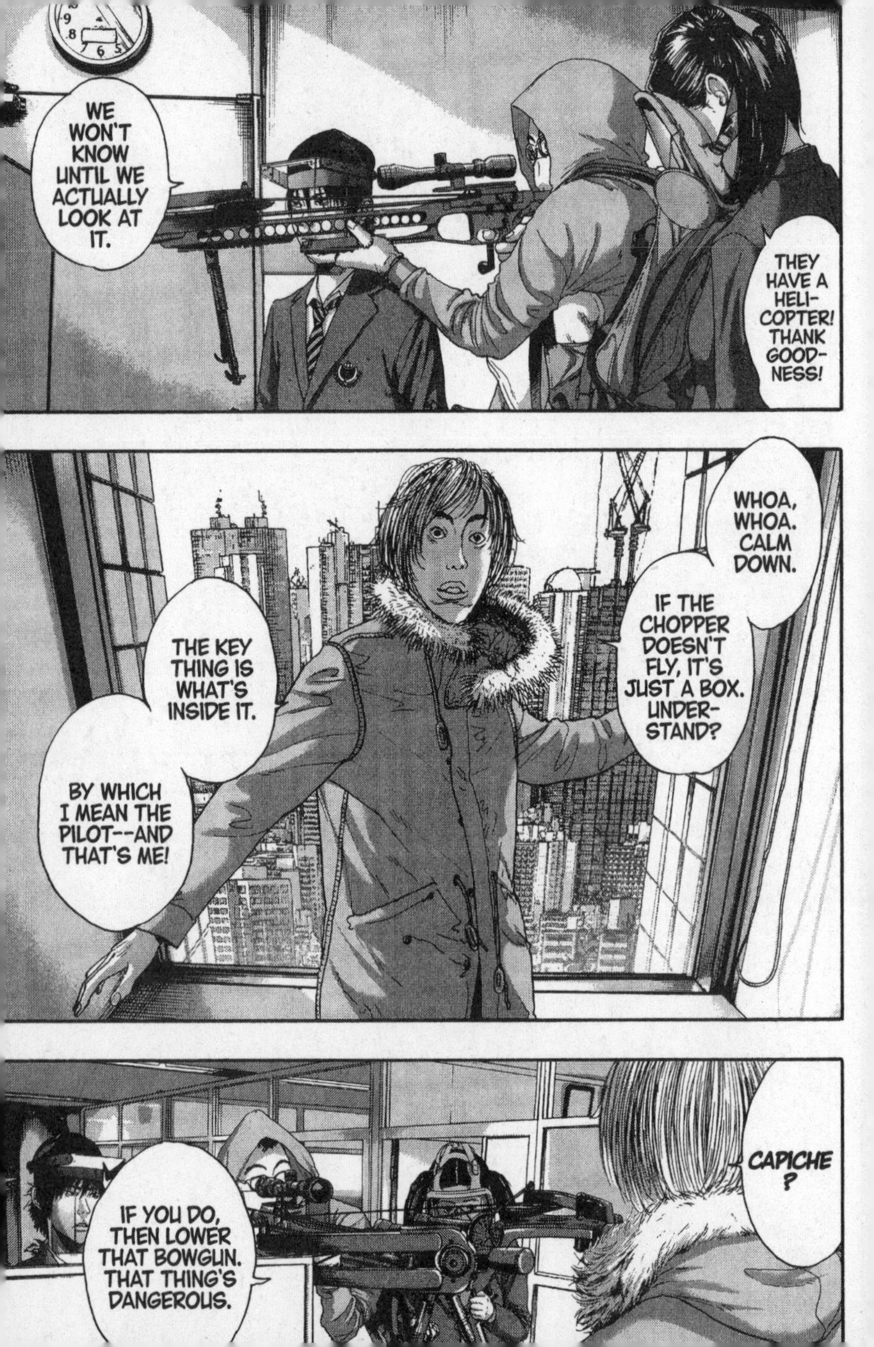
THEY HAVE A HELI-COPTER! THANK GOOD-NESS!
WE WON'T KNOW UNTIL WE ACTUALLY LOOK AT IT.
WHOA, WHOA. CALM DOWN.
IF THE CHOPPER DOESN'T FLY, IT'S JUST A BOX. UNDER-STAND?
THE KEY THING IS WHAT'S INSIDE IT.
BY WHICH I MEAN THE PILOT--AND THAT'S ME!
CAPICHE?
IF YOU DO, THEN LOWER THAT BOWGUN. THAT THING'S DANGEROUS.

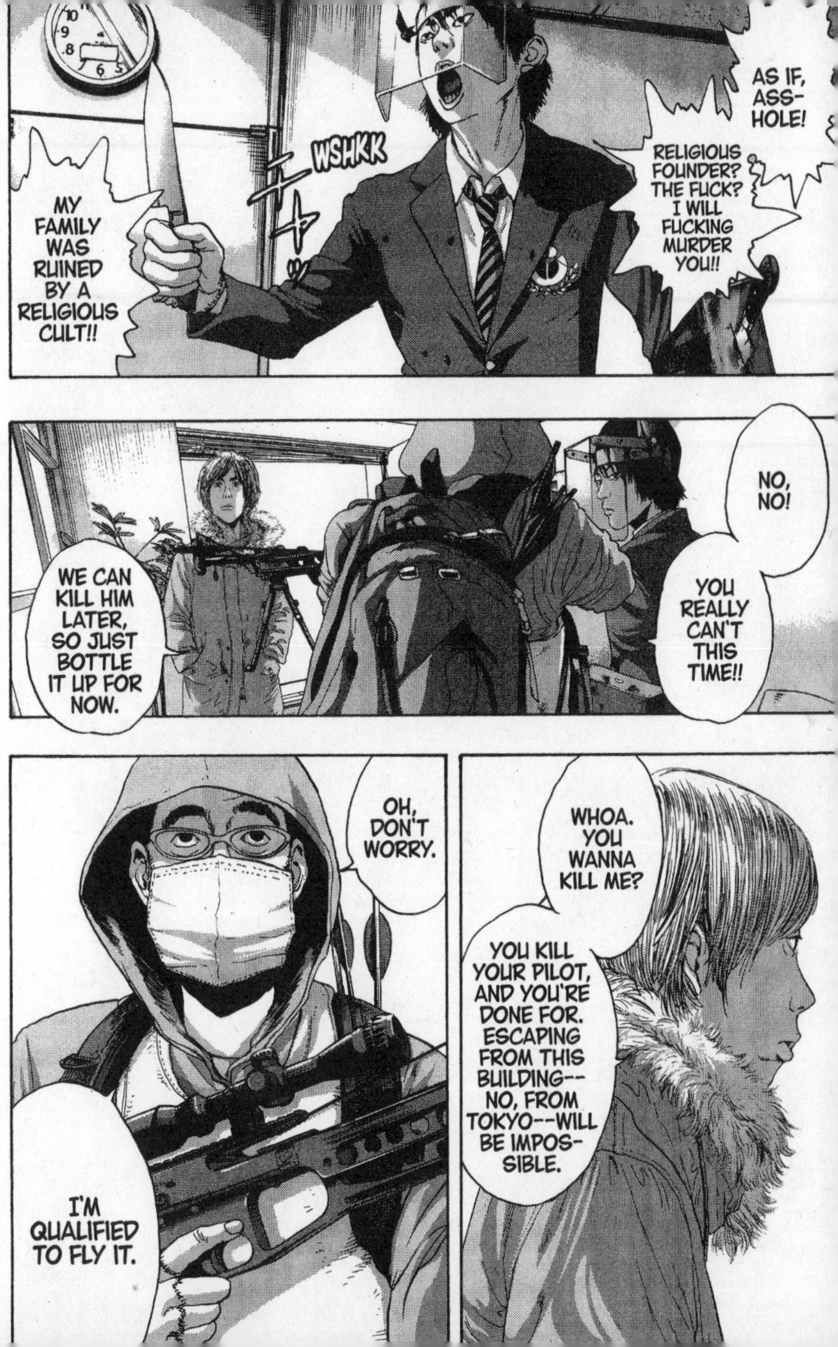
AS IF, ASS-HOLE!
RELIGIOUS FOUNDER? THE FUCK? I WILL FUCKING MURDER YOU!!
WSHKK
MY FAMILY WAS RUINED BY A RELIGIOUS CULT!!
NO, NO!
YOU REALLY CAN'T THIS TIME!!
WE CAN KILL HIM LATER, SO JUST BOTTLE IT UP FOR NOW.
WHOA. YOU WANNA KILL ME?
YOU KILL YOUR PILOT, AND YOU'RE DONE FOR. ESCAPING FROM THIS BUILDING--NO, FROM TOKYO--WILL BE IMPOS-SIBLE.
OH, DON'T WORRY.
I'M QUALIFIED TO FLY IT.

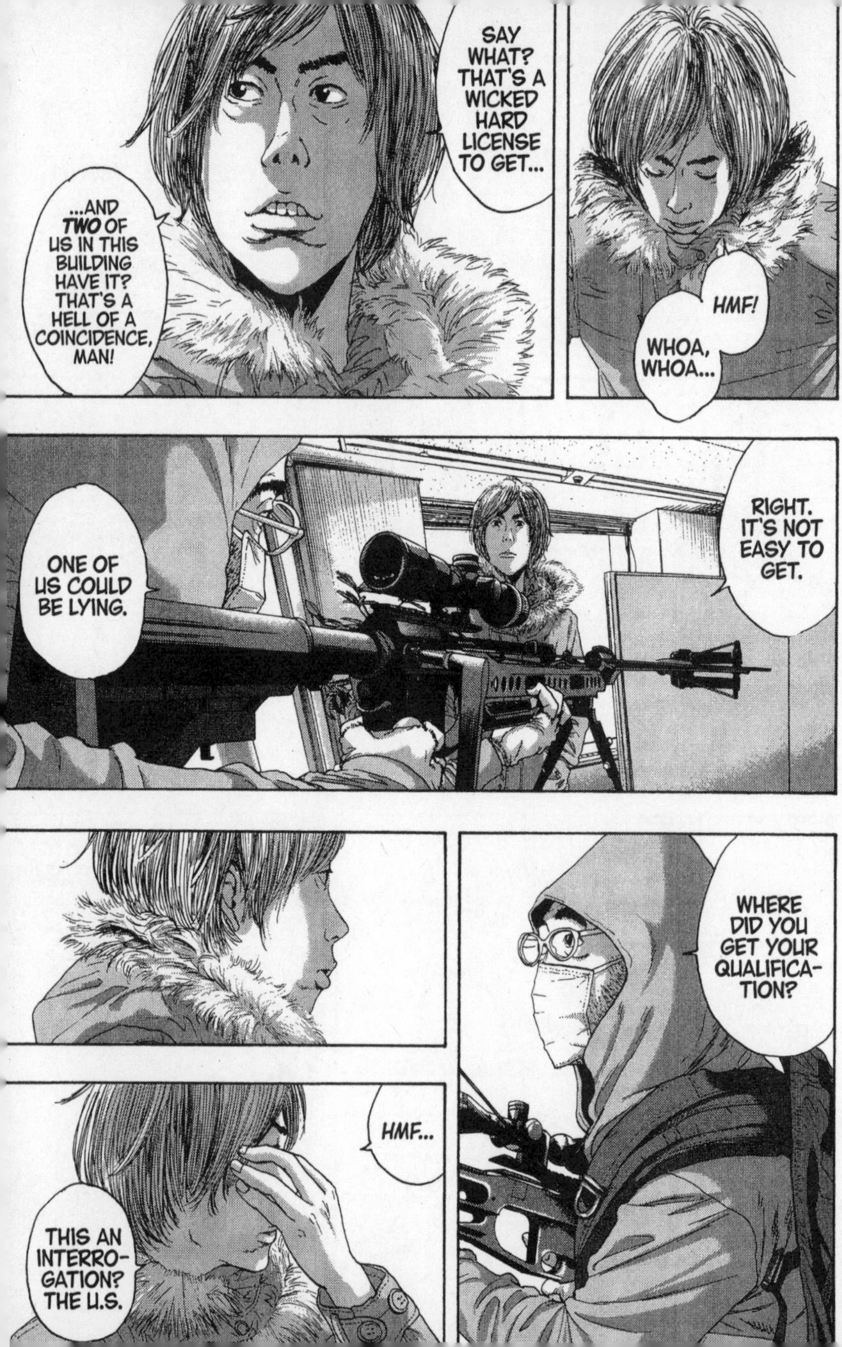
HMF!
WHOA, WHOA...
SAY WHAT? THAT'S A WICKED HARD LICENSE TO GET...
...AND *TWO* OF US IN THIS BUILDING HAVE IT? THAT'S A HELL OF A COINCIDENCE, MAN!
RIGHT. IT'S NOT EASY TO GET.
ONE OF US COULD BE LYING.
WHERE DID YOU GET YOUR QUALIFICA-TION?
HMF...
THIS AN INTERRO-GATION? THE U.S.

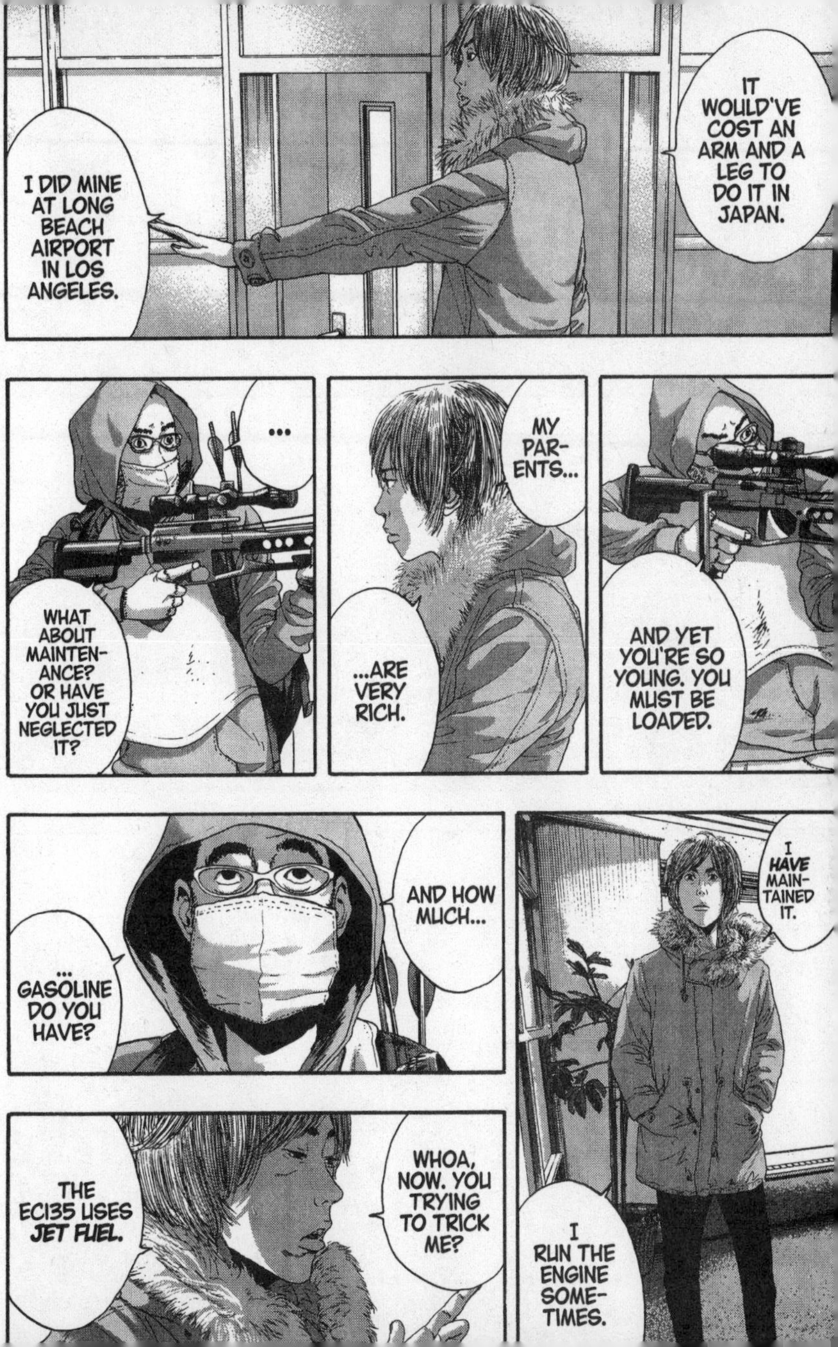
IT WOULD'VE COST AN ARM AND A LEG TO DO IT IN JAPAN.
I DID MINE AT LONG BEACH AIRPORT IN LOS ANGELES.
AND YET YOU'RE SO YOUNG. YOU MUST BE LOADED.
MY PARENTS...
...ARE VERY RICH.
...
WHAT ABOUT MAINTENANCE? OR HAVE YOU JUST NEGLECTED IT?
I *HAVE* MAINTAINED IT.
I RUN THE ENGINE SOMETIMES.
AND HOW MUCH...
...GASOLINE DO YOU HAVE?
WHOA, NOW. YOU TRYING TO TRICK ME?
THE EC135 USES **JET FUEL.**

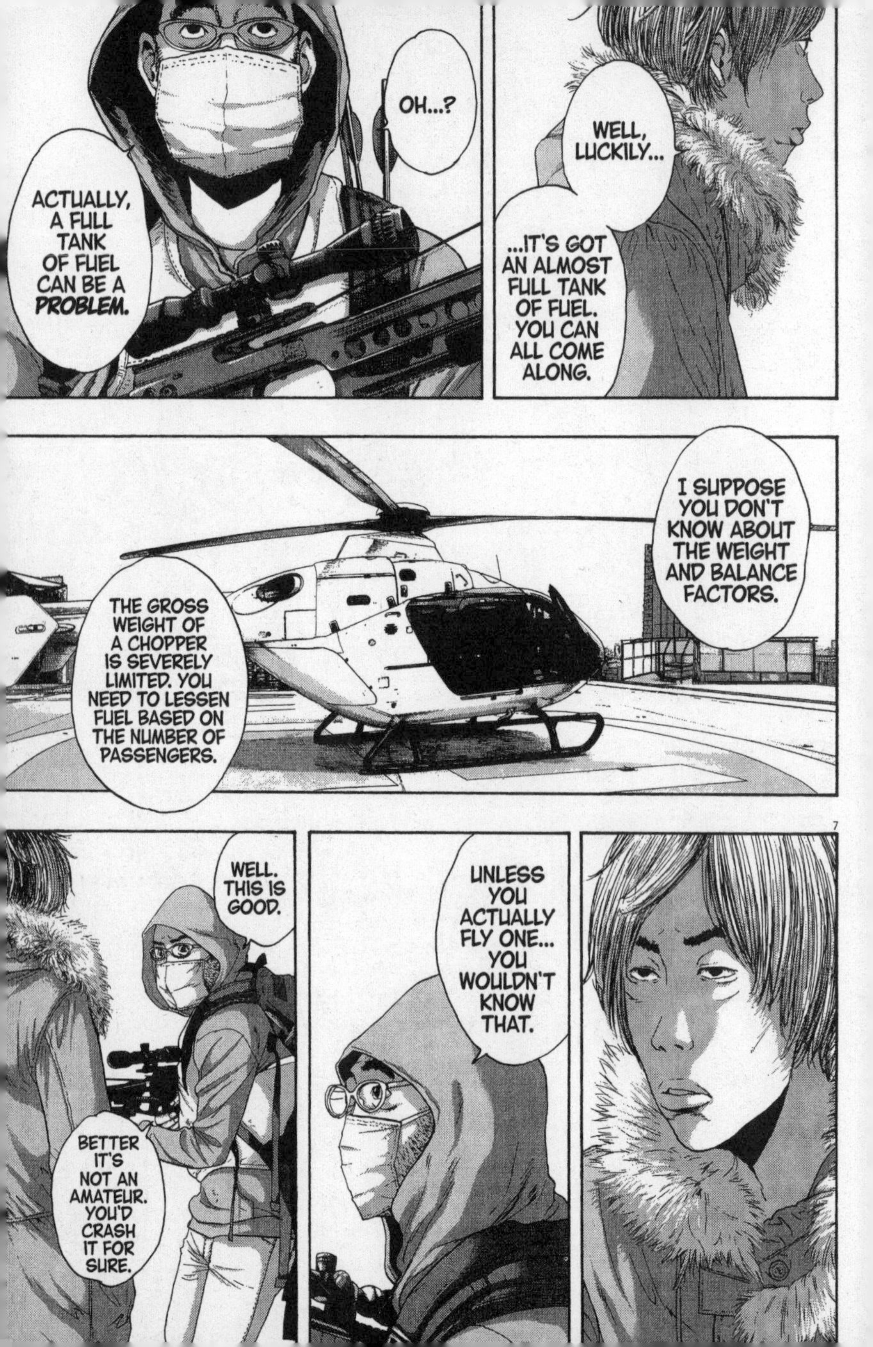
WELL, LUCKILY...
...IT'S GOT AN ALMOST FULL TANK OF FUEL. YOU CAN ALL COME ALONG.
OH...?
ACTUALLY, A FULL TANK OF FUEL CAN BE A *PROBLEM*.
I SUPPOSE YOU DON'T KNOW ABOUT THE WEIGHT AND BALANCE FACTORS.
THE GROSS WEIGHT OF A CHOPPER IS SEVERELY LIMITED. YOU NEED TO LESSEN FUEL BASED ON THE NUMBER OF PASSENGERS.
UNLESS YOU ACTUALLY FLY ONE... YOU WOULDN'T KNOW THAT.
WELL. THIS IS GOOD.
BETTER IT'S NOT AN AMATEUR. YOU'D CRASH IT FOR SURE.

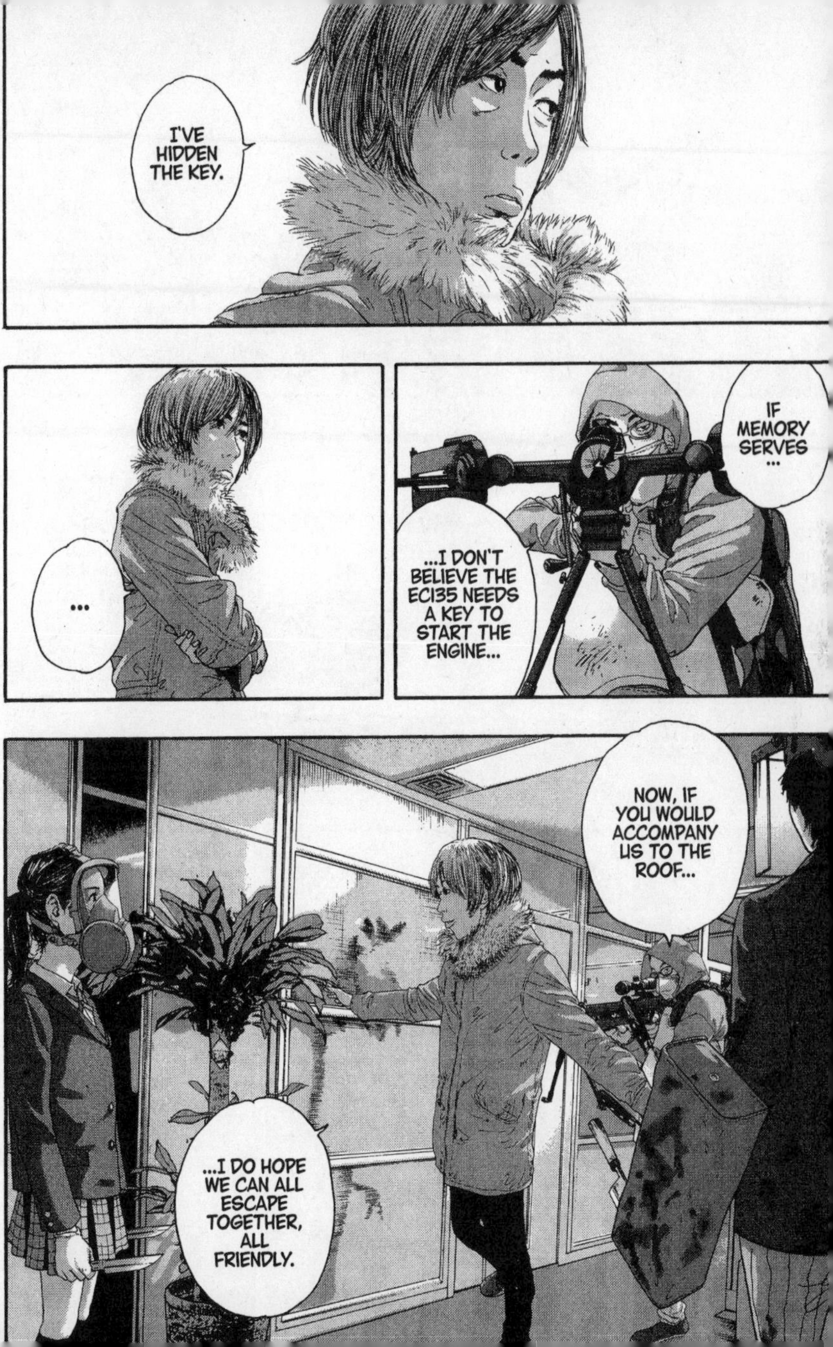
I'VE HIDDEN THE KEY.
IF MEMORY SERVES...
...I DON'T BELIEVE THE EC135 NEEDS A KEY TO START THE ENGINE...
...
NOW, IF YOU WOULD ACCOMPANY US TO THE ROOF...
...I DO HOPE WE CAN ALL ESCAPE TOGETHER, ALL FRIENDLY.

HEY, DUDE! THIS IS THE FIRST I'VE HEARD ABOUT THIS WEIGHT STUFF.

HOW MANY'LL BE ABLE TO FLY AWAY IN THE END?

WE'LL HAVE TO ACTUALLY CHECK IT OUT TO KNOW FOR SURE. LET'S GO!

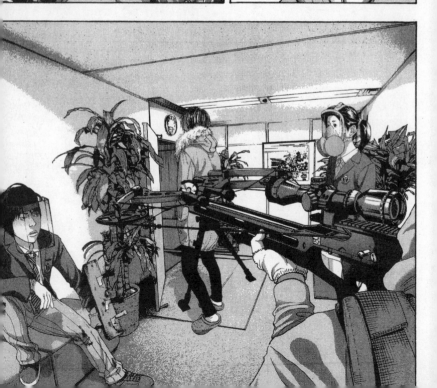

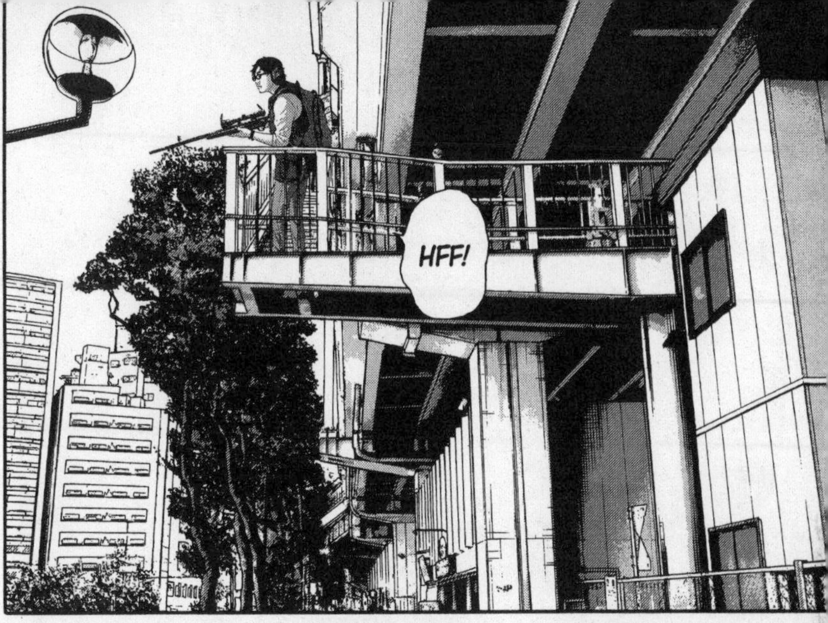
HFF!

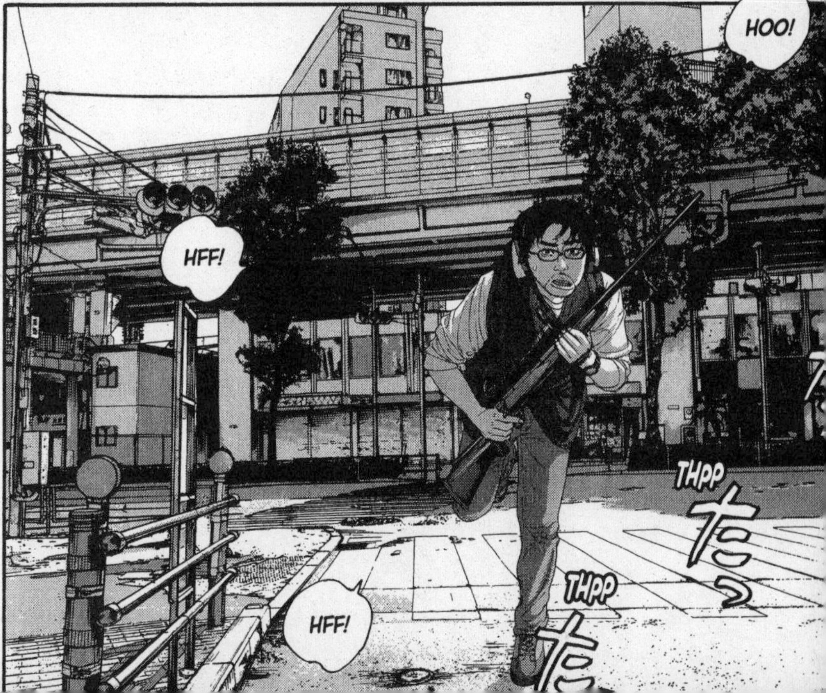
HOO!
THPP
たっ
HFF!
THPP
HFF!

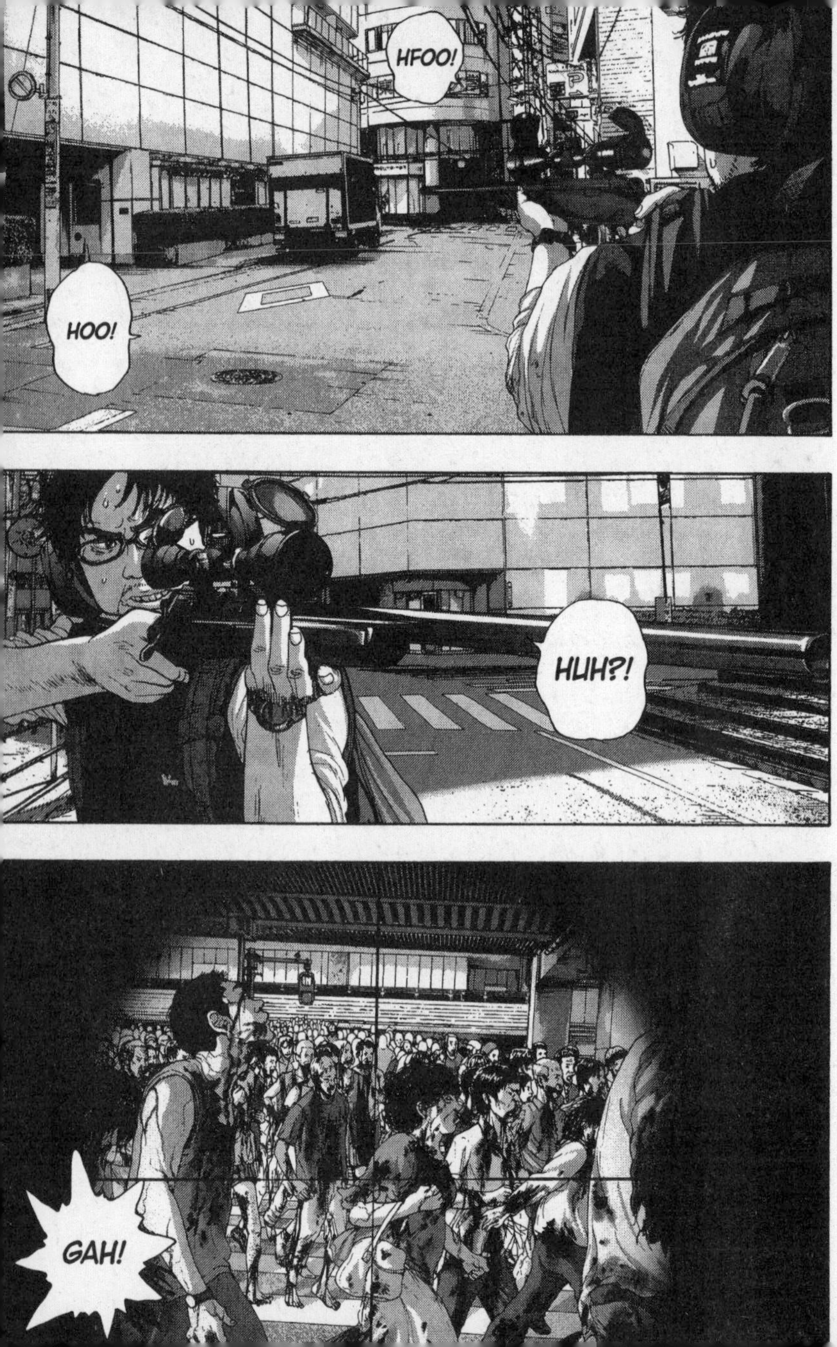
HFOO!
HOO!
HUH?!
GAH!

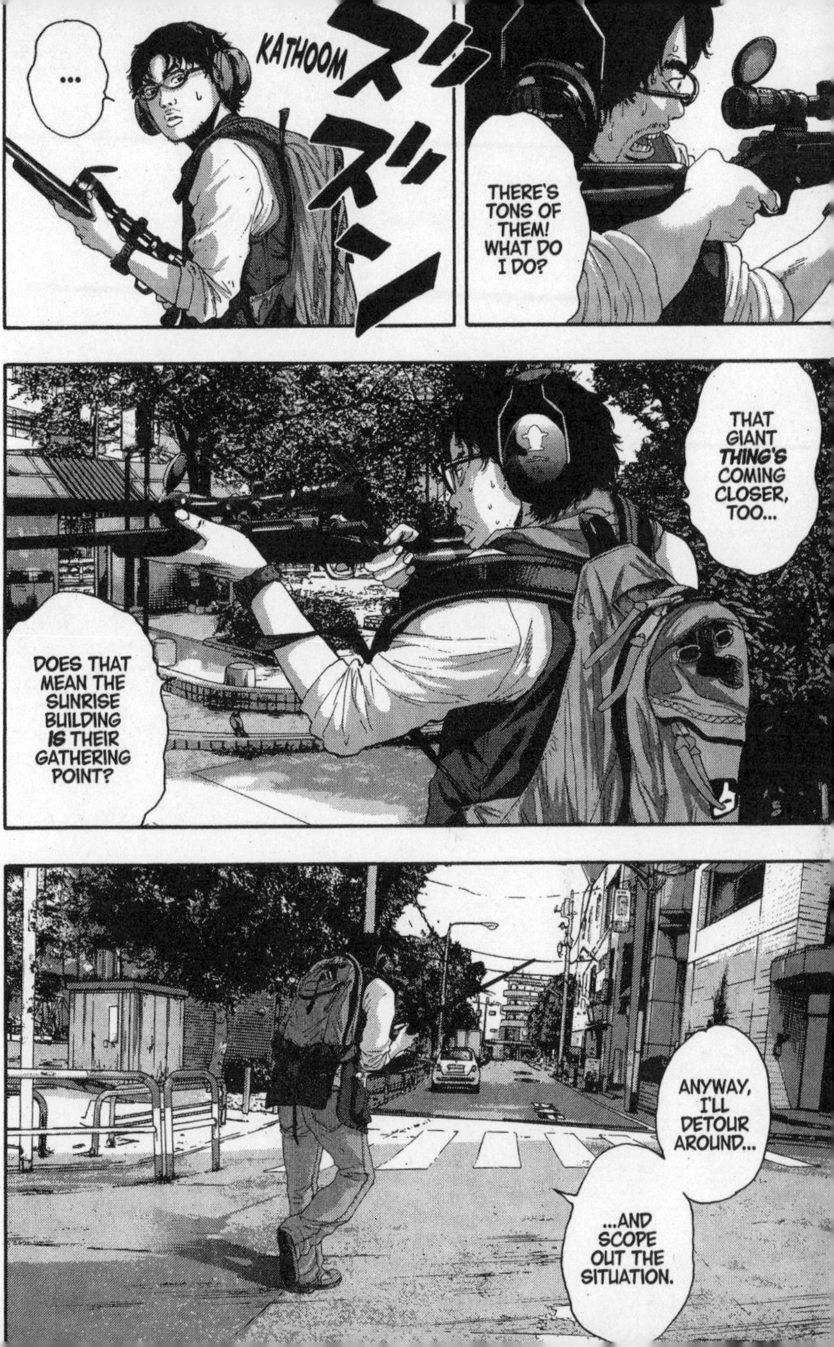

THERE'S TONS OF THEM! WHAT DO I DO?
KATHOOM
...
THAT GIANT THING'S COMING CLOSER, TOO...
DOES THAT MEAN THE SUNRISE BUILDING IS THEIR GATHERING POINT?
ANYWAY, I'LL DETOUR AROUND...
...AND SCOPE OUT THE SITUATION.

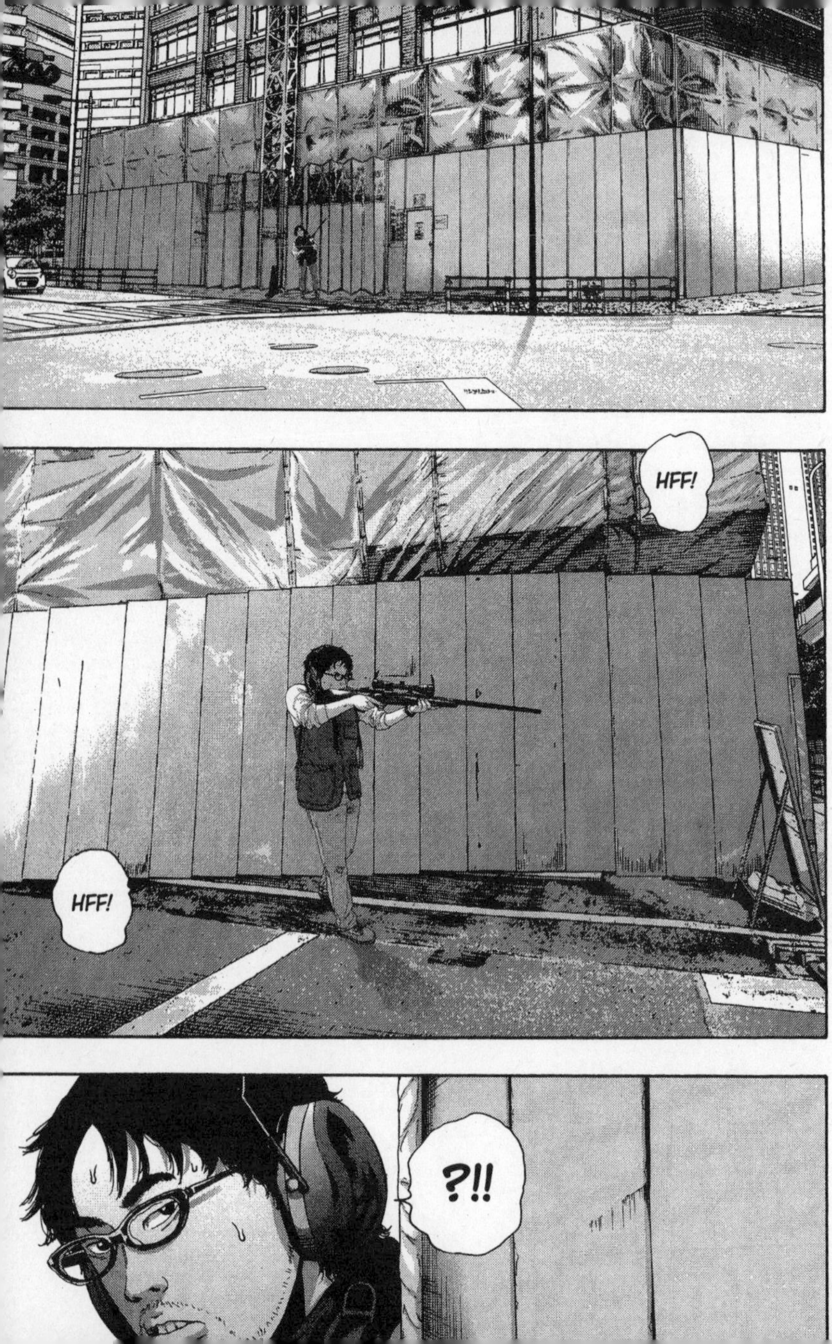
HFF!
HFF!
?!!

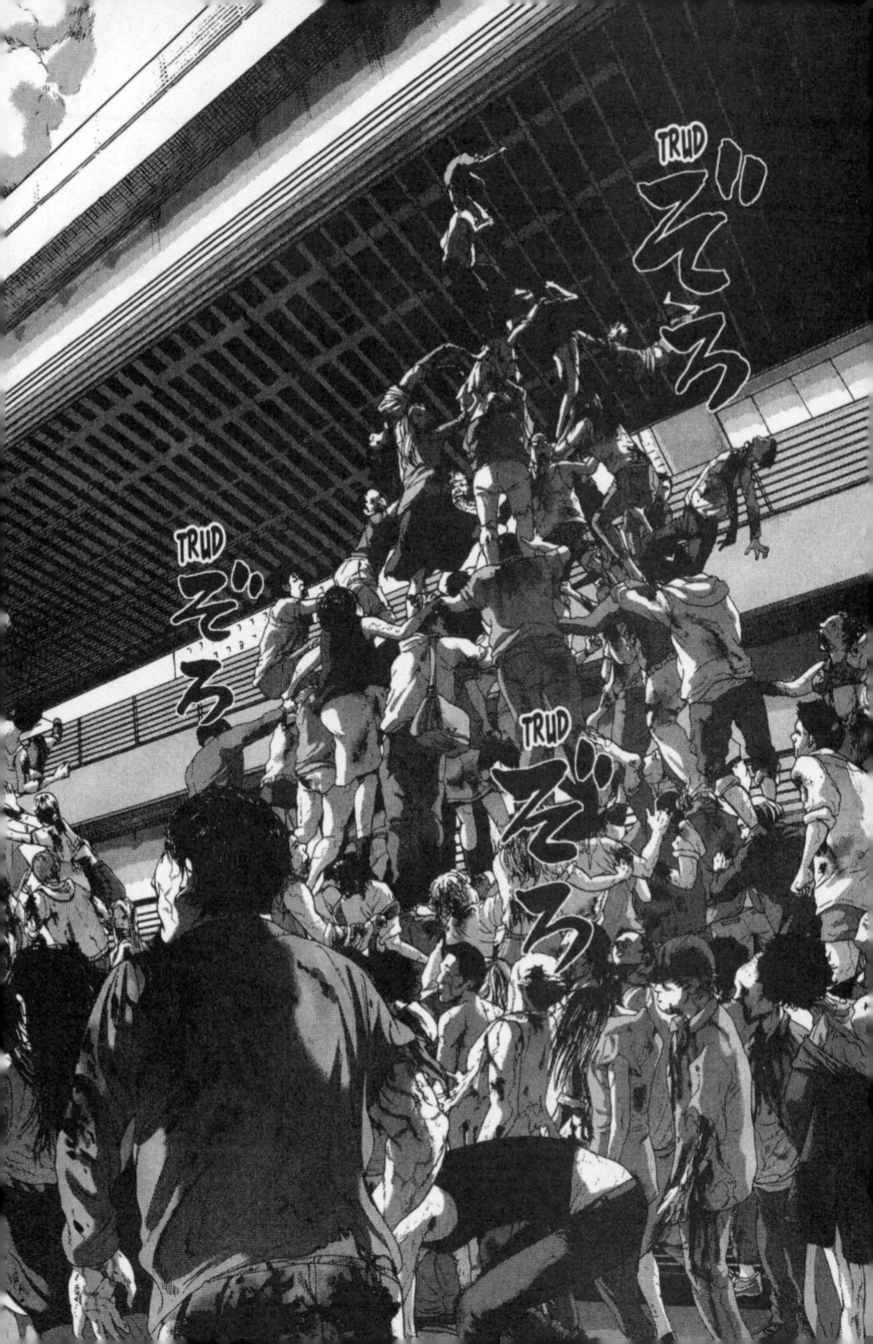
TRUD
ぞろ
TRUD
ぞろ
TRUD
ぞろ

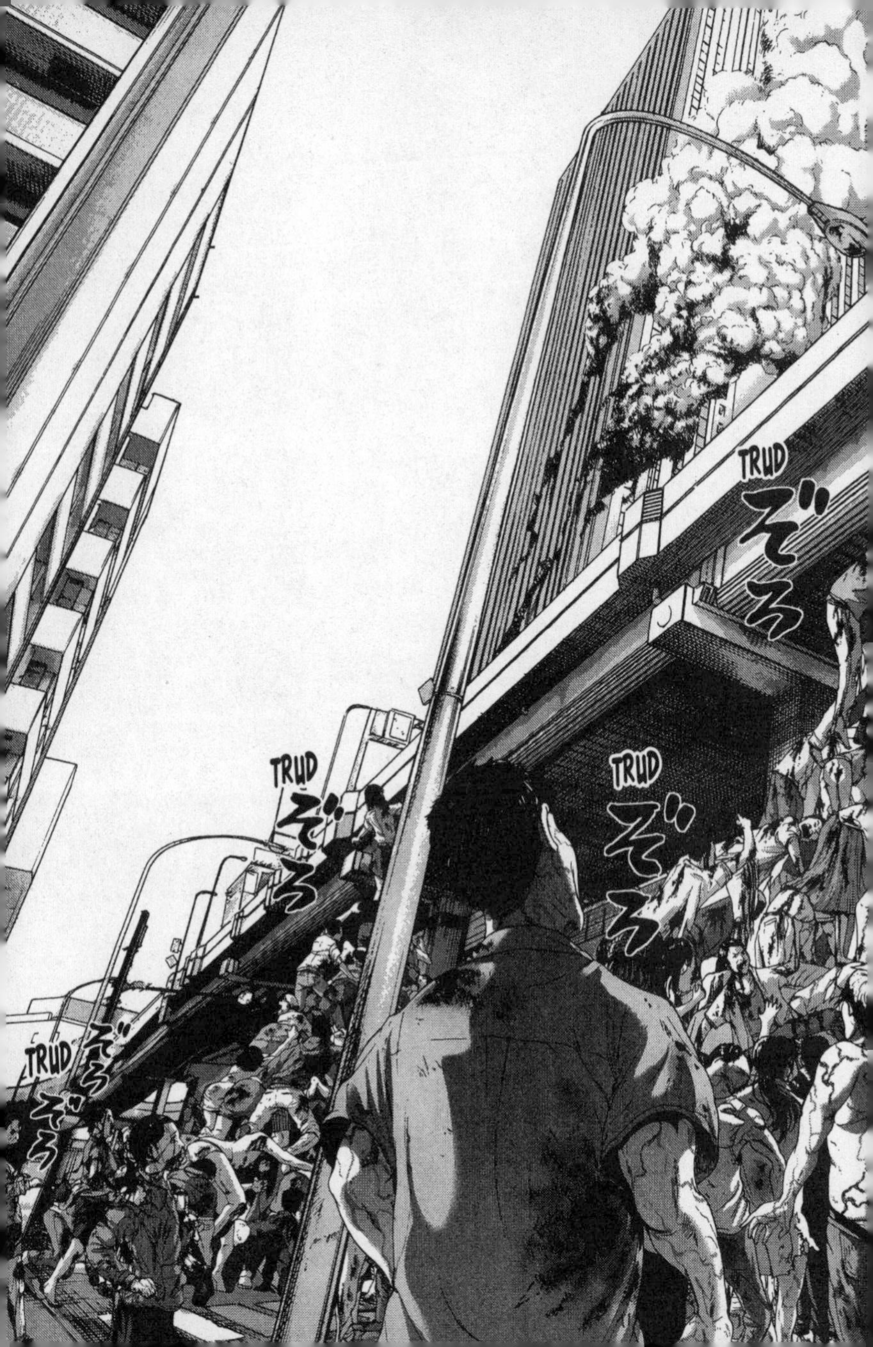
TRUD
ぞろ
TRUD
ぞろ
TRUD
ぞろ
TRUD
ぞろぞろ

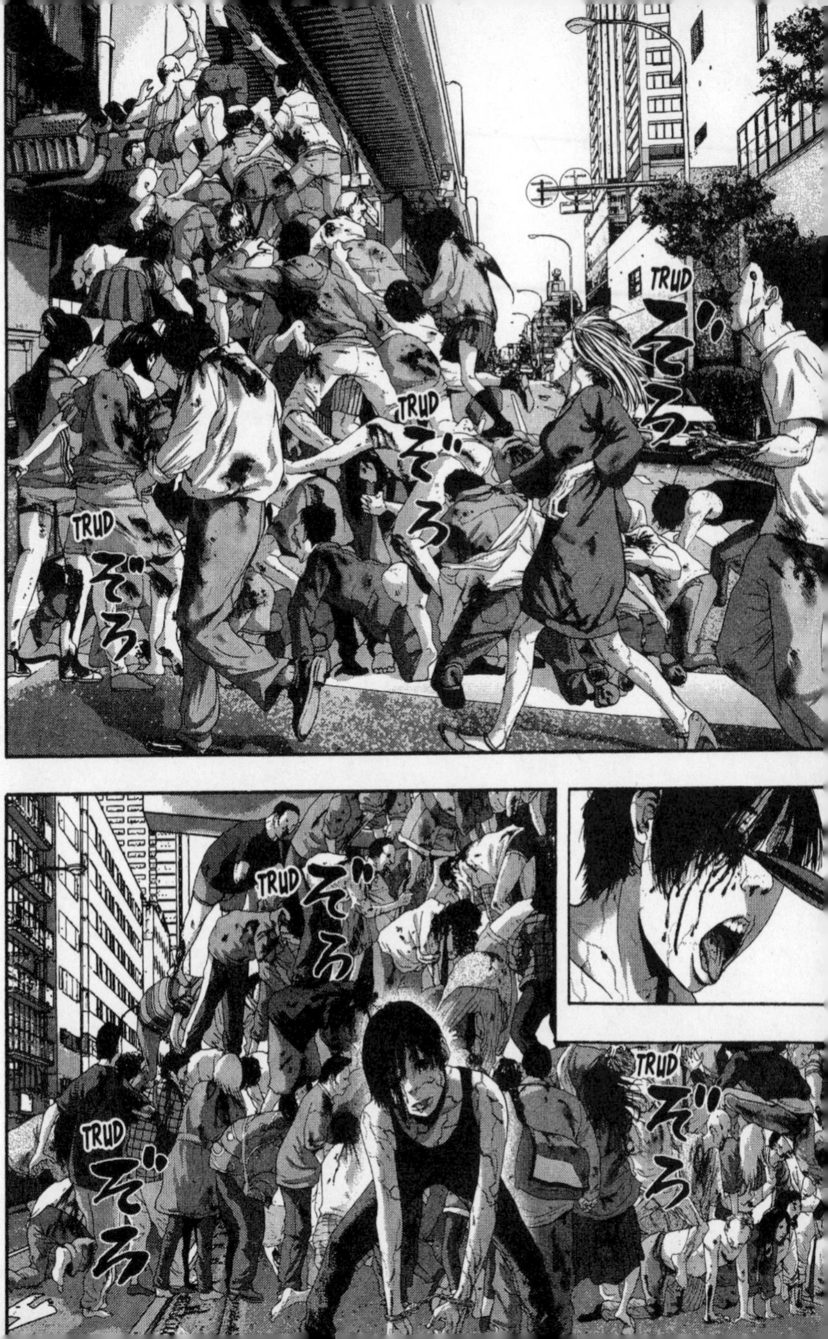
TRUD
ぞろ
TRUD
ぞろ
TRUD
ぞろ
TRUD
ぞろ
TRUD
ぞろ
TRUD
ぞろ

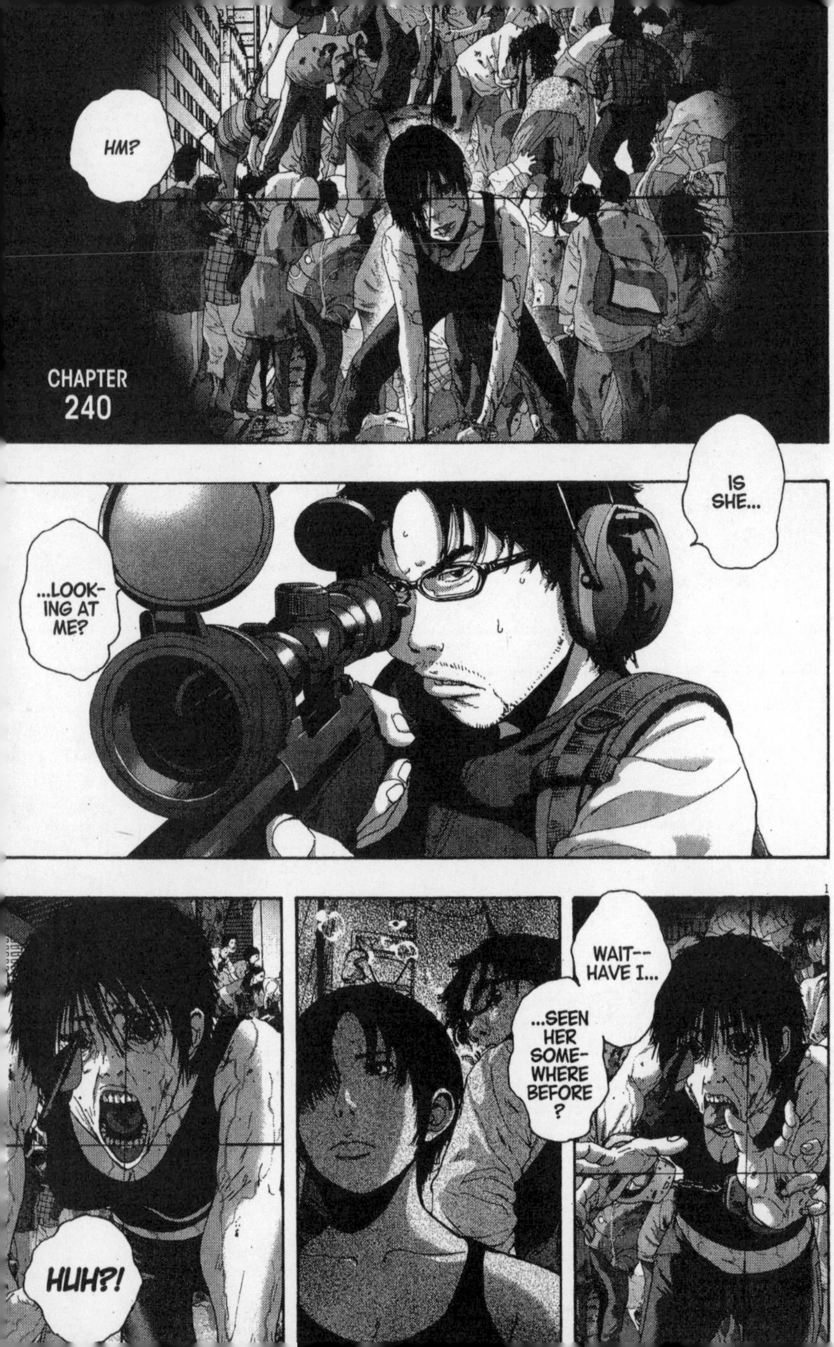
HM?
CHAPTER 240
IS SHE...
...LOOKING AT ME?
WAIT-- HAVE I...
...SEEN HER SOMEWHERE BEFORE?
HUH?!

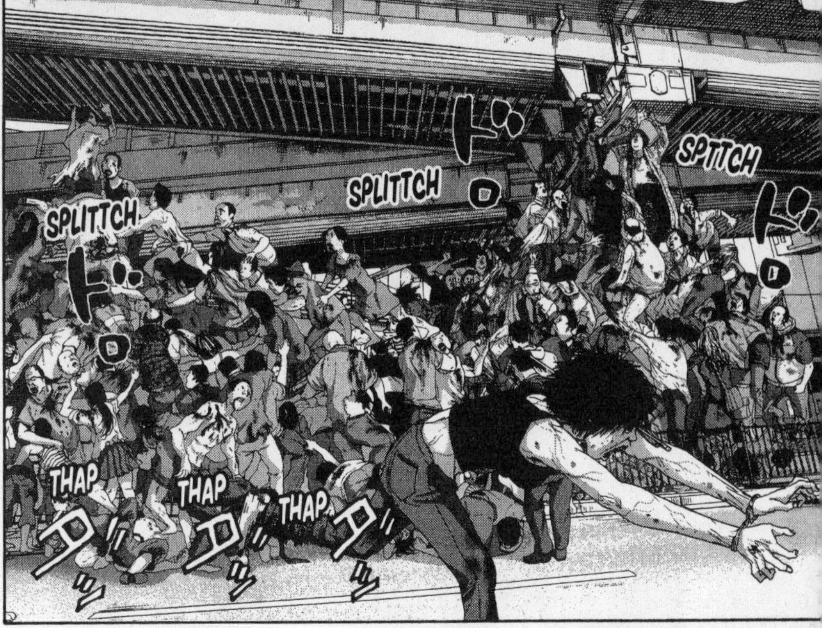
SPTTCH
SPLITTCH
SPLITTCH
THAP
THAP
THAP

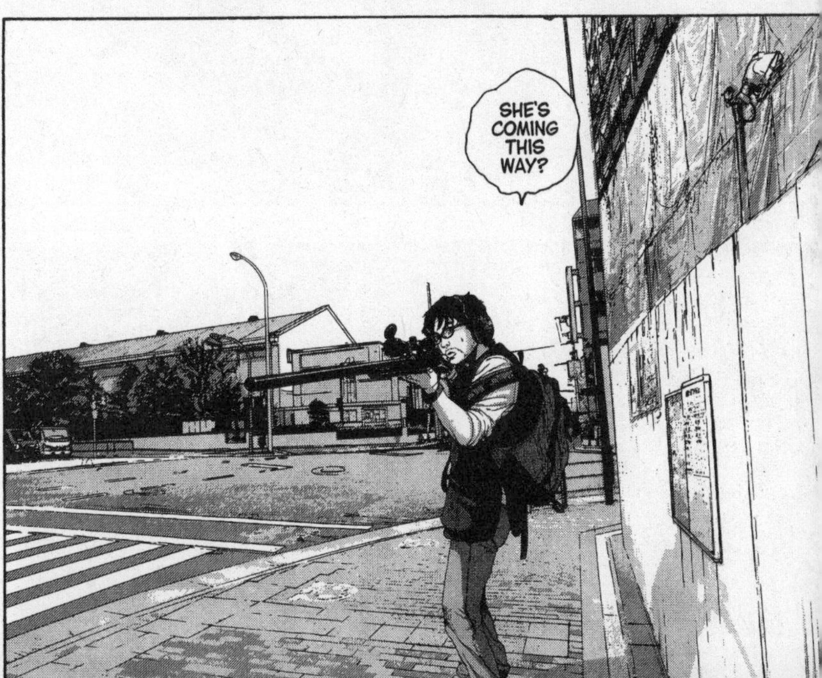
SHE'S COMING THIS WAY?

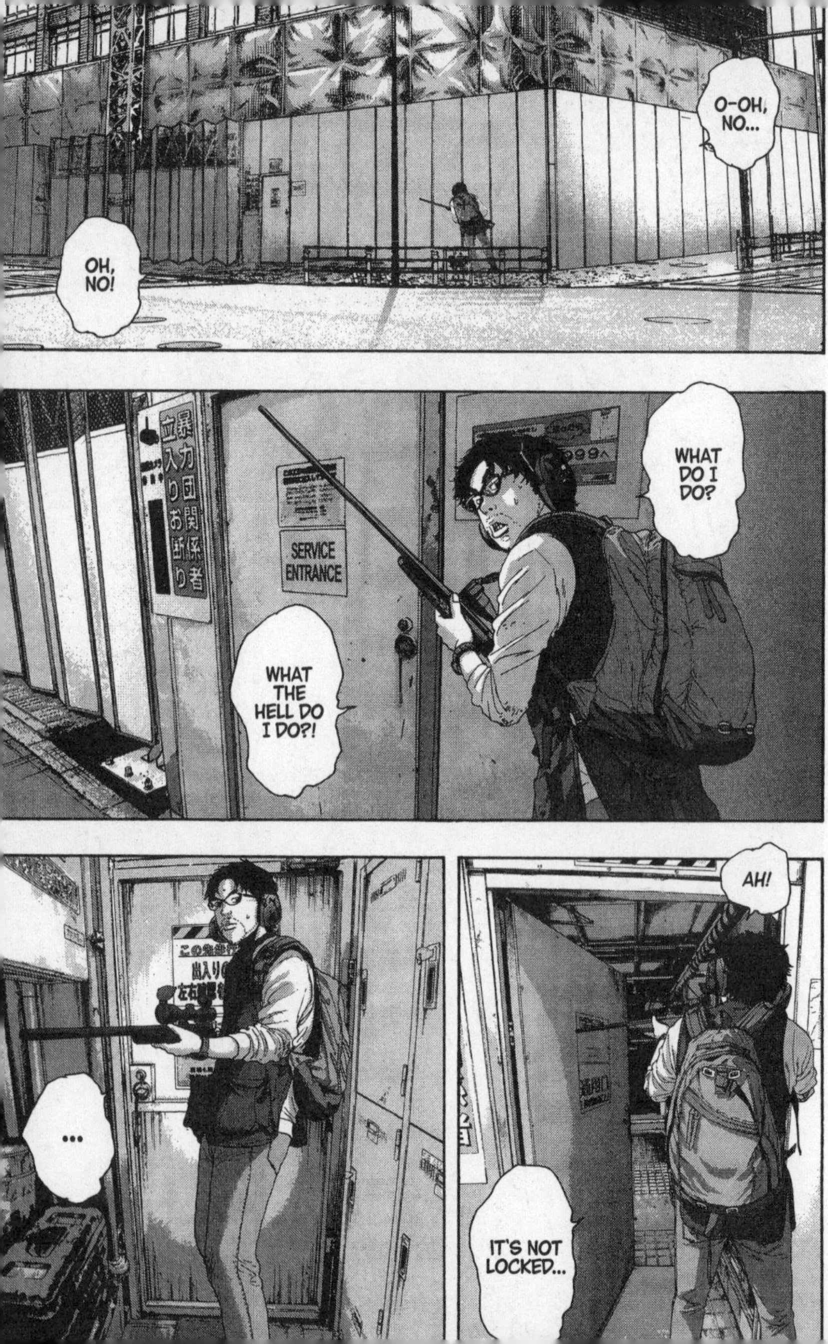
O-OH, NO...
OH, NO!
WHAT DO I DO?
暴力団関係者立入りお断り
SERVICE ENTRANCE
WHAT THE HELL DO I DO?!
AH!
IT'S NOT LOCKED...
...

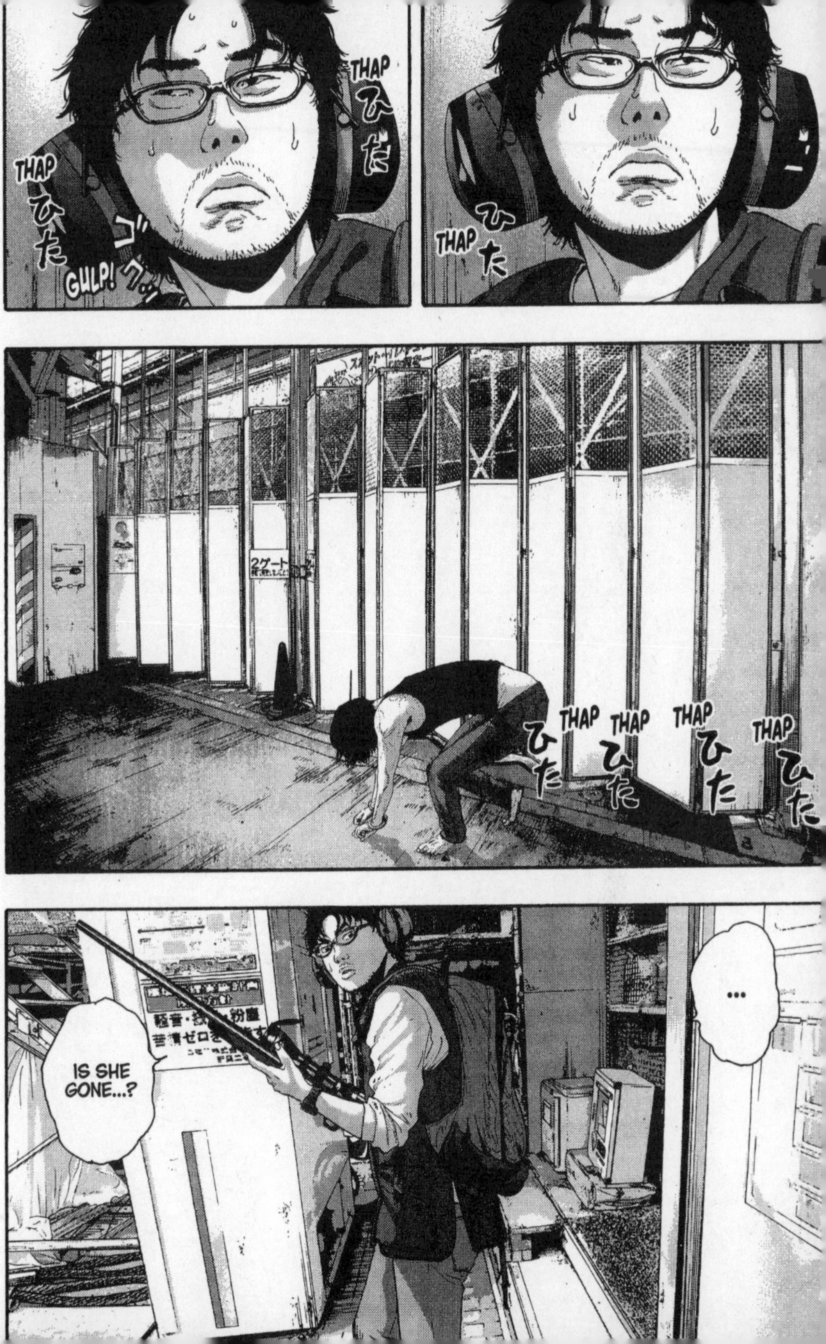

THAP
ひた
THAP
ひだ
THAP
ひた
GULP!
ゴクッ
THAP
ひた
THAP
ひた
THAP
ひた
THAP
ひた
2ゲート
...
IS SHE GONE...?

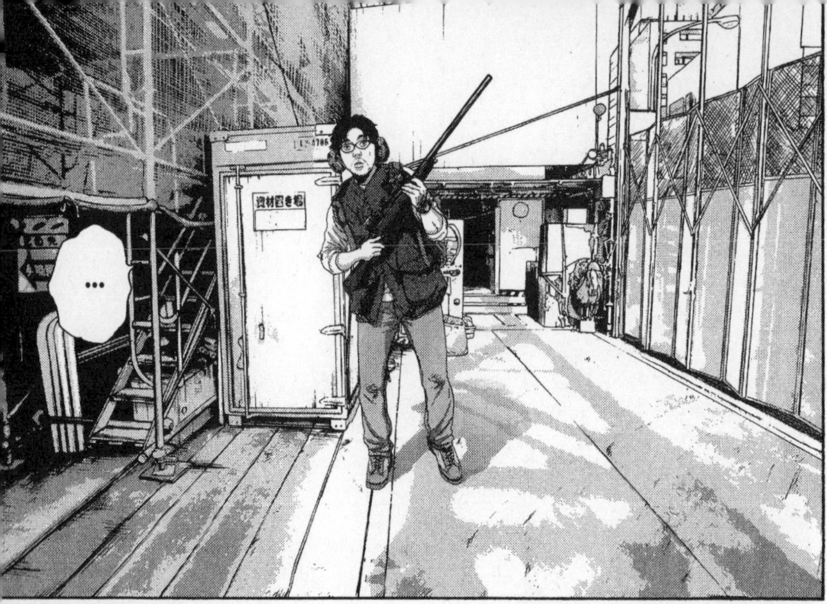
...
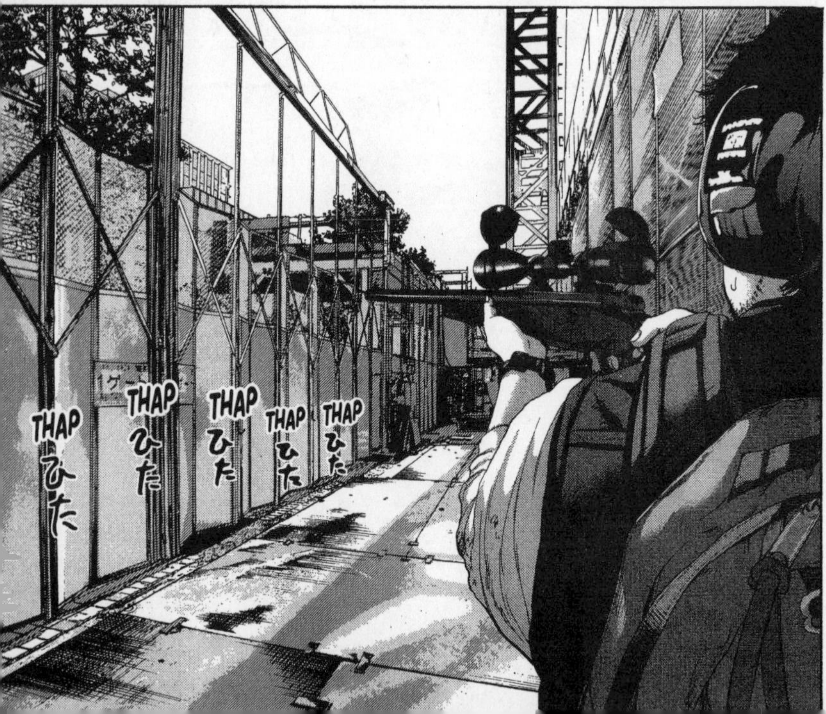
THAP ひた
THAP ひた
THAP ひた
THAP ひた
THAP ひた

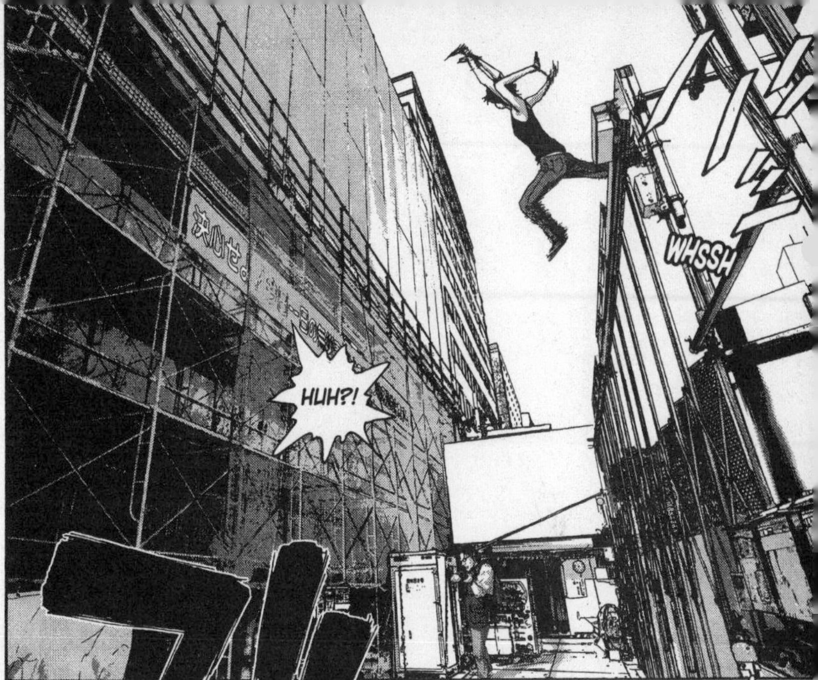
WHSSH
HUH?!
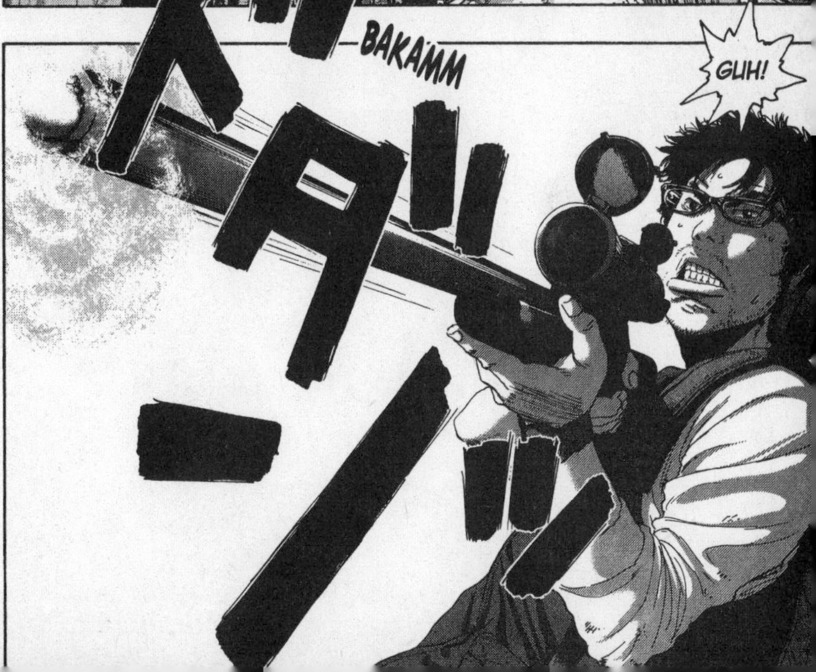
GUH!
BAKAMM

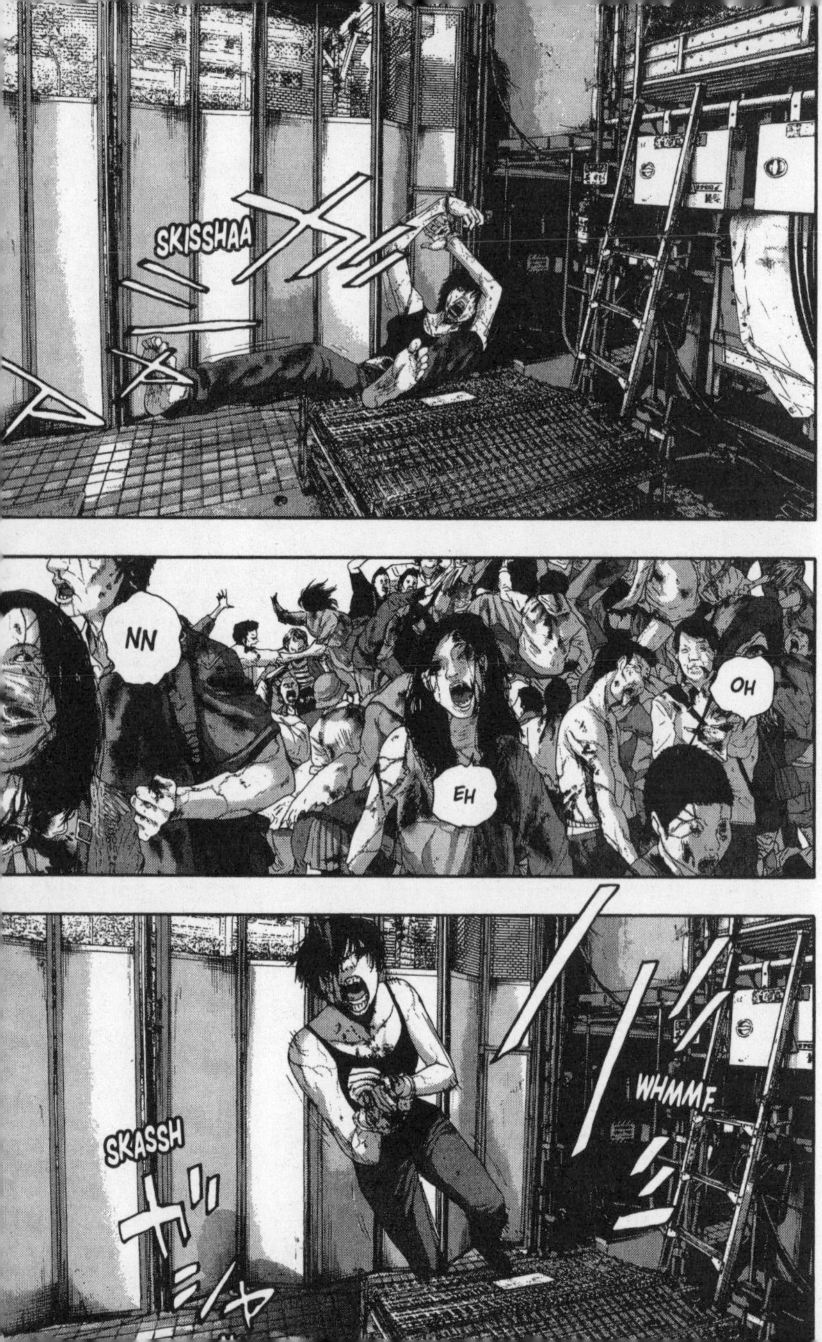
SKISSHAA
OH
EH
NN
WHMMF
SKASSH

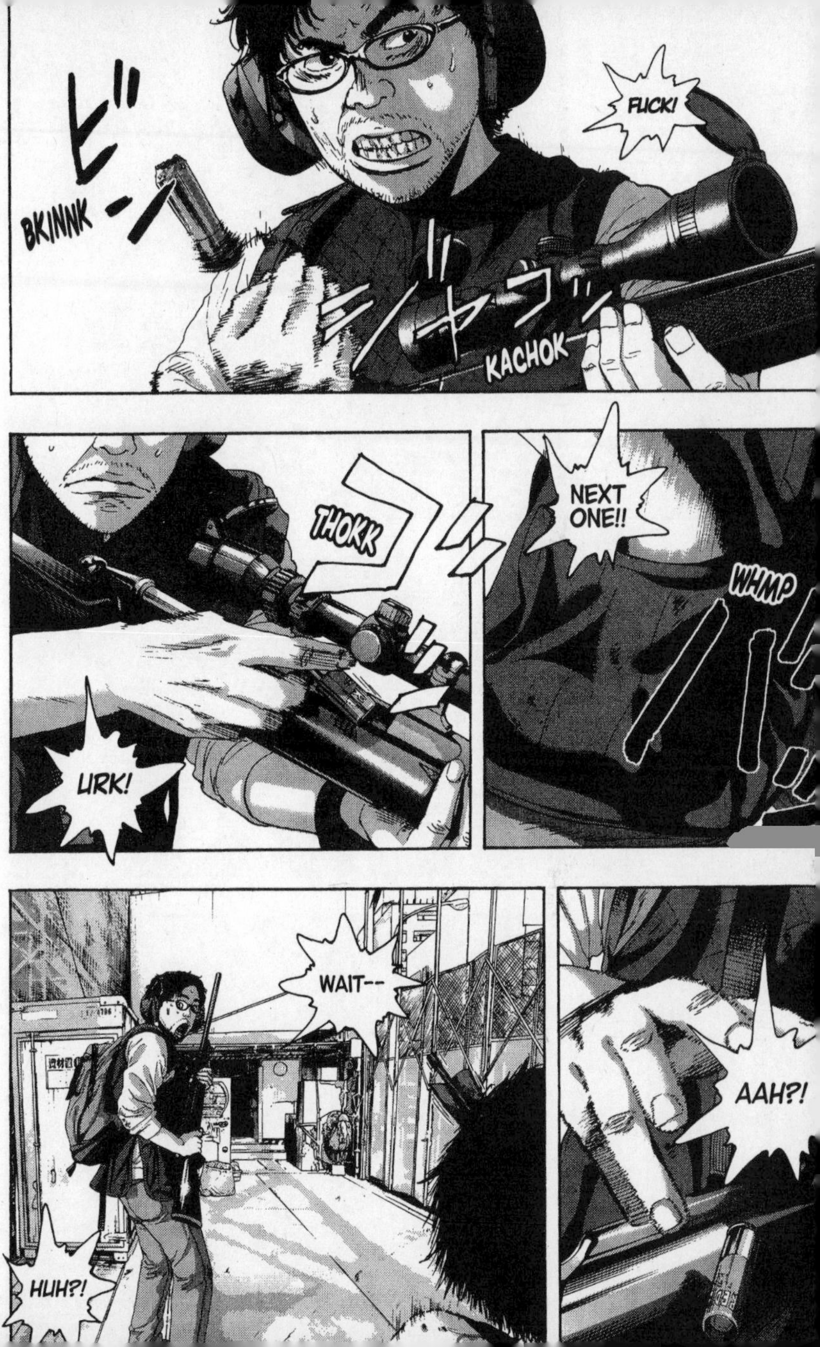
FUCK!
KACHOK
BKINNK
NEXT ONE!!
WHMP
THOKK
URK!
AAH?!
WAIT--
HUH?!

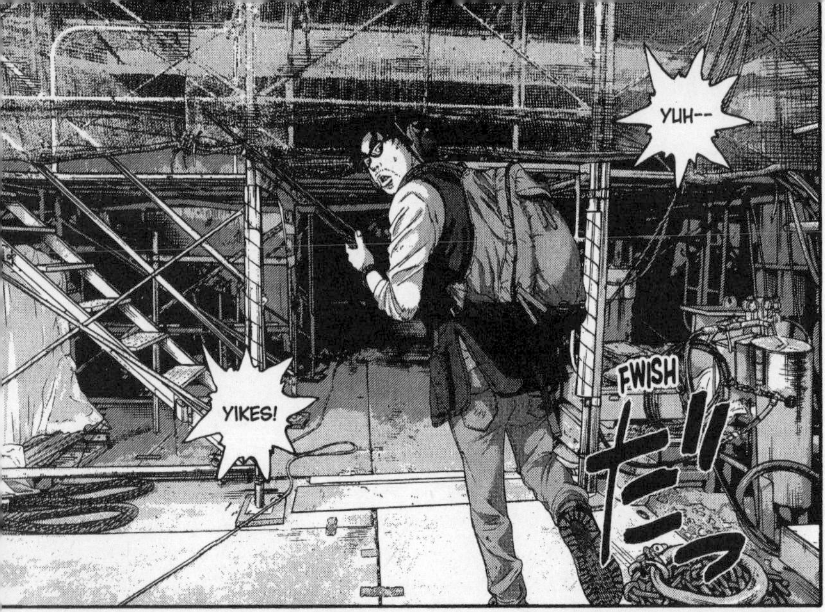
YUH--
FWISH
YIKES!
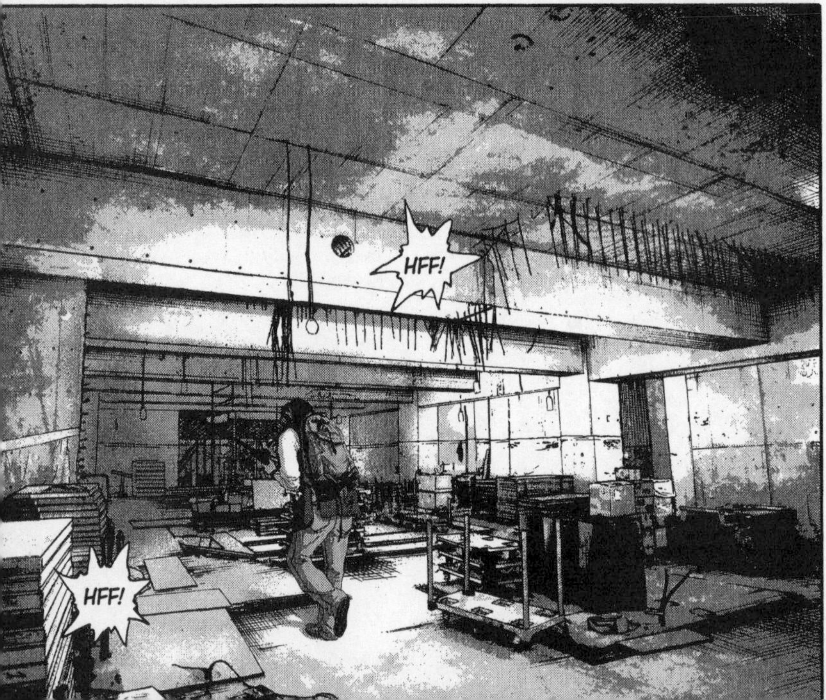
HFF!
HFF!

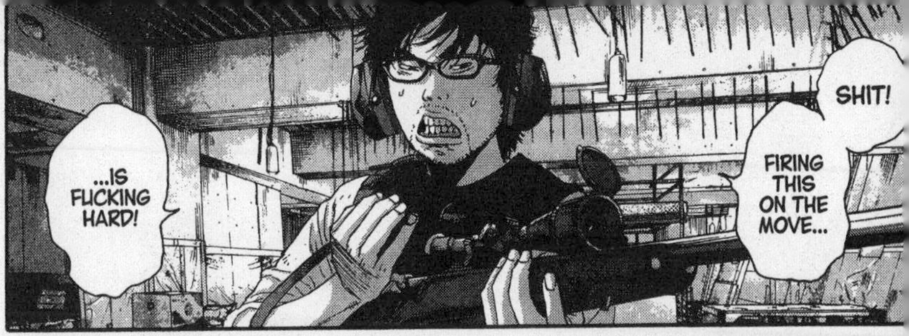
SHIT!
FIRING THIS ON THE MOVE...
...IS FUCKING HARD!
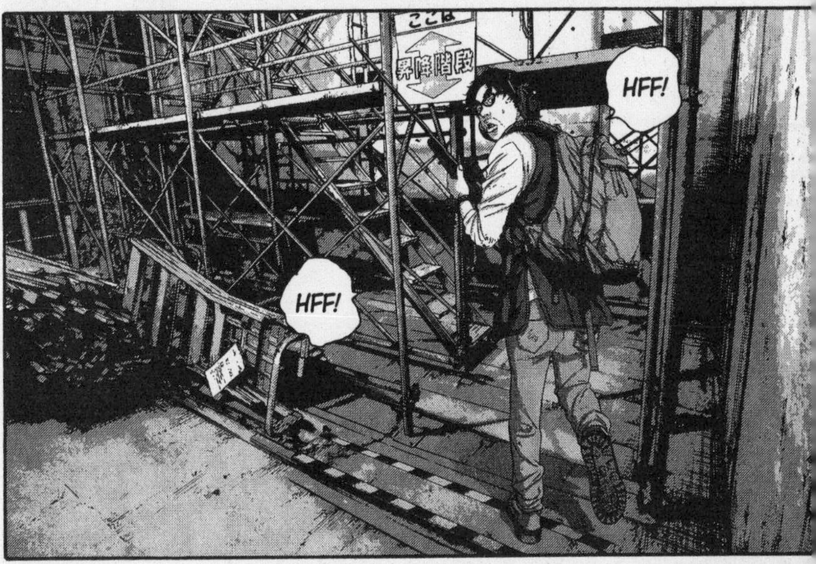
ここは
昇降階段
HFF!
HFF!
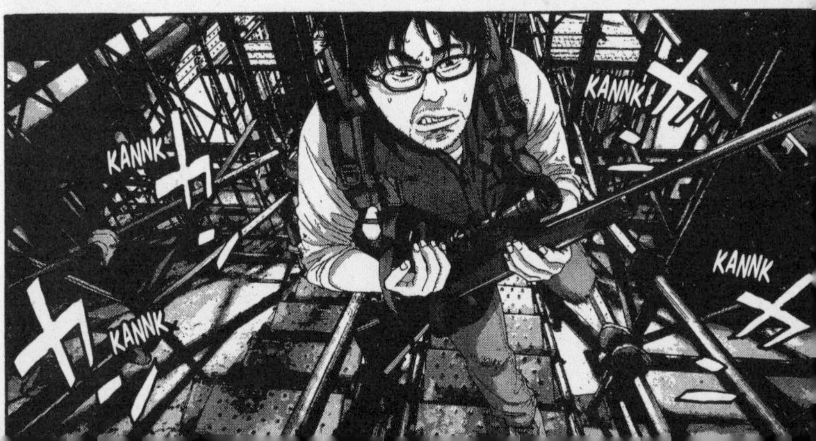
KANNK
KANNK
KANNK
KANNK

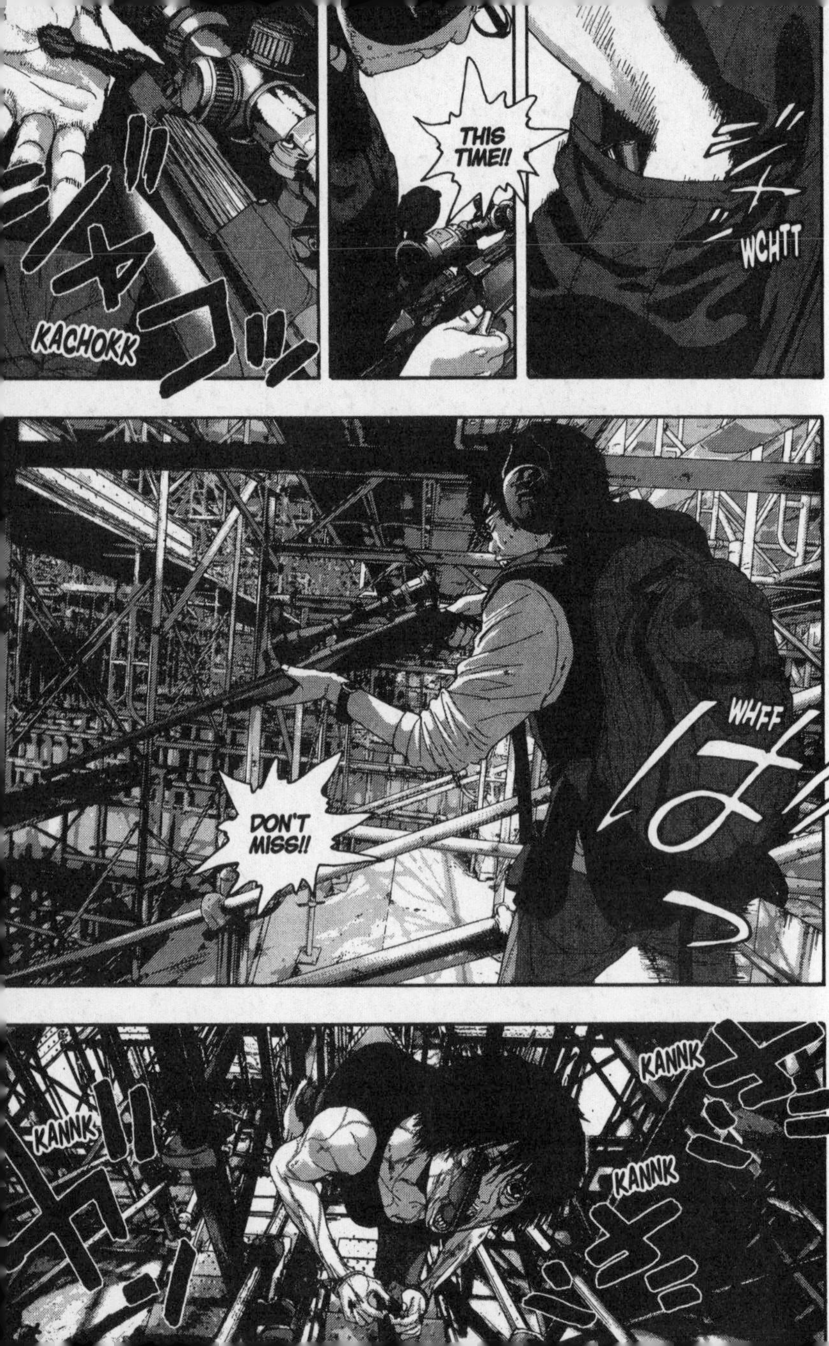
WCHTT
THIS TIME!!
KACHOKK
WHFF
DON'T MISS!!
KANNK
KANNK
KANNK

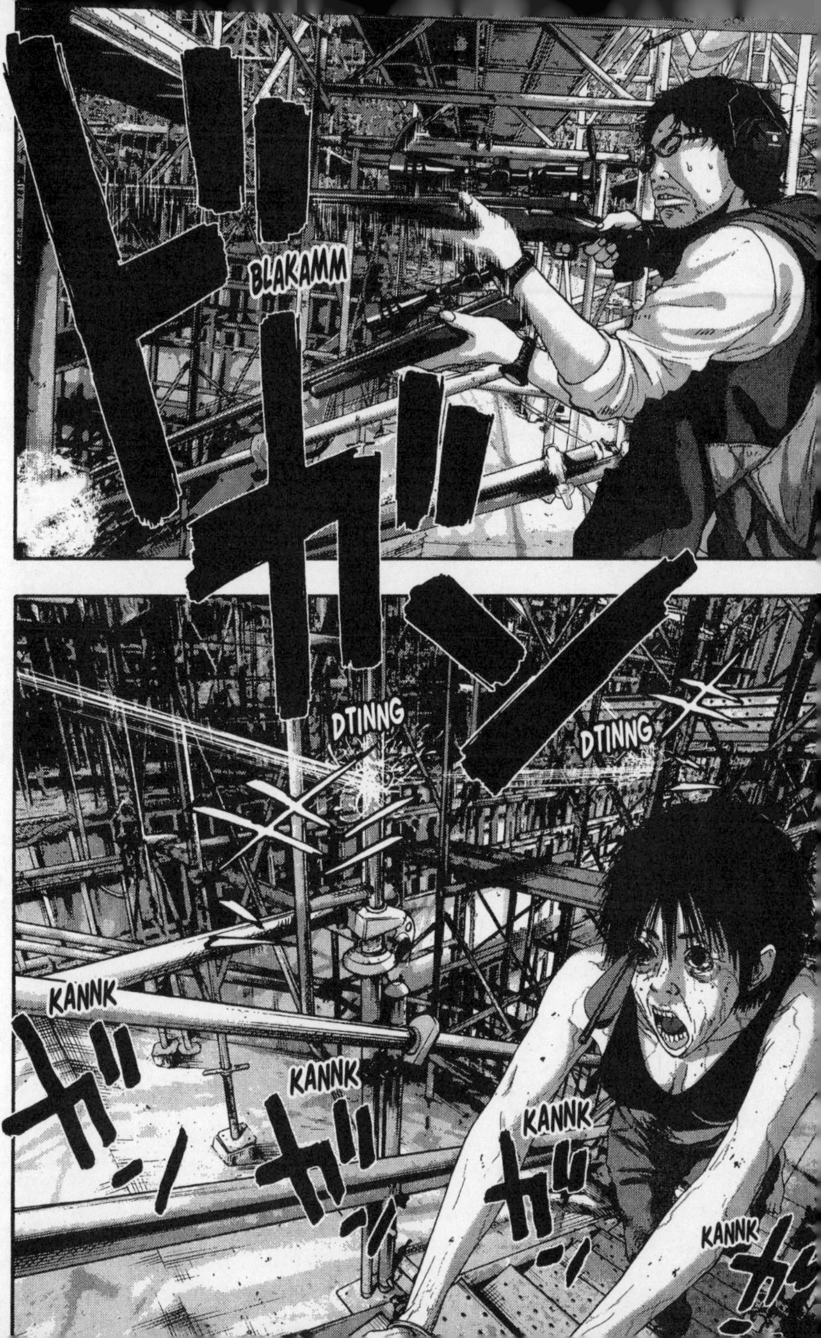
BLAKAMM
DTINNG
DTINNG
KANNK
KANNK
KANNK
KANNK

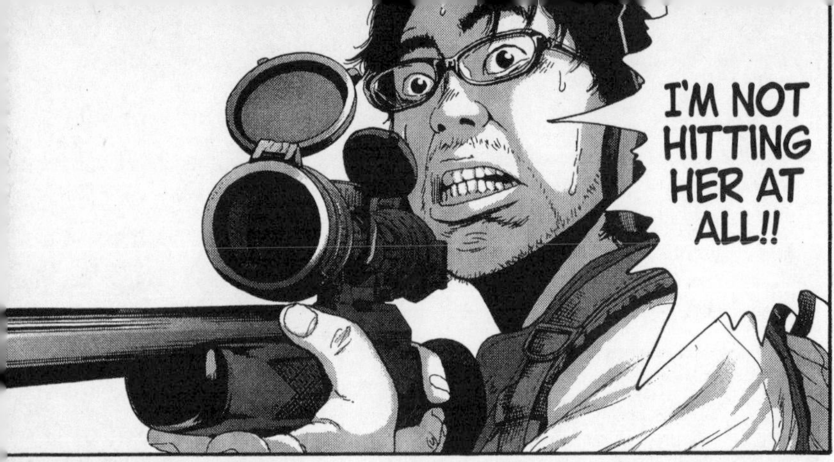
I'M NOT HITTING HER AT ALL!!

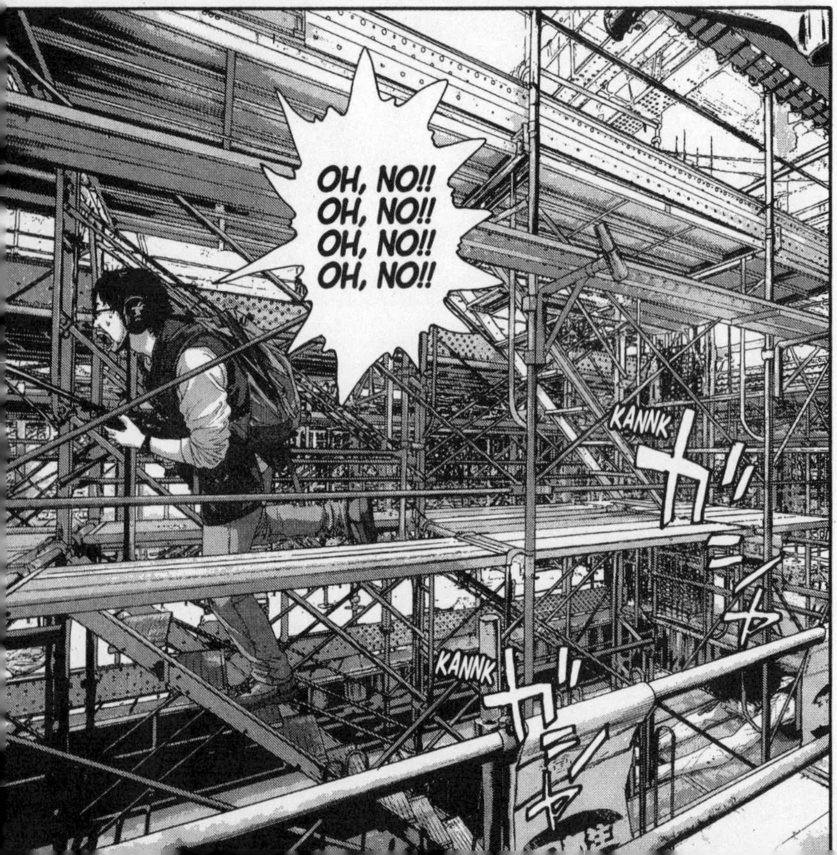
OH, NO!! OH, NO!! OH, NO!! OH, NO!!
KANNK
KANNK

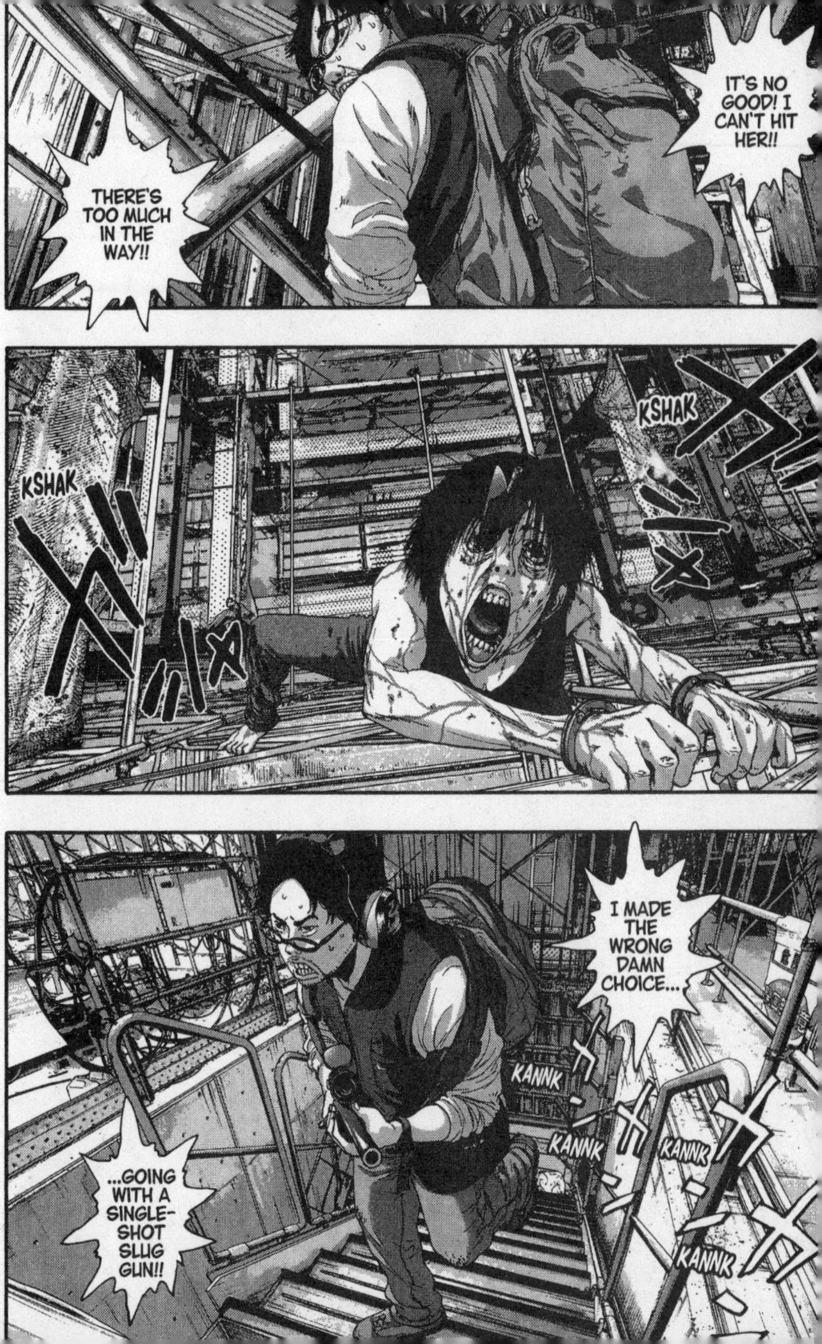
IT'S NO GOOD! I CAN'T HIT HER!!
THERE'S TOO MUCH IN THE WAY!!
KSHAK
KSHAK
I MADE THE WRONG DAMN CHOICE...
KANNK
KANNK
KANNK
KANNK
...GOING WITH A SINGLE-SHOT SLUG GUN!!

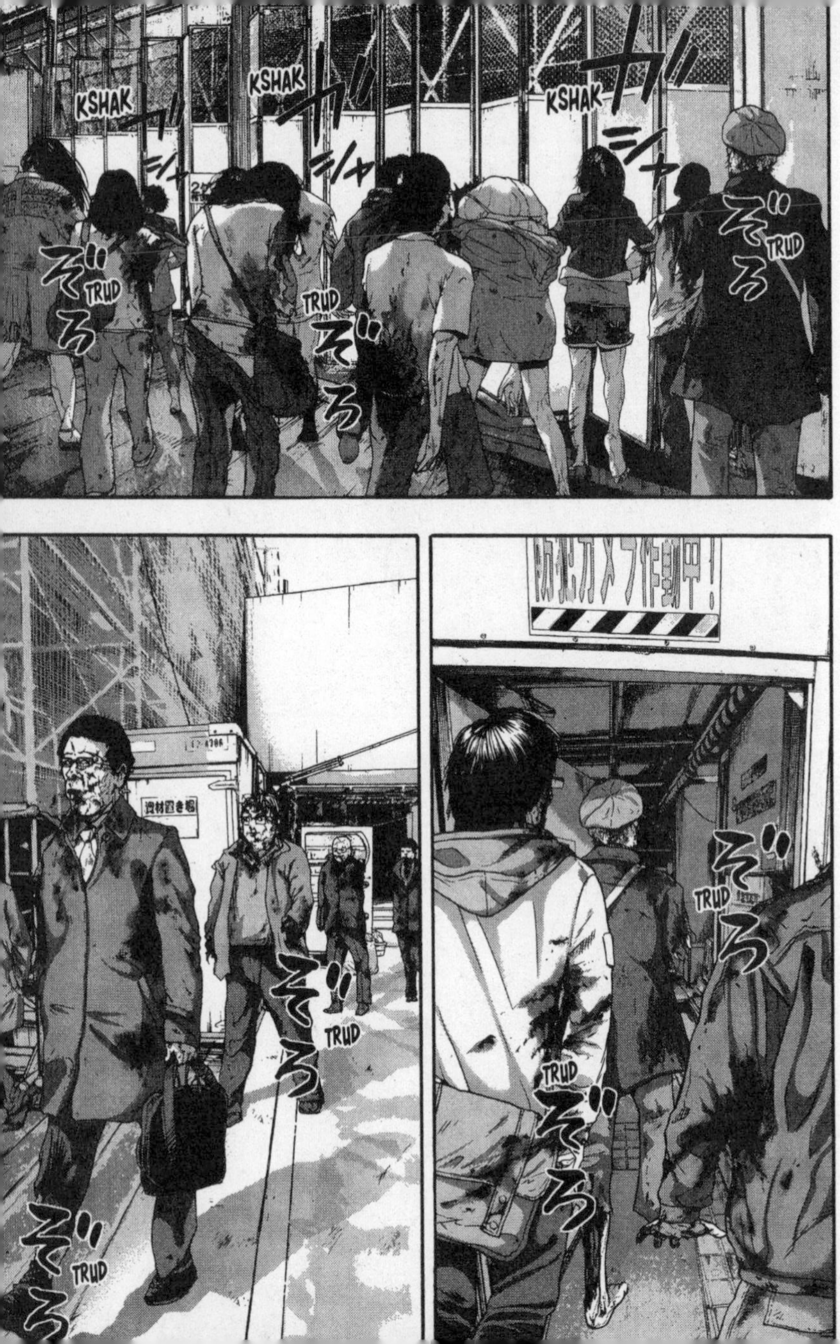
KSHAK
ガシャ
TRUD
ぞろ
KSHAK
ガシャ
TRUD
ぞろ
KSHAK
ガシャ
TRUD
ぞろ
防犯カメラ作動中！
TRUD
ぞろ
TRUD
ぞろ
資材置き場
TRUD
ぞろ
TRUD
ぞろ

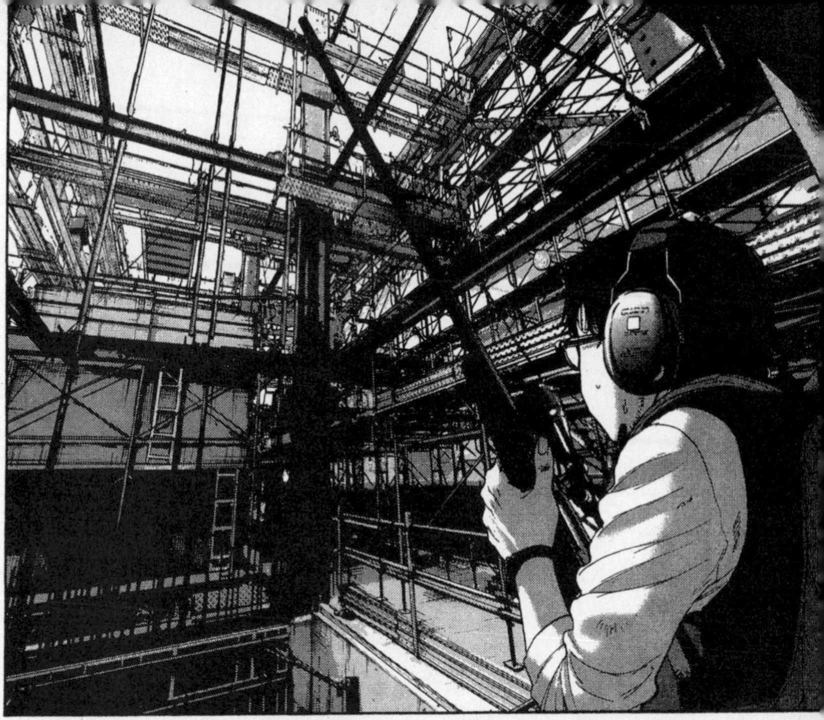

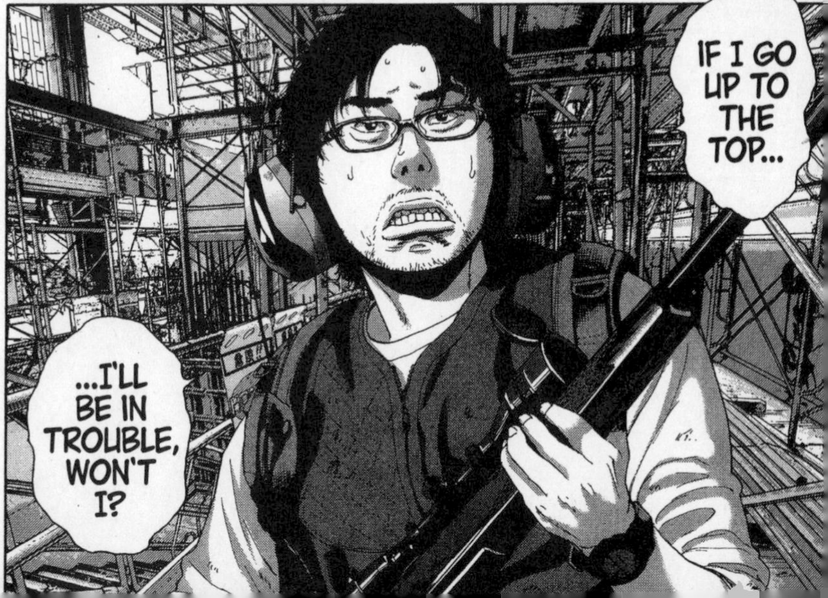
IF I GO UP TO THE TOP...
...I'LL BE IN TROUBLE, WON'T I?

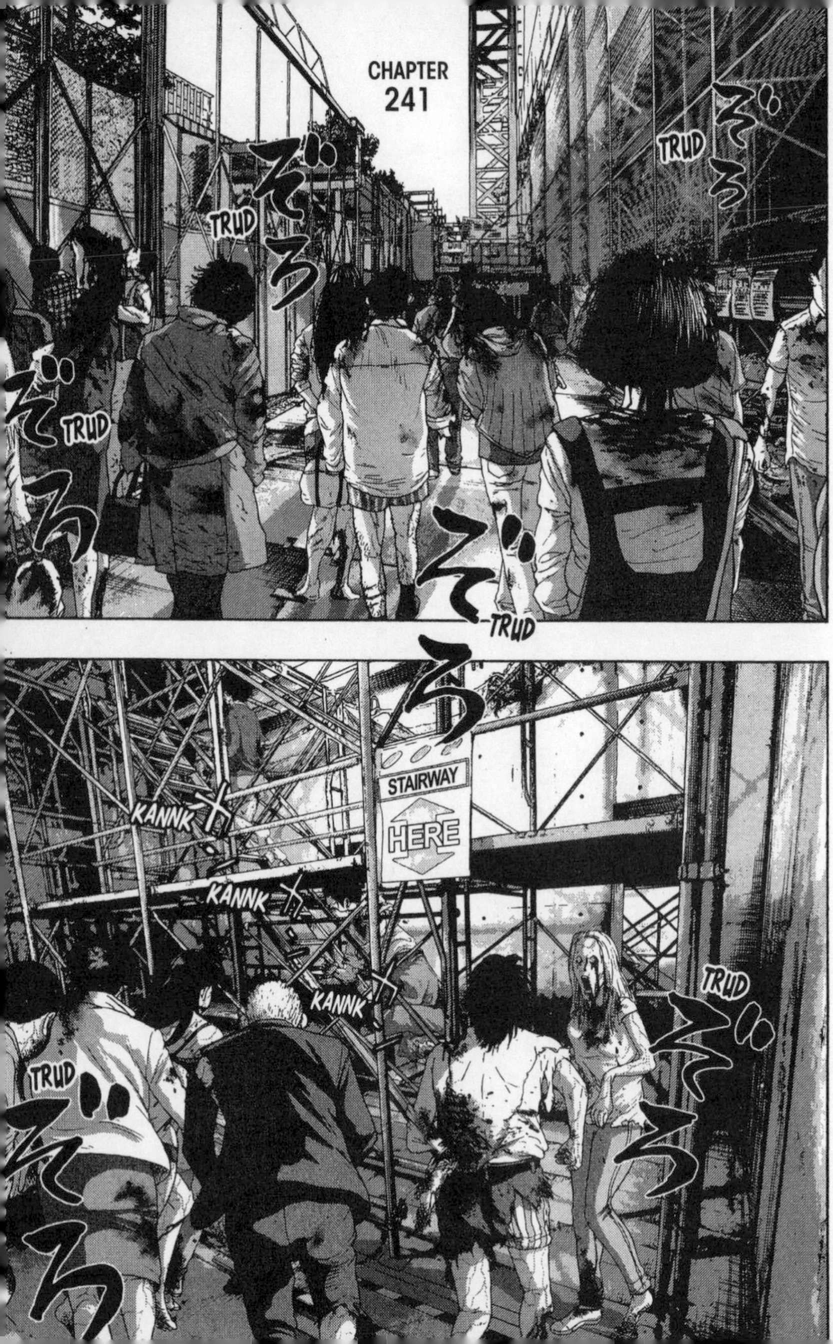
CHAPTER
241
ぞろ
TRUD
ぞろ
TRUD
ぞろ
TRUD
ぞろ
TRUD
ぞろ
TRUD
STAIRWAY
HERE
KANNK
KANNK
KANNK
ぞろ
TRUD

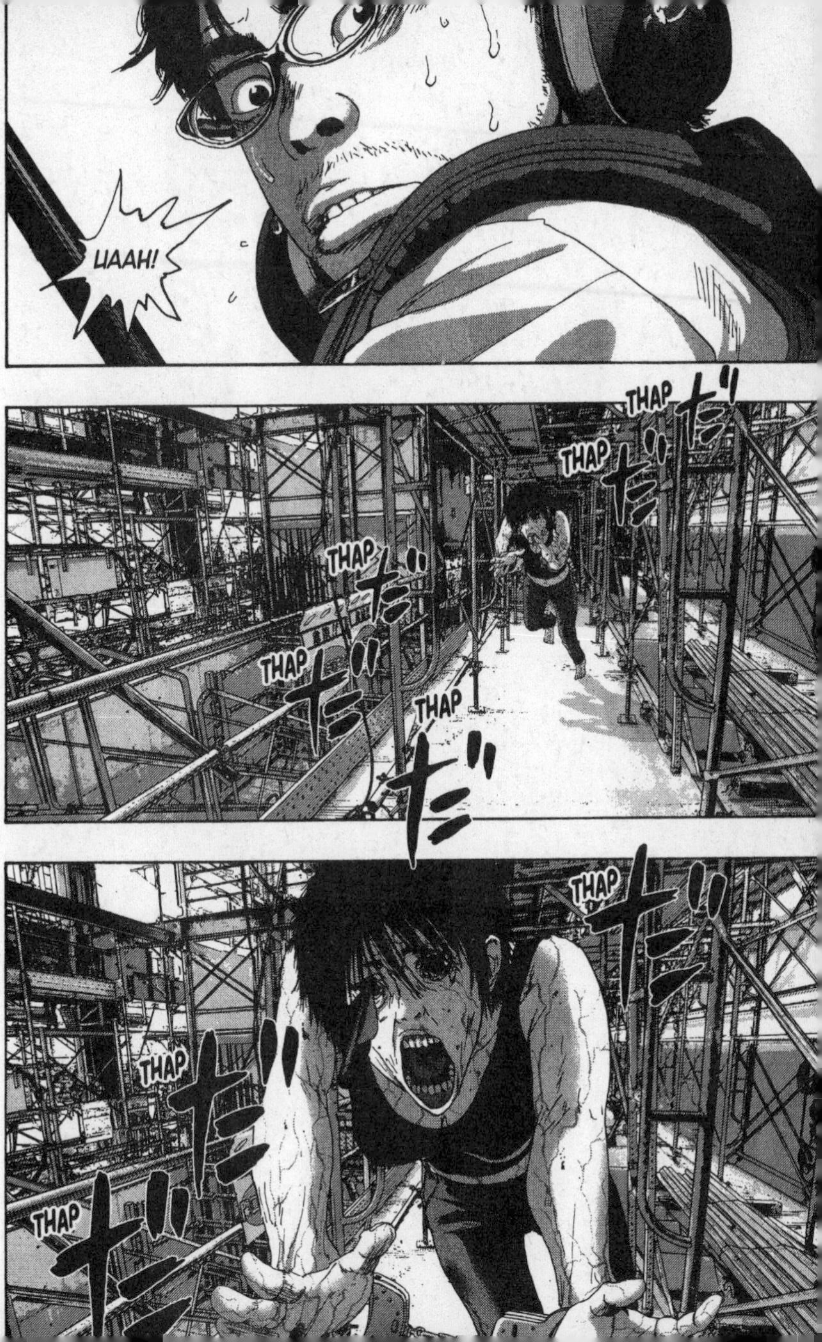
UAAH!
THAP
THAP
THAP
THAP
THAP
THAP
THAP
THAP
THAP

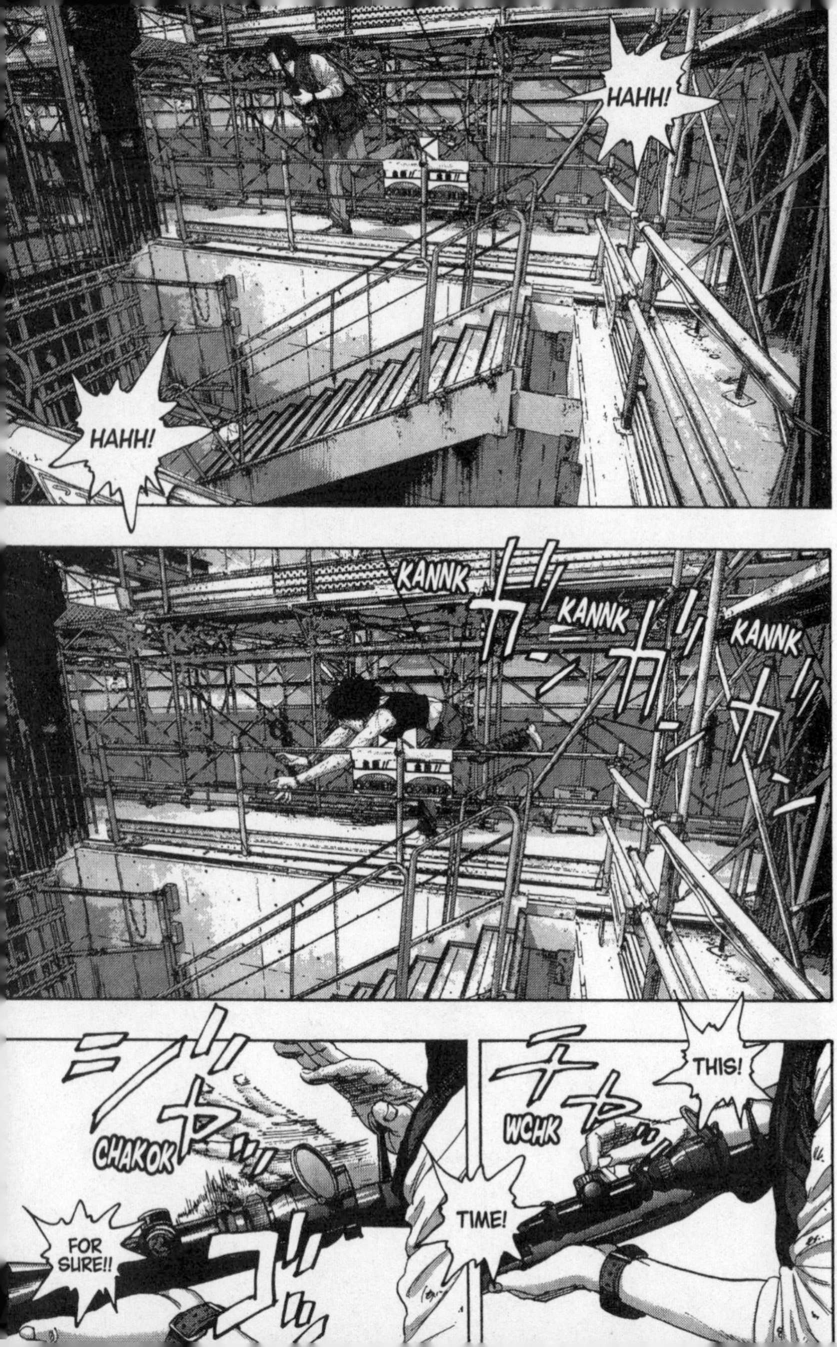
HAHH!
HAHH!
KANNK
KANNK
KANNK
THIS!
WCHK
TIME!
CHAKOK
FOR SURE!!

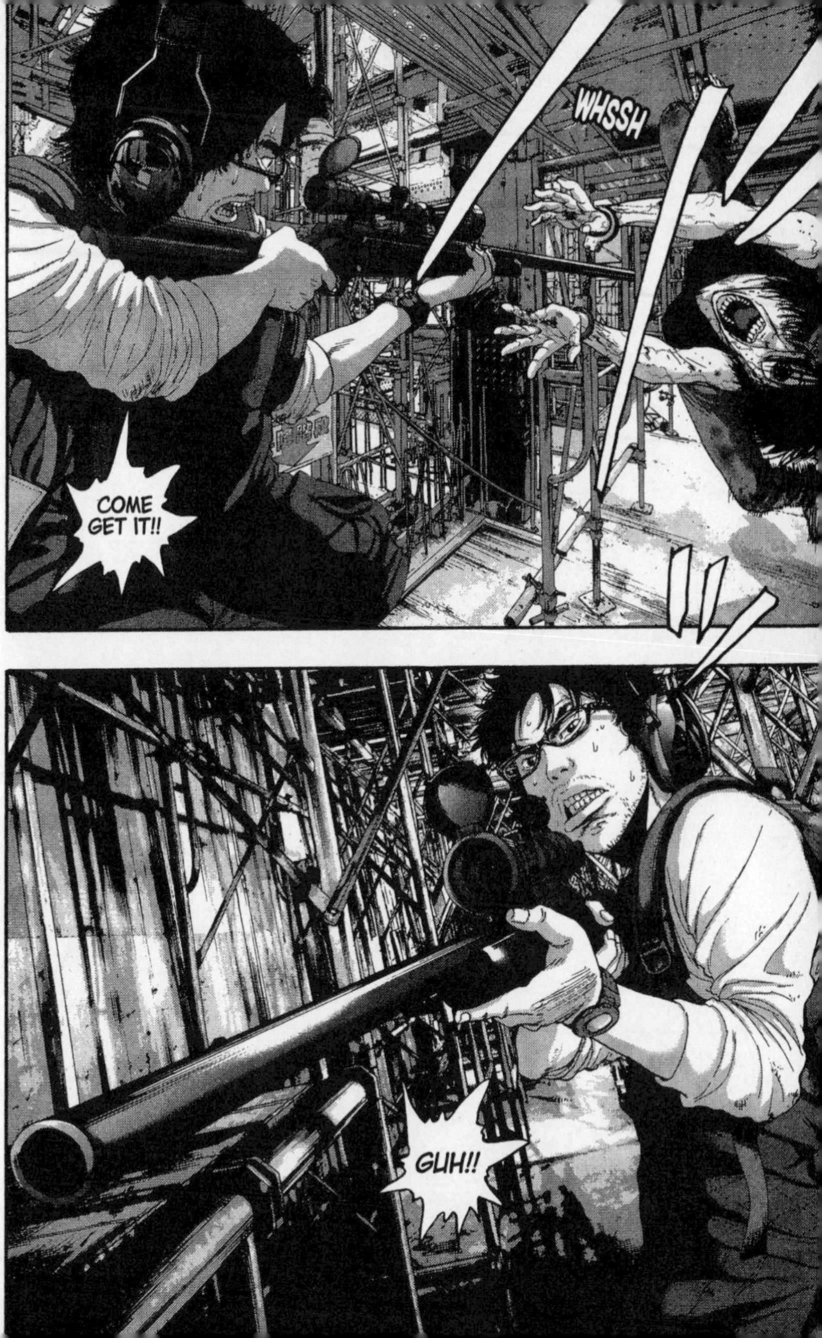
WHSSH
COME GET IT!!
GUH!!

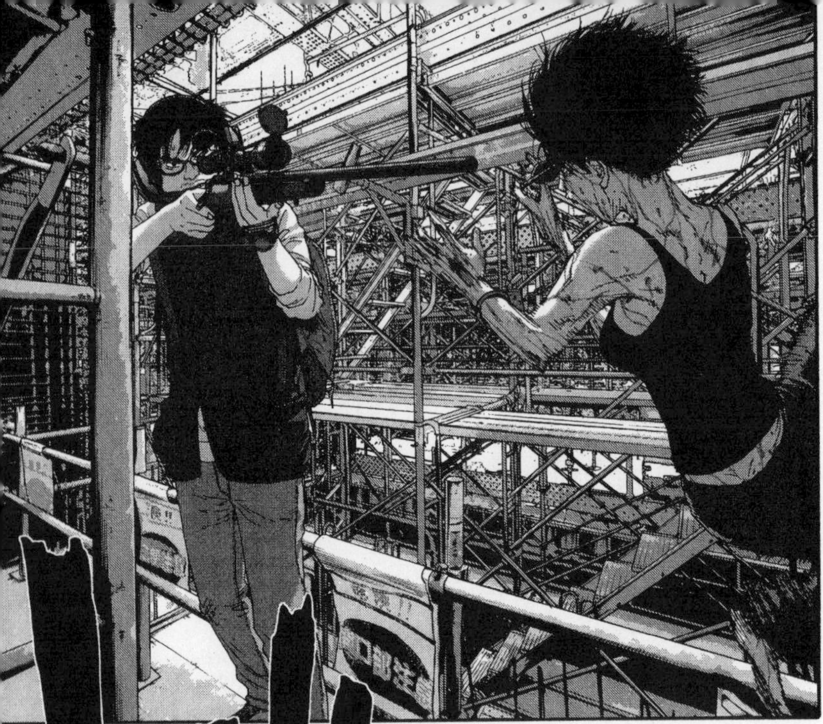

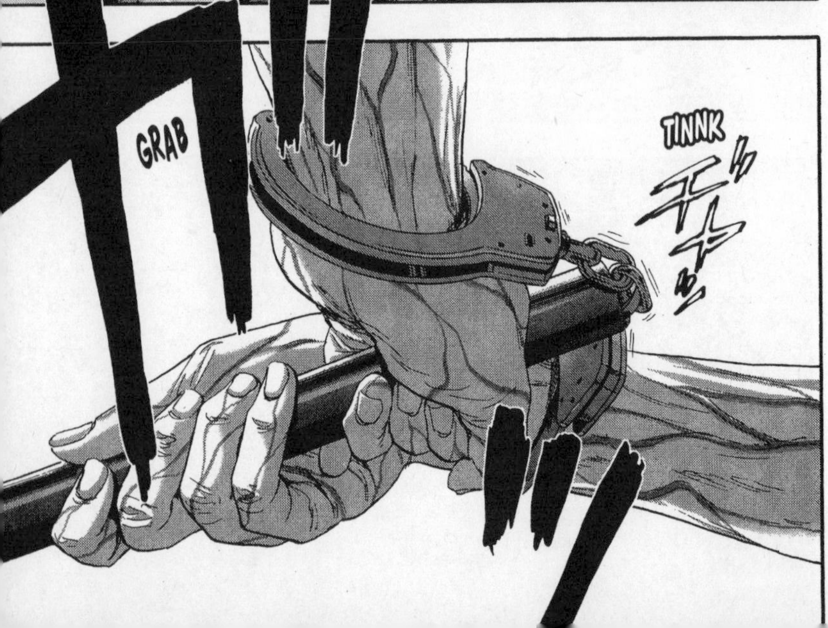
TINNK
GRAB

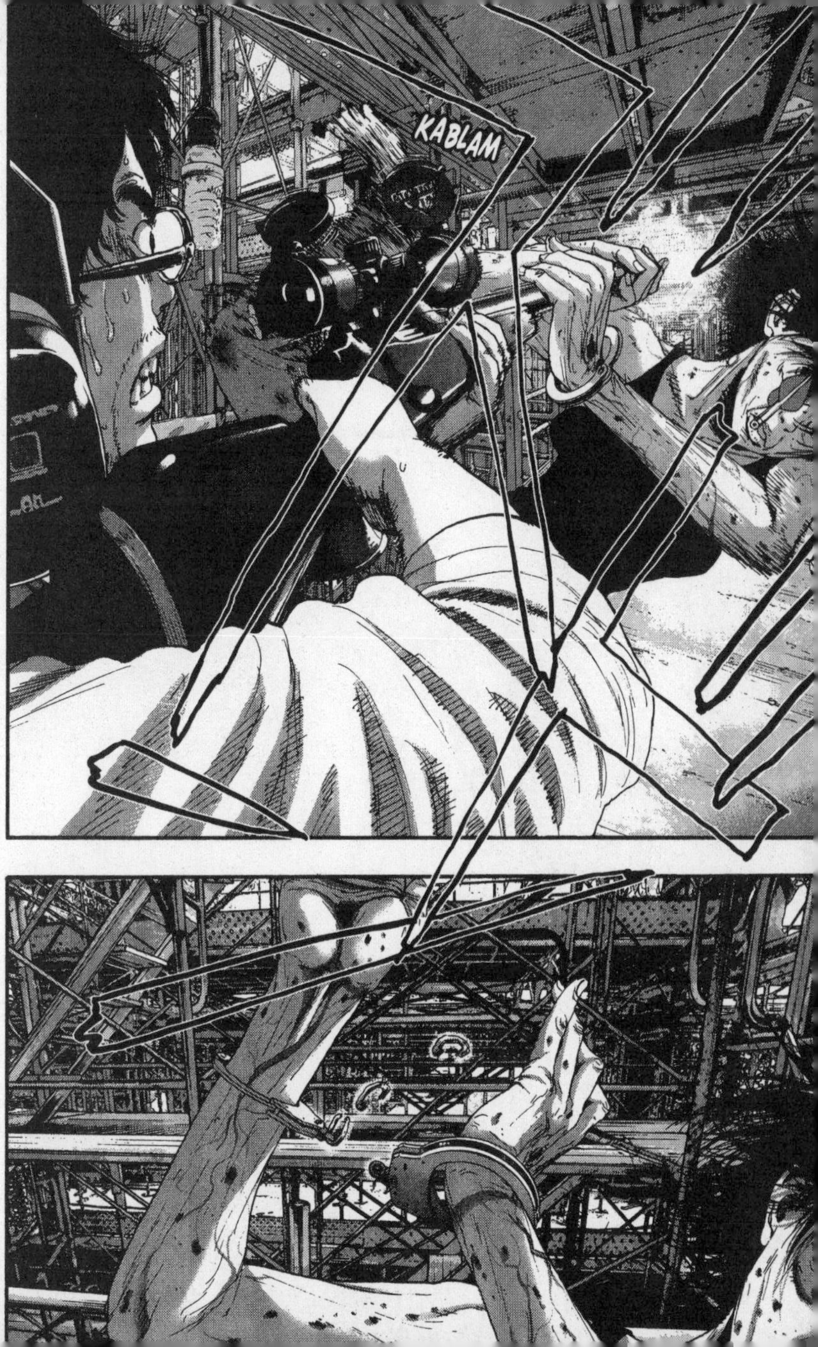
KABLAM

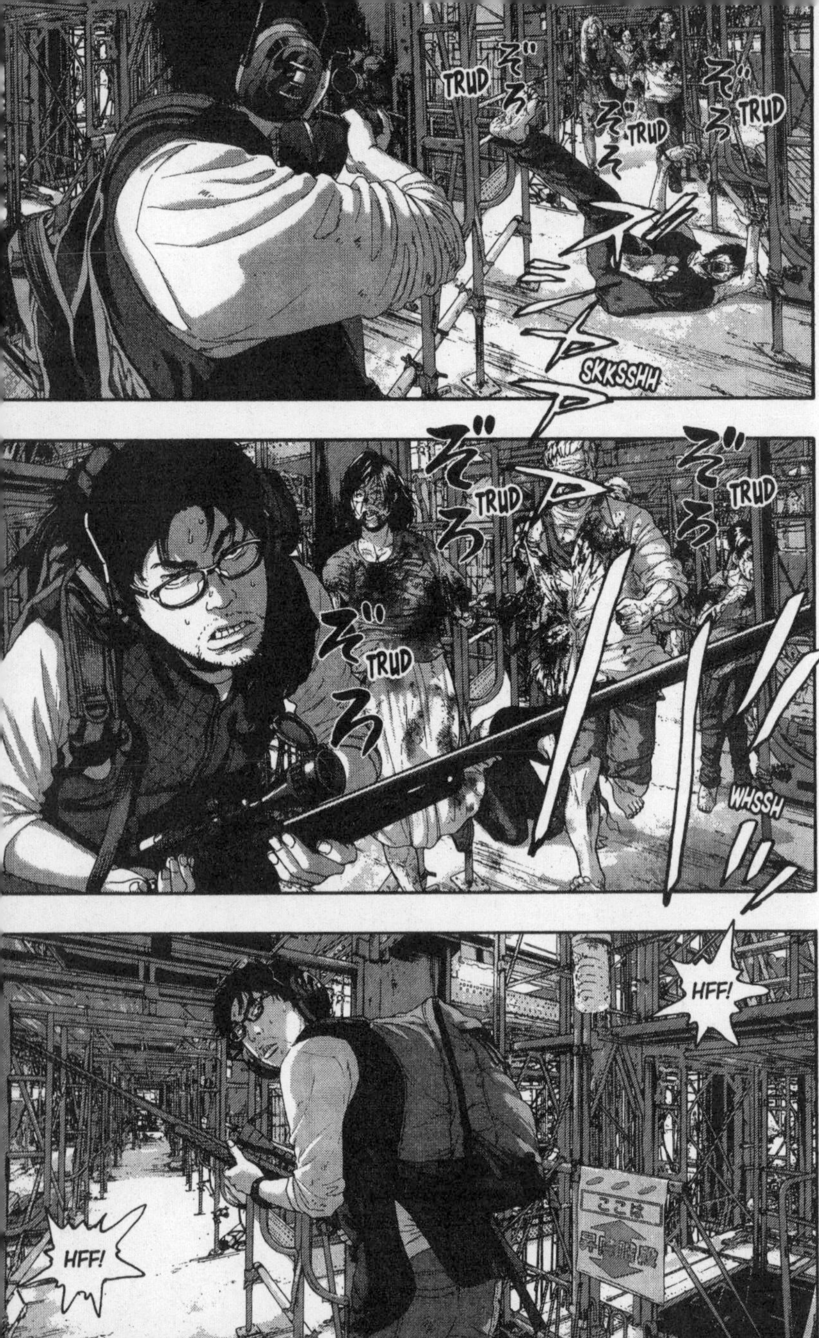
ぞろ
TRUD
ぞろ
TRUD
ぞろ
TRUD
SKKSSHH
ぞろ
TRUD
ぞろ
TRUD
ぞろ
TRUD
WHSSH
HFF!
ここは
HFF!

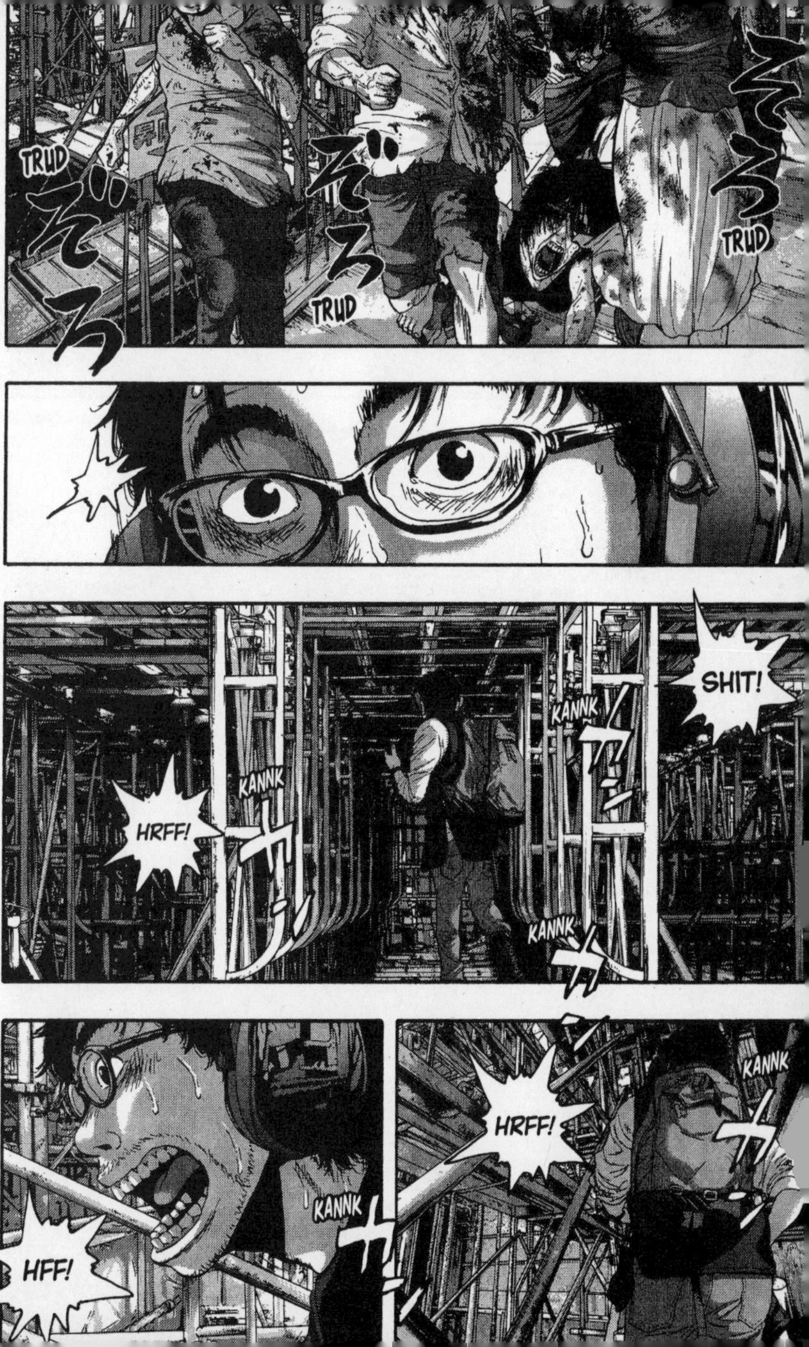
TRUD
TRUD
TRUD
SHIT!
KANNK
KANNK
KANNK
HRFF!
KANNK
HRFF!
KANNK
HFF!

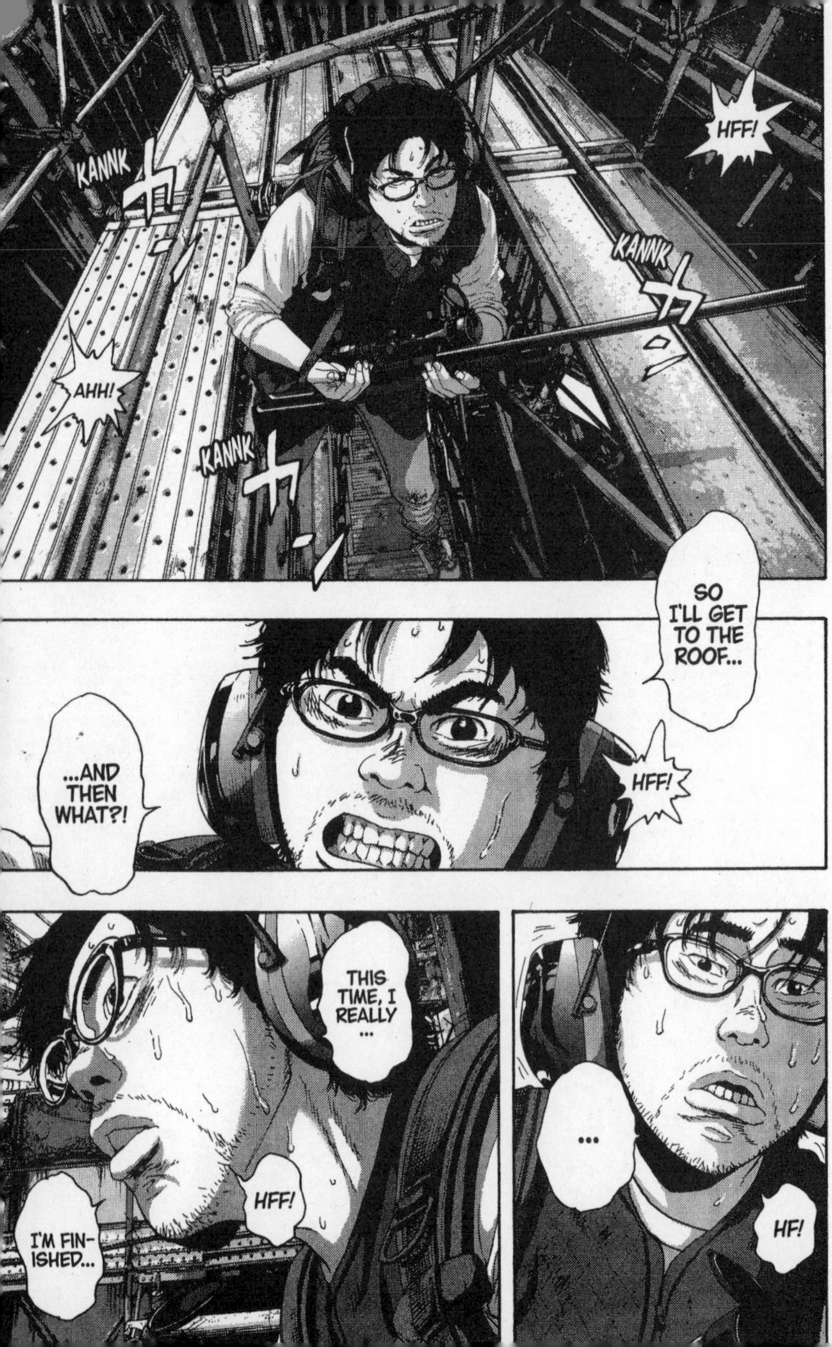
HFF!
KANNK
KANNK
AHH!
KANNK
SO I'LL GET TO THE ROOF...
HFF!
...AND THEN WHAT?!
...
HF!
THIS TIME, I REALLY ...
HFF!
I'M FIN- ISHED...

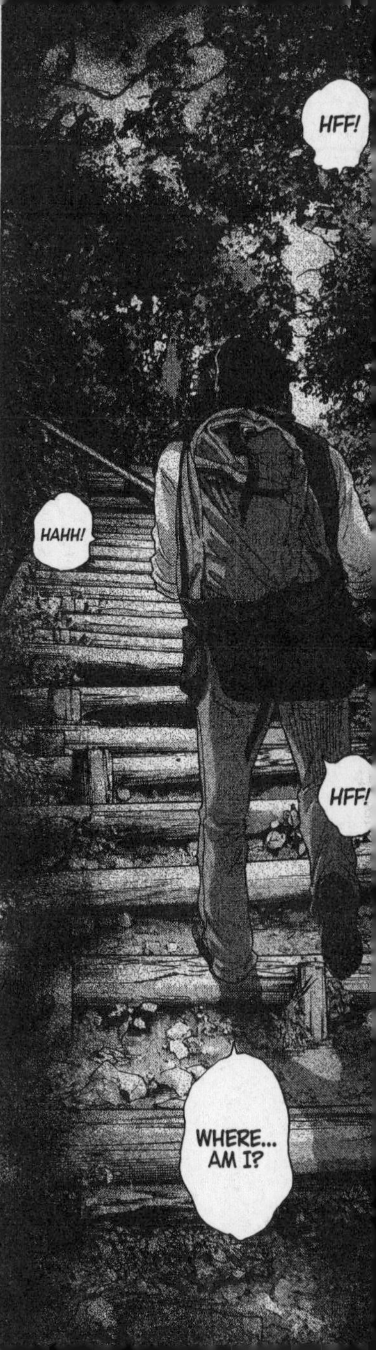
HFF!
HAHH!
HFF!
WHERE... AM I?
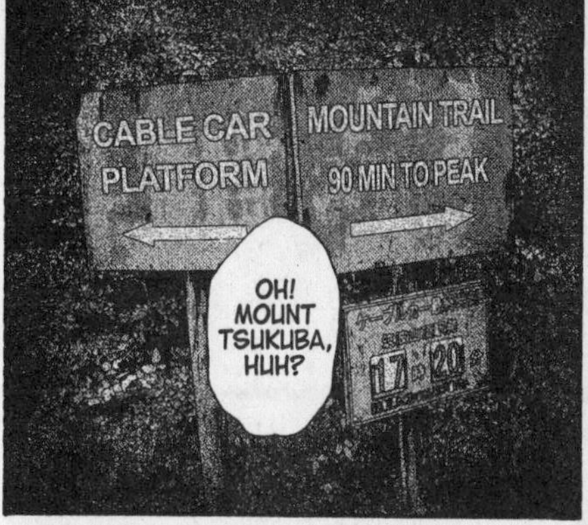
MOUNTAIN TRAIL 90 MIN TO PEAK
CABLE CAR PLATFORM
OH! MOUNT TSUKUBA, HUH?
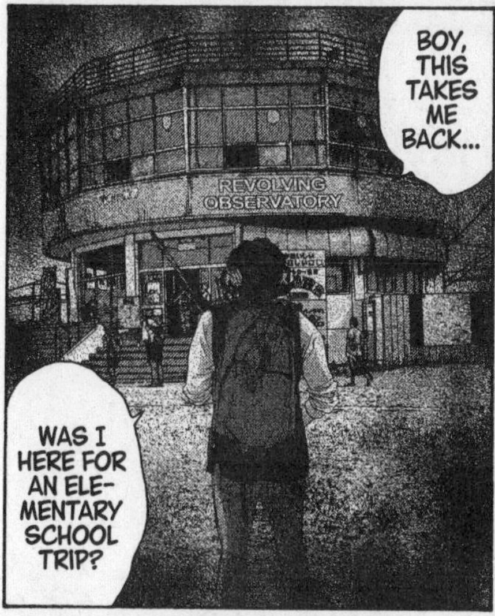
BOY, THIS TAKES ME BACK...
REVOLVING OBSERVATORY
WAS I HERE FOR AN ELE-MENTARY SCHOOL TRIP?
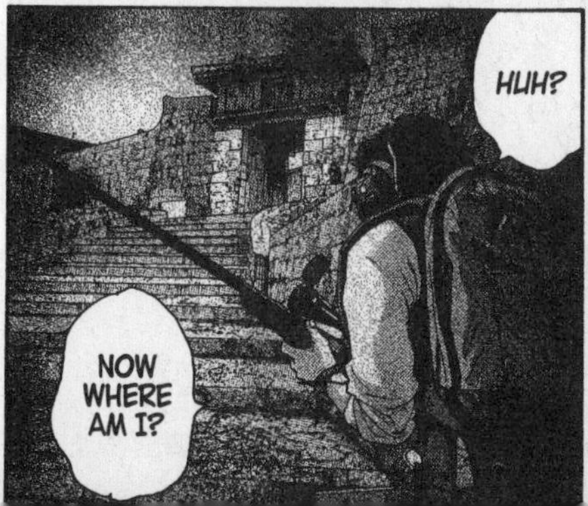
HUH?
NOW WHERE AM I?

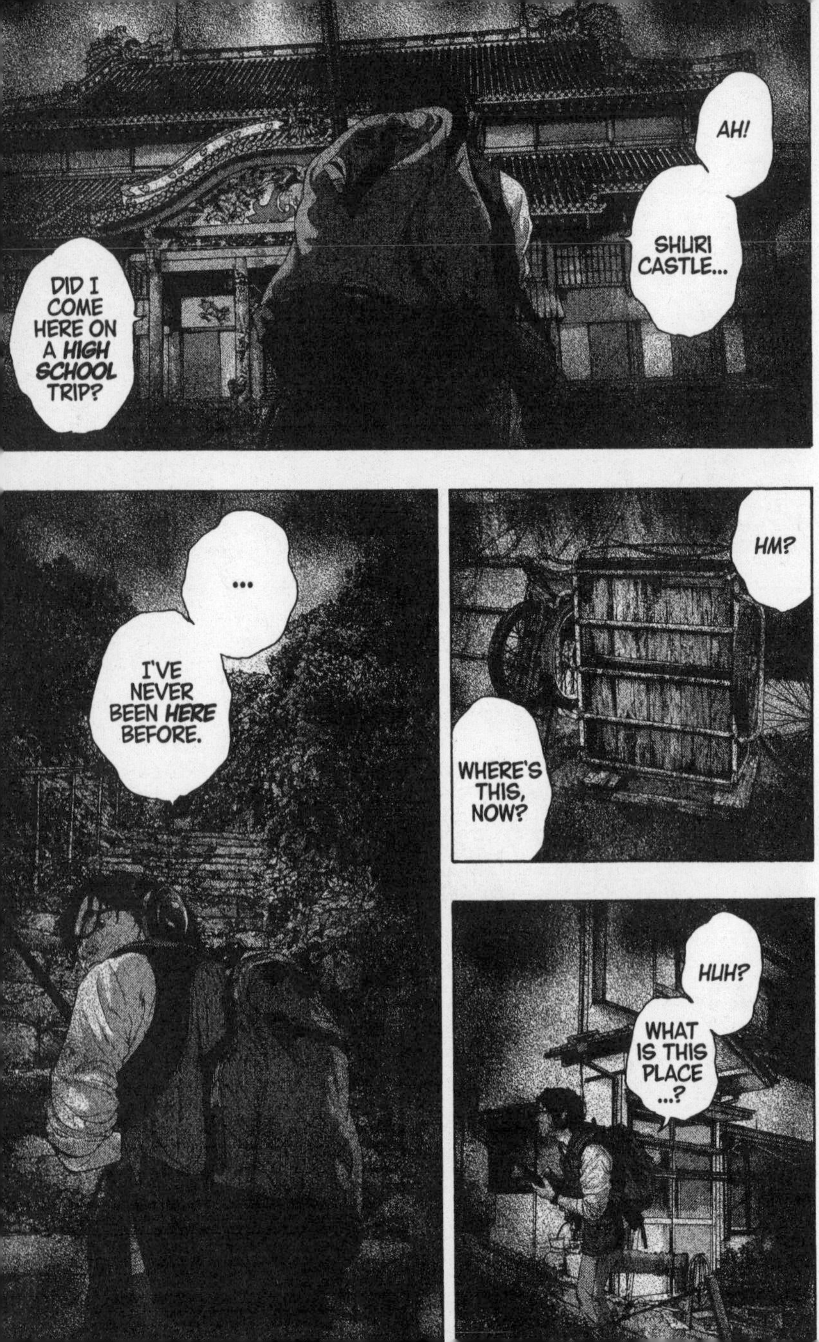
AH!
SHURI CASTLE...
DID I COME HERE ON A HIGH SCHOOL TRIP?
HM?
WHERE'S THIS, NOW?
HUH?
WHAT IS THIS PLACE ...?
...
I'VE NEVER BEEN HERE BEFORE.

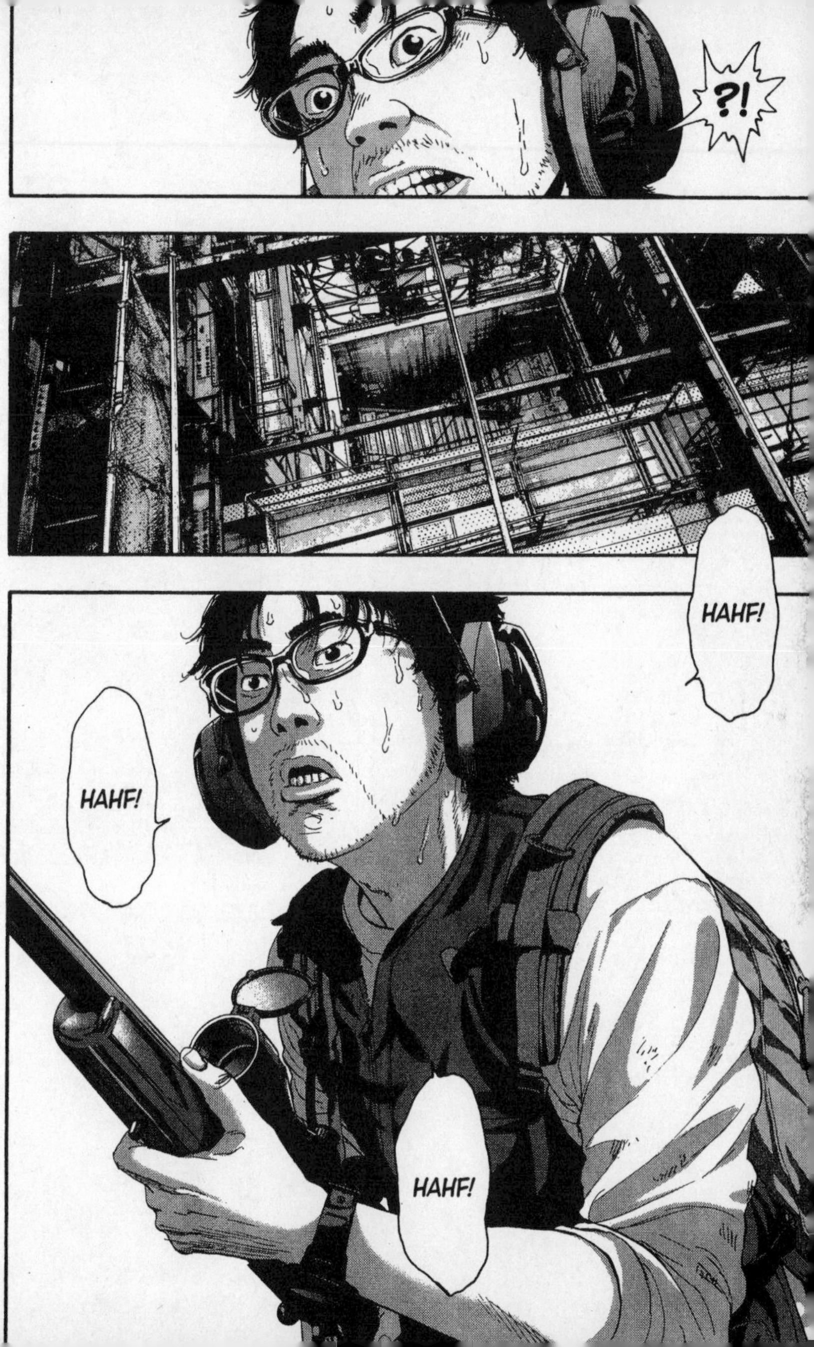
?!
HAHF!
HAHF!
HAHF!

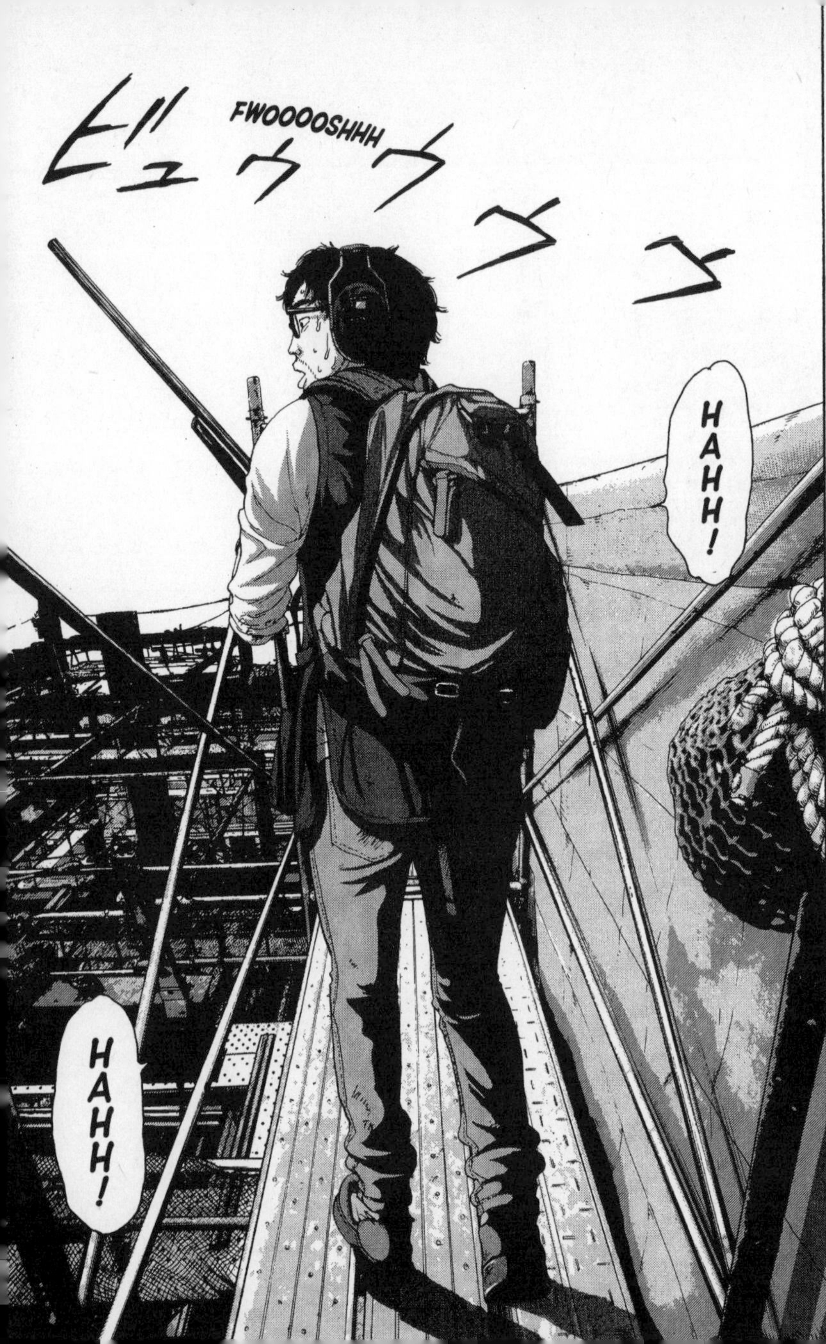
FWOOOOSHHH
HAHH!
HAHH!

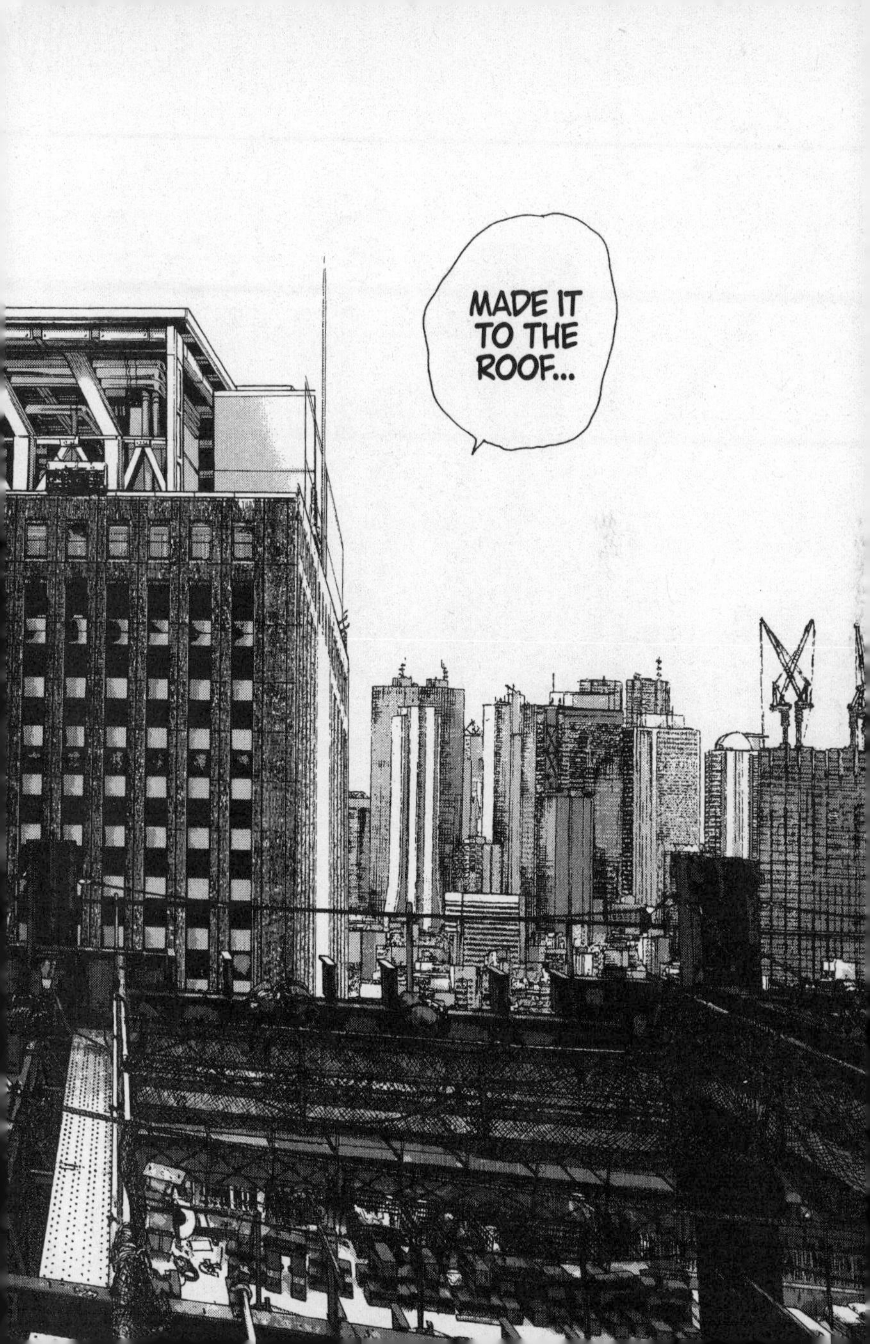
MADE IT TO THE ROOF...

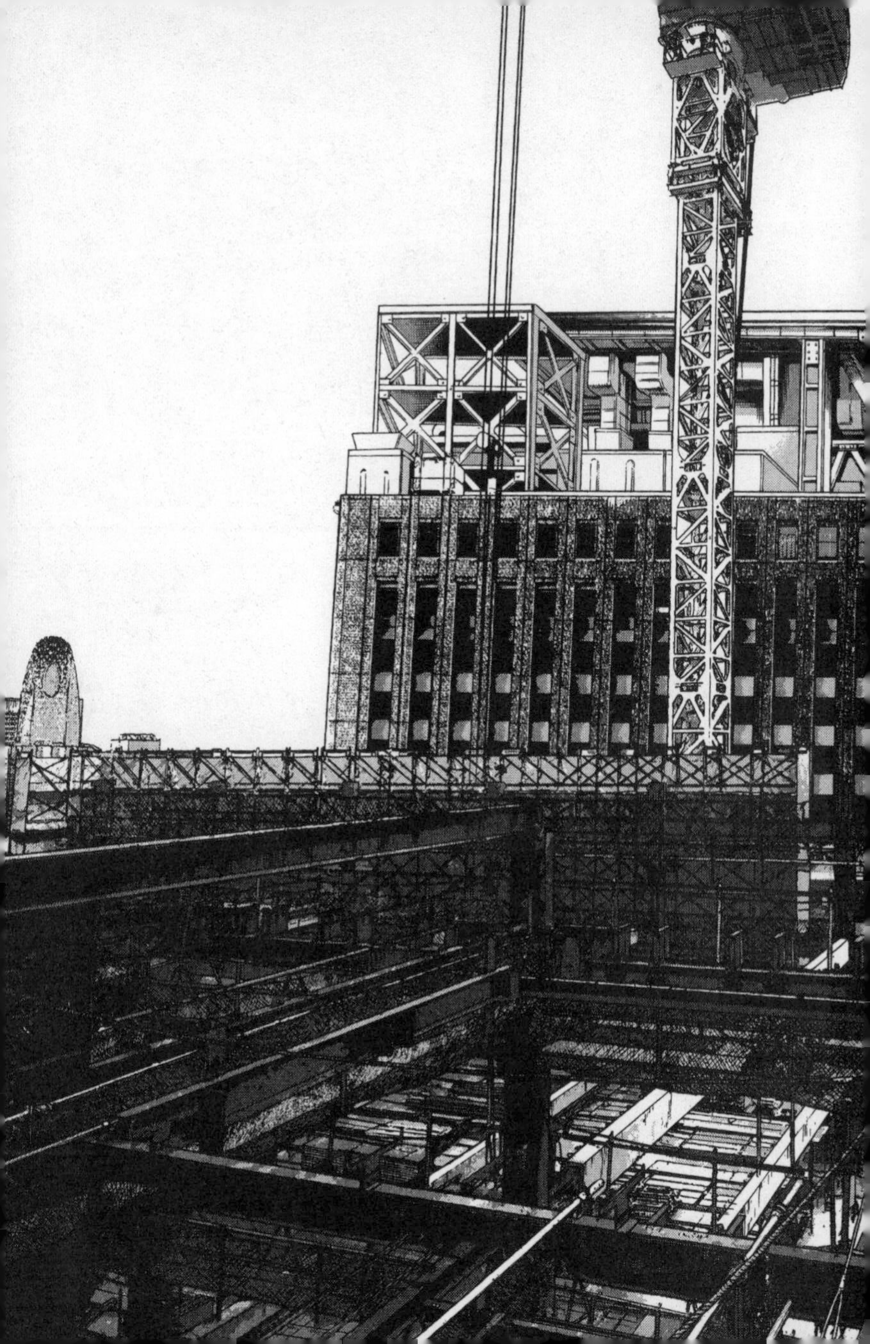

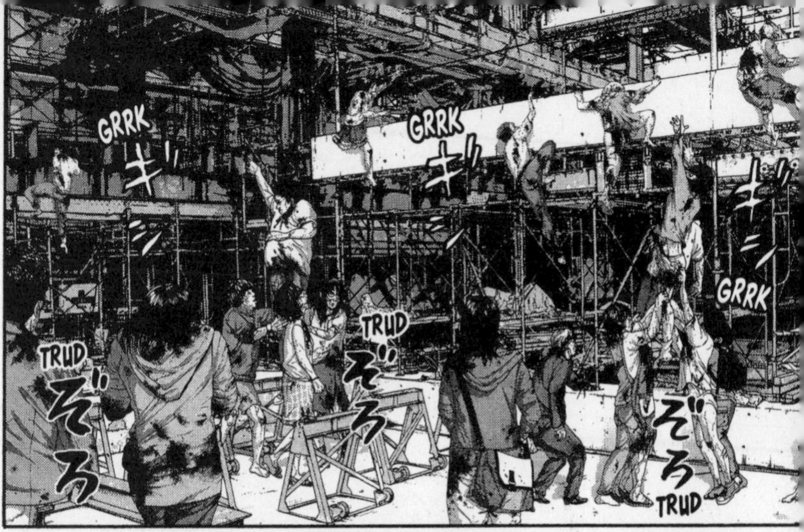
GRRK
GRRK
GRRK
TRUD
ぞろ
TRUD
ぞろ
TRUD
ぞろ
TRUD
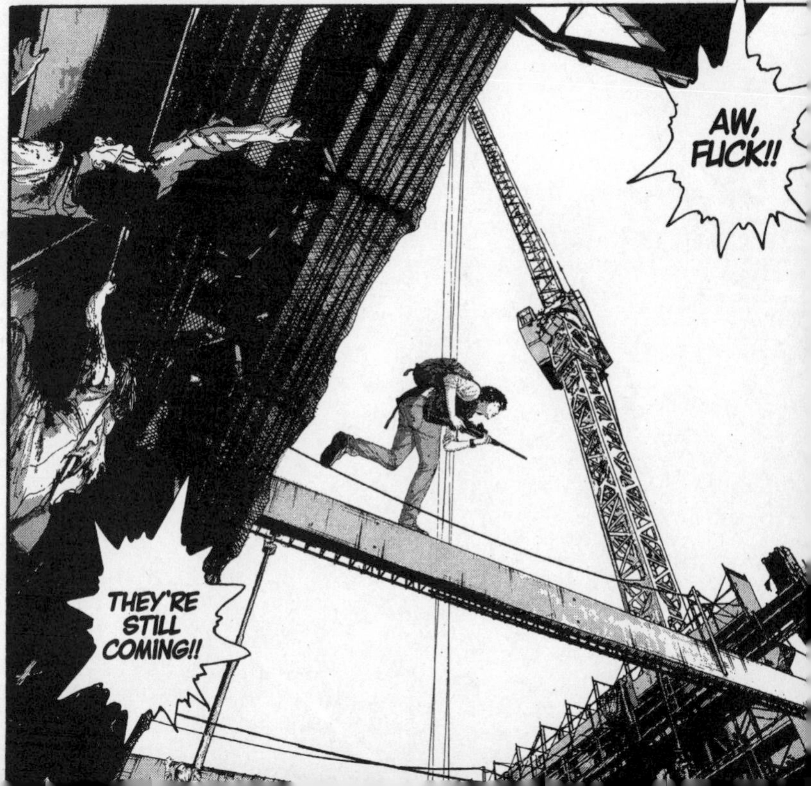
AW, FUCK!!
THEY'RE STILL COMING!!

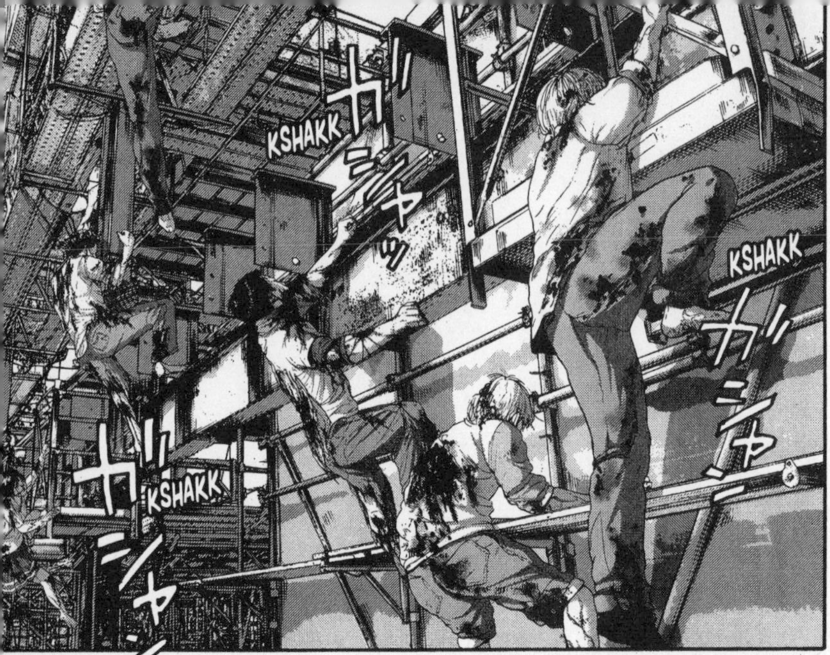
KSHAKK
KSHAKK
KSHAKK

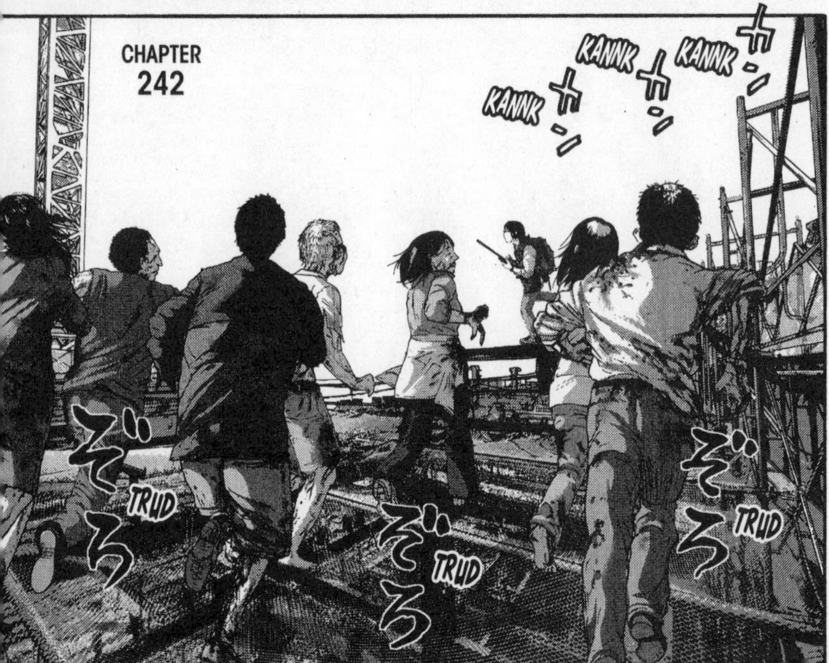
CHAPTER 242
カーン
KANNK
カーン
KANNK
カーン
KANNK
ぞろ
TRUD
ぞろ
TRUD
ぞろ
TRUD

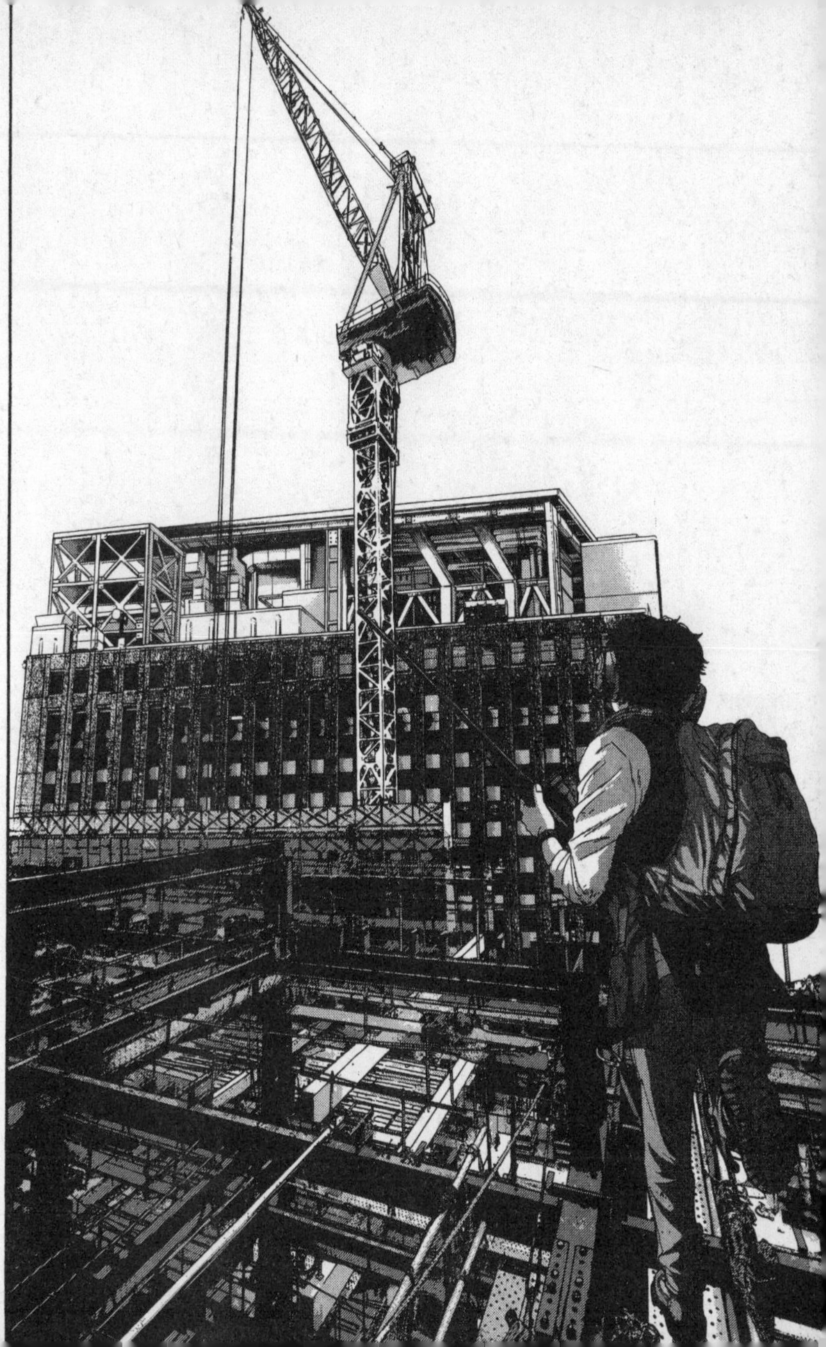

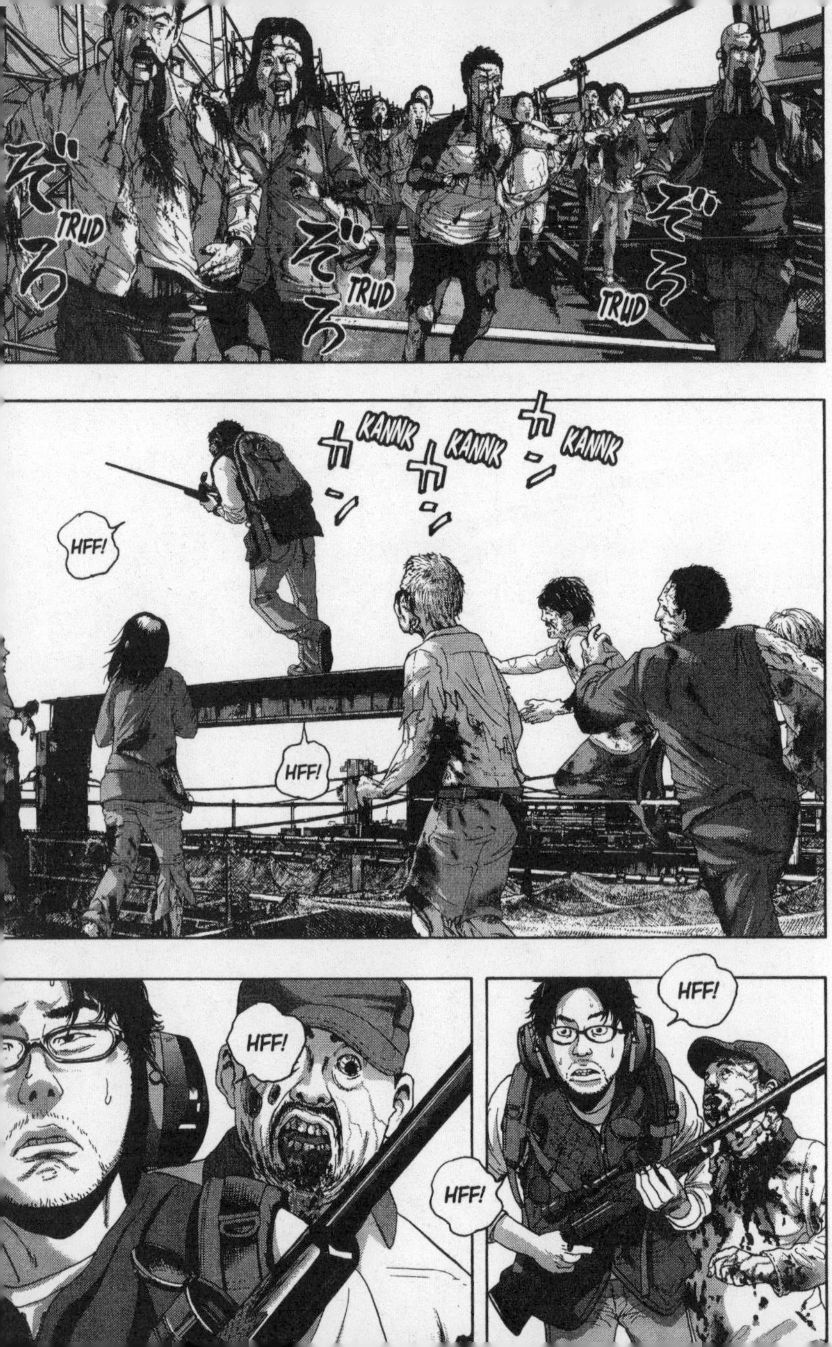
ぞろ
TRUD
ぞろ
TRUD
ぞろ
TRUD
カーン
KANNK
カーン
KANNK
カーン
KANNK
HFF!
HFF!
HFF!
HFF!
HFF!

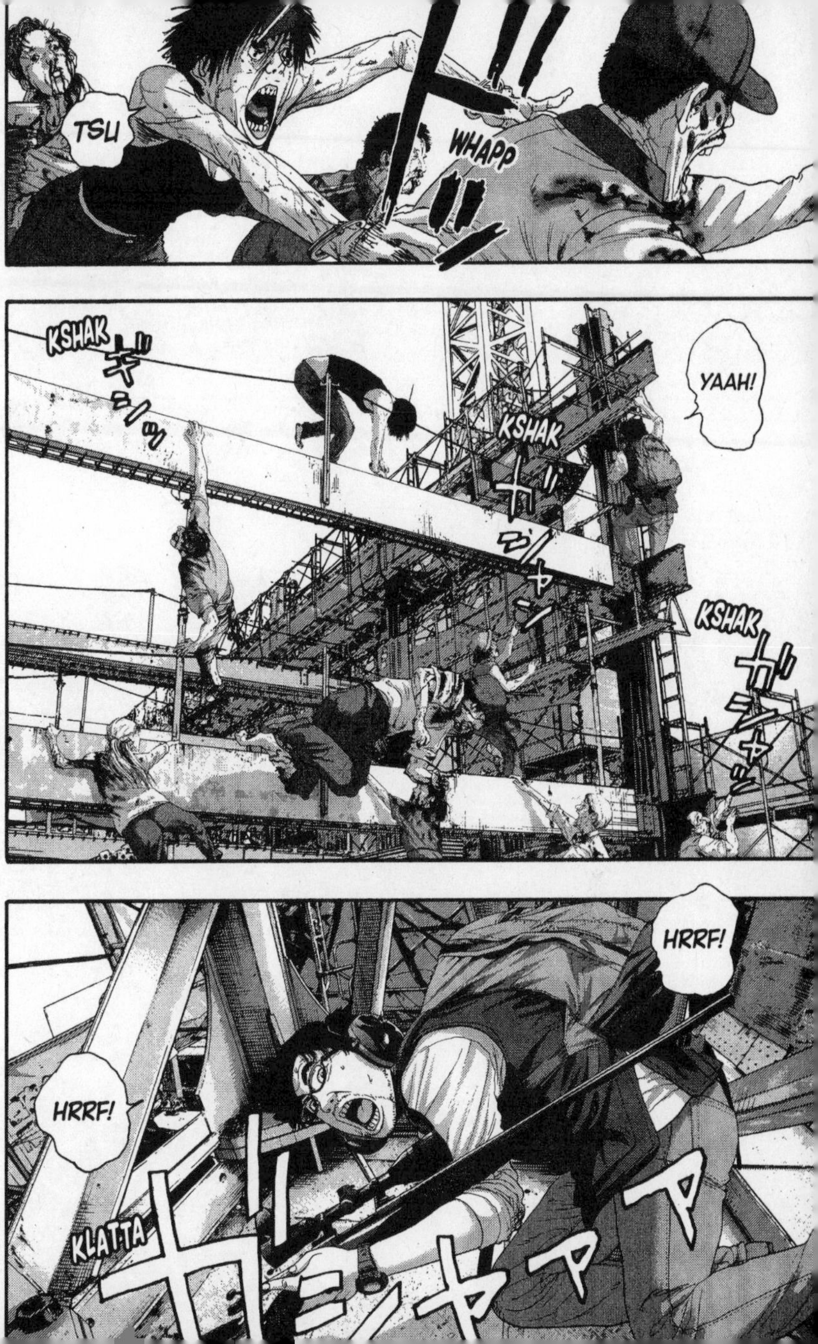
WHAPP
TSU
YAAH!
KSHAK
KSHAK
KSHAK
HRRF!
HRRF!
KLATTA

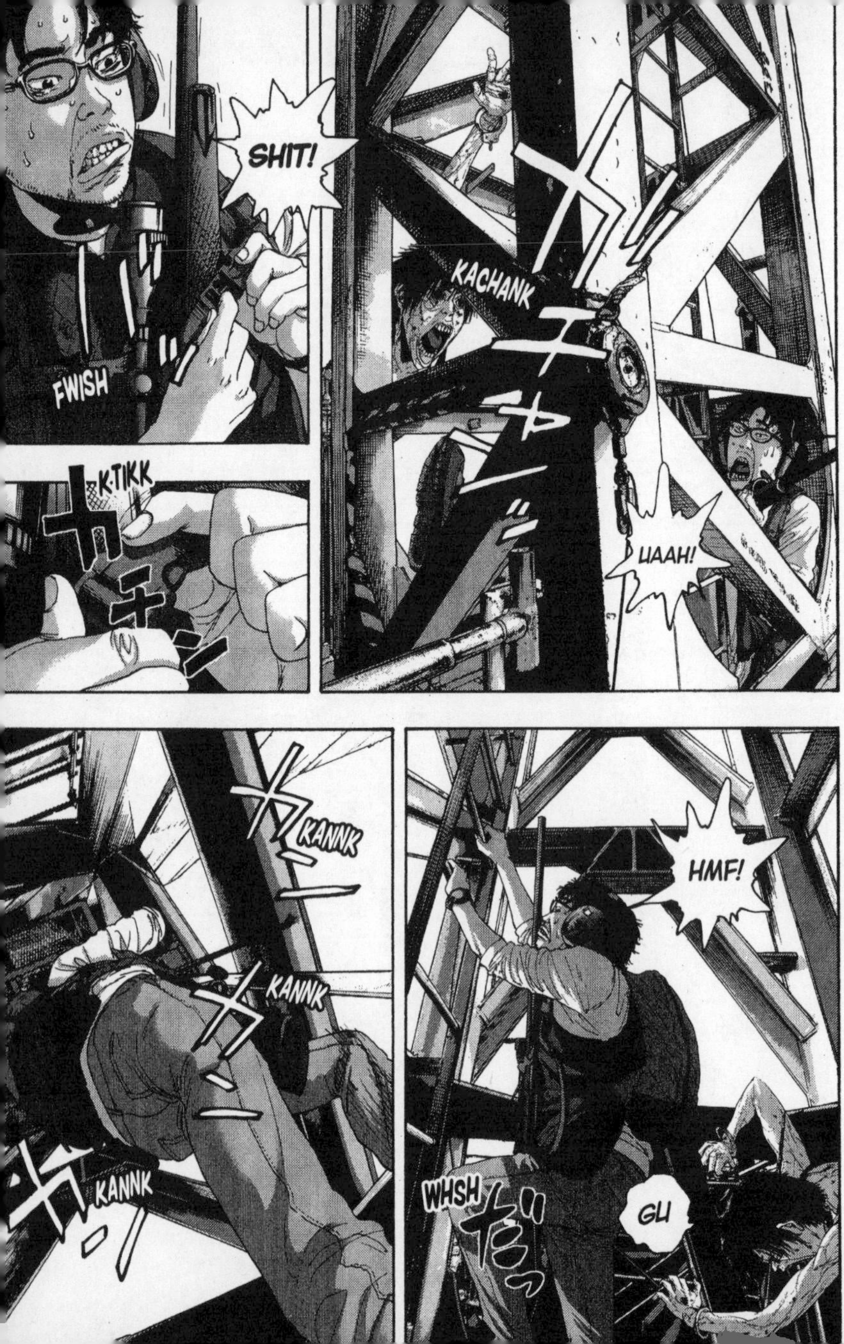
KACHANK
UAAH!
SHIT!
FWISH
K-TIKK
HMF!
GU
WHSH
KANNK
KANNK
KANNK

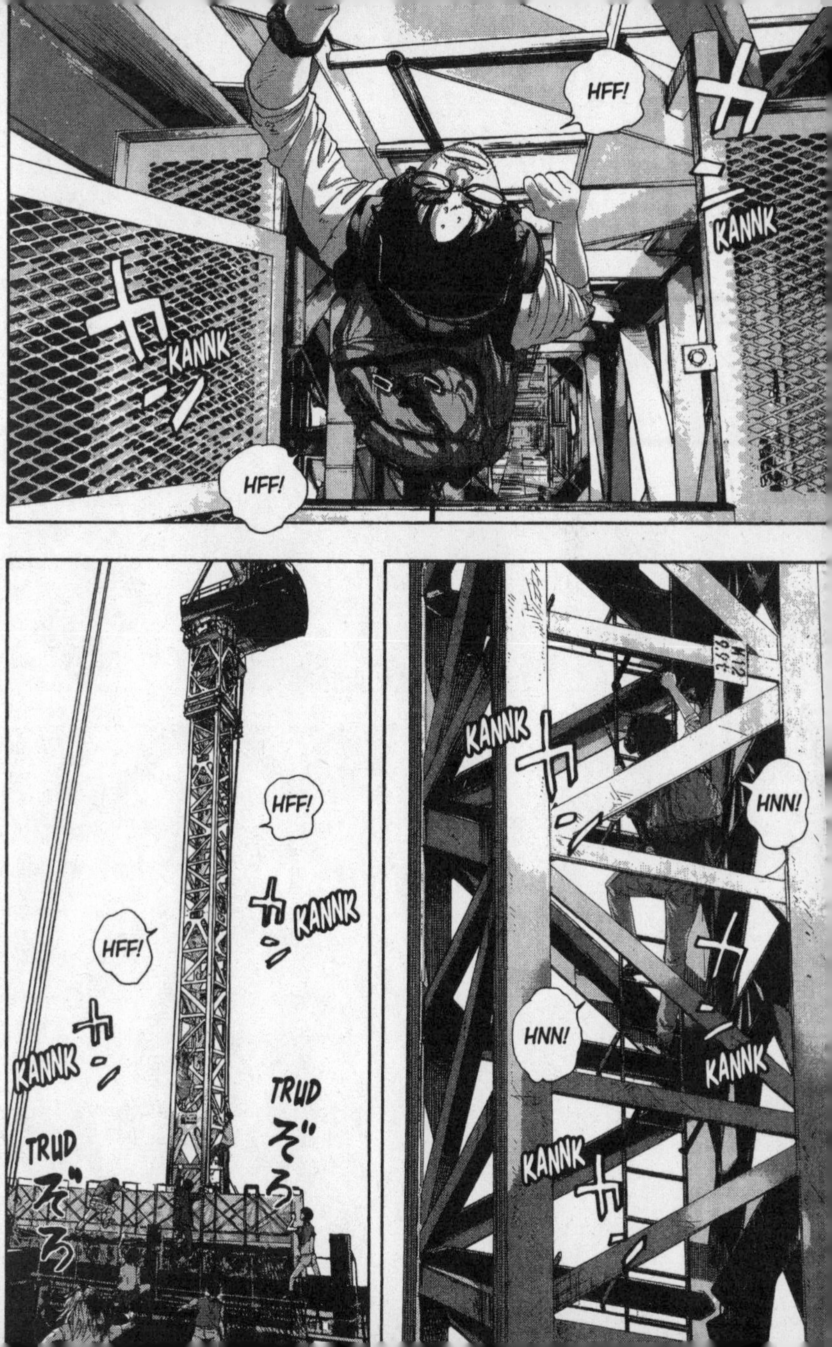
HFF!
KANNK
KANNK
HFF!
KANNK
HNN!
HNN!
KANNK
KANNK
HFF!
KANNK
HFF!
KANNK
TRUD
ぞろ
TRUD
ぞろ

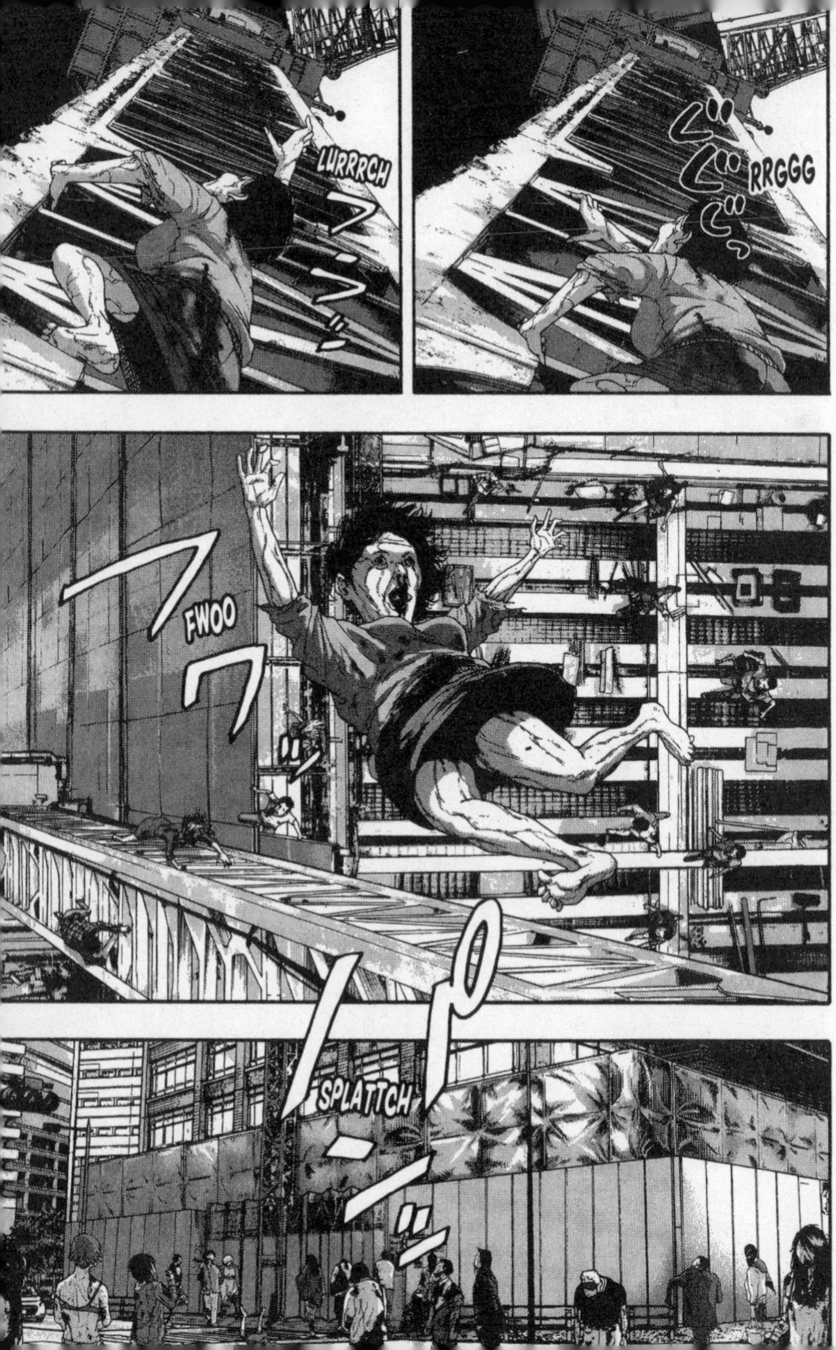
RRGGG
LURRRCH
FWOO
SPLATTCH

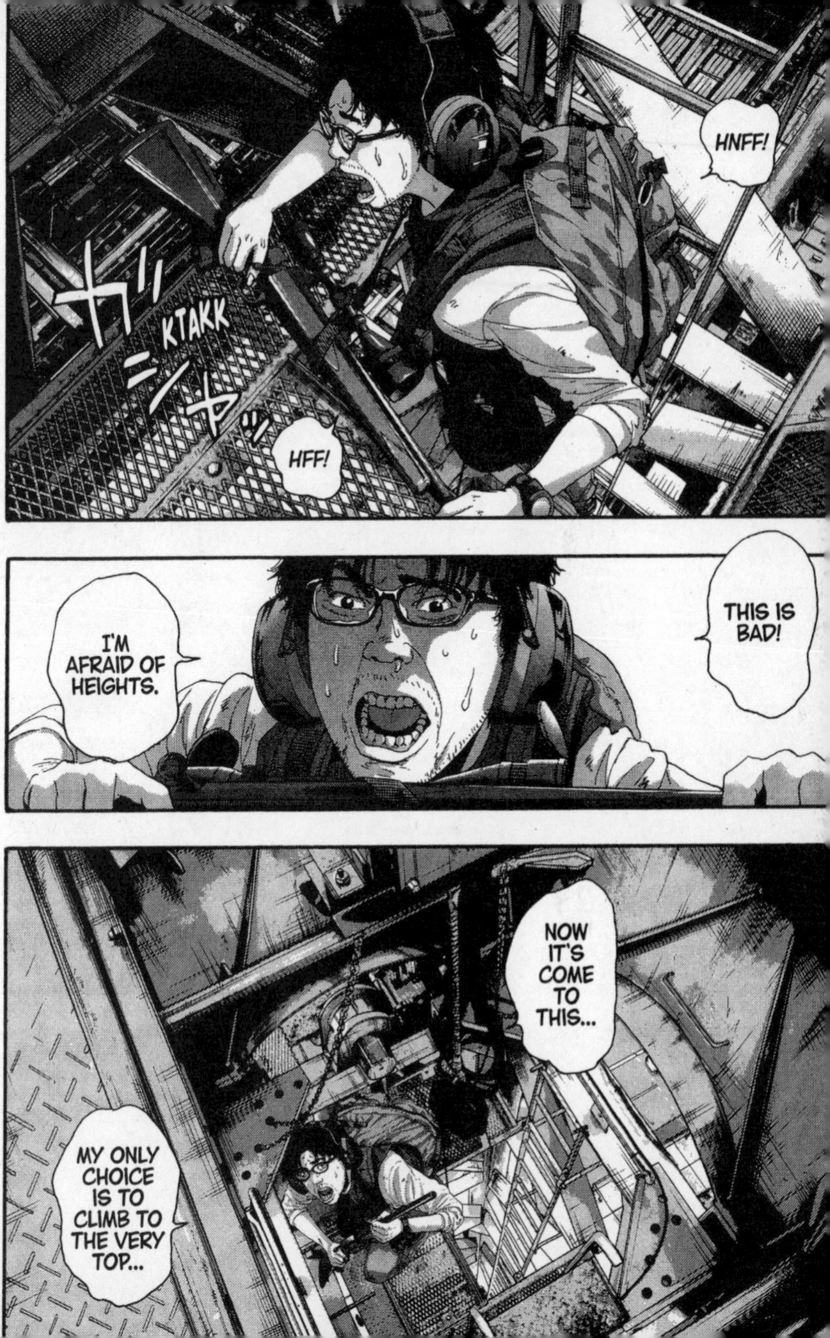
HNFF!
KTAKK
HFF!
THIS IS BAD!
I'M AFRAID OF HEIGHTS.
NOW IT'S COME TO THIS...
MY ONLY CHOICE IS TO CLIMB TO THE VERY TOP...

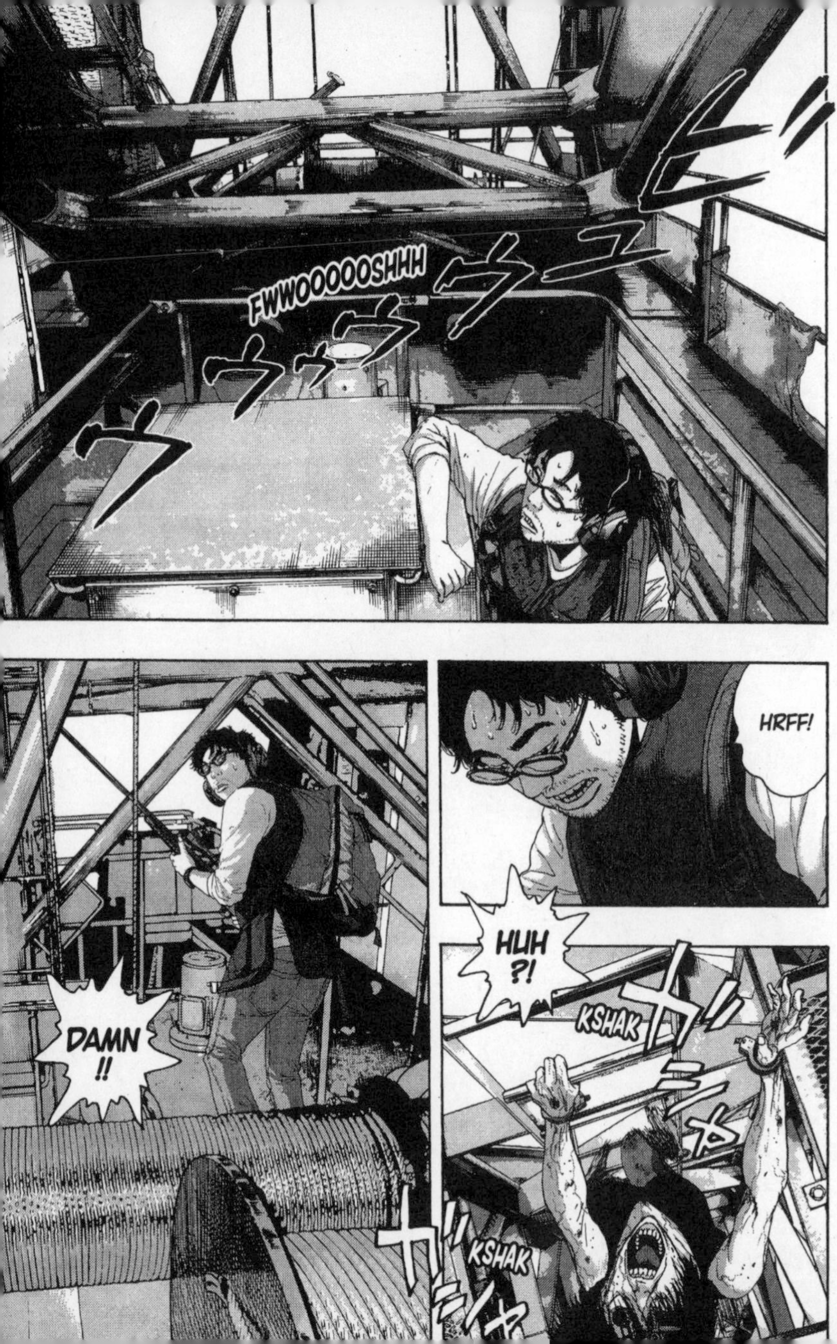
FWWOOOOOSHHH
HRFF!
HUH ?!
KSHAK
KSHAK
DAMN !!

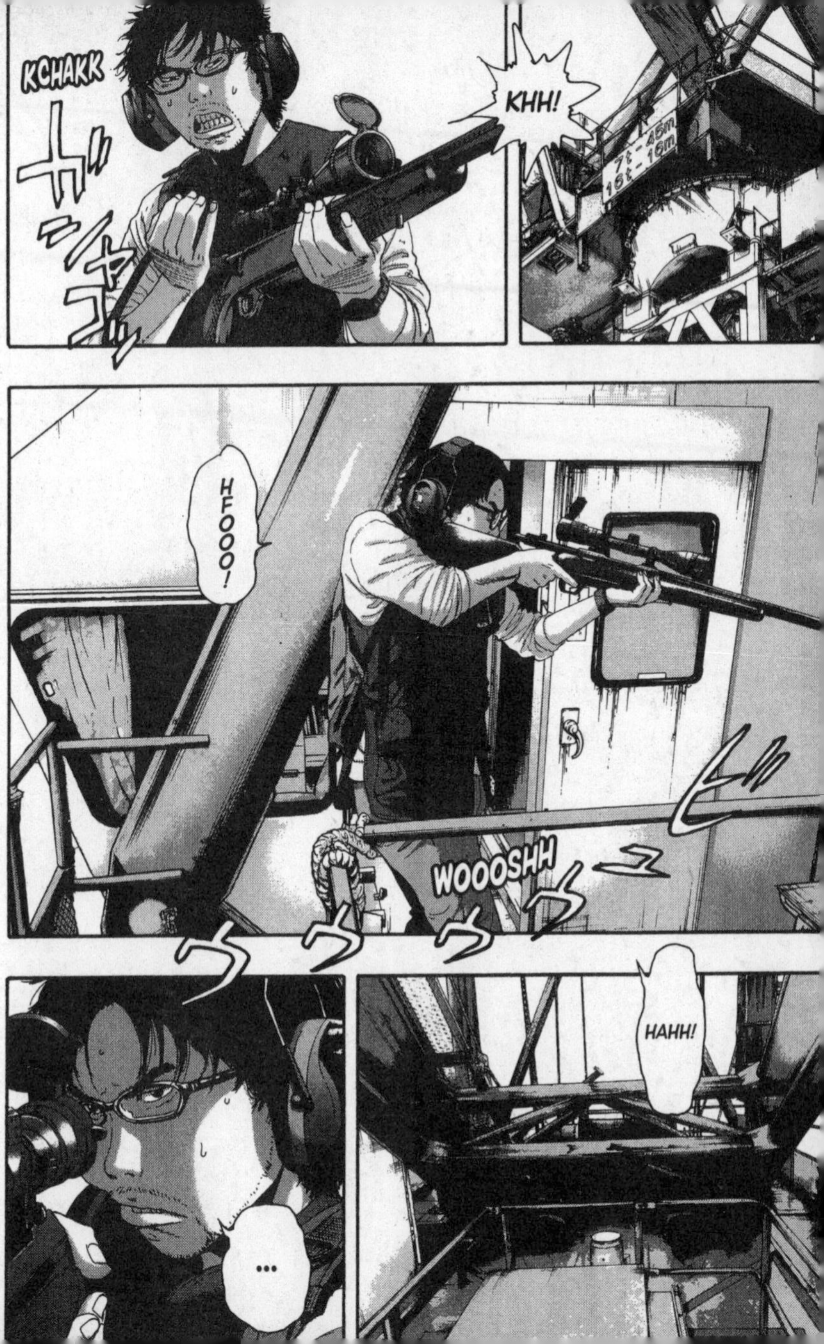
KHH!
KCHAKK
HFOOO!
WOOOSHH
HAHH!
...

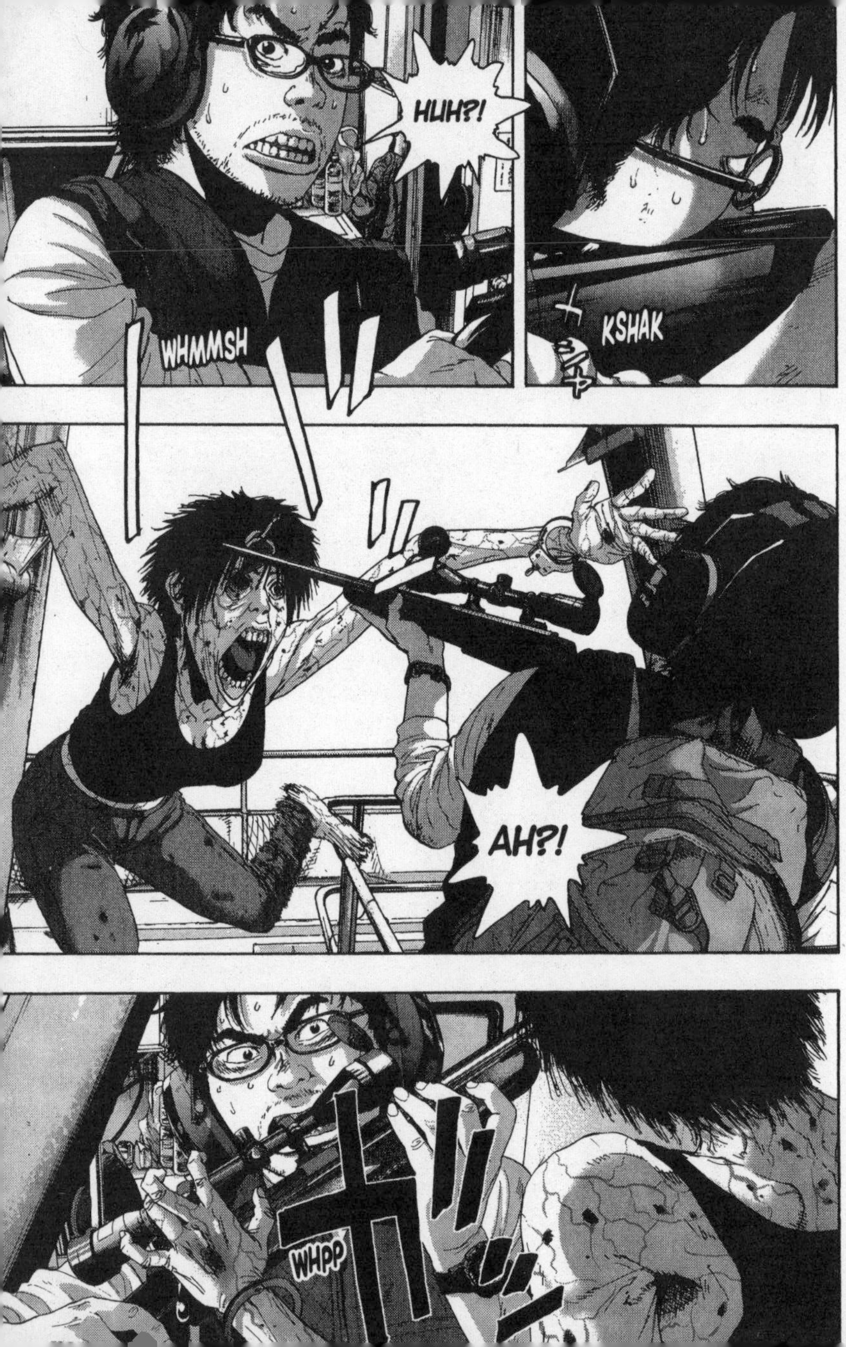
KSHAK
HUH?!
WHMMSH
AH?!
WHPP

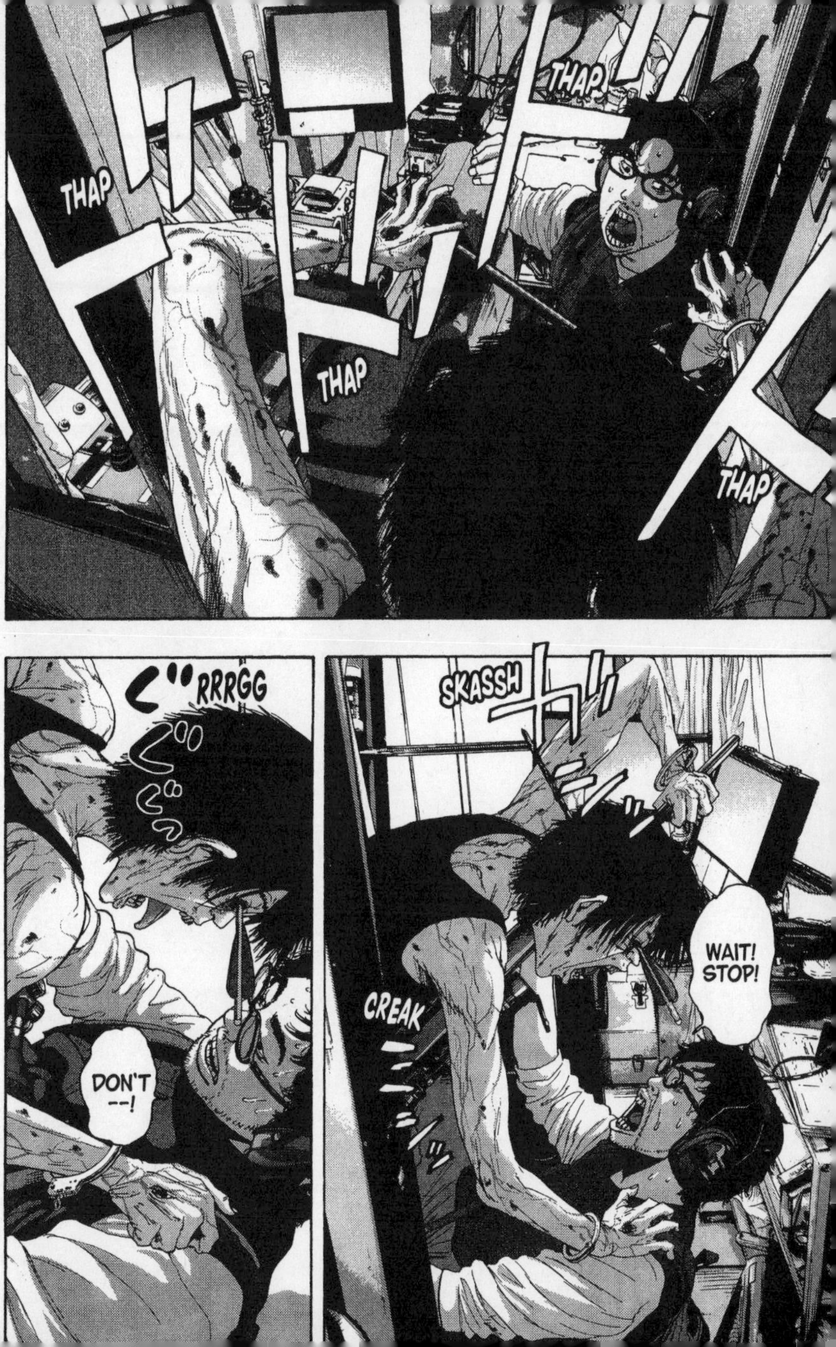
THAP
THAP
THAP
THAP
SKASSH
WAIT! STOP!
CREAK
RRRGG
DON'T --!

MI
ぎしっ GRIK
ぎしっ GRIK
YOW! OW! OW!
ぎしっ GRIK
くっ KRIK
くっ KRIK
くっ KRIK
!!!
THIS TIME I'M GOING TO DIE!
I'M GOING TO DIE FOR SURE!
GRAHH
HELP M--

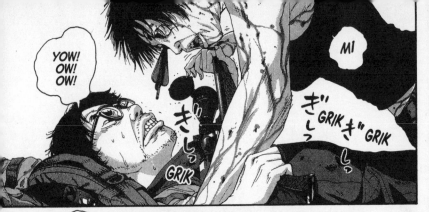

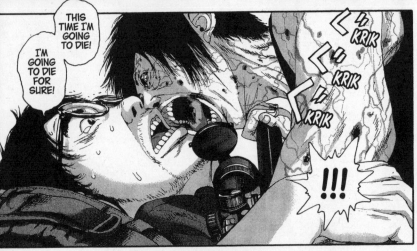

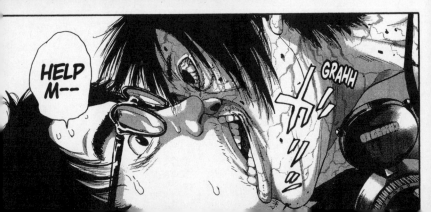

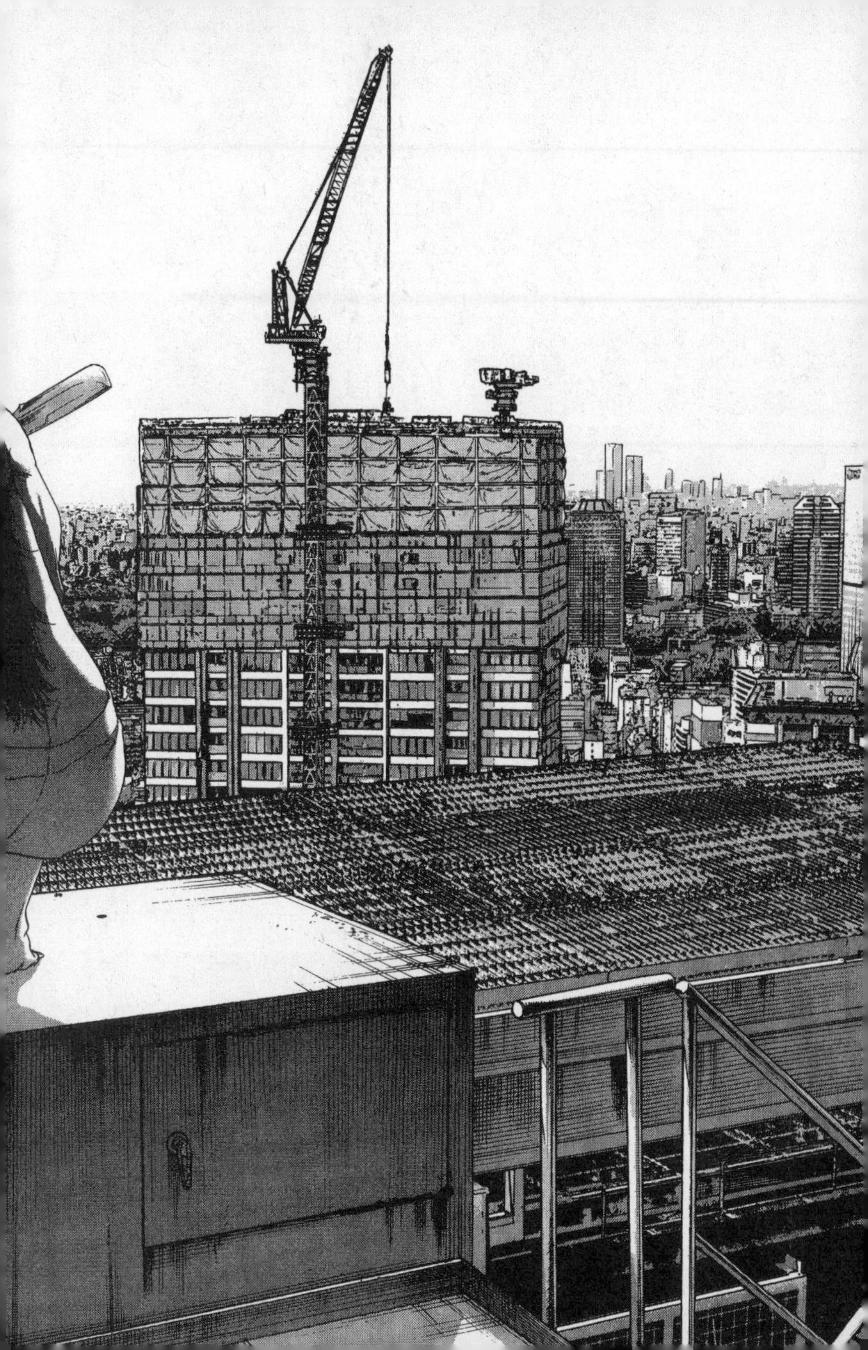

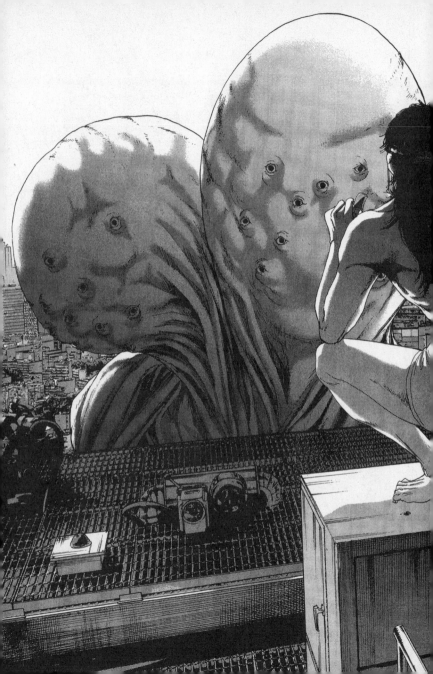

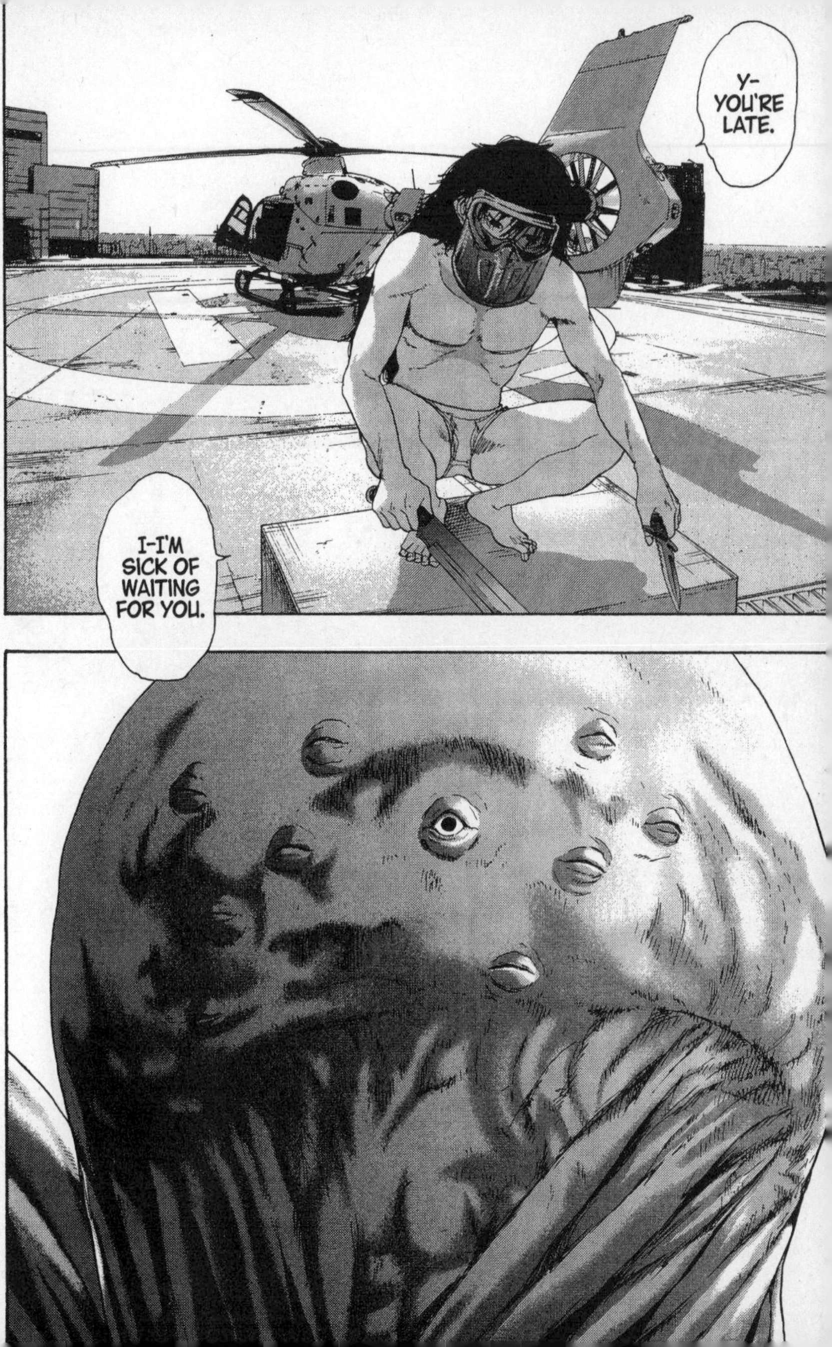
Y- YOU'RE LATE.
I-I'M SICK OF WAITING FOR YOU.

I AM
A HERO

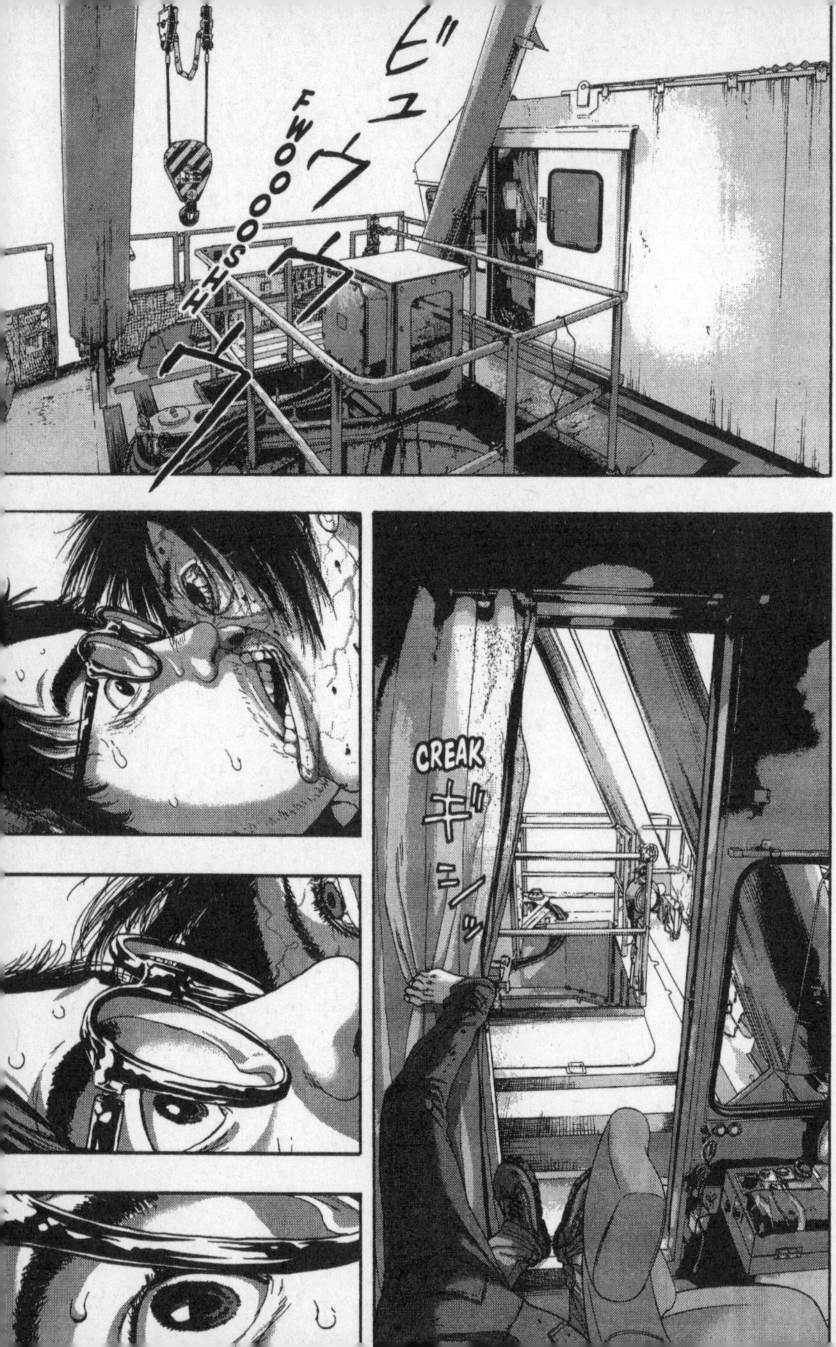
ビュウウウウ
FWOOOOSHH
CREAK

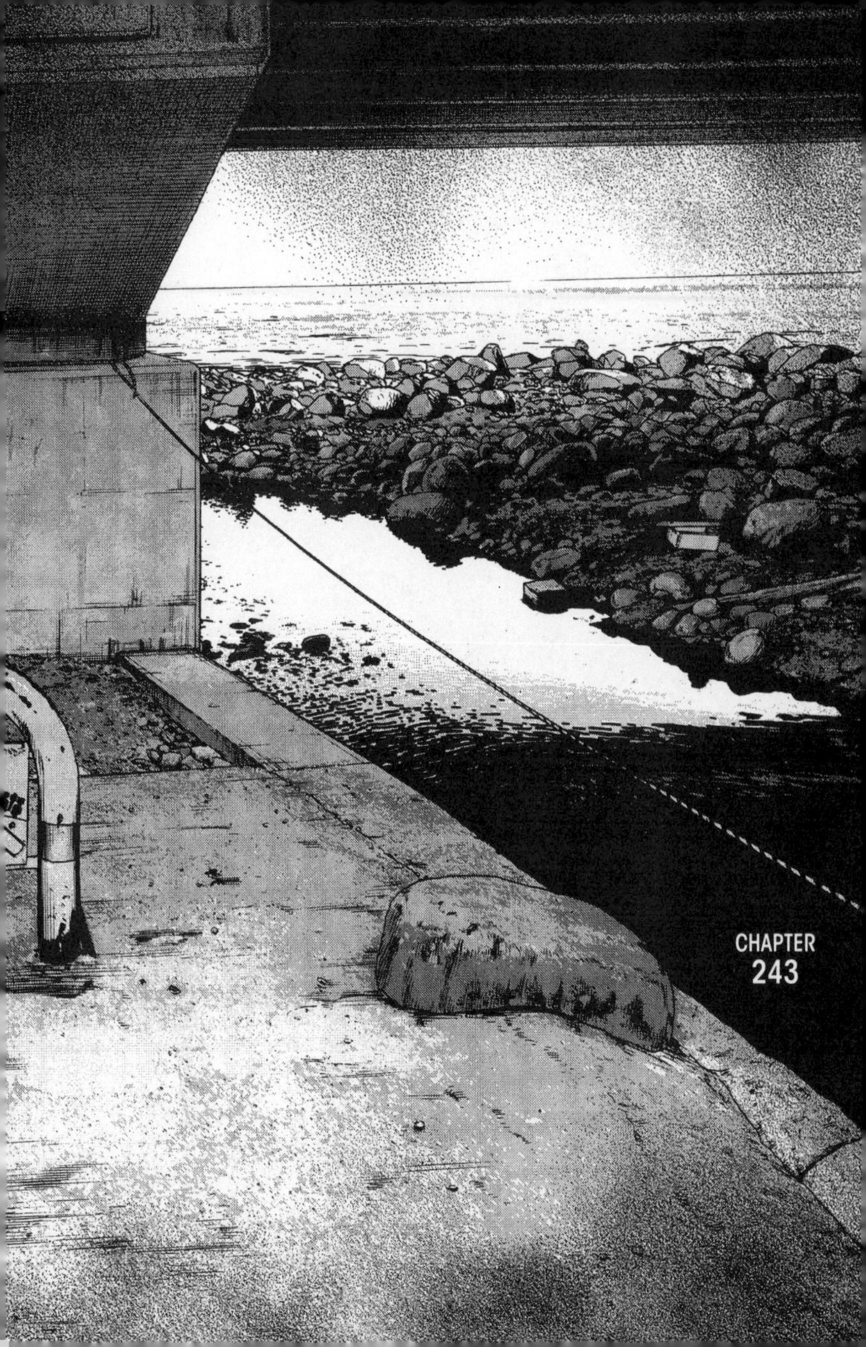
CHAPTER
243

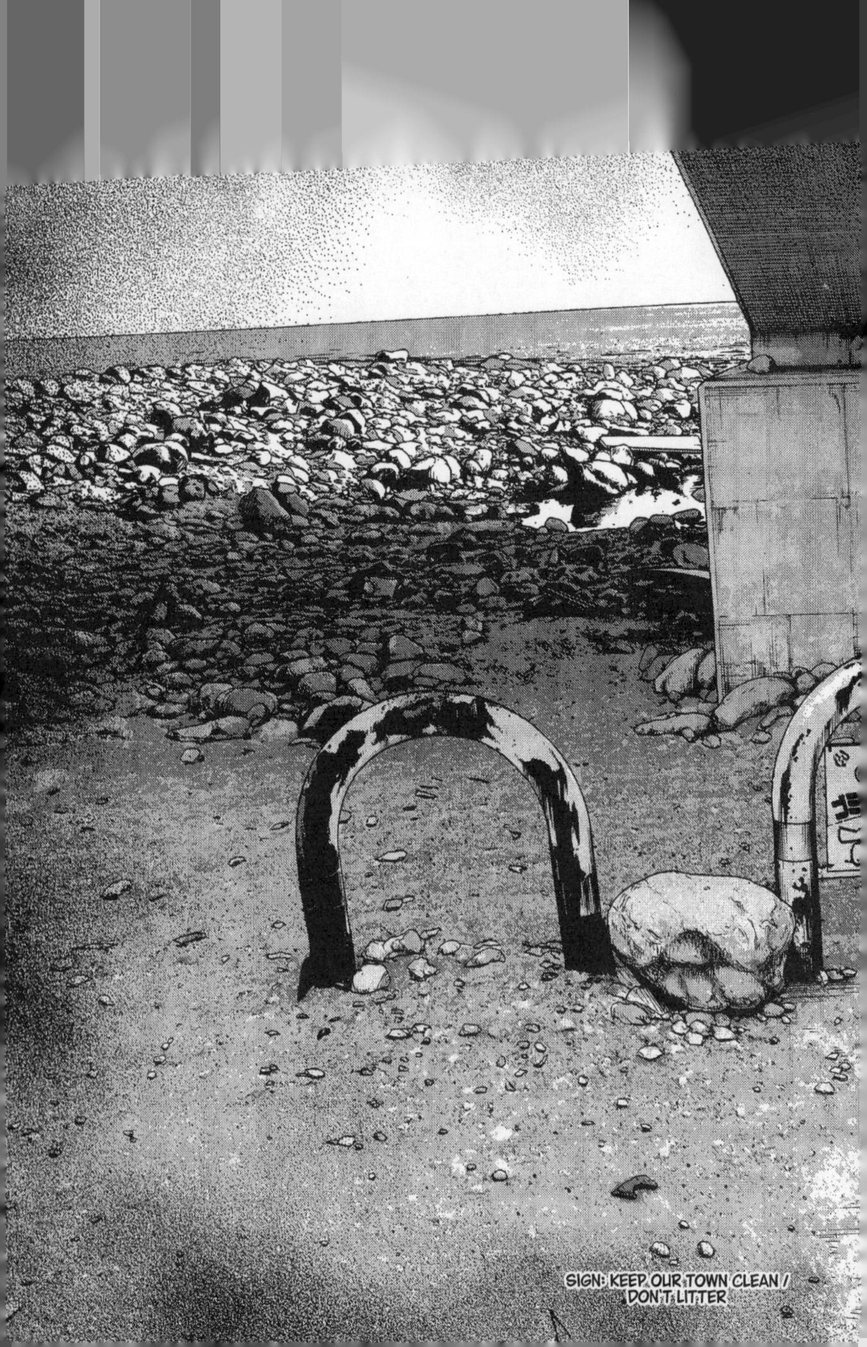
SIGN: KEEP OUR TOWN CLEAN / DON'T LITTER

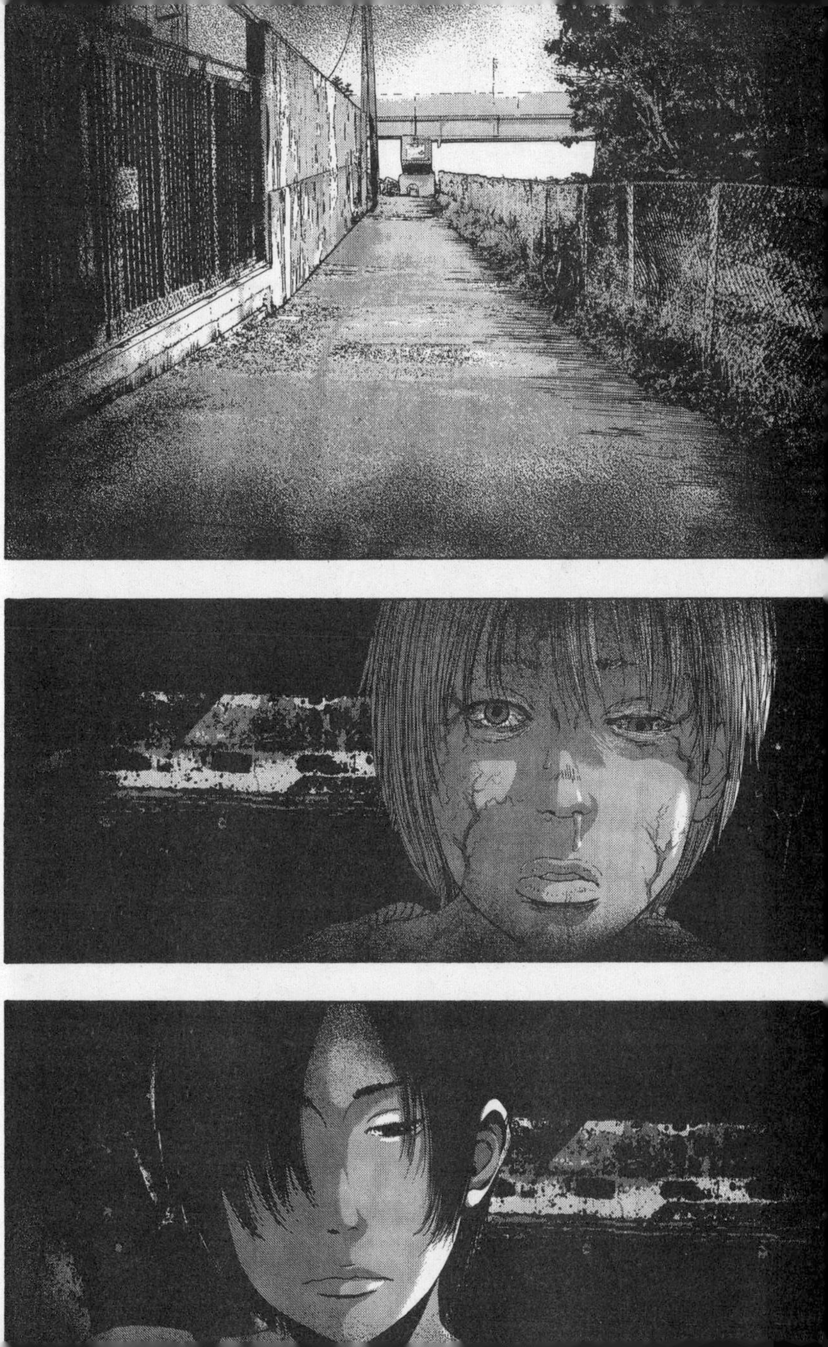

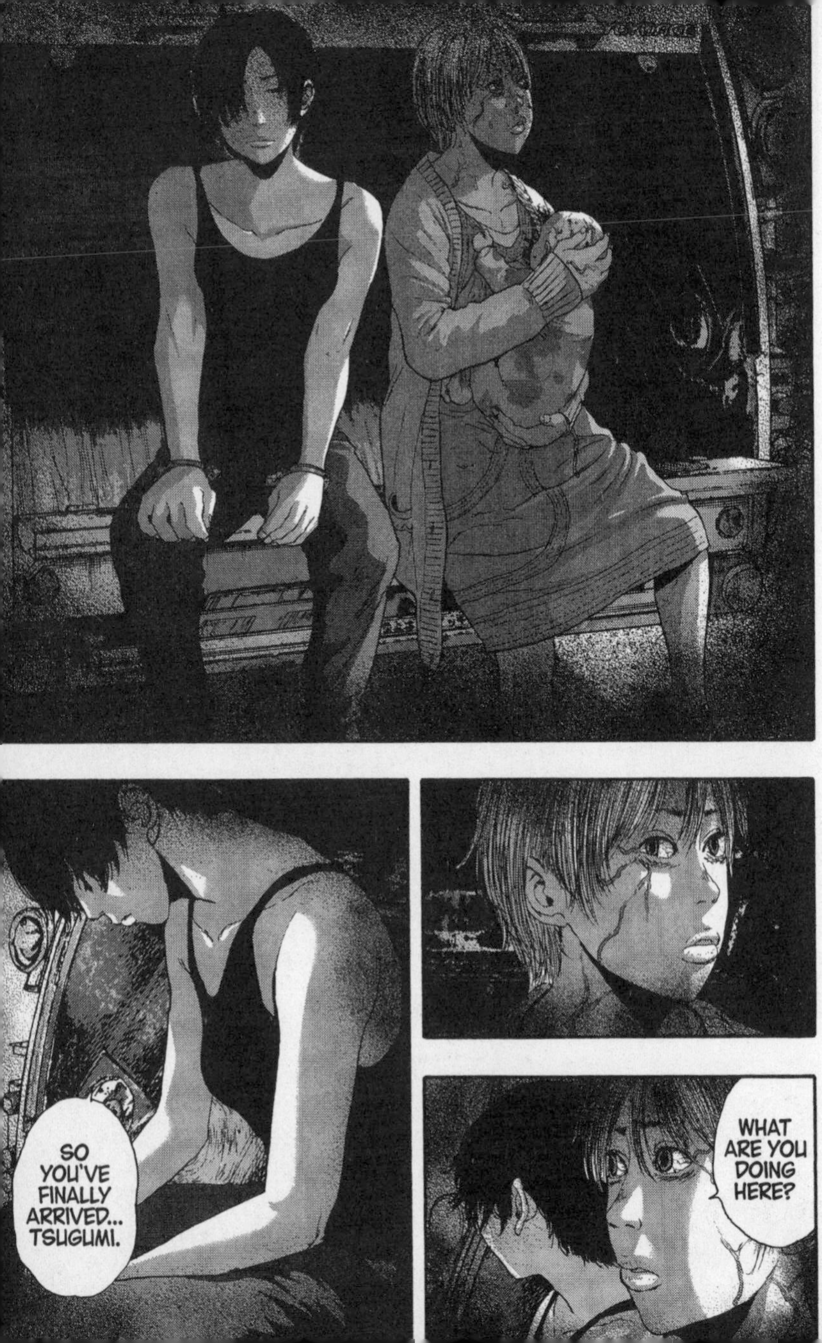
WHAT ARE YOU DOING HERE?
SO YOU'VE FINALLY ARRIVED... TSUGUMI.

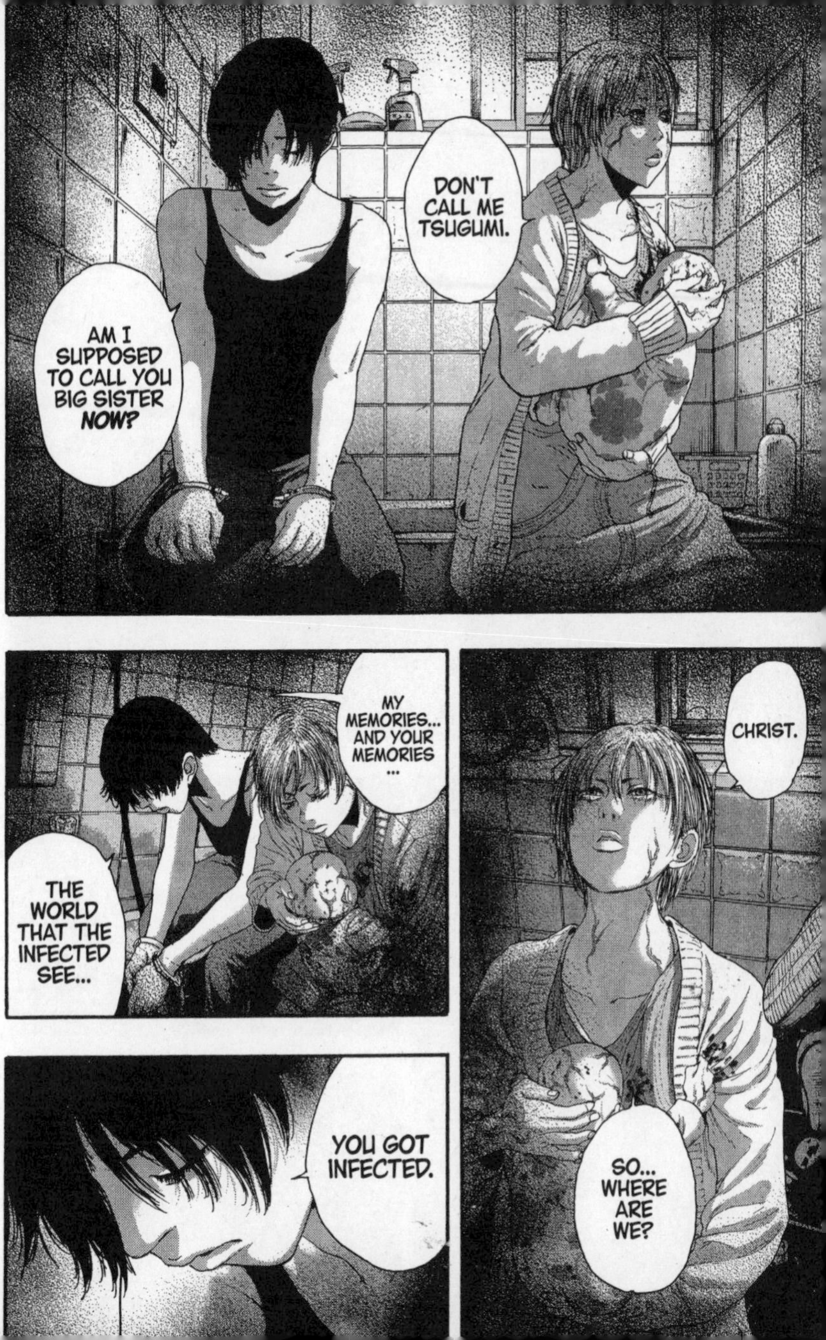
DON'T CALL ME TSUGUMI.
AM I SUPPOSED TO CALL YOU BIG SISTER *NOW?*
CHRIST.
SO... WHERE ARE WE?
MY MEMORIES... AND YOUR MEMORIES ...
THE WORLD THAT THE INFECTED SEE...
YOU GOT INFECTED.

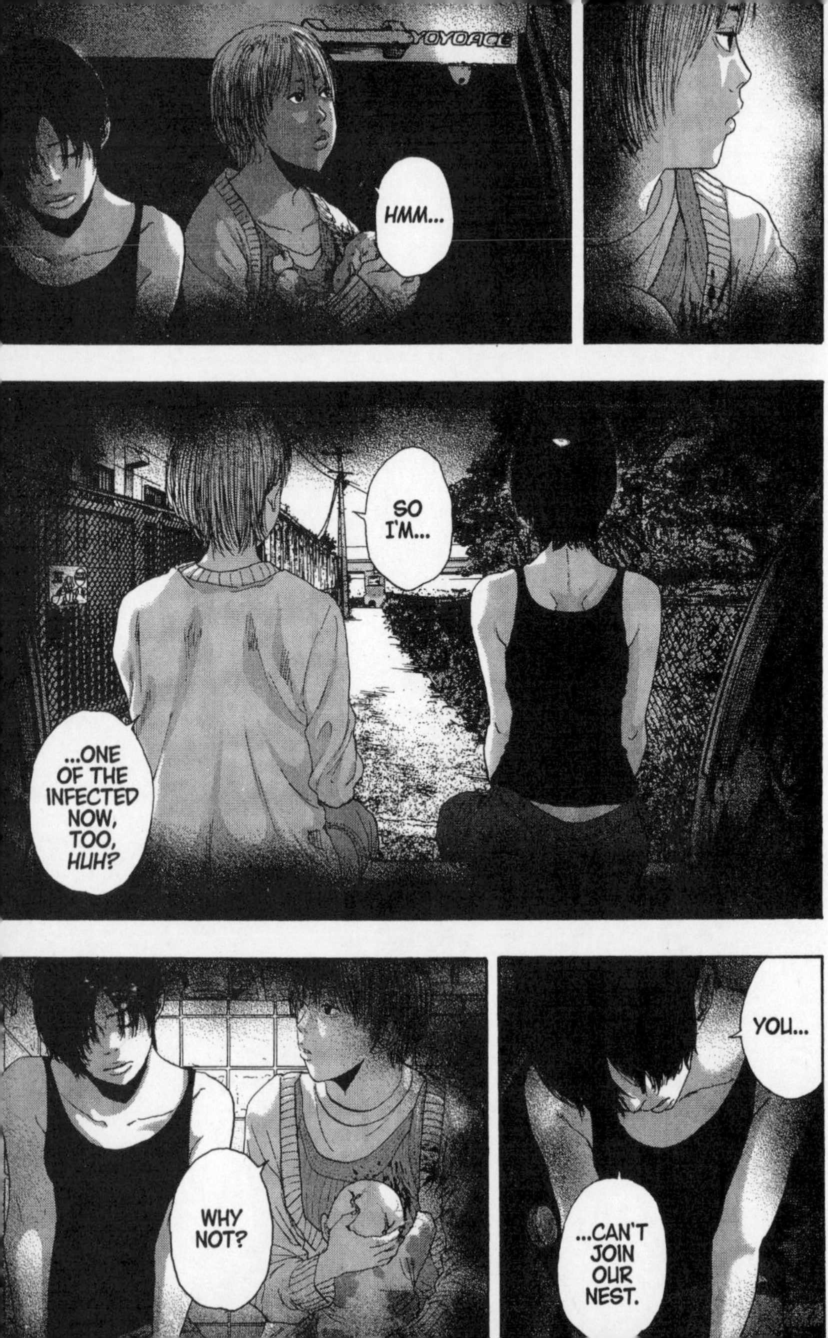
YOYOACE
HMM...
SO I'M...
...ONE OF THE INFECTED NOW, TOO, HUH?
YOU...
...CAN'T JOIN OUR NEST.
WHY NOT?

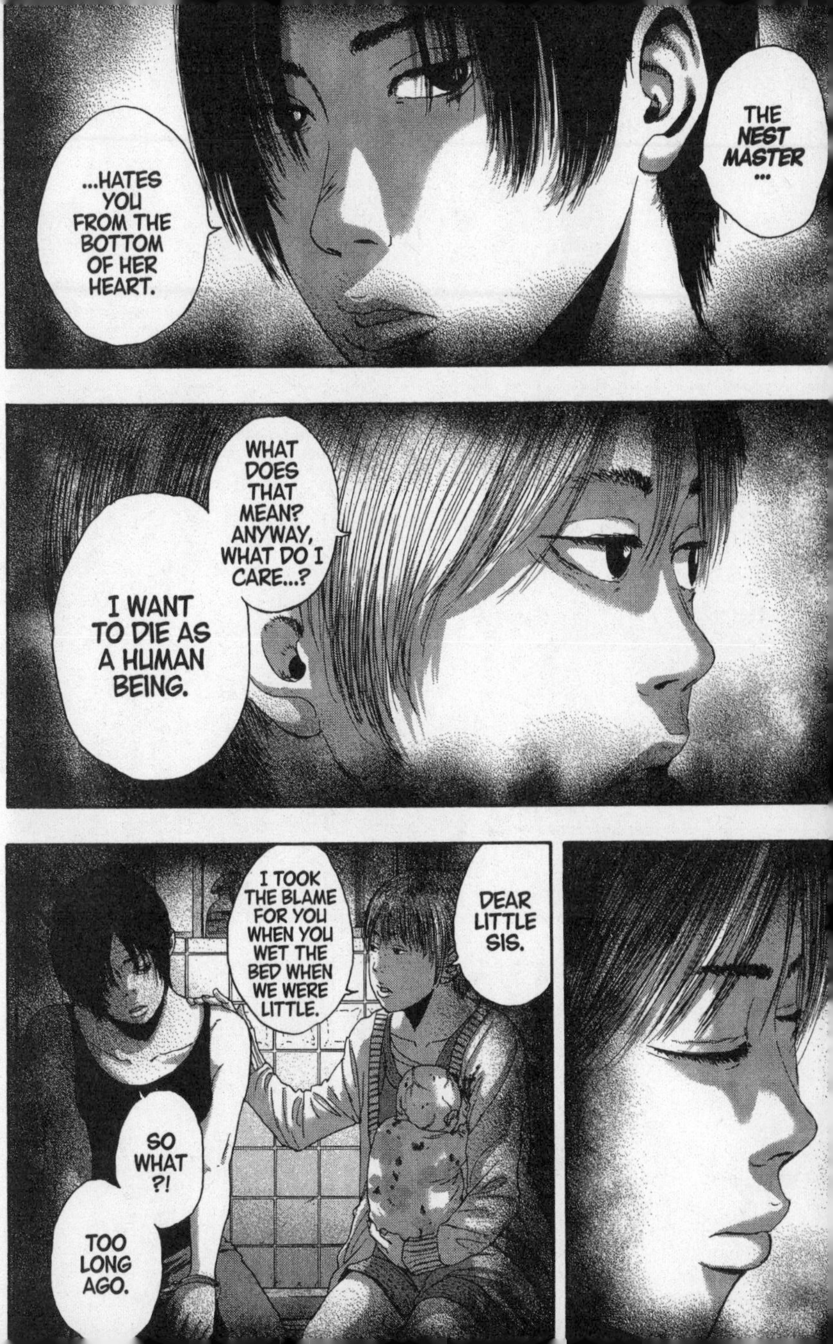
THE NEST MASTER...
...HATES YOU FROM THE BOTTOM OF HER HEART.
WHAT DOES THAT MEAN? ANYWAY, WHAT DO I CARE...?
I WANT TO DIE AS A HUMAN BEING.
DEAR LITTLE SIS.
I TOOK THE BLAME FOR YOU WHEN YOU WET THE BED WHEN WE WERE LITTLE.
SO WHAT?!
TOO LONG AGO.

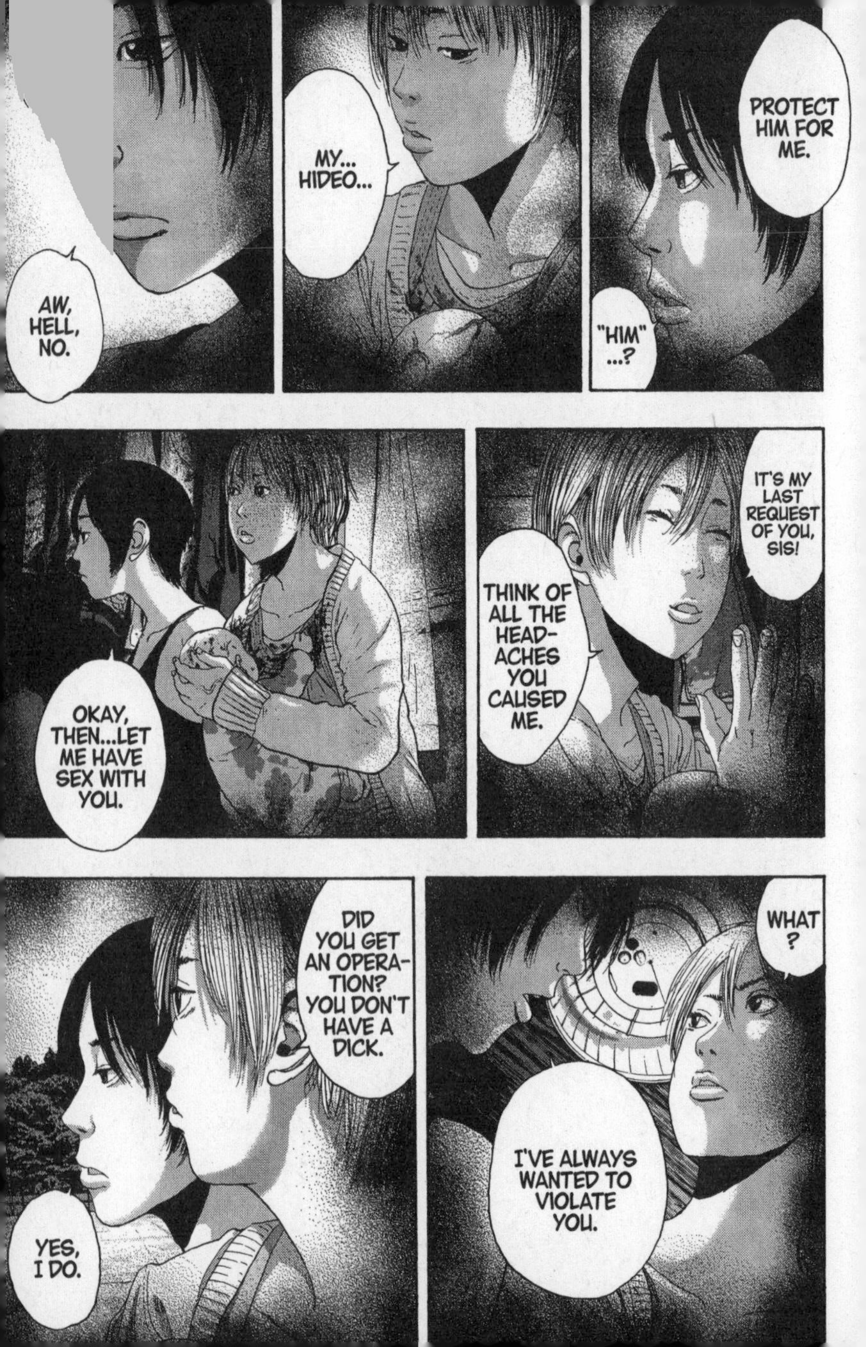
PROTECT HIM FOR ME.
"HIM" ...?
MY... HIDEO...
AW, HELL, NO.
IT'S MY LAST REQUEST OF YOU, SIS!
THINK OF ALL THE HEADACHES YOU CAUSED ME.
OKAY, THEN...LET ME HAVE SEX WITH YOU.
WHAT?
I'VE ALWAYS WANTED TO VIOLATE YOU.
DID YOU GET AN OPERATION? YOU DON'T HAVE A DICK.
YES, I DO.

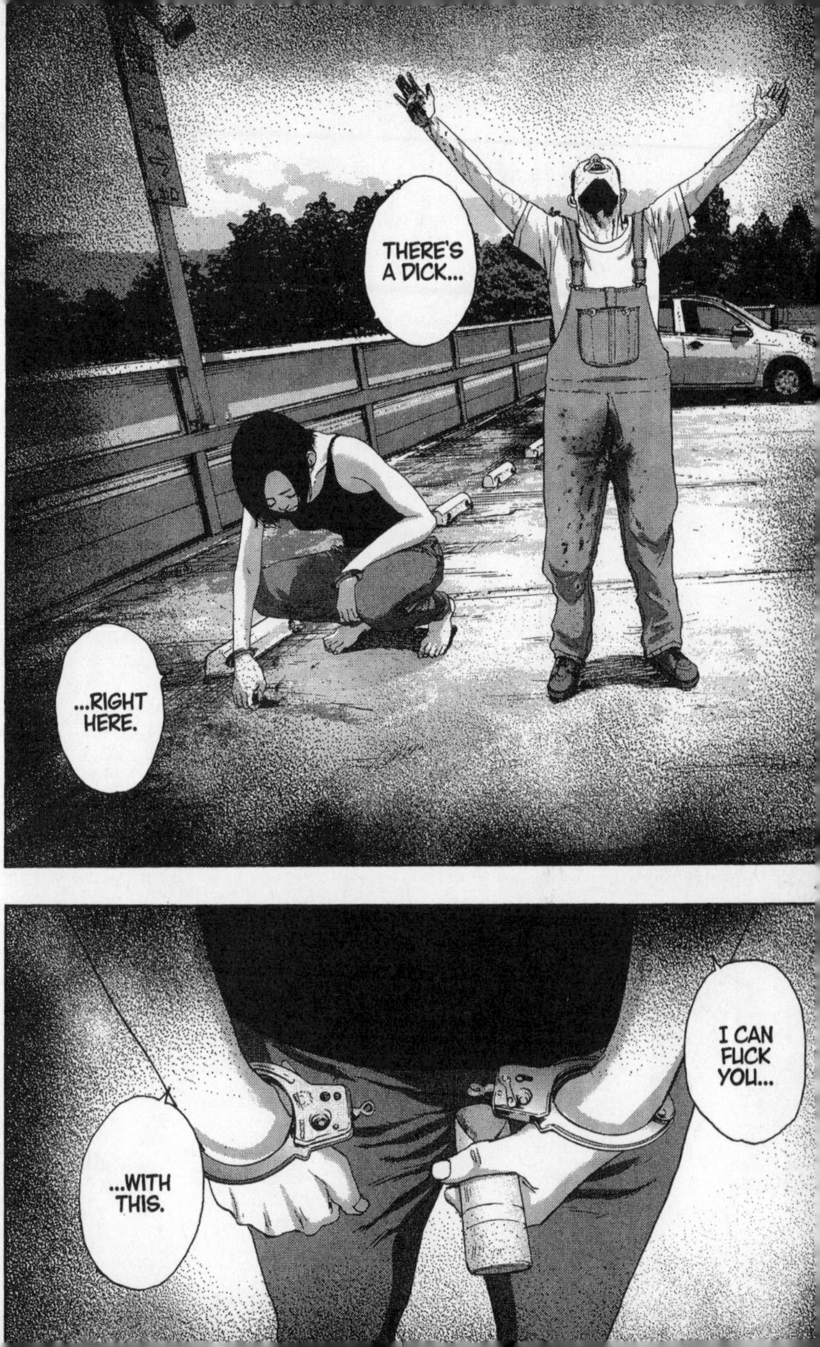
THERE'S A DICK...
...RIGHT HERE.
I CAN FUCK YOU...
...WITH THIS.

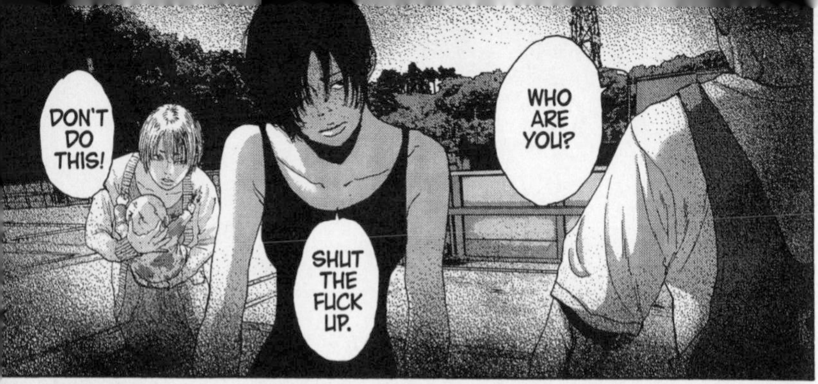
WHO ARE YOU?
SHUT THE FUCK UP.
DON'T DO THIS!

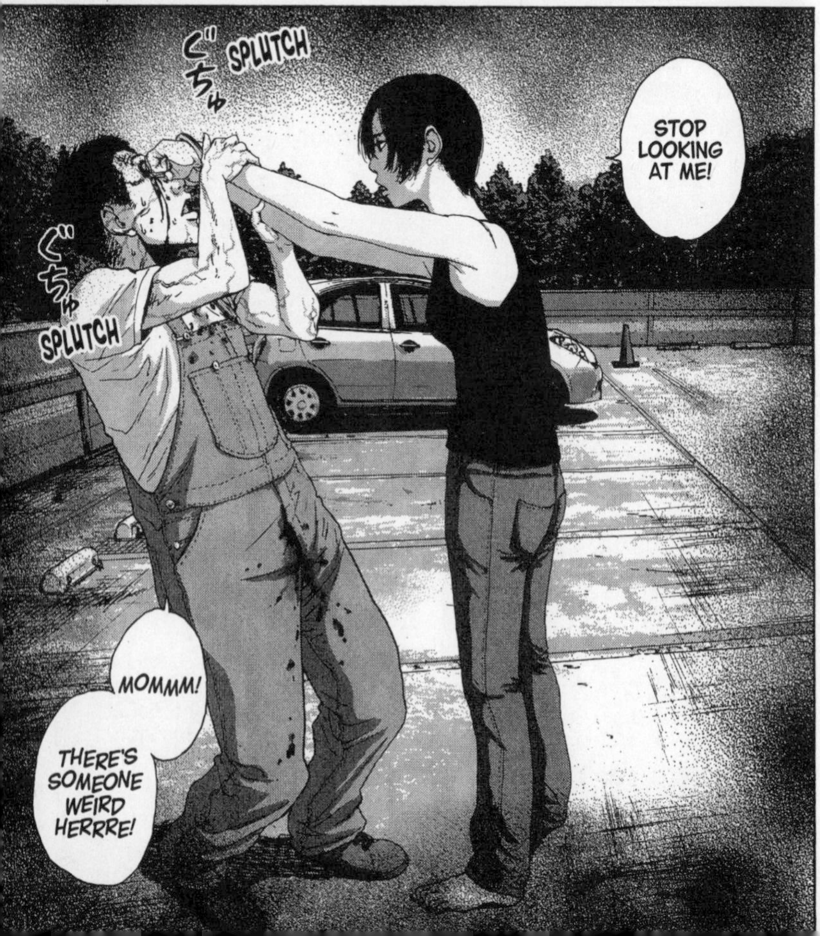
STOP LOOKING AT ME!
ぐちゅ SPLUTCH
ぐちゅ SPLUTCH
MOMMM!
THERE'S SOMEONE WEIRD HERRRE!

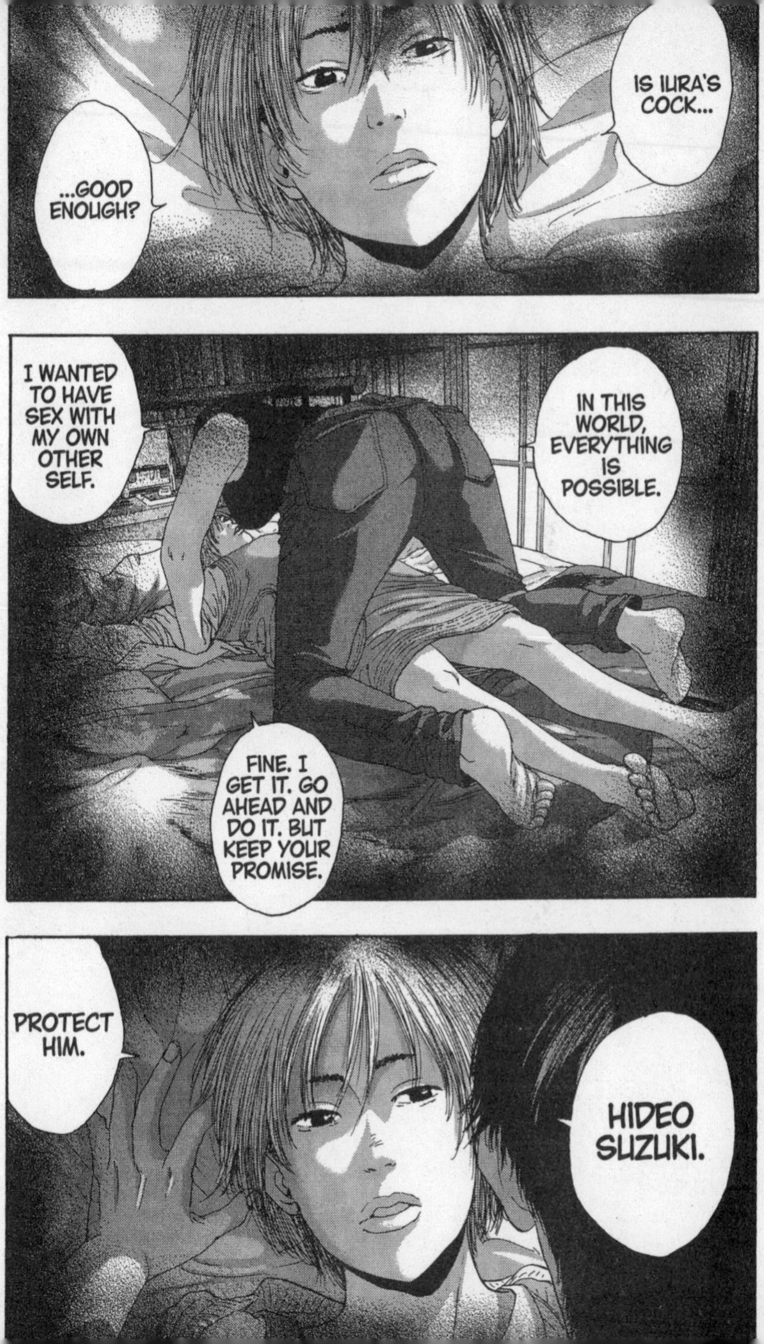
IS IURA'S COCK...
...GOOD ENOUGH?
IN THIS WORLD, EVERYTHING IS POSSIBLE.
I WANTED TO HAVE SEX WITH MY OWN OTHER SELF.
FINE. I GET IT. GO AHEAD AND DO IT. BUT KEEP YOUR PROMISE.
HIDEO SUZUKI.
PROTECT HIM.

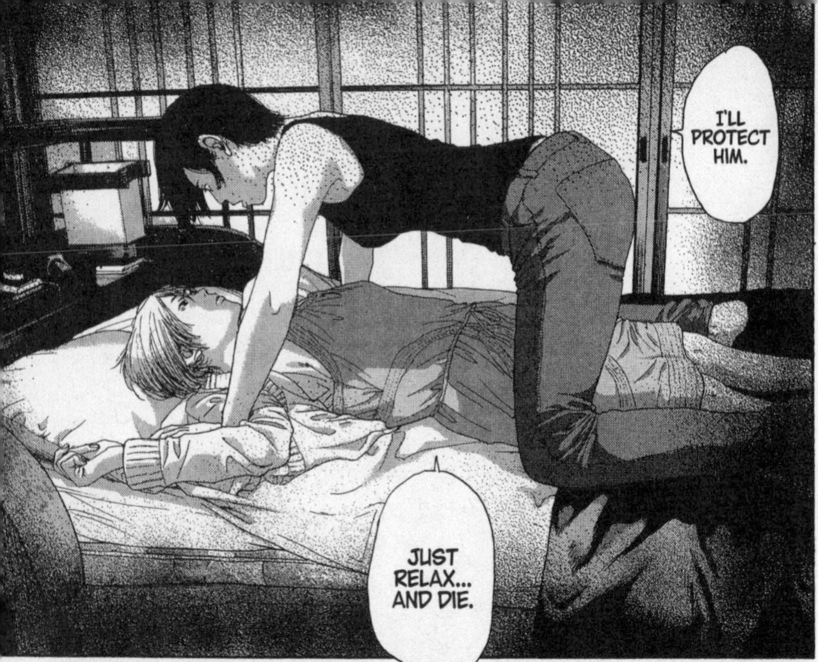
I'LL PROTECT HIM.
JUST RELAX... AND DIE.

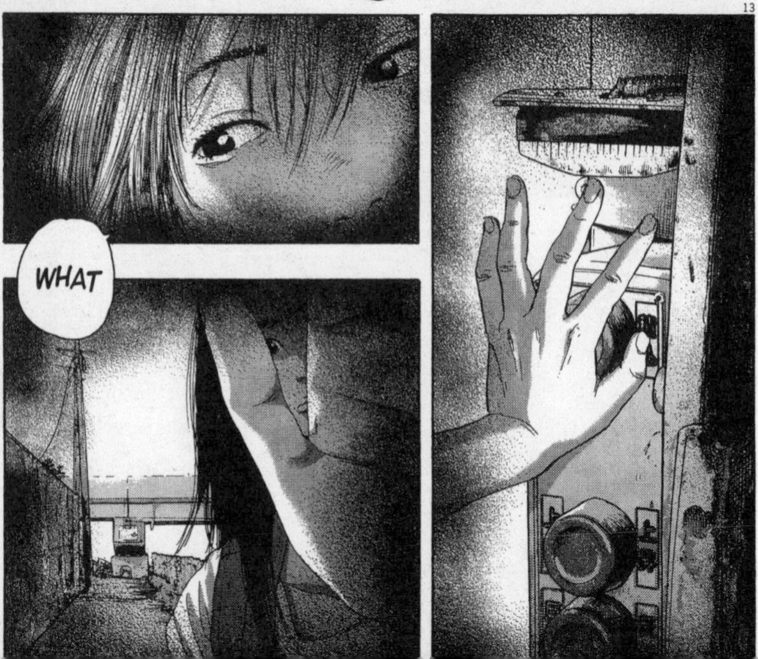
WHAT

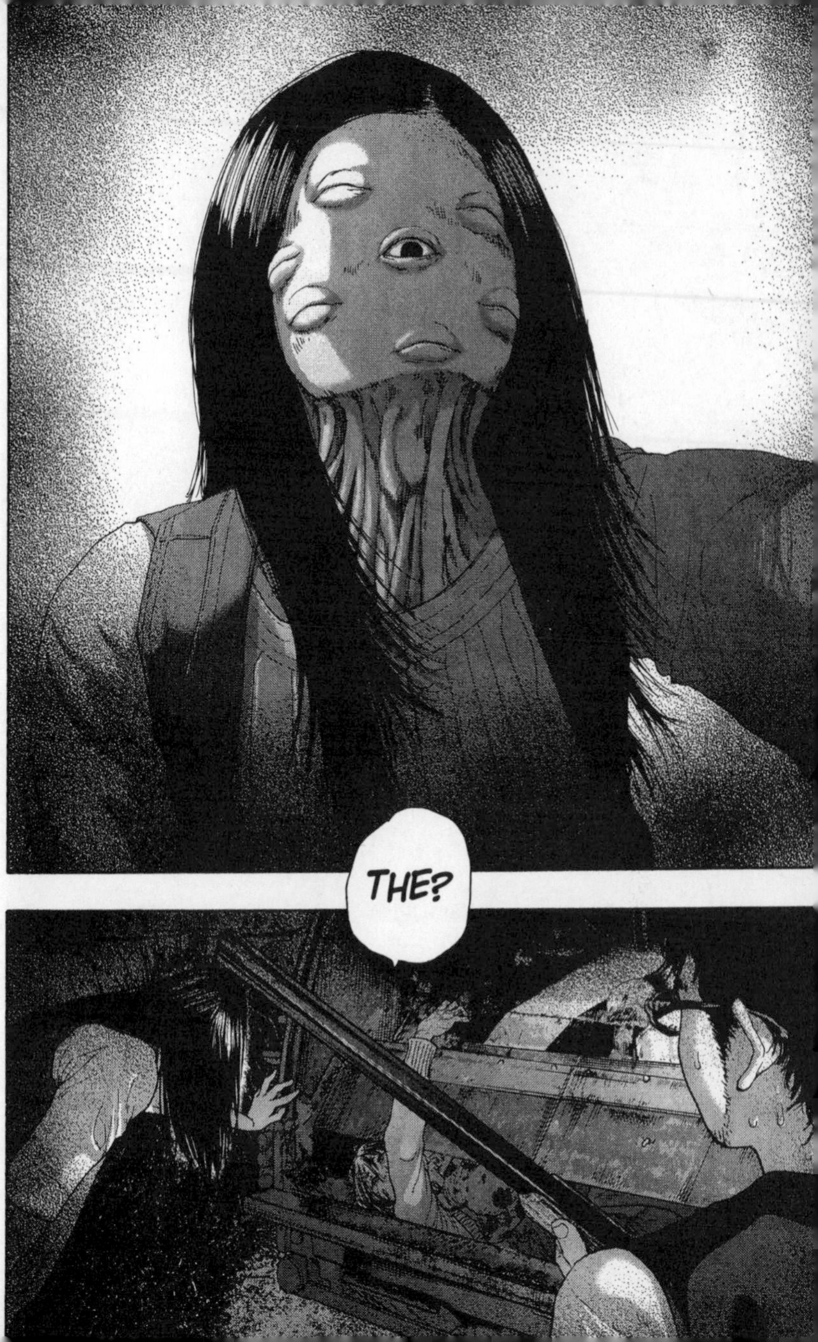
THE?

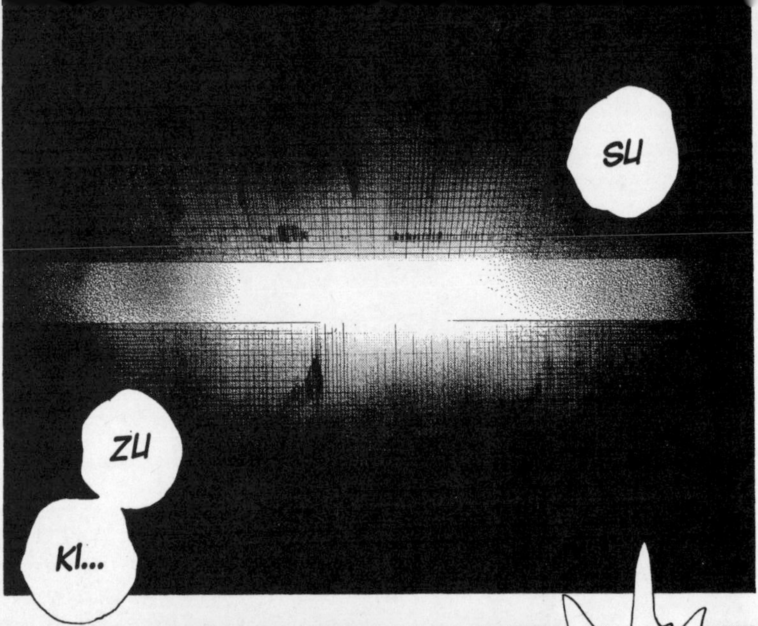
SU
ZU
KI...

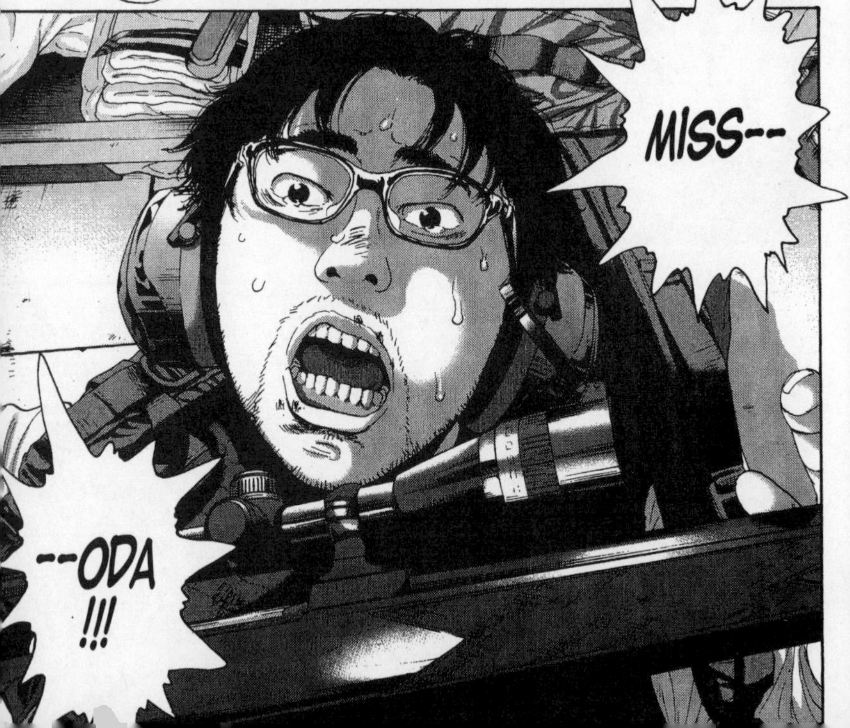
MISS--
--ODA !!!

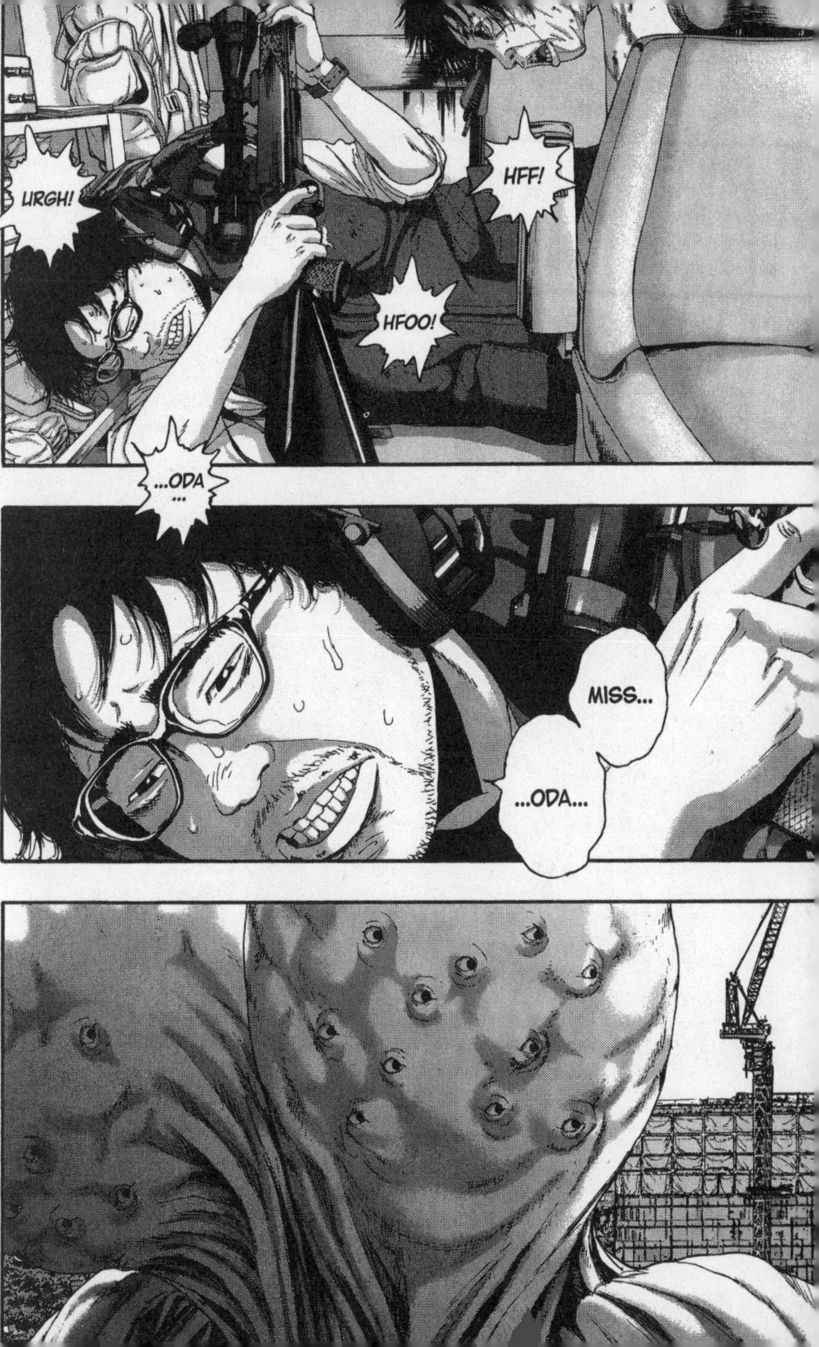
HFF!
URGH!
HFOO!
...ODA ...
MISS...
...ODA...

CHAPTER 244

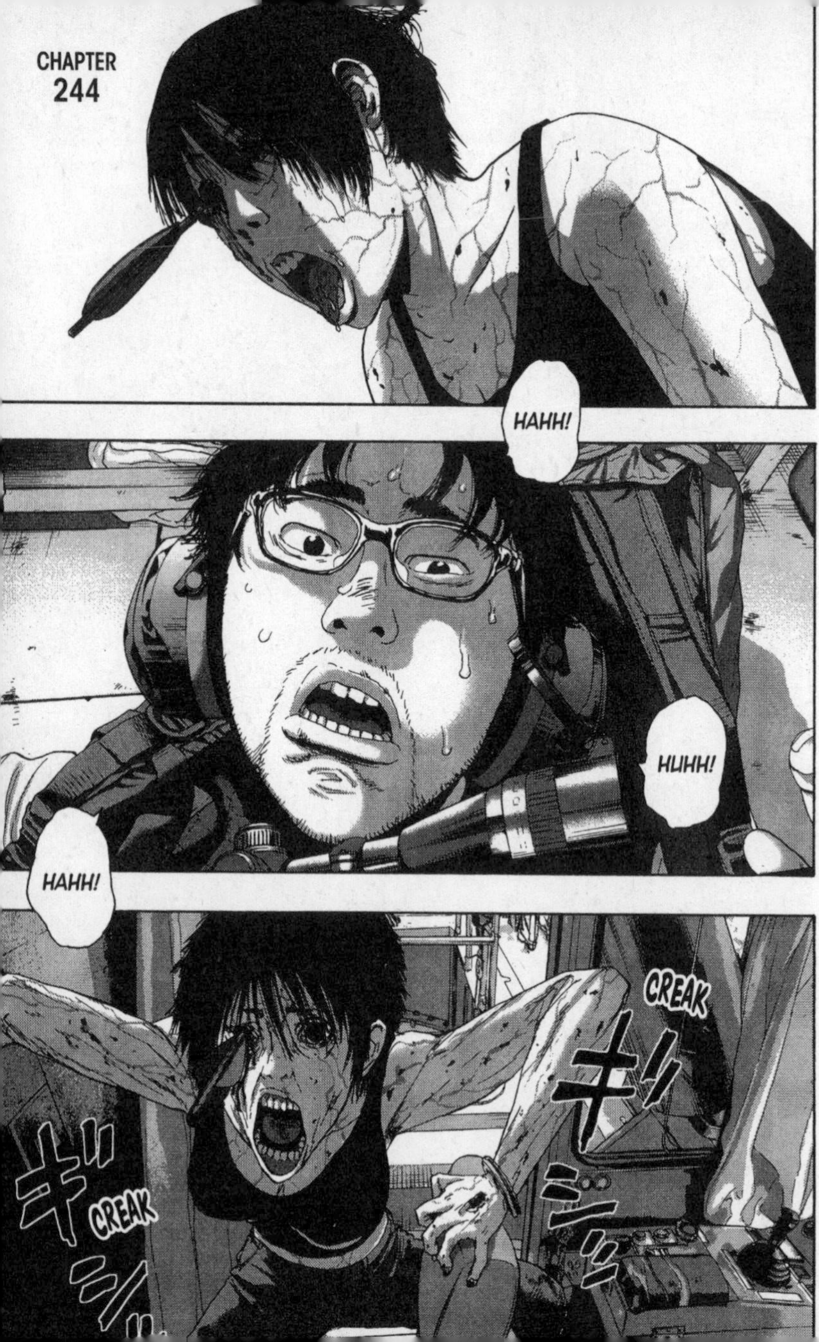
HAHH!
HUHH!
HAHH!
CREAK
CREAK

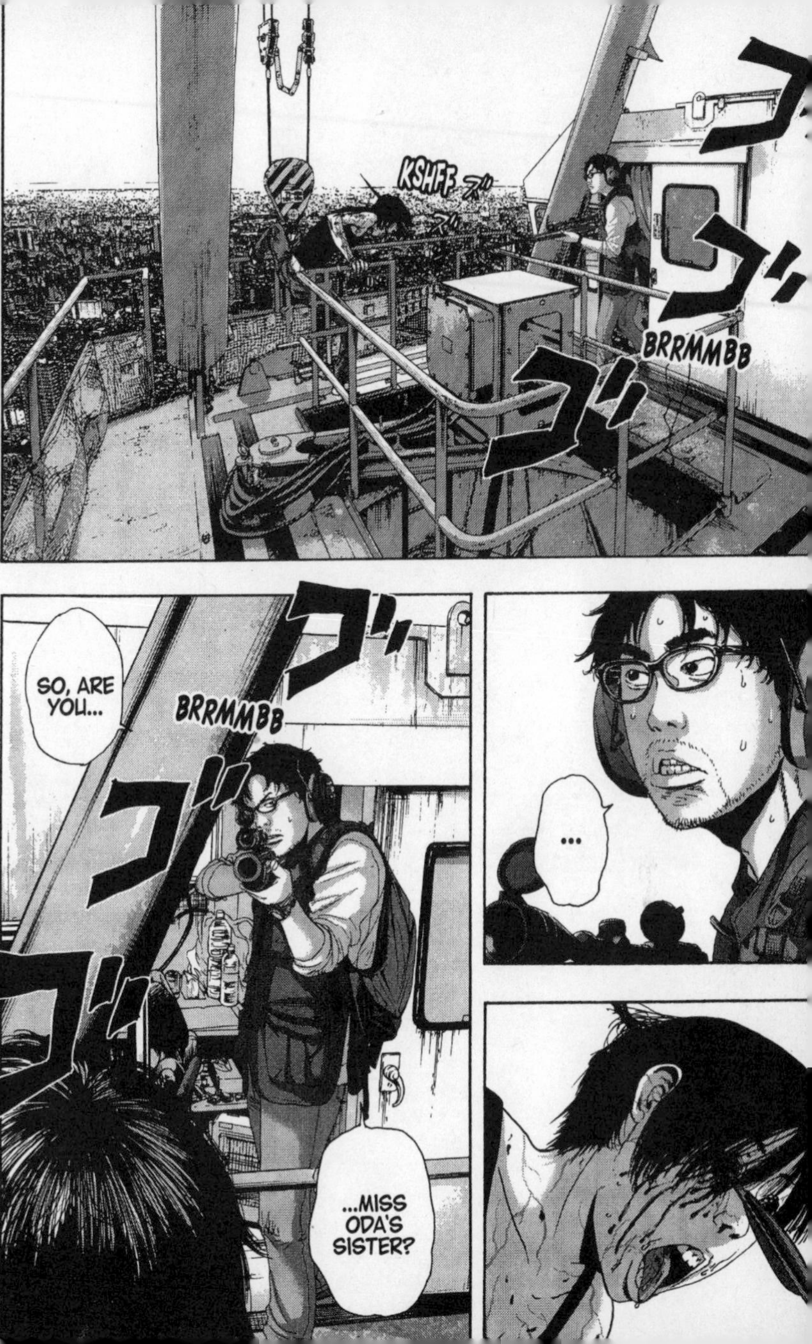
KSHFF ズ
ズ
ゴ
ゴ
BRRMMBB
ゴ
...
SO, ARE YOU...
ゴ
BRRMMBB
ゴ
ゴ
...MISS ODA'S SISTER?

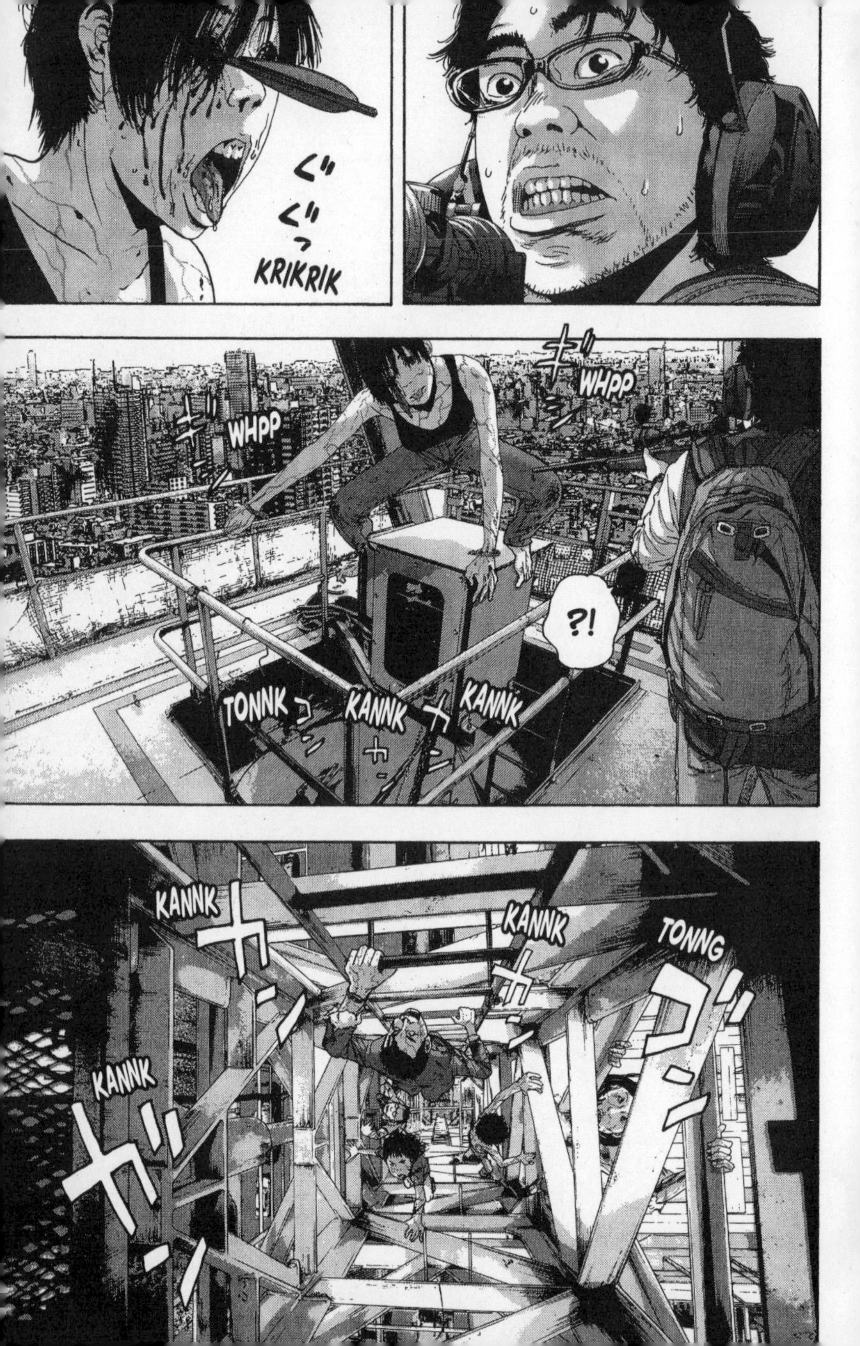

ぐぐっ
KRIKRIK
WHPP
WHPP
?!
KANNK
KANNK
TONNK
TONNG
KANNK
KANNK
KANNK

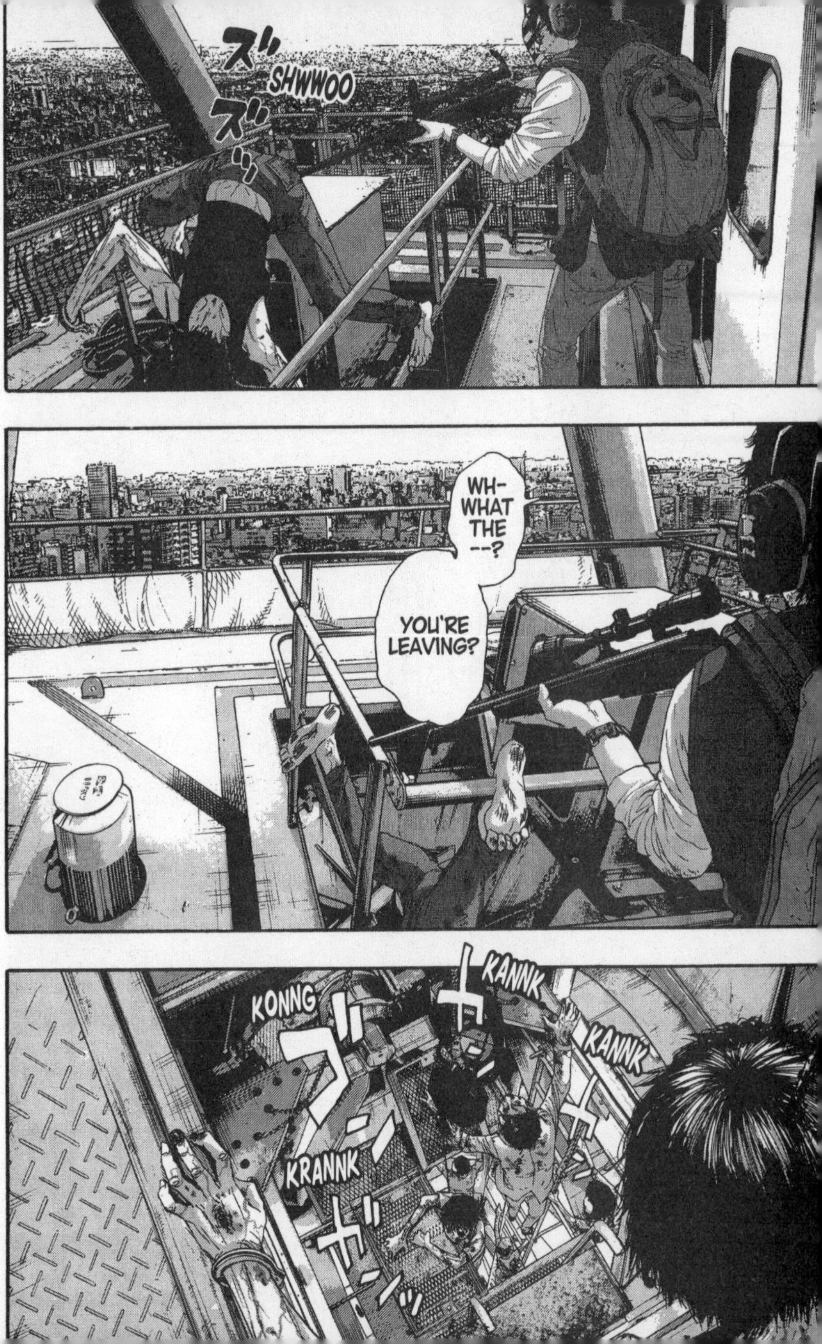
SHWWOO
WH-WHAT THE --?
YOU'RE LEAVING?
KANNK
KANNK
KONNG
KRANNK

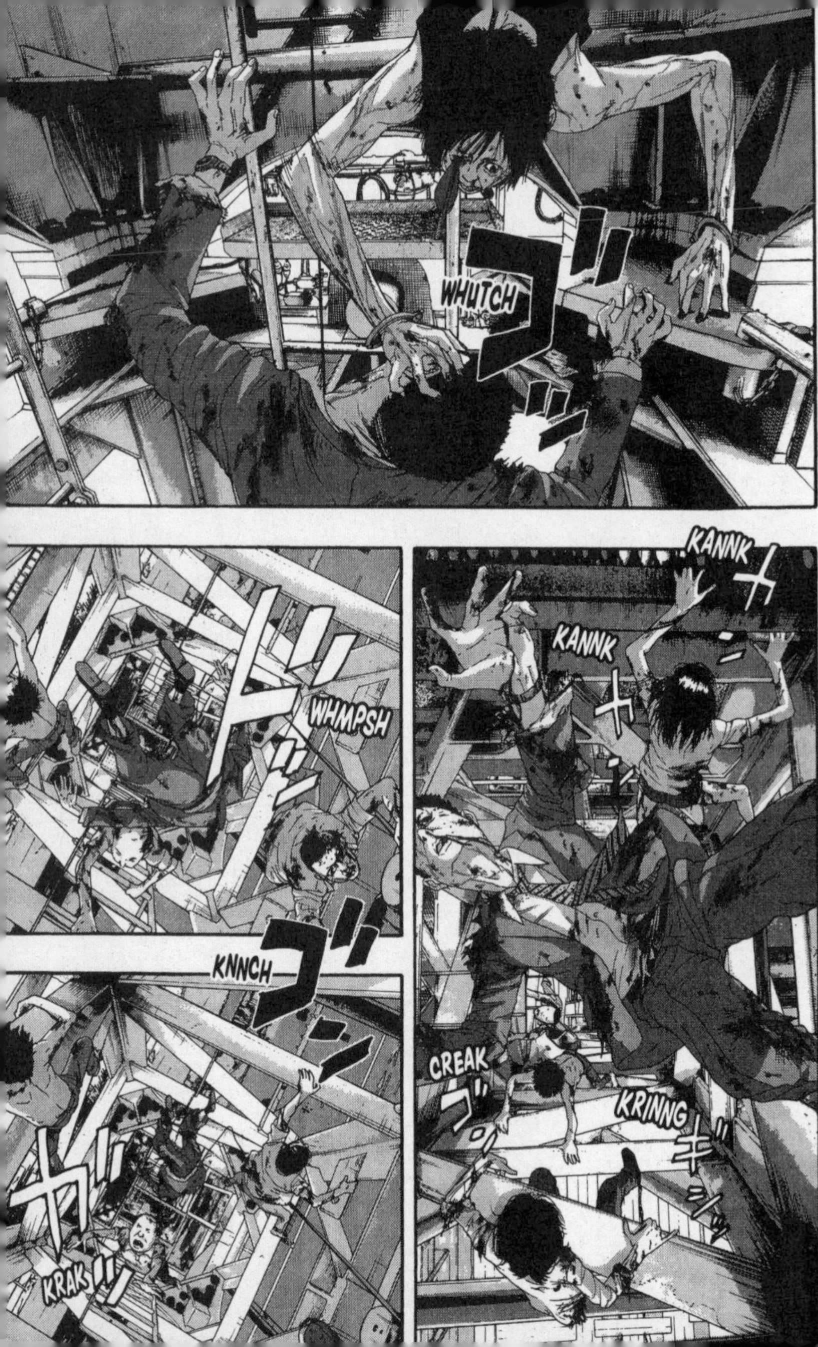
WHUTCH
KANNK
KANNK
CREAK
KRINNG
WHMPSH
KNNCH
KRAK

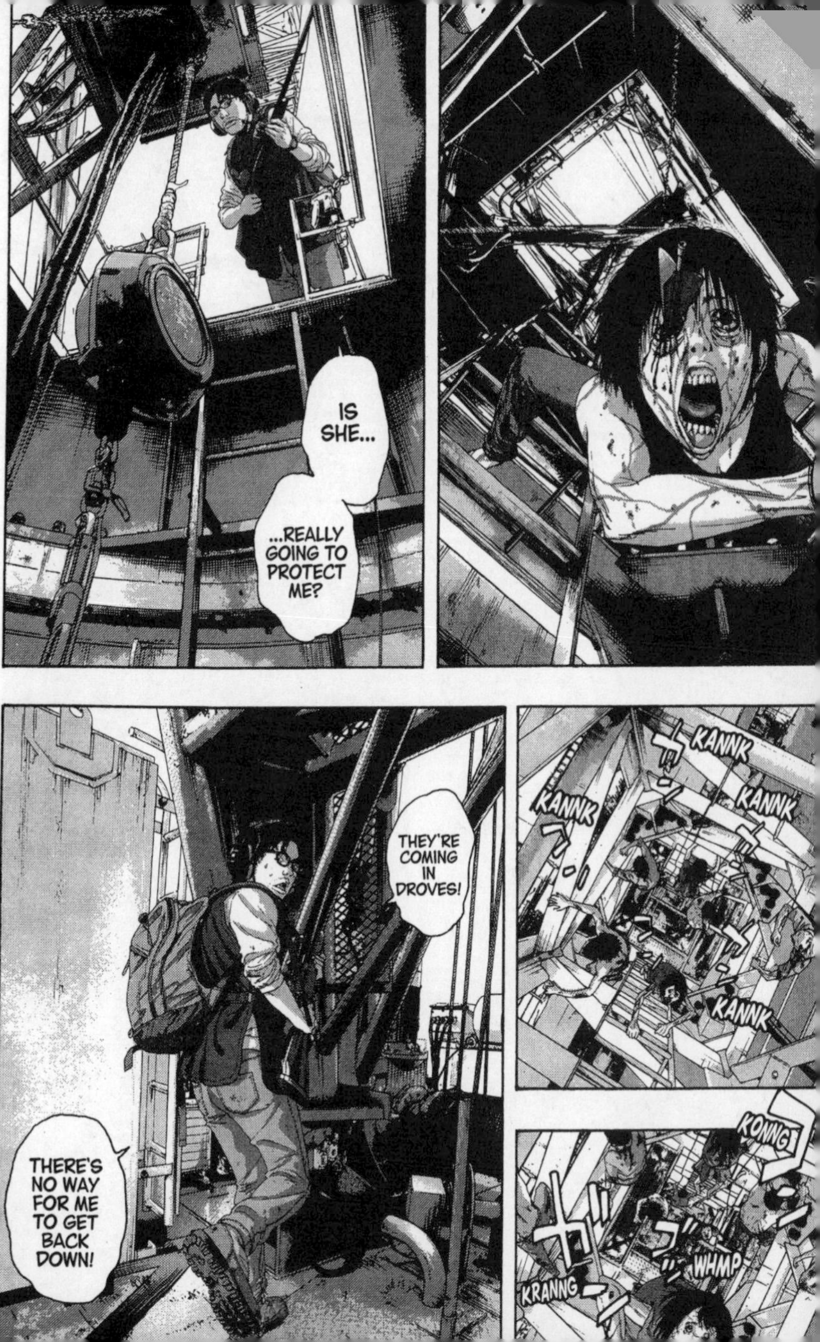
IS SHE...
...REALLY GOING TO PROTECT ME?
KANNK
KANNK
KANNK
KANNK
KONNG
WHMP
KRANNG
THEY'RE COMING IN DROVES!
THERE'S NO WAY FOR ME TO GET BACK DOWN!

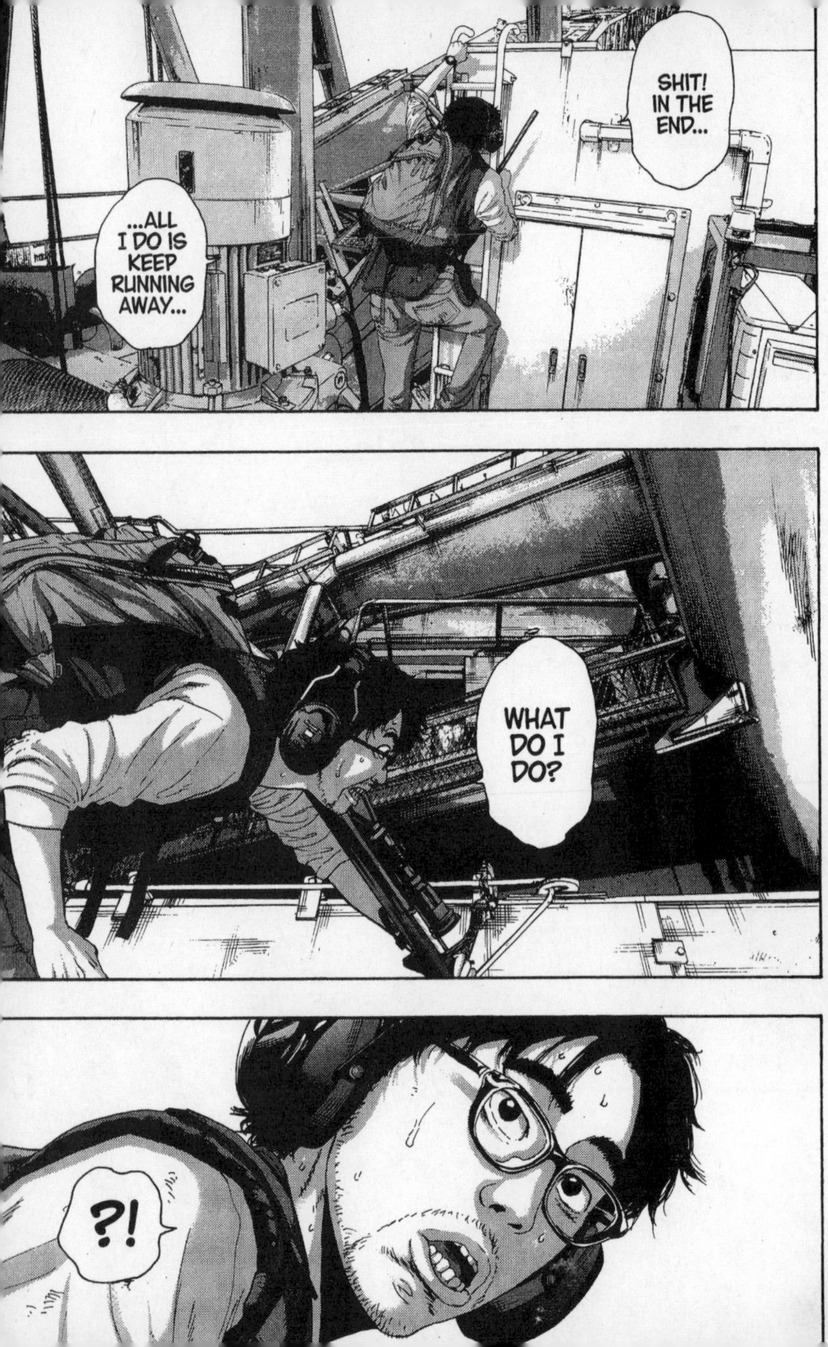
SHIT! IN THE END...
...ALL I DO IS KEEP RUNNING AWAY...
WHAT DO I DO?
?!

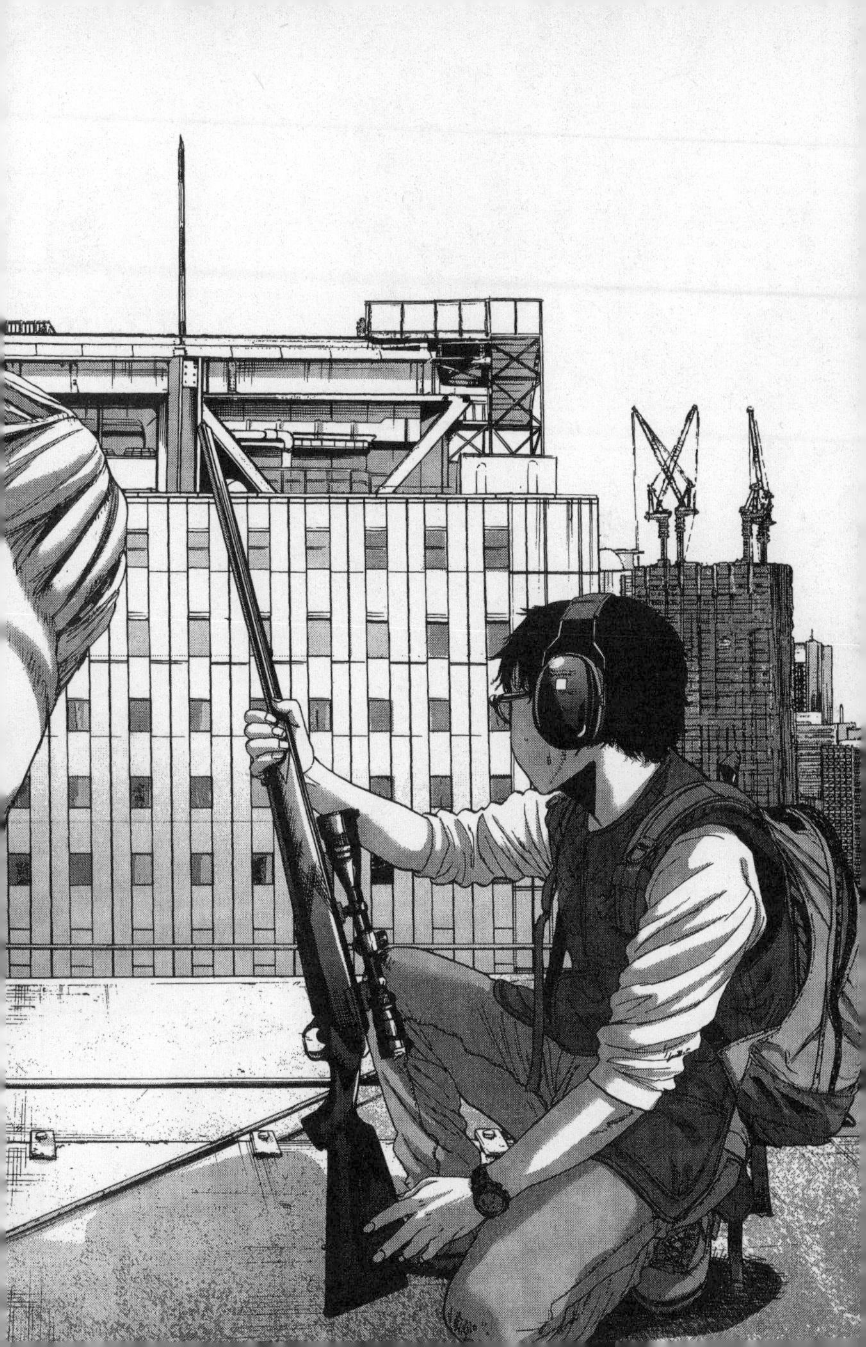

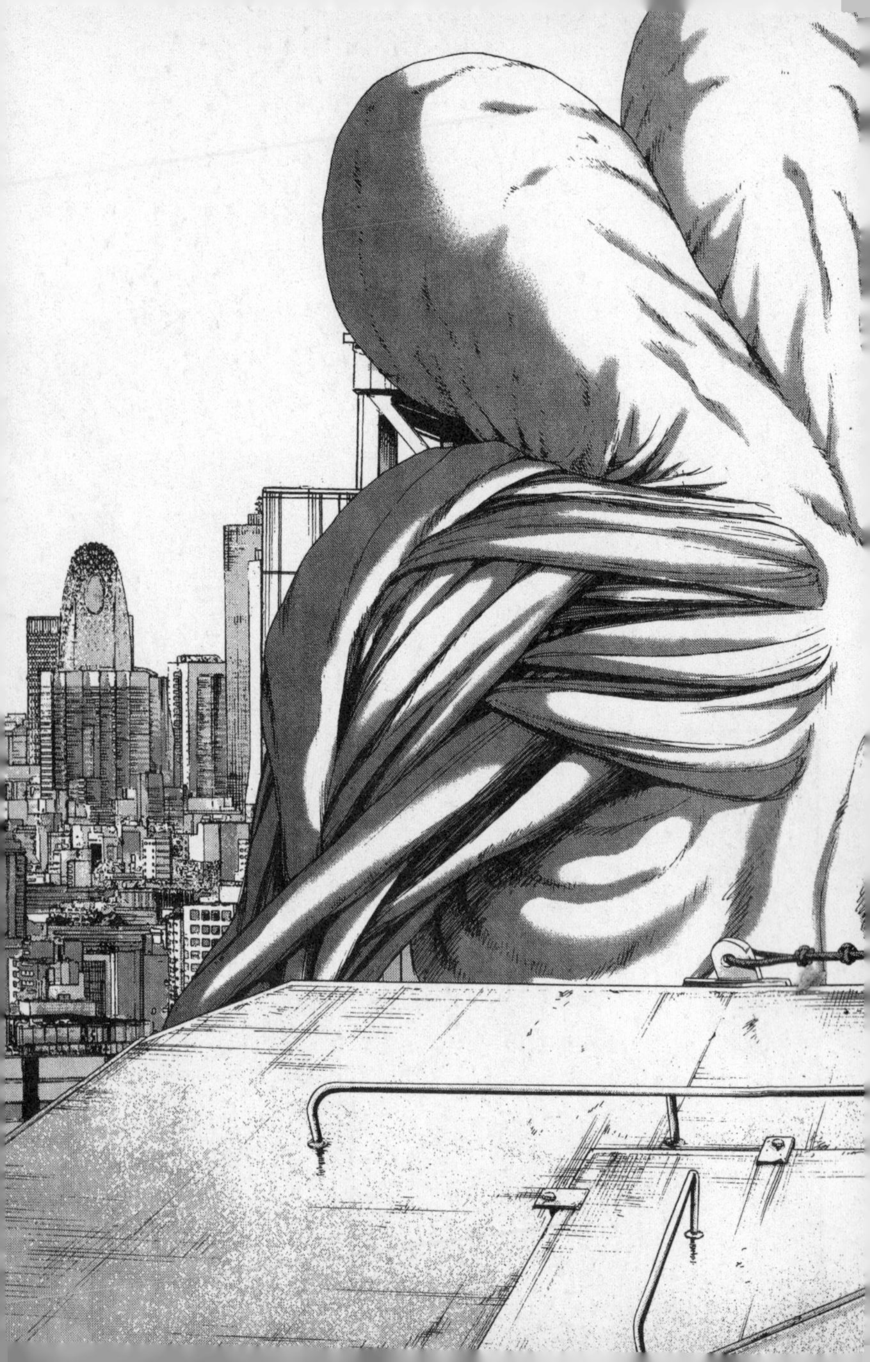

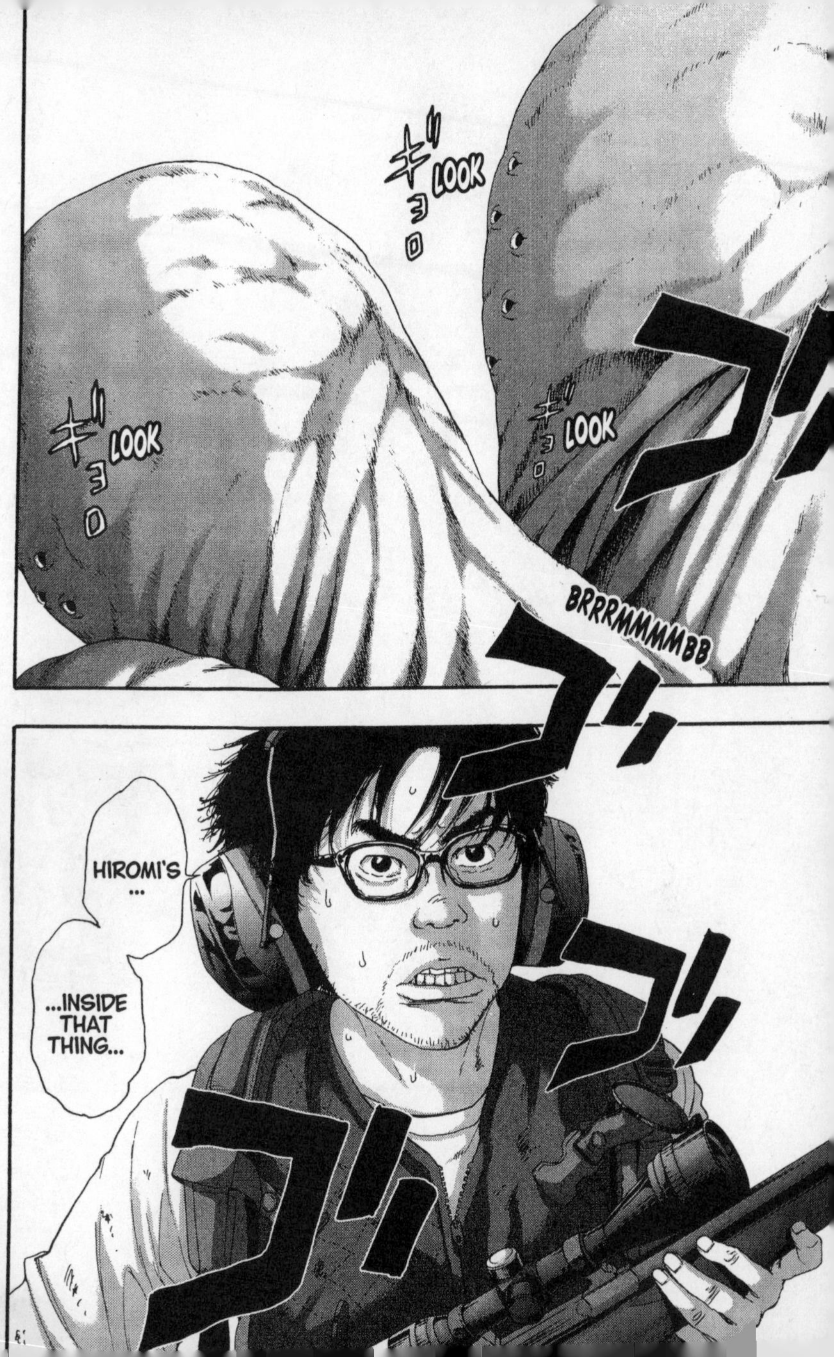

LOOK
LOOK
LOOK
BRRRMMMMBB
HIROMI'S ...
...INSIDE THAT THING...

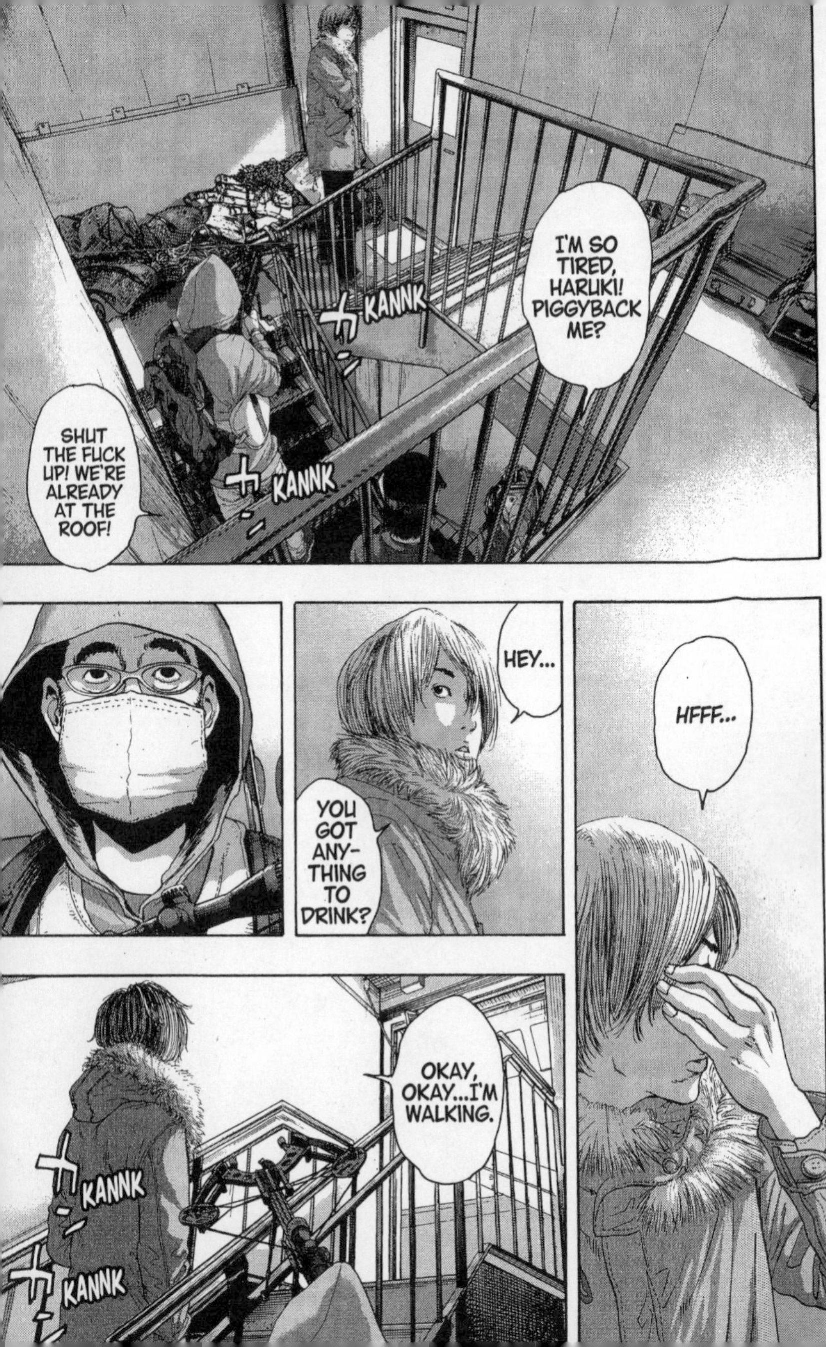
I'M SO TIRED, HARUKI! PIGGYBACK ME?
KANNK
SHUT THE FUCK UP! WE'RE ALREADY AT THE ROOF!
KANNK
HFFF...
HEY...
YOU GOT ANY-THING TO DRINK?
OKAY, OKAY...I'M WALKING.
KANNK
KANNK

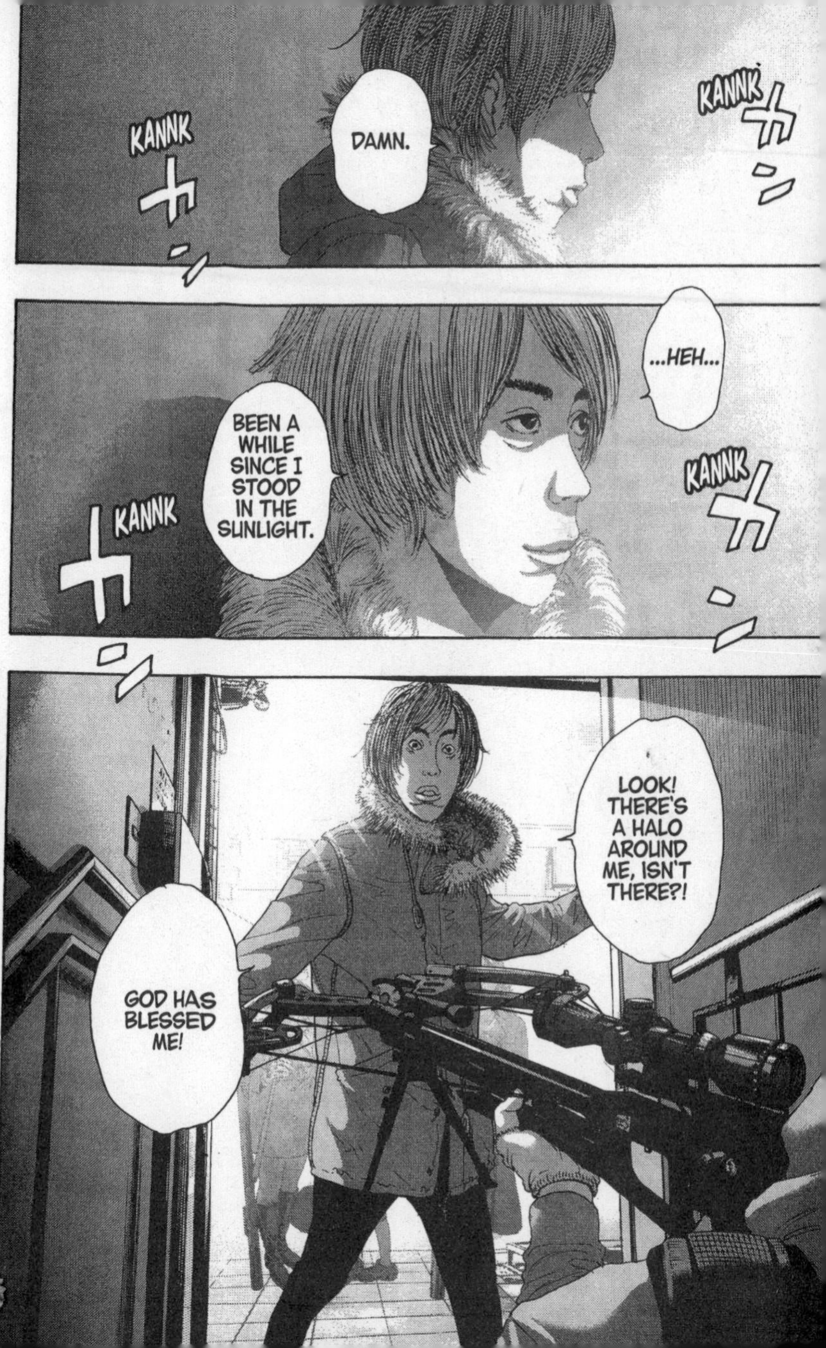
KANNK
DAMN.
KANNK
...HEH...
KANNK
BEEN A WHILE SINCE I STOOD IN THE SUNLIGHT.
KANNK
LOOK! THERE'S A HALO AROUND ME, ISN'T THERE?!
GOD HAS BLESSED ME!

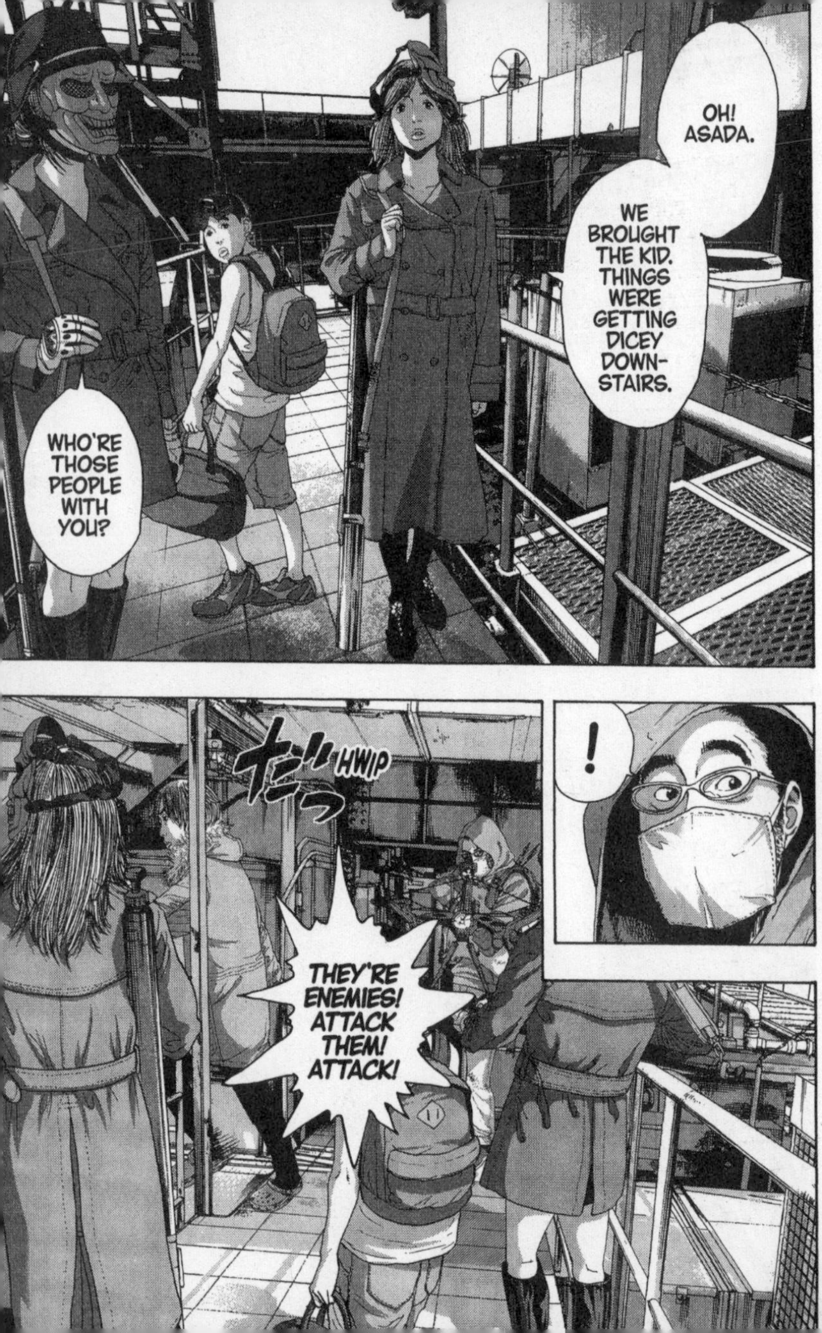
OH! ASADA.
WE BROUGHT THE KID. THINGS WERE GETTING DICEY DOWN-STAIRS.
WHO'RE THOSE PEOPLE WITH YOU?
!
HWIP
THEY'RE ENEMIES! ATTACK THEM! ATTACK!

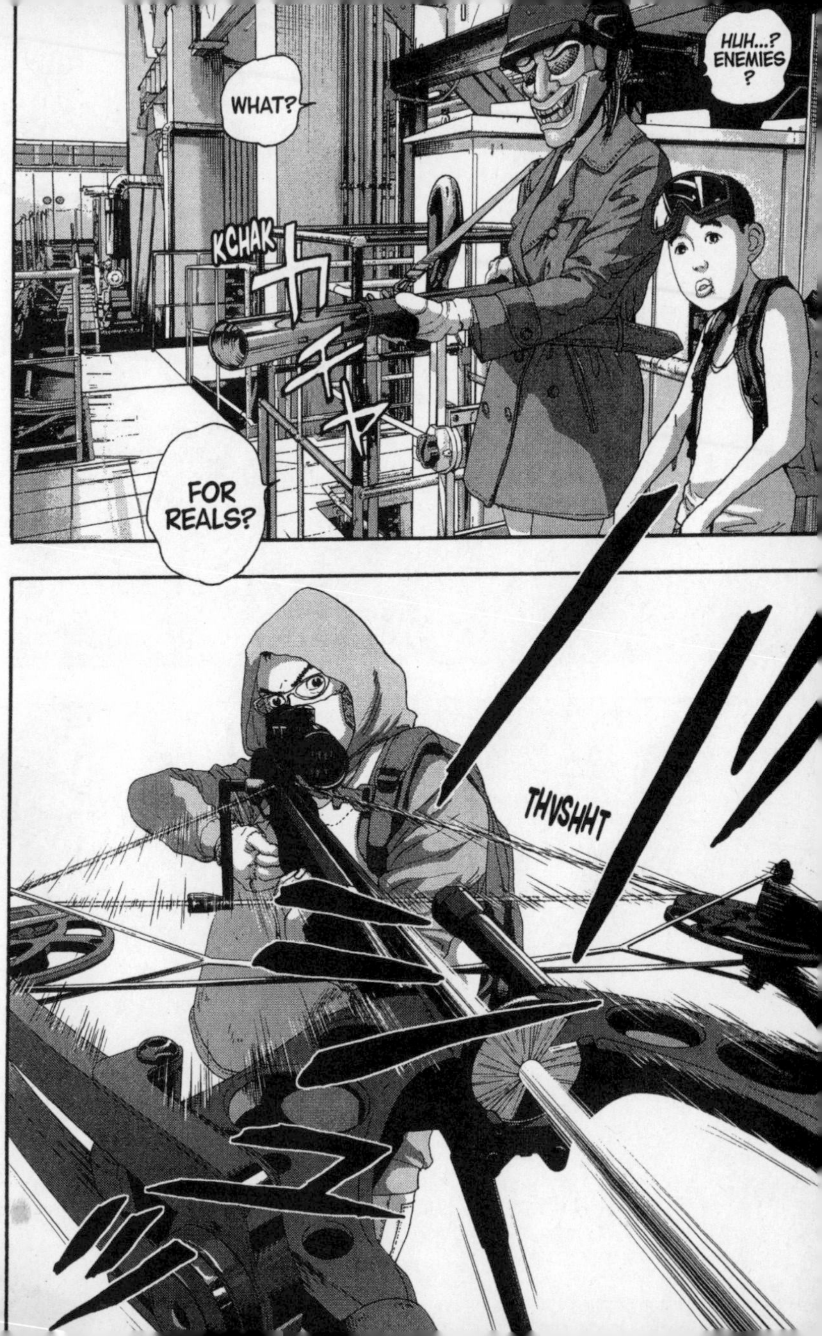
HUH...? ENEMIES ?
WHAT?
KCHAK
FOR REALS?
THVSHHT

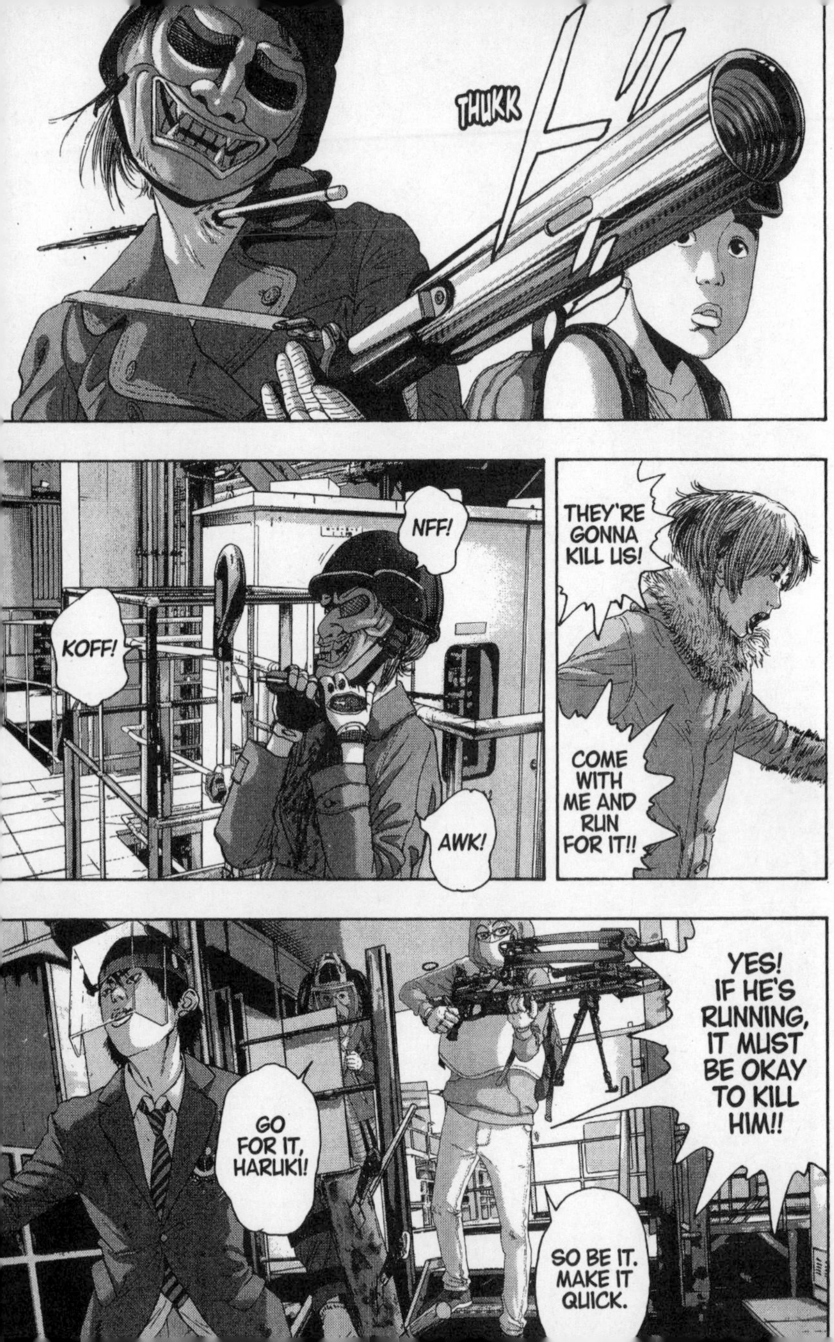
THUKK
THEY'RE GONNA KILL US!
COME WITH ME AND RUN FOR IT!!
NFF!
KOFF!
AWK!
YES! IF HE'S RUNNING, IT MUST BE OKAY TO KILL HIM!!
GO FOR IT, HARUKI!
SO BE IT. MAKE IT QUICK.

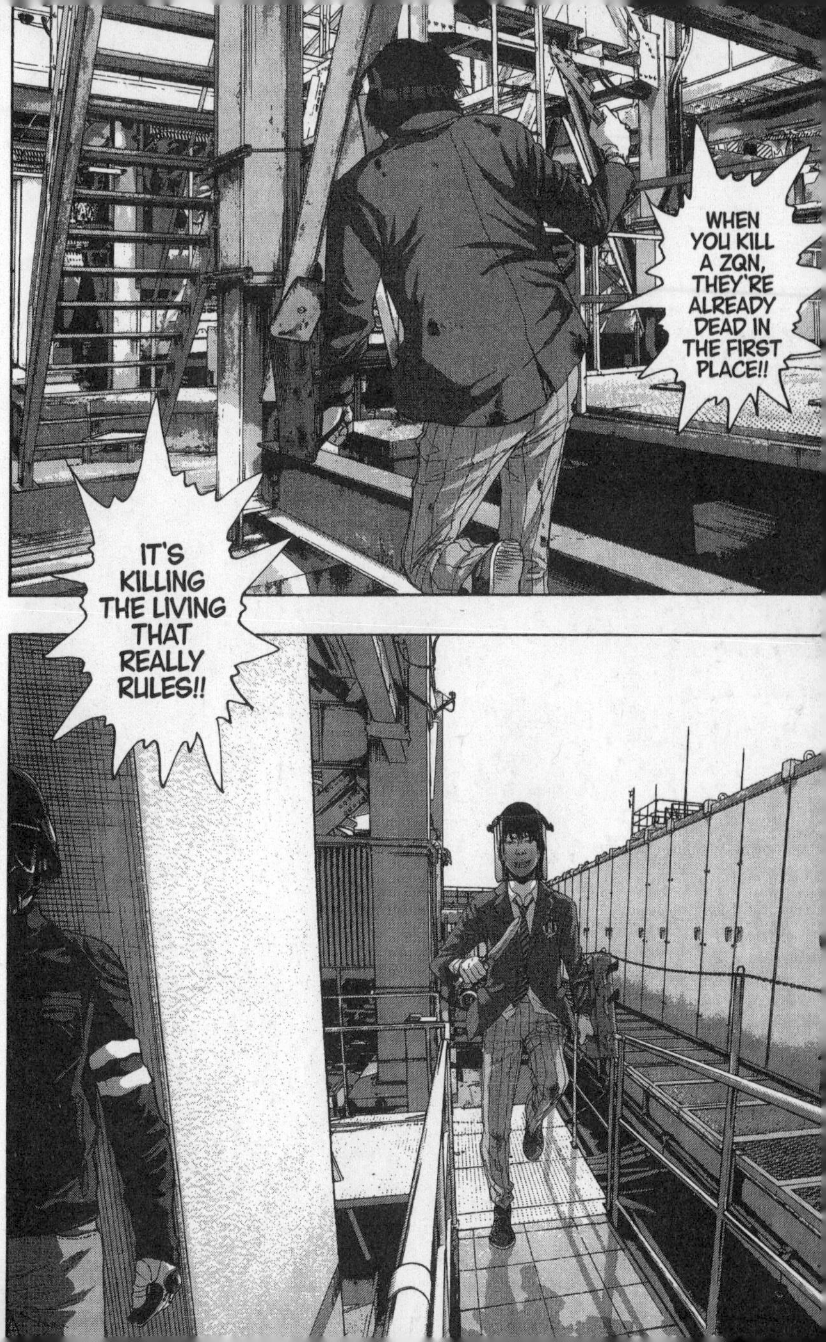
WHEN YOU KILL A ZQN, THEY'RE ALREADY DEAD IN THE FIRST PLACE!!
IT'S KILLING THE LIVING THAT REALLY RULES!!

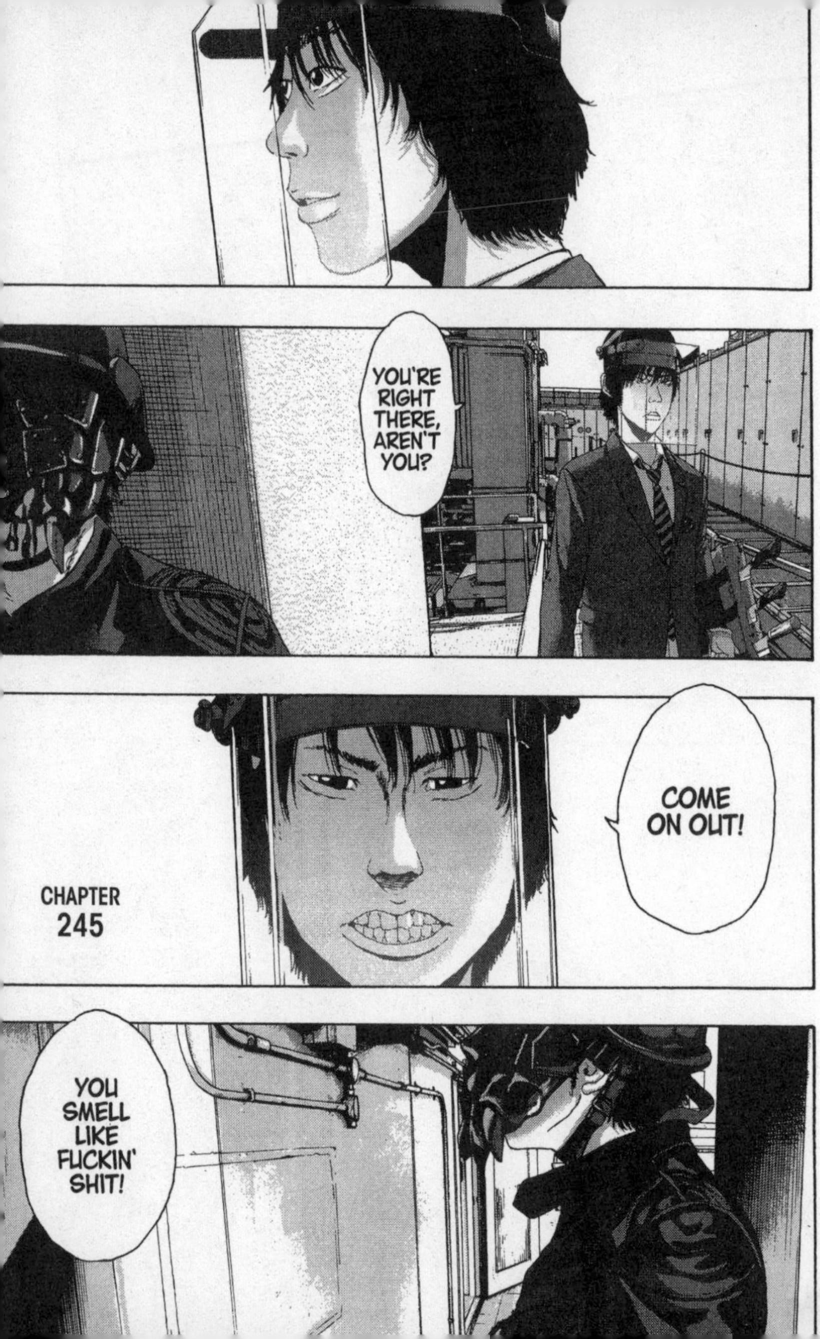
YOU'RE RIGHT THERE, AREN'T YOU?
COME ON OUT!
CHAPTER 245
YOU SMELL LIKE FUCKIN' SHIT!

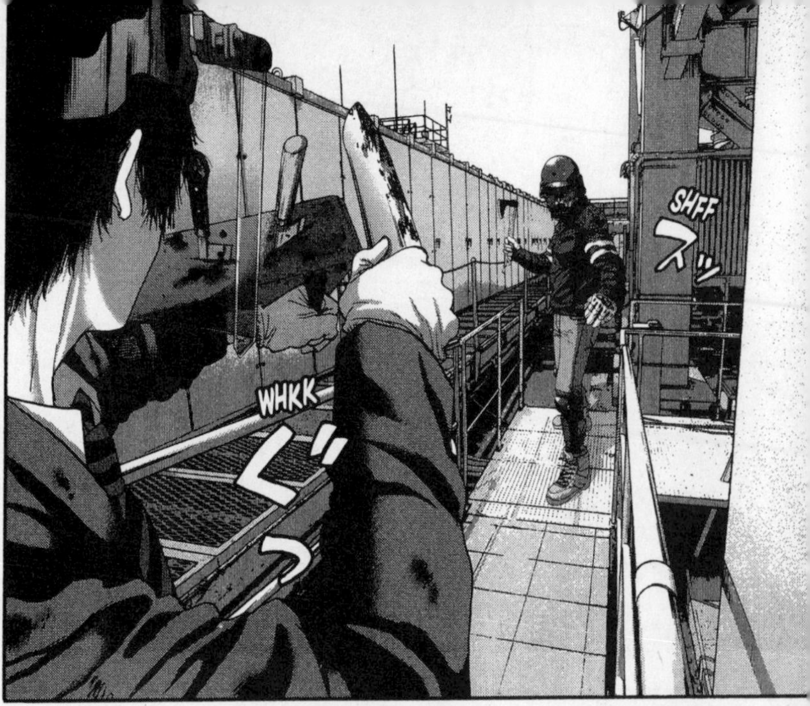
SHFF
スッ
WHKK

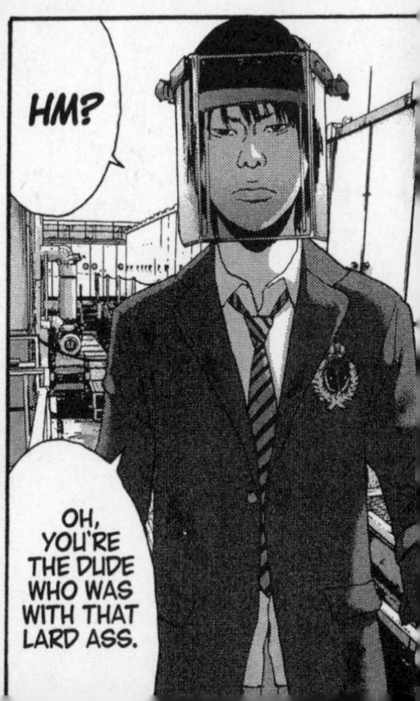
HM?
OH, YOU'RE THE DUDE WHO WAS WITH THAT LARD ASS.

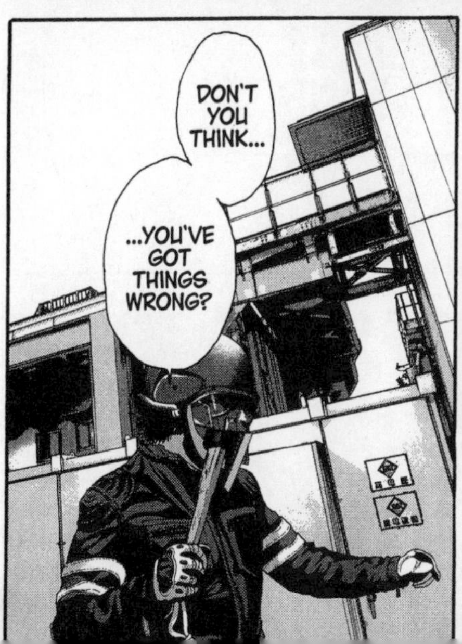
DON'T YOU THINK...
...YOU'VE GOT THINGS WRONG?

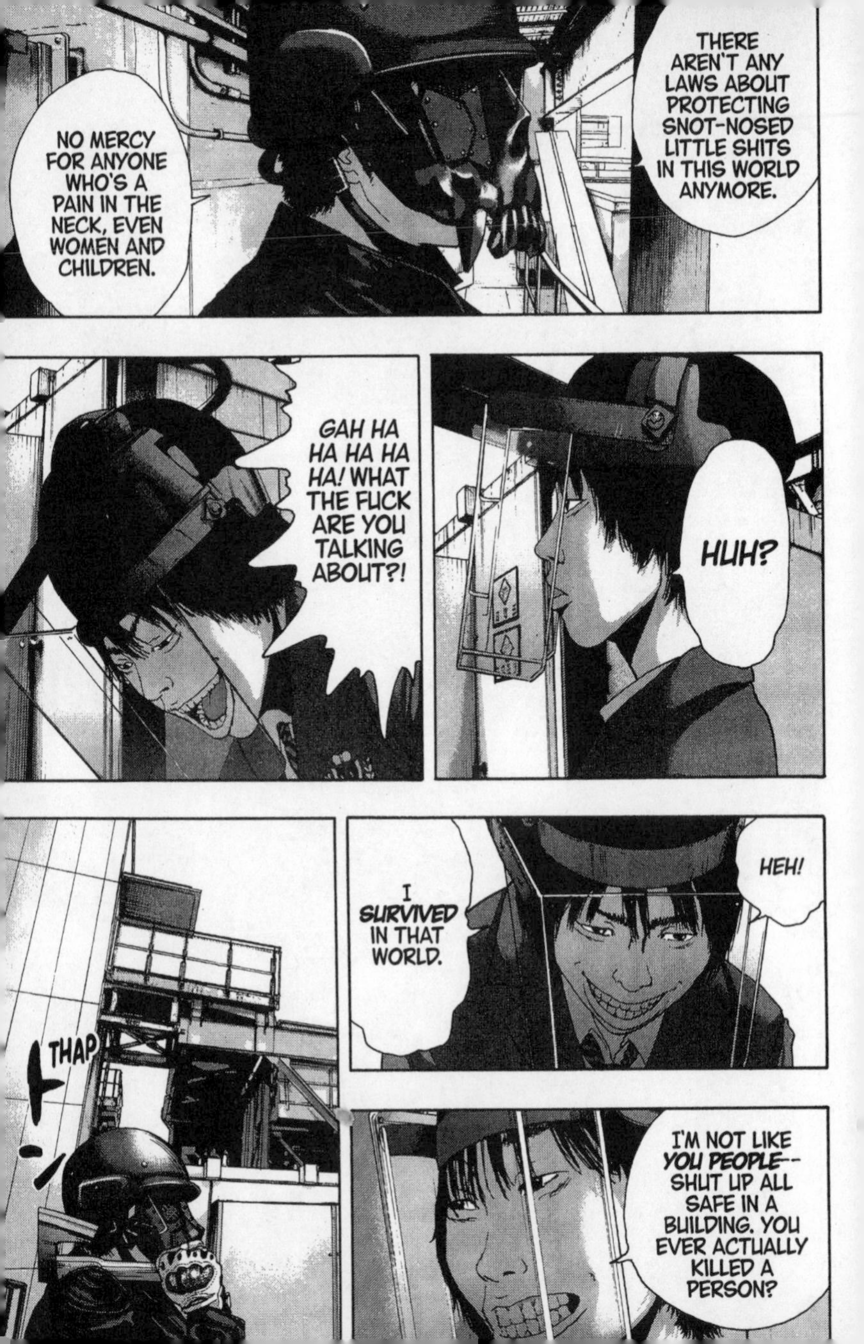
THERE AREN'T ANY LAWS ABOUT PROTECTING SNOT-NOSED LITTLE SHITS IN THIS WORLD ANYMORE.
NO MERCY FOR ANYONE WHO'S A PAIN IN THE NECK, EVEN WOMEN AND CHILDREN.
HUH?
GAH HA HA HA HA HA! WHAT THE FUCK ARE YOU TALKING ABOUT?!
HEH!
I *SURVIVED* IN THAT WORLD.
I'M NOT LIKE *YOU PEOPLE*--SHUT UP ALL SAFE IN A BUILDING. YOU EVER ACTUALLY KILLED A PERSON?
THAP

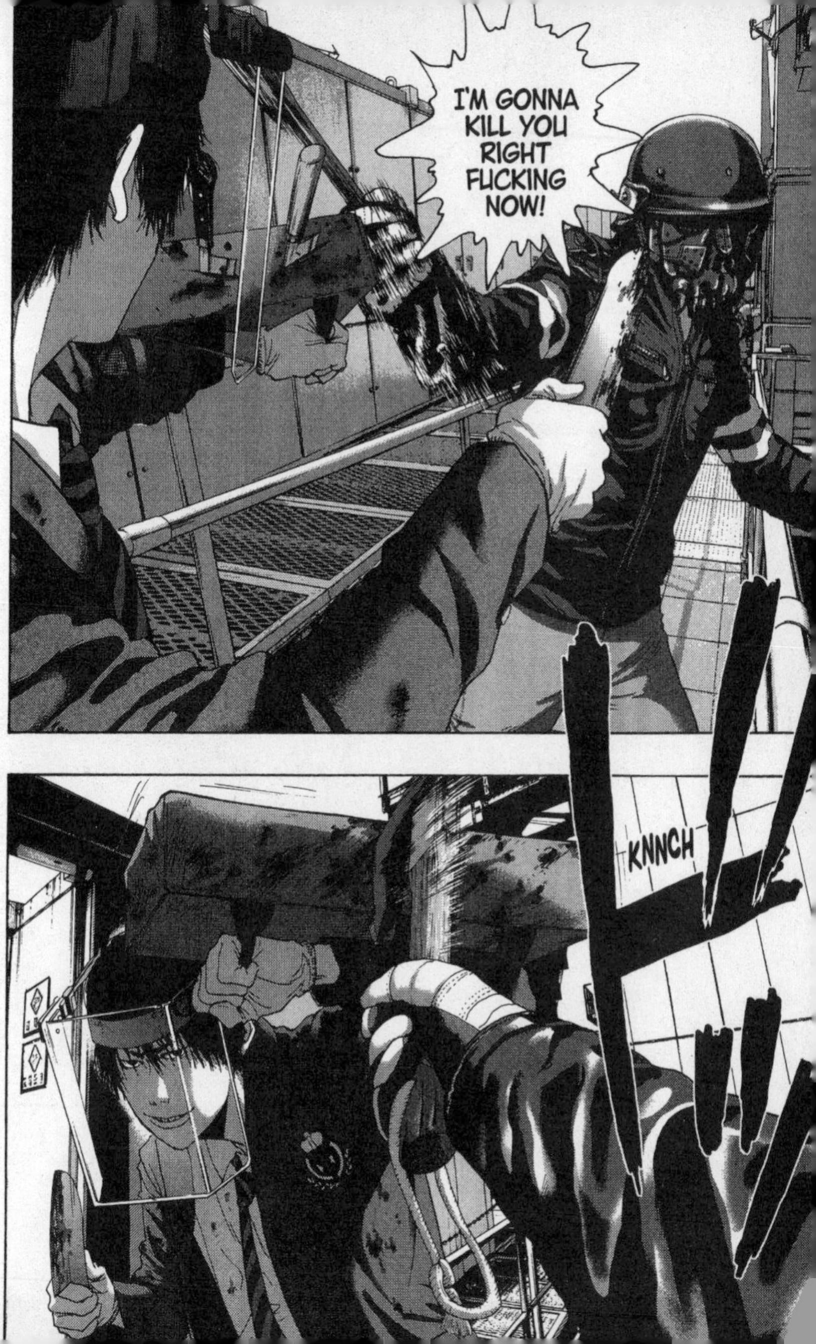
I'M GONNA KILL YOU RIGHT FUCKING NOW!
KNNCH

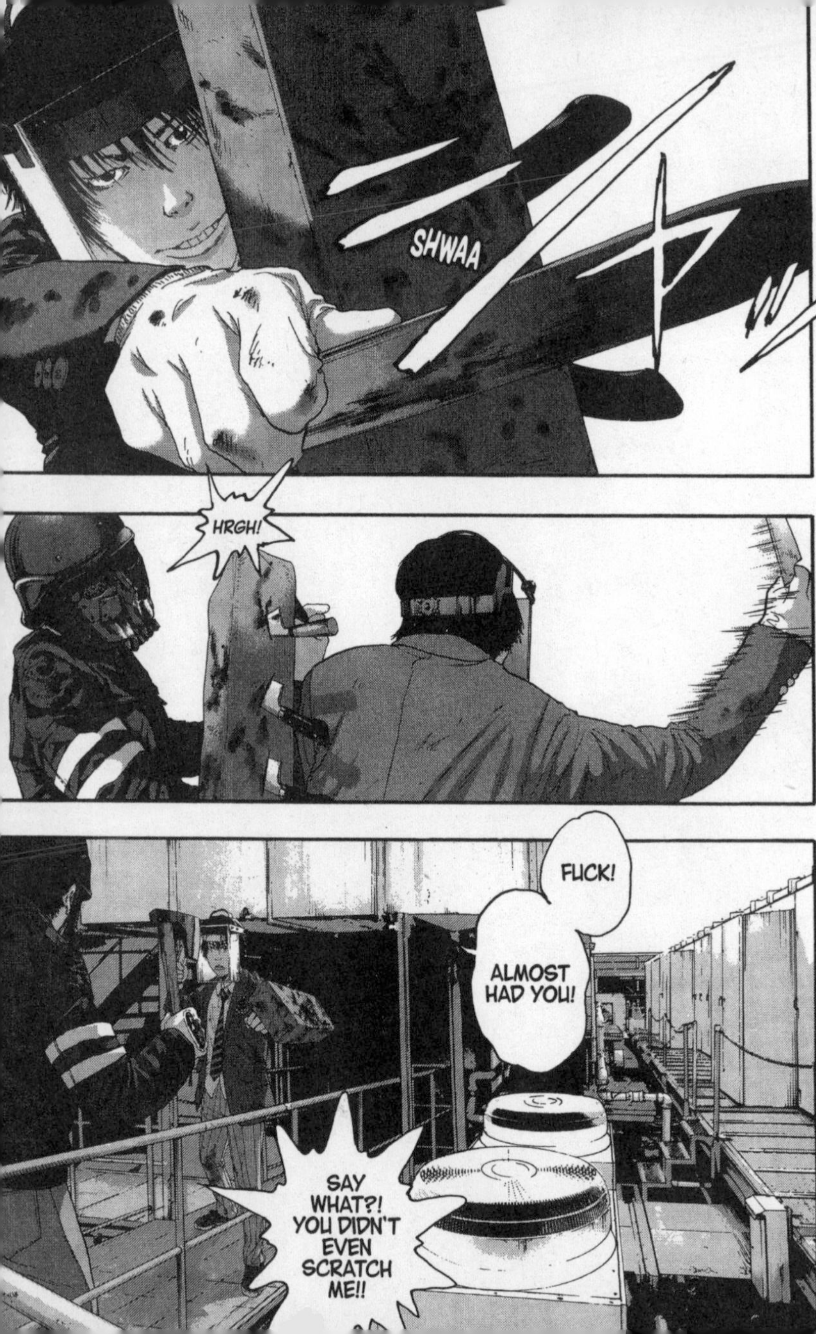
SHWAA
HRGH!
FUCK!
ALMOST HAD YOU!
SAY WHAT?! YOU DIDN'T EVEN SCRATCH ME!!

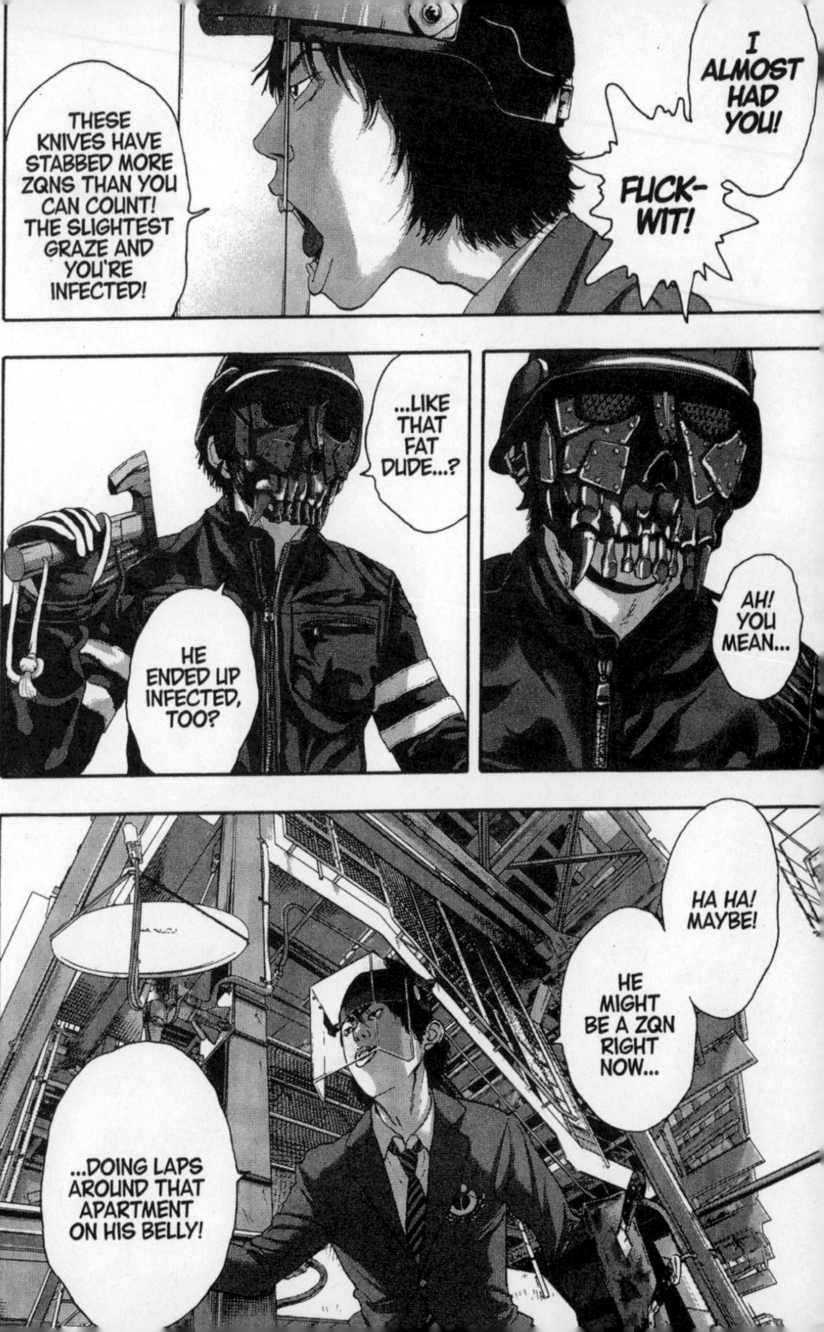
I ALMOST HAD YOU!
FUCK-WIT!
THESE KNIVES HAVE STABBED MORE ZQNS THAN YOU CAN COUNT! THE SLIGHTEST GRAZE AND YOU'RE INFECTED!
AH! YOU MEAN...
...LIKE THAT FAT DUDE...?
HE ENDED UP INFECTED, TOO?
HA HA! MAYBE!
HE MIGHT BE A ZQN RIGHT NOW...
...DOING LAPS AROUND THAT APARTMENT ON HIS BELLY!

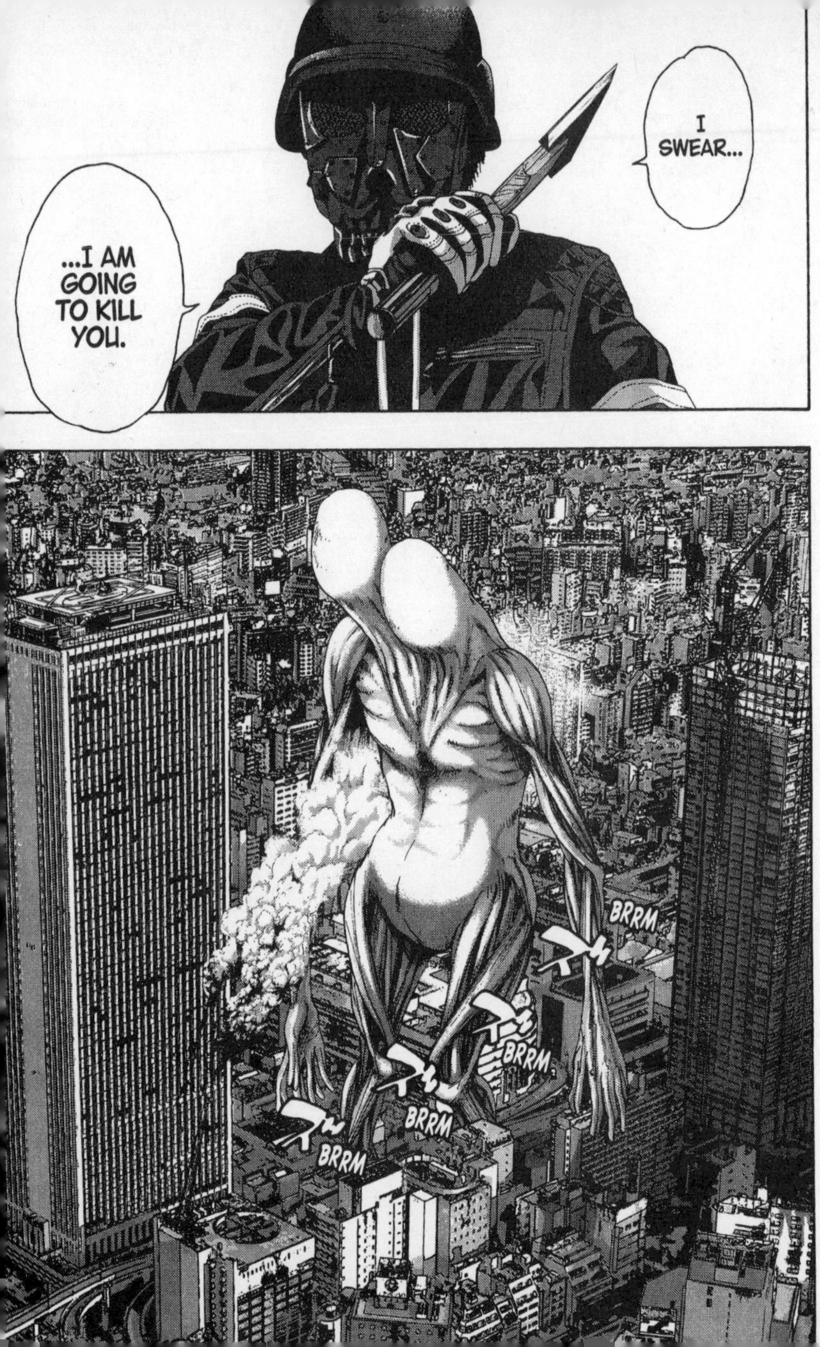
I SWEAR...
...I AM GOING TO KILL YOU.
BRRM
BRRM
BRRM
BRRM

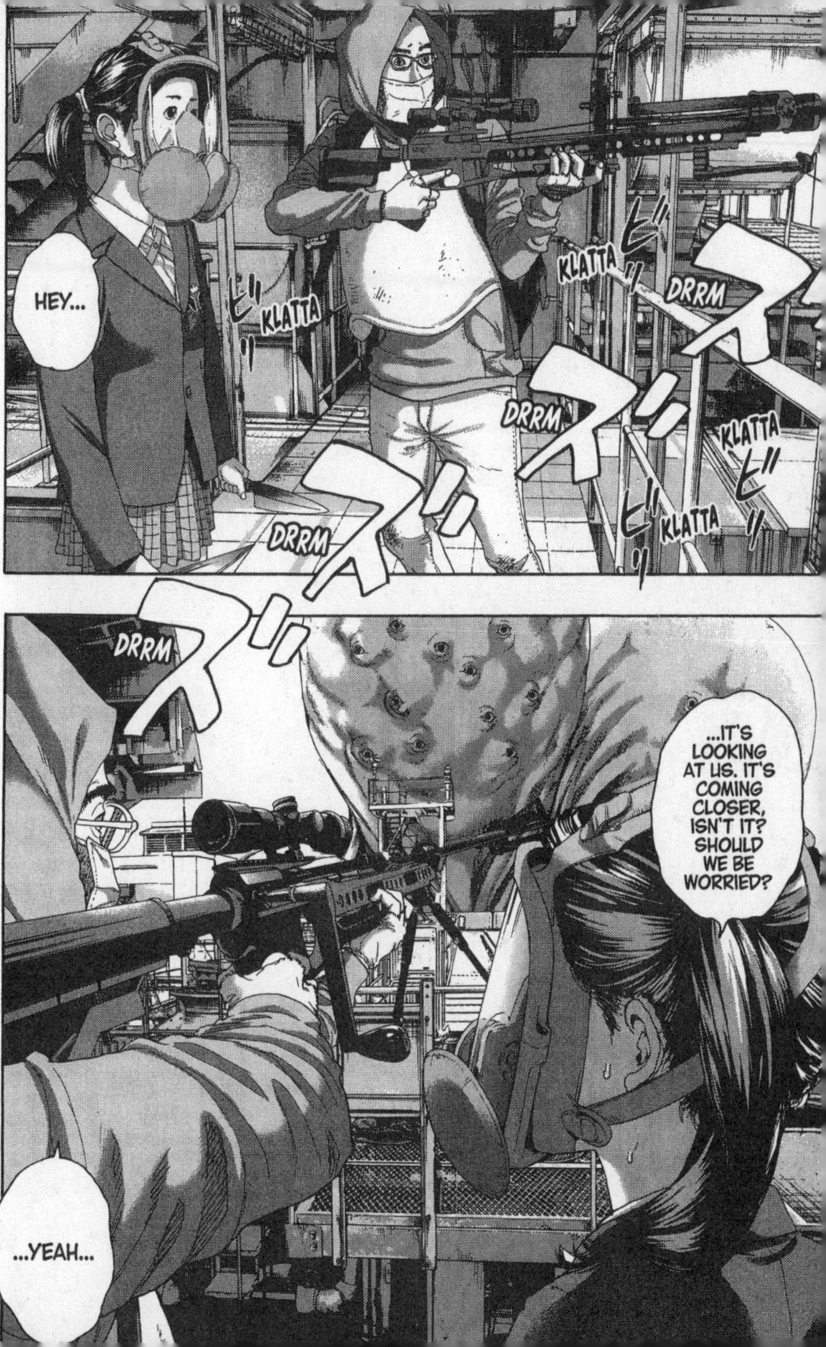
DRRM
KLATTA
KLATTA
KLATTA
DRRM
DRRM
KLATTA
HEY...
...IT'S LOOKING AT US. IT'S COMING CLOSER, ISN'T IT? SHOULD WE BE WORRIED?
DRRM
...YEAH...

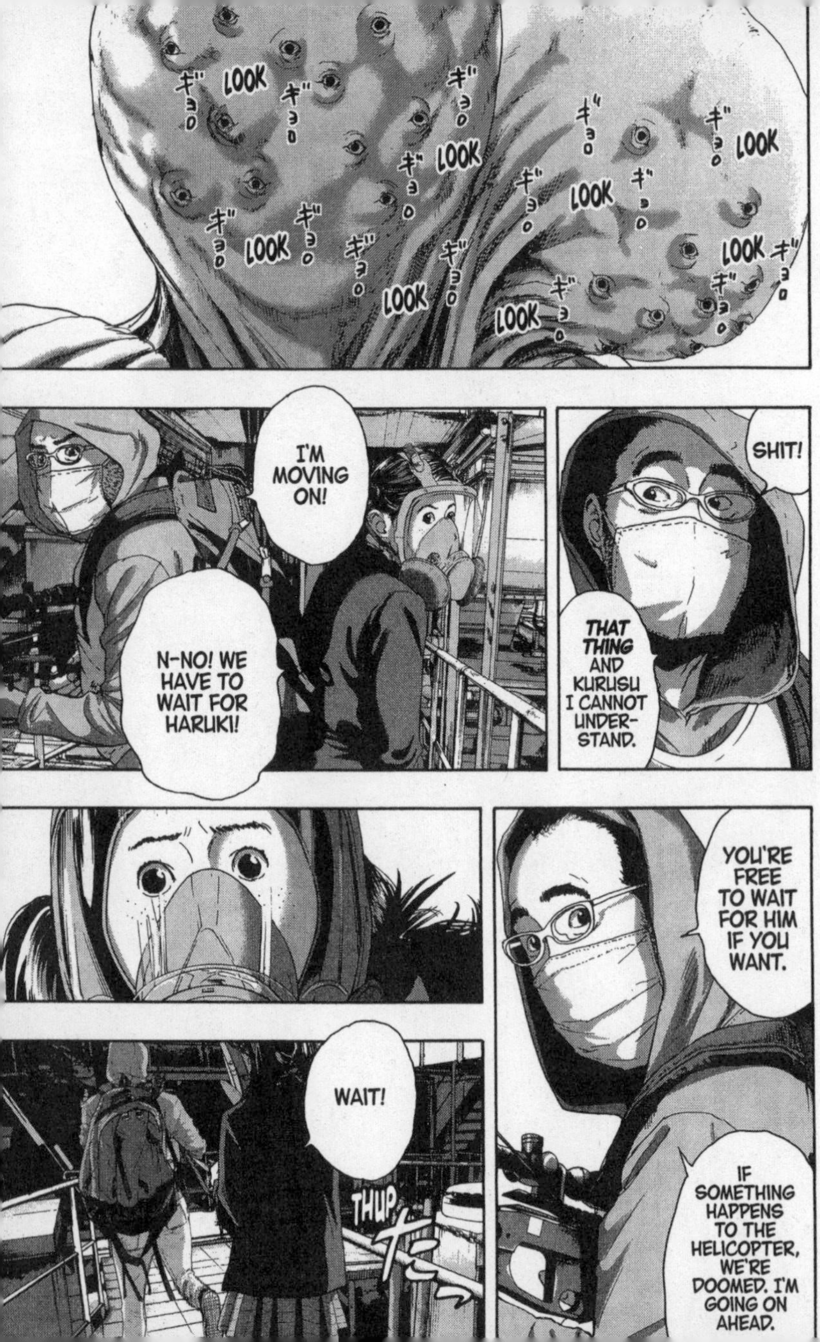

LOOK
ギョロ
LOOK
ギョロ
ギョロ
ギョロ
LOOK
ギョロ
ギョロ
LOOK
ギョロ
ギョロ
LOOK
ギョロ
ギョロ
LOOK
ギョロ
ギョロ
ギョロ
LOOK
ギョロ
LOOK
ギョロ
SHIT!
THAT THING AND KURUSU I CANNOT UNDERSTAND.
I'M MOVING ON!
N-NO! WE HAVE TO WAIT FOR HARUKI!
YOU'RE FREE TO WAIT FOR HIM IF YOU WANT.
IF SOMETHING HAPPENS TO THE HELICOPTER, WE'RE DOOMED. I'M GOING ON AHEAD.
WAIT!
THUP

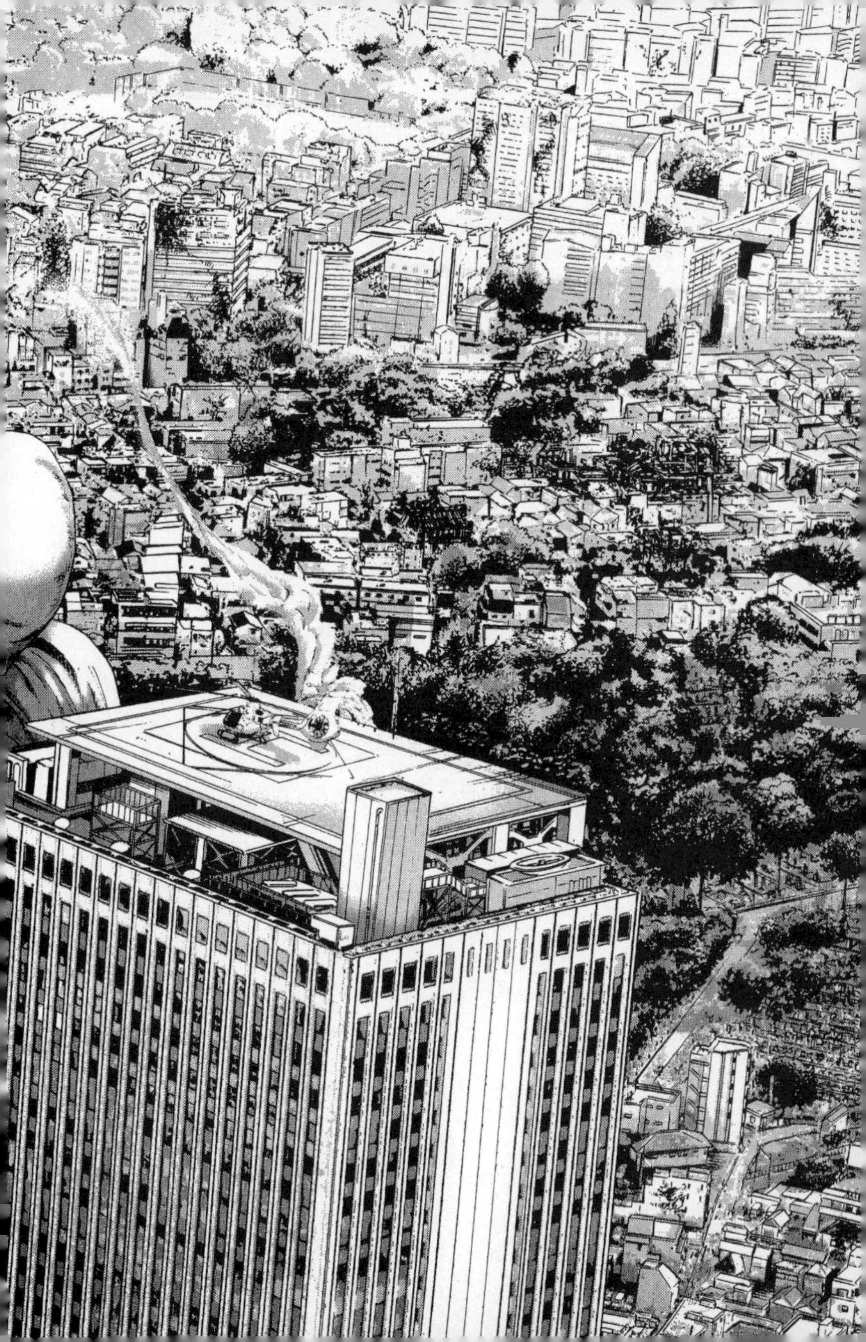

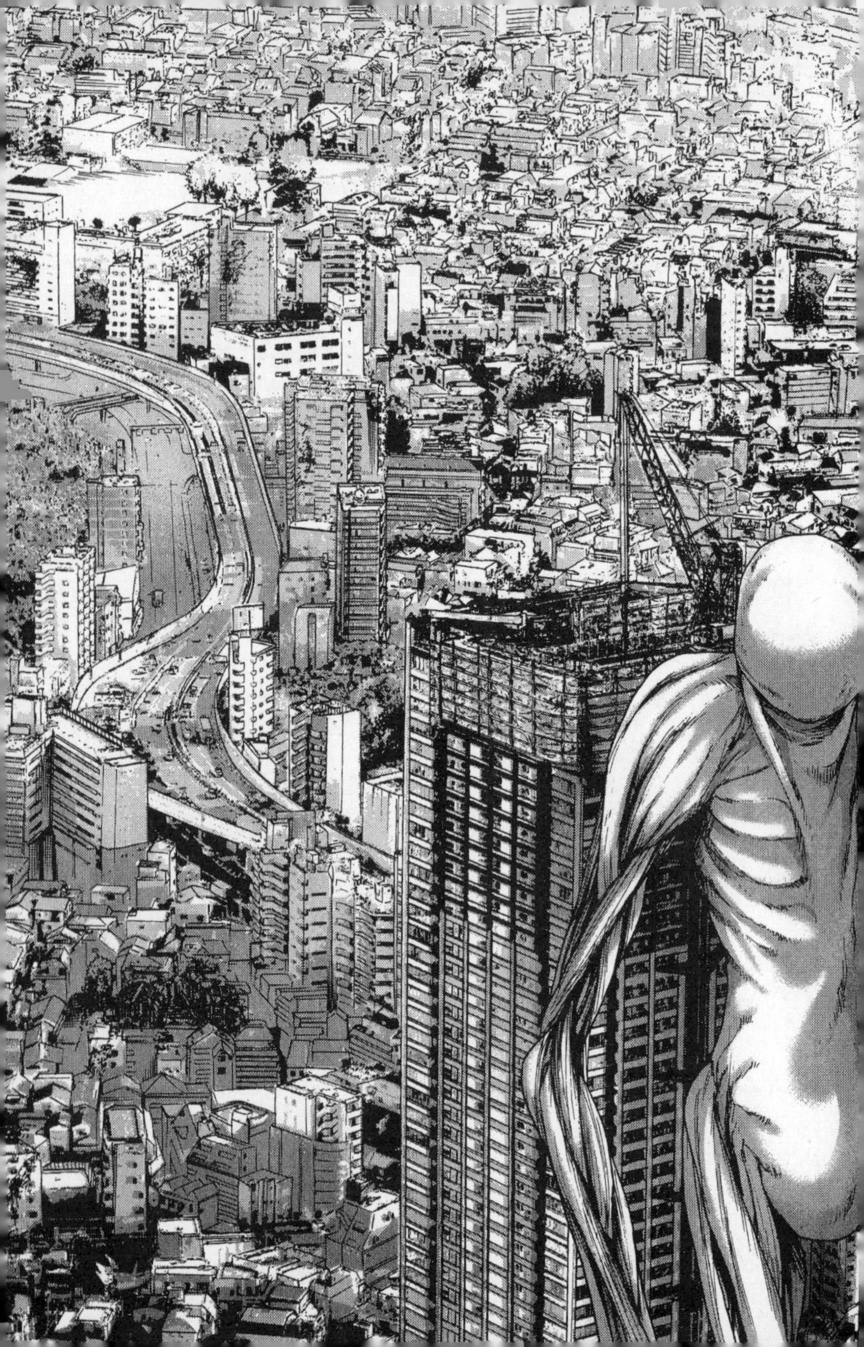

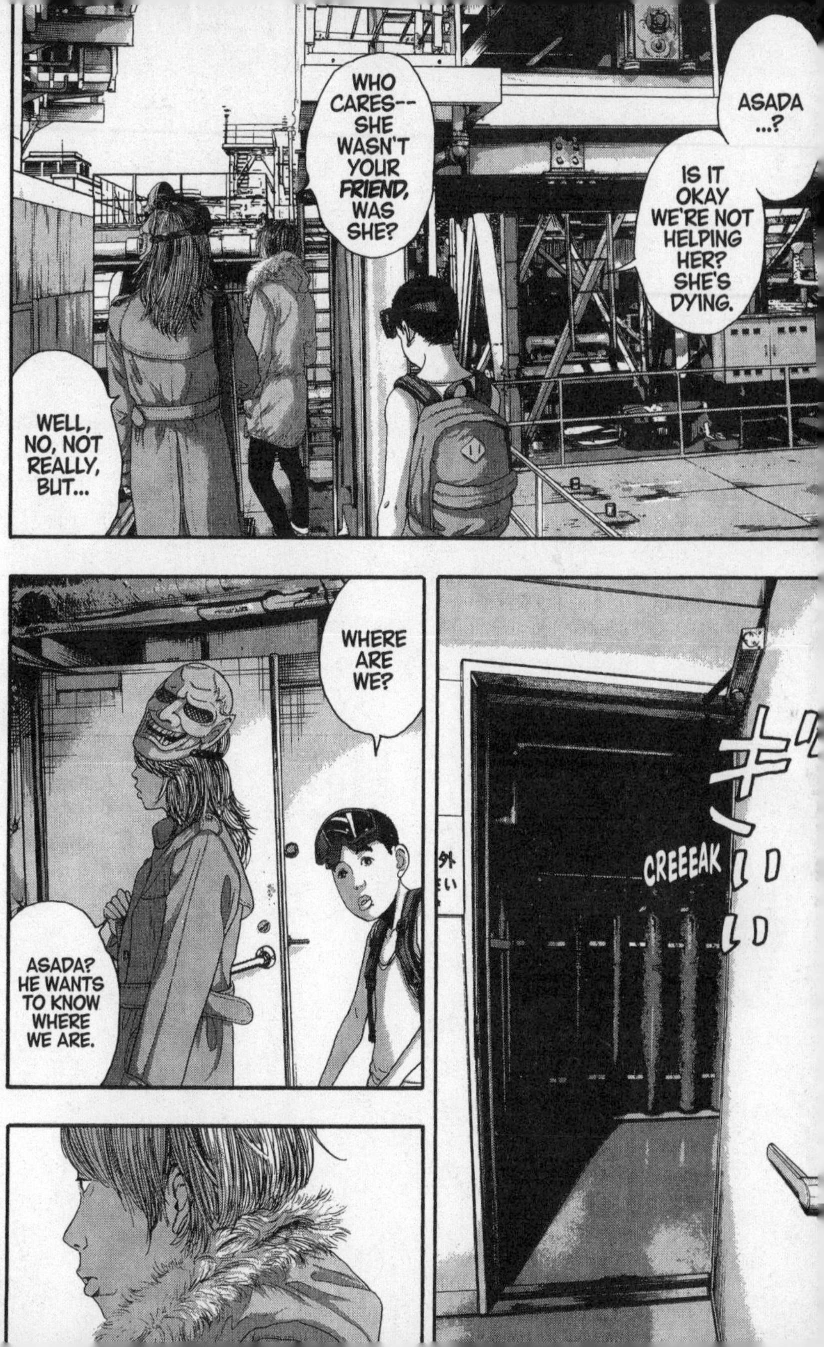
ASADA ...?
IS IT OKAY WE'RE NOT HELPING HER? SHE'S DYING.
WHO CARES-- SHE WASN'T YOUR FRIEND, WAS SHE?
WELL, NO, NOT REALLY, BUT...
CREEEAK
WHERE ARE WE?
ASADA? HE WANTS TO KNOW WHERE WE ARE.

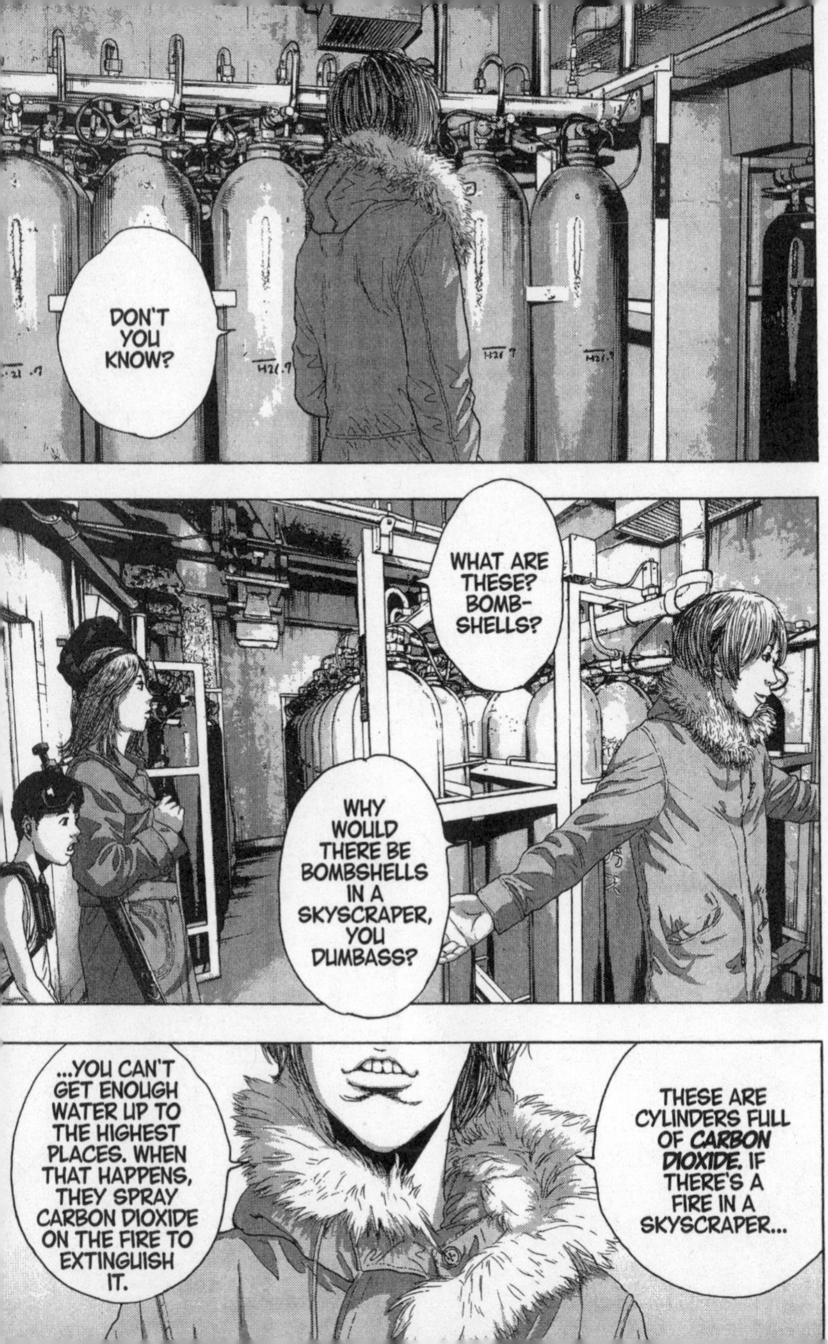
DON'T YOU KNOW?
WHAT ARE THESE? BOMB-SHELLS?
WHY WOULD THERE BE BOMBSHELLS IN A SKYSCRAPER, YOU DUMBASS?
THESE ARE CYLINDERS FULL OF *CARBON DIOXIDE.* IF THERE'S A FIRE IN A SKYSCRAPER...
...YOU CAN'T GET ENOUGH WATER UP TO THE HIGHEST PLACES. WHEN THAT HAPPENS, THEY SPRAY CARBON DIOXIDE ON THE FIRE TO EXTINGUISH IT.

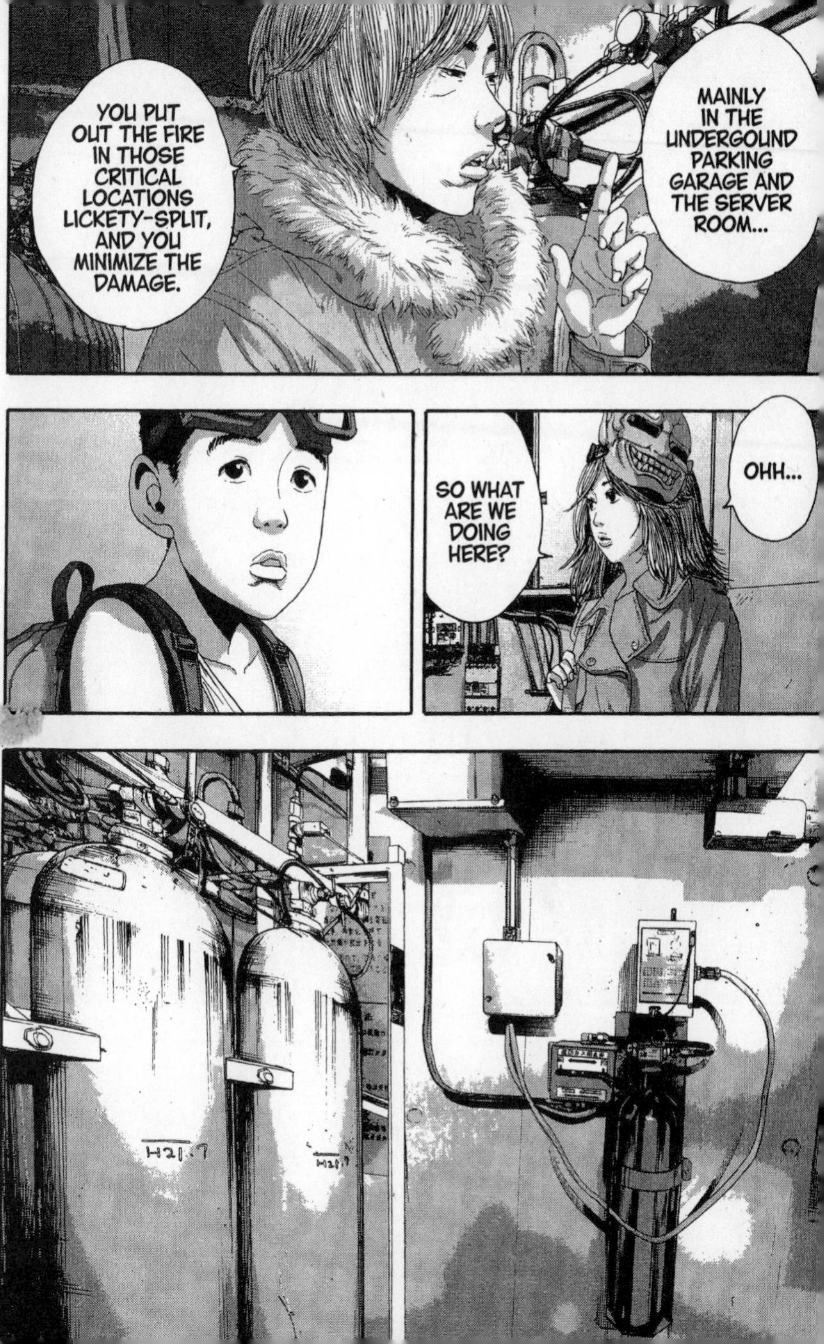
MAINLY IN THE UNDERGOUND PARKING GARAGE AND THE SERVER ROOM...
YOU PUT OUT THE FIRE IN THOSE CRITICAL LOCATIONS LICKETY-SPLIT, AND YOU MINIMIZE THE DAMAGE.
OHH...
SO WHAT ARE WE DOING HERE?

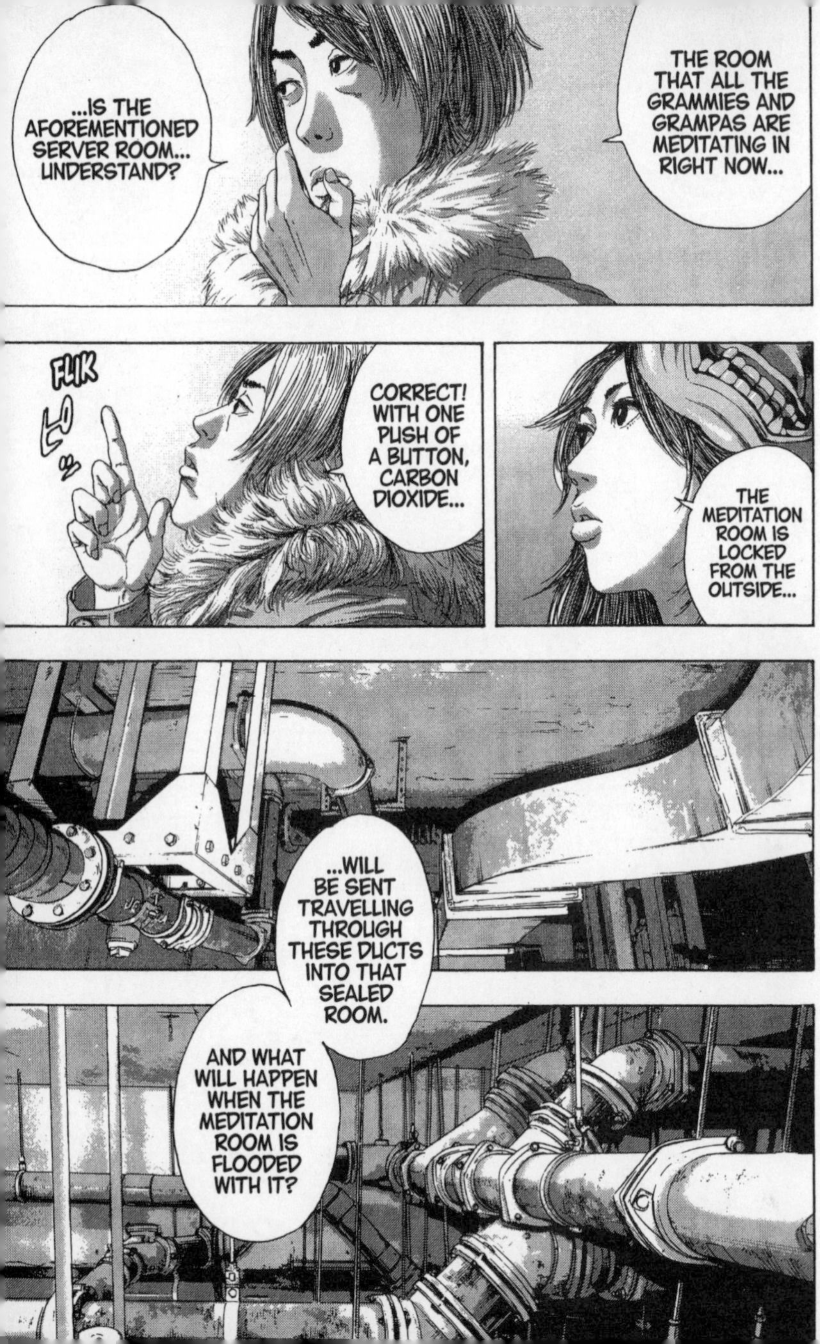
THE ROOM THAT ALL THE GRAMMIES AND GRAMPAS ARE MEDITATING IN RIGHT NOW...
...IS THE AFOREMENTIONED SERVER ROOM... UNDERSTAND?
THE MEDITATION ROOM IS LOCKED FROM THE OUTSIDE...
FLIK
CORRECT! WITH ONE PUSH OF A BUTTON, CARBON DIOXIDE...
...WILL BE SENT TRAVELLING THROUGH THESE DUCTS INTO THAT SEALED ROOM.
AND WHAT WILL HAPPEN WHEN THE MEDITATION ROOM IS FLOODED WITH IT?

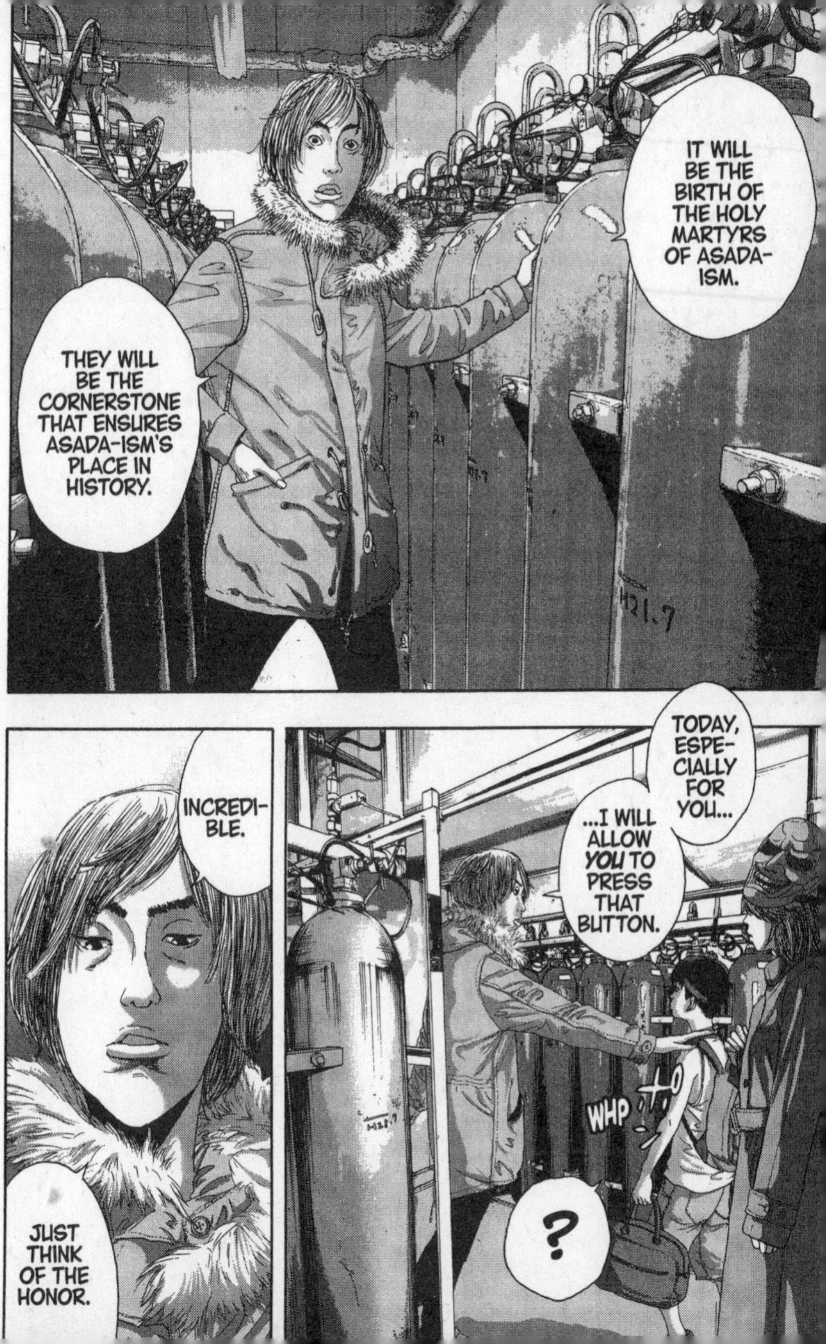
IT WILL BE THE BIRTH OF THE HOLY MARTYRS OF ASADA-ISM.
THEY WILL BE THE CORNERSTONE THAT ENSURES ASADA-ISM'S PLACE IN HISTORY.
TODAY, ESPECIALLY FOR YOU...
...I WILL ALLOW *YOU* TO PRESS THAT BUTTON.
WHP
?
INCREDIBLE.
JUST THINK OF THE HONOR.

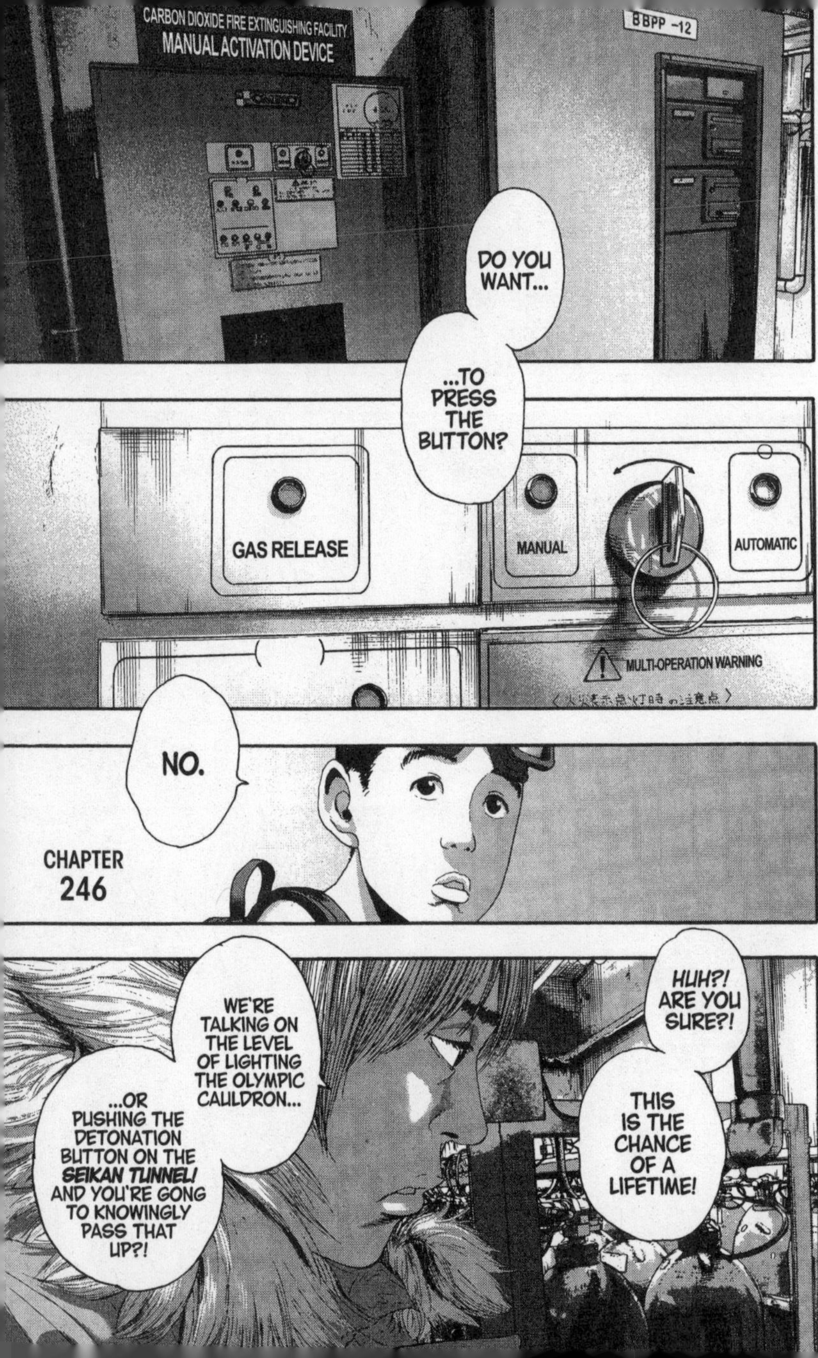
CARBON DIOXIDE FIRE EXTINGUISHING FACILITY
MANUAL ACTIVATION DEVICE
BBPP -12
DO YOU WANT...
...TO PRESS THE BUTTON?
GAS RELEASE
MANUAL
AUTOMATIC
MULTI-OPERATION WARNING
NO.
CHAPTER 246
HUH?! ARE YOU SURE?!
THIS IS THE CHANCE OF A LIFETIME!
WE'RE TALKING ON THE LEVEL OF LIGHTING THE OLYMPIC CAULDRON...
...OR PUSHING THE DETONATION BUTTON ON THE *SEIKAN TUNNEL!* AND YOU'RE GONG TO KNOWINGLY PASS THAT UP?!

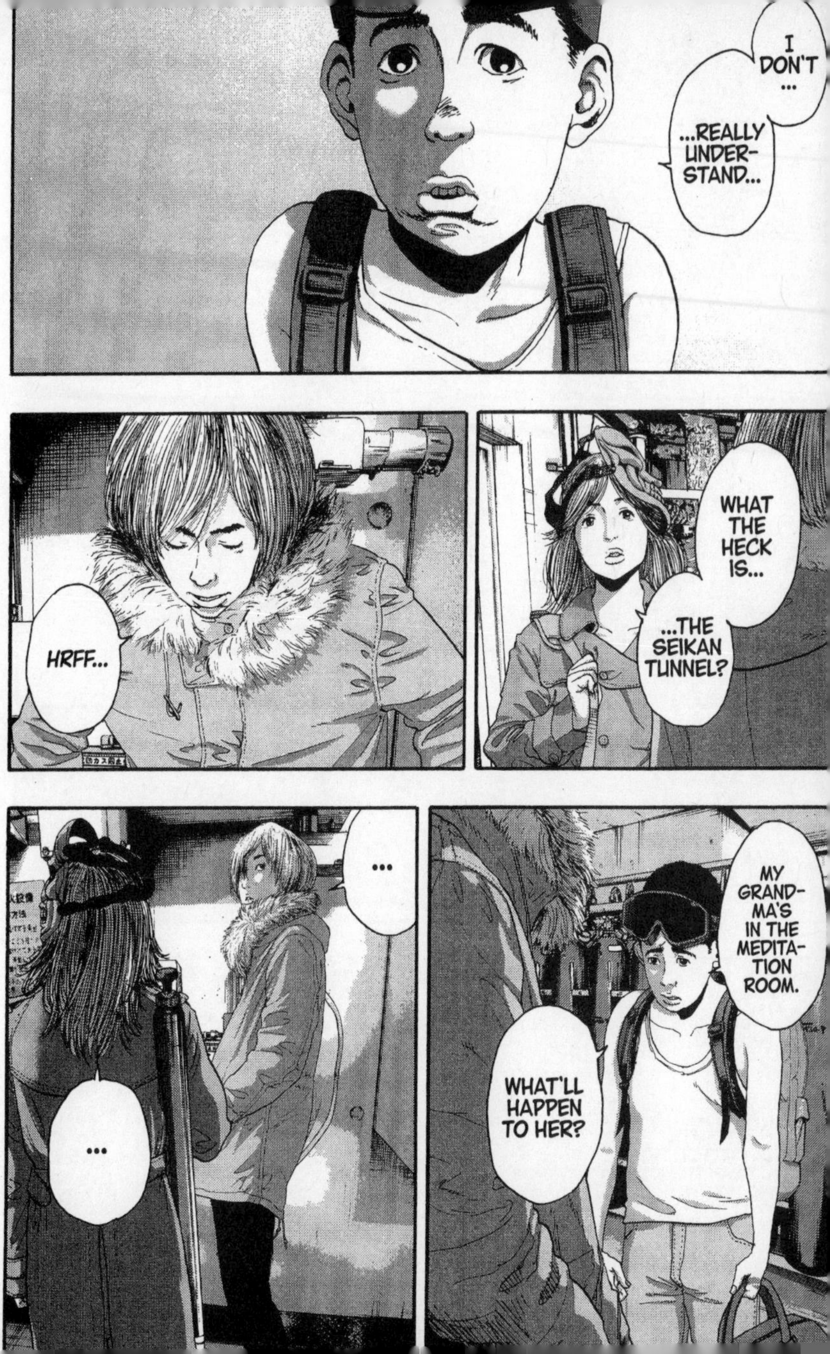
I DON'T ...
...REALLY UNDER-STAND...
WHAT THE HECK IS...
...THE SEIKAN TUNNEL?
HRFF...
MY GRAND-MA'S IN THE MEDITA-TION ROOM.
WHAT'LL HAPPEN TO HER?
...
...

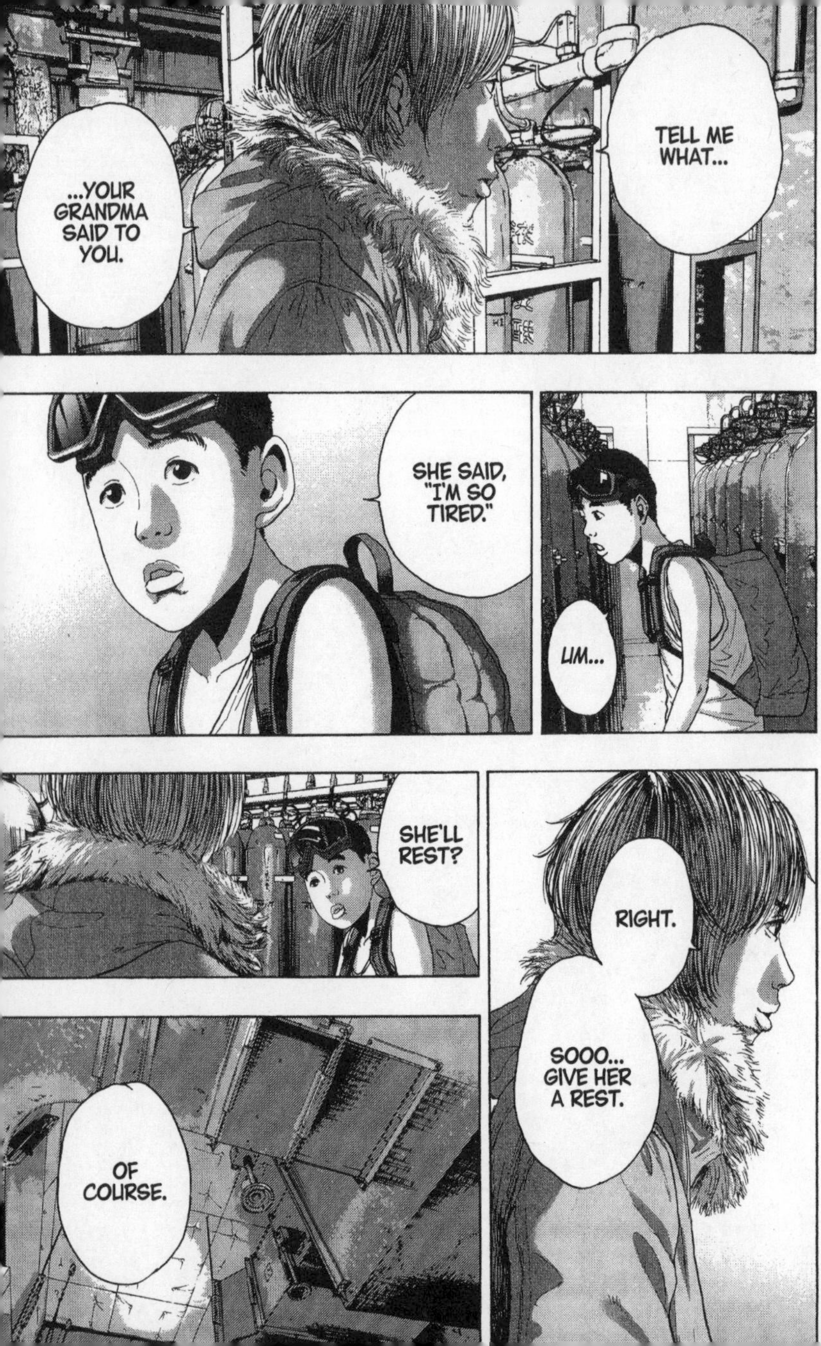
TELL ME WHAT...
...YOUR GRANDMA SAID TO YOU.
UM...
SHE SAID, "I'M SO TIRED."
RIGHT.
SOOO... GIVE HER A REST.
SHE'LL REST?
OF COURSE.

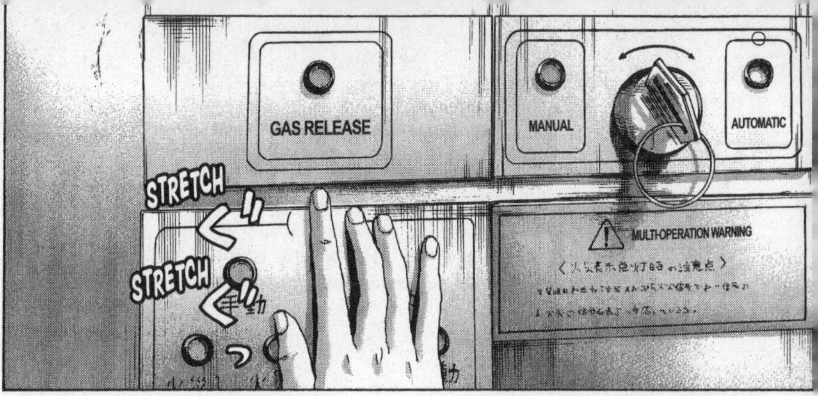
GAS RELEASE
MANUAL
AUTOMATIC
MULTI-OPERATION WARNING
STRETCH
STRETCH

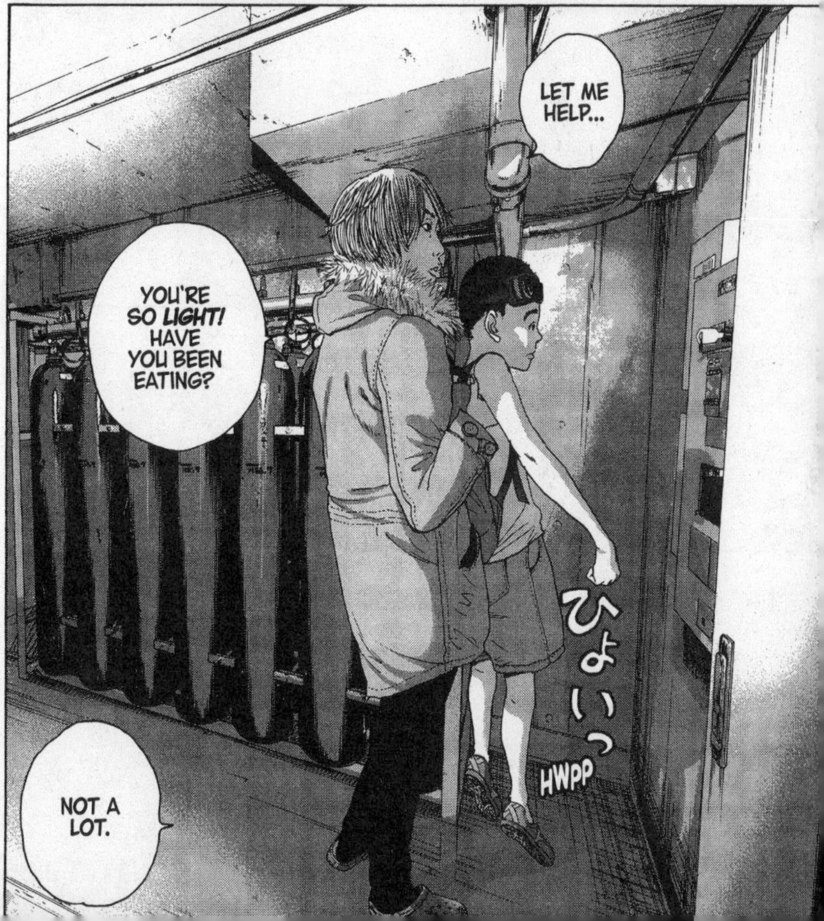
LET ME HELP...
YOU'RE SO *LIGHT!* HAVE YOU BEEN EATING?
ひょいっ
HWPP
NOT A LOT.

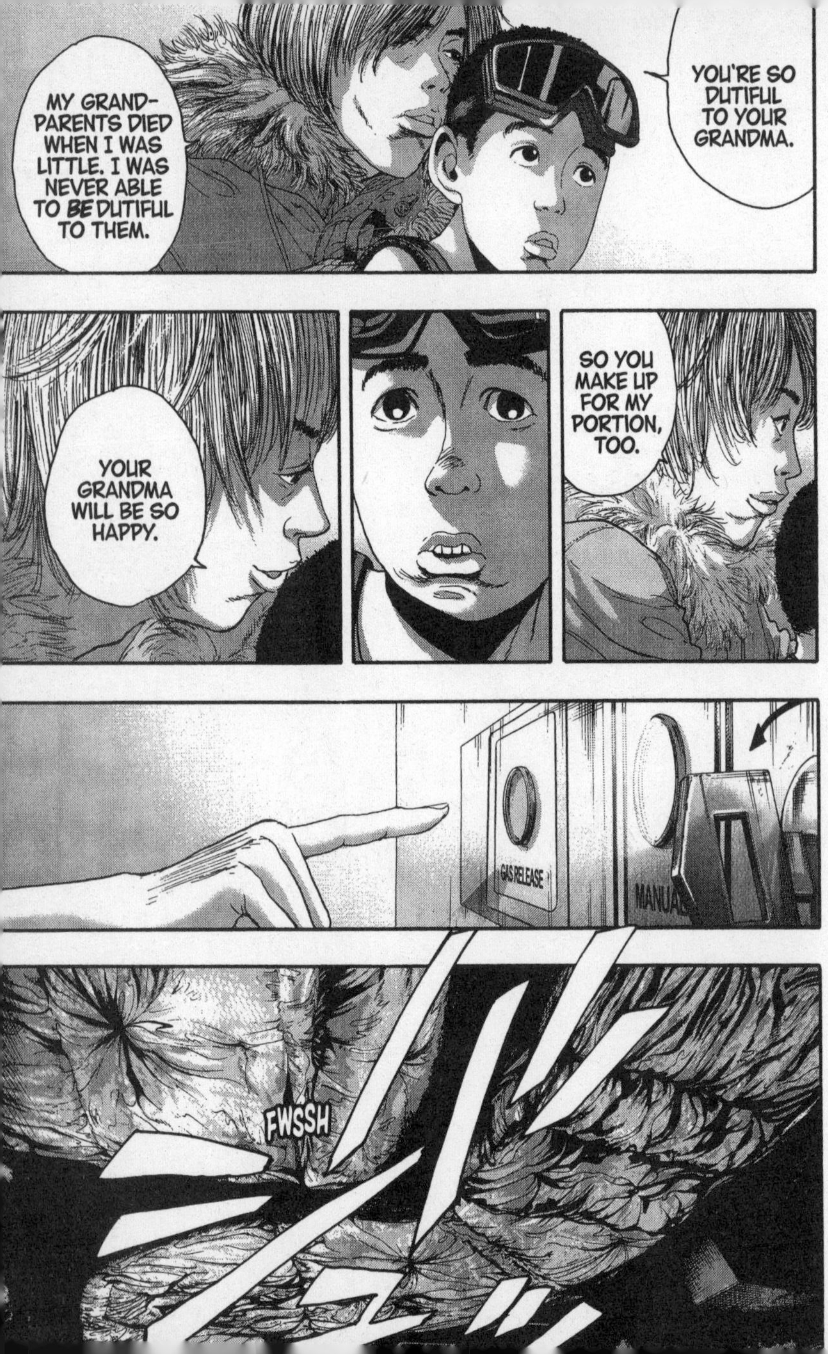
YOU'RE SO DUTIFUL TO YOUR GRANDMA.
MY GRAND-PARENTS DIED WHEN I WAS LITTLE. I WAS NEVER ABLE TO *BE* DUTIFUL TO THEM.
SO YOU MAKE UP FOR MY PORTION, TOO.
YOUR GRANDMA WILL BE SO HAPPY.
GAS RELEASE
MANUAL
FWSSH

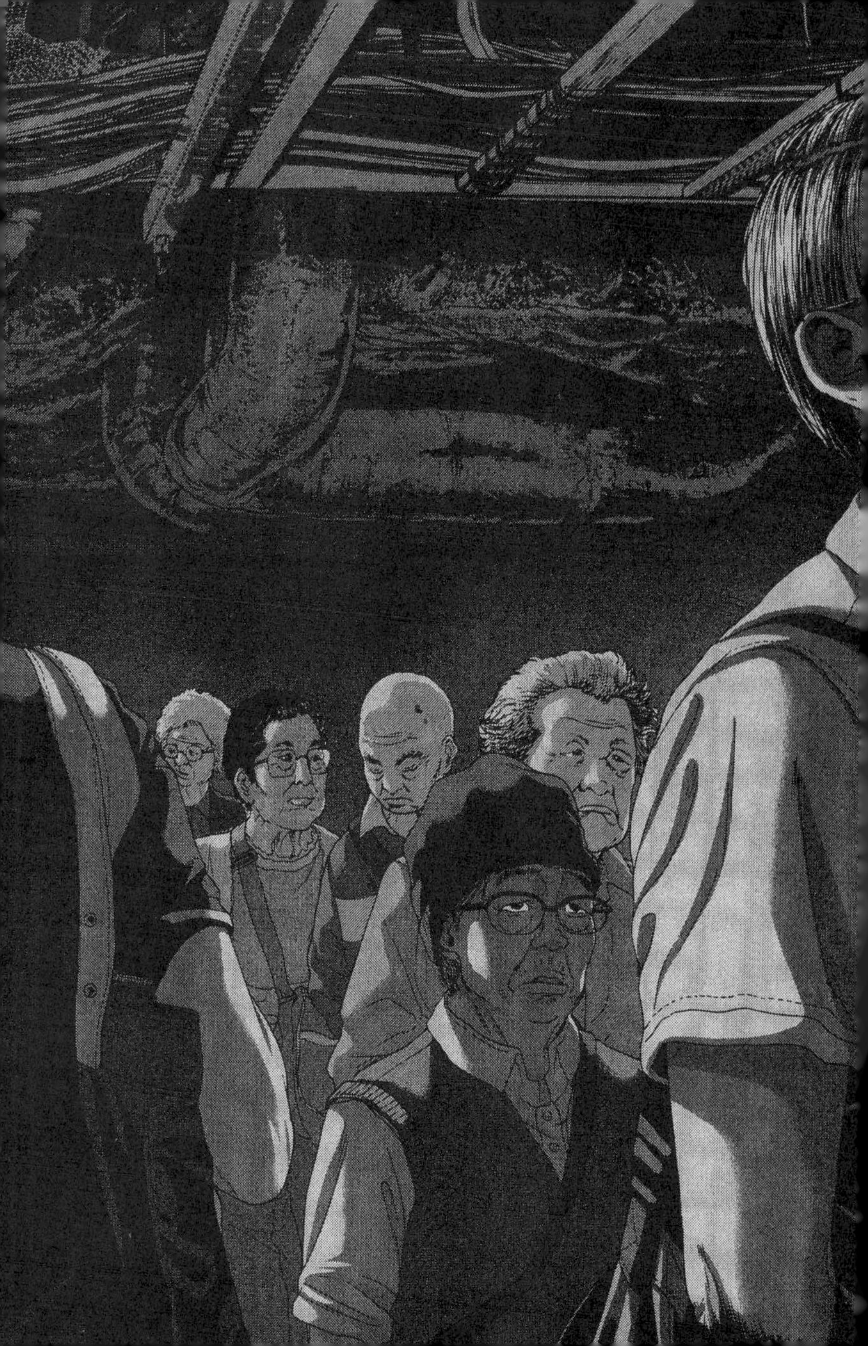

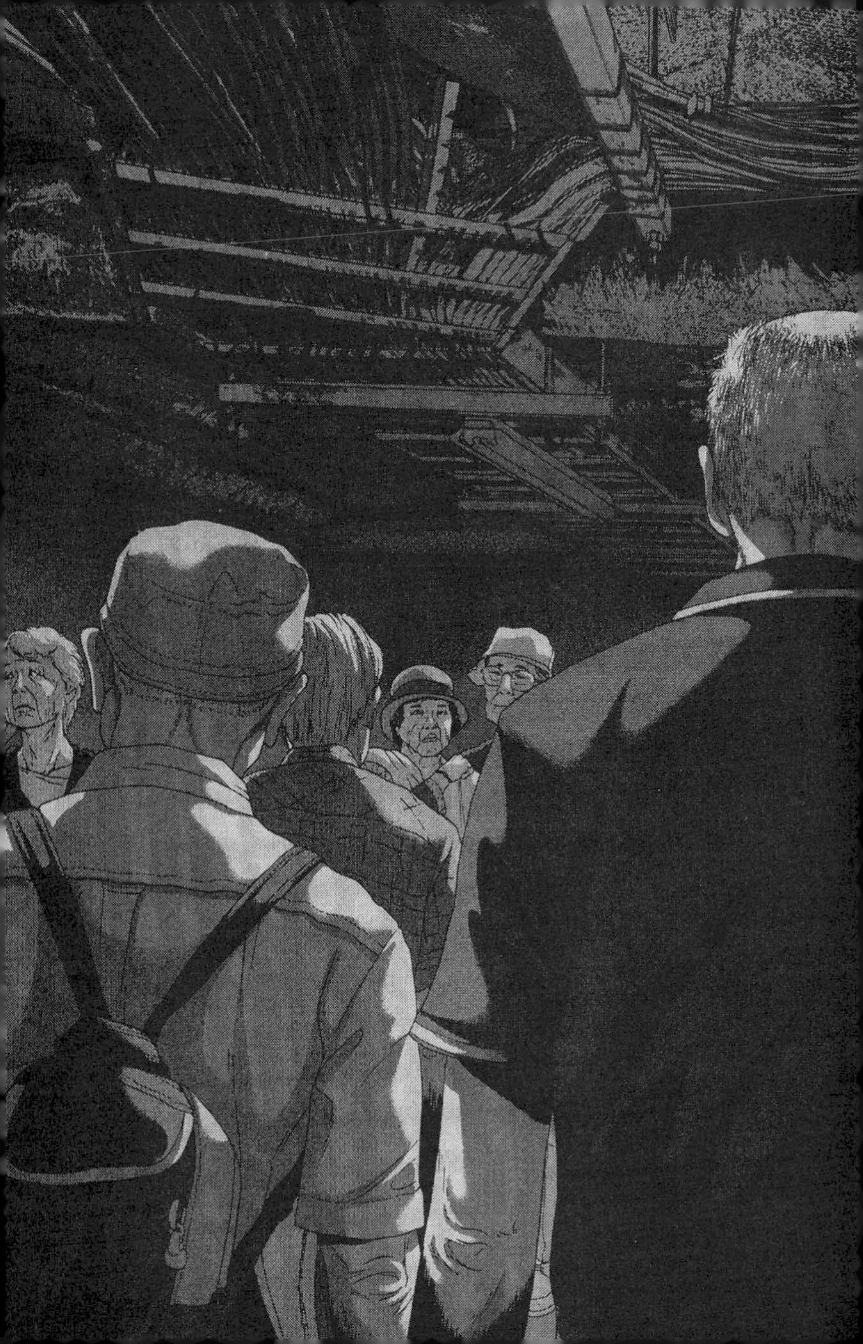

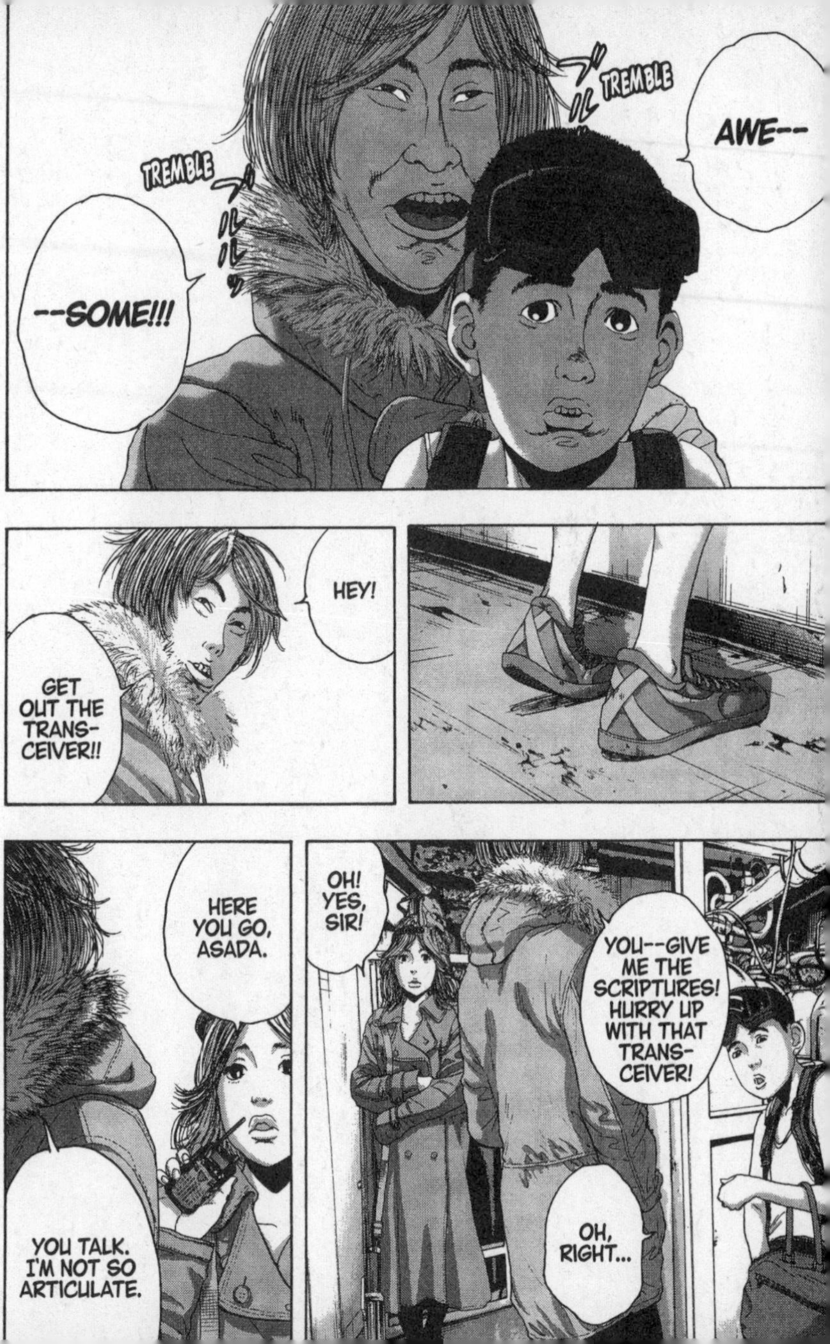
AWE--
ブル
TREMBLE
TREMBLE
ブルルッ
--SOME!!!
HEY!
GET OUT THE TRANS-CEIVER!!
YOU--GIVE ME THE SCRIPTURES! HURRY UP WITH THAT TRANS-CEIVER!
OH! YES, SIR!
OH, RIGHT...
HERE YOU GO, ASADA.
YOU TALK. I'M NOT SO ARTICULATE.

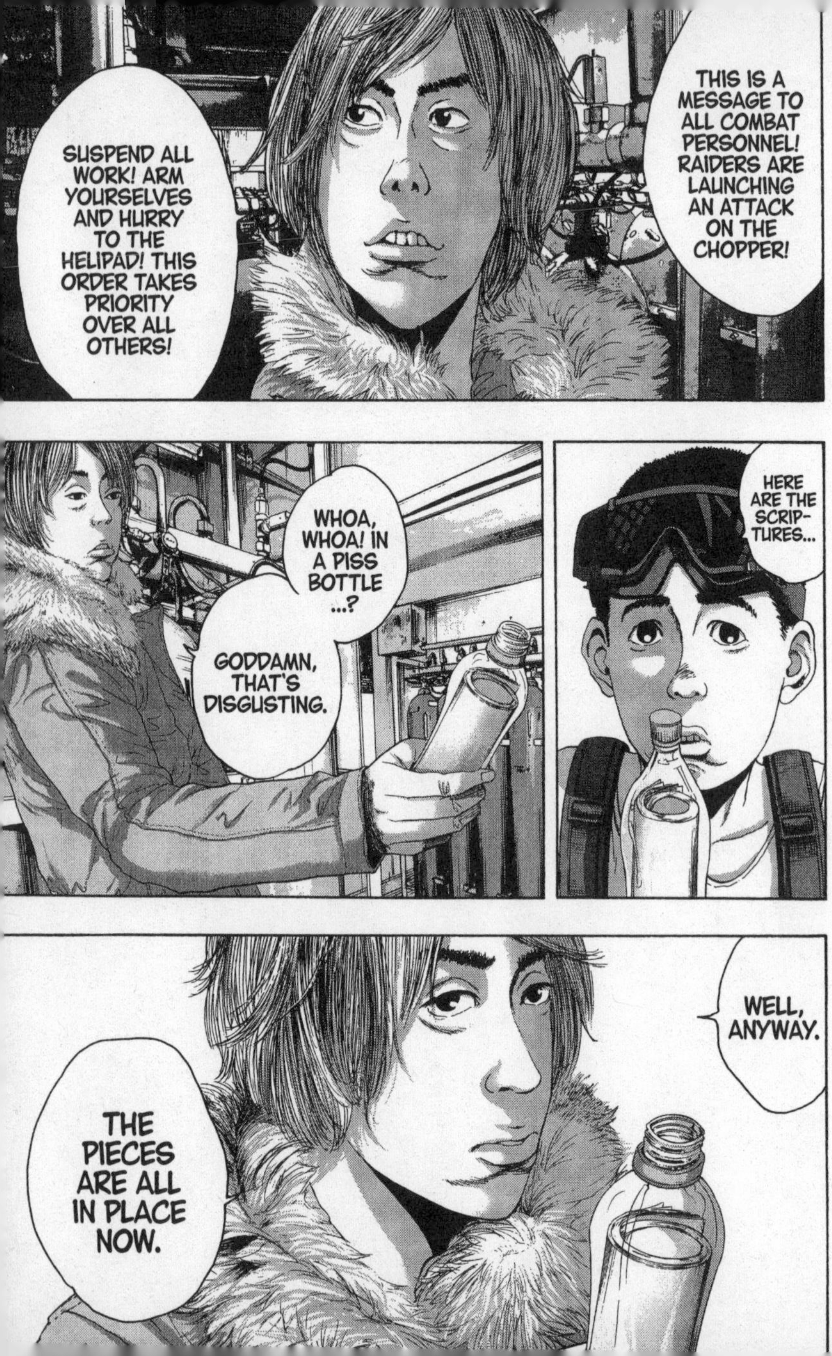
THIS IS A MESSAGE TO ALL COMBAT PERSONNEL! RAIDERS ARE LAUNCHING AN ATTACK ON THE CHOPPER!
SUSPEND ALL WORK! ARM YOURSELVES AND HURRY TO THE HELIPAD! THIS ORDER TAKES PRIORITY OVER ALL OTHERS!
HERE ARE THE SCRIP-TURES...
WHOA, WHOA! IN A PISS BOTTLE ...?
GODDAMN, THAT'S DISGUSTING.
WELL, ANYWAY.
THE PIECES ARE ALL IN PLACE NOW.

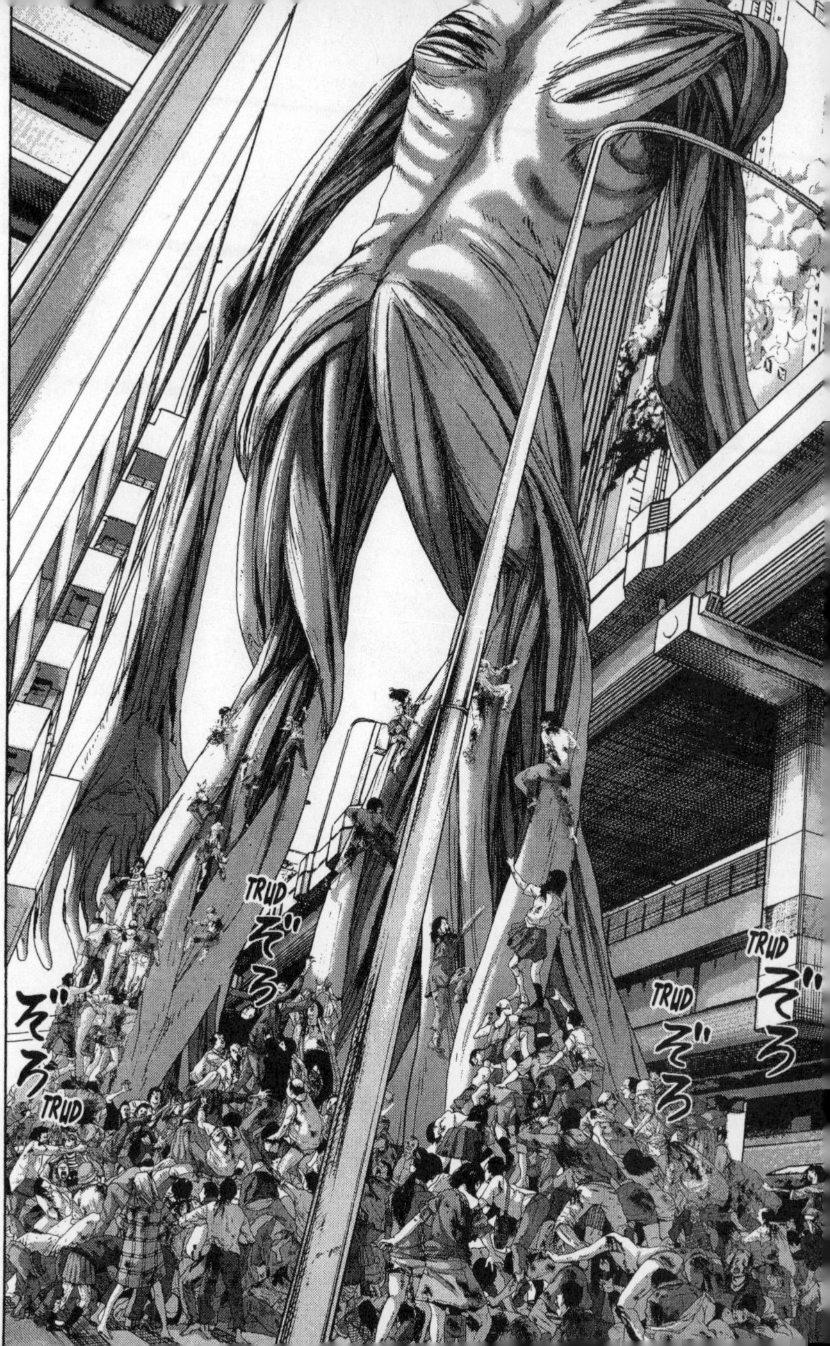
TRUD
ぞろ
TRUD
ぞろ
TRUD
ぞろ
ぞろ
TRUD

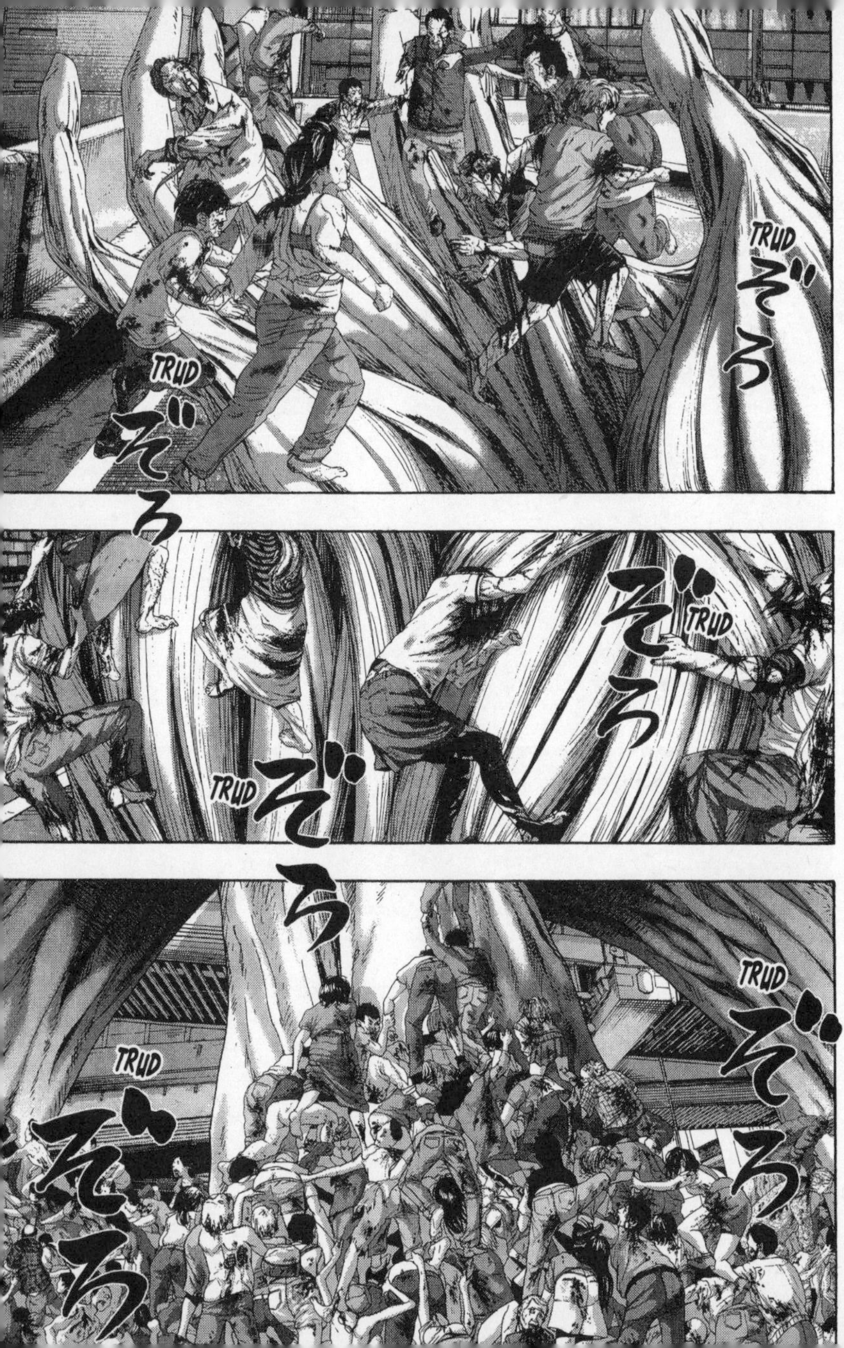
TRUD
ぞろ
TRUD
ぞろ
TRUD
ぞろ
TRUD
ぞろ
TRUD
ぞろ
TRUD
ぞろ

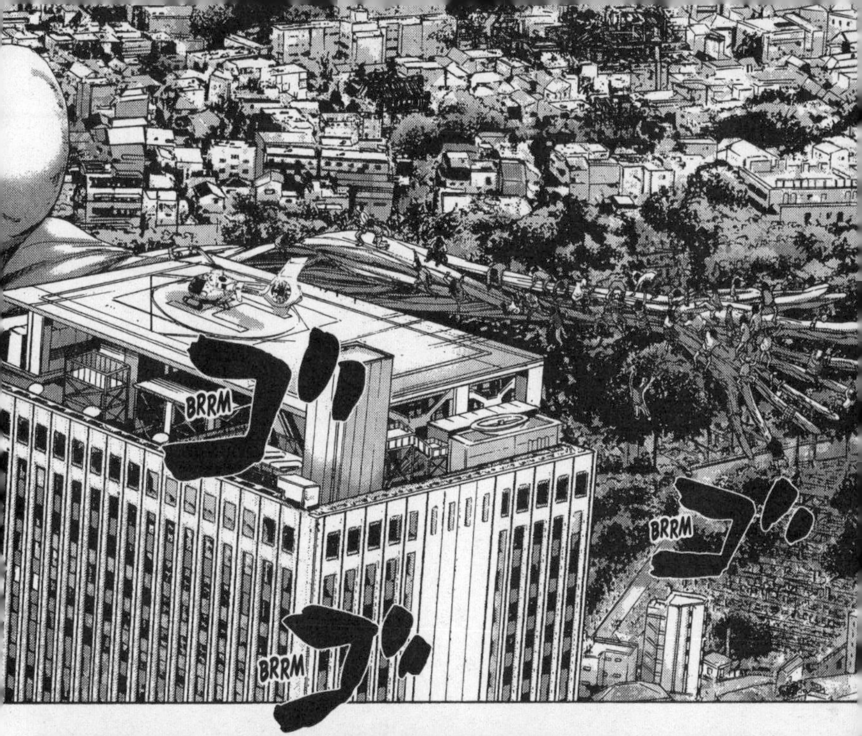
BRRM
BRRM
BRRM
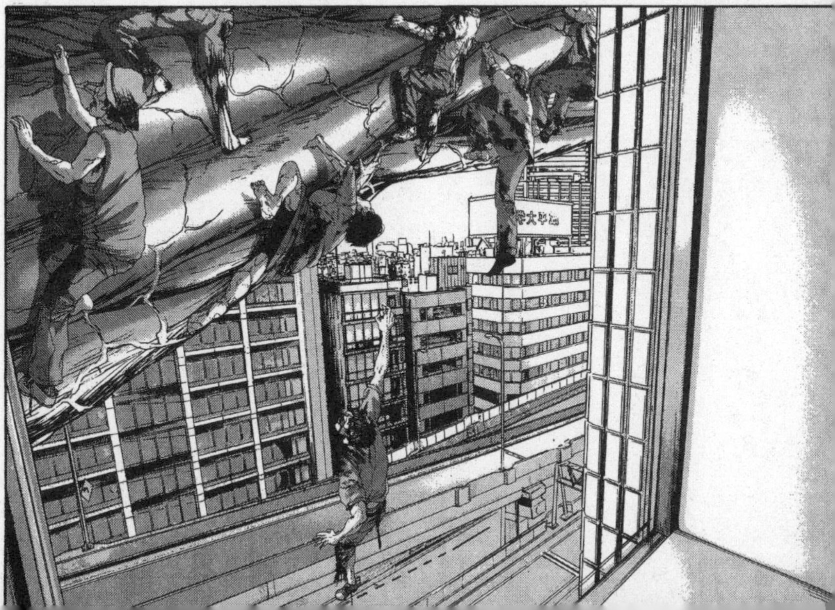

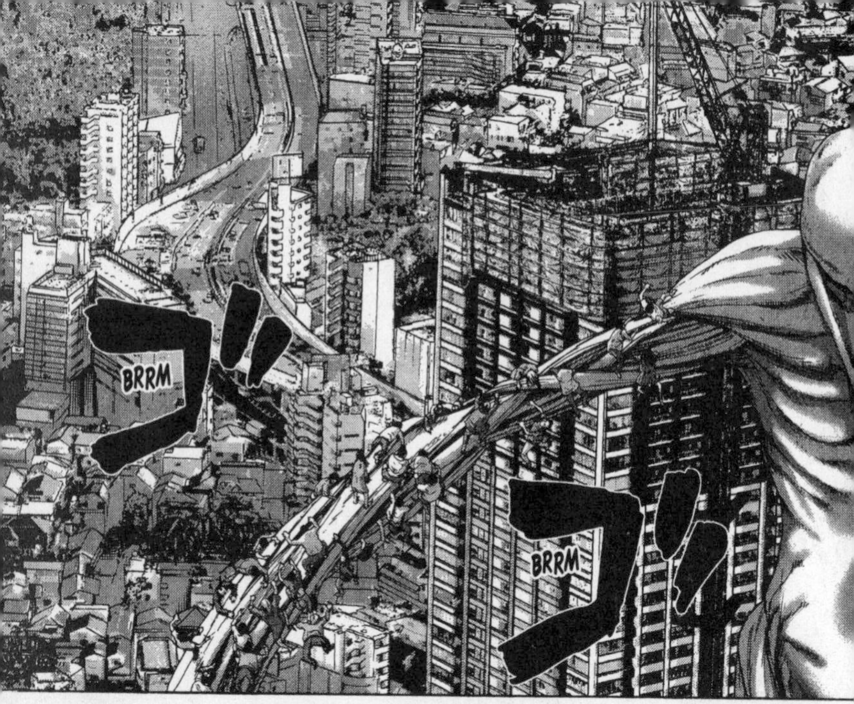
ゴ
BRRM
ゴ
BRRM
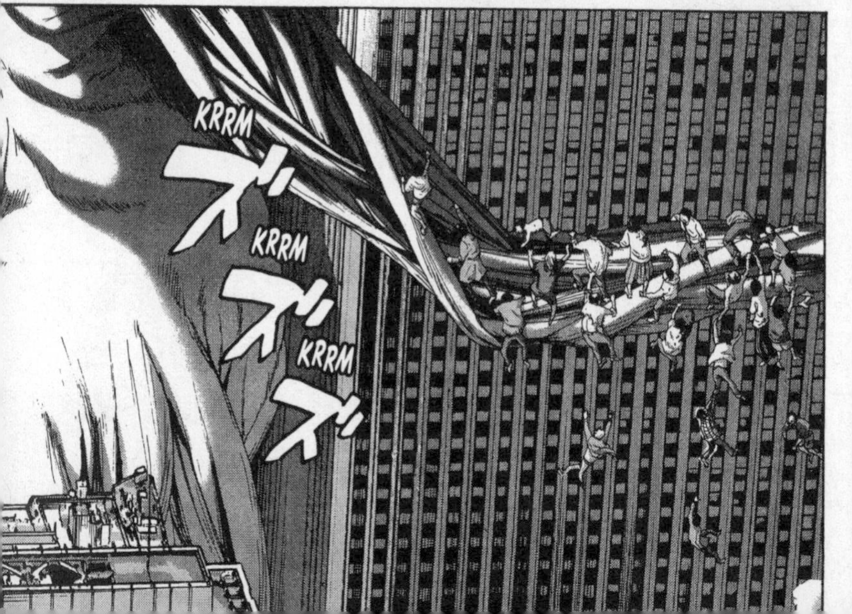
KRRM
ズ
KRRM
ズ
KRRM
ズ

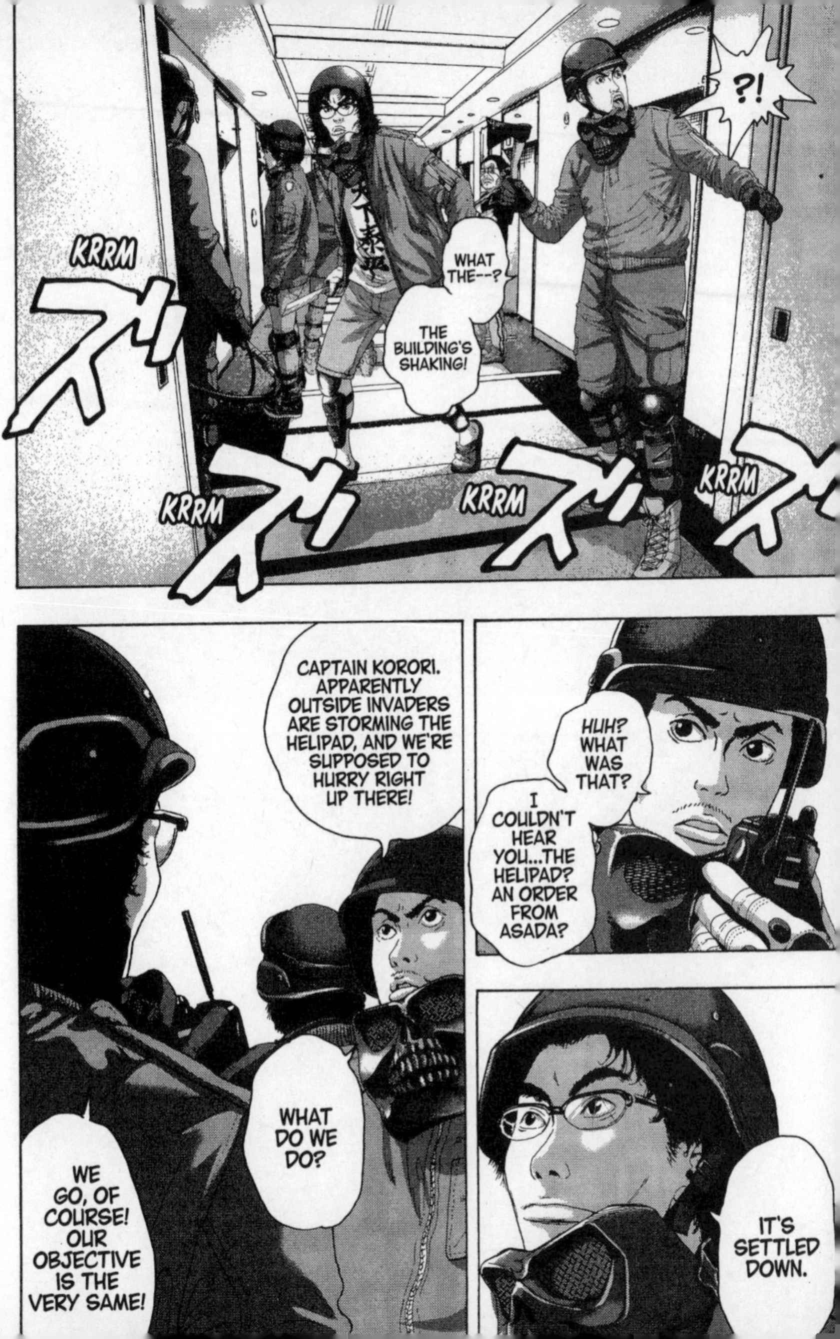
?!
WHAT THE--?
THE BUILDING'S SHAKING!
KRRM
ズ
KRRM
ズ
KRRM
ズ
KRRM
ズ
HUH? WHAT WAS THAT?
I COULDN'T HEAR YOU...THE HELIPAD? AN ORDER FROM ASADA?
IT'S SETTLED DOWN.
CAPTAIN KORORI. APPARENTLY OUTSIDE INVADERS ARE STORMING THE HELIPAD, AND WE'RE SUPPOSED TO HURRY RIGHT UP THERE!
WHAT DO WE DO?
WE GO, OF COURSE! OUR OBJECTIVE IS THE VERY SAME!

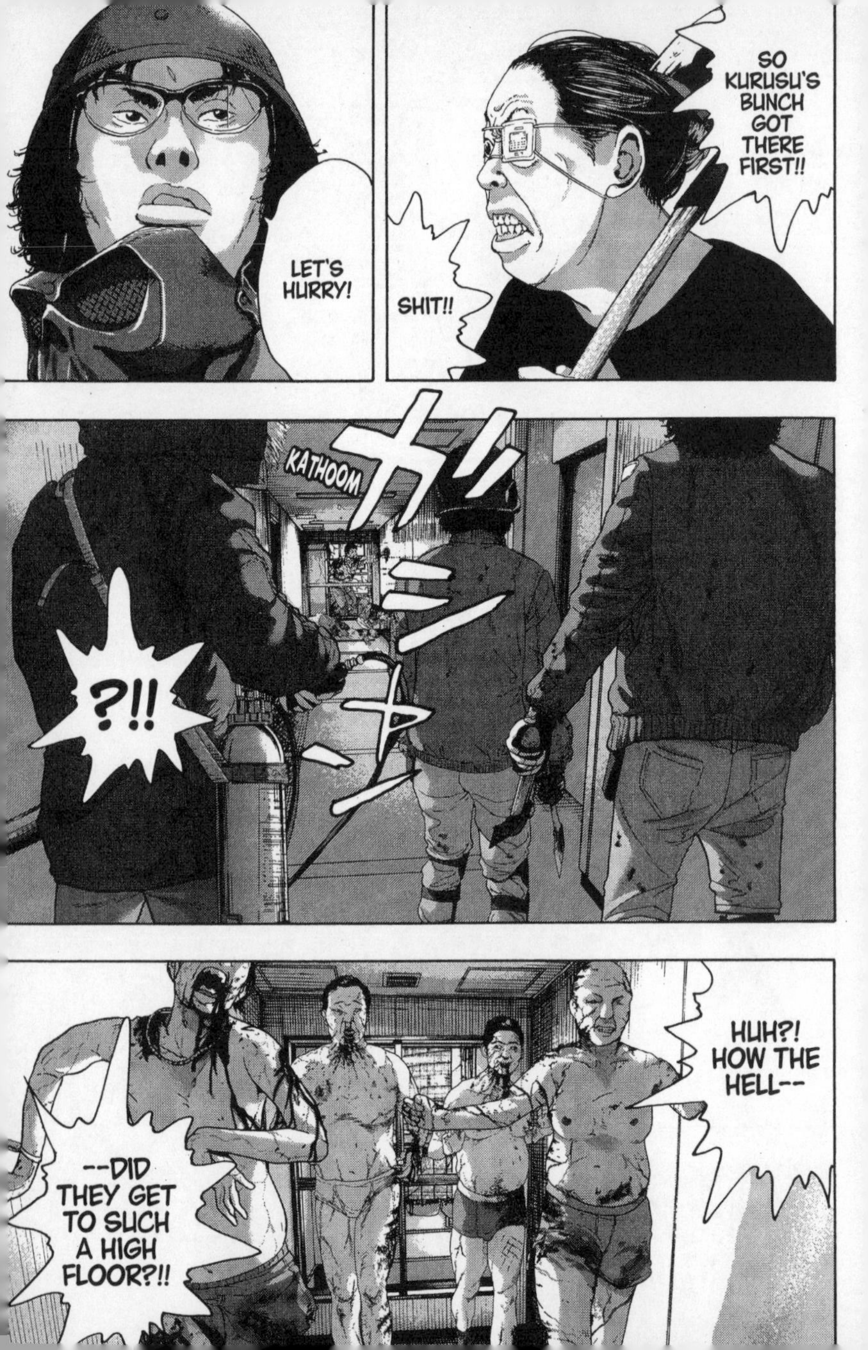
SO KURUSU'S BUNCH GOT THERE FIRST!!
SHIT!!
LET'S HURRY!
KATHOOM
?!!
HUH?! HOW THE HELL--
--DID THEY GET TO SUCH A HIGH FLOOR?!!

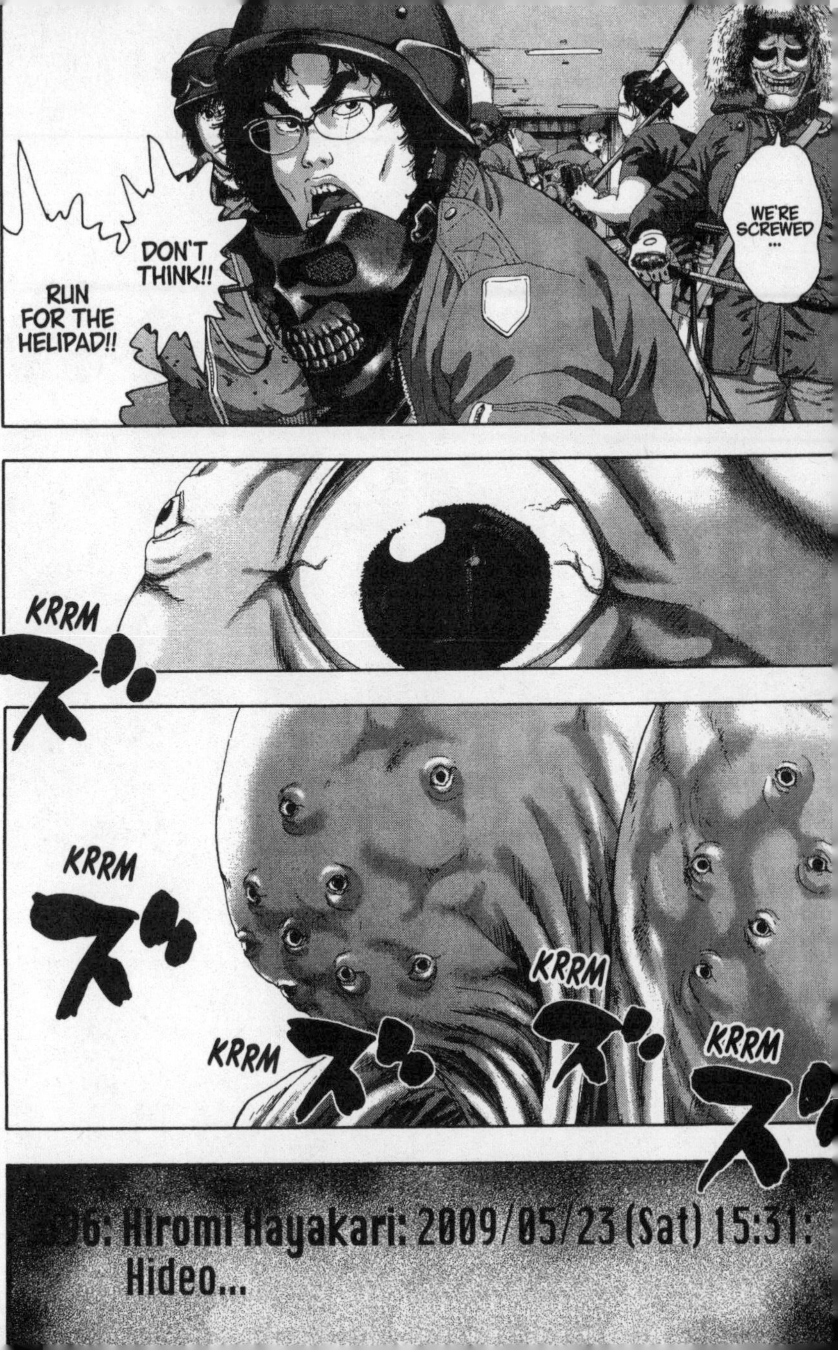
WE'RE SCREWED ...
DON'T THINK!!
RUN FOR THE HELIPAD!!
KRRM
ズッ
KRRM
ズッ
KRRM
ズッ
KRRM
ズッ
KRRM
ズッ
96: Hiromi Hayakari: 2009/05/23 (Sat) 15:31: Hideo...

697: Hiromi Hayakari: 2009/05/23 (Sat) 15:32:02 ID: hirohaya
    Hideo...
    Don't look at me like that...

CHAPTER
247

HIDEO...

: Hiromi Hayakari: 2009/05/2
I didn't really want to kill her
I had no choice.

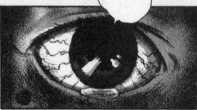

1

: Anonymous Integrated Mind: 2009/05/23 (Sat) 15:52:0
>> 698
Liar!
You killed her because you wanted to, isn't that right?
You wanted to kill her so bad, you pushed the button.
Isn't that right?

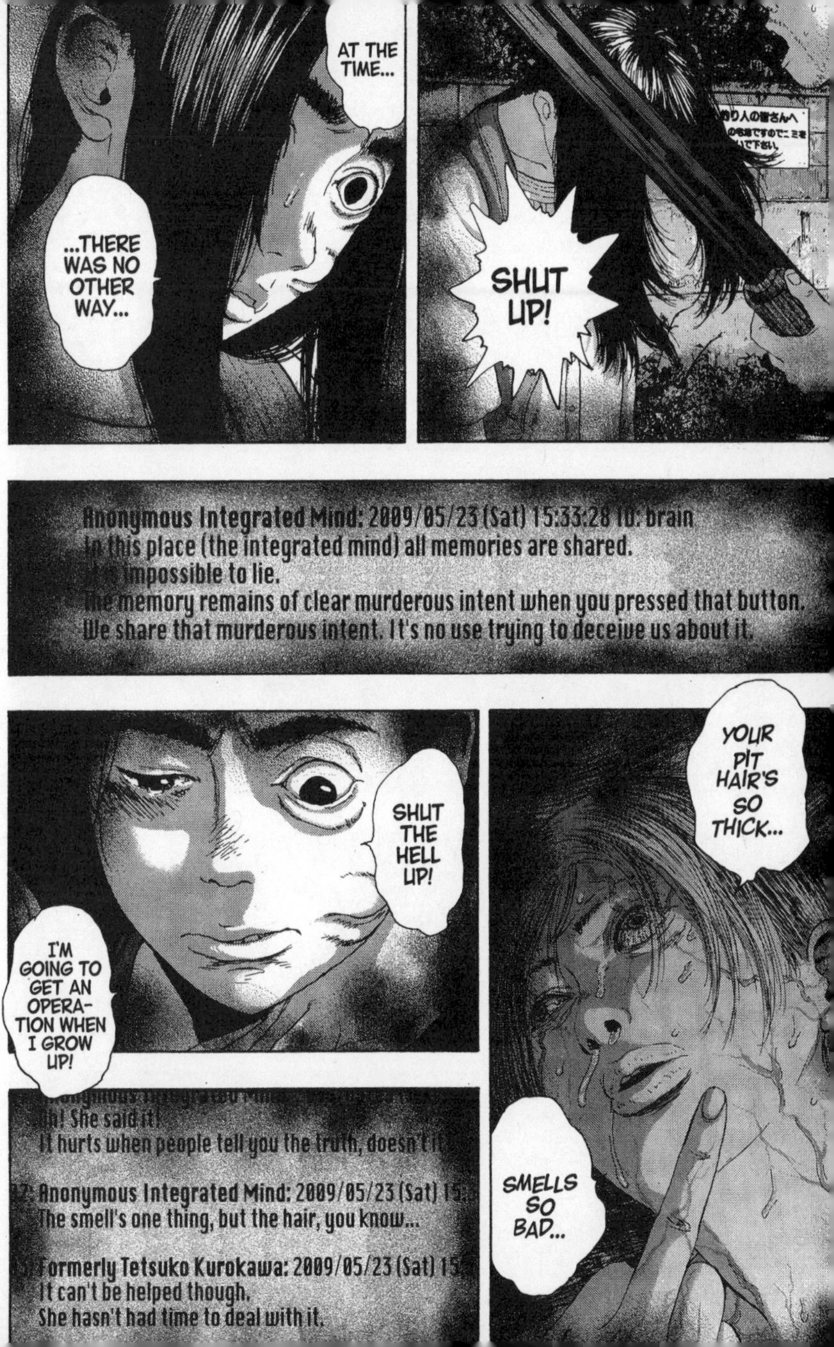
SHUT UP!
AT THE TIME...
...THERE WAS NO OTHER WAY...
Anonymous Integrated Mind: 2009/05/23 (Sat) 15:33:28 ID: brain
In this place (the integrated mind) all memories are shared.
It's impossible to lie.
The memory remains of clear murderous intent when you pressed that button.
We share that murderous intent. It's no use trying to deceive us about it.
YOUR PIT HAIR'S SO THICK...
SMELLS SO BAD...
SHUT THE HELL UP!
I'M GOING TO GET AN OPERATION WHEN I GROW UP!
Ah! She said it!
It hurts when people tell you the truth, doesn't it
Anonymous Integrated Mind: 2009/05/23 (Sat) 15
The smell's one thing, but the hair, you know...
Formerly Tetsuko Kurokawa: 2009/05/23 (Sat) 15
It can't be helped though.
She hasn't had time to deal with it.

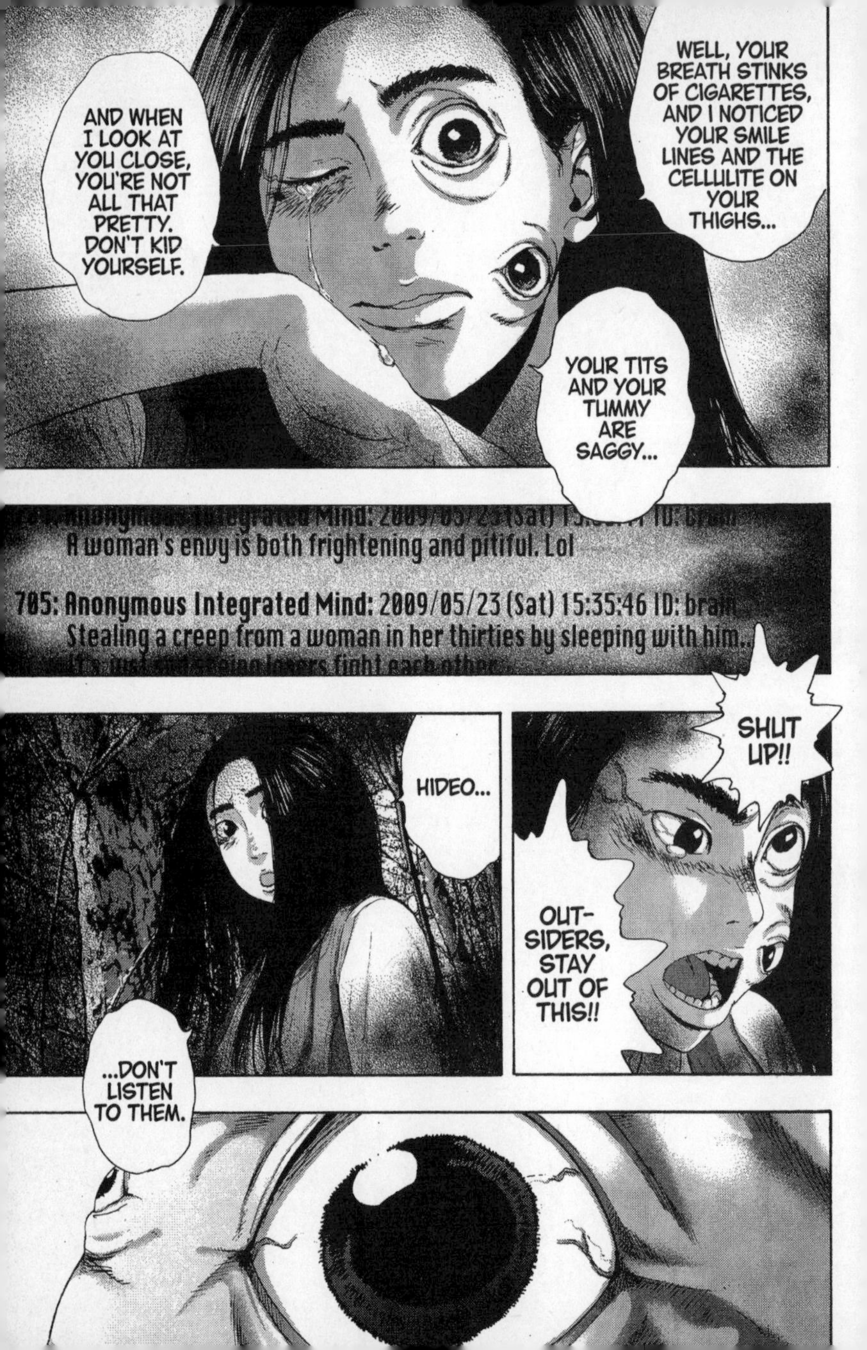
WELL, YOUR BREATH STINKS OF CIGARETTES, AND I NOTICED YOUR SMILE LINES AND THE CELLULITE ON YOUR THIGHS...
YOUR TITS AND YOUR TUMMY ARE SAGGY...
AND WHEN I LOOK AT YOU CLOSE, YOU'RE NOT ALL THAT PRETTY. DON'T KID YOURSELF.
A woman's envy is both frightening and pitiful. Lol
705: Anonymous Integrated Mind: 2009/05/23 (Sat) 15:35:46 ID: brain
Stealing a creep from a woman in her thirties by sleeping with him..
SHUT UP!!
OUT-SIDERS, STAY OUT OF THIS!!
HIDEO...
...DON'T LISTEN TO THEM.

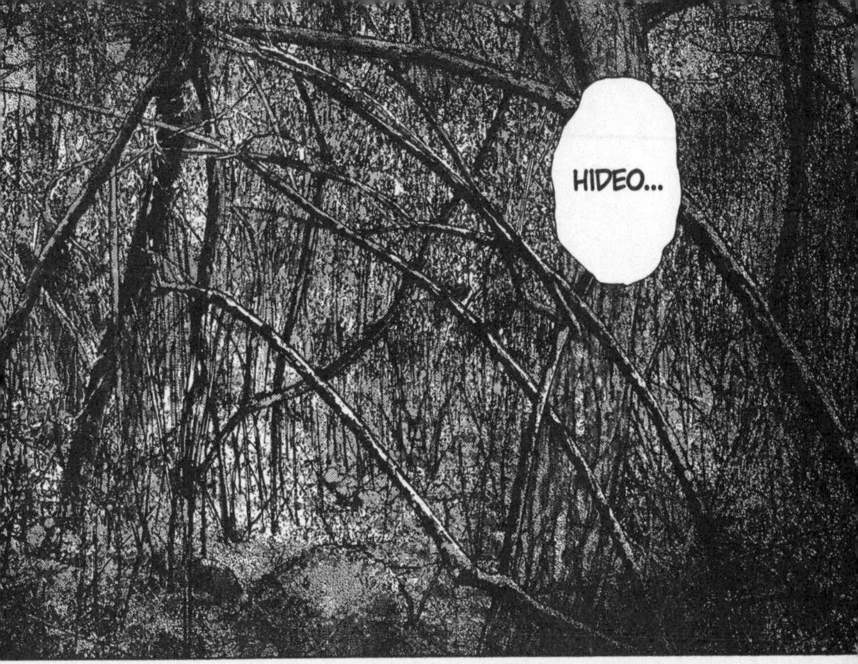
HIDEO...
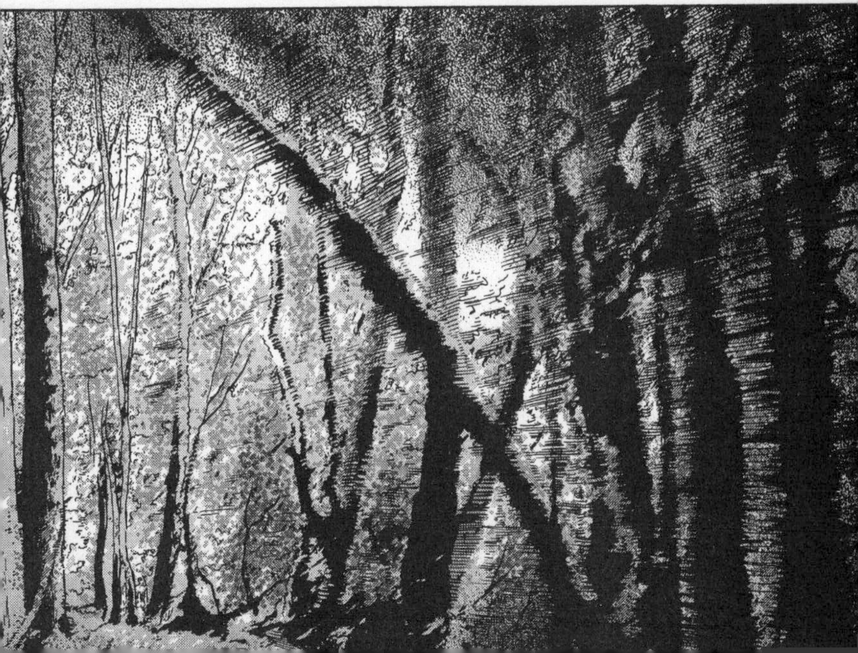

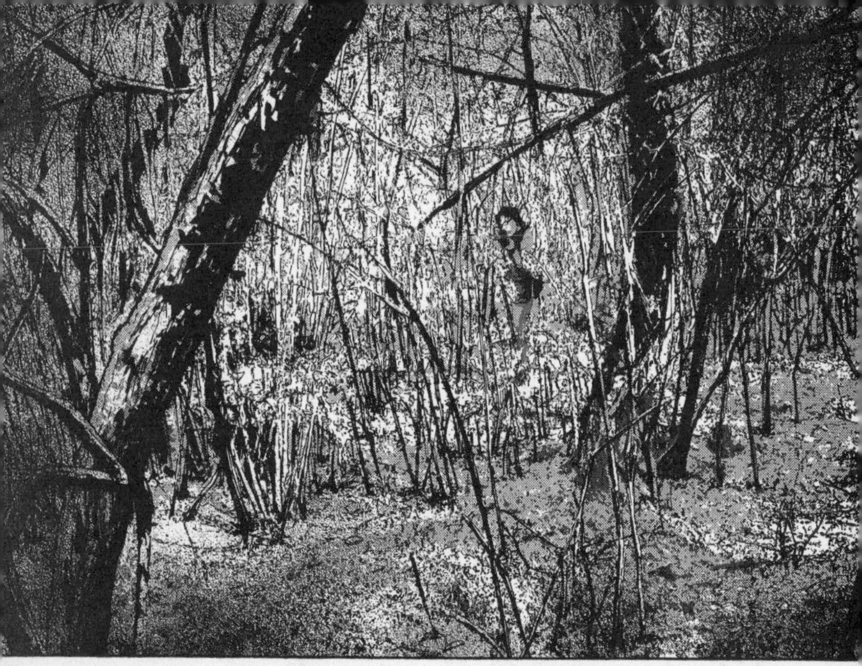

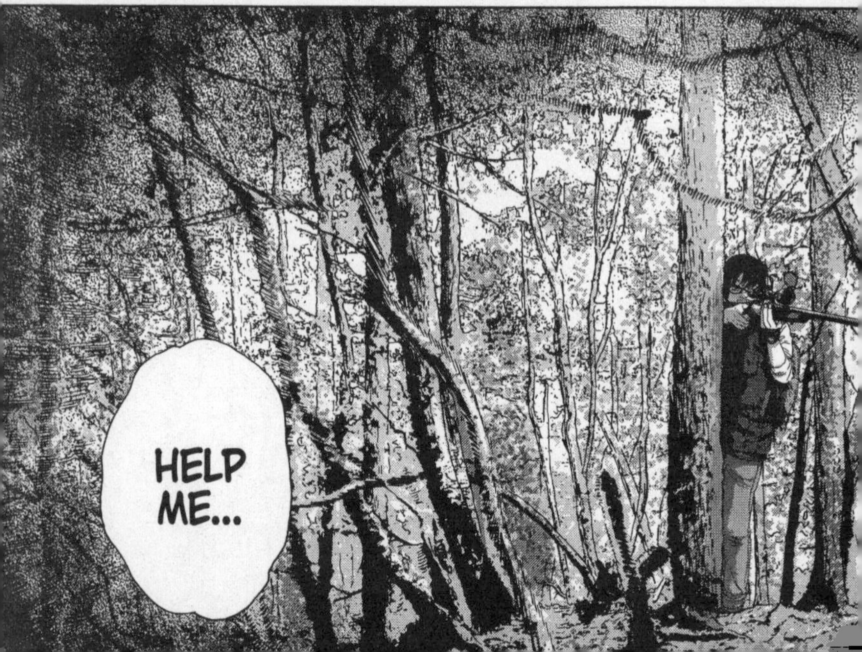
HELP ME...

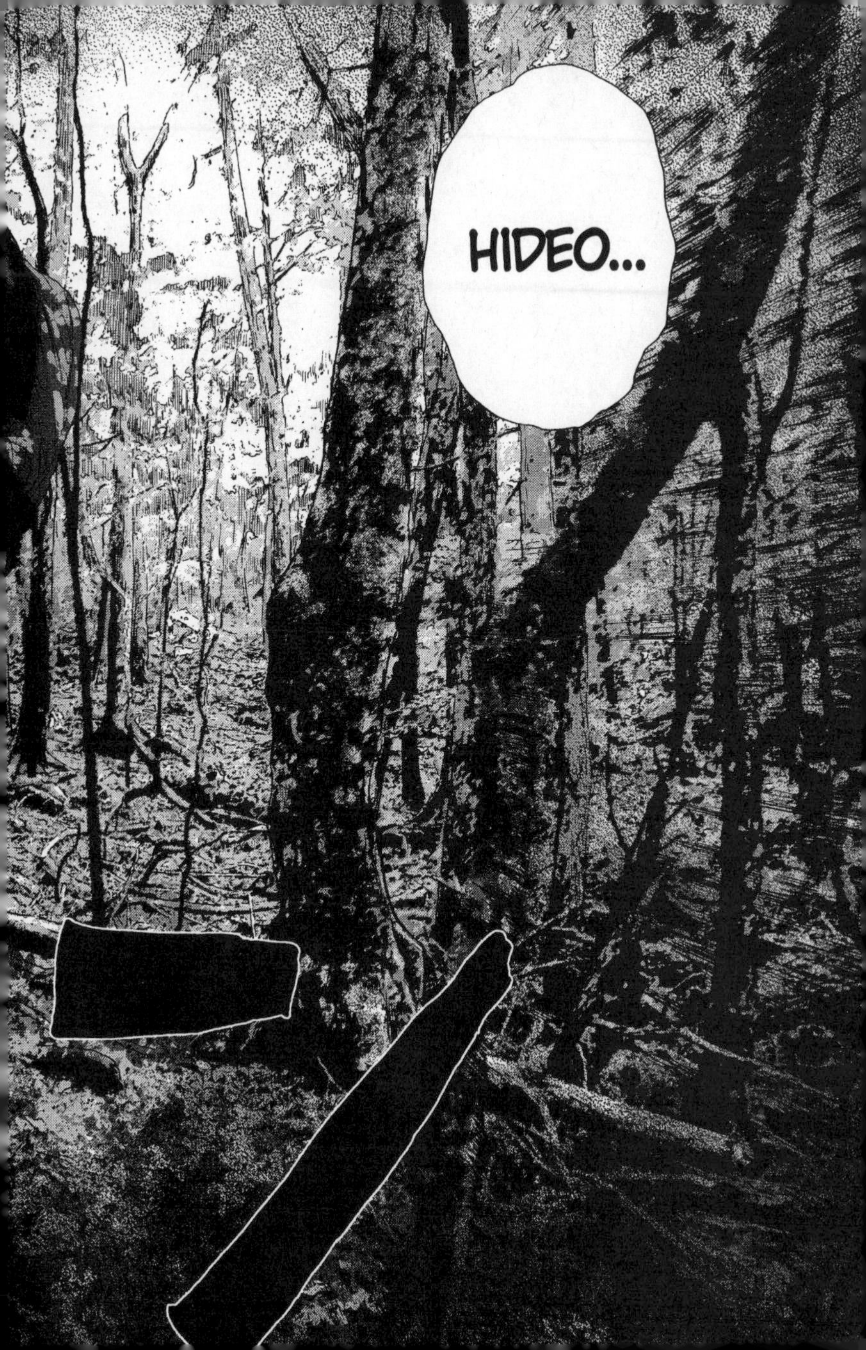
HIDEO...

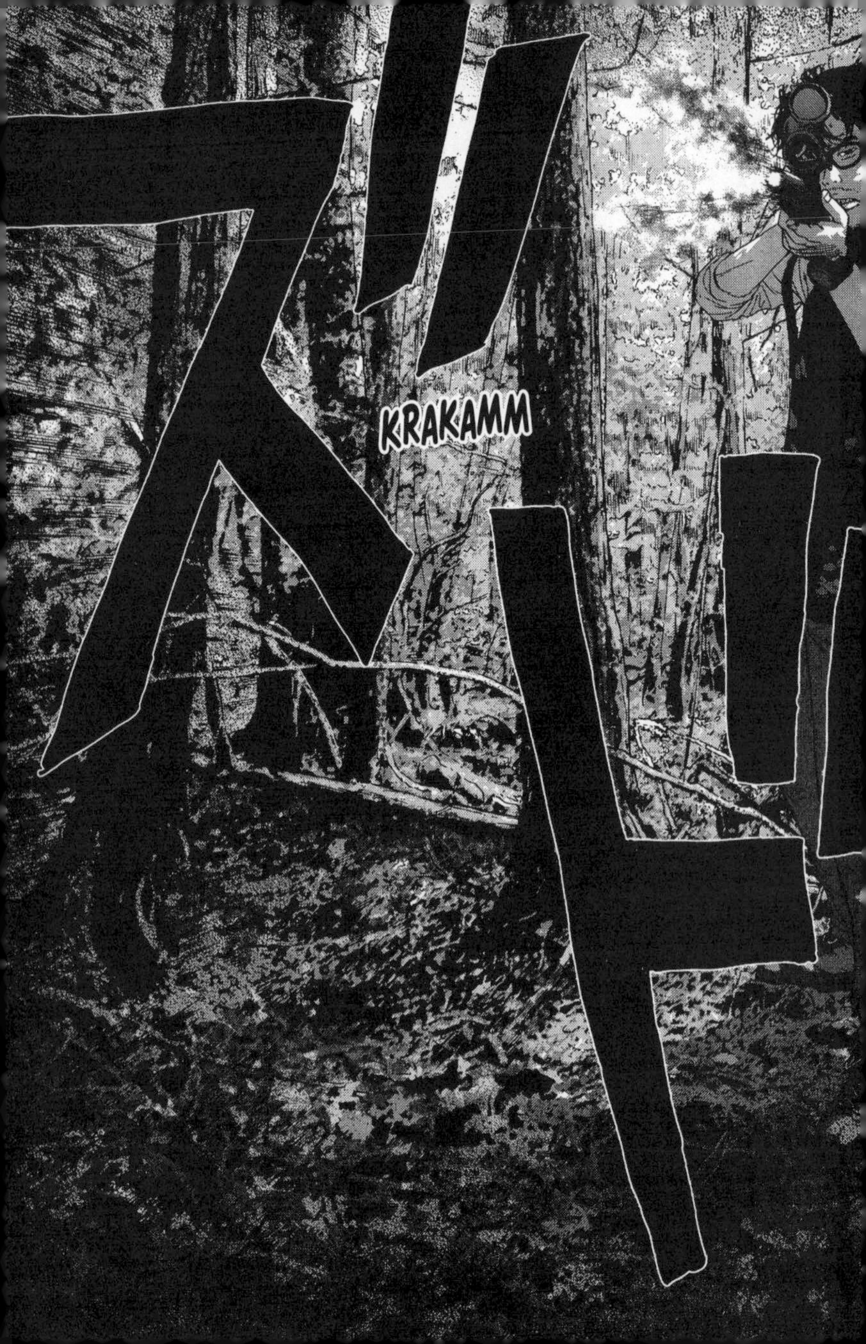
KRAKAMM

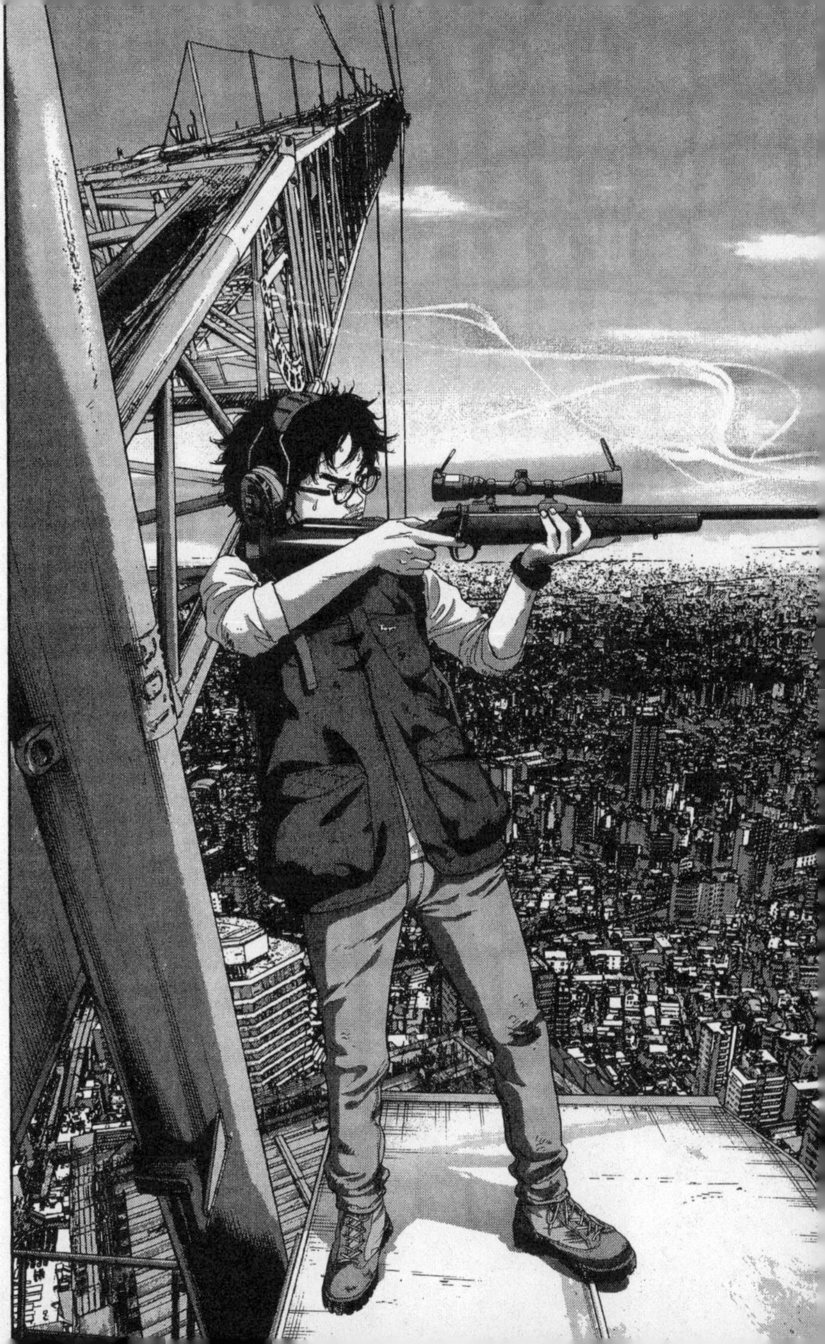

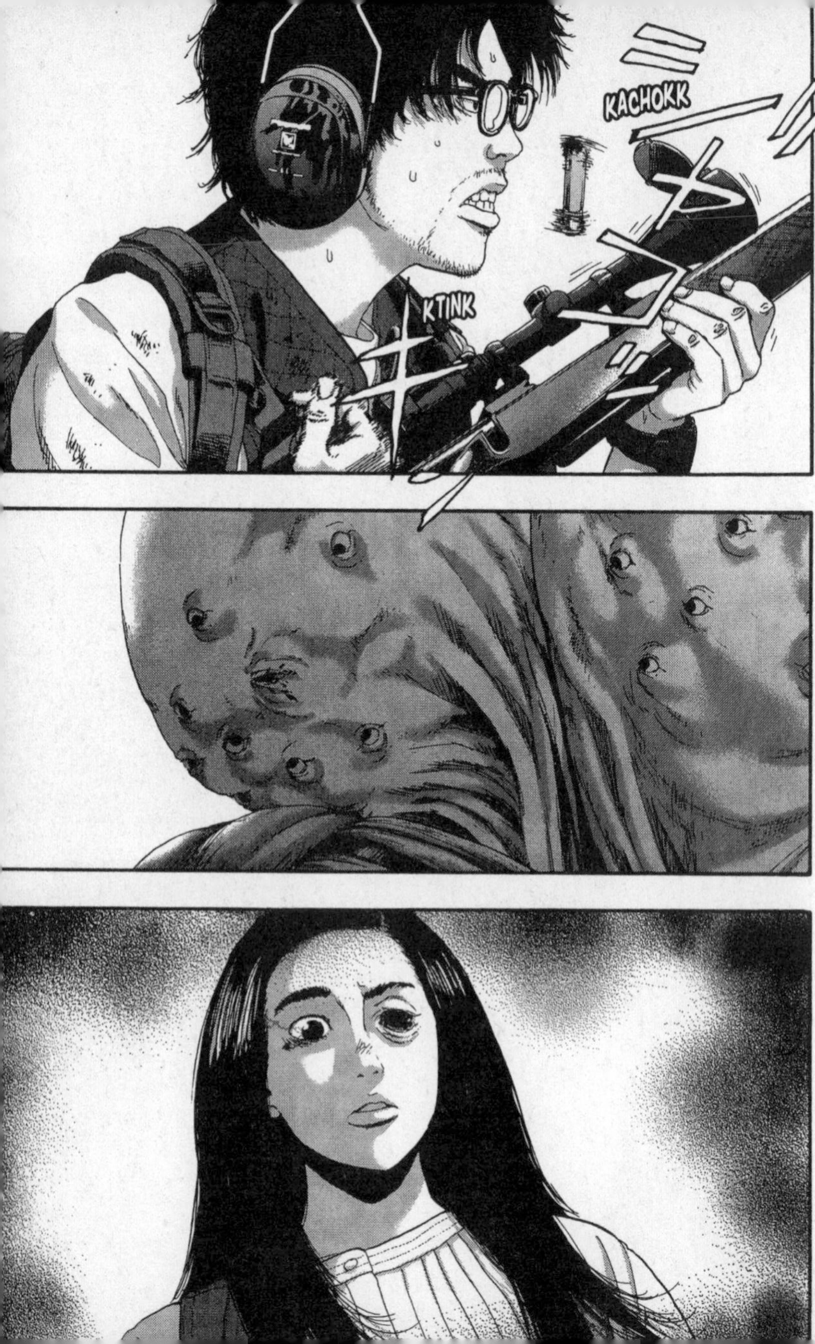
KACHOKK
KTINK

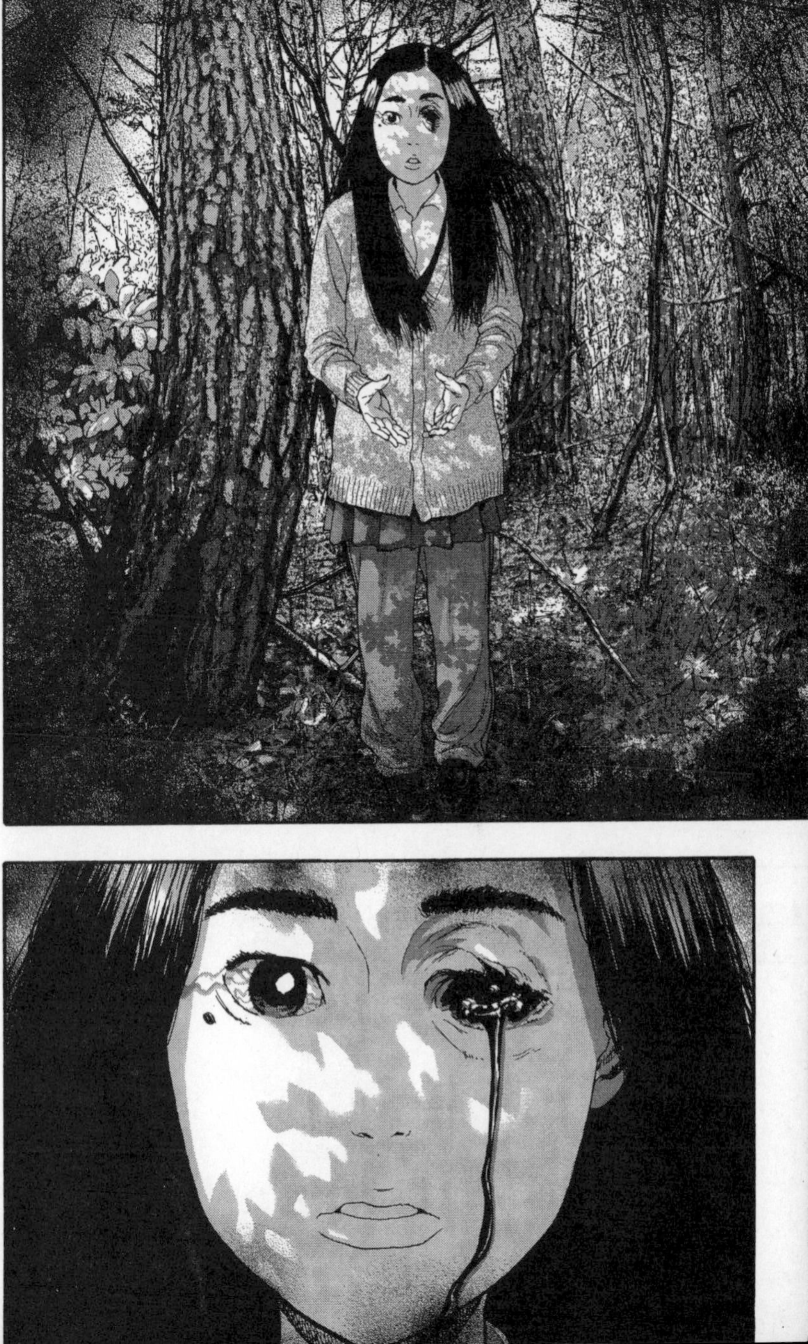

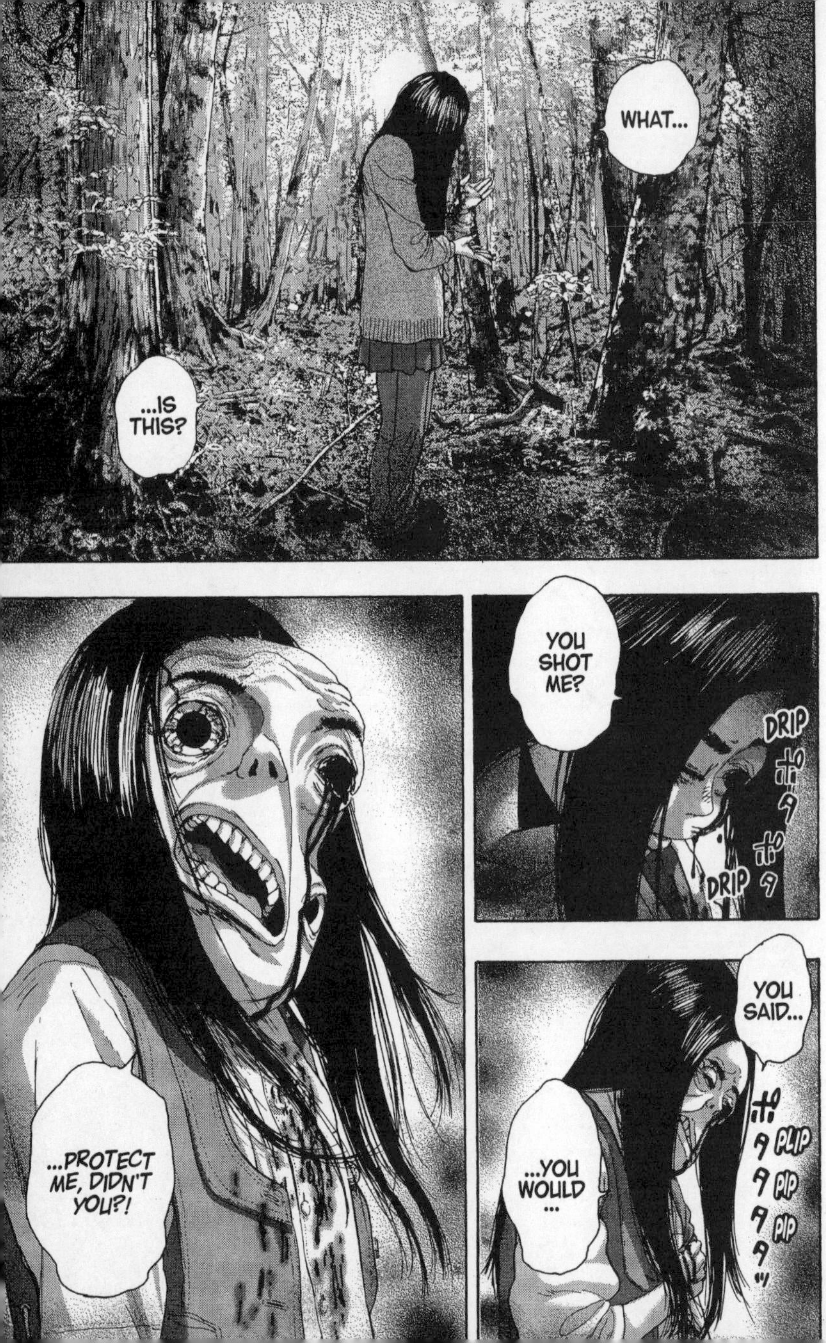
WHAT...
...IS THIS?
YOU SHOT ME?
DRIP
ポタポタ
DRIP
YOU SAID...
...YOU WOULD ...
ポタタタタッ
PLIP
PIP
PIP
PIP
...PROTECT ME, DIDN'T YOU?!

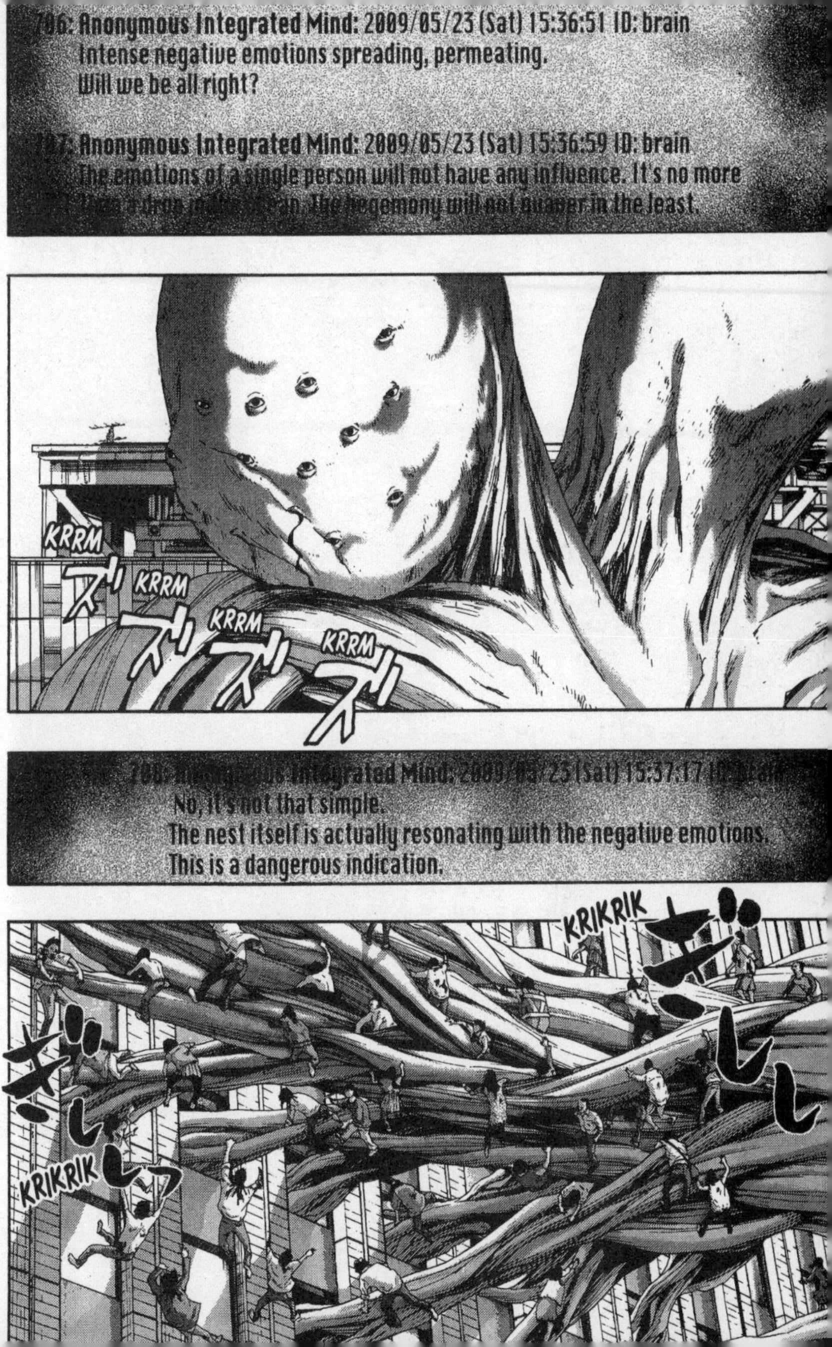
786: Anonymous Integrated Mind: 2009/05/23 (Sat) 15:36:51 ID: brain
Intense negative emotions spreading, permeating.
Will we be all right?
787: Anonymous Integrated Mind: 2009/05/23 (Sat) 15:36:59 ID: brain
The emotions of a single person will not have any influence. It's no more
than a drop in the ocean. The hegemony will not quaver in the least.
KRRM
KRRM
KRRM
KRRM
788: Anonymous Integrated Mind: 2009/05/23 (Sat) 15:37:17 ID: brain
No, it's not that simple.
The nest itself is actually resonating with the negative emotions.
This is a dangerous indication.
KRIKRIK
KRIKRIK

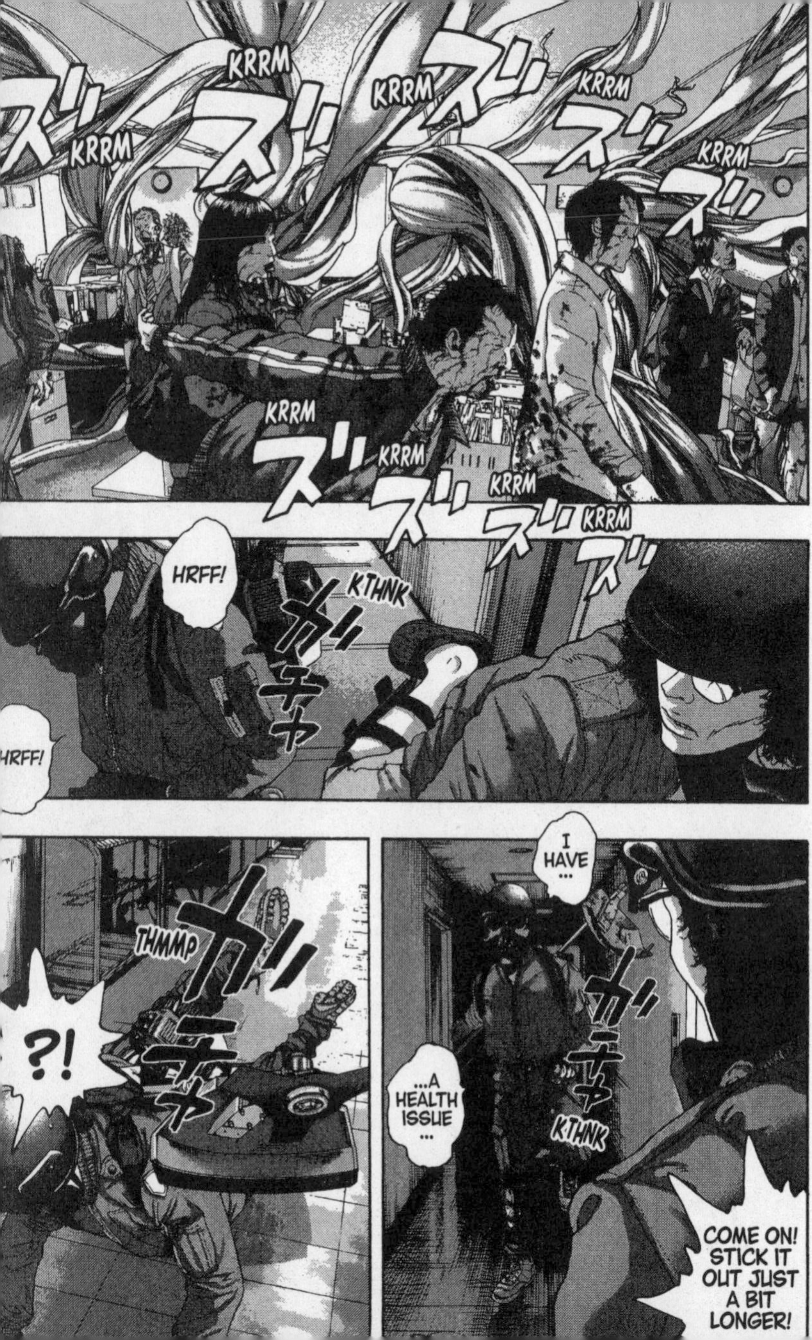
KRRM
KRRM
KRRM
KRRM
KRRM
KRRM
KRRM
KRRM
KRRM
HRFF!
KTHNK
HRFF!
I HAVE ...
...A HEALTH ISSUE ...
KTHNK
COME ON! STICK IT OUT JUST A BIT LONGER!
THMMP
?!

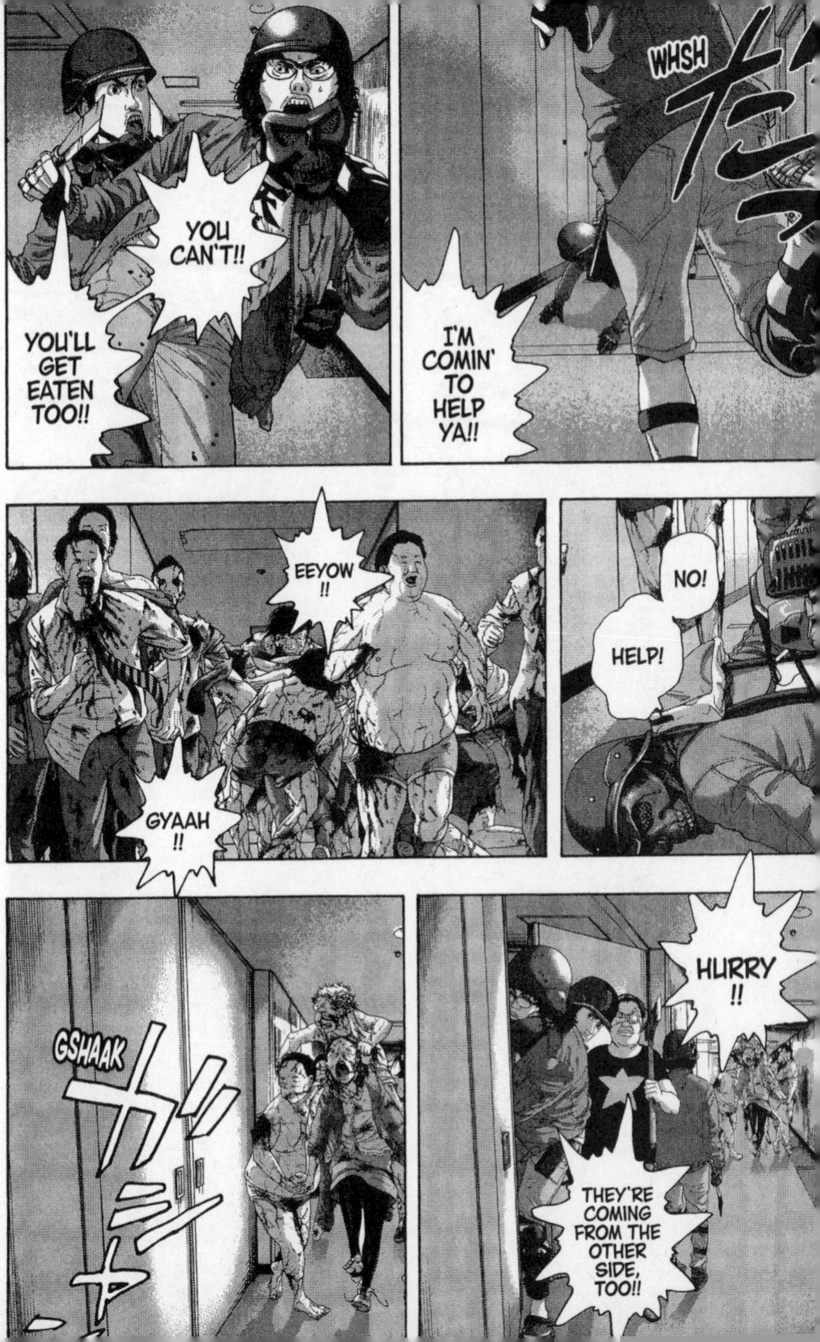
WHSH
I'M COMIN' TO HELP YA!!
YOU CAN'T!!
YOU'LL GET EATEN TOO!!
NO!
HELP!
EEYOW !!
GYAAH !!
HURRY !!
THEY'RE COMING FROM THE OTHER SIDE, TOO!!
GSHAAK

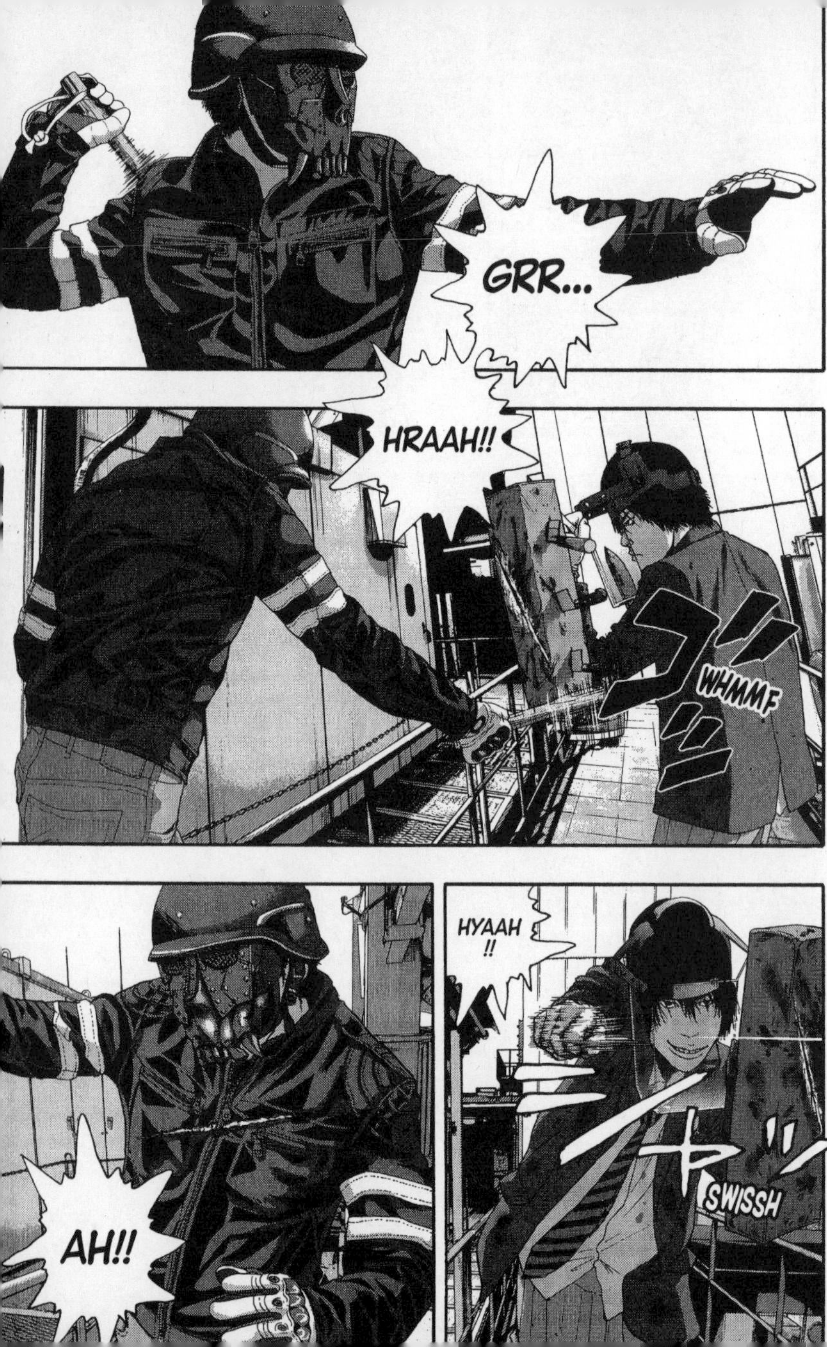
GRR...
HRAAH!!
WHMMF
HYAAH!!
SWISSH
AH!!

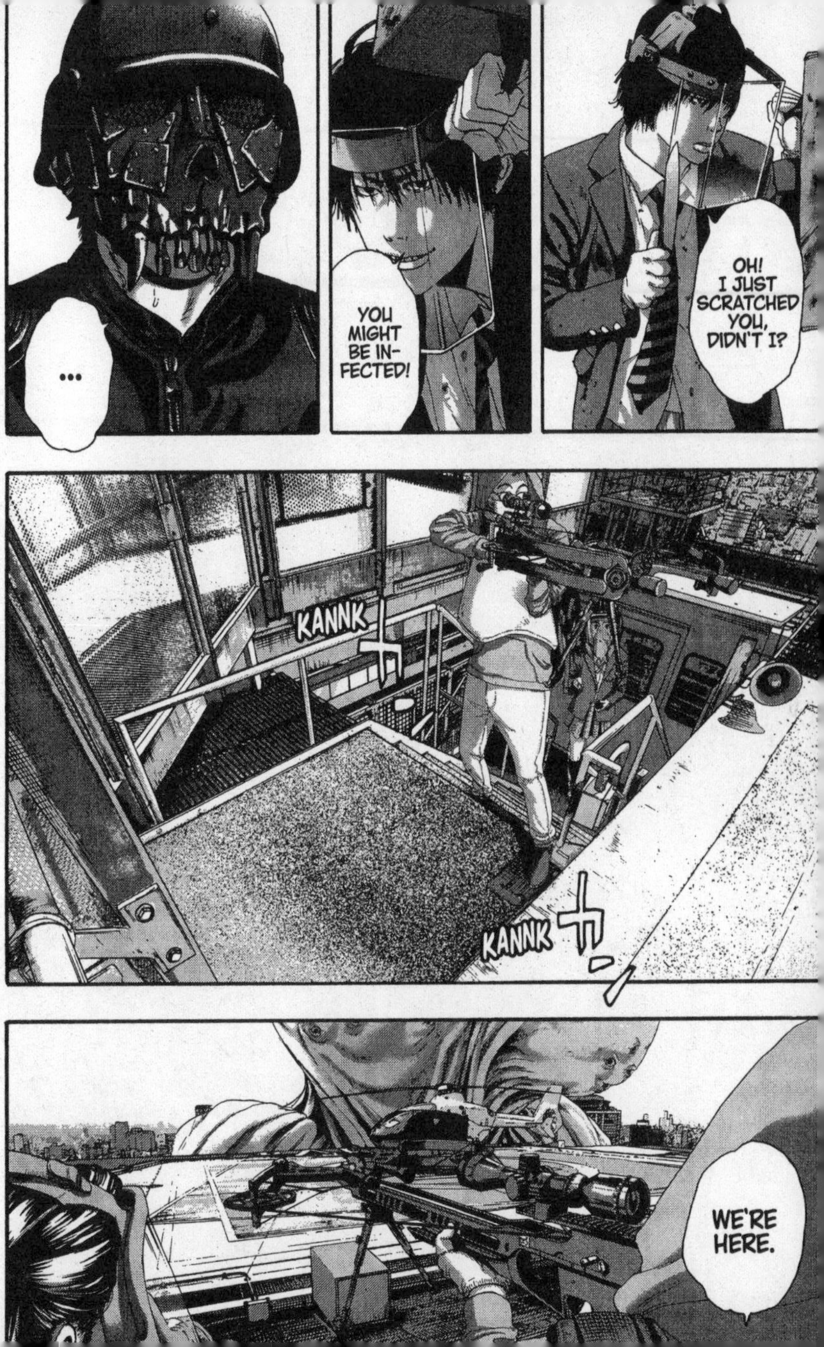
OH! I JUST SCRATCHED YOU, DIDN'T I?
YOU MIGHT BE IN-FECTED!
...
KANNK
KANNK
WE'RE HERE.

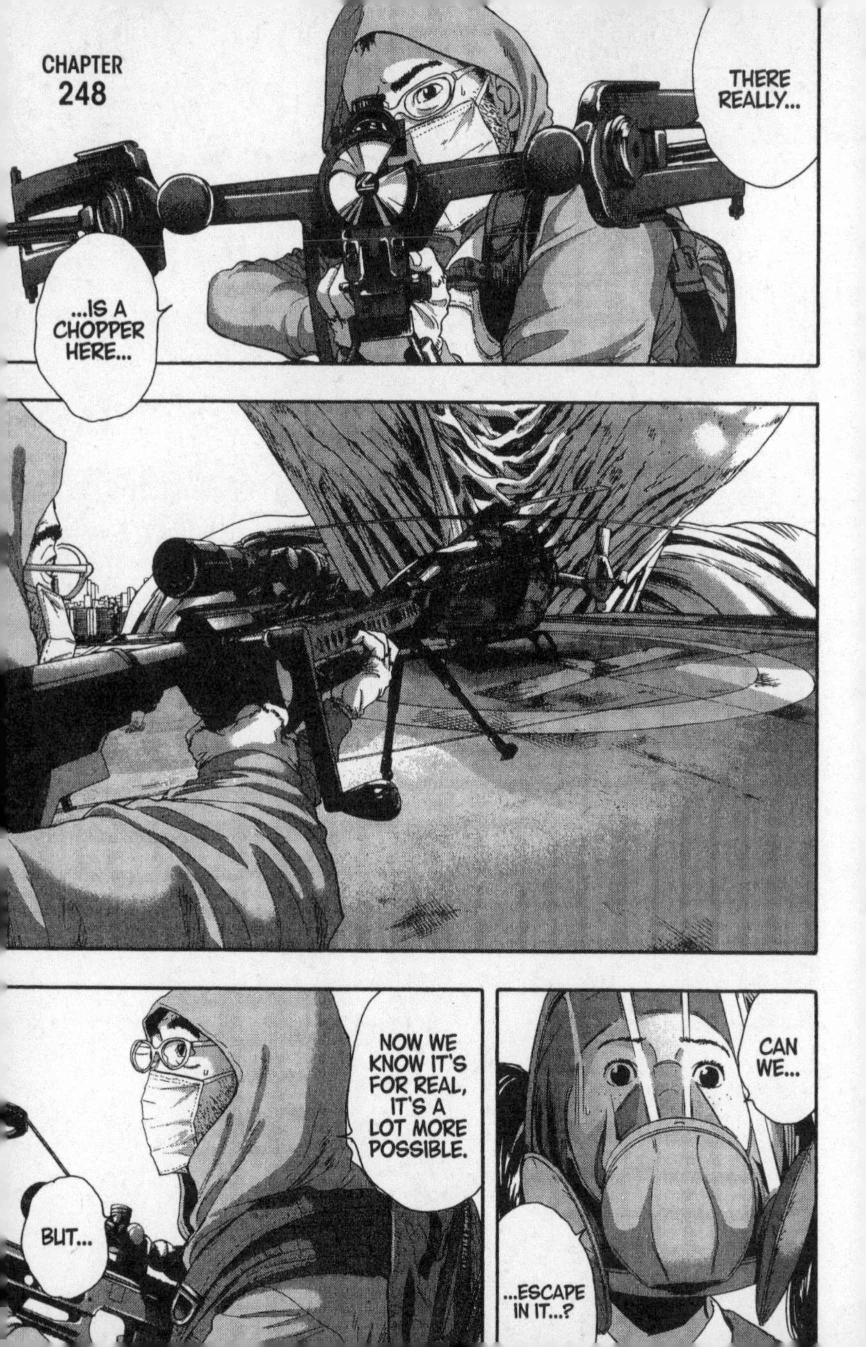
CHAPTER 248
THERE REALLY...
...IS A CHOPPER HERE...
CAN WE...
...ESCAPE IN IT...?
NOW WE KNOW IT'S FOR REAL, IT'S A LOT MORE POSSIBLE.
BUT...

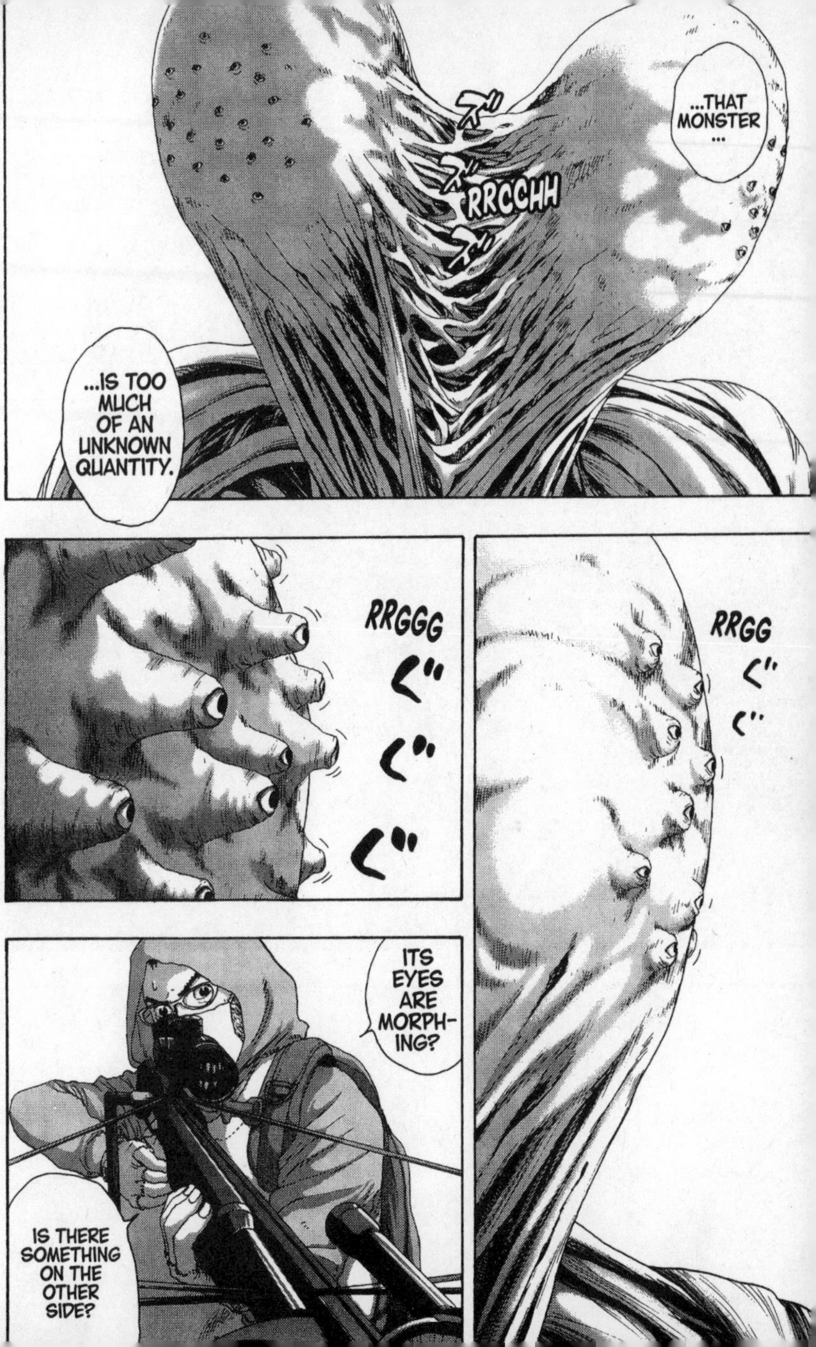
...THAT MONSTER ...
RRCCHH
...IS TOO MUCH OF AN UNKNOWN QUANTITY.
RRGG
ぐ ぐ
RRGGG
ぐ ぐ ぐ
ITS EYES ARE MORPH-ING?
IS THERE SOMETHING ON THE OTHER SIDE?

WHAT THE--?

BLOOD'S COMING OUT OF ONE OF THEM...

ACTUALLY, I HEARD SOMETHING LIKE GUNSHOTS BEFORE...

COULD SOMEBODY HAVE SHOT IT?

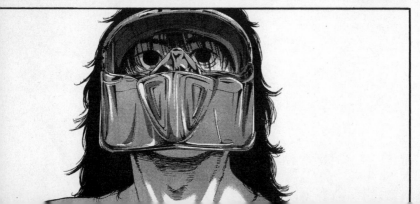

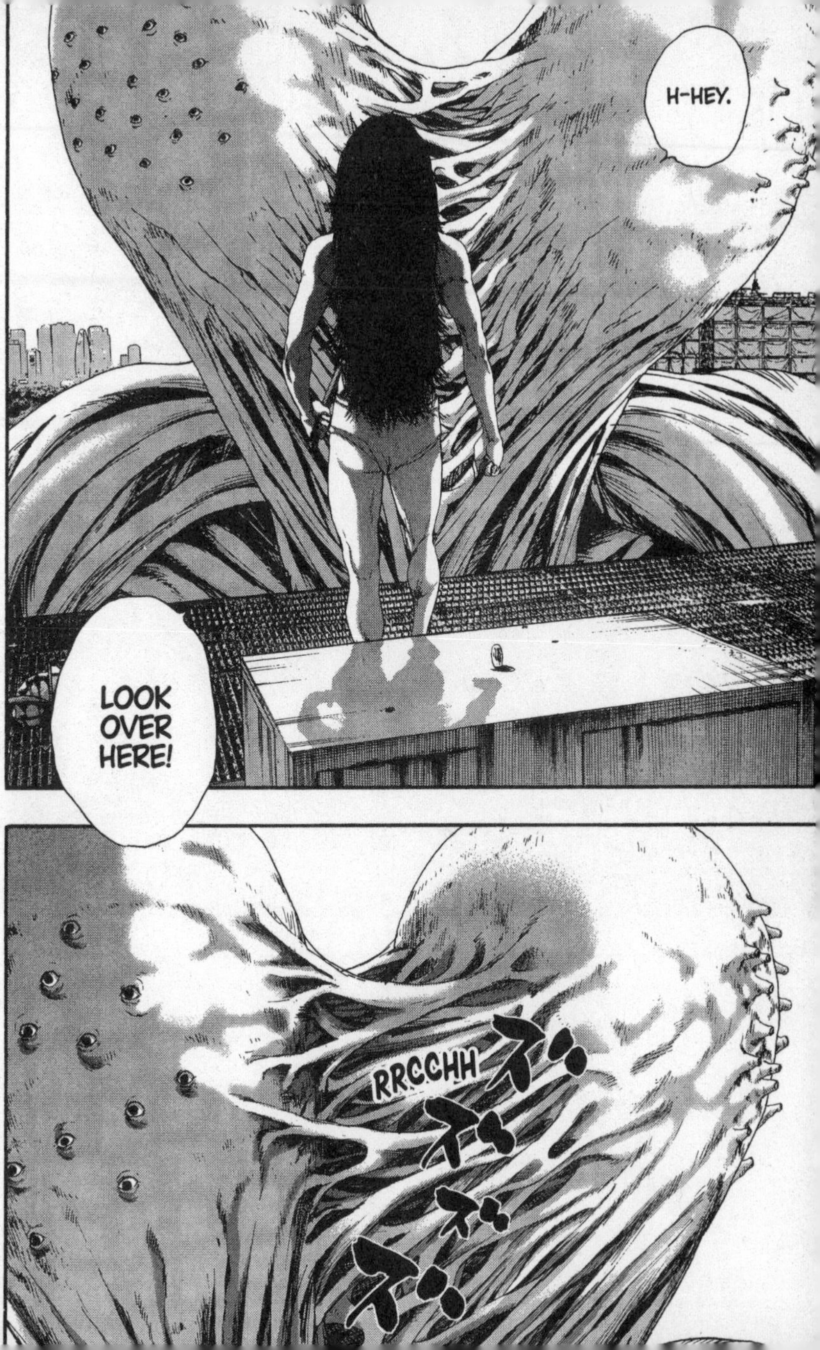
H-HEY.
LOOK OVER HERE!
RRCCHH
ズズズズ

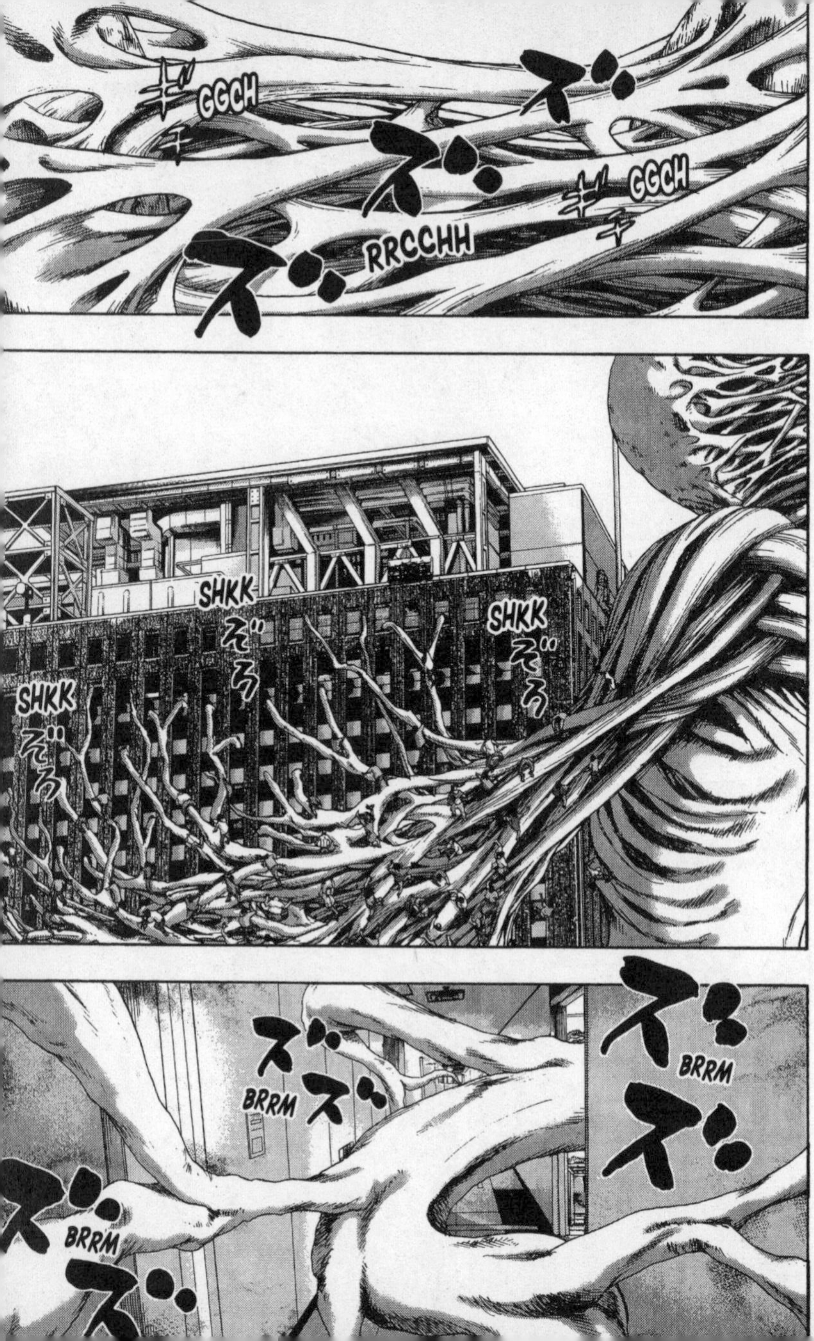
ズ
GGCH
ギギ
ズ
ズ
RRCCHH
GGCH
ギギ
SHKK
ぞろ
SHKK
ぞろ
SHKK
ぞろ
ズズ
BRRM
ズズ
BRRM
ズズ
BRRM

ゴオオオオ
CCHHRRRR
ズズズズ
BRRM
BRRM
BRRM
BRRM
FIRE EXTINGUISHER
ガ
FWHPP

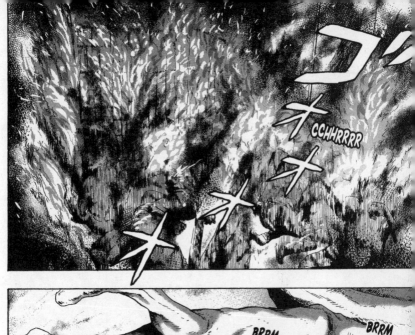

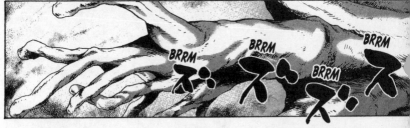

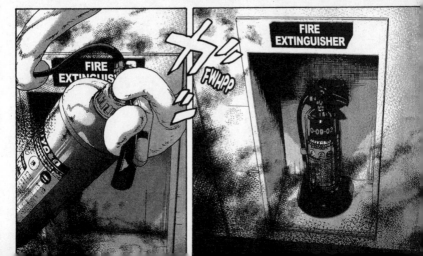

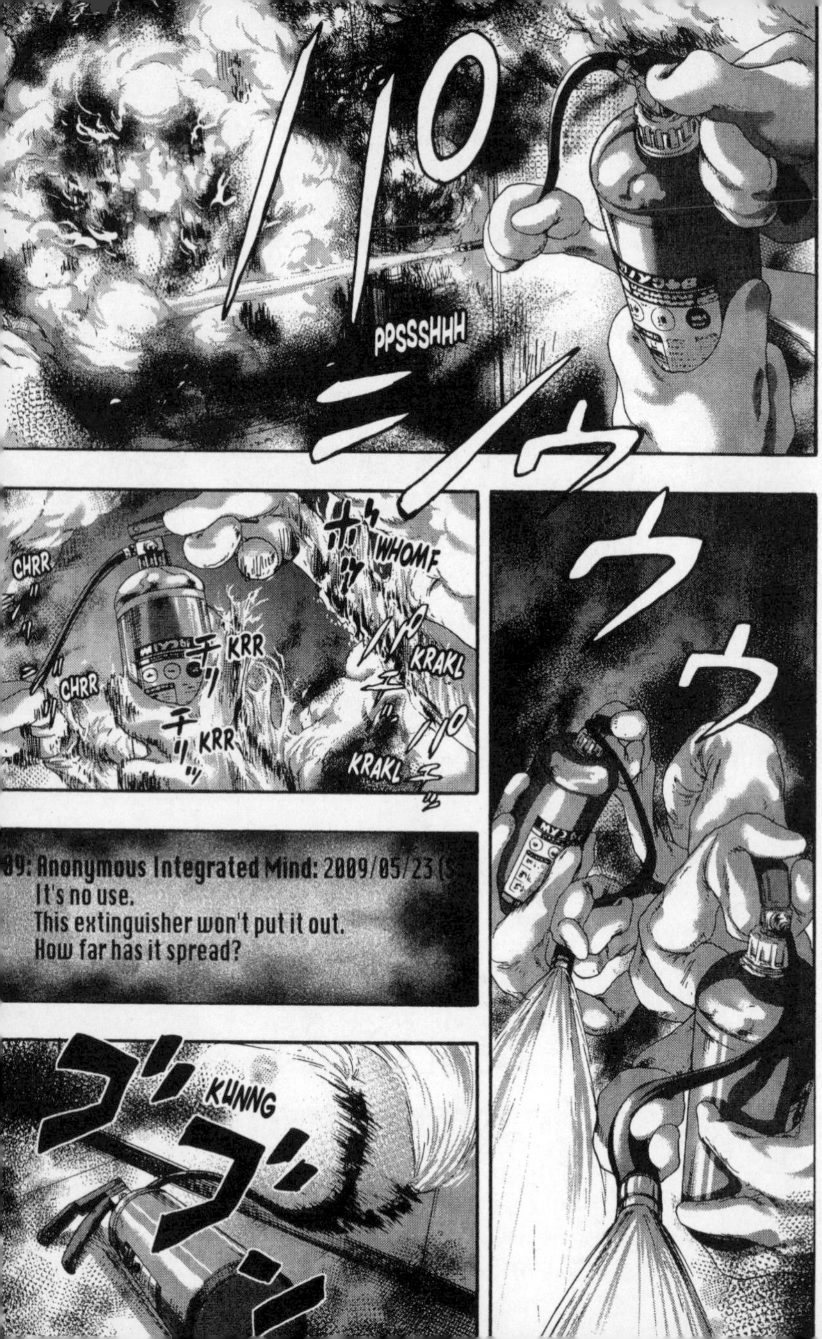
PPSSSHHH
WHOMF
KRAKL
KRAKL
KRR
KRR
CHRR
CHRR
09: Anonymous Integrated Mind: 2009/05/23 (S
It's no use.
This extinguisher won't put it out.
How far has it spread?
KUNNG

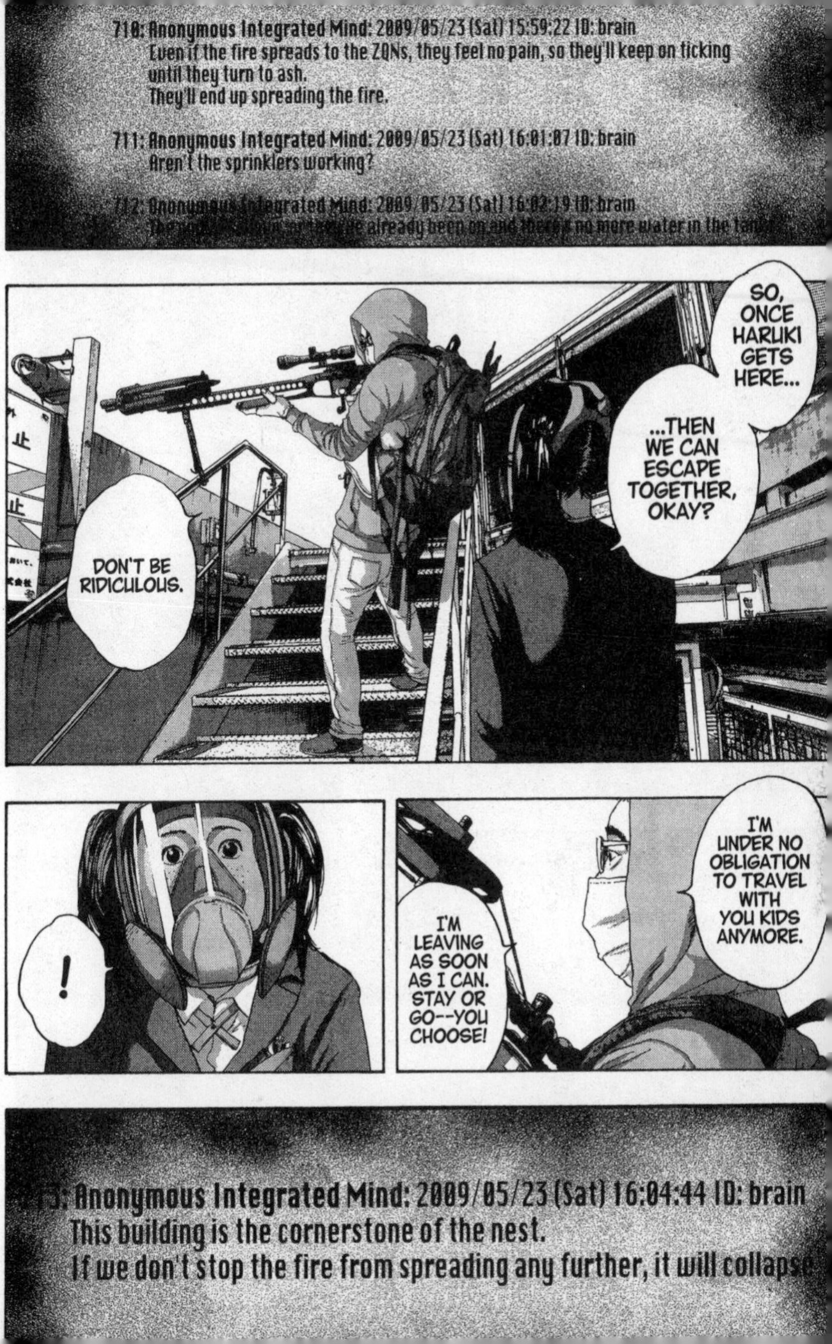
710: Anonymous Integrated Mind: 2009/05/23 (Sat) 15:59:22 ID: brain
Even if the fire spreads to the ZQNs, they feel no pain, so they'll keep on ticking until they turn to ash.
They'll end up spreading the fire.
711: Anonymous Integrated Mind: 2009/05/23 (Sat) 16:01:07 ID: brain
Aren't the sprinklers working?
712: Anonymous Integrated Mind: 2009/05/23 (Sat) 16:02:19 ID: brain
SO, ONCE HARUKI GETS HERE...
...THEN WE CAN ESCAPE TOGETHER, OKAY?
DON'T BE RIDICULOUS.
I'M UNDER NO OBLIGATION TO TRAVEL WITH YOU KIDS ANYMORE.
I'M LEAVING AS SOON AS I CAN. STAY OR GO--YOU CHOOSE!
!
Anonymous Integrated Mind: 2009/05/23 (Sat) 16:04:44 ID: brain
This building is the cornerstone of the nest.
If we don't stop the fire from spreading any further, it will collapse.

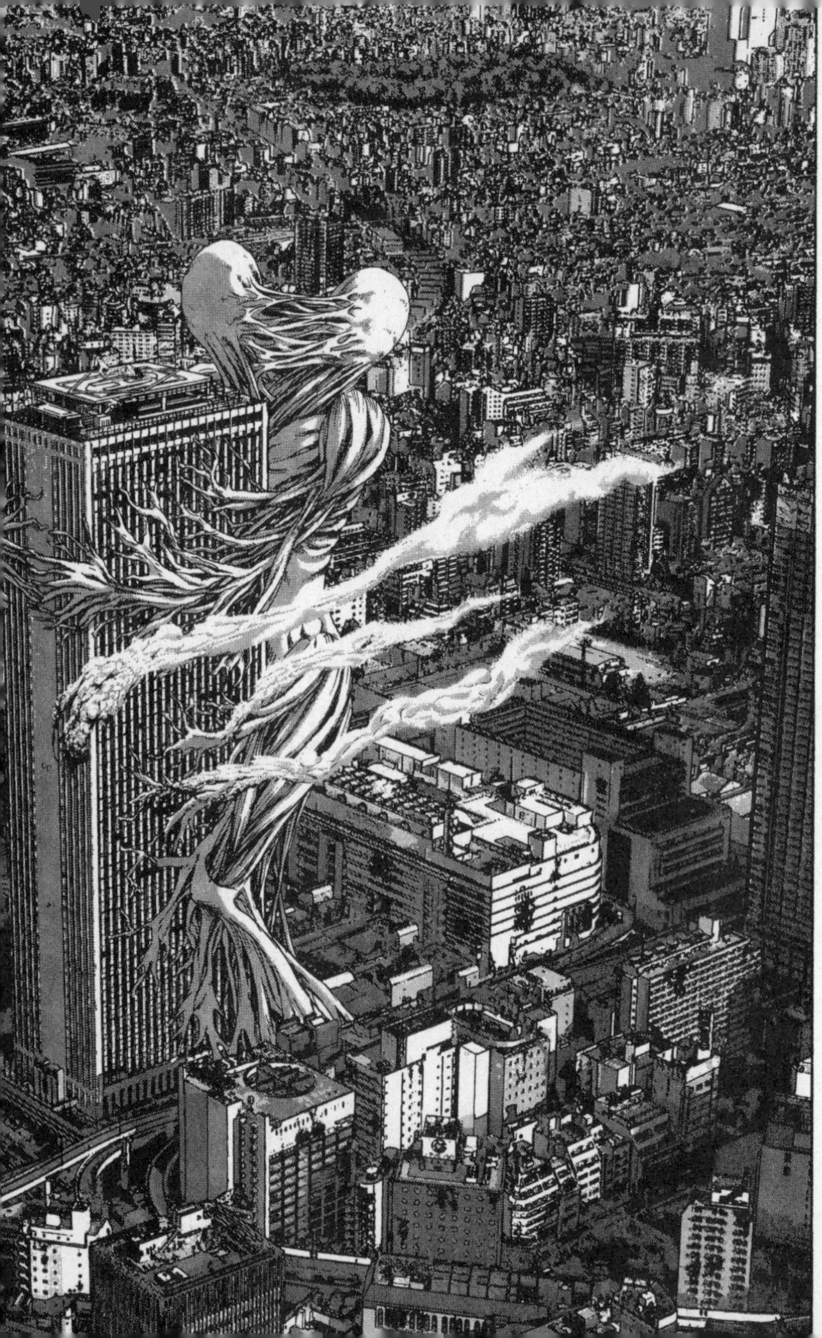

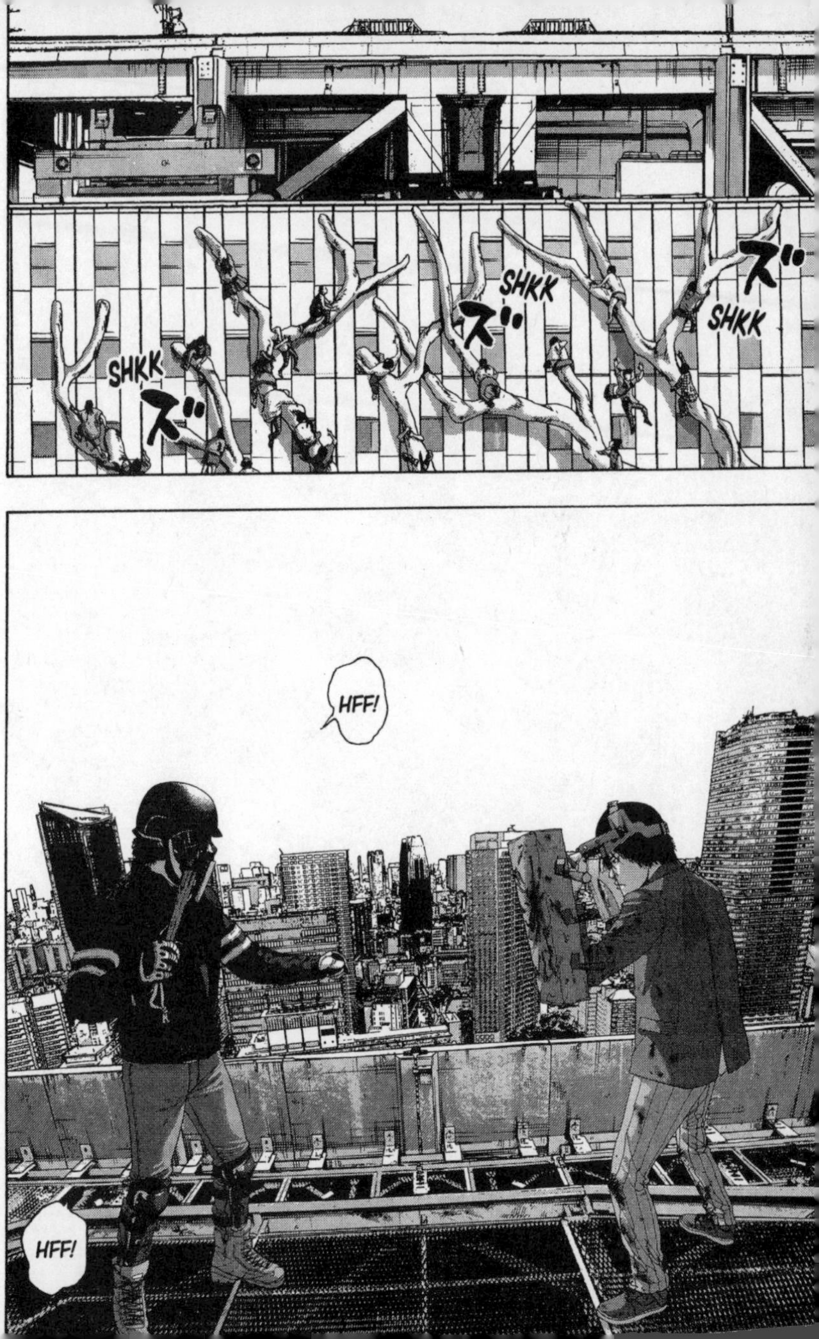
ズ
SHKK
SHKK
ズ
SHKK
ズ
HFF!
HFF!

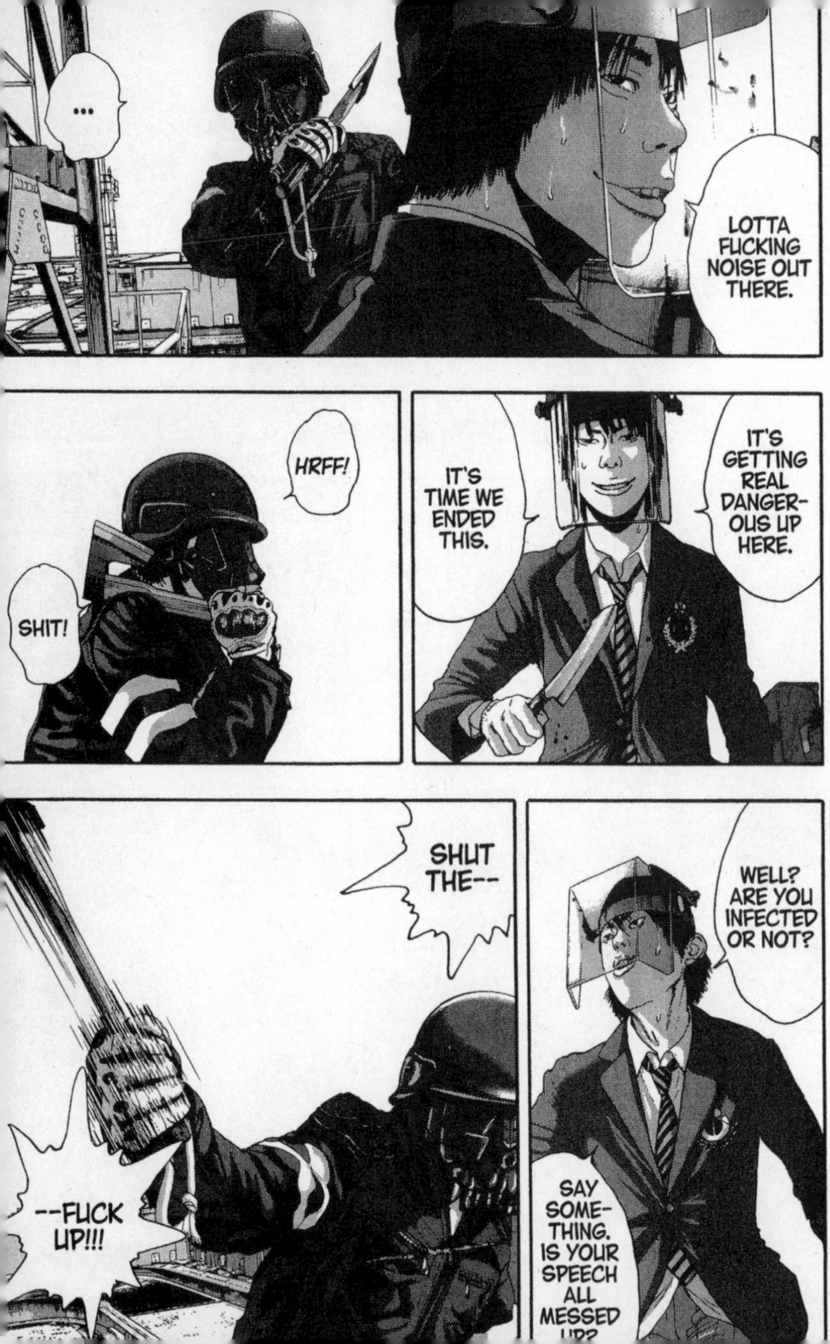
LOTTA FUCKING NOISE OUT THERE.
...
IT'S GETTING REAL DANGER-OUS UP HERE.
IT'S TIME WE ENDED THIS.
HRFF!
SHIT!
WELL? ARE YOU INFECTED OR NOT?
SAY SOME-THING. IS YOUR SPEECH ALL MESSED
SHUT THE--
--FUCK UP!!!

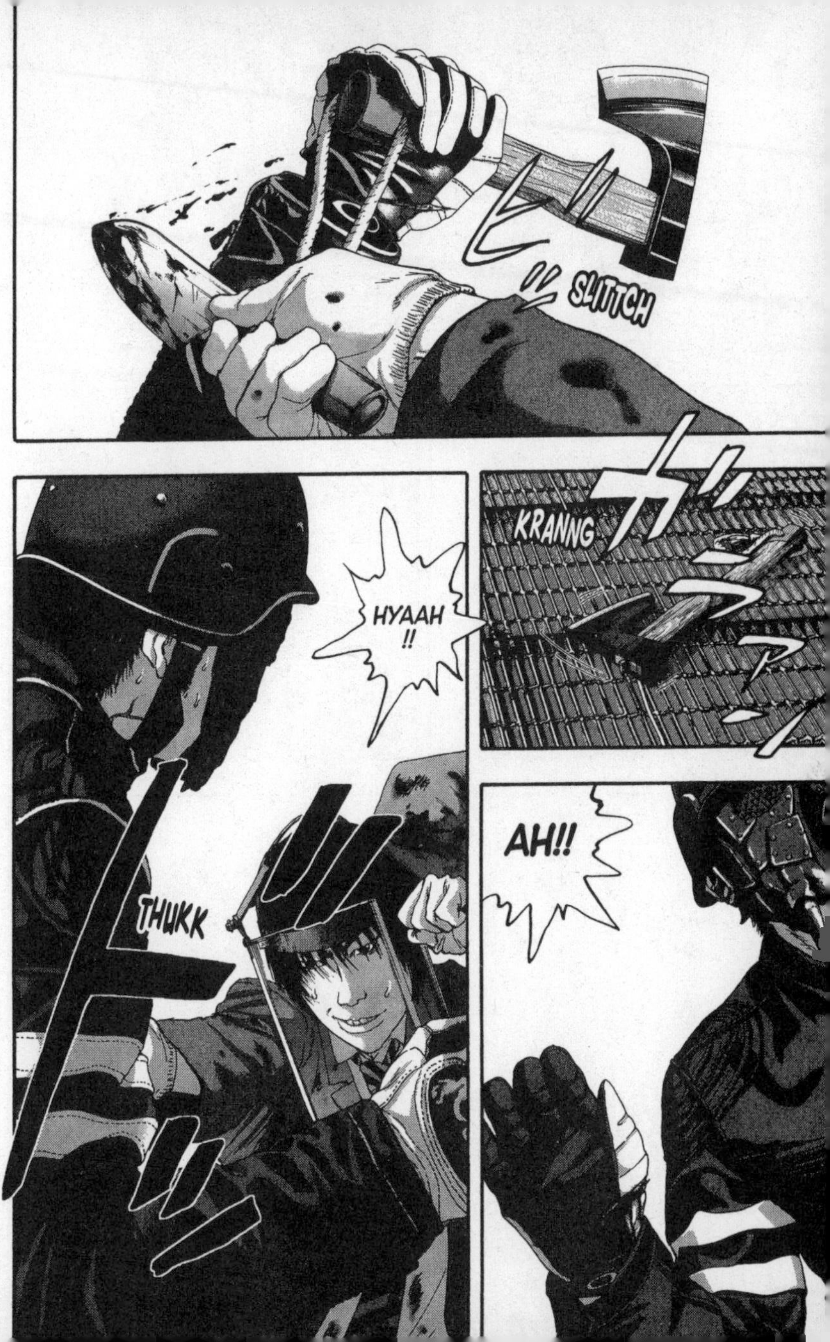
SLITTCH
KRANNG
AH!!
HYAAH!!
THUKK

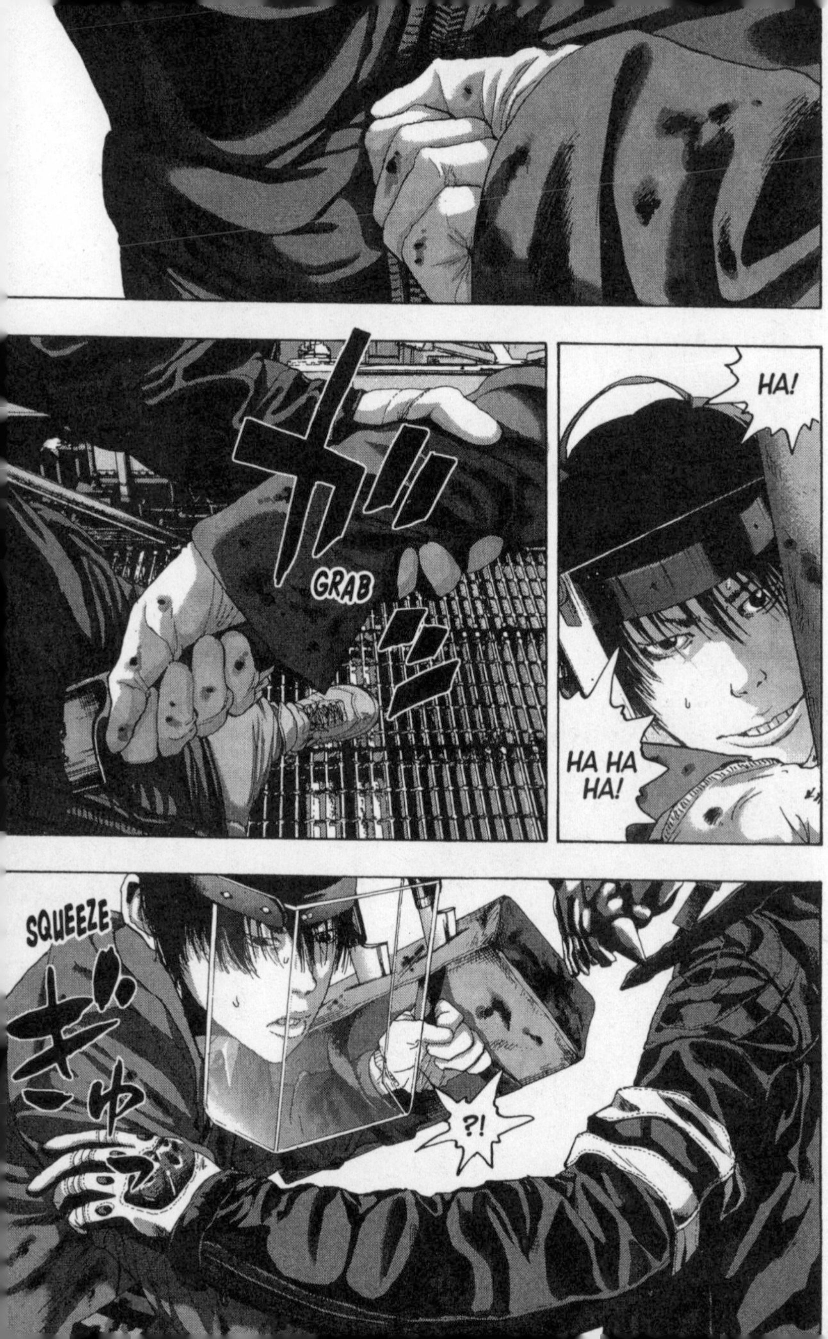
HA!
HA HA HA!
GRAB
SQUEEZE
?!

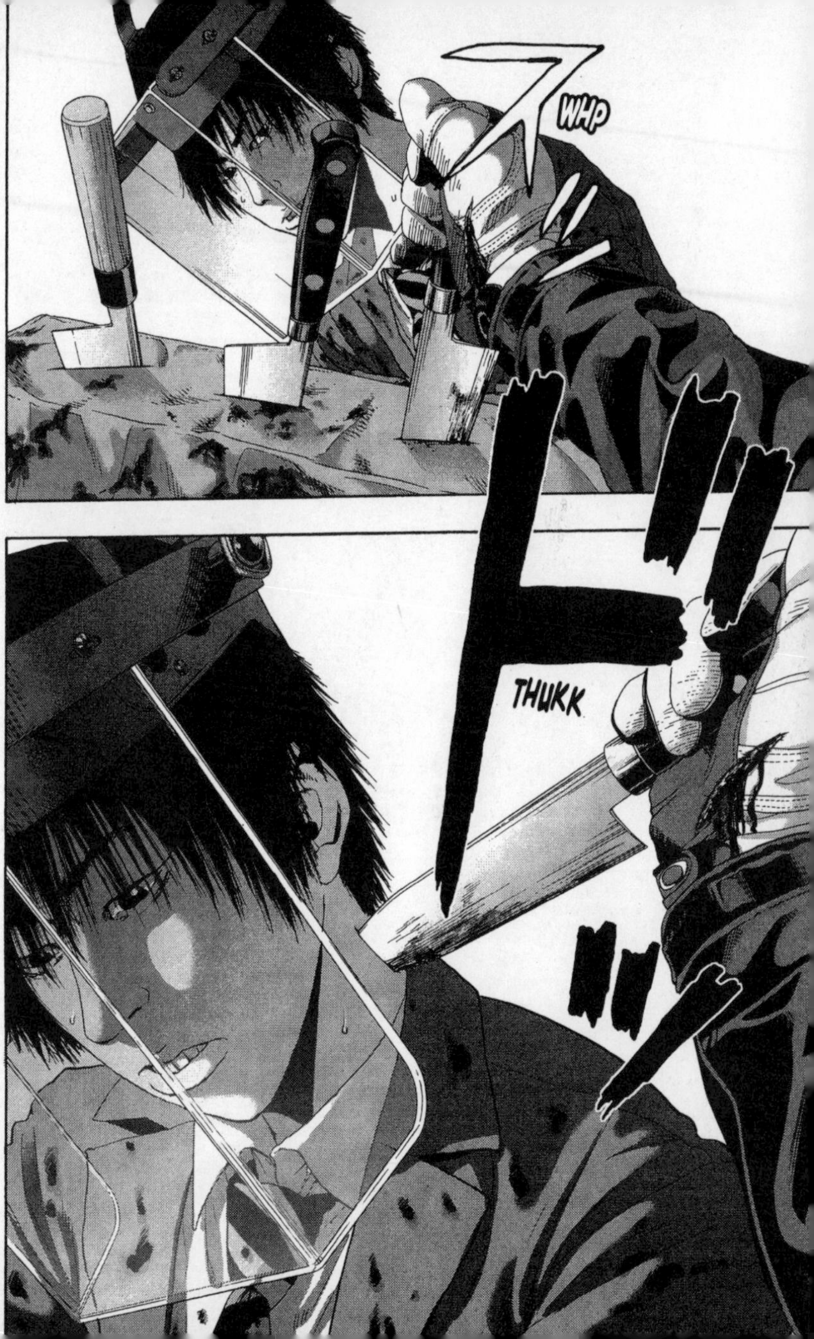
WHP
THUKK

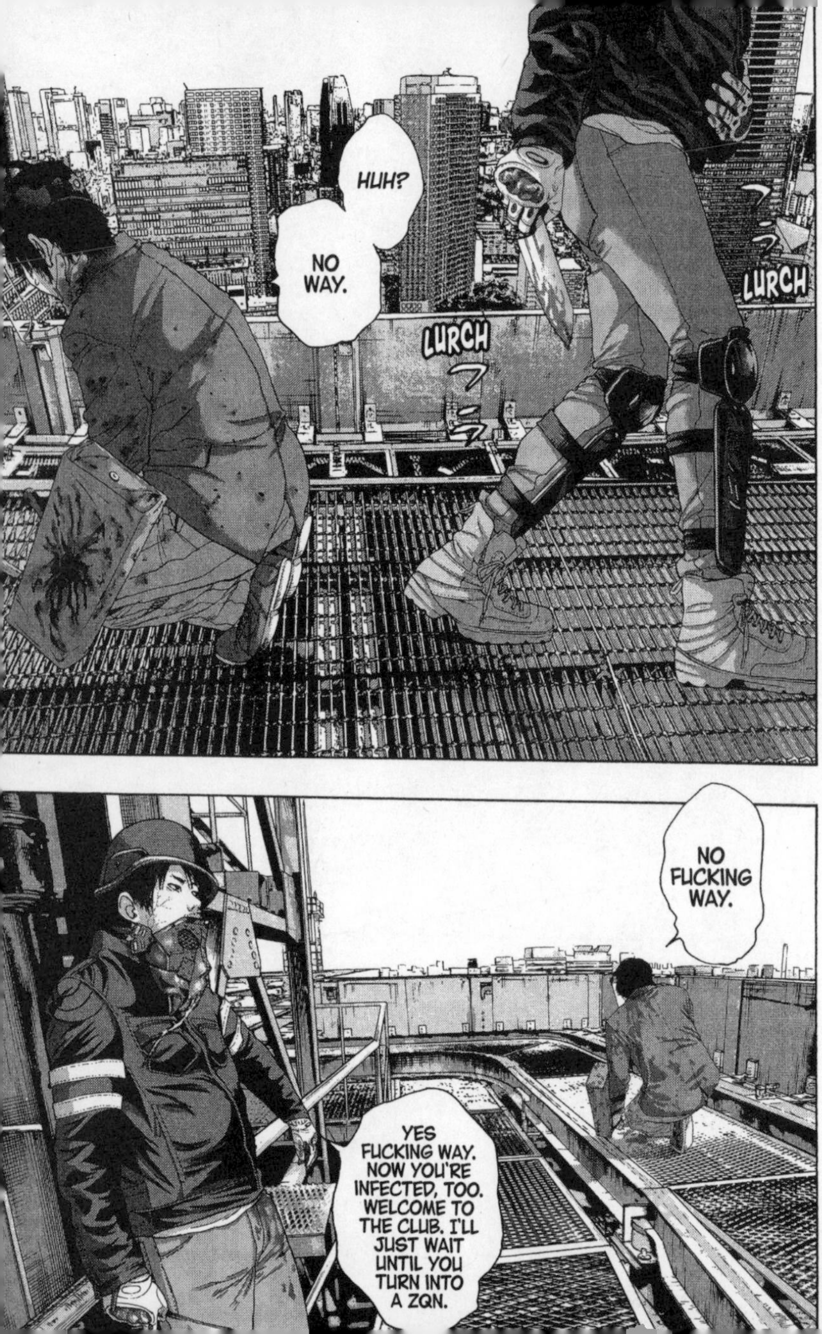
LURCH
HUH?
NO WAY.
LURCH
NO FUCKING WAY.
YES FUCKING WAY. NOW YOU'RE INFECTED, TOO. WELCOME TO THE CLUB. I'LL JUST WAIT UNTIL YOU TURN INTO A ZQN.

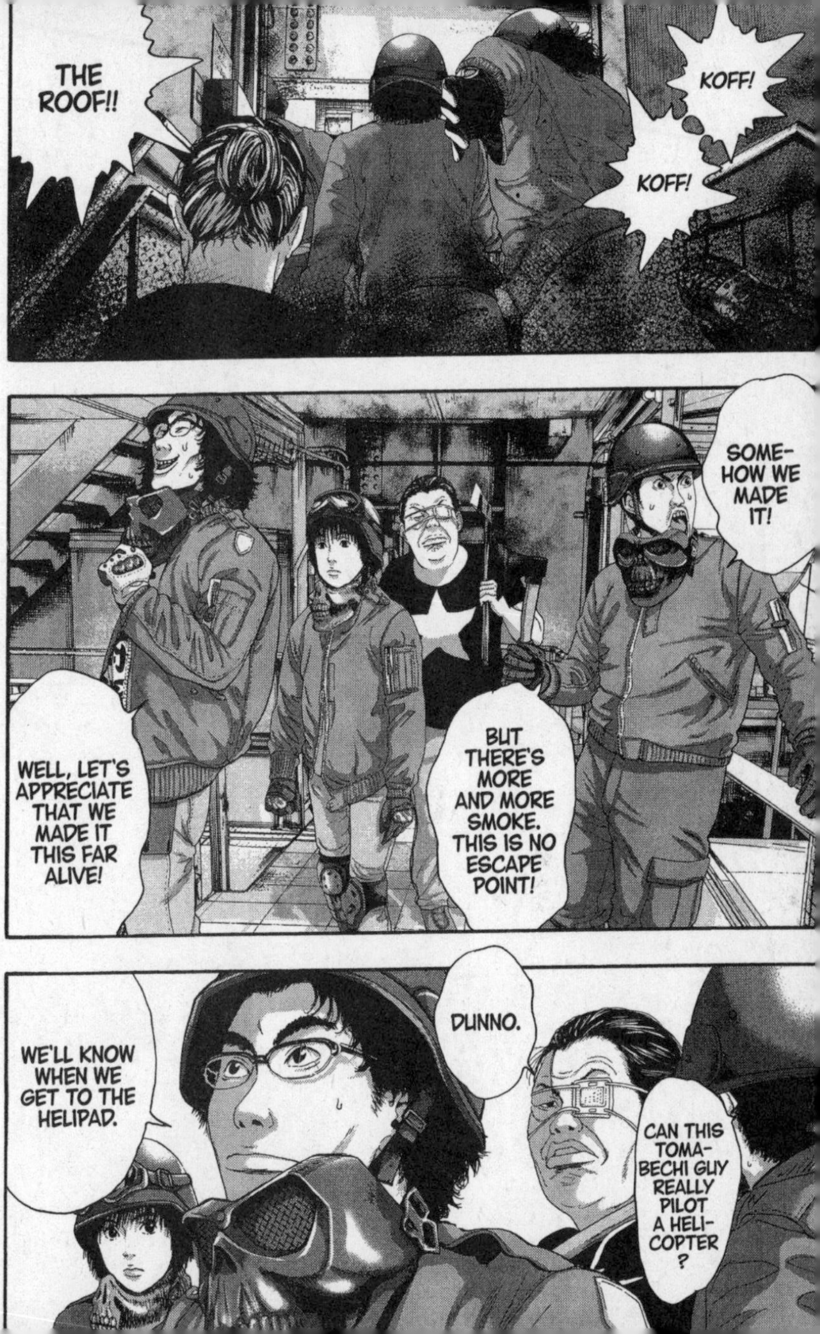
KOFF!
KOFF!
THE ROOF!!
SOMEHOW WE MADE IT!
BUT THERE'S MORE AND MORE SMOKE. THIS IS NO ESCAPE POINT!
WELL, LET'S APPRECIATE THAT WE MADE IT THIS FAR ALIVE!
CAN THIS TOMABECHI GUY REALLY PILOT A HELICOPTER?
DUNNO.
WE'LL KNOW WHEN WE GET TO THE HELIPAD.

I AM
A HERO

CHAPTER 249

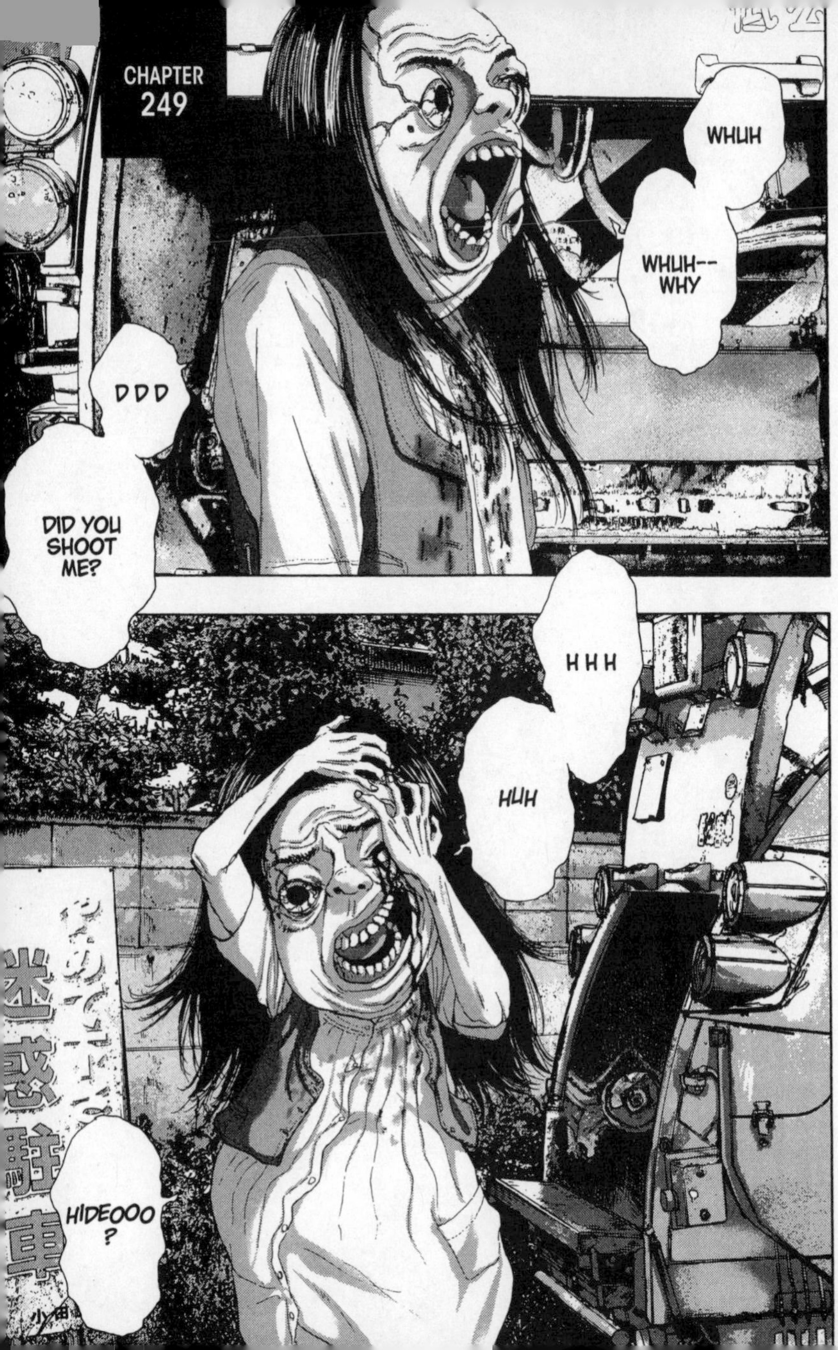
WHUH
WHUH-- WHY
DDD
DID YOU SHOOT ME?
HHH
HUH
HIDEOOO?

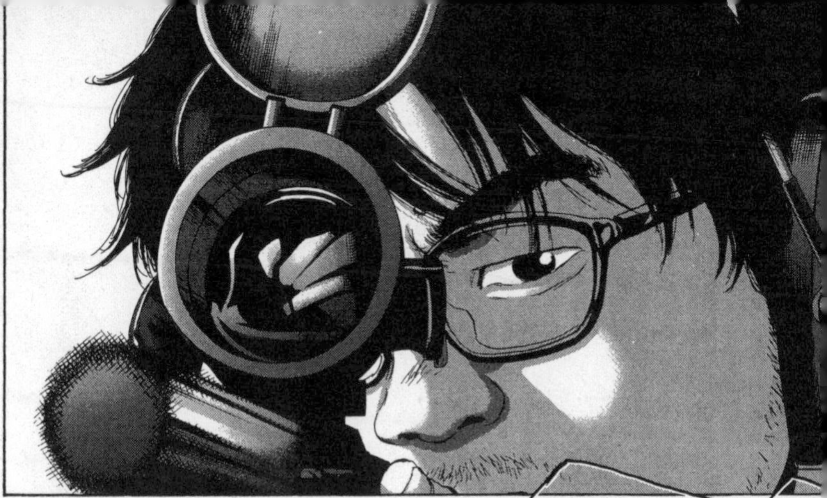

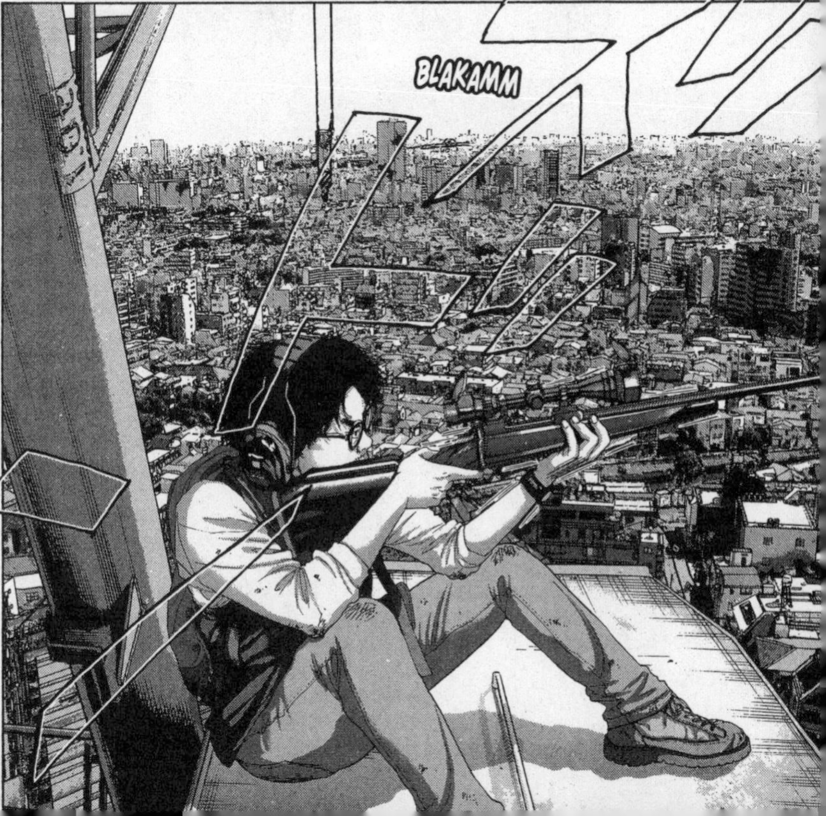
BLAKAMM

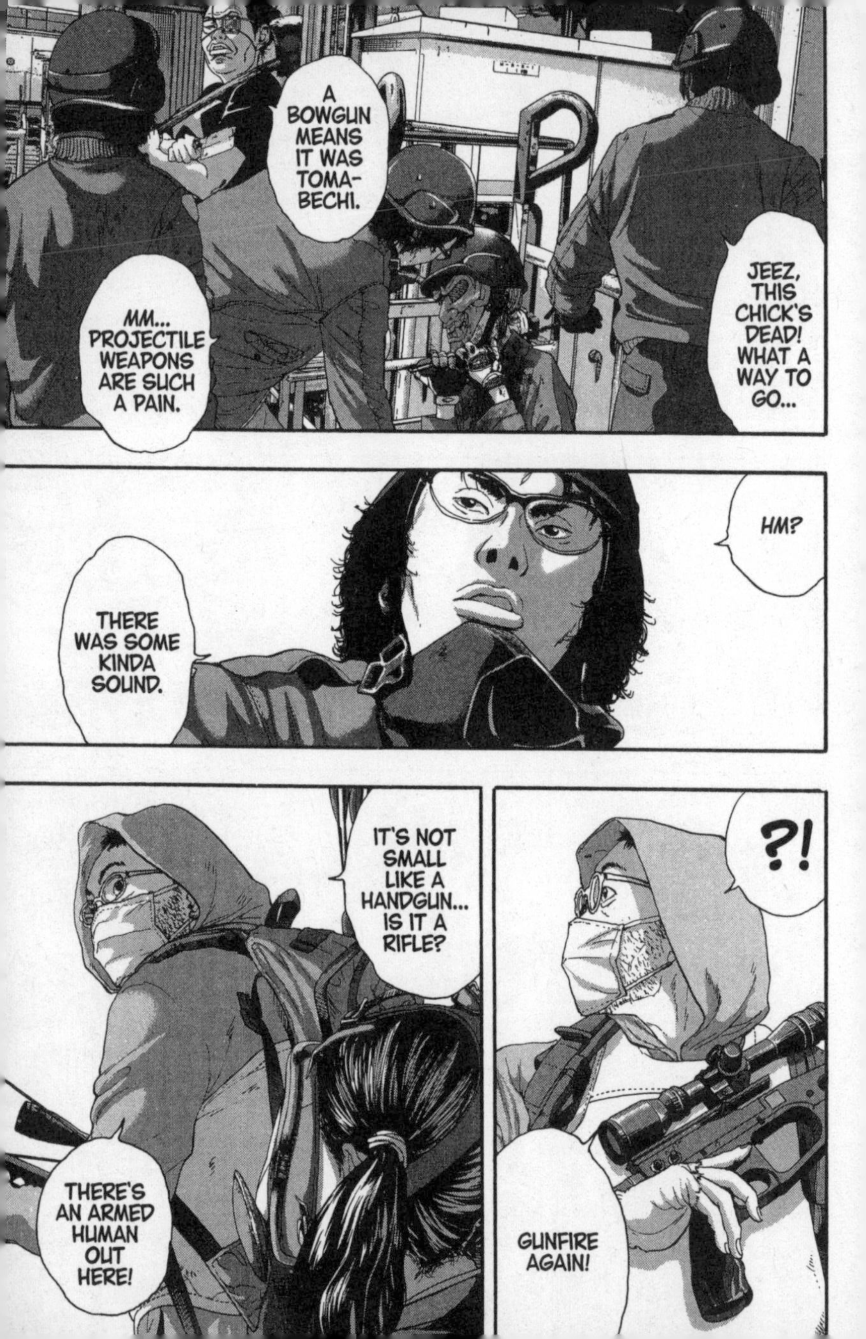
JEEZ, THIS CHICK'S DEAD! WHAT A WAY TO GO...
A BOWGUN MEANS IT WAS TOMA-BECHI.
MM... PROJECTILE WEAPONS ARE SUCH A PAIN.
HM?
THERE WAS SOME KINDA SOUND.
?!
GUNFIRE AGAIN!
IT'S NOT SMALL LIKE A HANDGUN... IS IT A RIFLE?
THERE'S AN ARMED HUMAN OUT HERE!

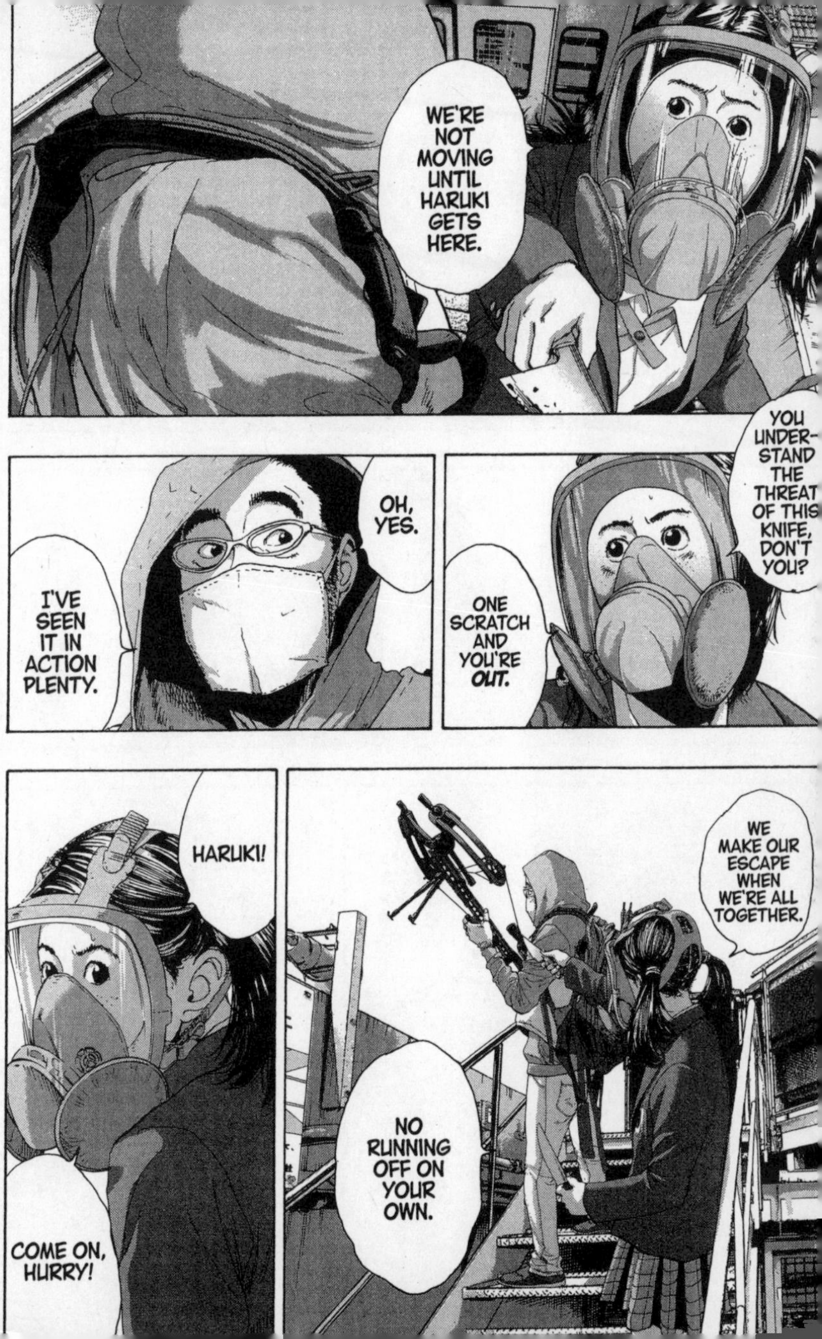
WE'RE NOT MOVING UNTIL HARUKI GETS HERE.
YOU UNDER-STAND THE THREAT OF THIS KNIFE, DON'T YOU?
ONE SCRATCH AND YOU'RE *OUT*.
OH, YES.
I'VE SEEN IT IN ACTION PLENTY.
WE MAKE OUR ESCAPE WHEN WE'RE ALL TOGETHER.
NO RUNNING OFF ON YOUR OWN.
HARUKI!
COME ON, HURRY!

GRRK

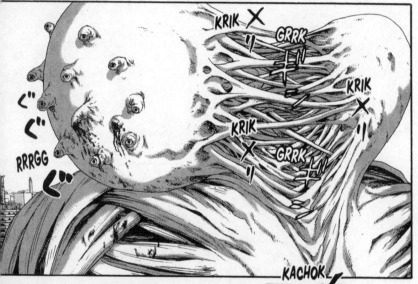

KRIK

GRRK

KRIK

KRIK

GRRK

RRRGG

KACHOK

PTINK

YES! IT'S WORKING!!

MAYBE!!

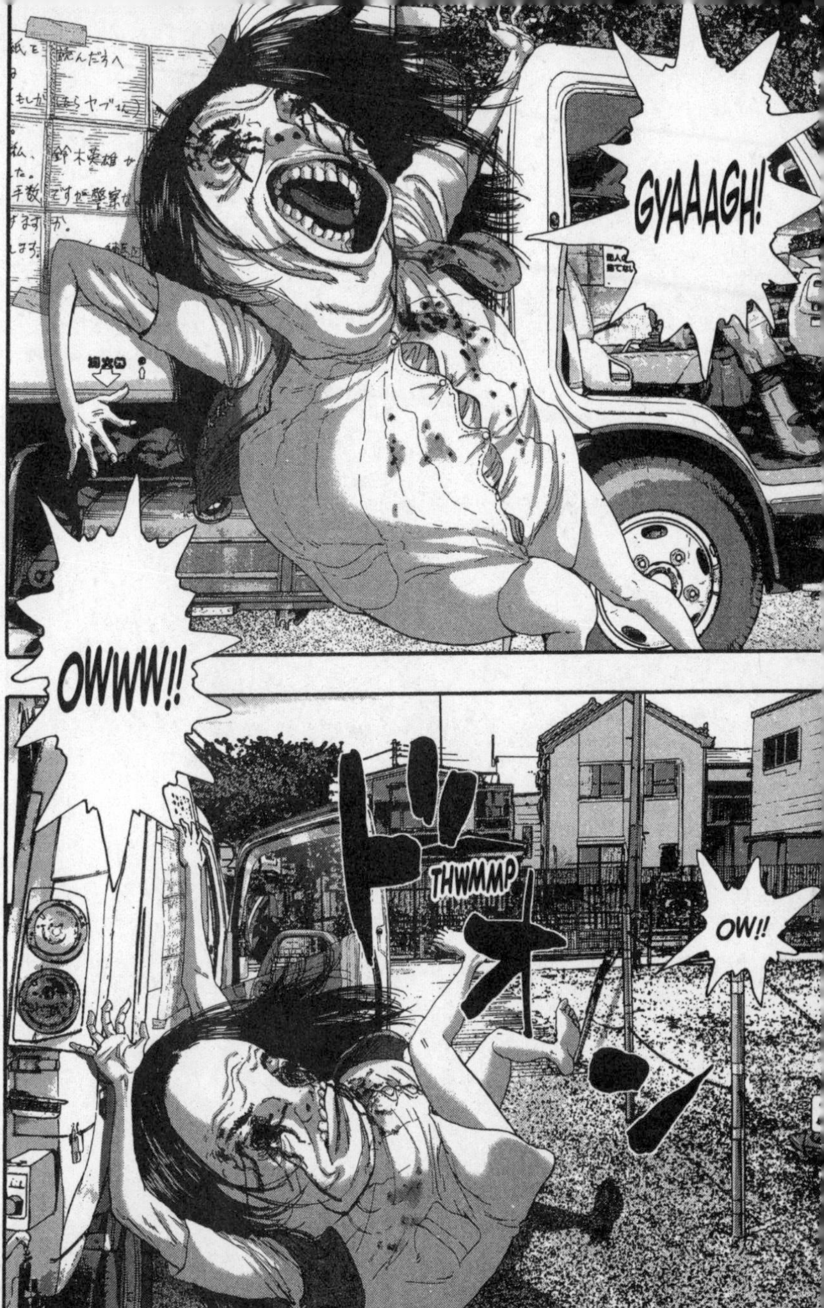
GYAAAGH!
OWWW!!
THWMMP
OW!!

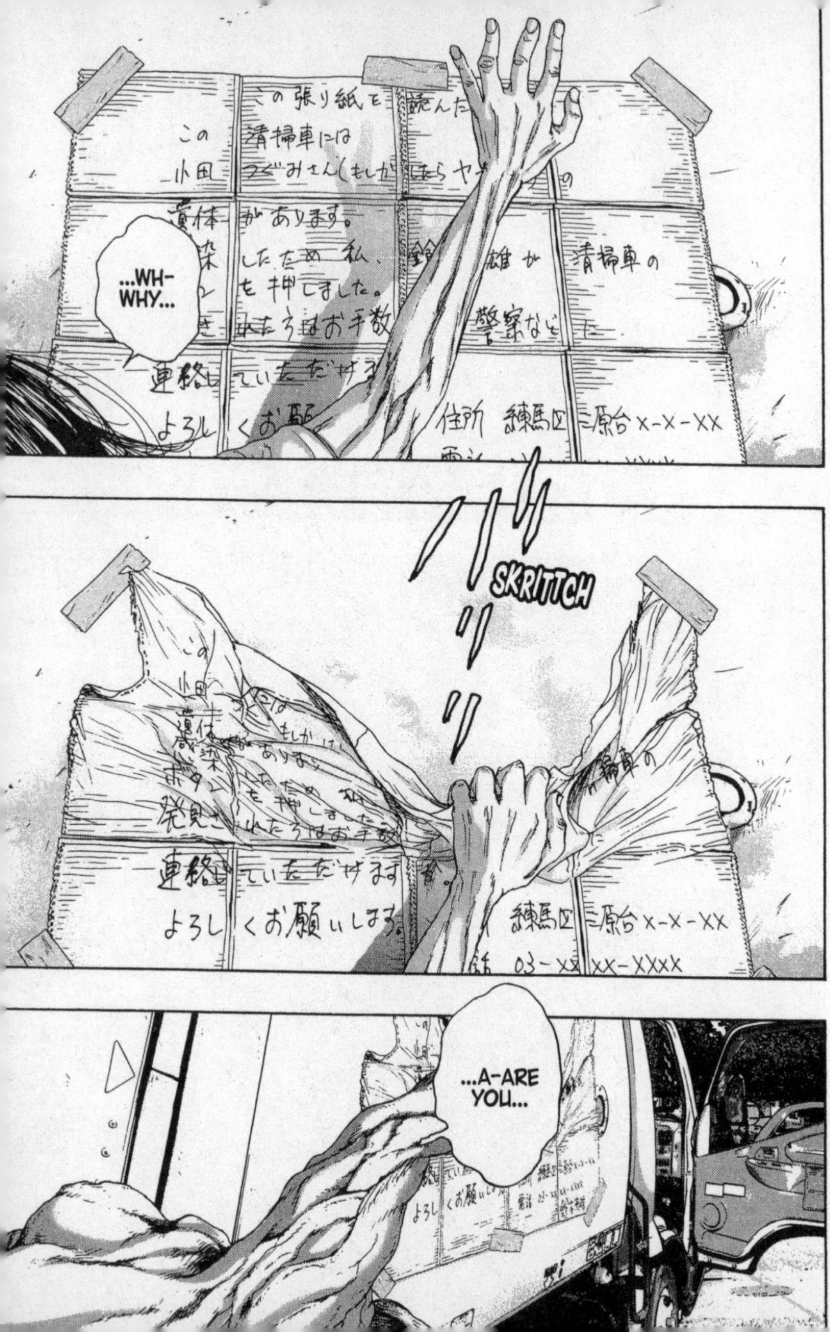
...WH-WHY...
SKRITTCH
...A-ARE YOU...

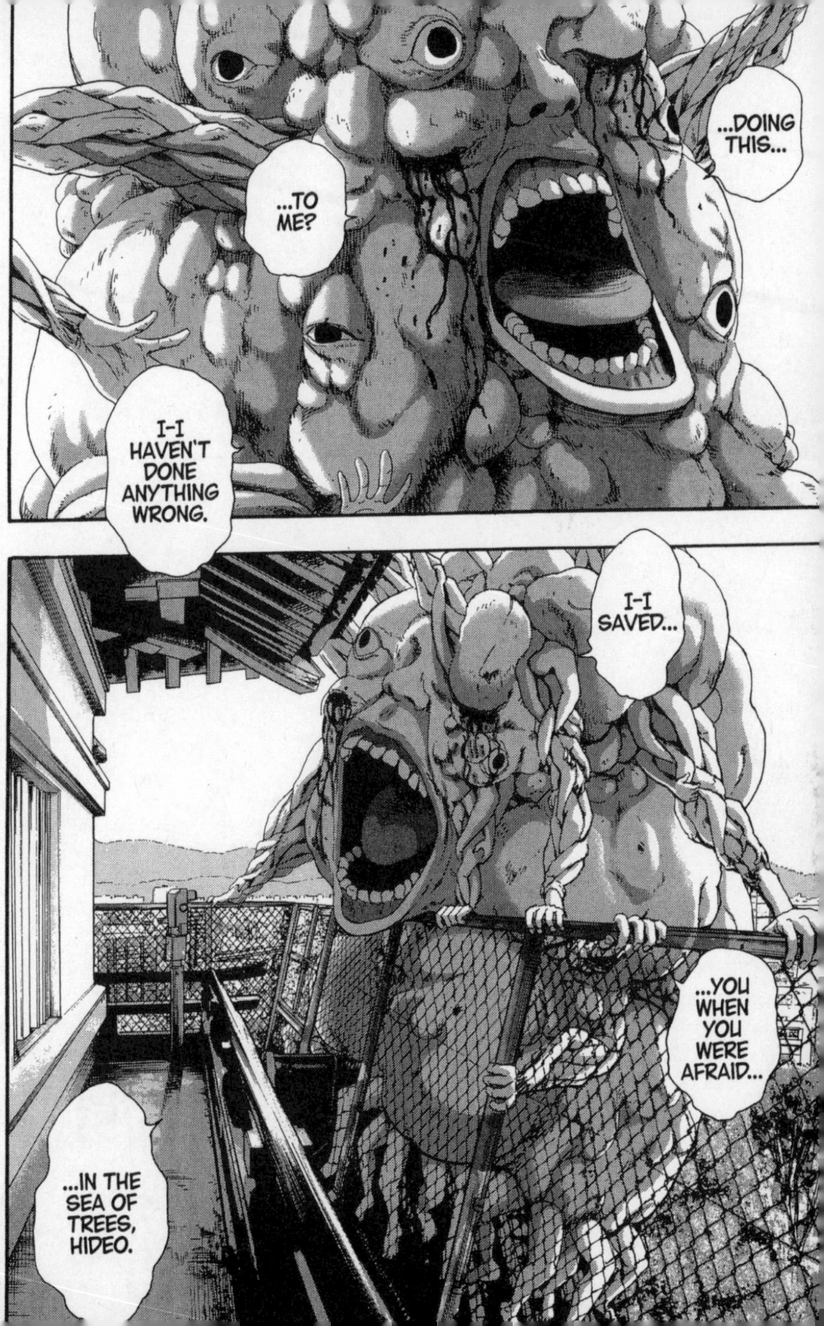
...DOING THIS...
...TO ME?
I-I HAVEN'T DONE ANYTHING WRONG.
I-I SAVED...
...YOU WHEN YOU WERE AFRAID...
...IN THE SEA OF TREES, HIDEO.

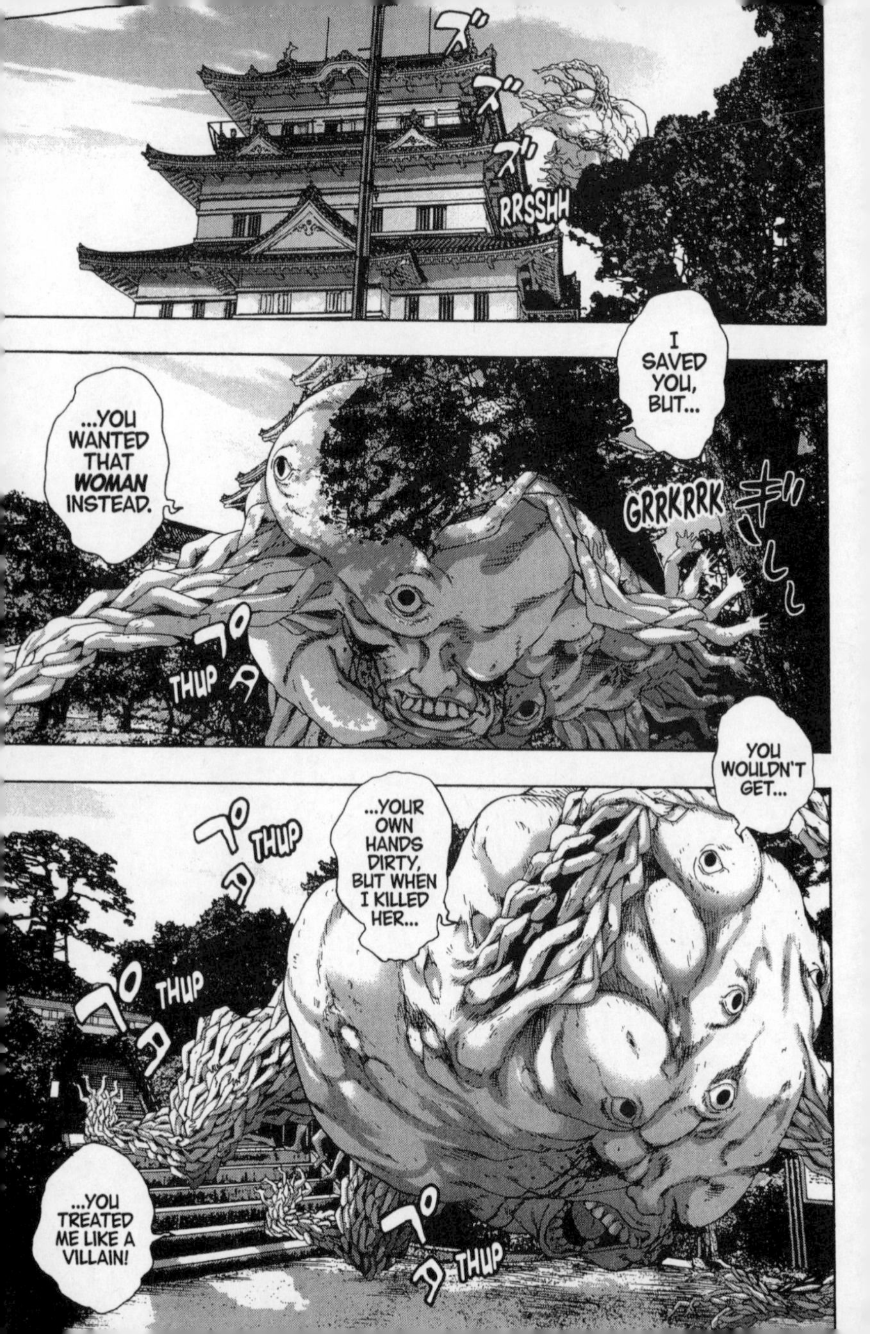

RRSSHH
I SAVED YOU, BUT...
GRRKRRK
...YOU WANTED THAT WOMAN INSTEAD.
THUP
YOU WOULDN'T GET...
...YOUR OWN HANDS DIRTY, BUT WHEN I KILLED HER...
THUP
THUP
...YOU TREATED ME LIKE A VILLAIN!
THUP

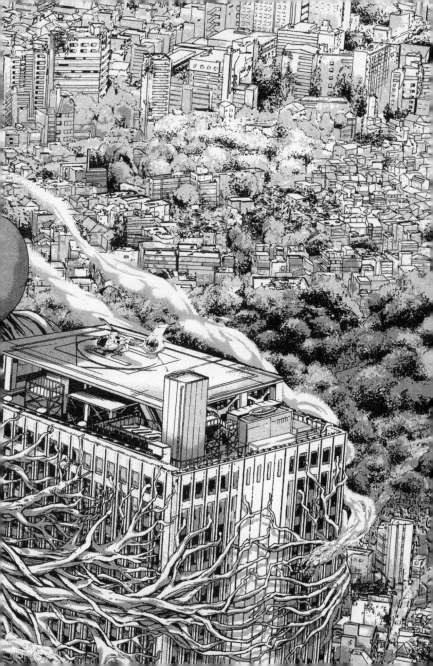

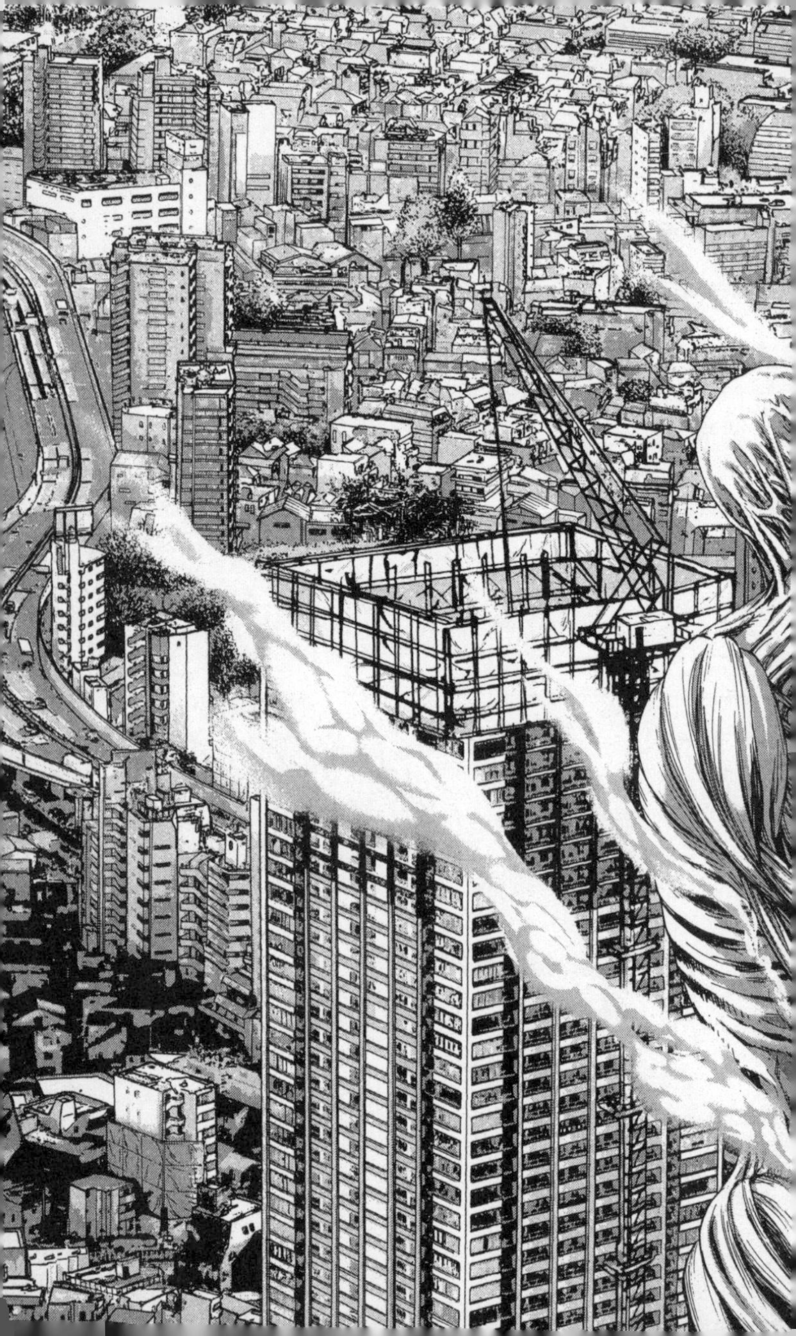

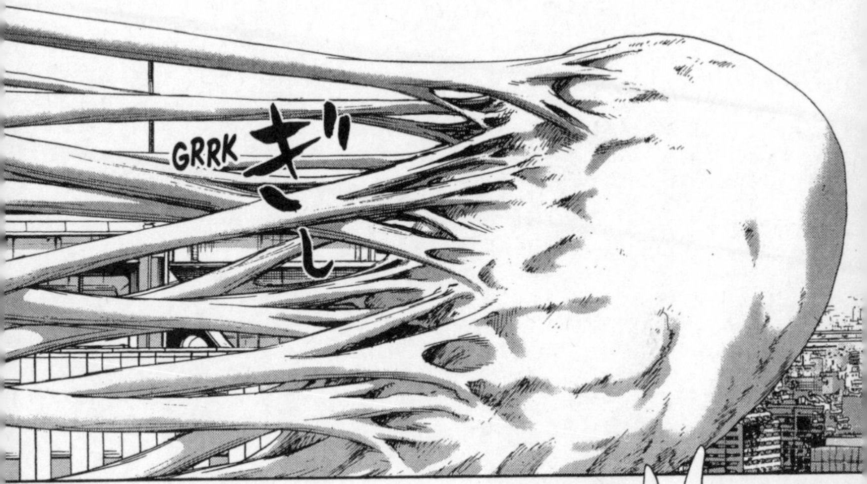
GRRK
ぎし

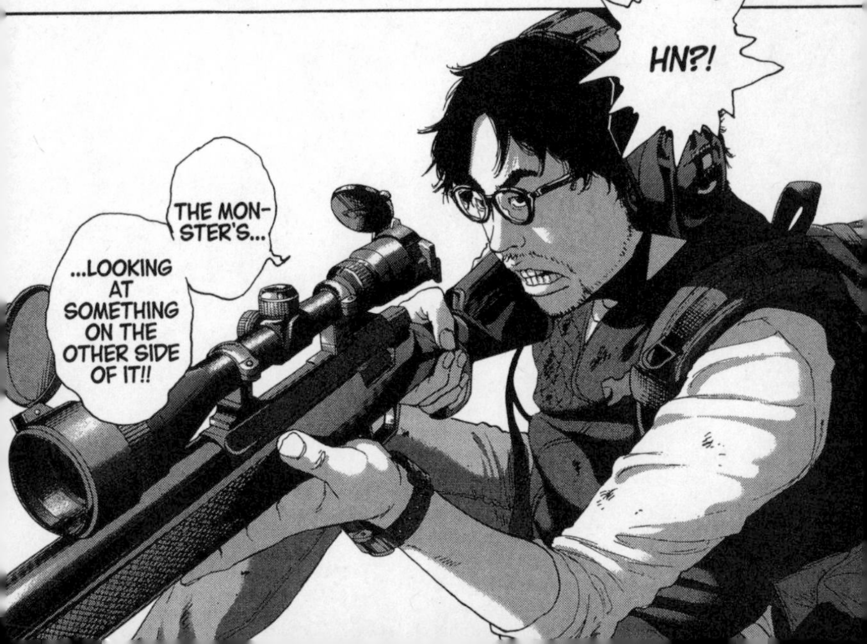
HN?!
THE MON-STER'S...
...LOOKING AT SOMETHING ON THE OTHER SIDE OF IT!!

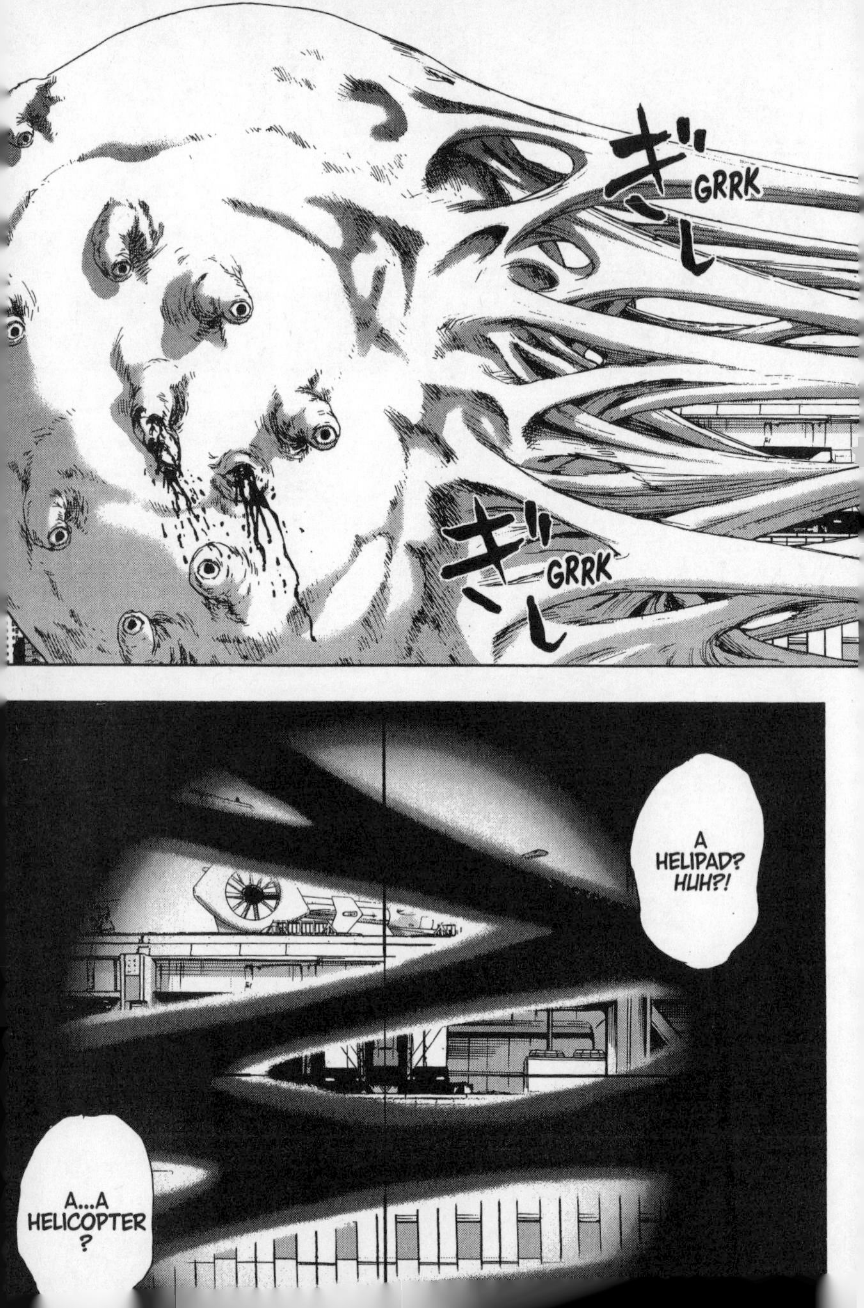

ぎし
GRRK
ぎし
GRRK
A HELIPAD? HUH?!
A...A HELICOPTER ?

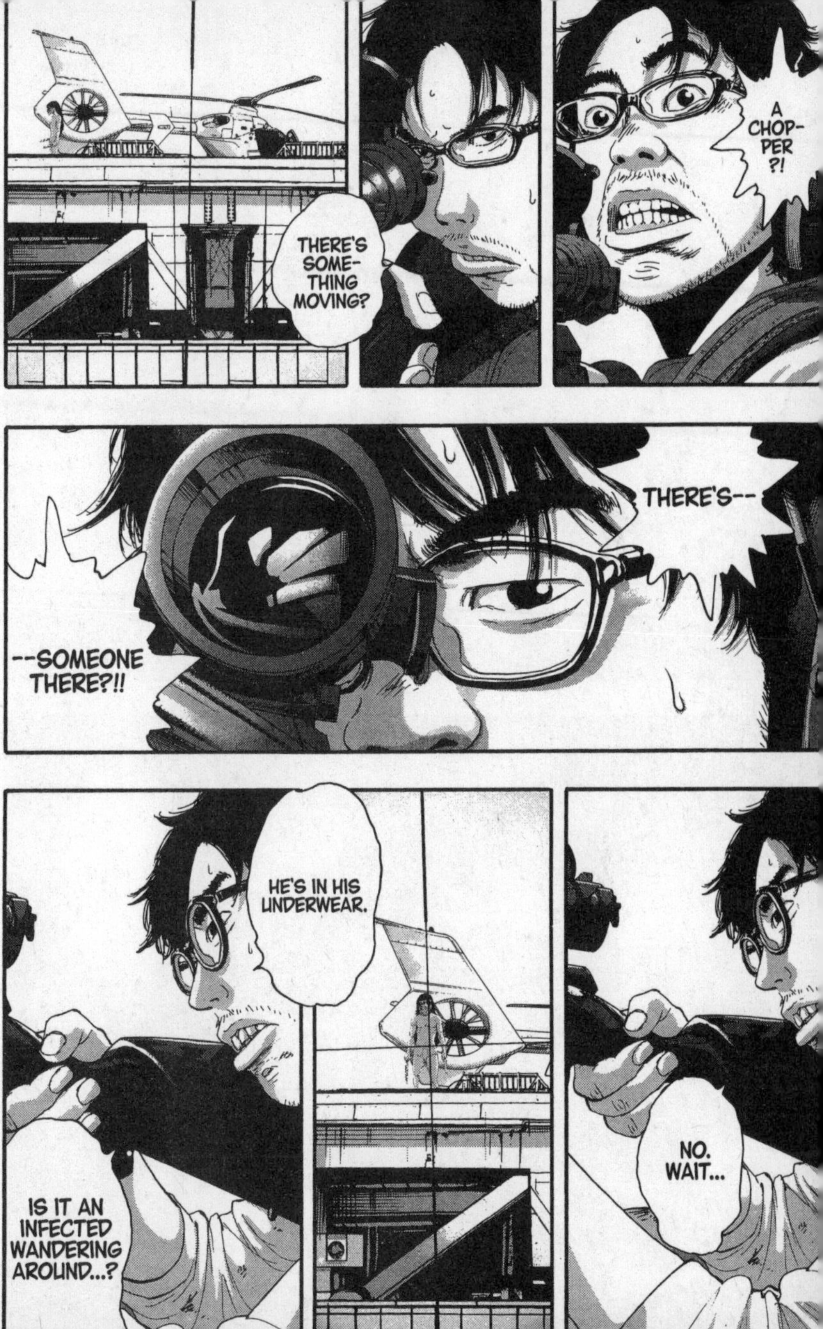
A CHOP-PER?!
THERE'S SOME-THING MOVING?
THERE'S--
--SOMEONE THERE?!!
NO. WAIT...
HE'S IN HIS UNDERWEAR.
IS IT AN INFECTED WANDERING AROUND...?

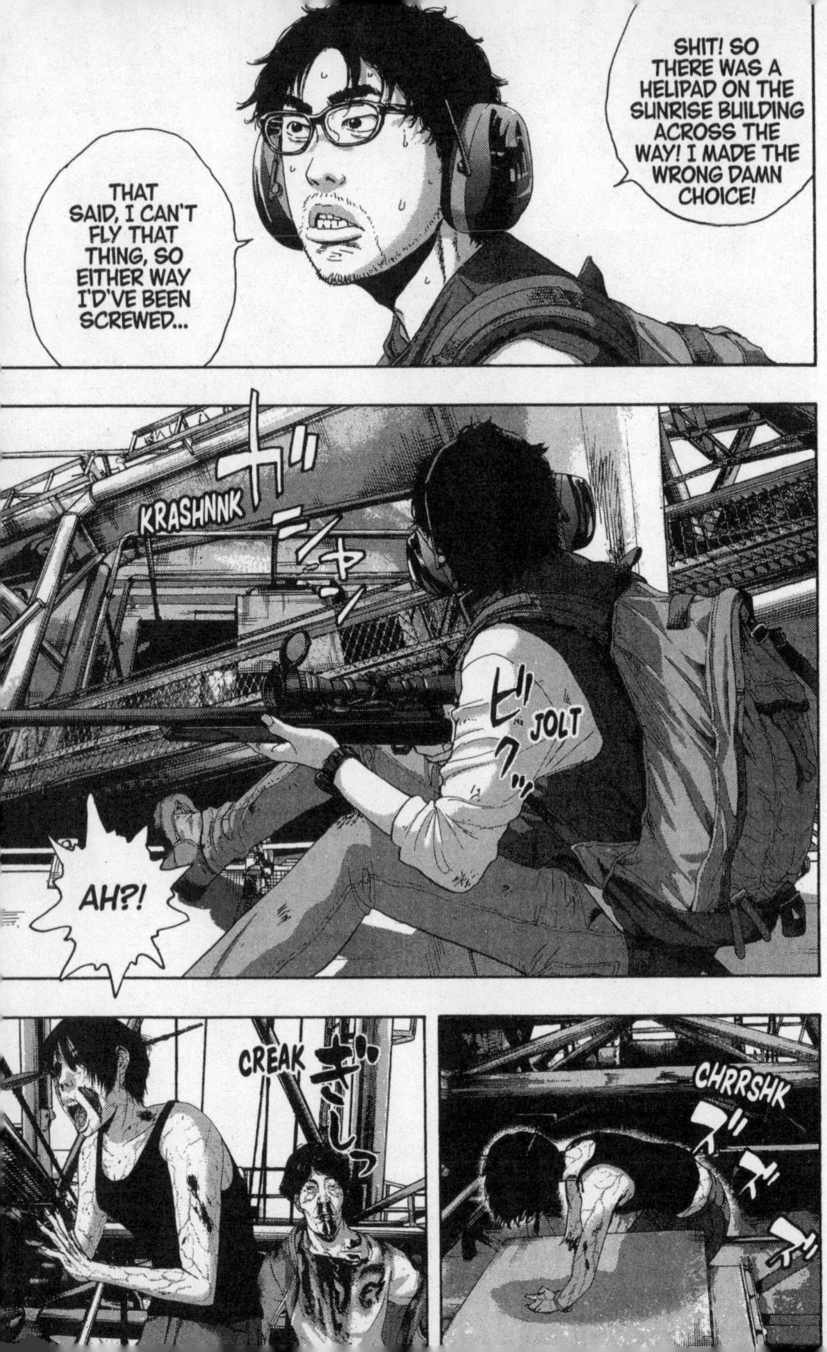
SHIT! SO THERE WAS A HELIPAD ON THE SUNRISE BUILDING ACROSS THE WAY! I MADE THE WRONG DAMN CHOICE!
THAT SAID, I CAN'T FLY THAT THING, SO EITHER WAY I'D'VE BEEN SCREWED...
ガッシャン
KRASHNNK
ビクッ
JOLT
AH?!
CHRRSHK
ズズズ
CREAK
ぎしっ

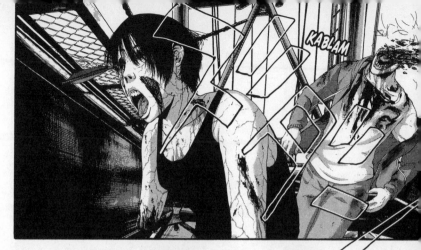

KABLAM

...

G--

GET OVER HERE!!!

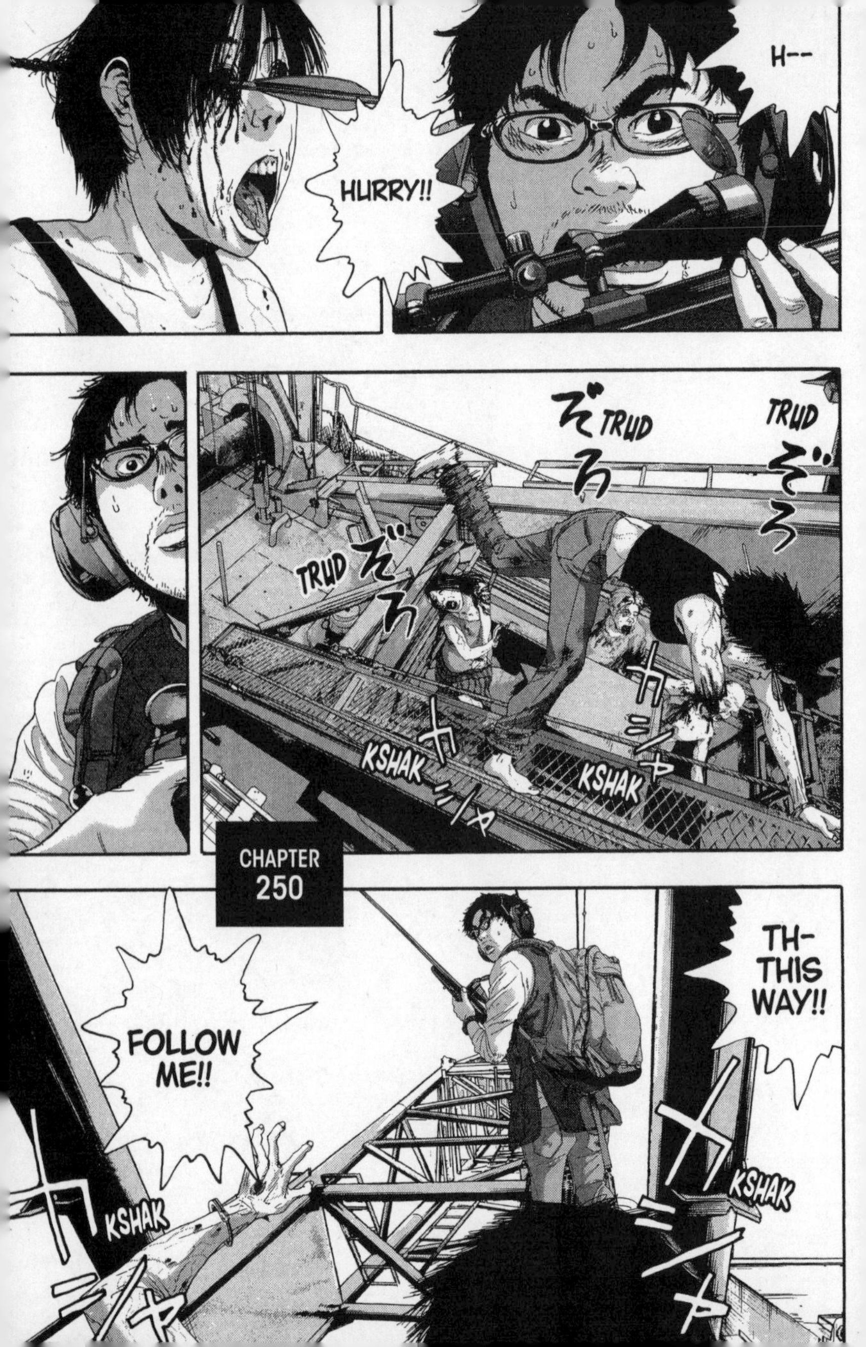
H--
HURRY!!
TRUD
ぞろ
TRUD
ぞろ
TRUD
ぞろ
KSHAK
KSHAK
CHAPTER 250
TH- THIS WAY!!
KSHAK
FOLLOW ME!!
KSHAK

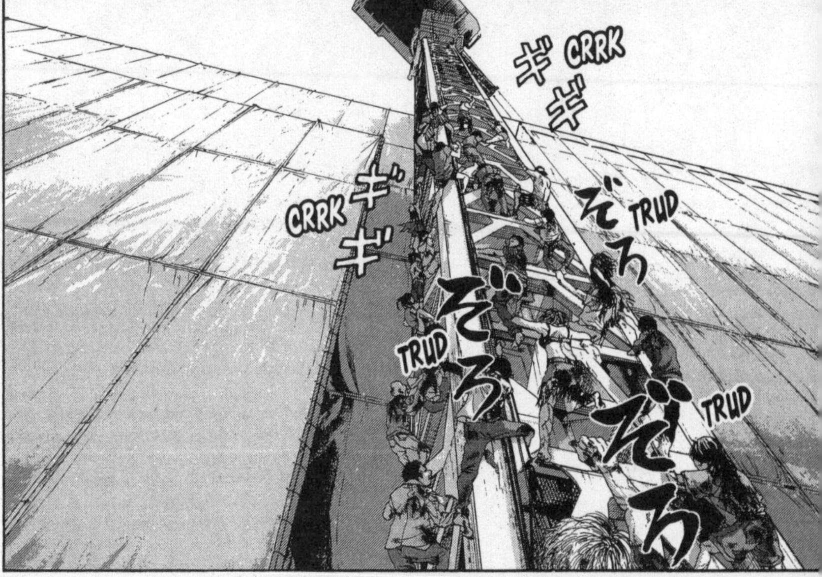
ギギ
CRRK
ぞろぞろ
TRUD
ギギ
CRRK
ぞろぞろ
TRUD
ぞろぞろ
TRUD

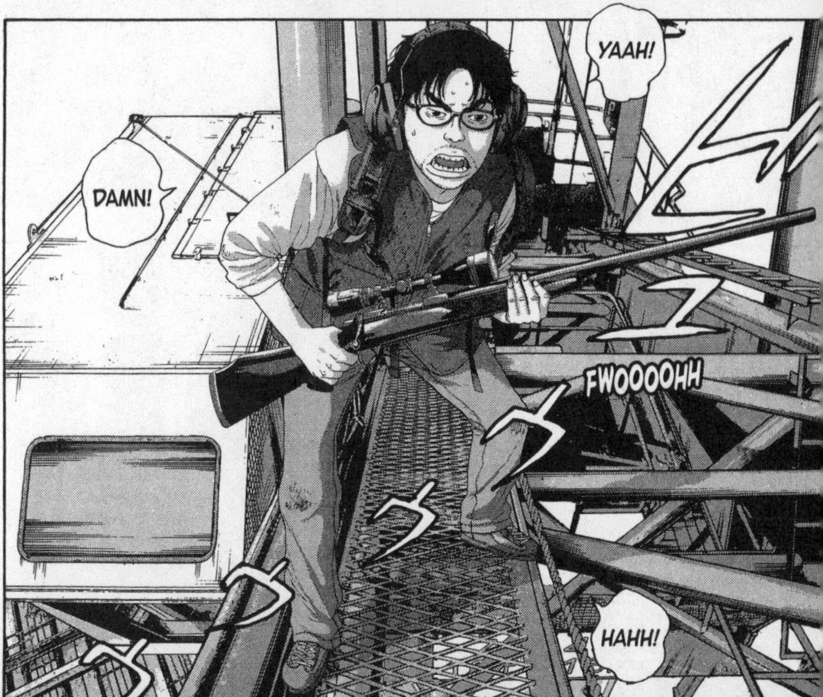
YAAH!
DAMN!
FWOOOOHH
HAHH!

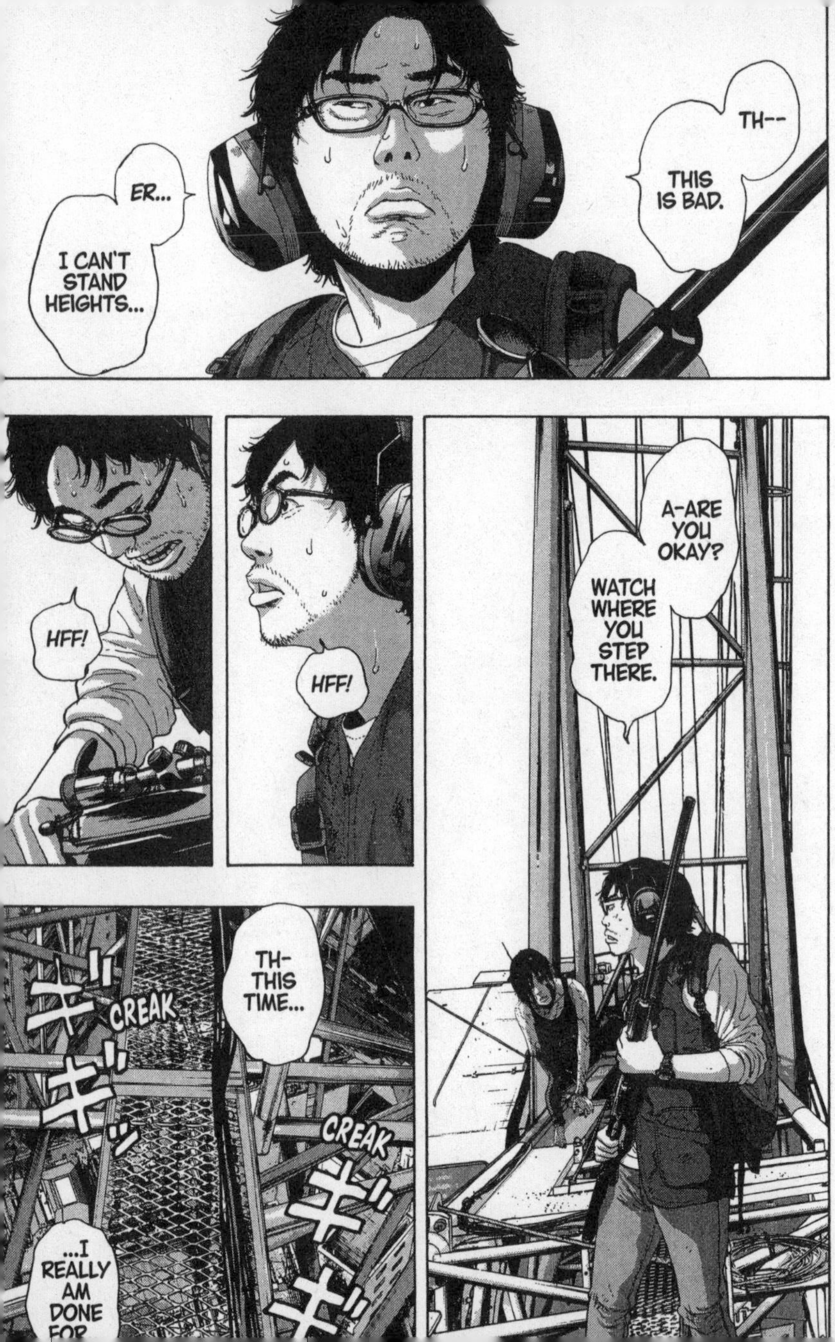
TH--
THIS IS BAD.
ER...
I CAN'T STAND HEIGHTS...
A-ARE YOU OKAY?
WATCH WHERE YOU STEP THERE.
HFF!
HFF!
TH- THIS TIME...
CREAK
CREAK
...I REALLY AM DONE FOR

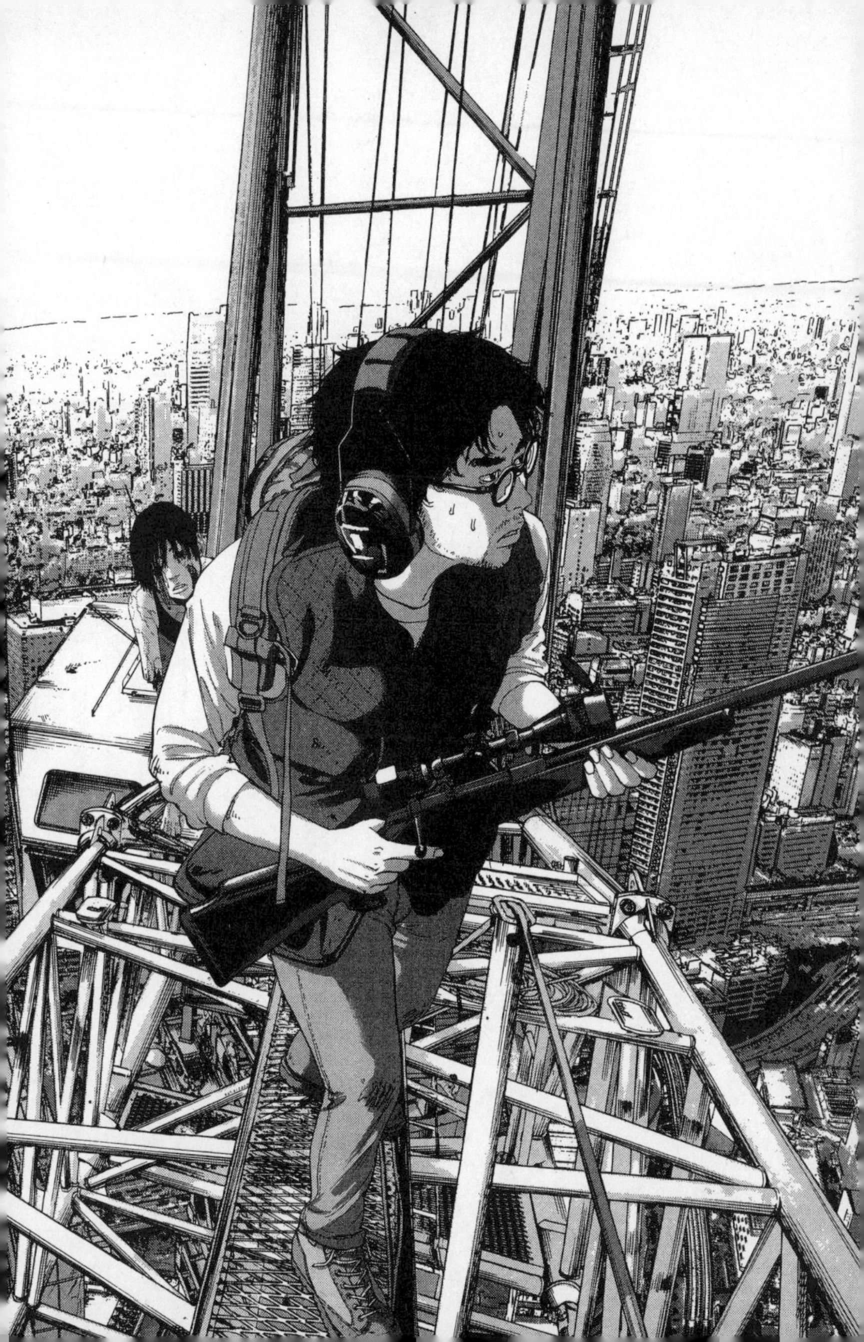

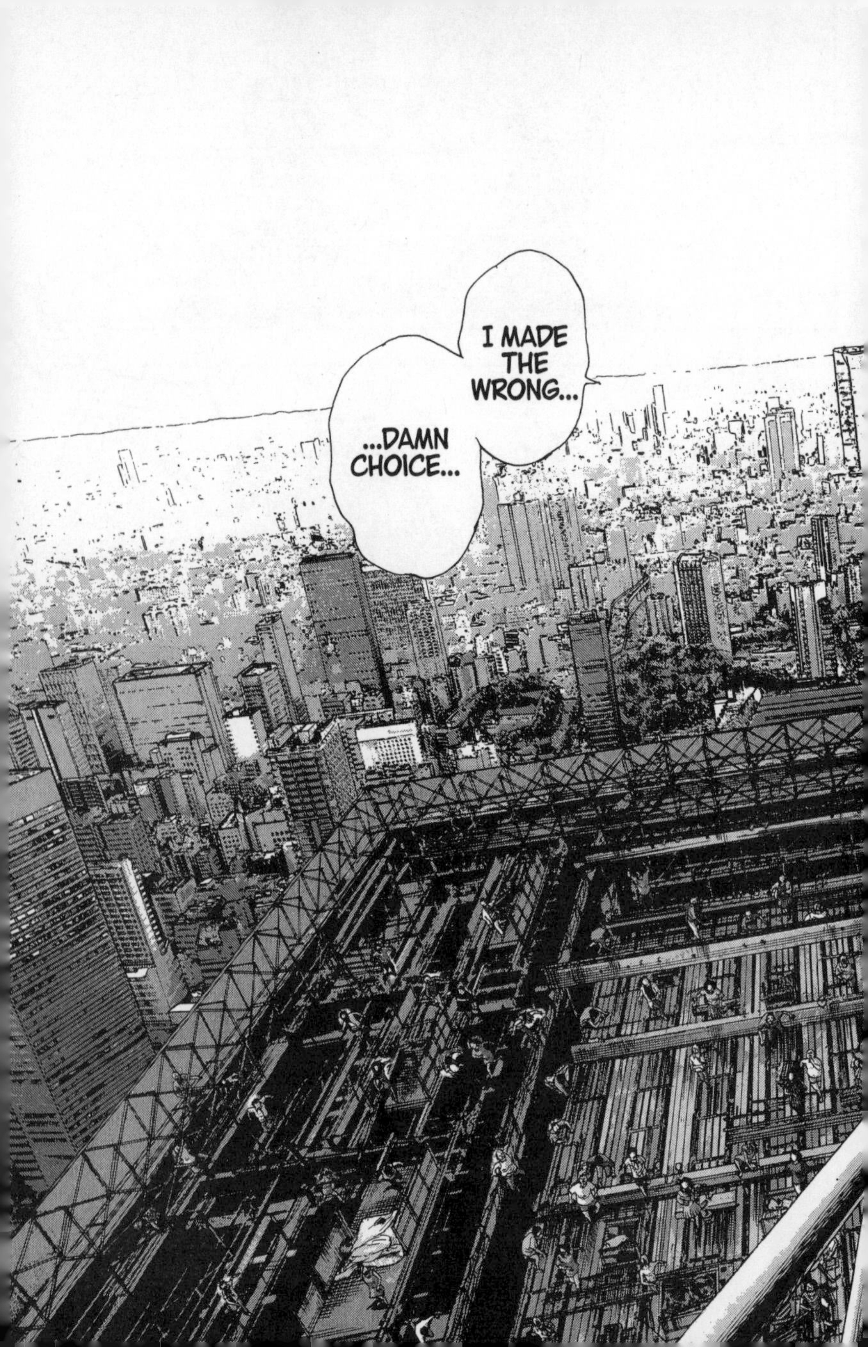
I MADE THE WRONG...
...DAMN CHOICE...

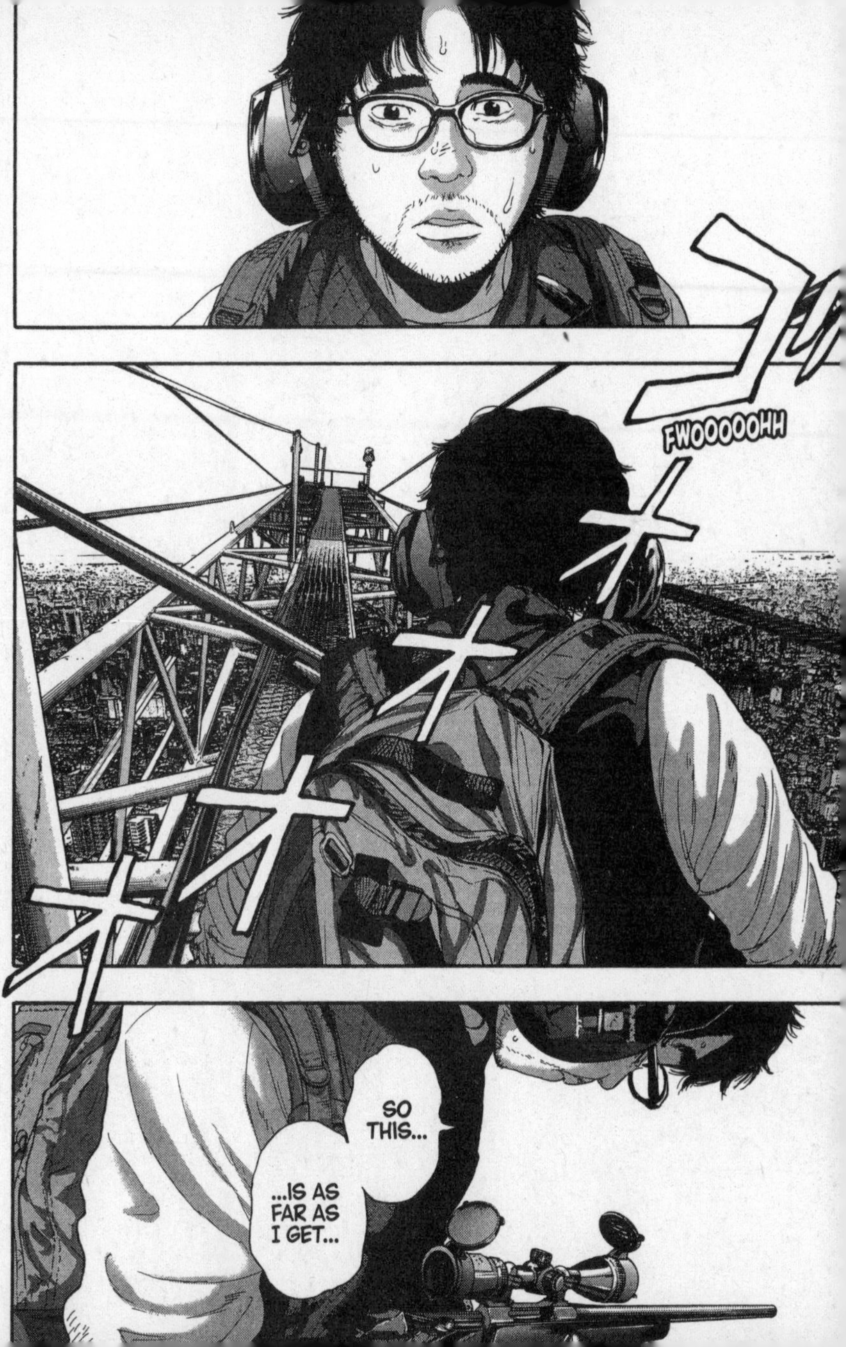
FWOOOOOHH
SO THIS...
...IS AS FAR AS I GET...

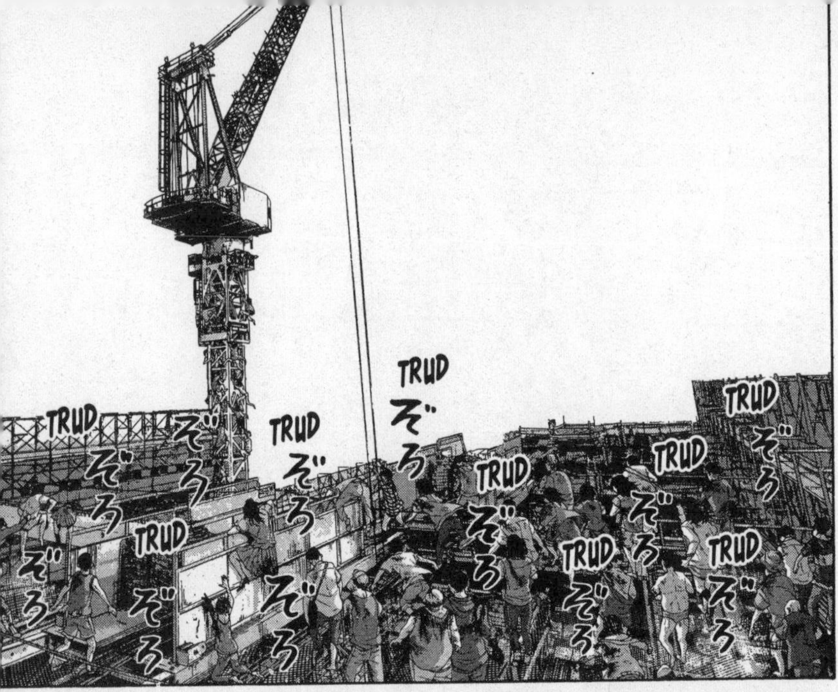
TRUD
ぞろ
TRUD
ぞろ
TRUD
ぞろ
TRUD
ぞろ
TRUD
ぞろ
TRUD
ぞろ
TRUD
ぞろ
ぞろ
TRUD
ぞろ
TRUD
ぞろ
ぞろ
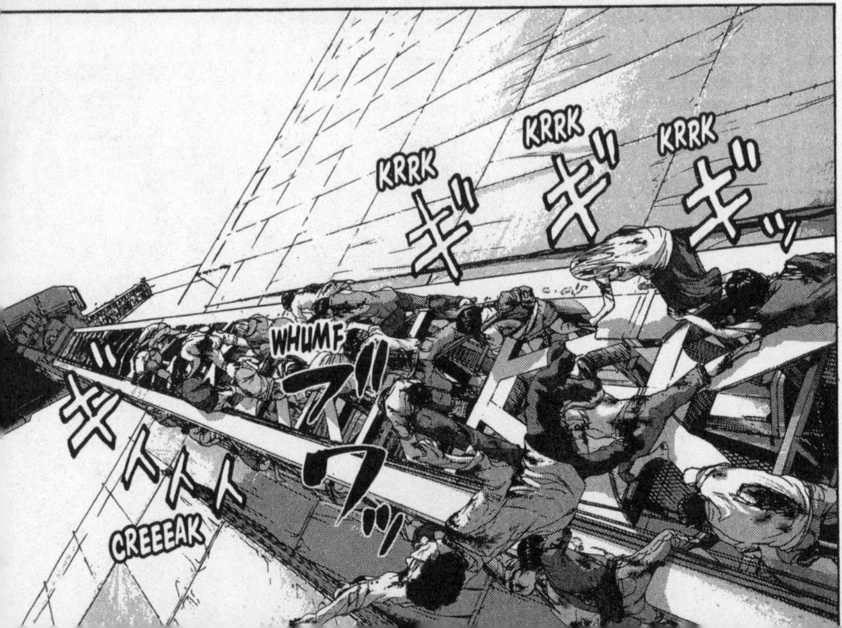
KRRK
ギッ
KRRK
ギリ
KRRK
ギリ
WHUMF
ブワッ
CREEEAK
ギイイイッ

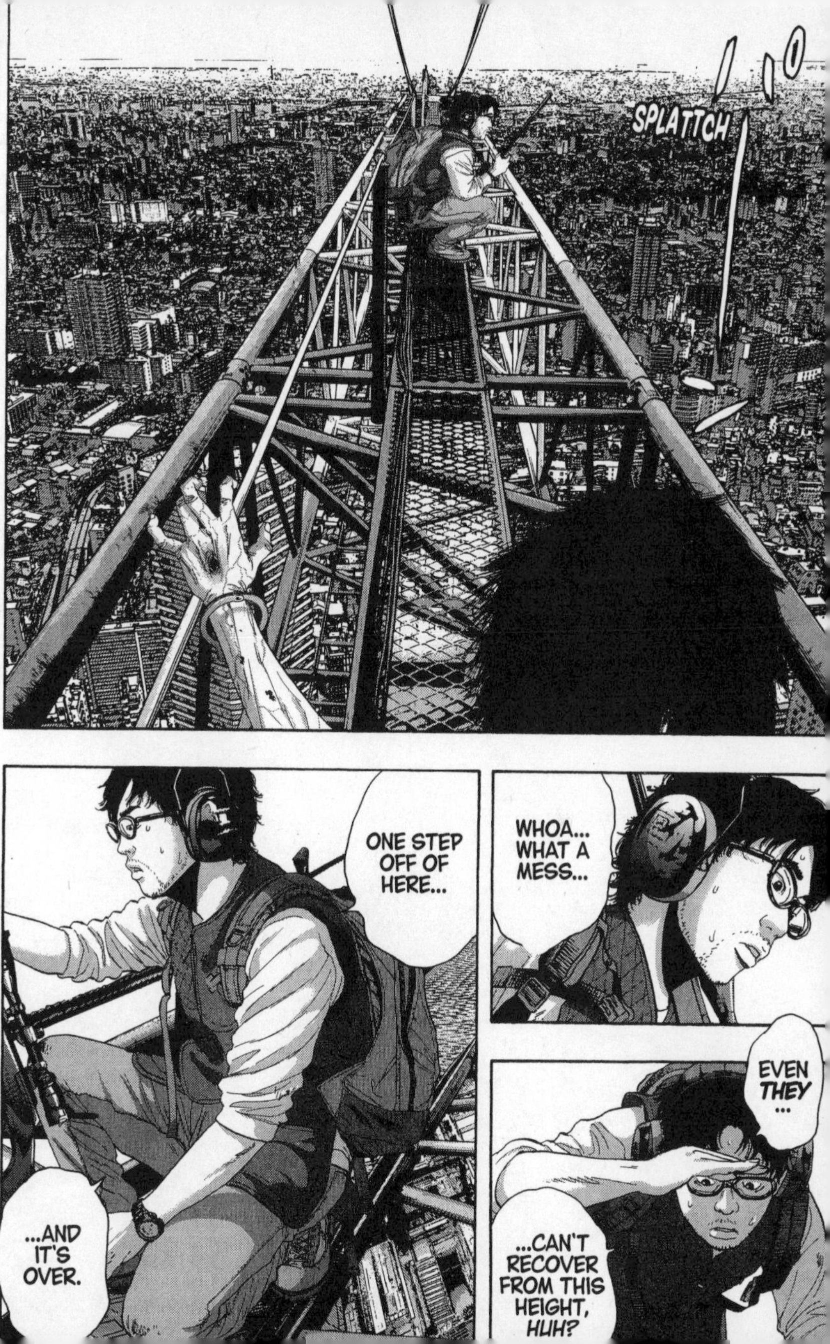
SPLATTCH
WHOA... WHAT A MESS...
EVEN THEY...
...CAN'T RECOVER FROM THIS HEIGHT, HUH?
ONE STEP OFF OF HERE...
...AND IT'S OVER.

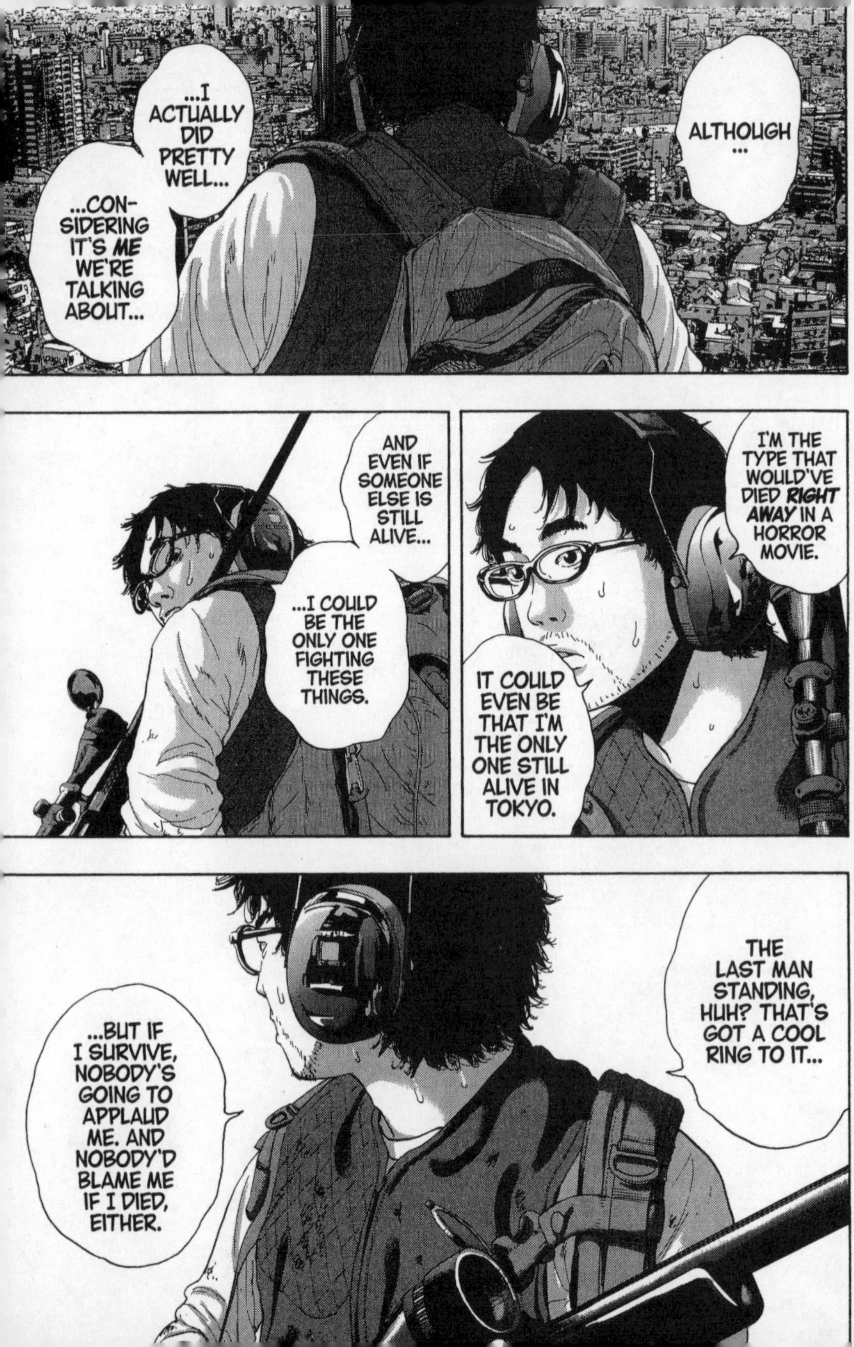
ALTHOUGH...
...I ACTUALLY DID PRETTY WELL...
...CONSIDERING IT'S *ME* WE'RE TALKING ABOUT...
I'M THE TYPE THAT WOULD'VE DIED ***RIGHT AWAY*** IN A HORROR MOVIE.
IT COULD EVEN BE THAT I'M THE ONLY ONE STILL ALIVE IN TOKYO.
AND EVEN IF SOMEONE ELSE IS STILL ALIVE...
...I COULD BE THE ONLY ONE FIGHTING THESE THINGS.
THE LAST MAN STANDING, HUH? THAT'S GOT A COOL RING TO IT...
...BUT IF I SURVIVE, NOBODY'S GOING TO APPLAUD ME. AND NOBODY'D BLAME ME IF I DIED, EITHER.

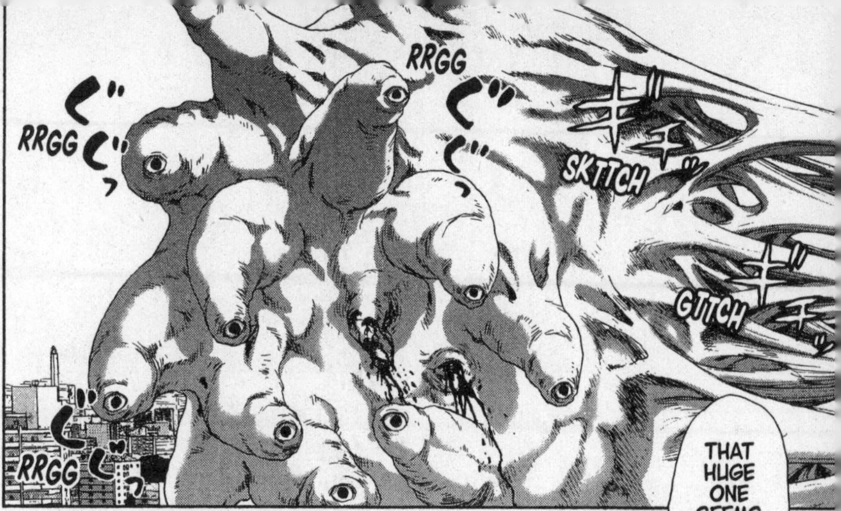
SKTTCH
GTTCH
RRGG
RRGG
RRGG
THAT HUGE ONE SEEMS TO BE...
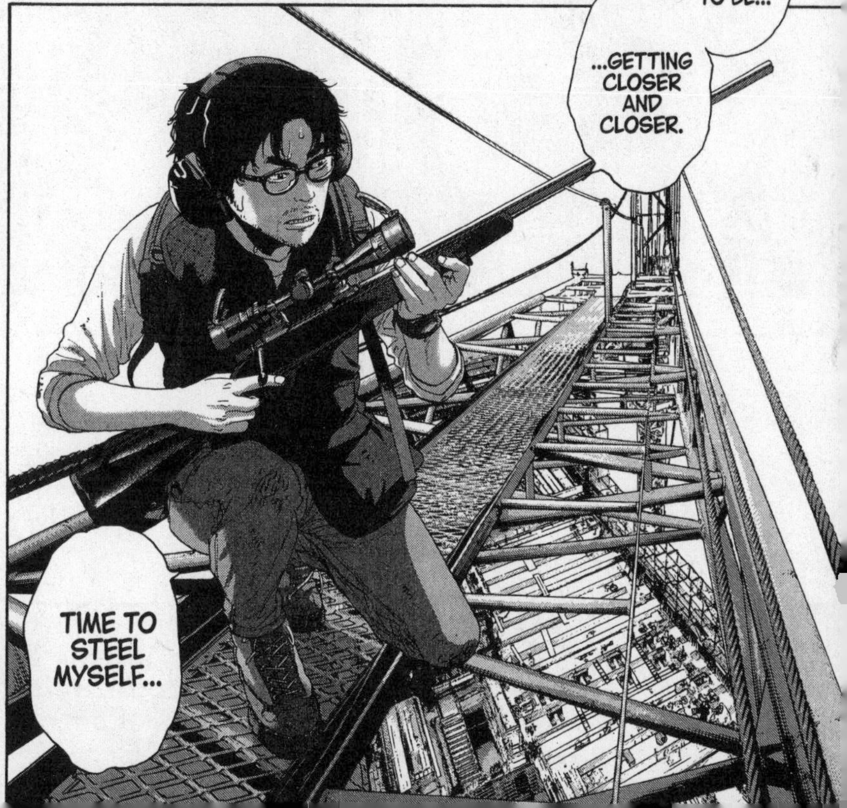
...GETTING CLOSER AND CLOSER.
TIME TO STEEL MYSELF...

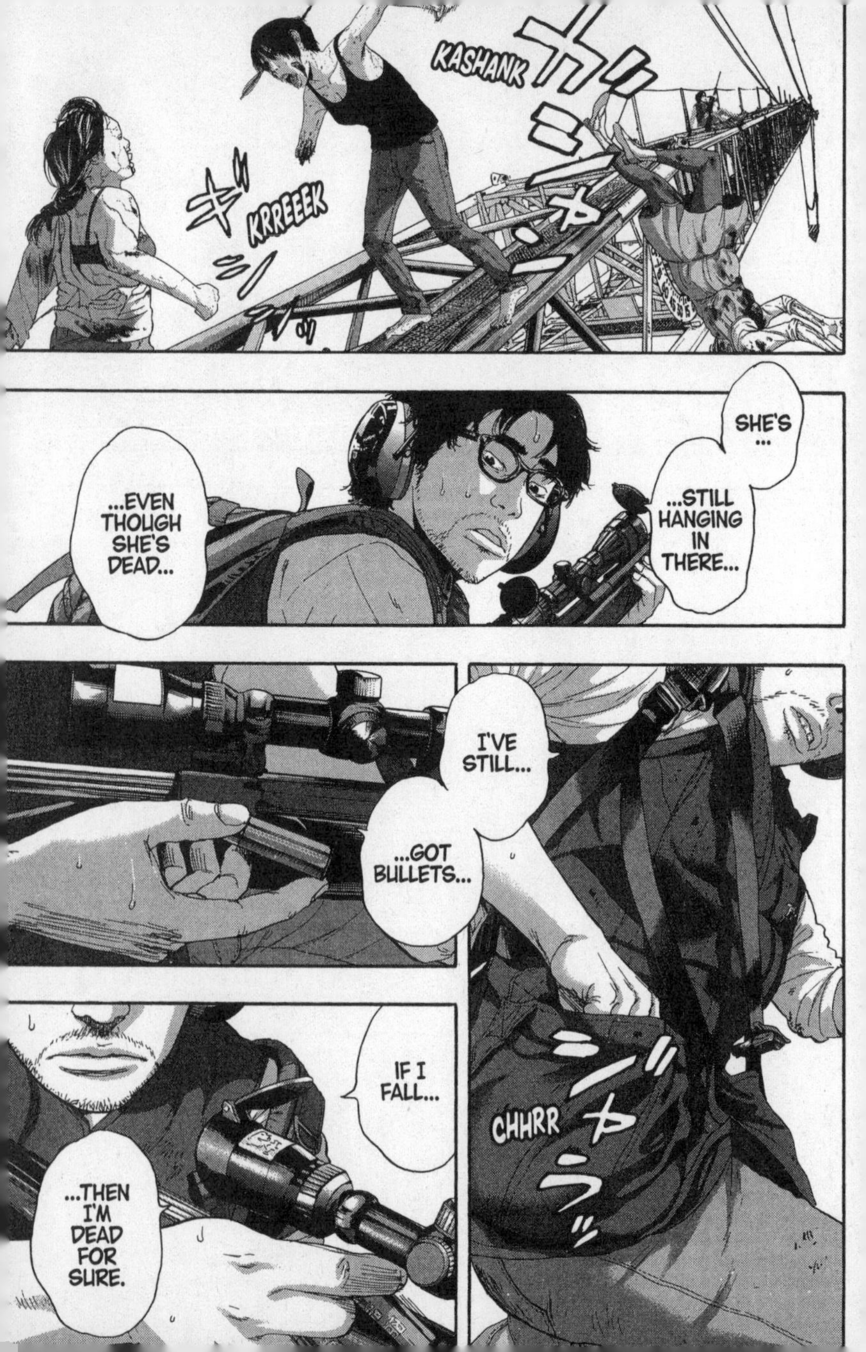
KASHANK
KRREEEK
SHE'S ...
...STILL HANGING IN THERE...
...EVEN THOUGH SHE'S DEAD...
I'VE STILL...
...GOT BULLETS...
CHHRR
IF I FALL...
...THEN I'M DEAD FOR SURE.

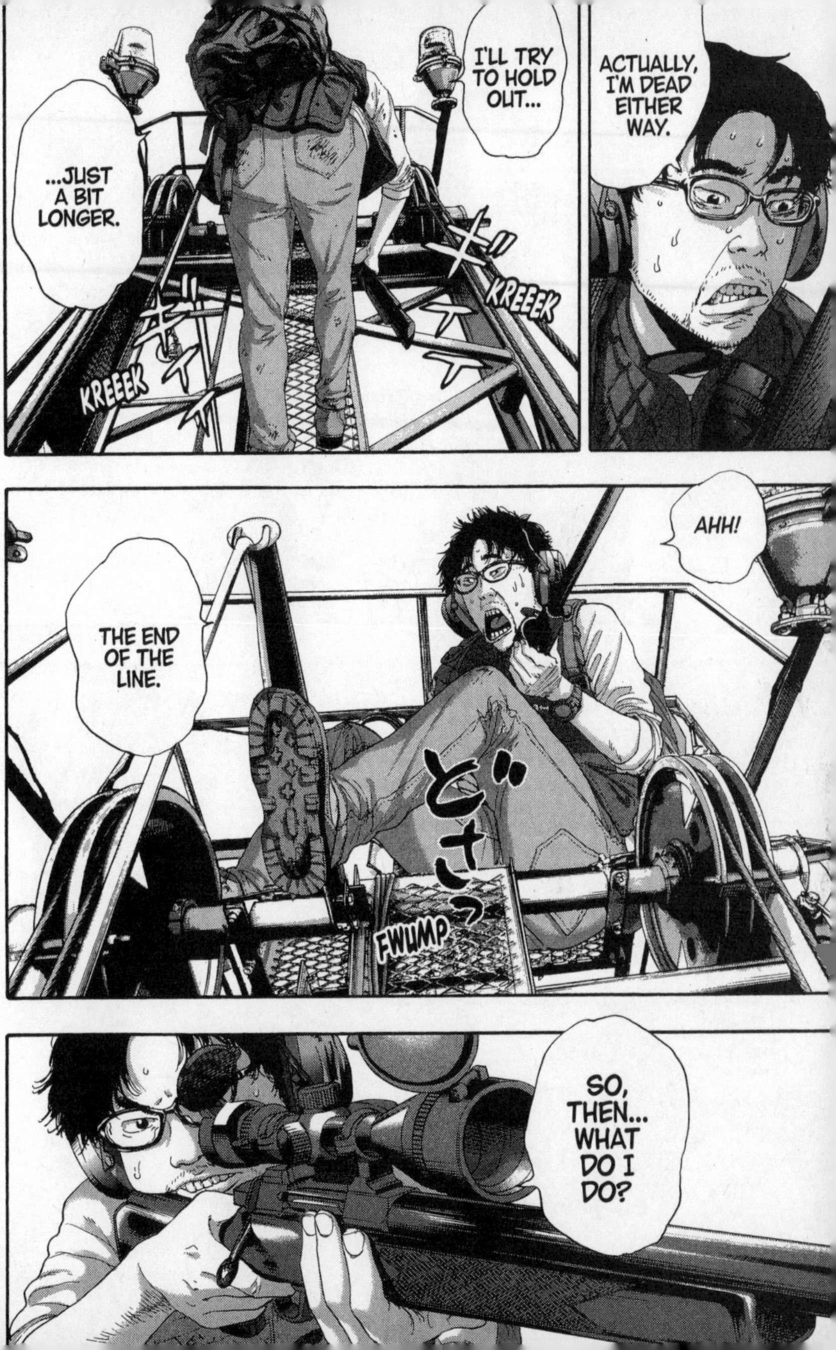
ACTUALLY, I'M DEAD EITHER WAY.
I'LL TRY TO HOLD OUT...
...JUST A BIT LONGER.
KREEEK
KREEEK
AHH!
THE END OF THE LINE.
どさっ
FWUMP
SO, THEN... WHAT DO I DO?

WHERE'D HE GO?

WHAT THE?

HE'S GONE.

I'LL JUST ADJUST...

KLIK

KLIK

KLIK

...THE MAGNIFICA-TION...

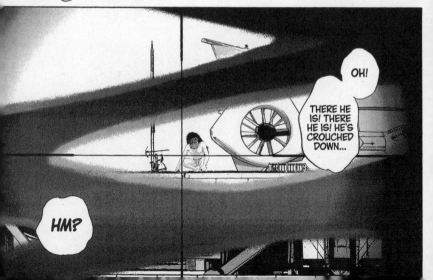

OH!

THERE HE IS! THERE HE IS! HE'S CROUCHED DOWN...

HM?

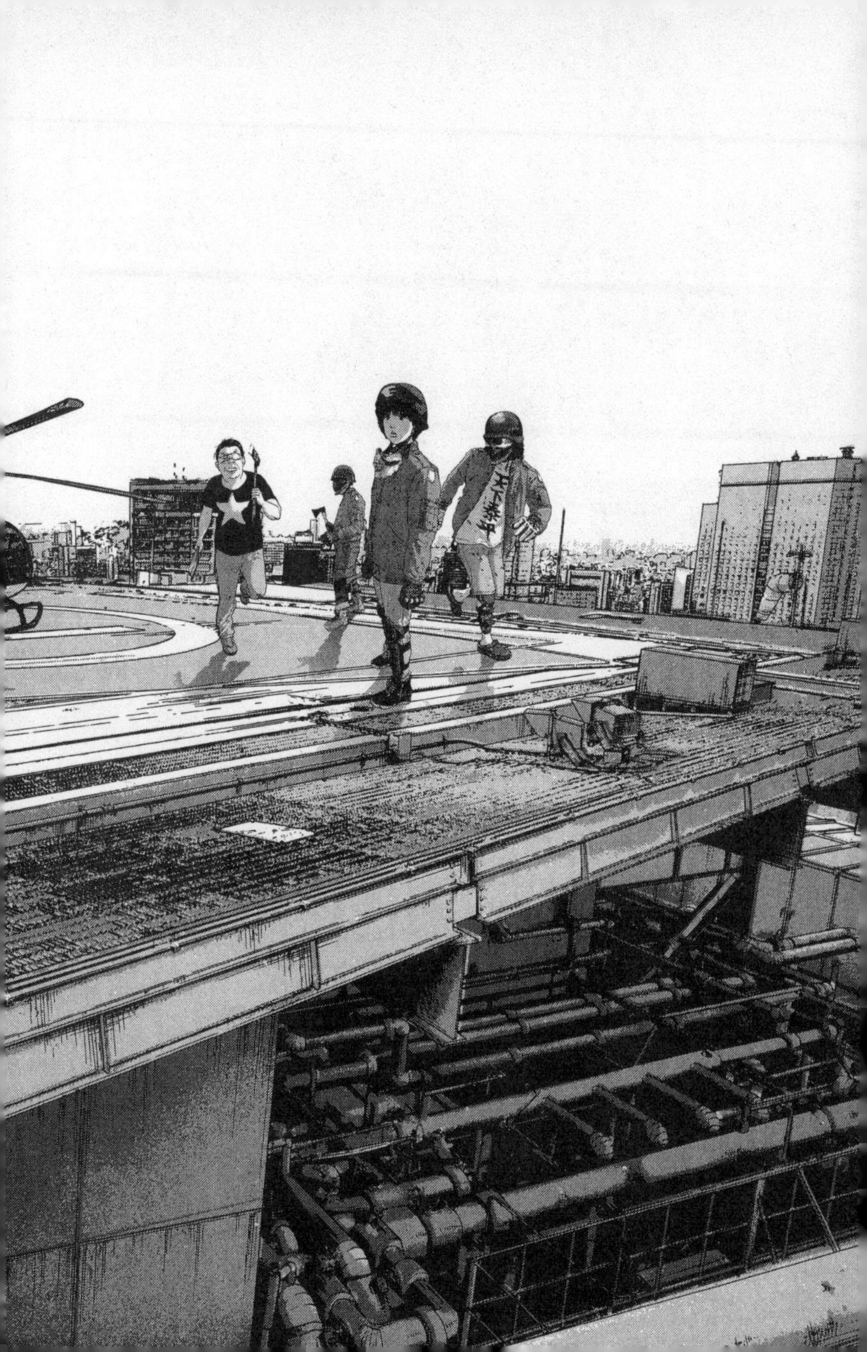
天下泰平

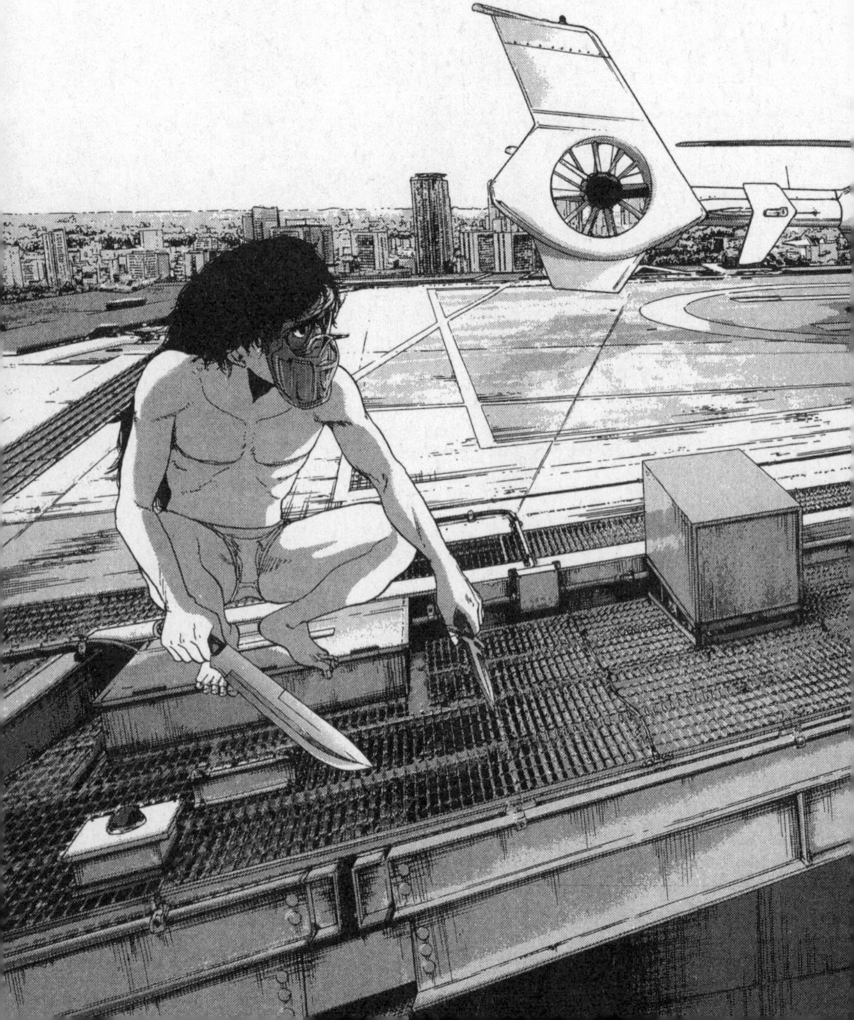

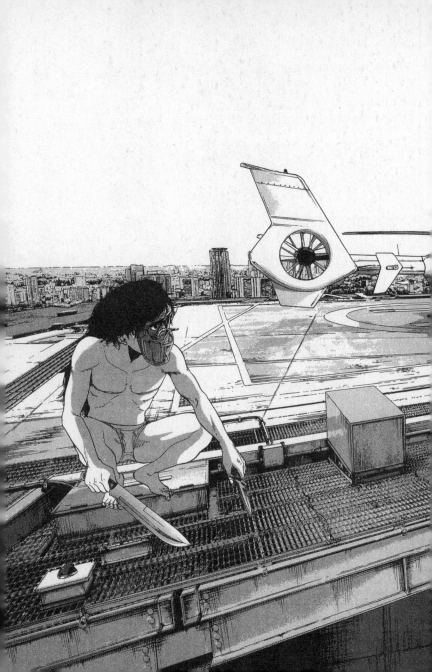

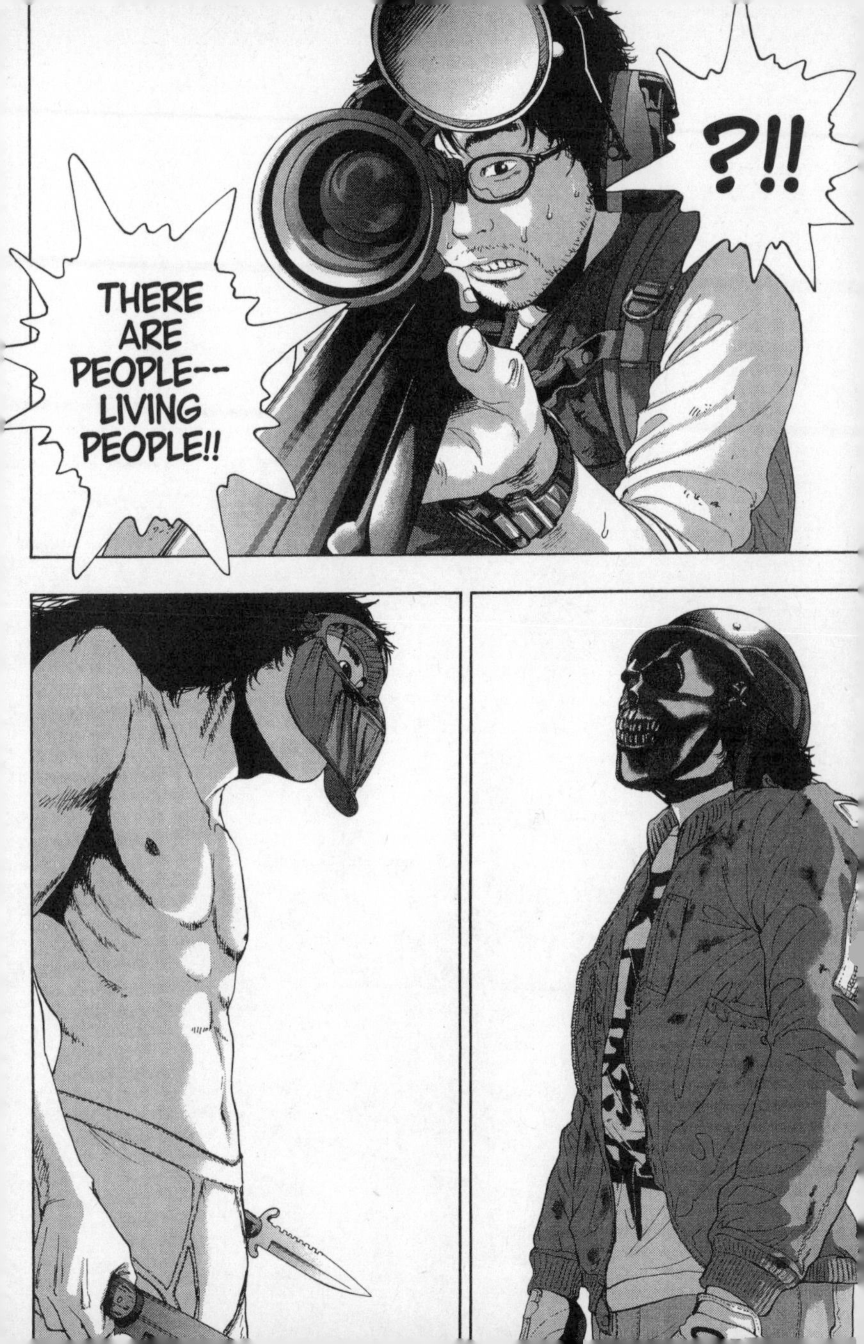
?!!
THERE ARE PEOPLE-- LIVING PEOPLE!!

CHAPTER 251

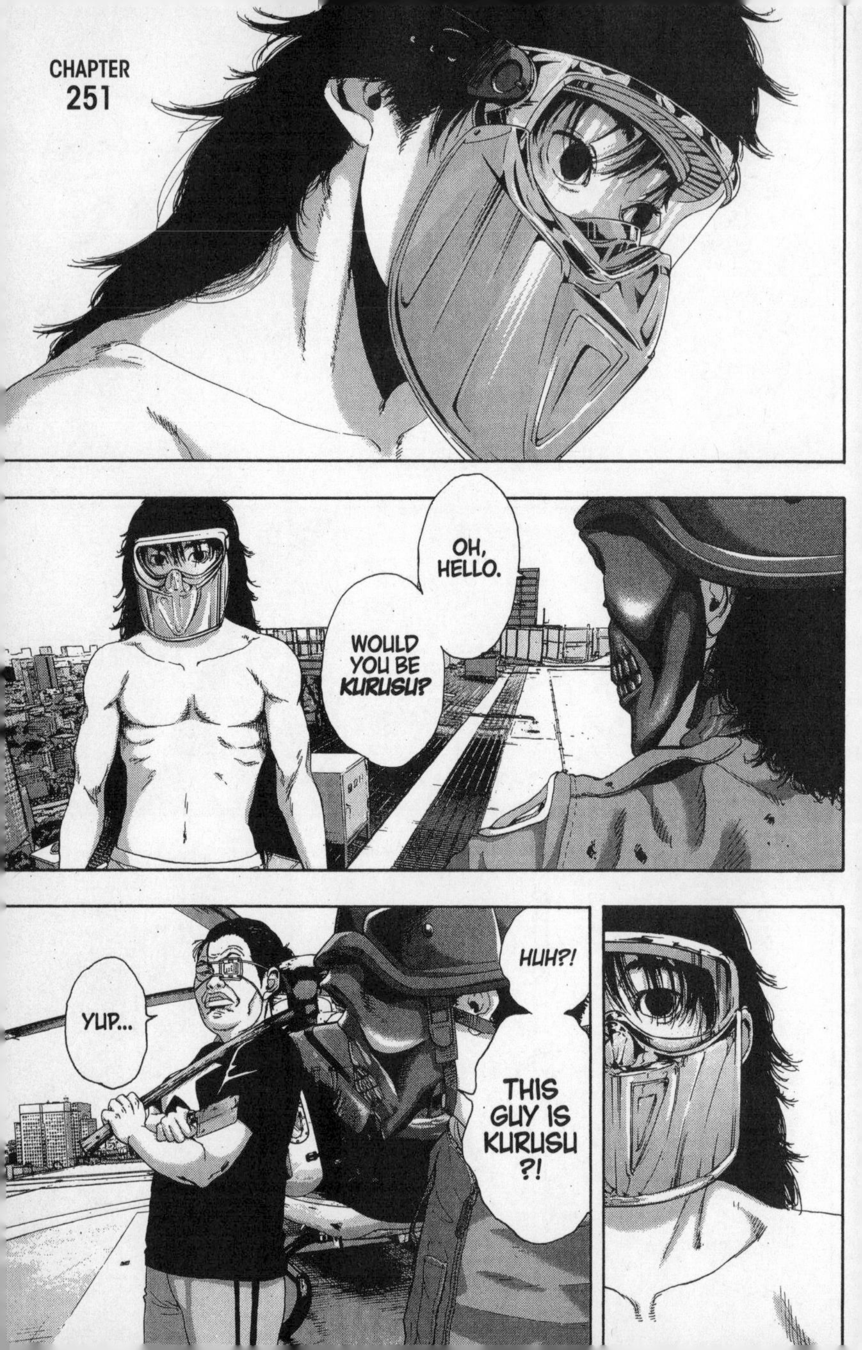
OH, HELLO.
WOULD YOU BE KURUSU?
YUP...
HUH?!
THIS GUY IS KURUSU?!

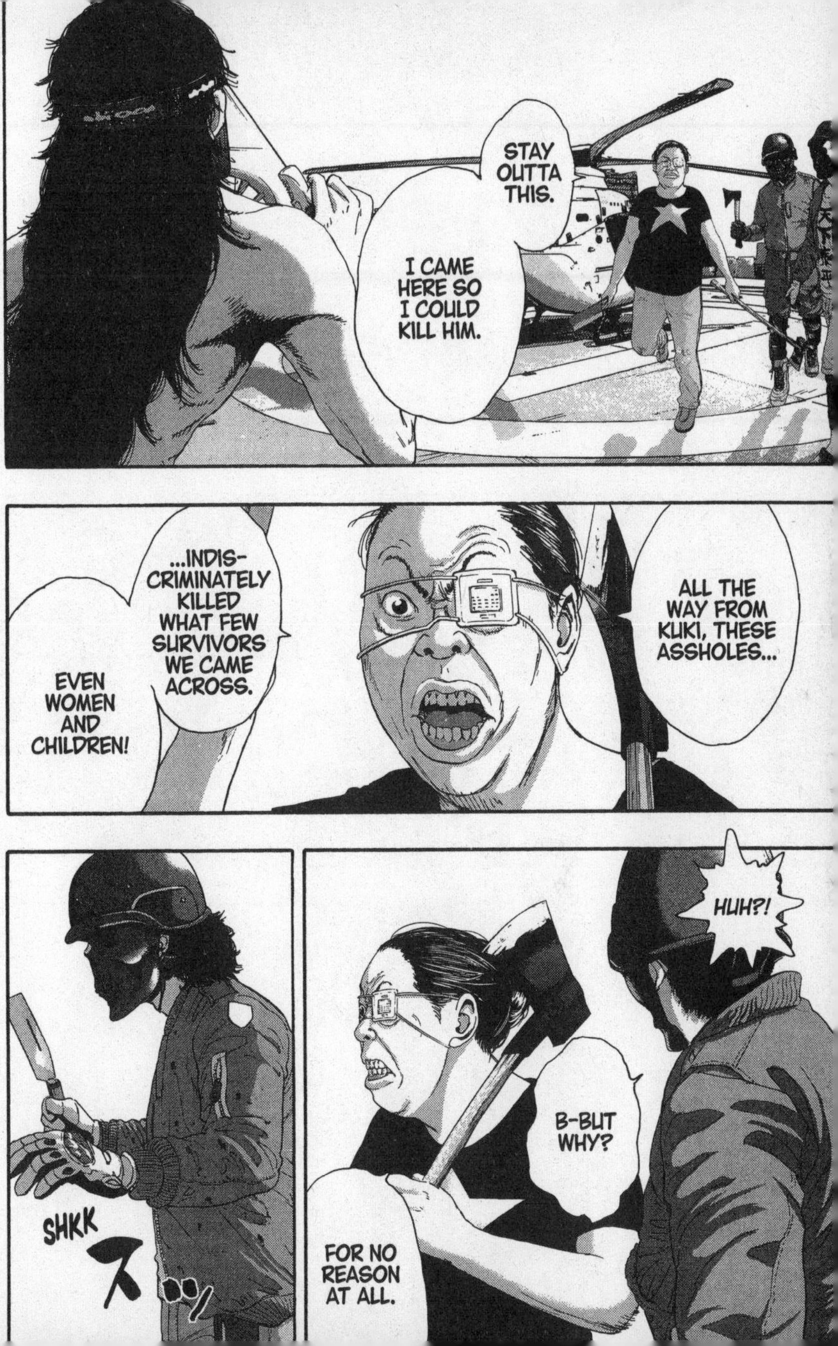
STAY OUTTA THIS.
I CAME HERE SO I COULD KILL HIM.
ALL THE WAY FROM KUKI, THESE ASSHOLES...
...INDIS-CRIMINATELY KILLED WHAT FEW SURVIVORS WE CAME ACROSS.
EVEN WOMEN AND CHILDREN!
HUH?!
B-BUT WHY?
FOR NO REASON AT ALL.
SHKK

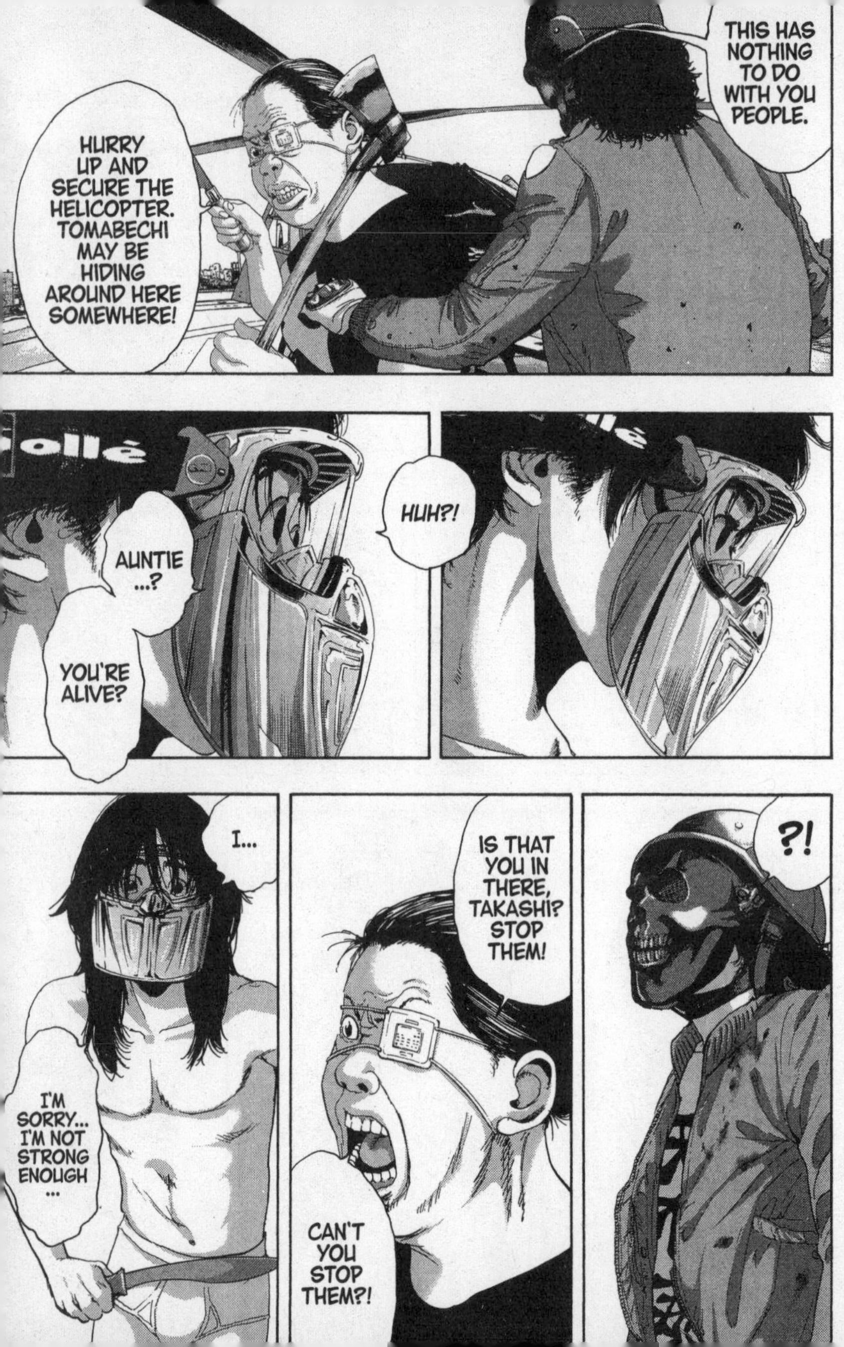
THIS HAS NOTHING TO DO WITH YOU PEOPLE.
HURRY UP AND SECURE THE HELICOPTER. TOMABECHI MAY BE HIDING AROUND HERE SOMEWHERE!
HUH?!
AUNTIE ...?
YOU'RE ALIVE?
?!
IS THAT YOU IN THERE, TAKASHI? STOP THEM!
CAN'T YOU STOP THEM?!
I...
I'M SORRY... I'M NOT STRONG ENOUGH ...

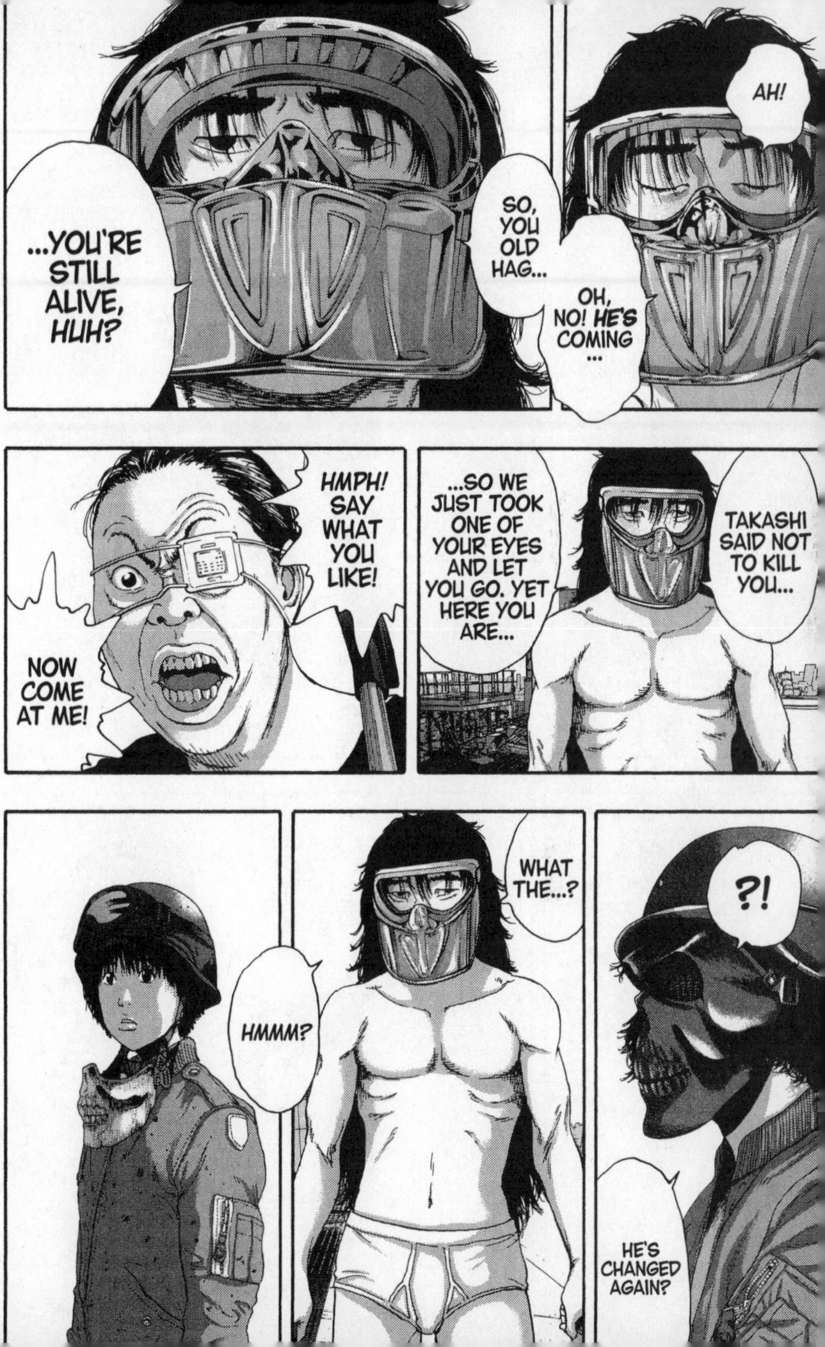
AH!
SO, YOU OLD HAG...
OH, NO! HE'S COMING...
...YOU'RE STILL ALIVE, HUH?
TAKASHI SAID NOT TO KILL YOU...
...SO WE JUST TOOK ONE OF YOUR EYES AND LET YOU GO. YET HERE YOU ARE...
HMPH! SAY WHAT YOU LIKE!
NOW COME AT ME!
?!
HE'S CHANGED AGAIN?
WHAT THE...?
HMMM?

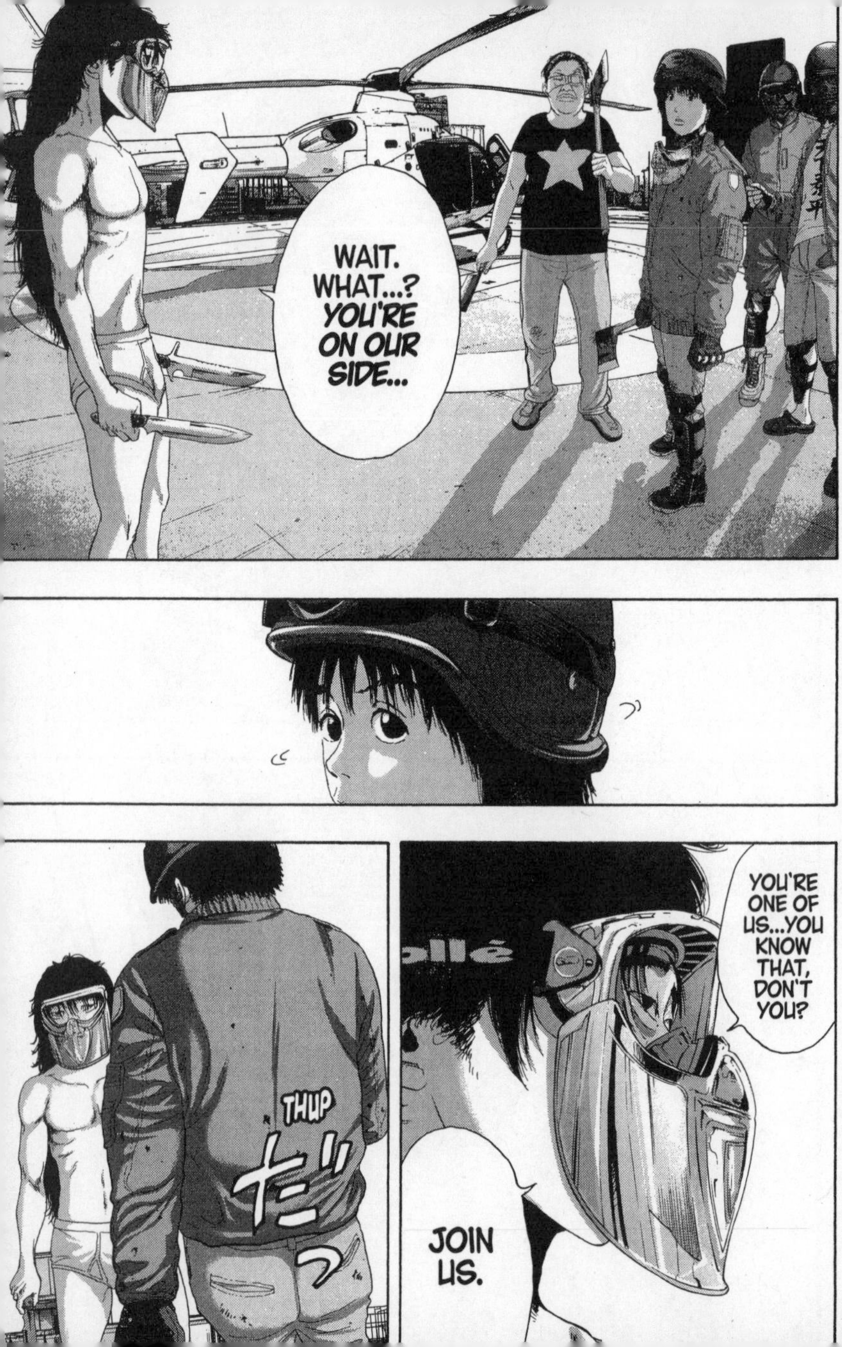
WAIT. WHAT...? YOU'RE ON OUR SIDE...
YOU'RE ONE OF US...YOU KNOW THAT, DON'T YOU?
JOIN US.
THUP

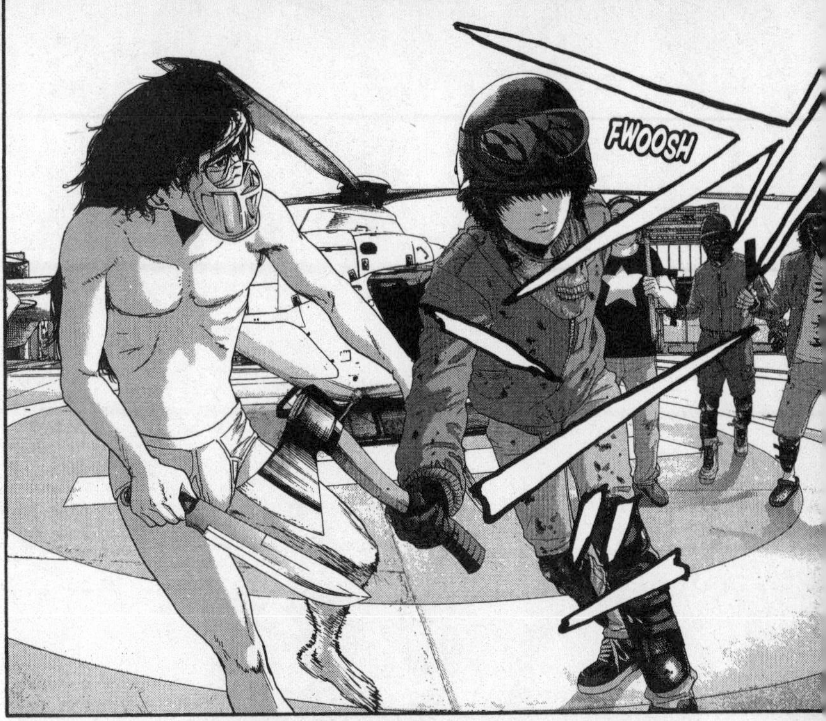
FWOOSH

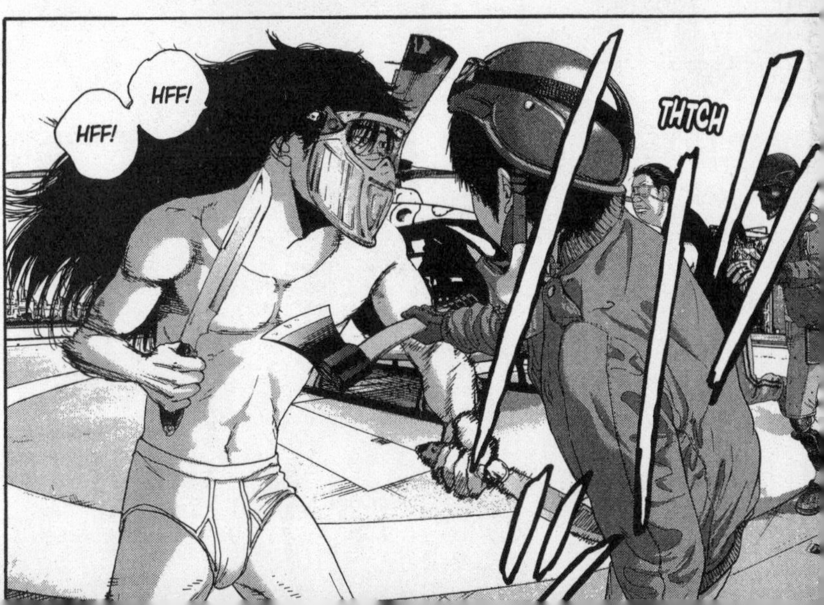
THTCH
HFF!
HFF!

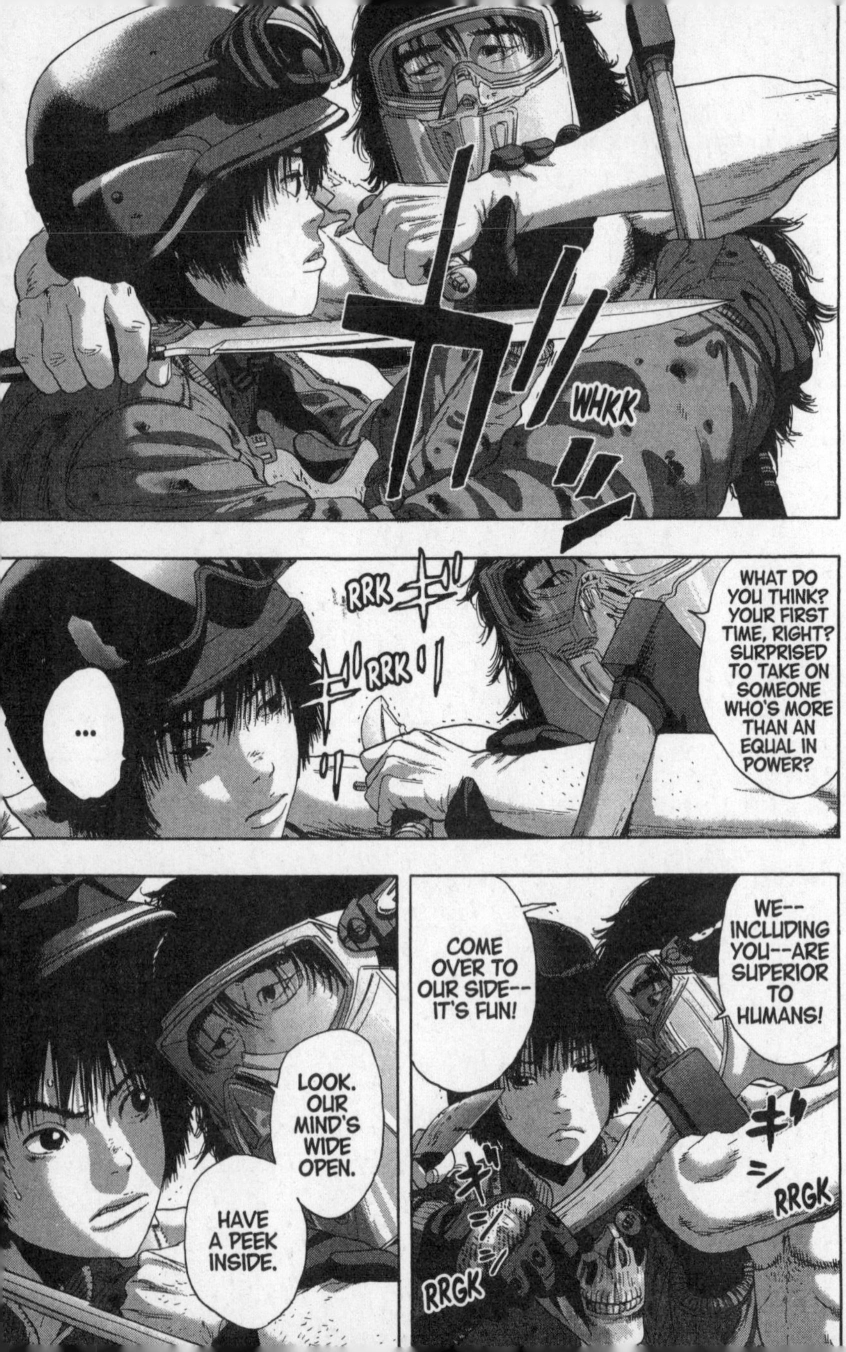
WHKK
WHAT DO YOU THINK? YOUR FIRST TIME, RIGHT? SURPRISED TO TAKE ON SOMEONE WHO'S MORE THAN AN EQUAL IN POWER?
RRK
RRK
...
WE-- INCLUDING YOU--ARE SUPERIOR TO HUMANS!
COME OVER TO OUR SIDE-- IT'S FUN!
RRGK
RRGK
LOOK. OUR MIND'S WIDE OPEN.
HAVE A PEEK INSIDE.

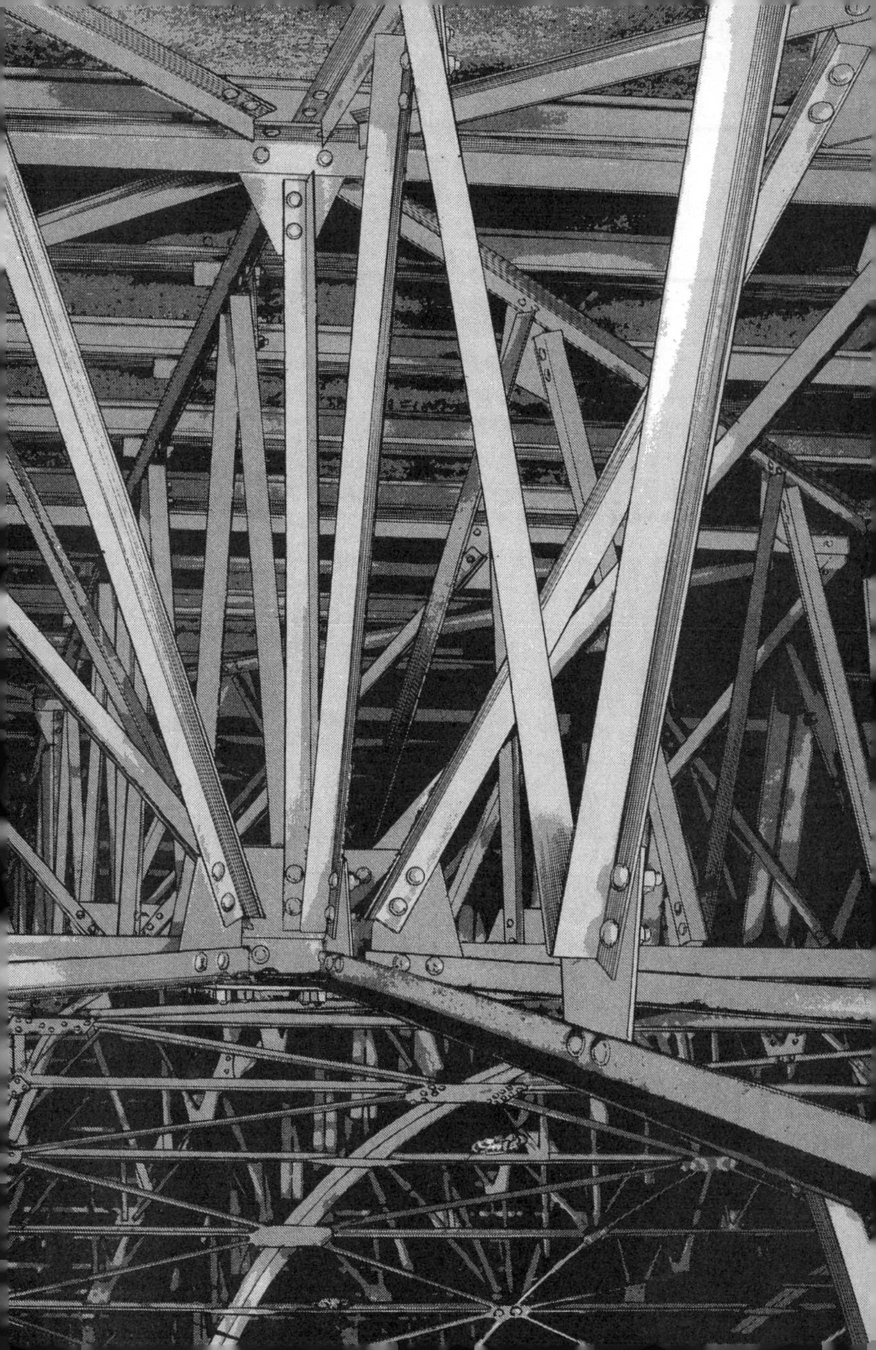

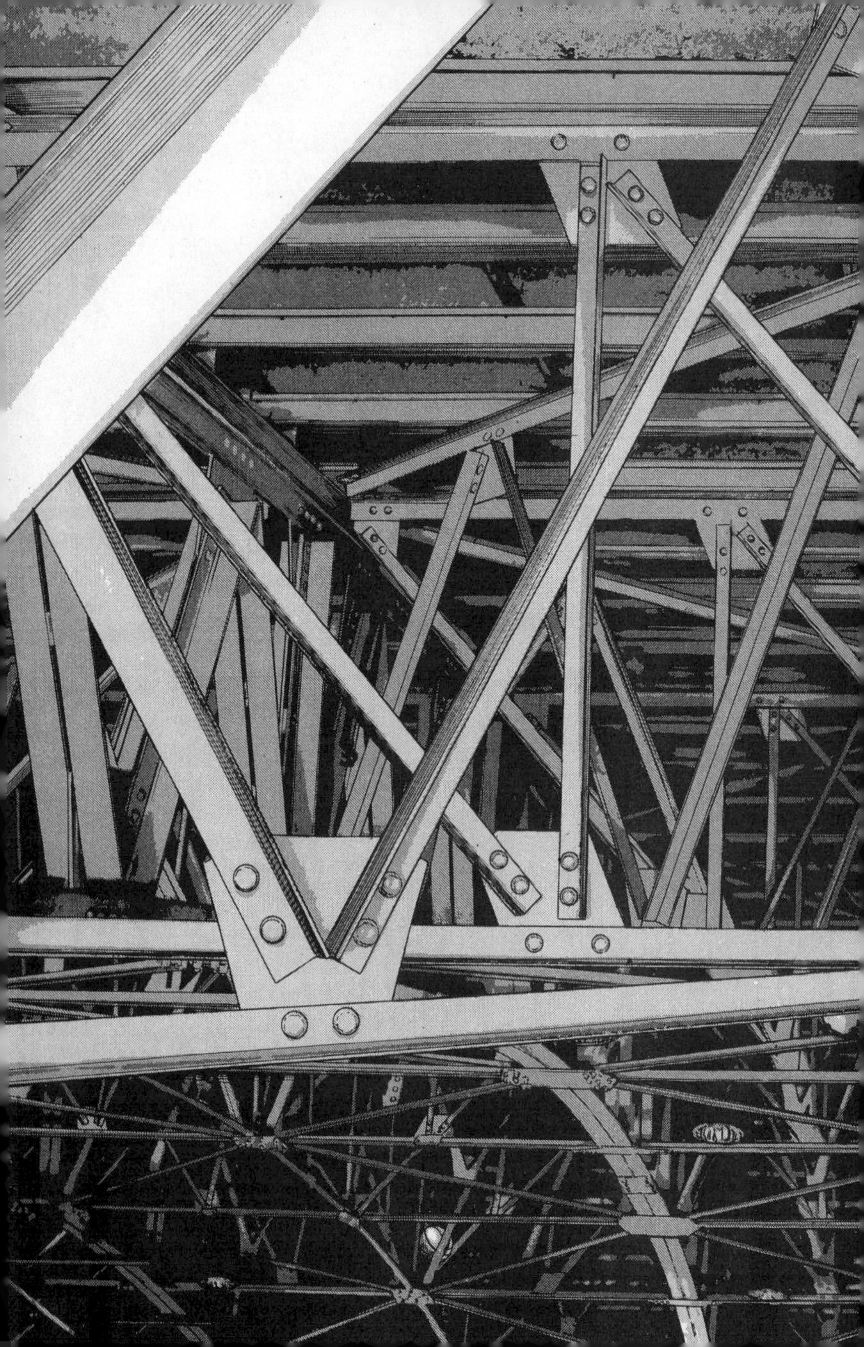

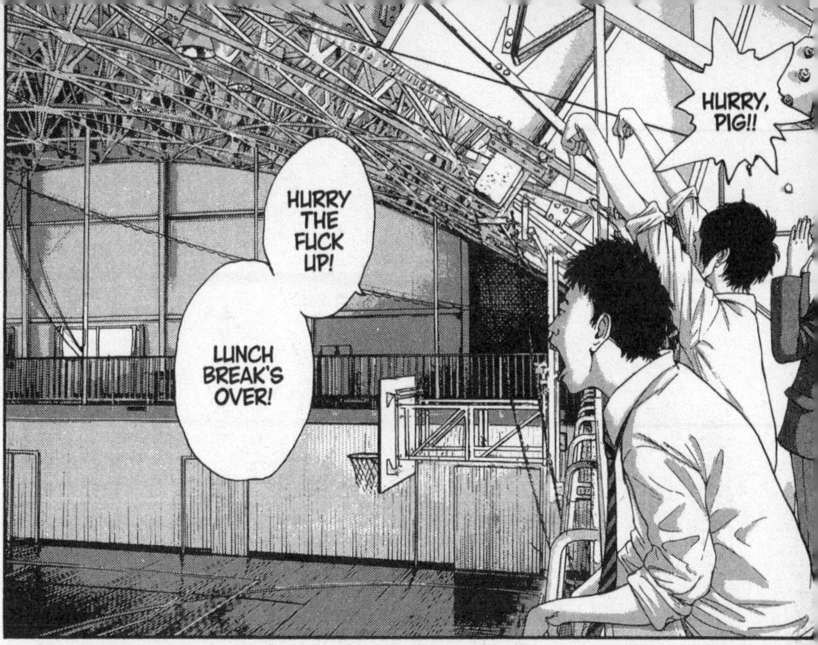
HURRY, PIG!!
HURRY THE FUCK UP!
LUNCH BREAK'S OVER!

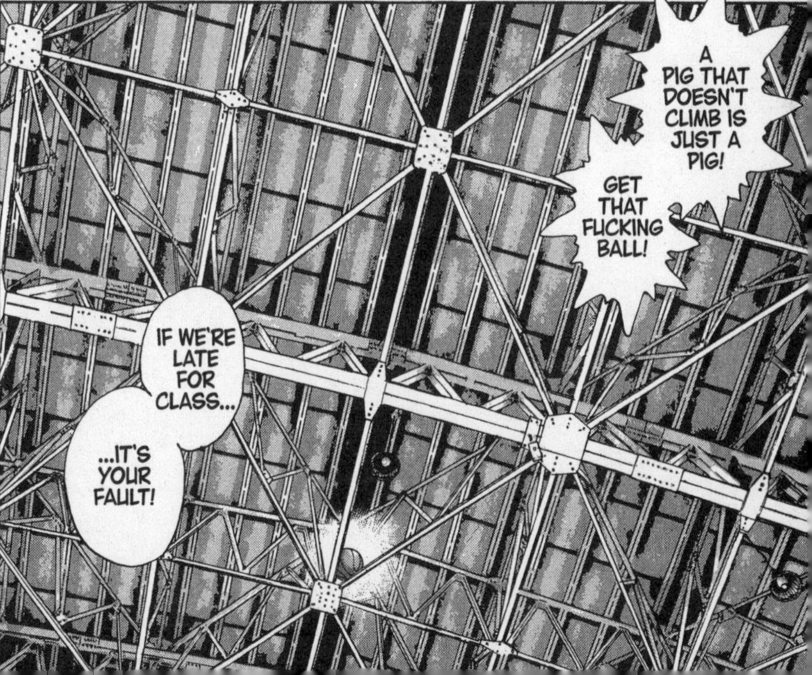
A PIG THAT DOESN'T CLIMB IS JUST A PIG!
GET THAT FUCKING BALL!
IF WE'RE LATE FOR CLASS...
...IT'S YOUR FAULT!

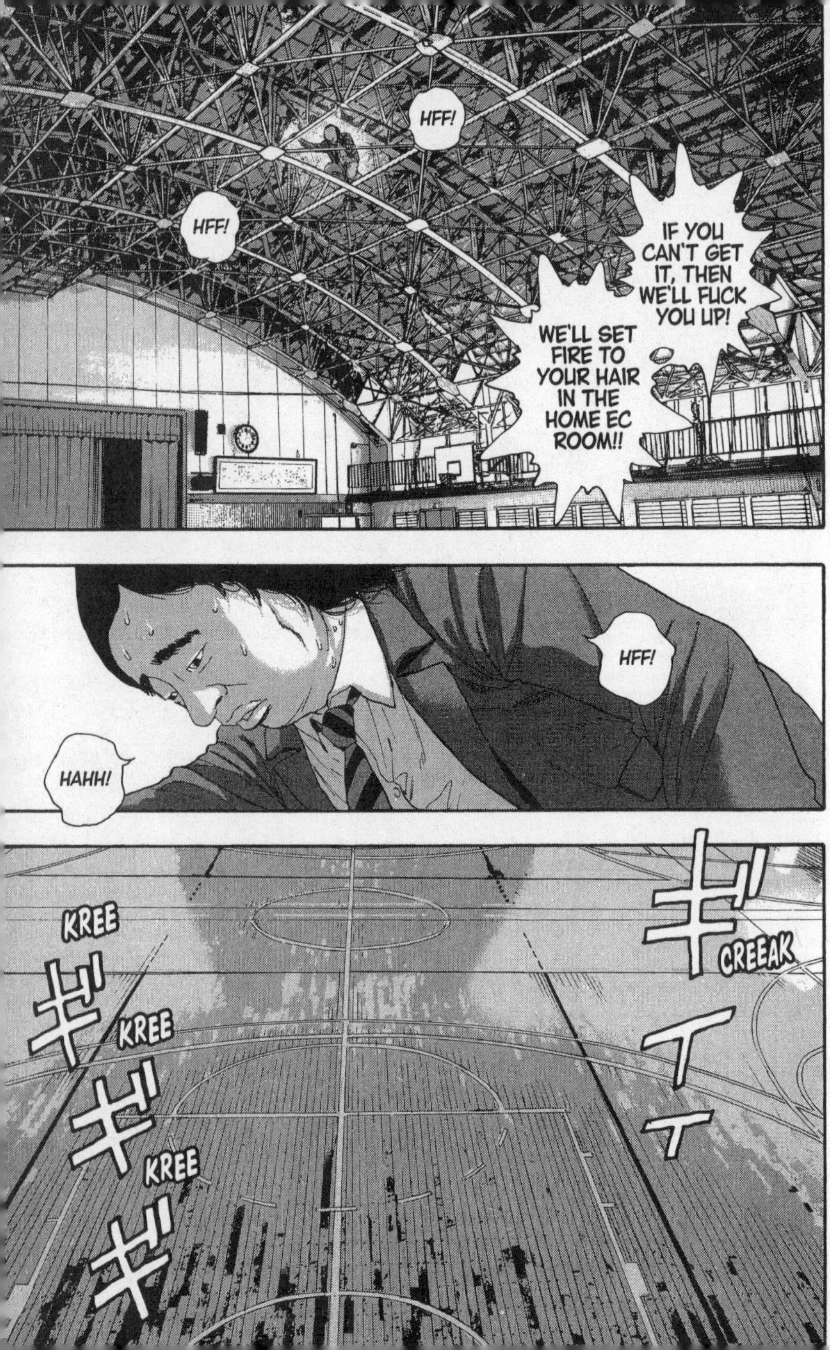
IF YOU CAN'T GET IT, THEN WE'LL FUCK YOU UP!
WE'LL SET FIRE TO YOUR HAIR IN THE HOME EC ROOM!!
HFF!
HFF!
HFF!
HAHH!
CREEAK
KREE
KREE
KREE

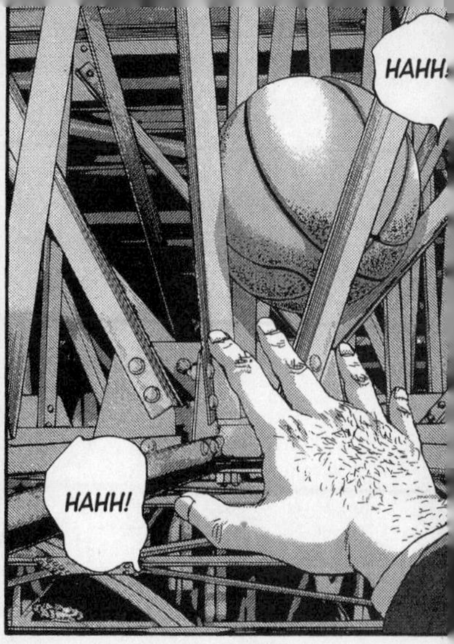
HAHH
HAHH!
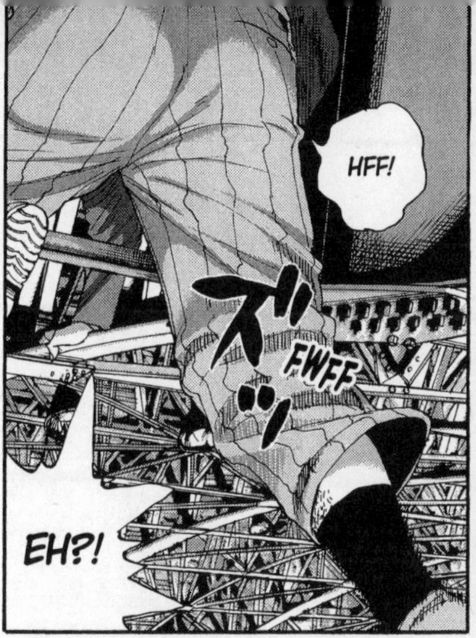
HFF!
FWFF
EH?!
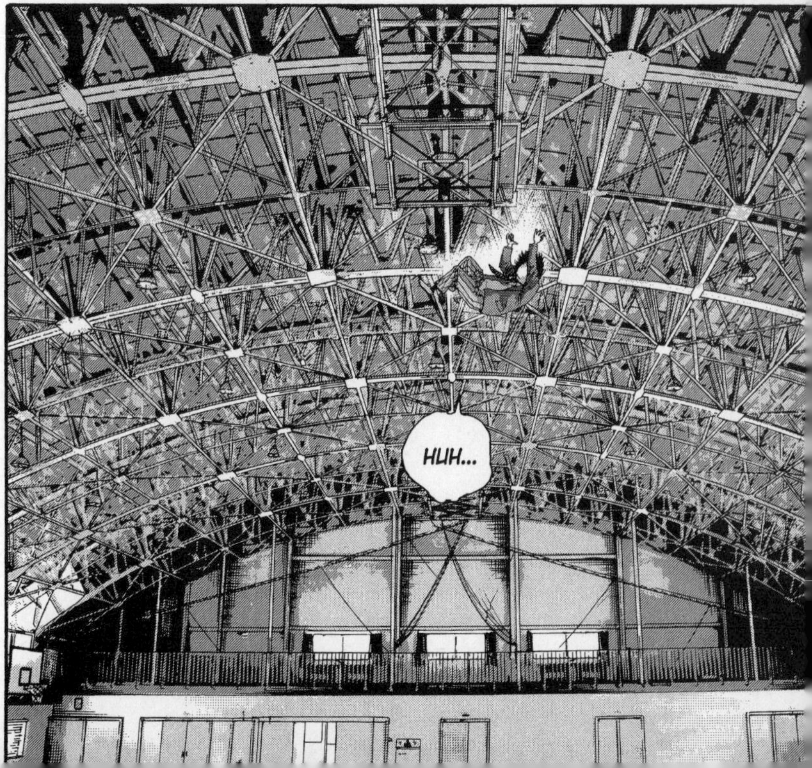
HUH...

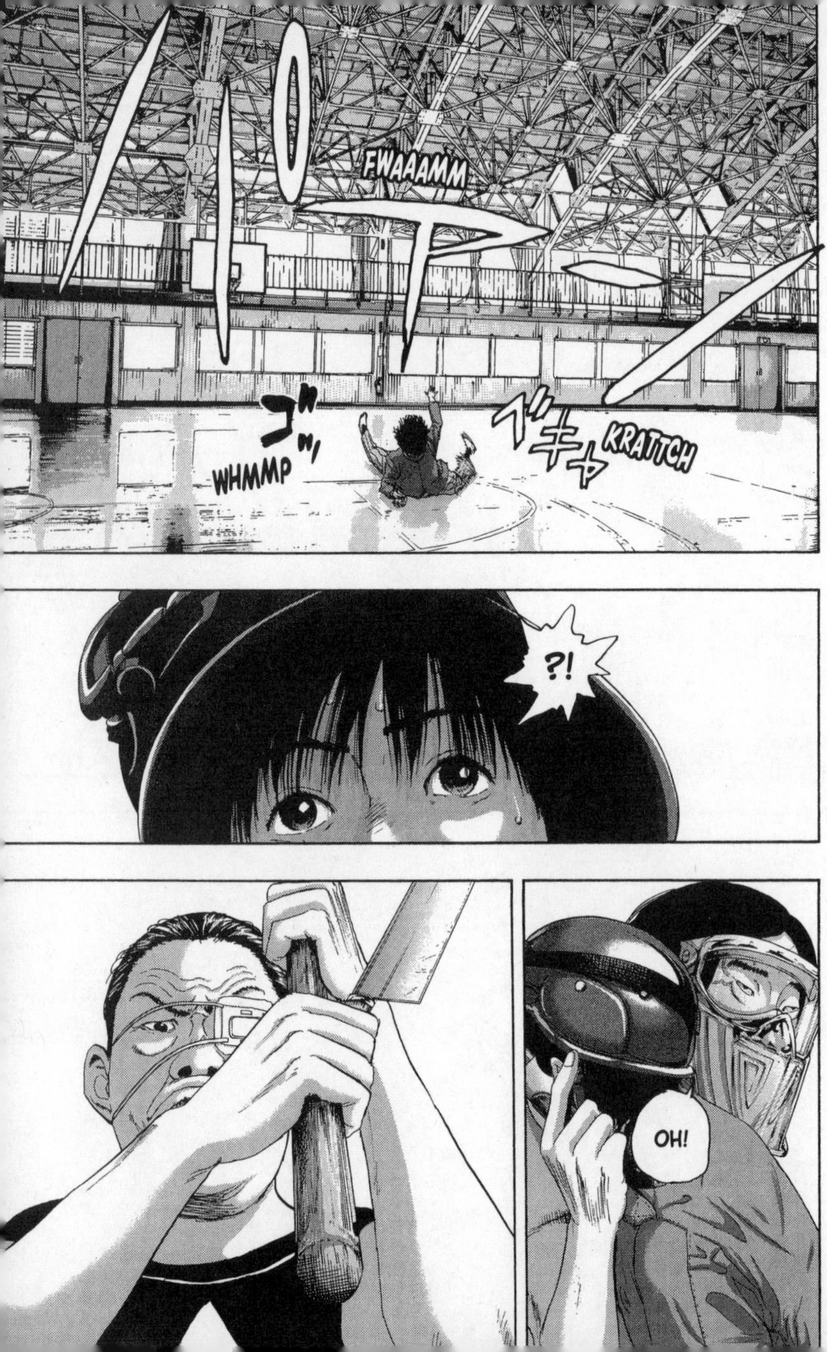
FWAAAMM
KRATTCH
WHMMP
?!
OH!

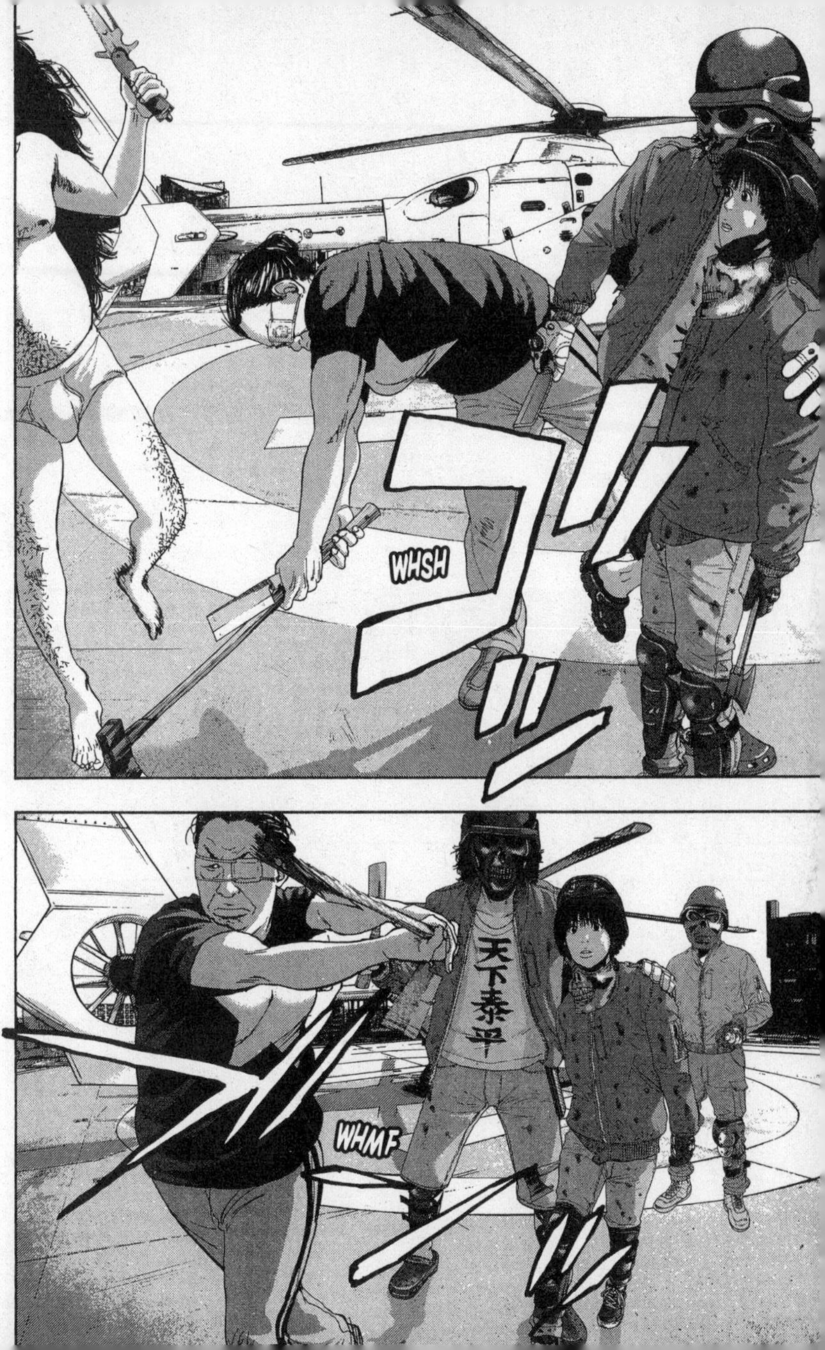
WHSH
天下泰平
WHMF

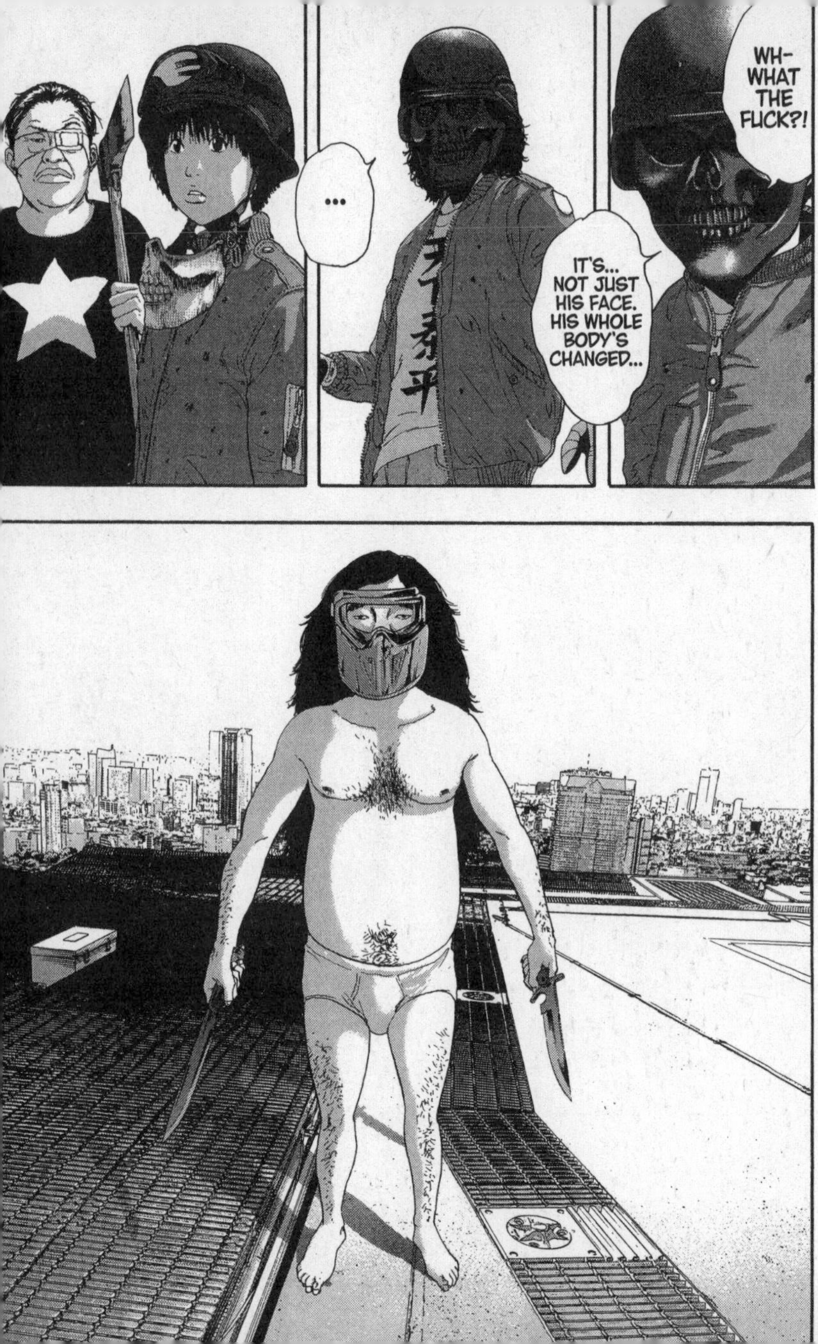
WH- WHAT THE FUCK?!
IT'S... NOT JUST HIS FACE. HIS WHOLE BODY'S CHANGED...
...

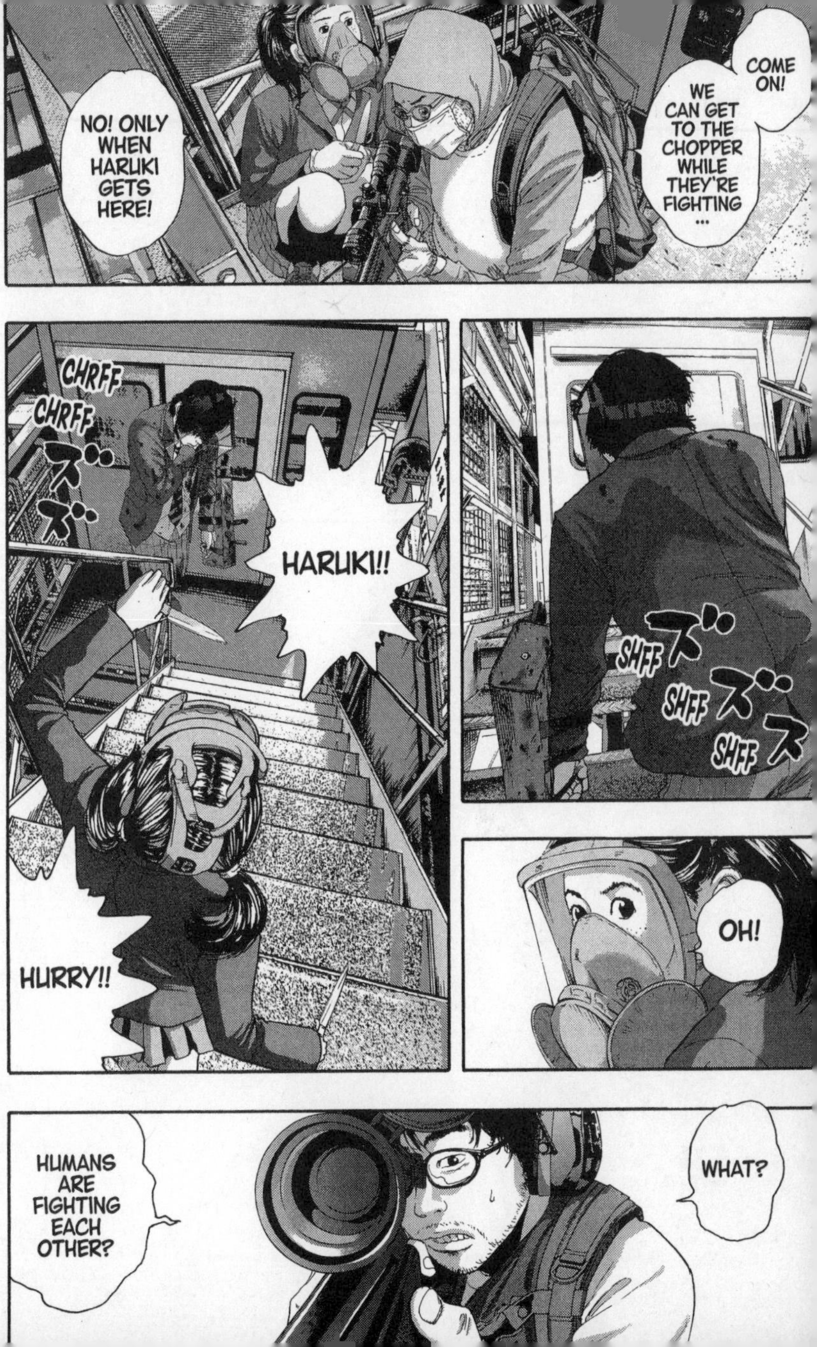
COME ON!
WE CAN GET TO THE CHOPPER WHILE THEY'RE FIGHTING ...
NO! ONLY WHEN HARUKI GETS HERE!
SHFF ズ
SHFF ズ
SHFF ス
OH!
CHRFF CHRFF ズズ
HARUKI!!
HURRY!!
WHAT?
HUMANS ARE FIGHTING EACH OTHER?

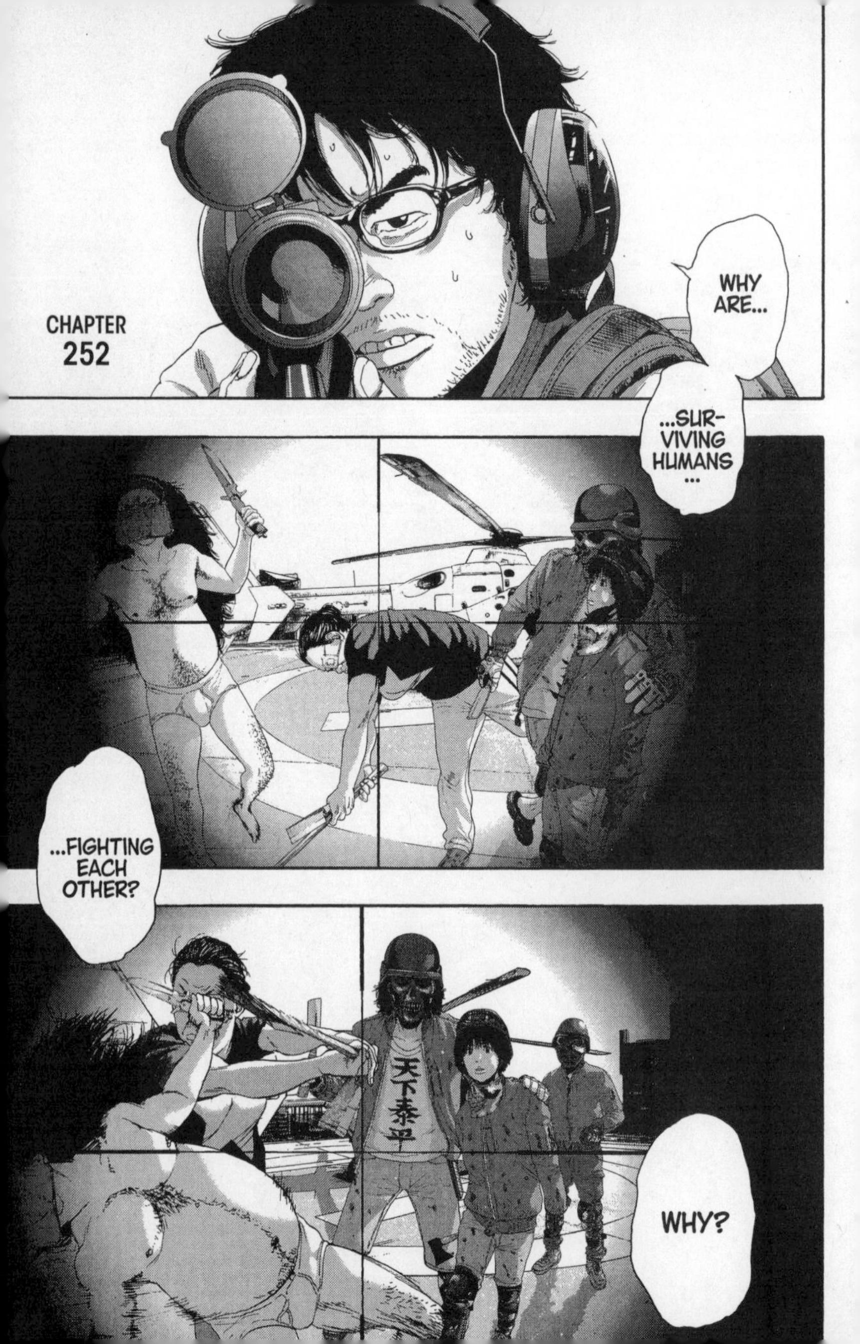
CHAPTER 252
WHY ARE...
...SUR-VIVING HUMANS...
...FIGHTING EACH OTHER?
天下泰平
WHY?

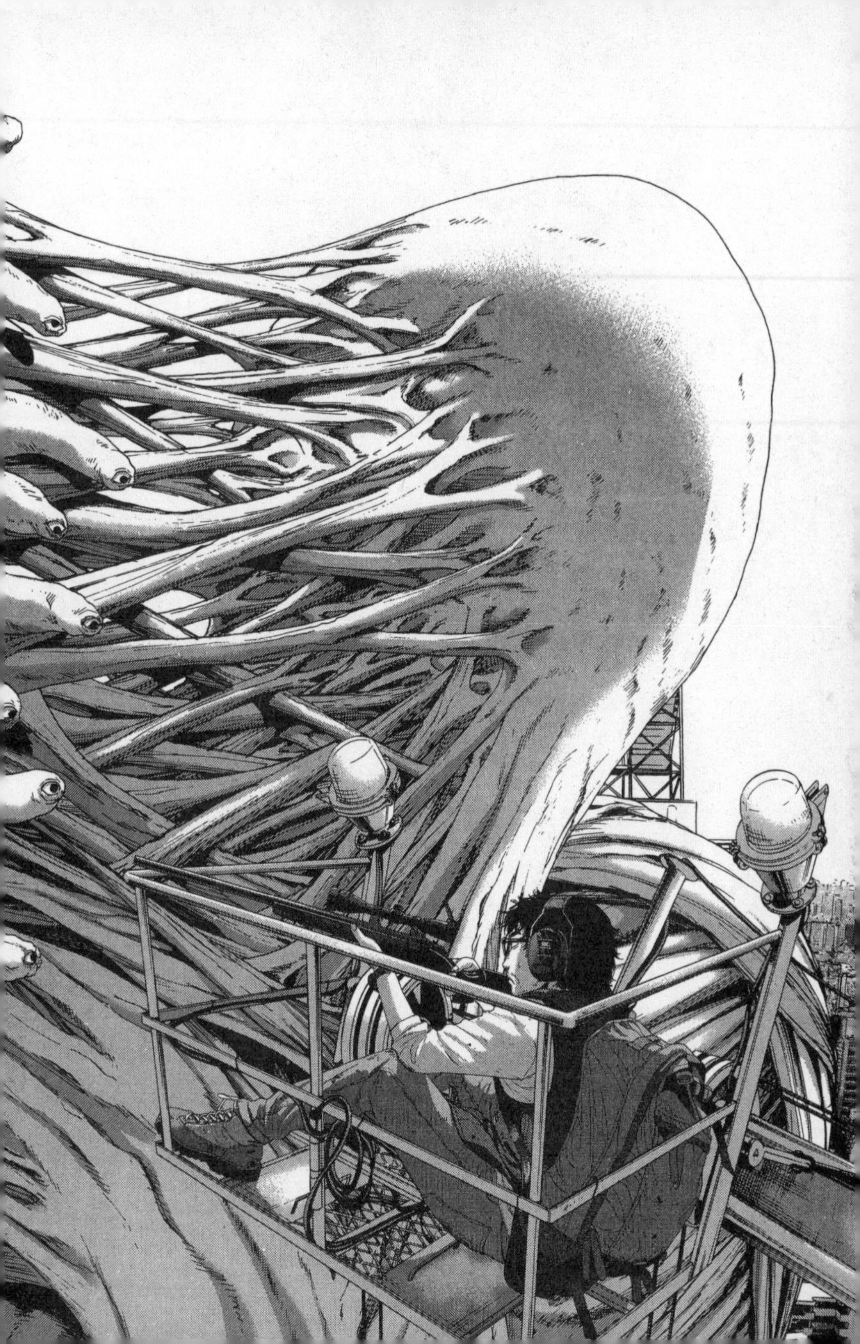

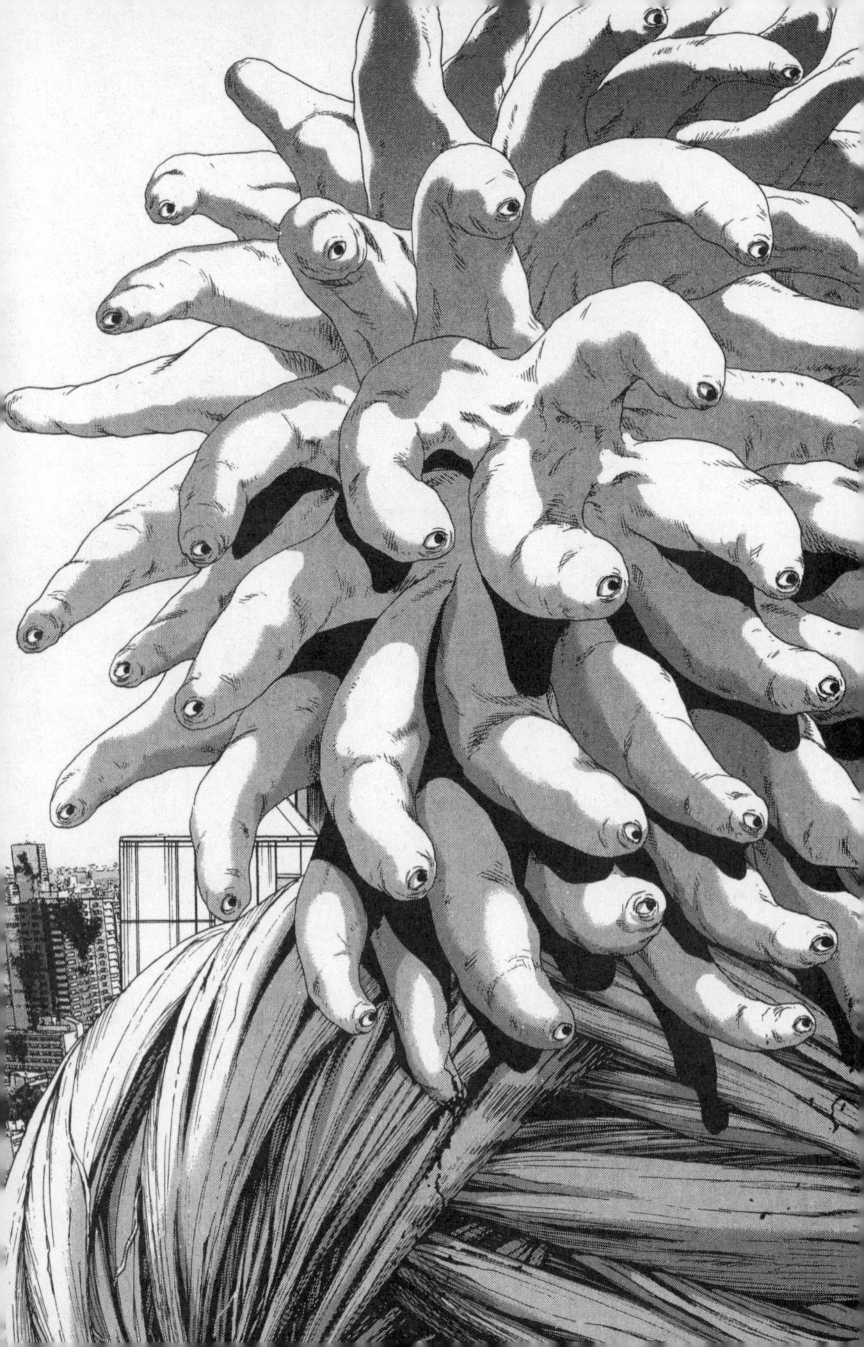

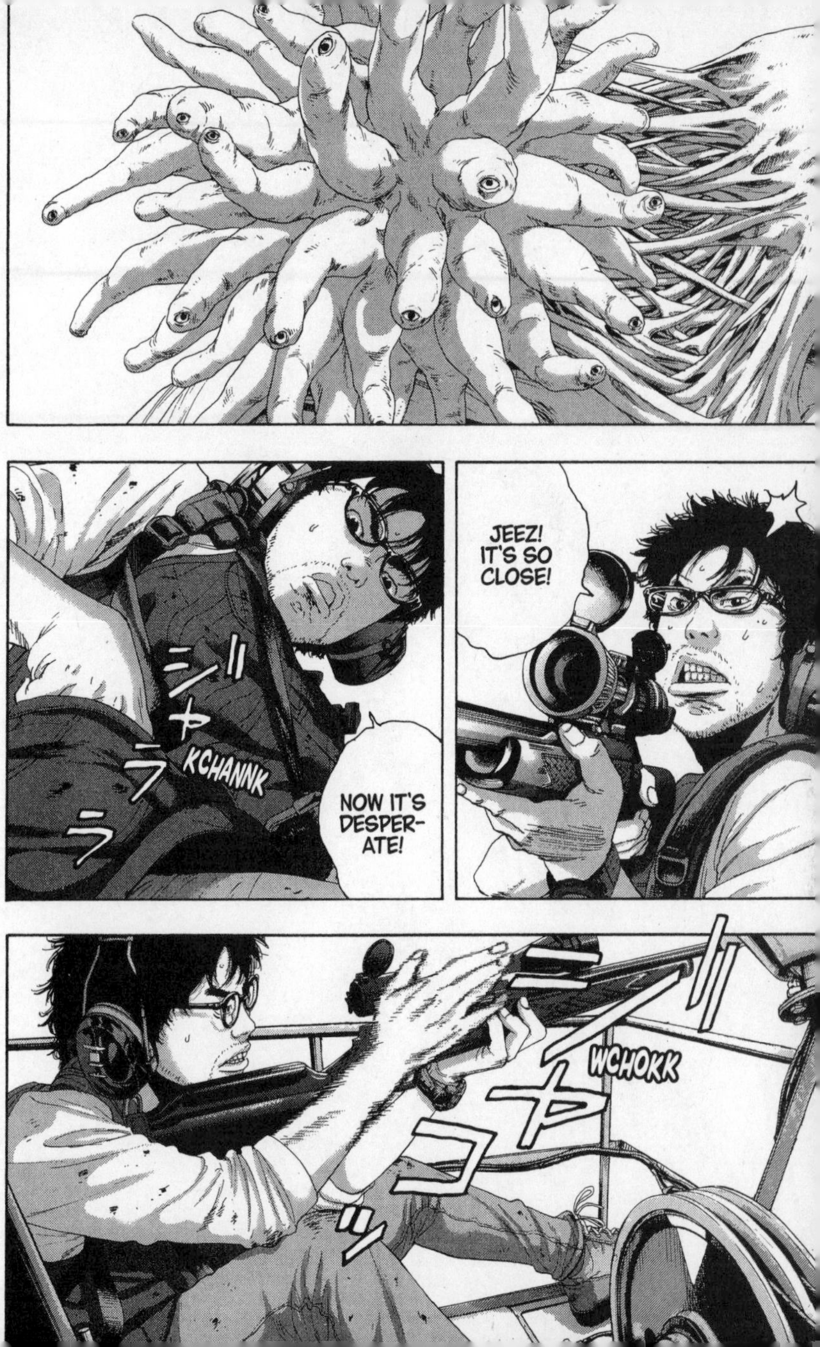
JEEZ! IT'S SO CLOSE!
KCHANNK
NOW IT'S DESPERATE!
WCHOKK

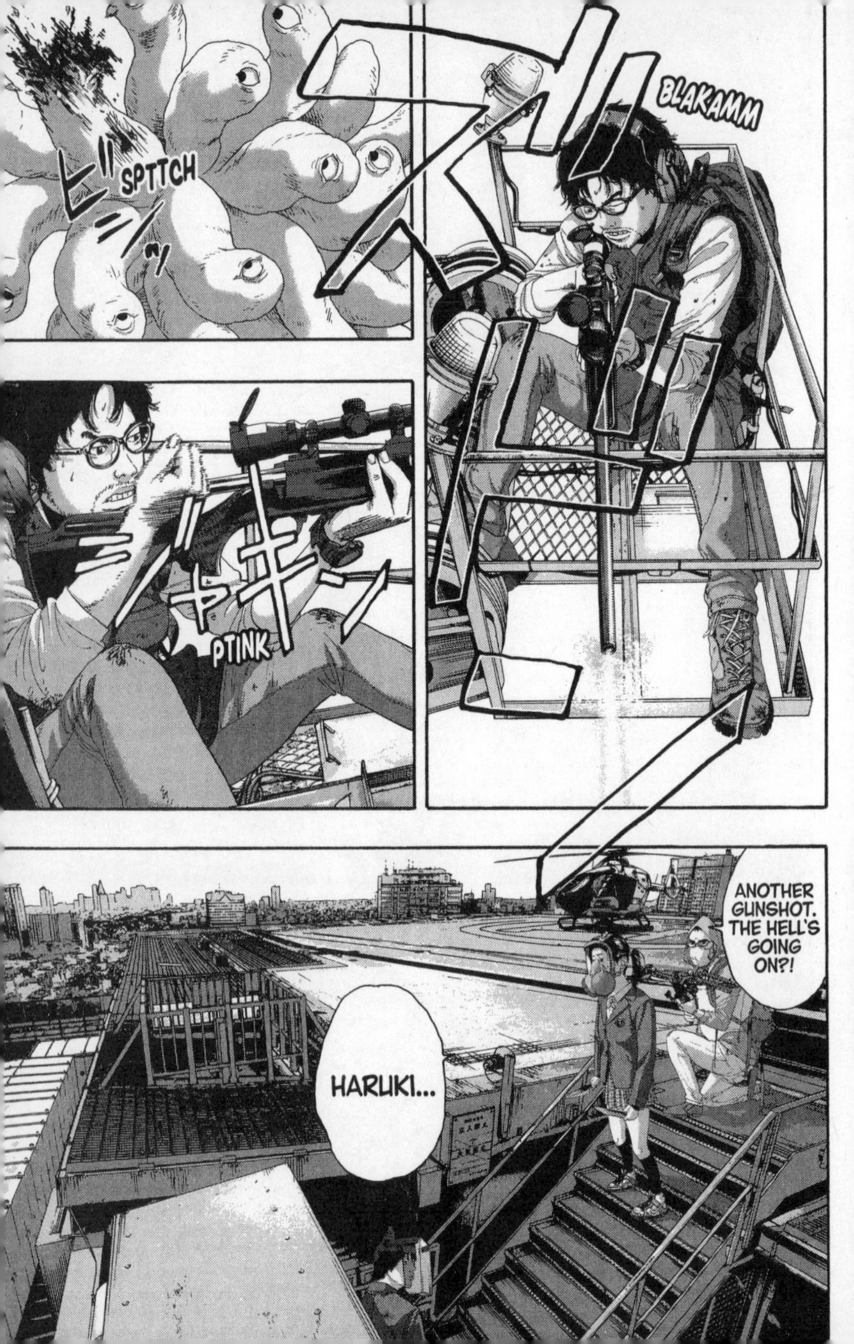
BLAKAMM
SPTTCH
PTINK
ANOTHER GUNSHOT. THE HELL'S GOING ON?!
HARUKI...

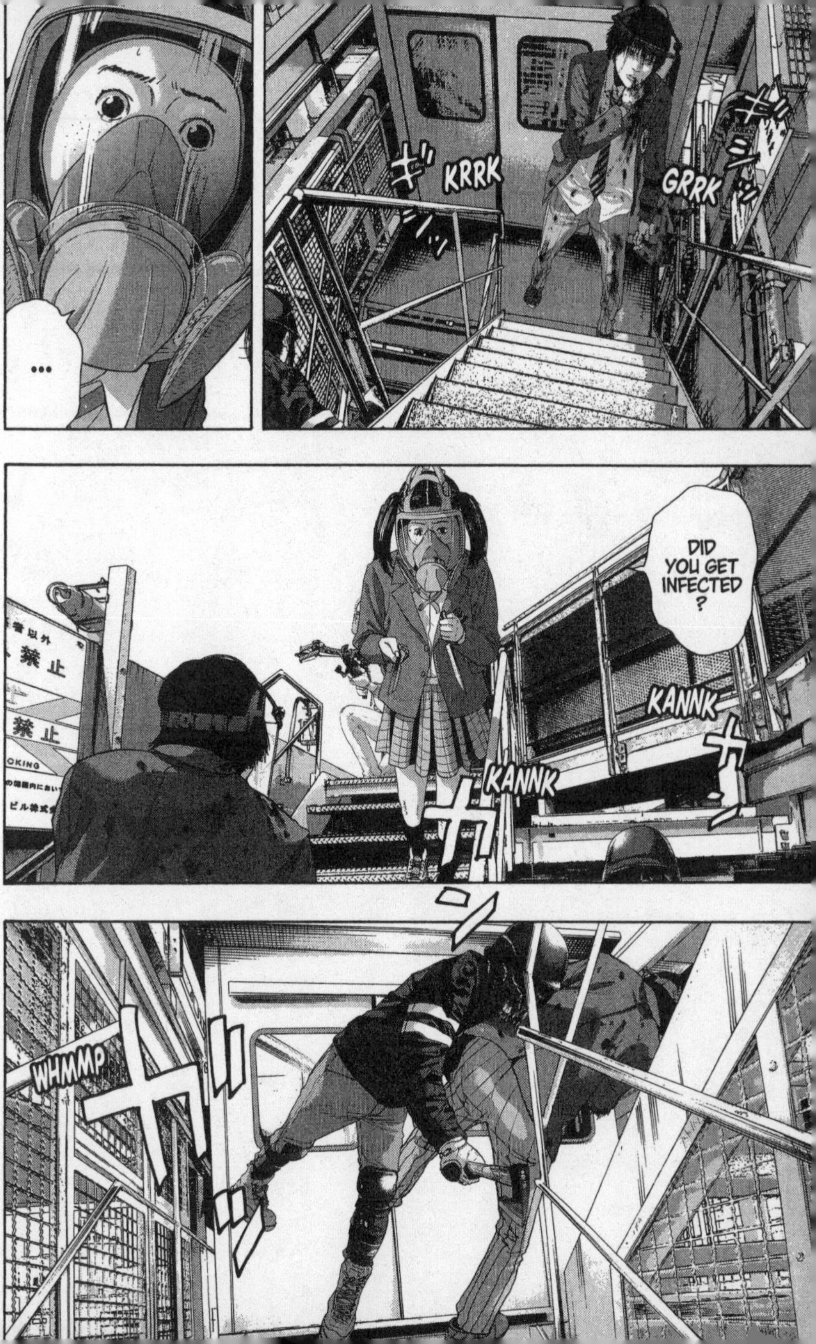
GRRK
KRRK
...
DID YOU GET INFECTED ?
KANNK
KANNK
WHMMP

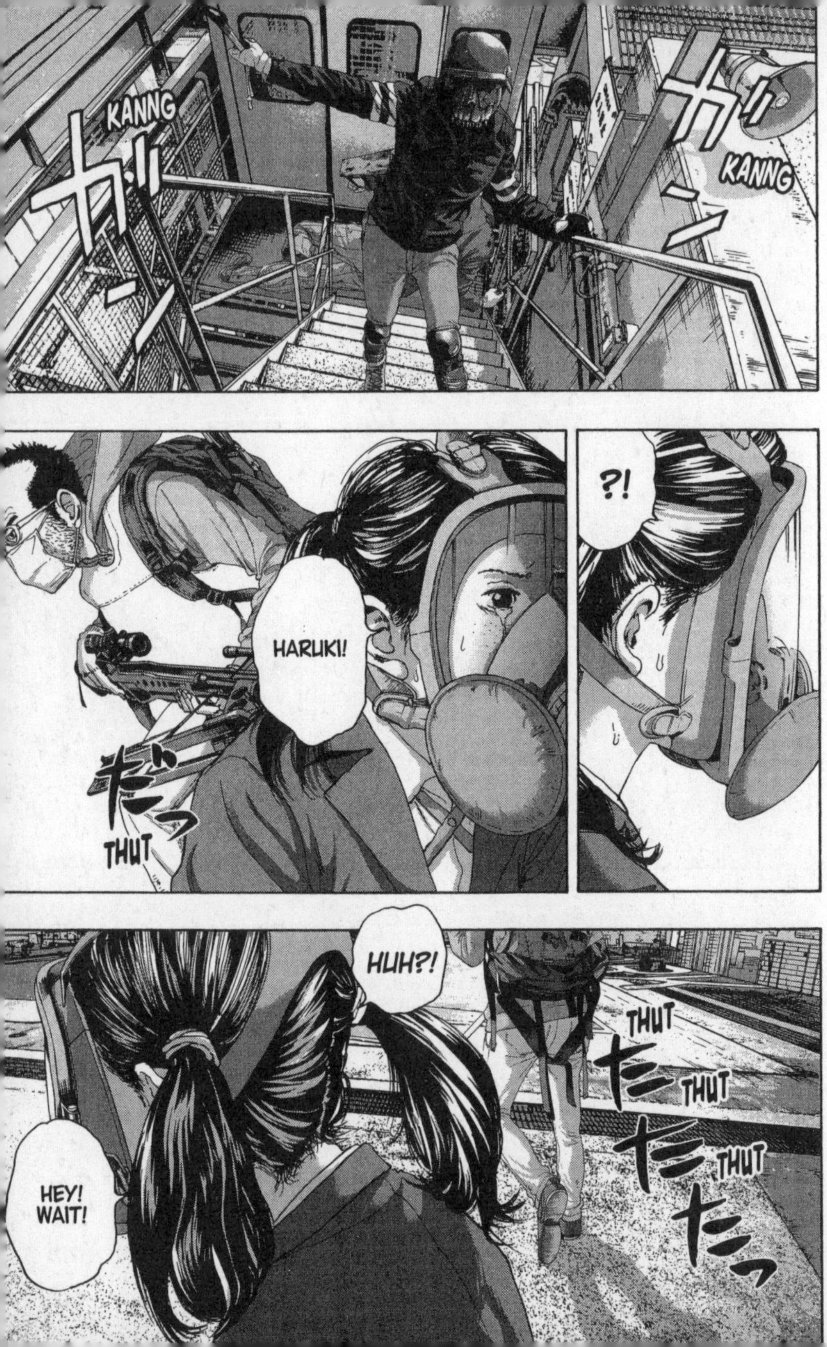
KANNG
KANNG
?!
HARUKI!
THUT
HUH?!
THUT
THUT
THUT
HEY! WAIT!

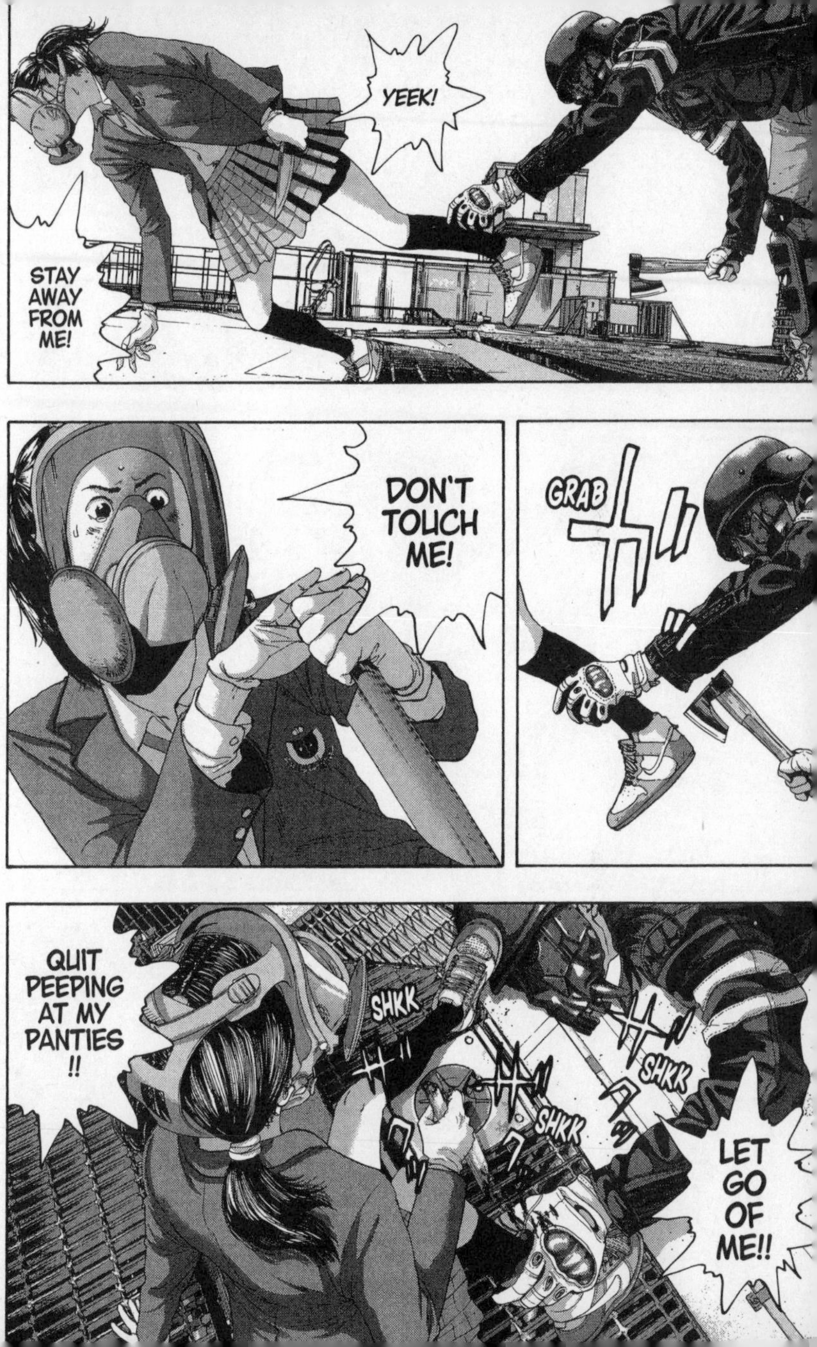
YEEK!
STAY AWAY FROM ME!
GRAB
DON'T TOUCH ME!
SHKK
SHKK
SHKK
LET GO OF ME!!
QUIT PEEPING AT MY PANTIES !!

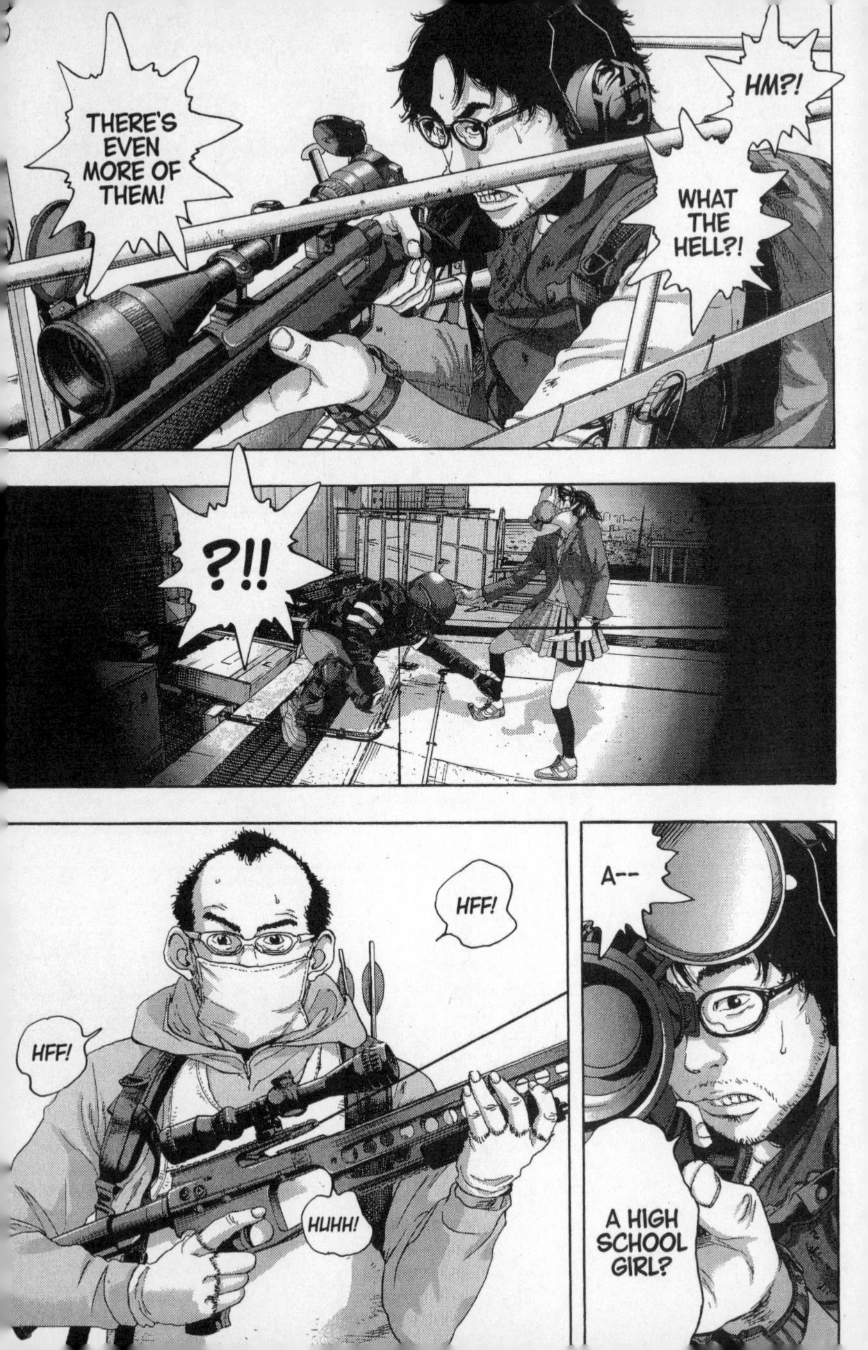
HM?!
WHAT THE HELL?!
THERE'S EVEN MORE OF THEM!
?!!
A--
A HIGH SCHOOL GIRL?
HFF!
HFF!
HUHH!

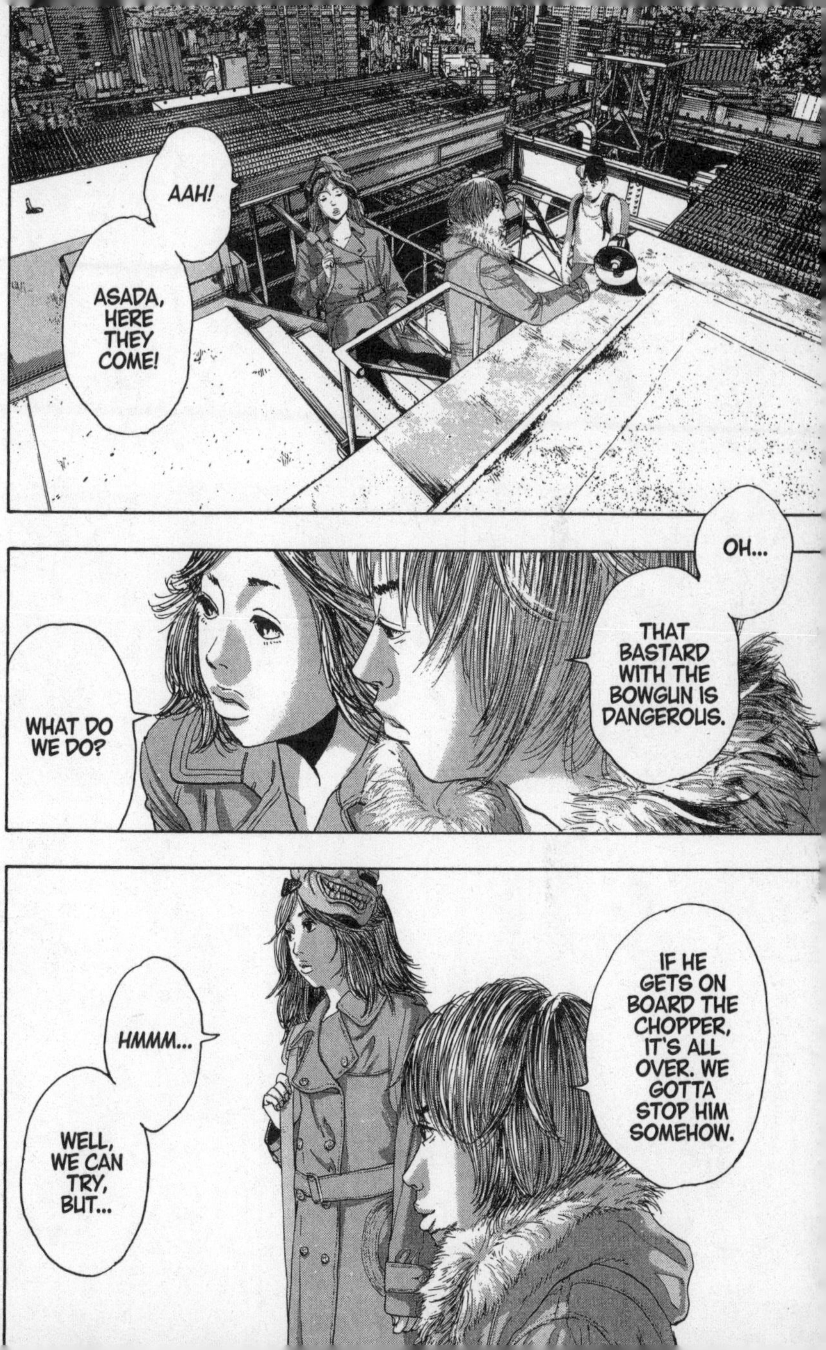
AAH!
ASADA, HERE THEY COME!
OH...
THAT BASTARD WITH THE BOWGUN IS DANGEROUS.
WHAT DO WE DO?
IF HE GETS ON BOARD THE CHOPPER, IT'S ALL OVER. WE GOTTA STOP HIM SOMEHOW.
HMMM...
WELL, WE CAN TRY, BUT...

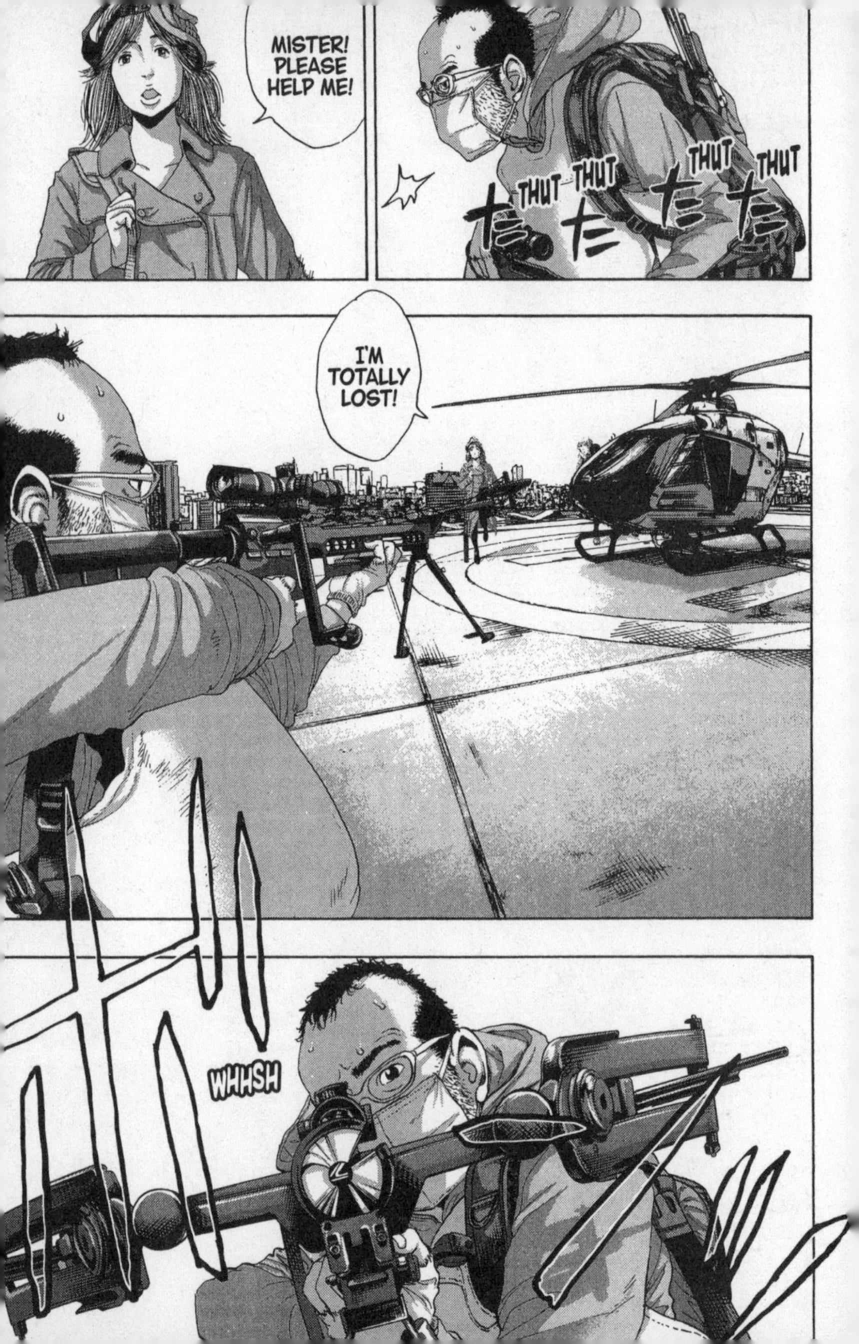
THUT THUT THUT THUT
MISTER! PLEASE HELP ME!
I'M TOTALLY LOST!
WHHSH

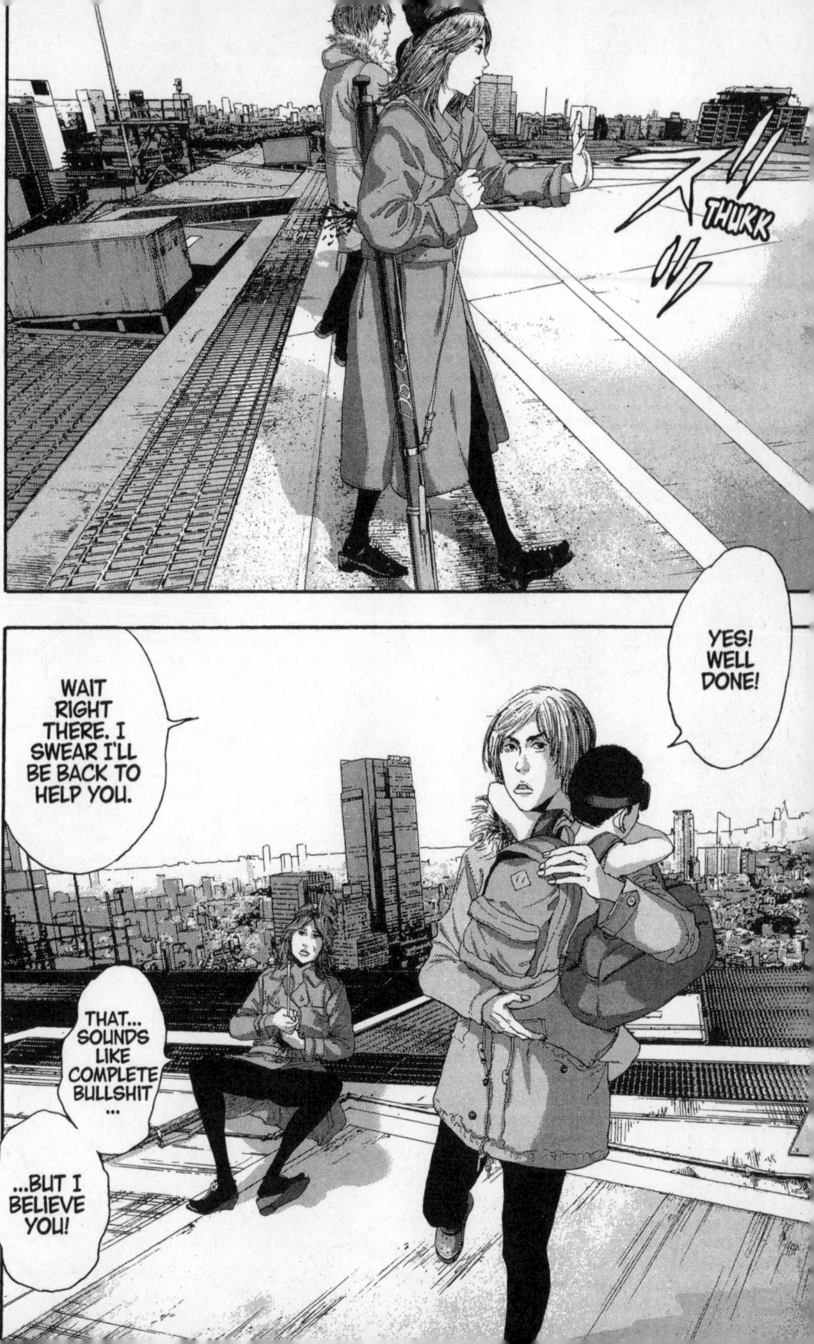
THUKK
YES! WELL DONE!
WAIT RIGHT THERE. I SWEAR I'LL BE BACK TO HELP YOU.
THAT... SOUNDS LIKE COMPLETE BULLSHIT ...
...BUT I BELIEVE YOU!

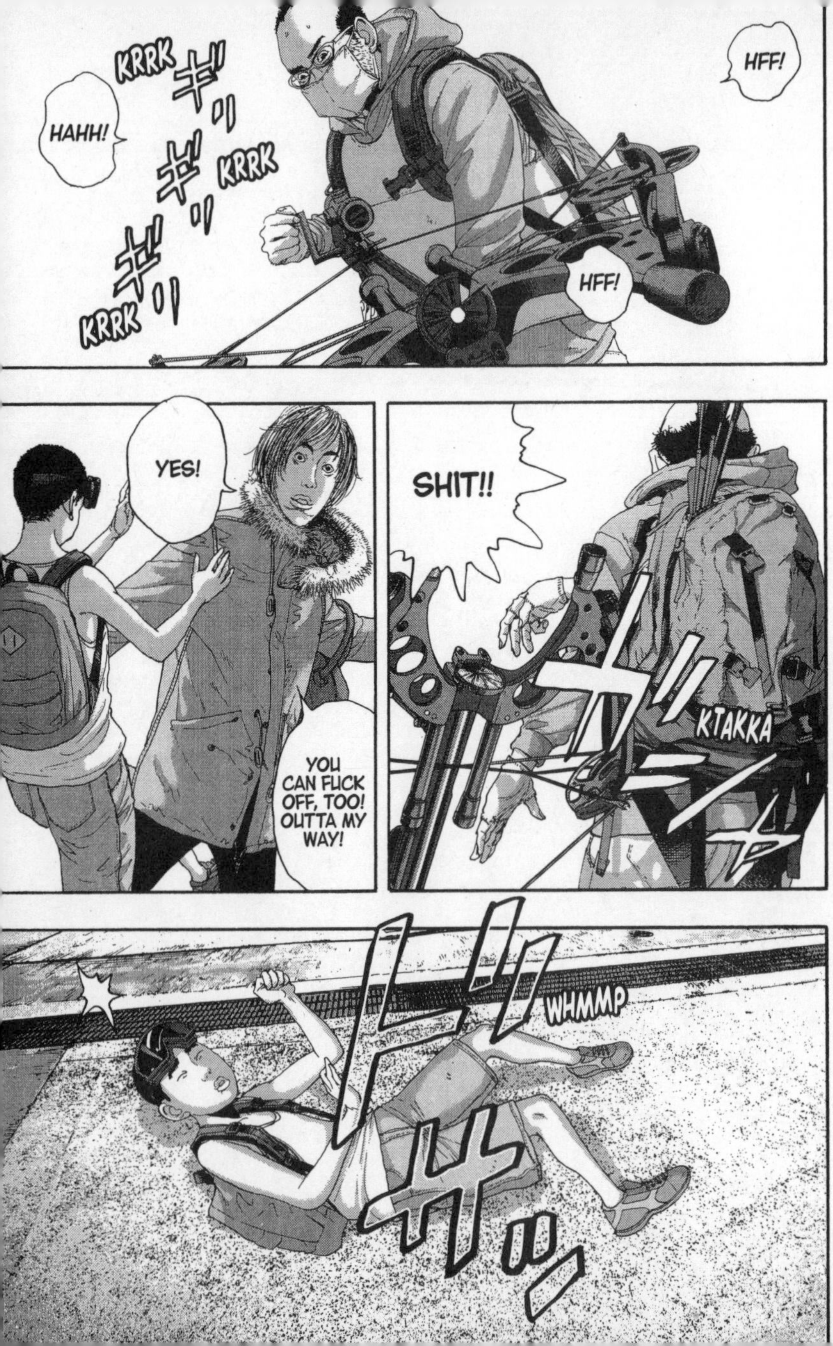

HFF!
KRRK
HAHH!
KRRK
HFF!
KRRK
SHIT!!
KTAKKA
YES!
YOU CAN FUCK OFF, TOO! OUTTA MY WAY!
WHMMP

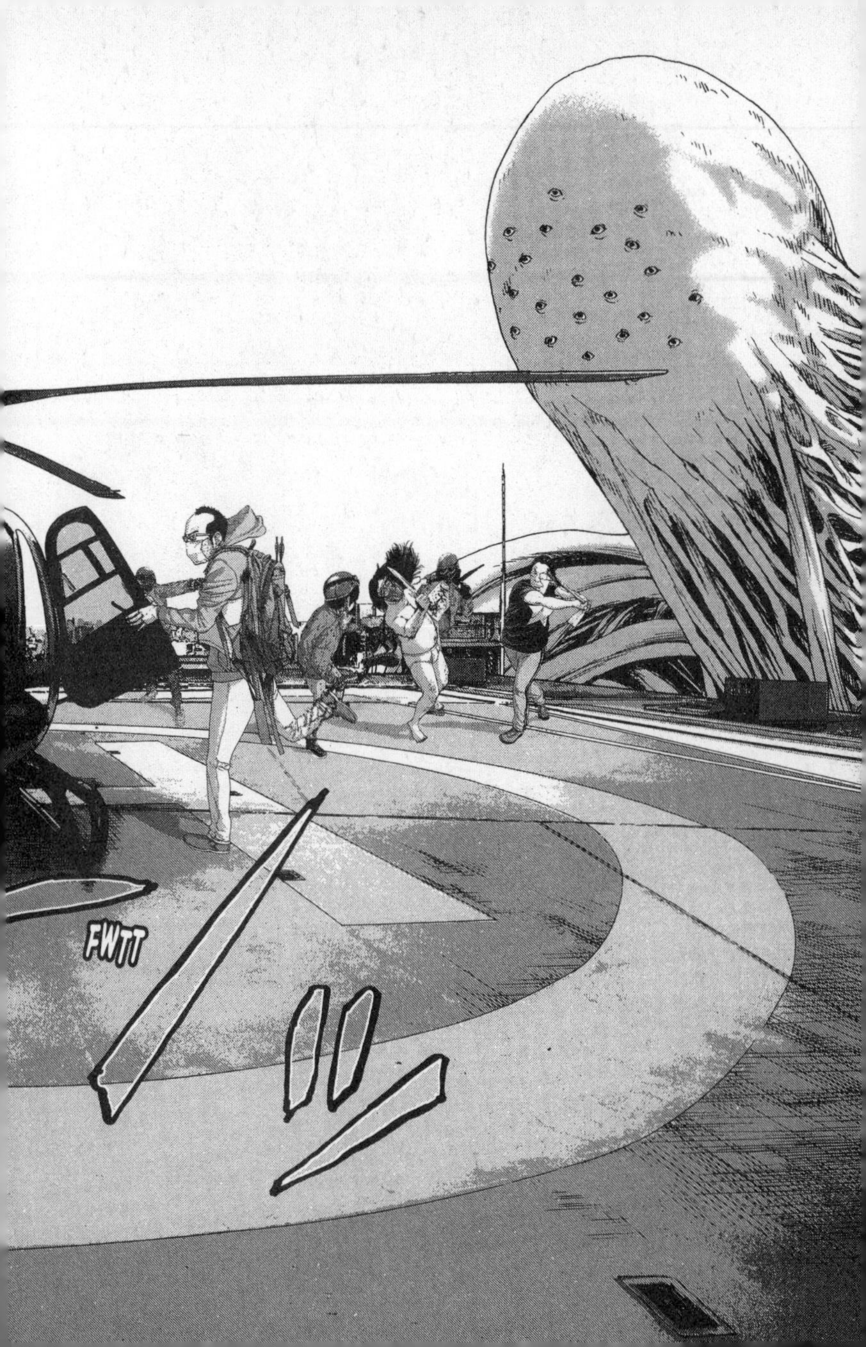
FWTT

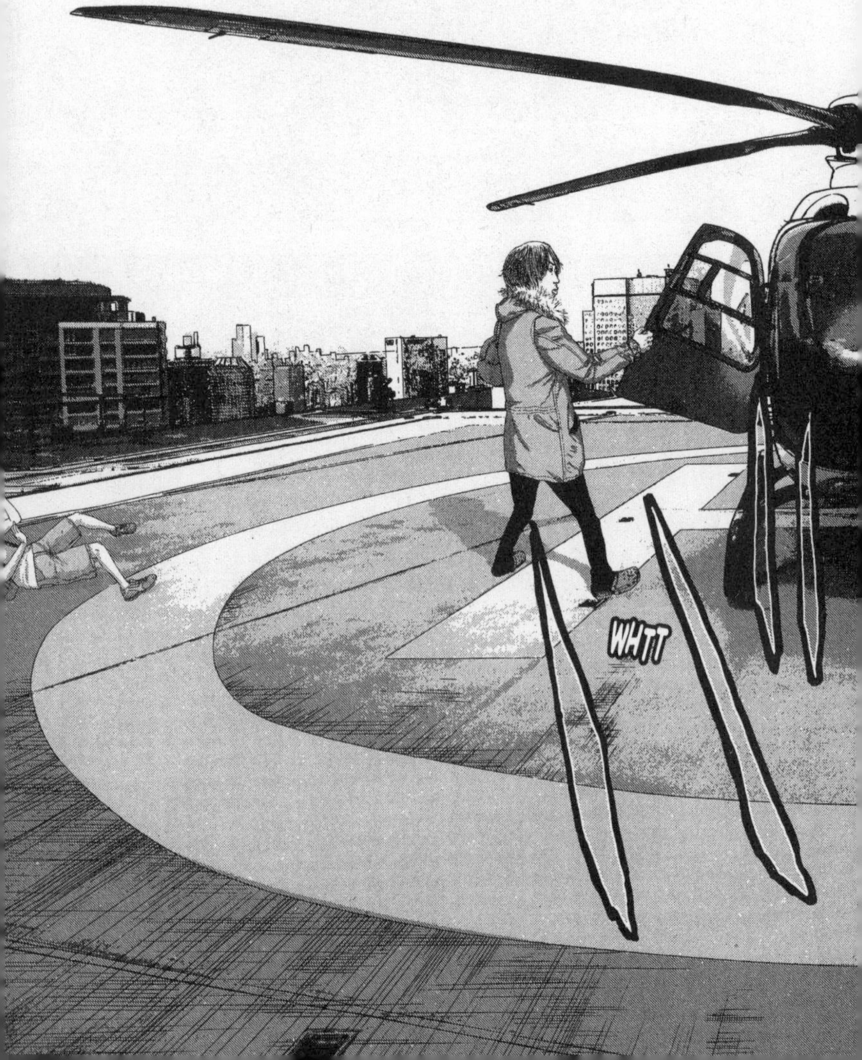
WHTT

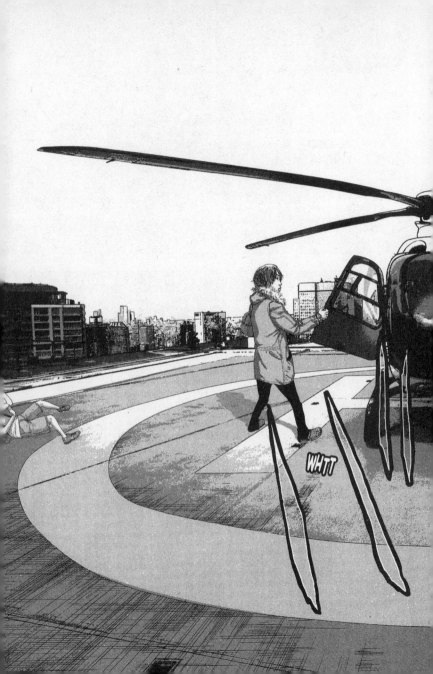

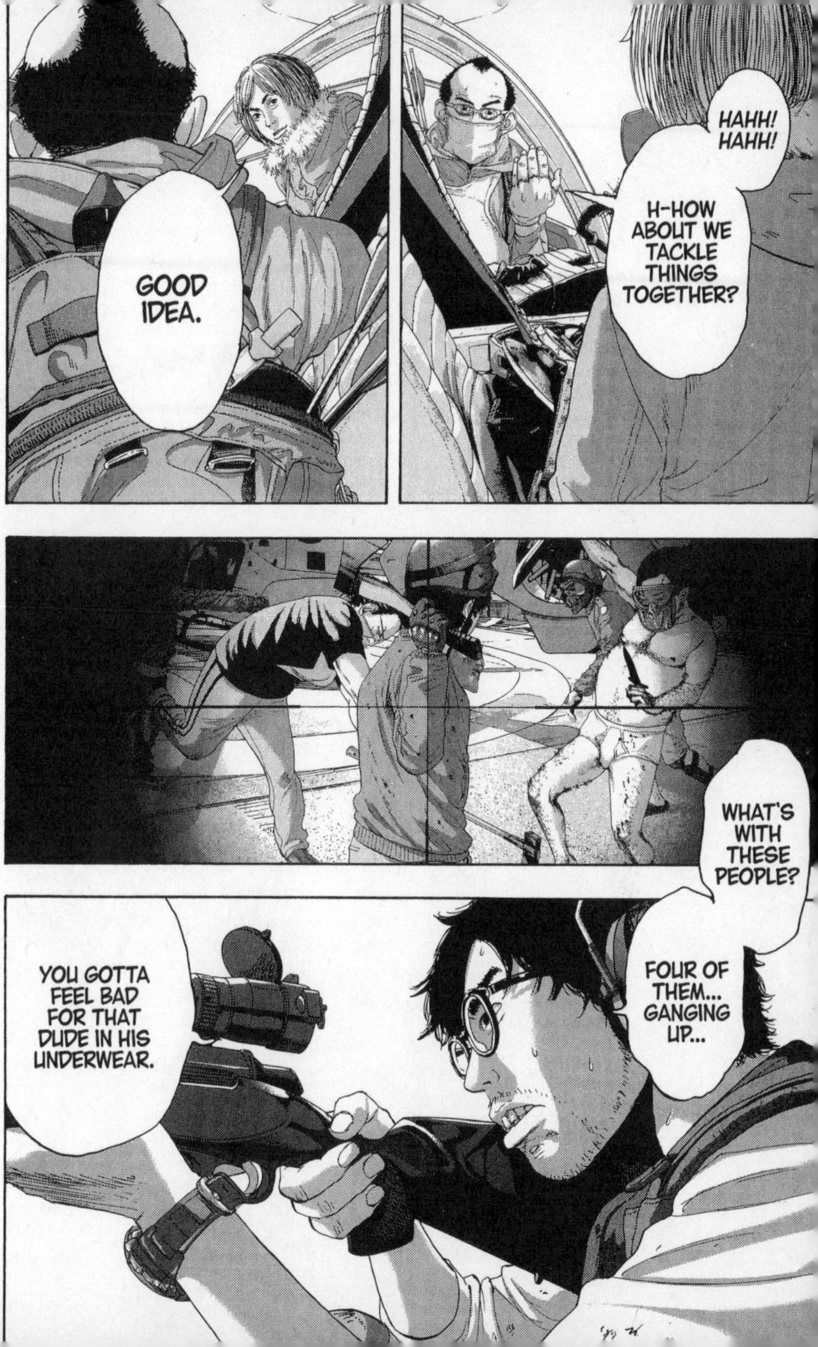
HAHH! HAHH!
H-HOW ABOUT WE TACKLE THINGS TOGETHER?
GOOD IDEA.
WHAT'S WITH THESE PEOPLE?
FOUR OF THEM... GANGING UP...
YOU GOTTA FEEL BAD FOR THAT DUDE IN HIS UNDERWEAR.

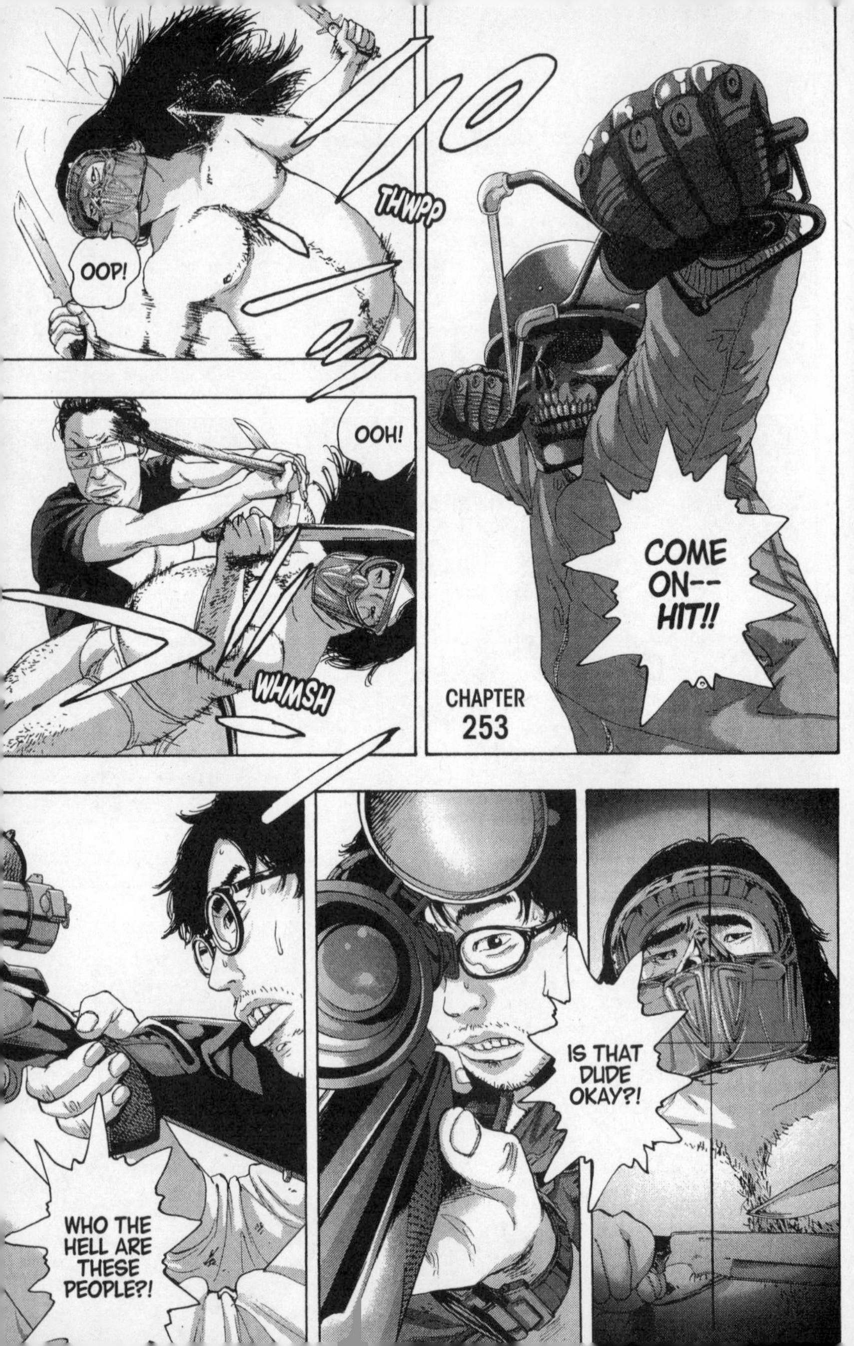

COME ON-- HIT!!
CHAPTER 253
THWPP
OOP!
OOH!
WHMSH
IS THAT DUDE OKAY?!
WHO THE HELL ARE THESE PEOPLE?!

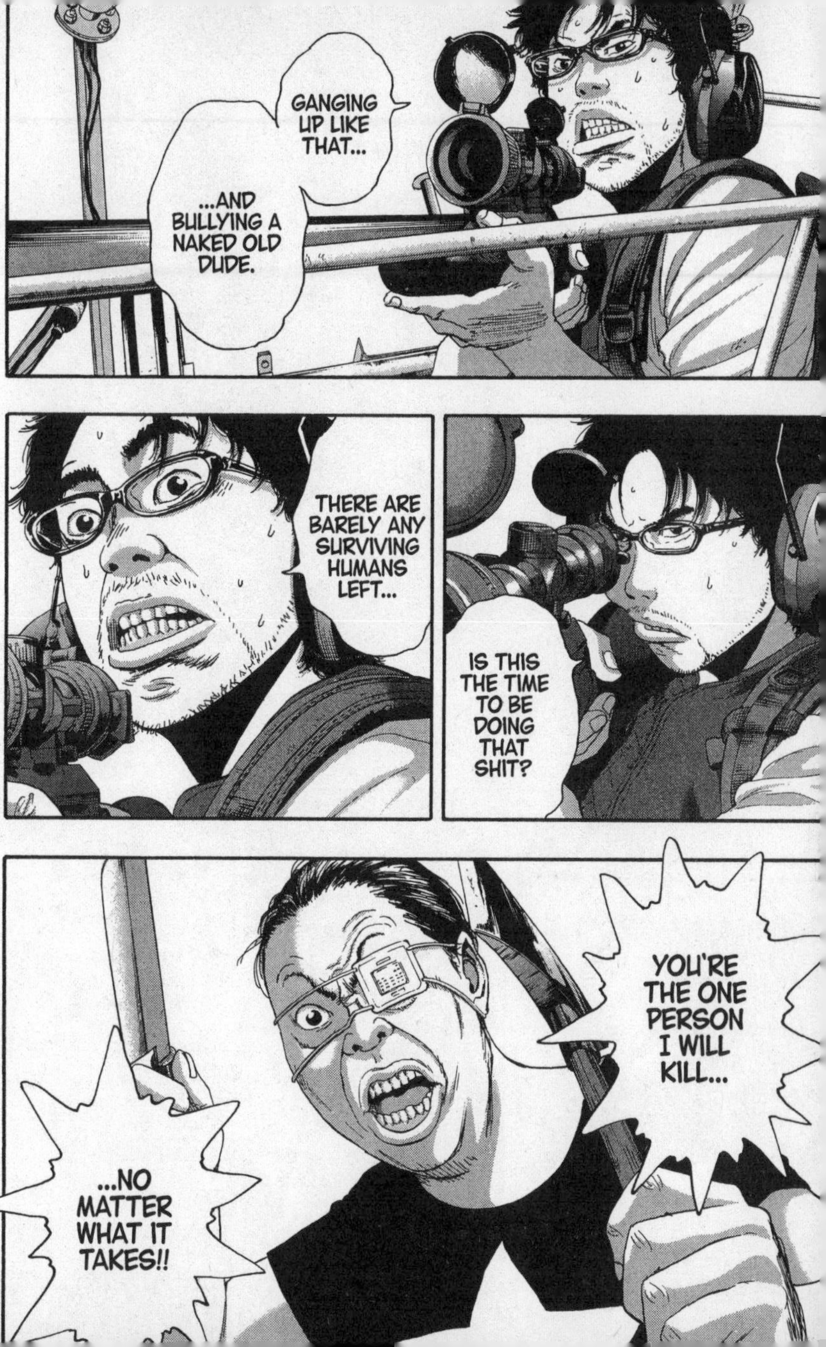
GANGING UP LIKE THAT...
...AND BULLYING A NAKED OLD DUDE.
THERE ARE BARELY ANY SURVIVING HUMANS LEFT...
IS THIS THE TIME TO BE DOING THAT SHIT?
YOU'RE THE ONE PERSON I WILL KILL...
...NO MATTER WHAT IT TAKES!!

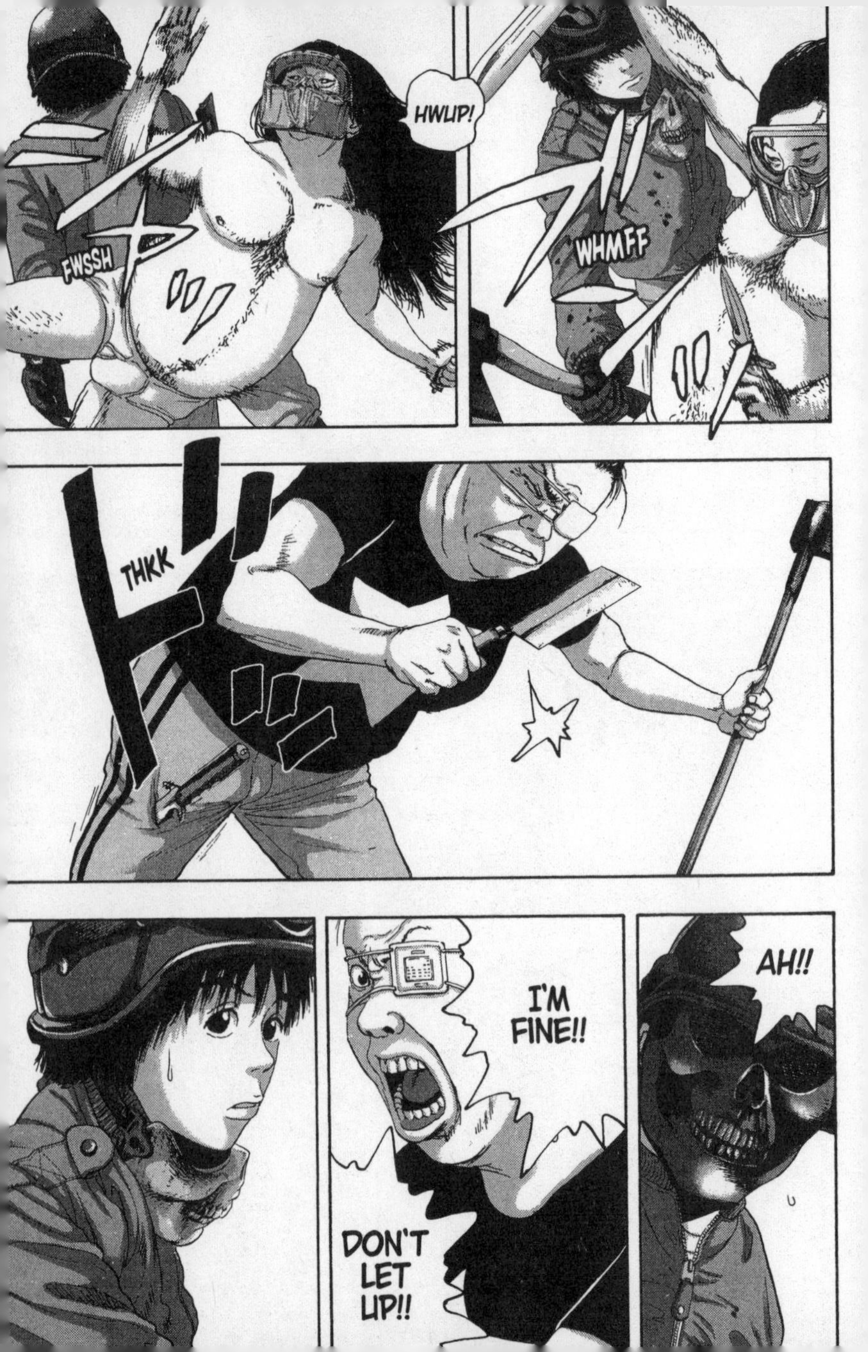
WHMFF
HWUP!
FWSSH
THKK
AH!!
I'M FINE!!
DON'T LET UP!!

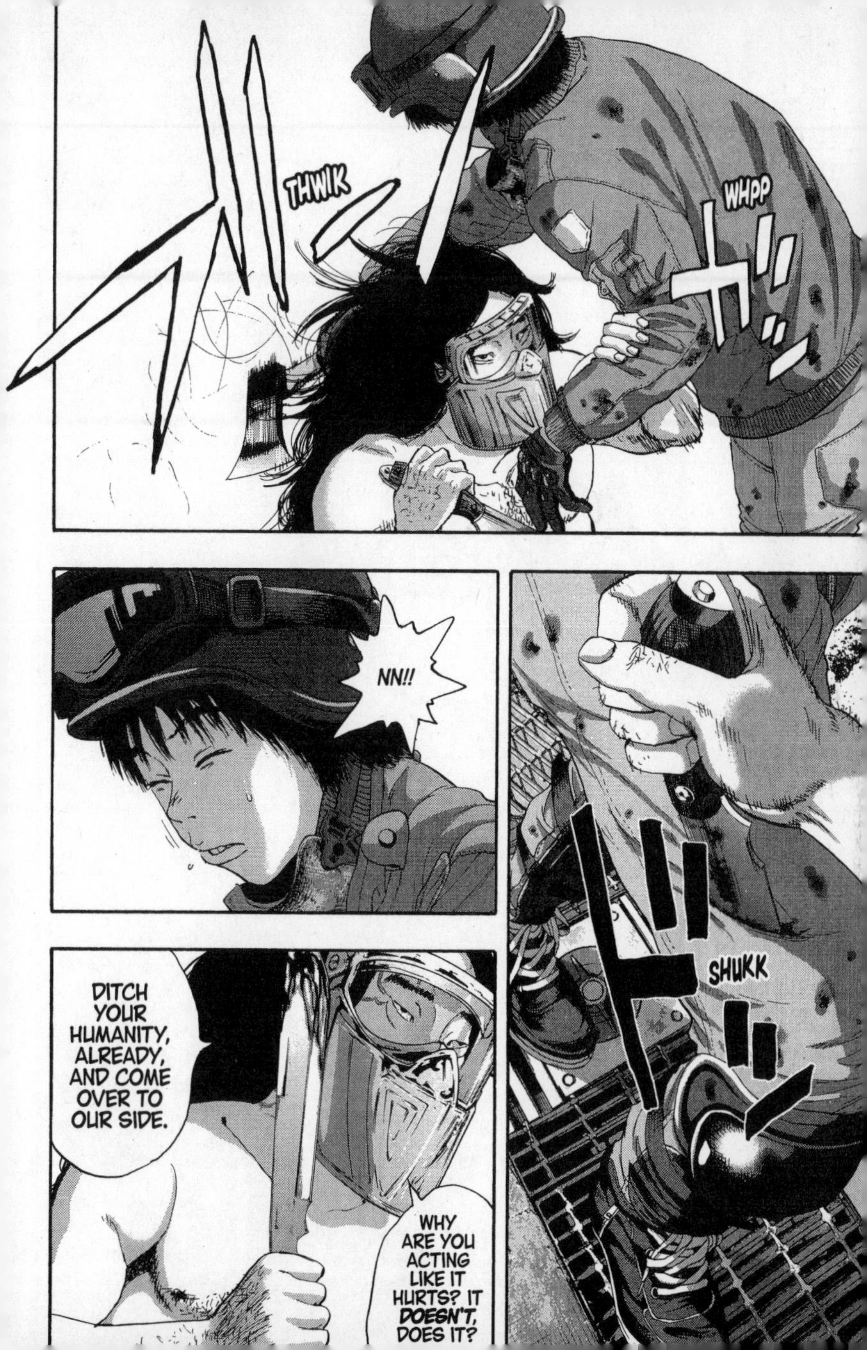
WHPP
THWIK
SHUKK
NN!!
DITCH YOUR HUMANITY, ALREADY, AND COME OVER TO OUR SIDE.
WHY ARE YOU ACTING LIKE IT HURTS? IT DOESN'T, DOES IT?

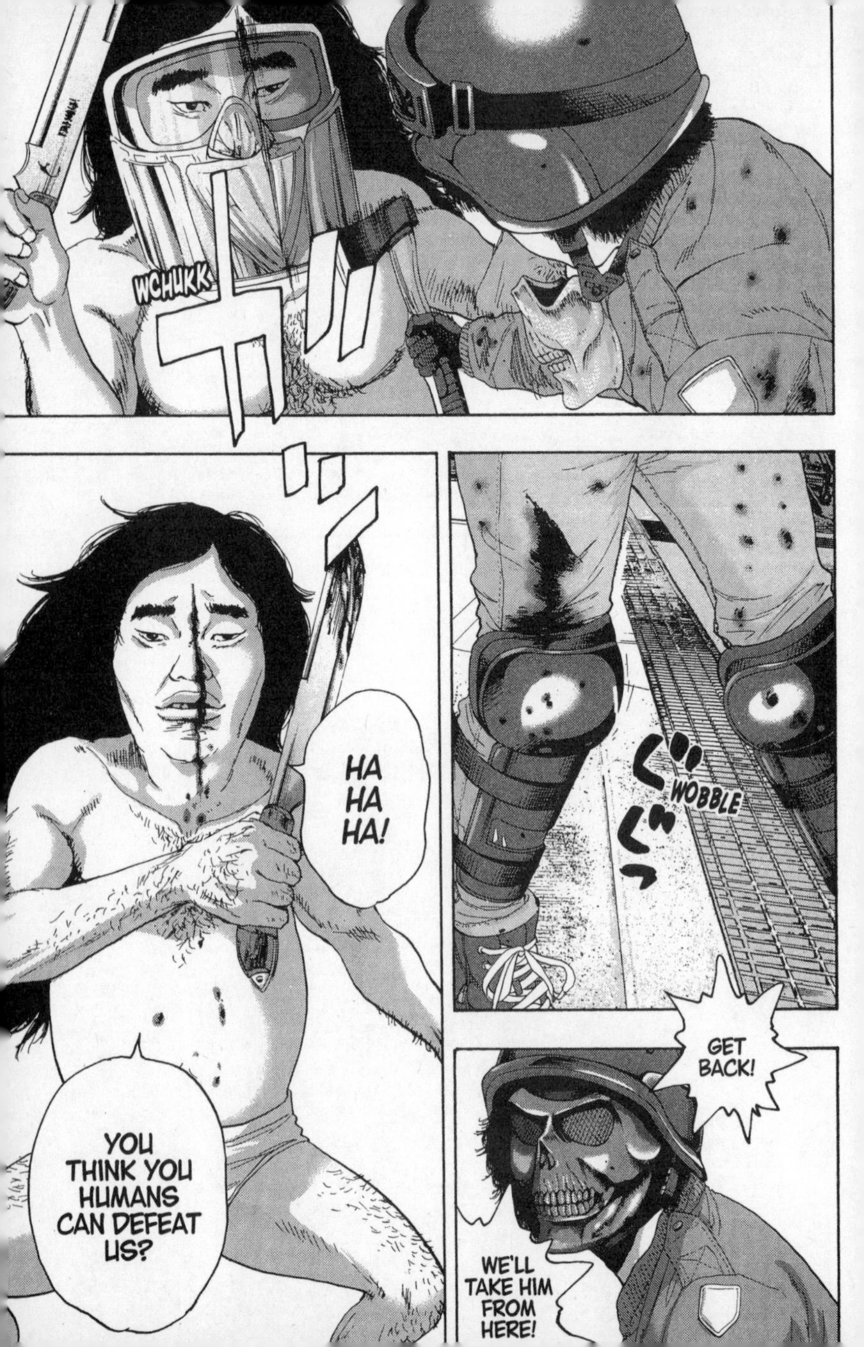
WCHUKK
WOBBLE
GET BACK!
WE'LL TAKE HIM FROM HERE!
HA HA HA!
YOU THINK YOU HUMANS CAN DEFEAT US?

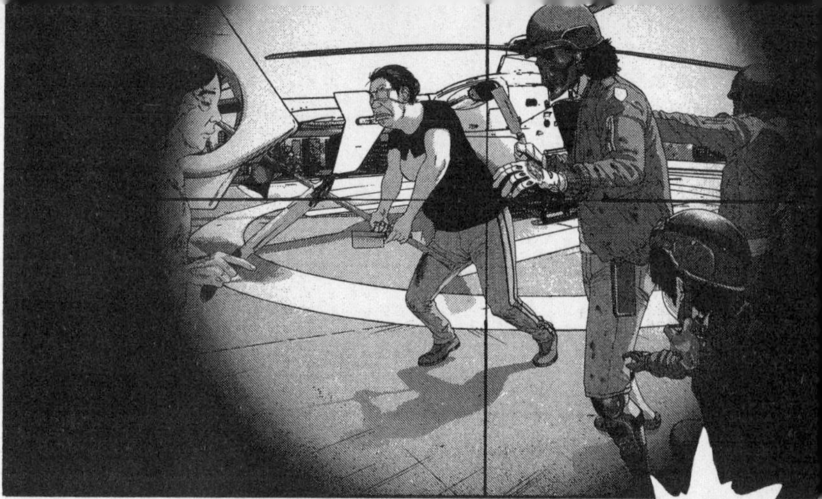
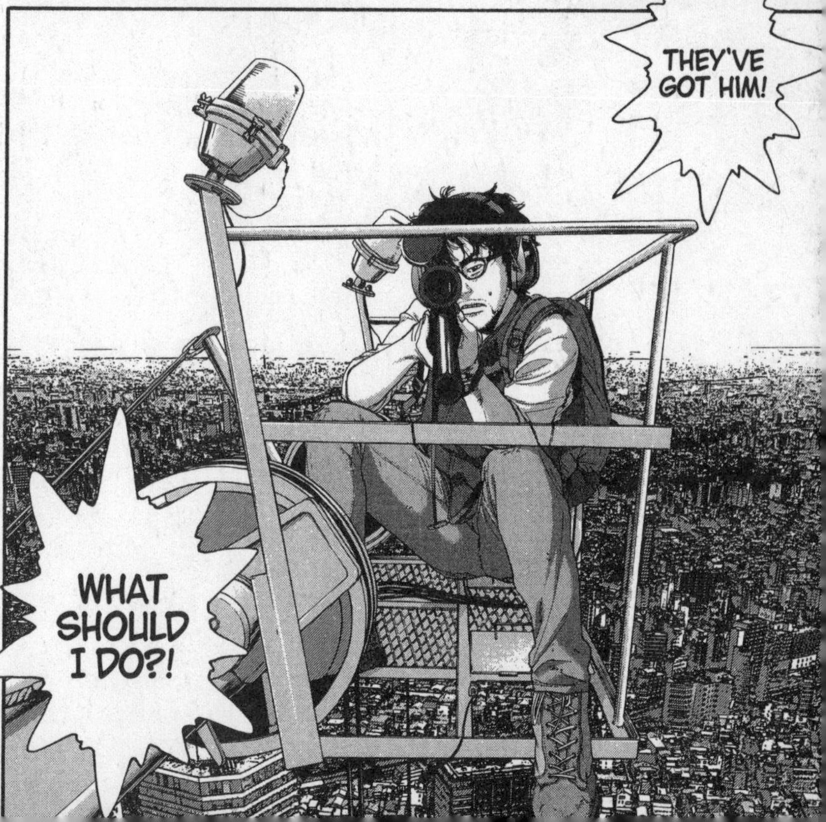
THEY'VE GOT HIM!
WHAT SHOULD I DO?!

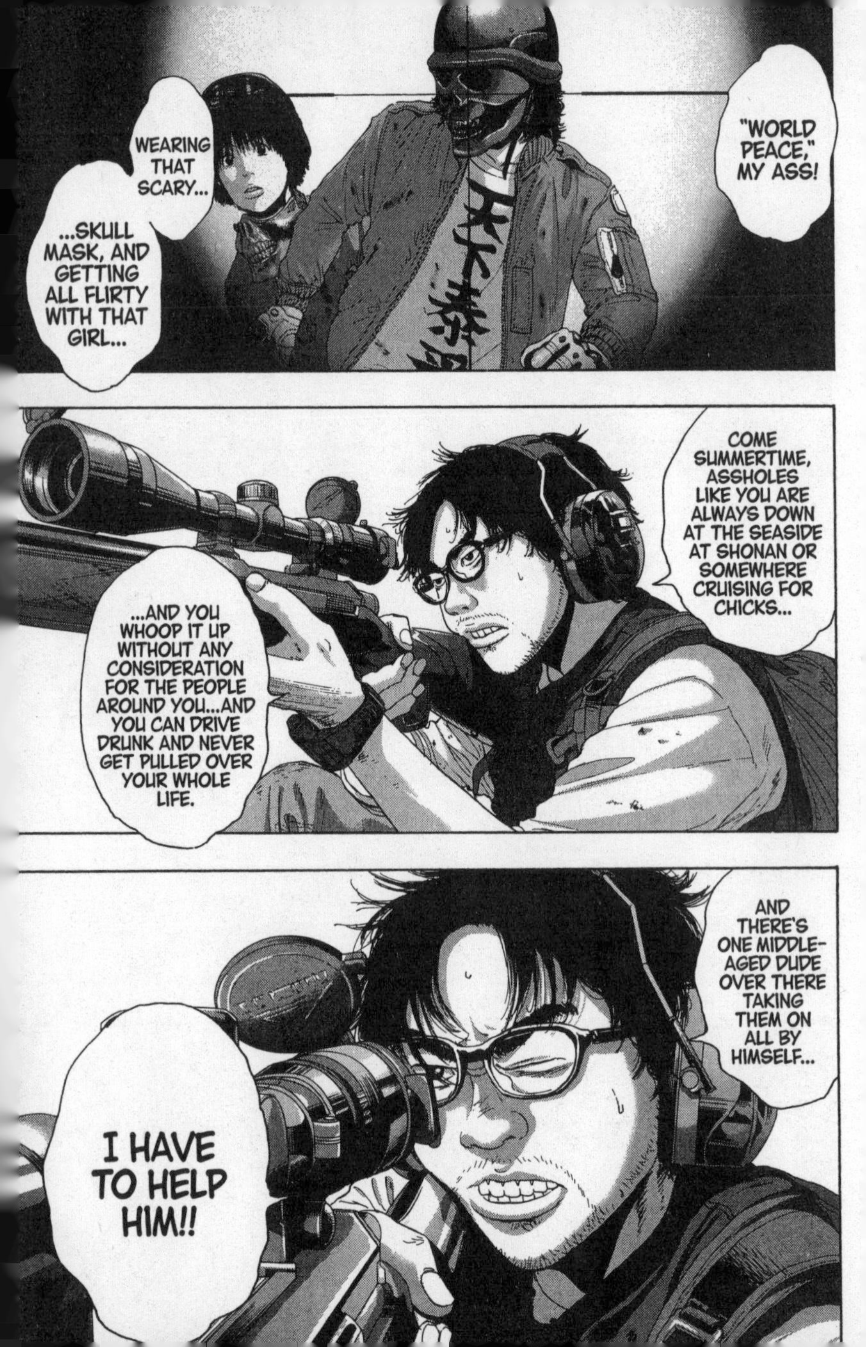
"WORLD PEACE," MY ASS!
WEARING THAT SCARY...
...SKULL MASK, AND GETTING ALL FLIRTY WITH THAT GIRL...
COME SUMMERTIME, ASSHOLES LIKE YOU ARE ALWAYS DOWN AT THE SEASIDE AT SHONAN OR SOMEWHERE CRUISING FOR CHICKS...
...AND YOU WHOOP IT UP WITHOUT ANY CONSIDERATION FOR THE PEOPLE AROUND YOU...AND YOU CAN DRIVE DRUNK AND NEVER GET PULLED OVER YOUR WHOLE LIFE.
AND THERE'S ONE MIDDLE-AGED DUDE OVER THERE TAKING THEM ON ALL BY HIMSELF...
I HAVE TO HELP HIM!!

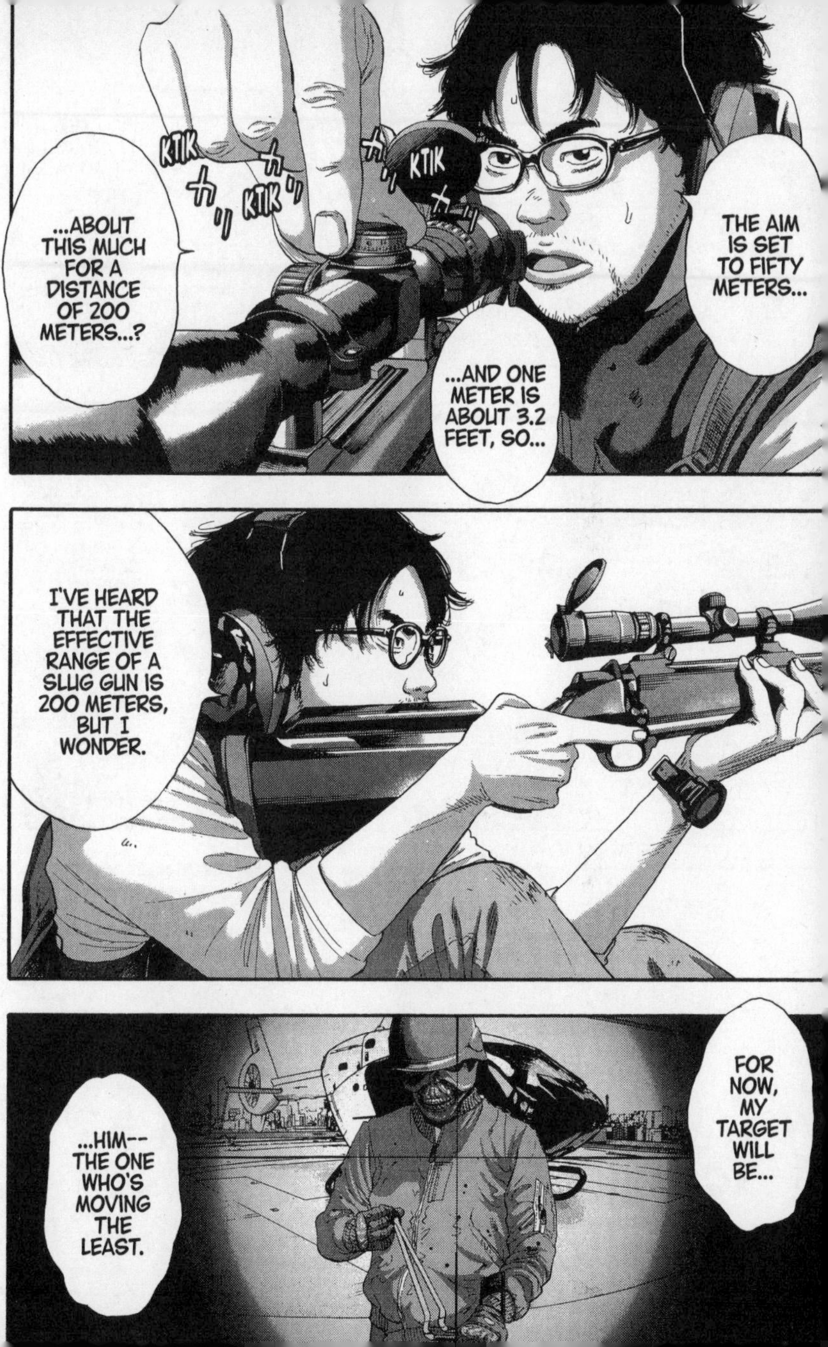
THE AIM IS SET TO FIFTY METERS...
KTIK
...AND ONE METER IS ABOUT 3.2 FEET, SO...
KTIK
KTIK
...ABOUT THIS MUCH FOR A DISTANCE OF 200 METERS...?
I'VE HEARD THAT THE EFFECTIVE RANGE OF A SLUG GUN IS 200 METERS, BUT I WONDER.
FOR NOW, MY TARGET WILL BE...
...HIM-- THE ONE WHO'S MOVING THE LEAST.

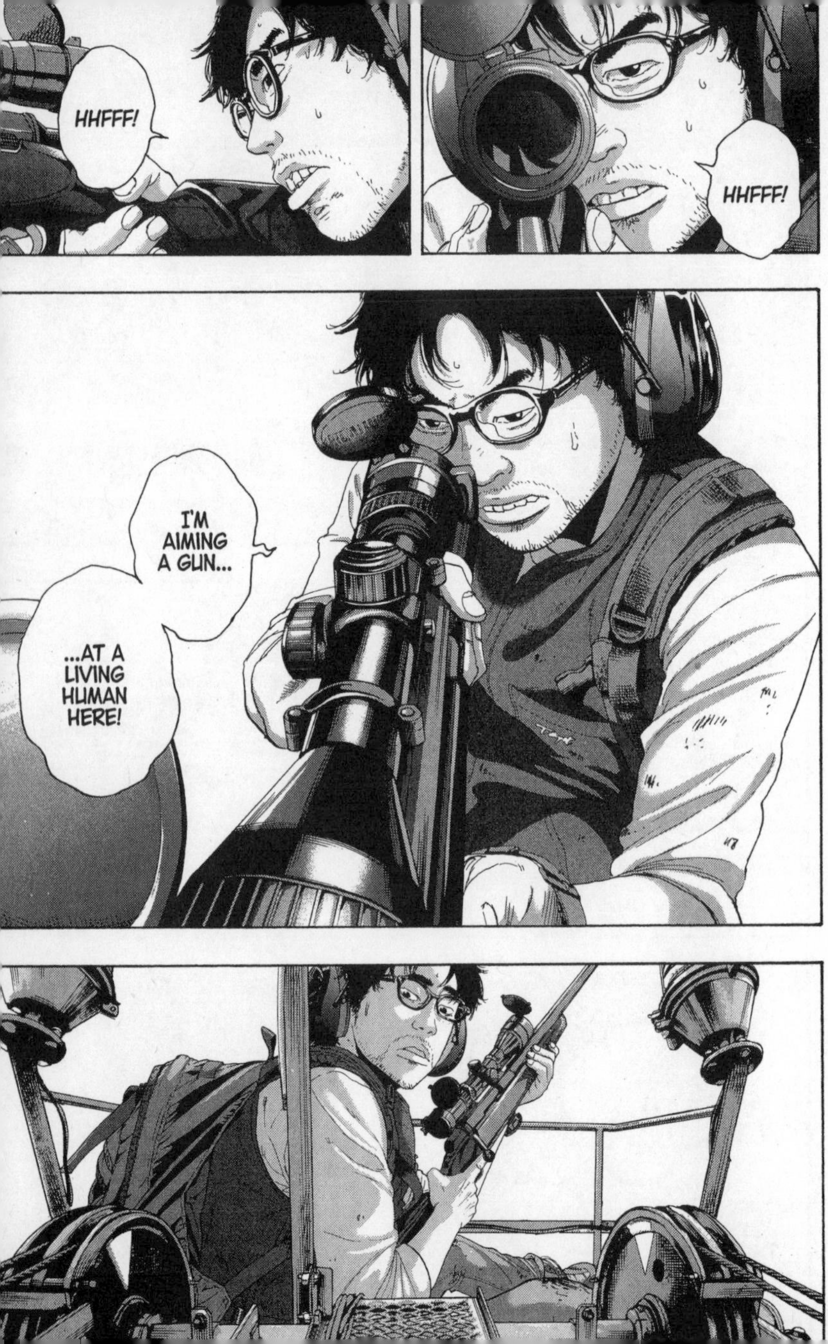
HHFFF!
HHFFF!
I'M AIMING A GUN...
...AT A LIVING HUMAN HERE!

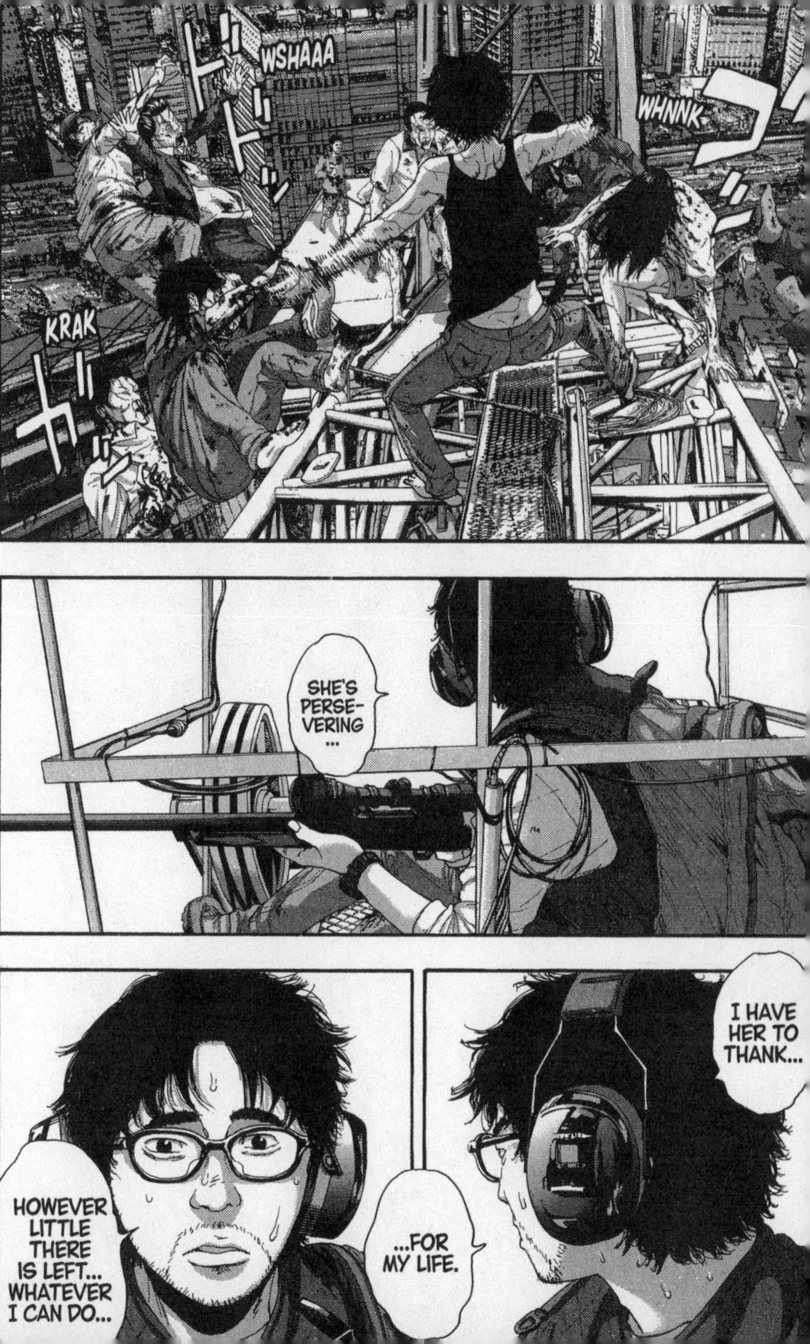
WHNNK
WSHAAA
KRAK
SHE'S PERSE-VERING ...
I HAVE HER TO THANK...
...FOR MY LIFE.
HOWEVER LITTLE THERE IS LEFT... WHATEVER I CAN DO...

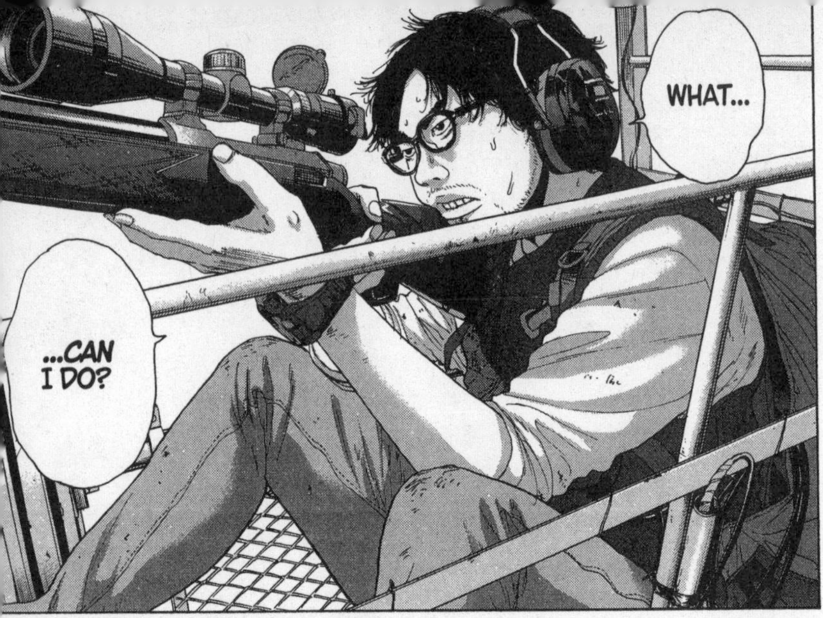
WHAT...
...CAN I DO?
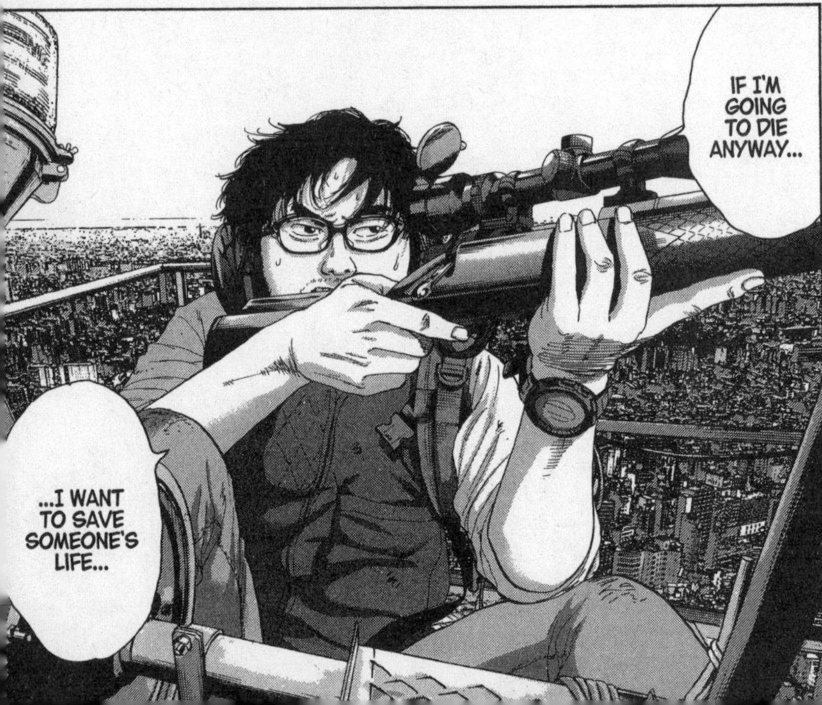
IF I'M GOING TO DIE ANYWAY...
...I WANT TO SAVE SOMEONE'S LIFE...

AH!

SHE'S IN TROUBLE!!

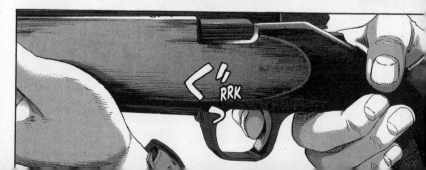

RRK

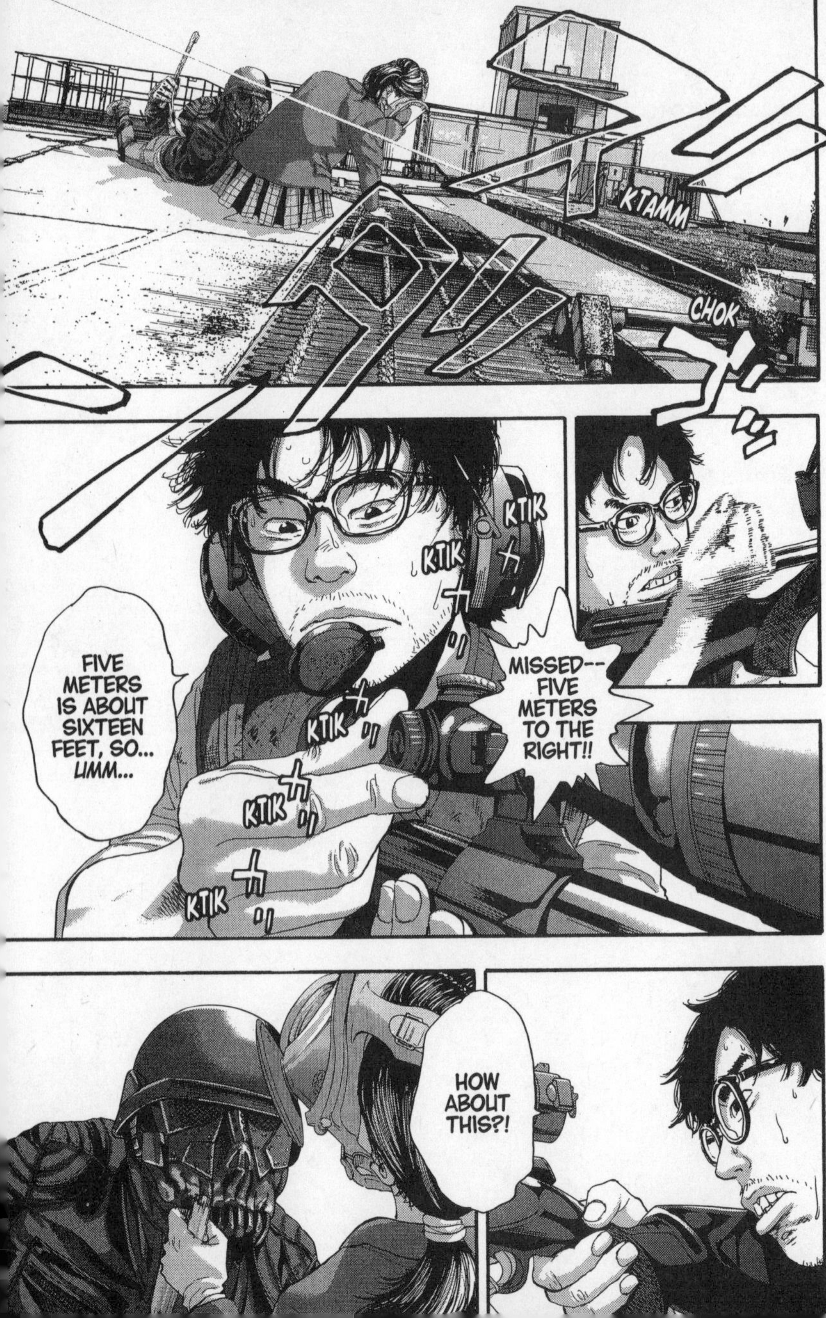
KTAMM
CHOK
KTIK
KTIK
MISSED-- FIVE METERS TO THE RIGHT!!
FIVE METERS IS ABOUT SIXTEEN FEET, SO... UMM...
KTIK
KTIK
KTIK
HOW ABOUT THIS?!

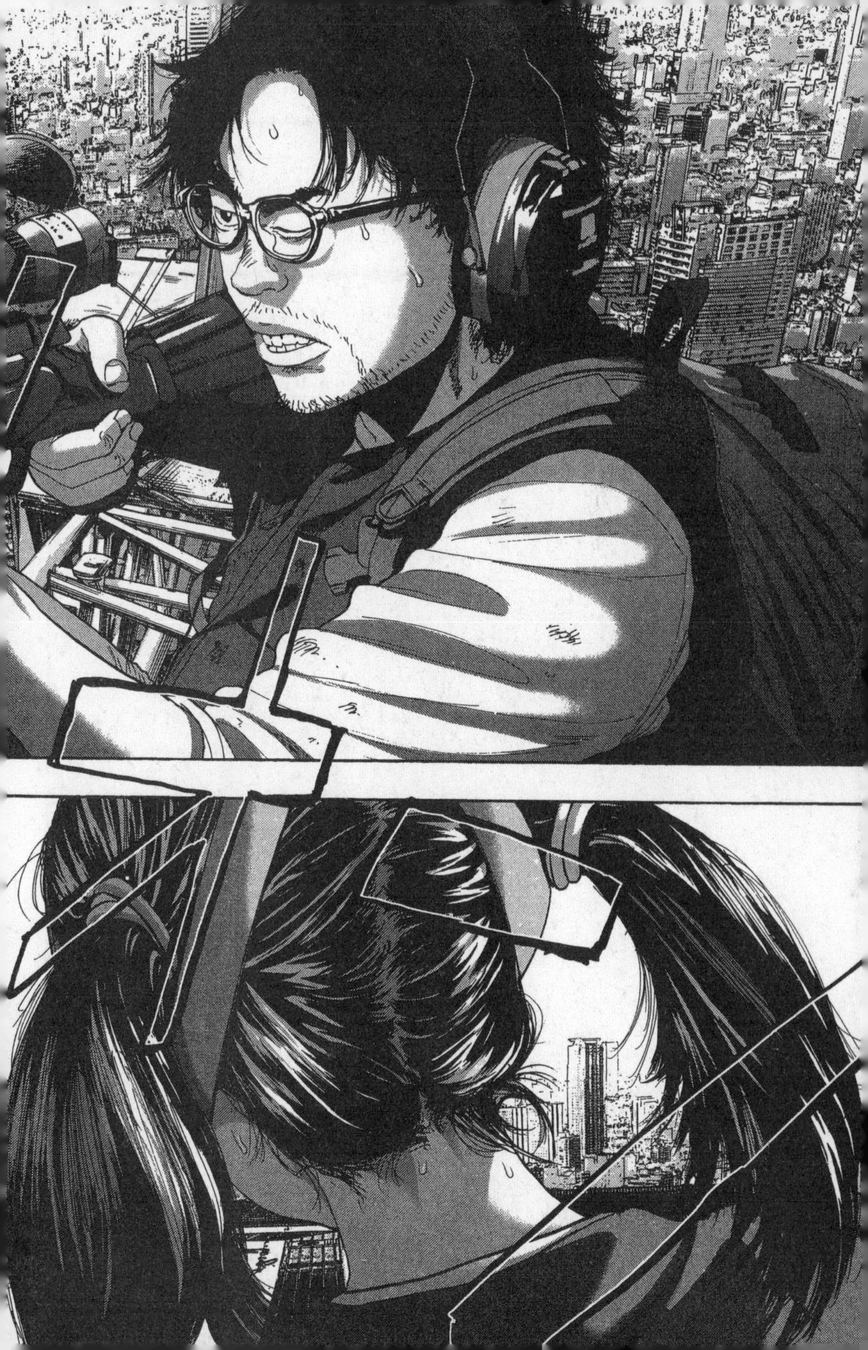

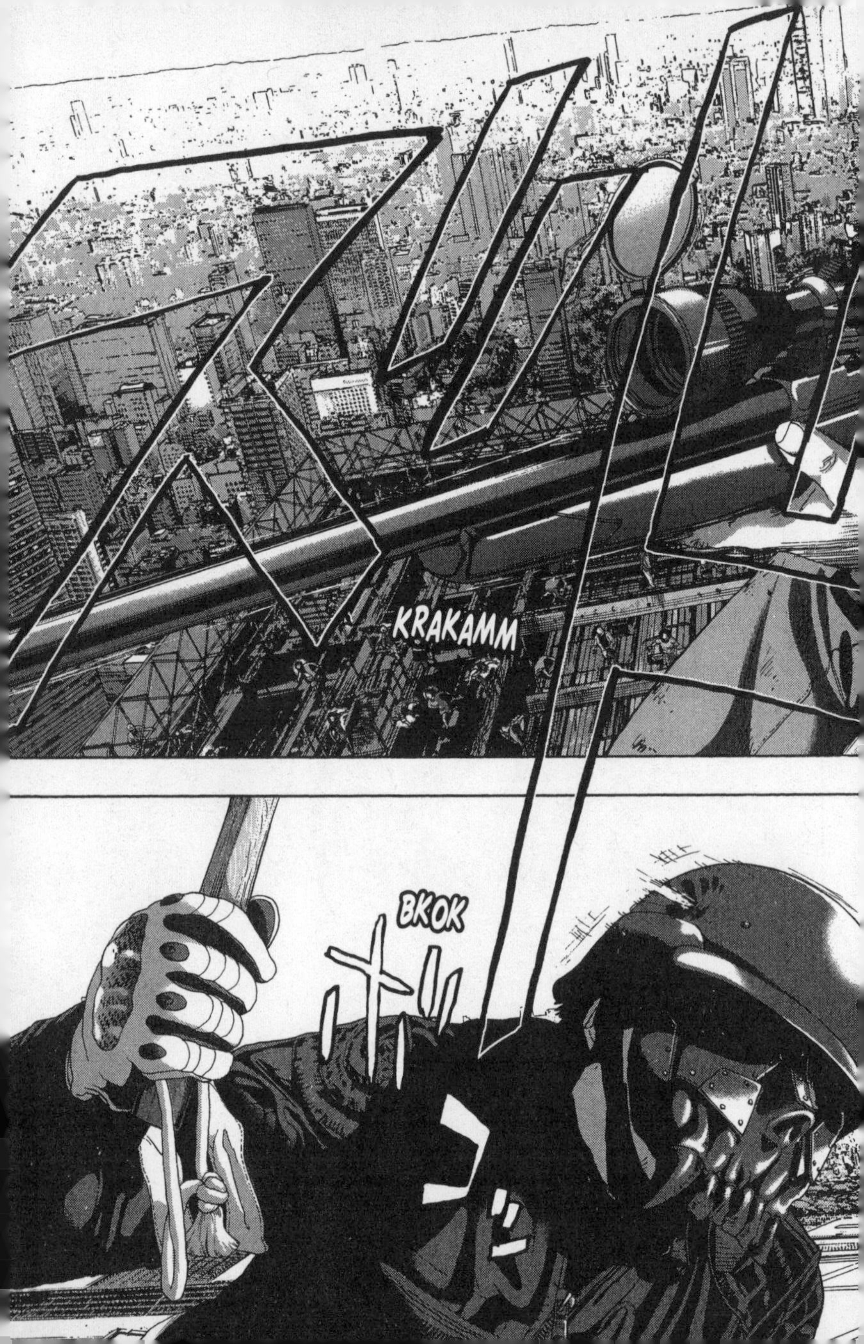
KRAKAMM
BKOK

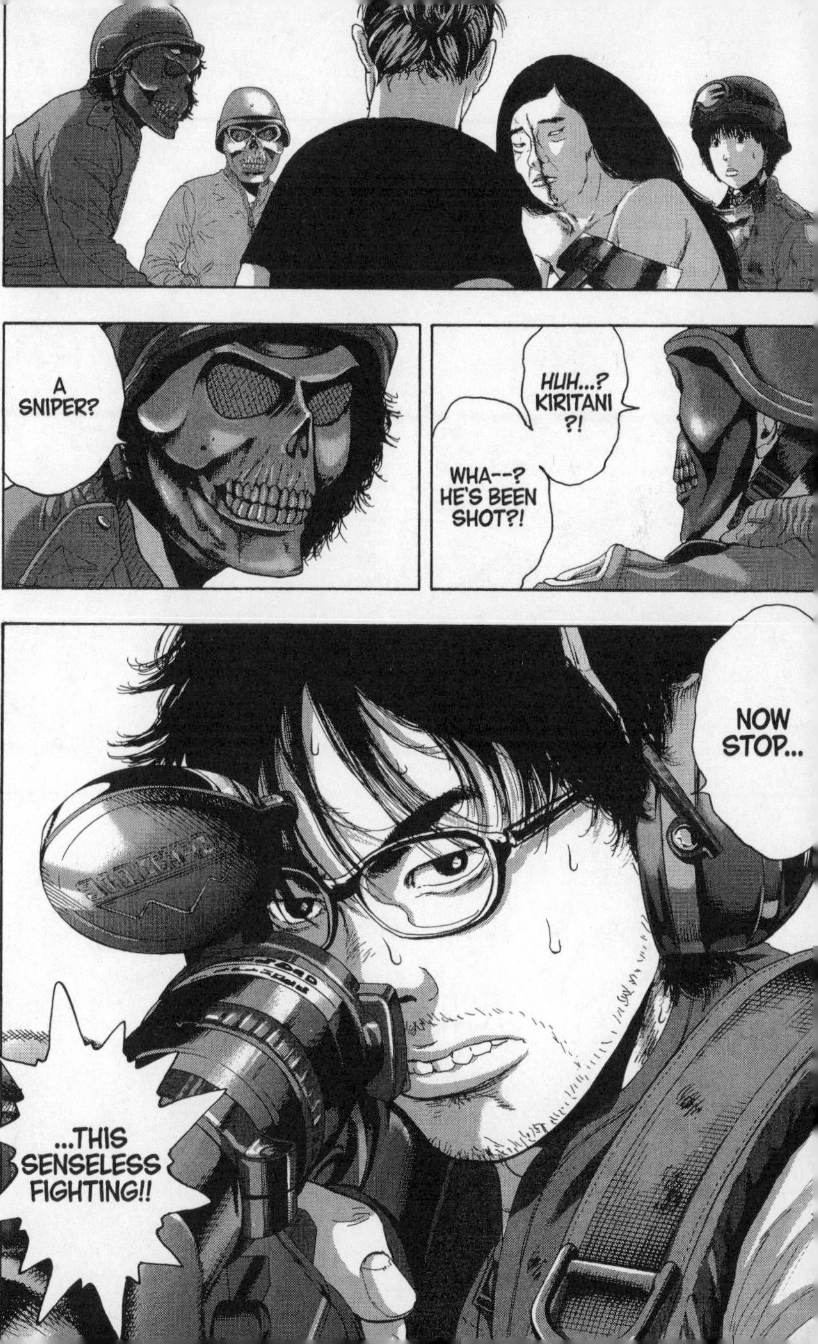
HUH...? KIRITANI ?!
WHA--? HE'S BEEN SHOT?!
A SNIPER?
NOW STOP...
...THIS SENSELESS FIGHTING!!

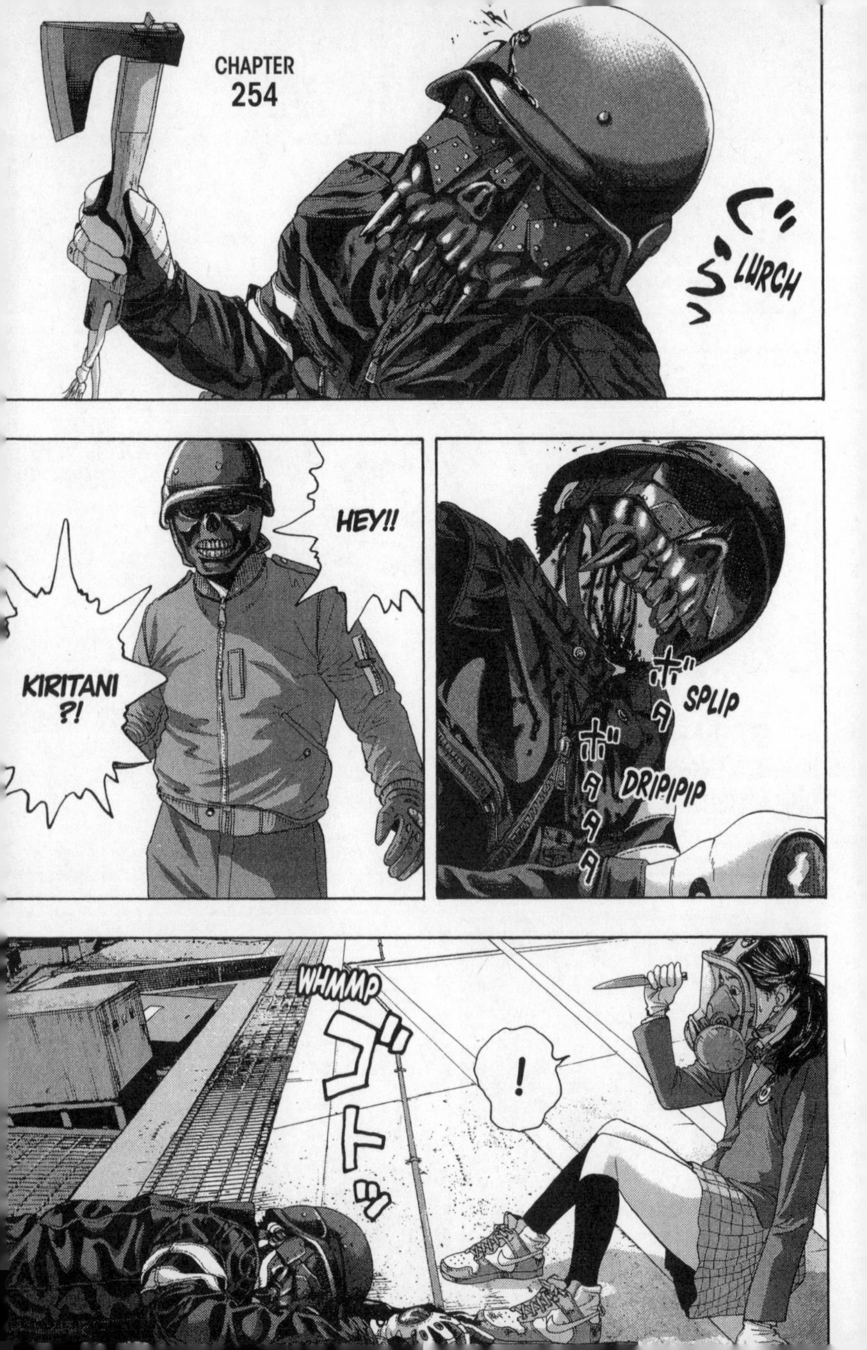
CHAPTER
254
LURCH
ボタ
ボタタタ
SPLIP
DRIPIPIP
HEY!!
KIRITANI
?!
WHMMP
ゴトッ
!

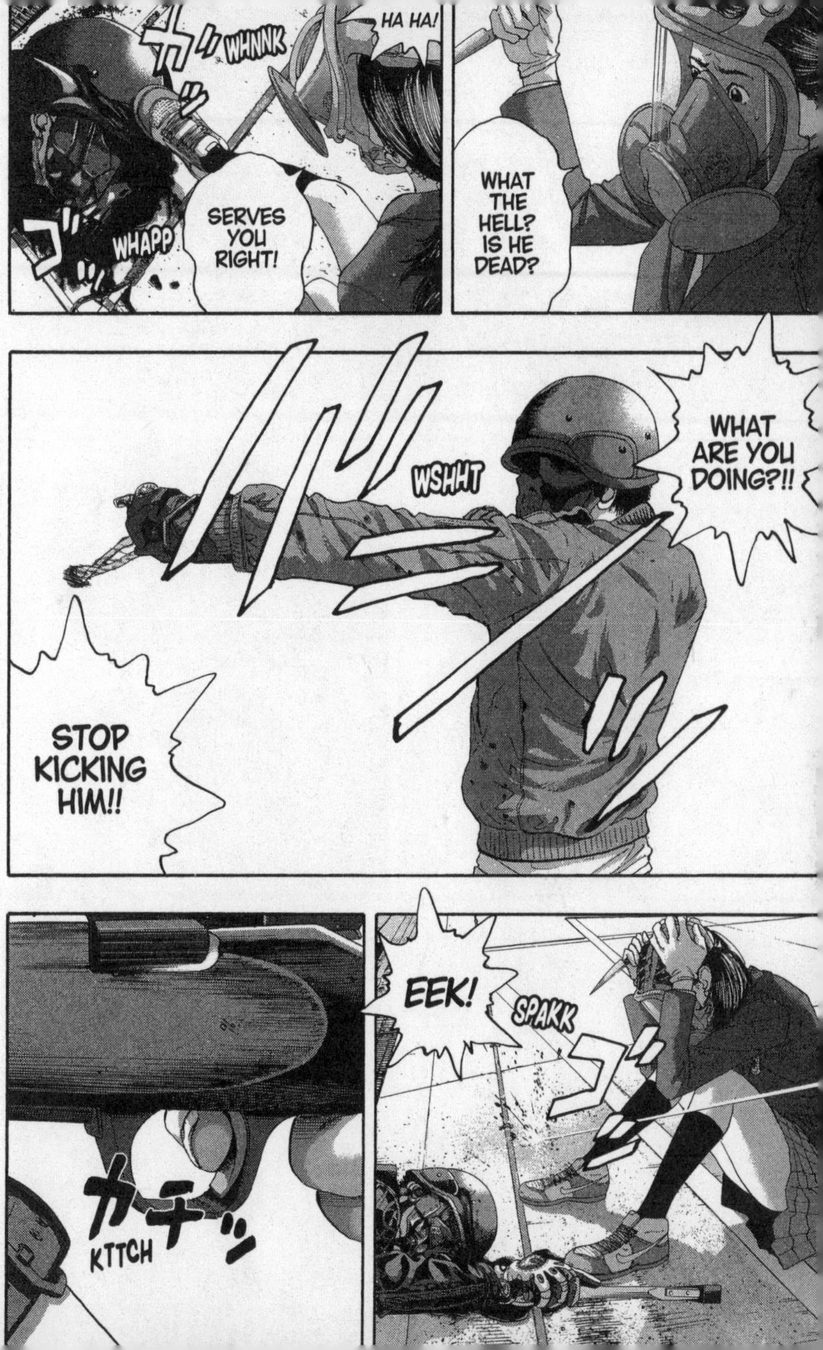
WHAT THE HELL? IS HE DEAD?
HA HA!
WHNNK
SERVES YOU RIGHT!
WHAPP
WHAT ARE YOU DOING?!!
WSHHT
STOP KICKING HIM!!
EEK!
SPAKK
KTTCH

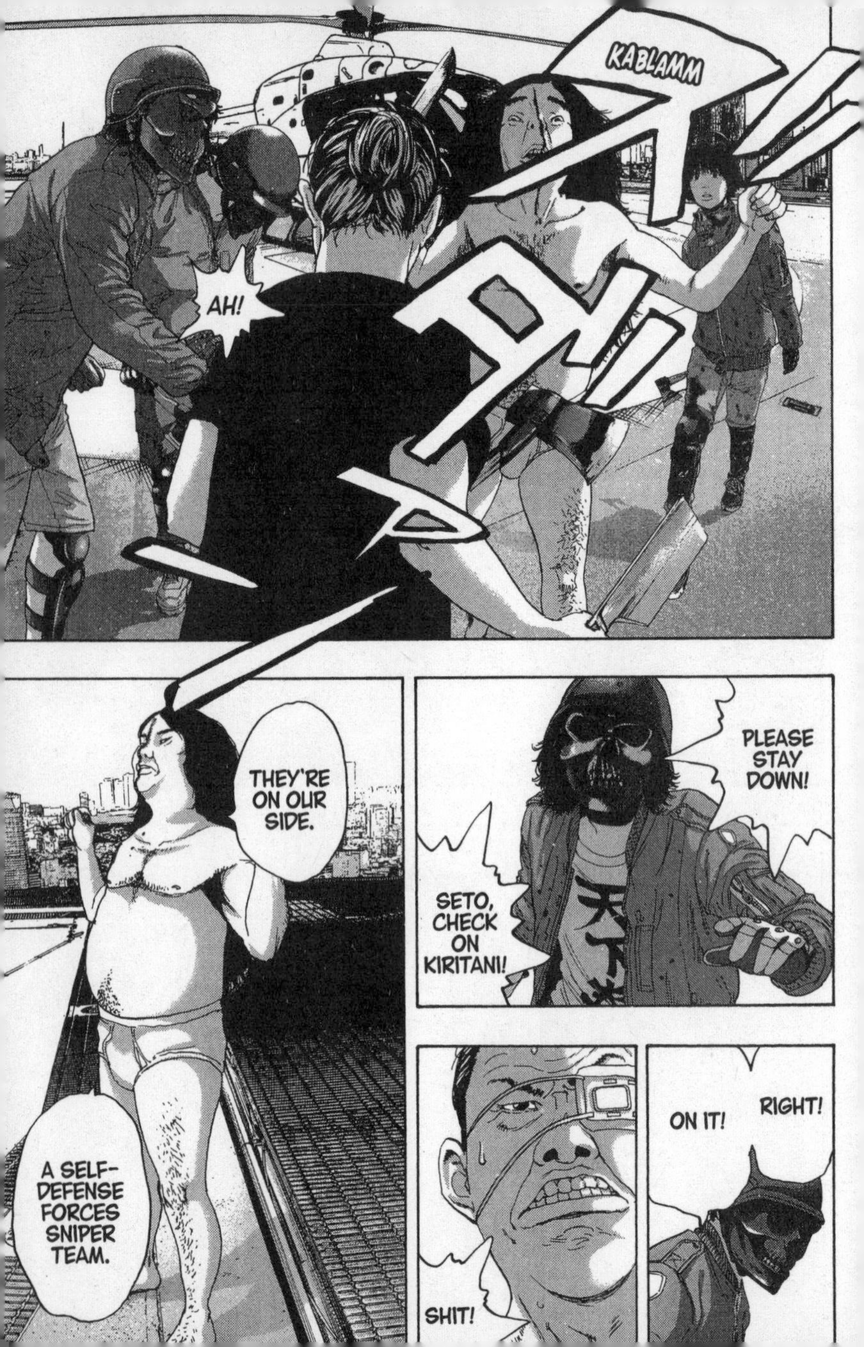
KABLAMM
AH!
PLEASE STAY DOWN!
SETO, CHECK ON KIRITANI!
RIGHT!
ON IT!
SHIT!
THEY'RE ON OUR SIDE.
A SELF-DEFENSE FORCES SNIPER TEAM.

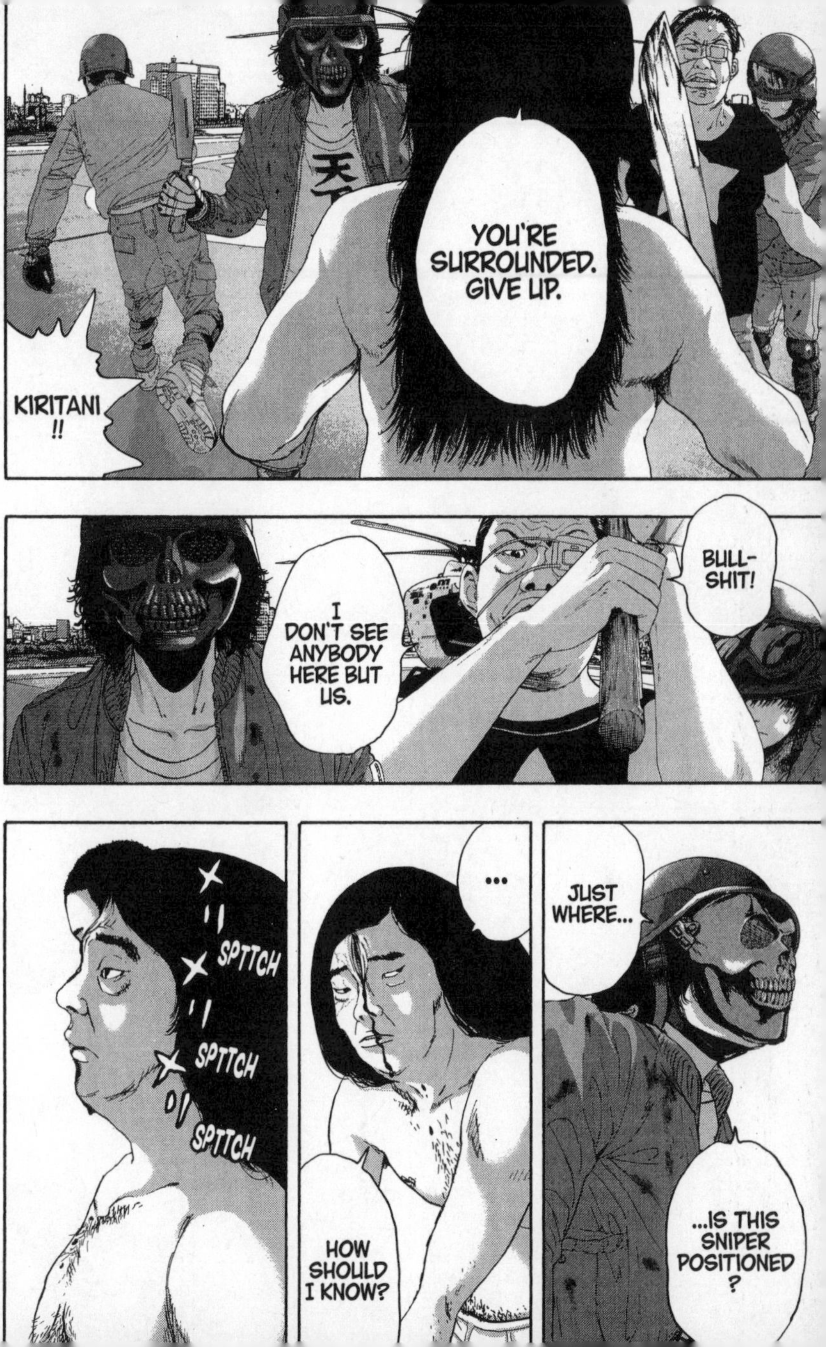
YOU'RE SURROUNDED. GIVE UP.
KIRITANI !!
BULL-SHIT!
I DON'T SEE ANYBODY HERE BUT US.
JUST WHERE...
...IS THIS SNIPER POSITIONED ?
...
HOW SHOULD I KNOW?
SPTTCH
SPTTCH
SPTTCH

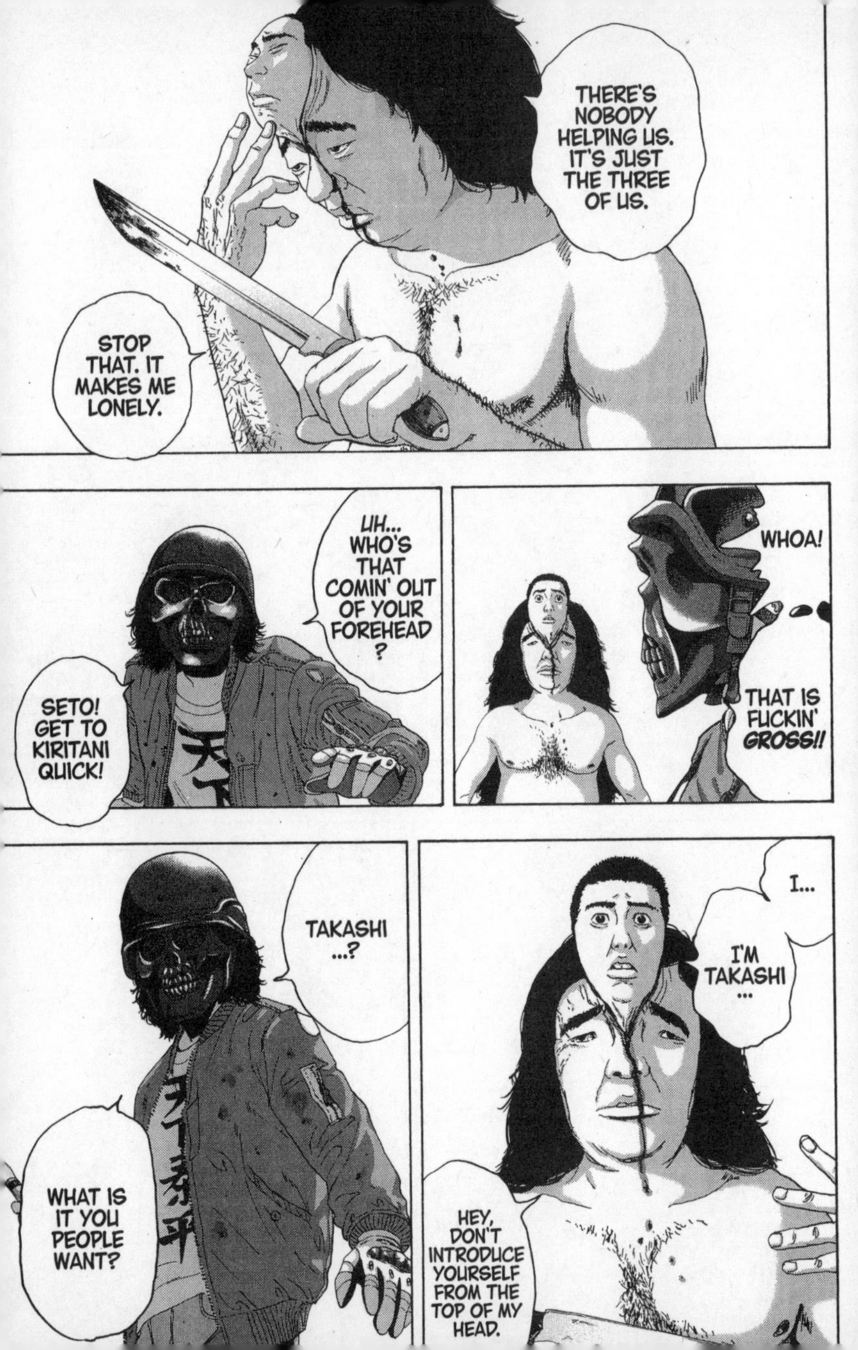
THERE'S NOBODY HELPING US. IT'S JUST THE THREE OF US.
STOP THAT. IT MAKES ME LONELY.
WHOA!
THAT IS FUCKIN' GROSS!!
UH... WHO'S THAT COMIN' OUT OF YOUR FOREHEAD ?
SETO! GET TO KIRITANI QUICK!
I...
I'M TAKASHI ...
HEY, DON'T INTRODUCE YOURSELF FROM THE TOP OF MY HEAD.
TAKASHI ...?
WHAT IS IT YOU PEOPLE WANT?

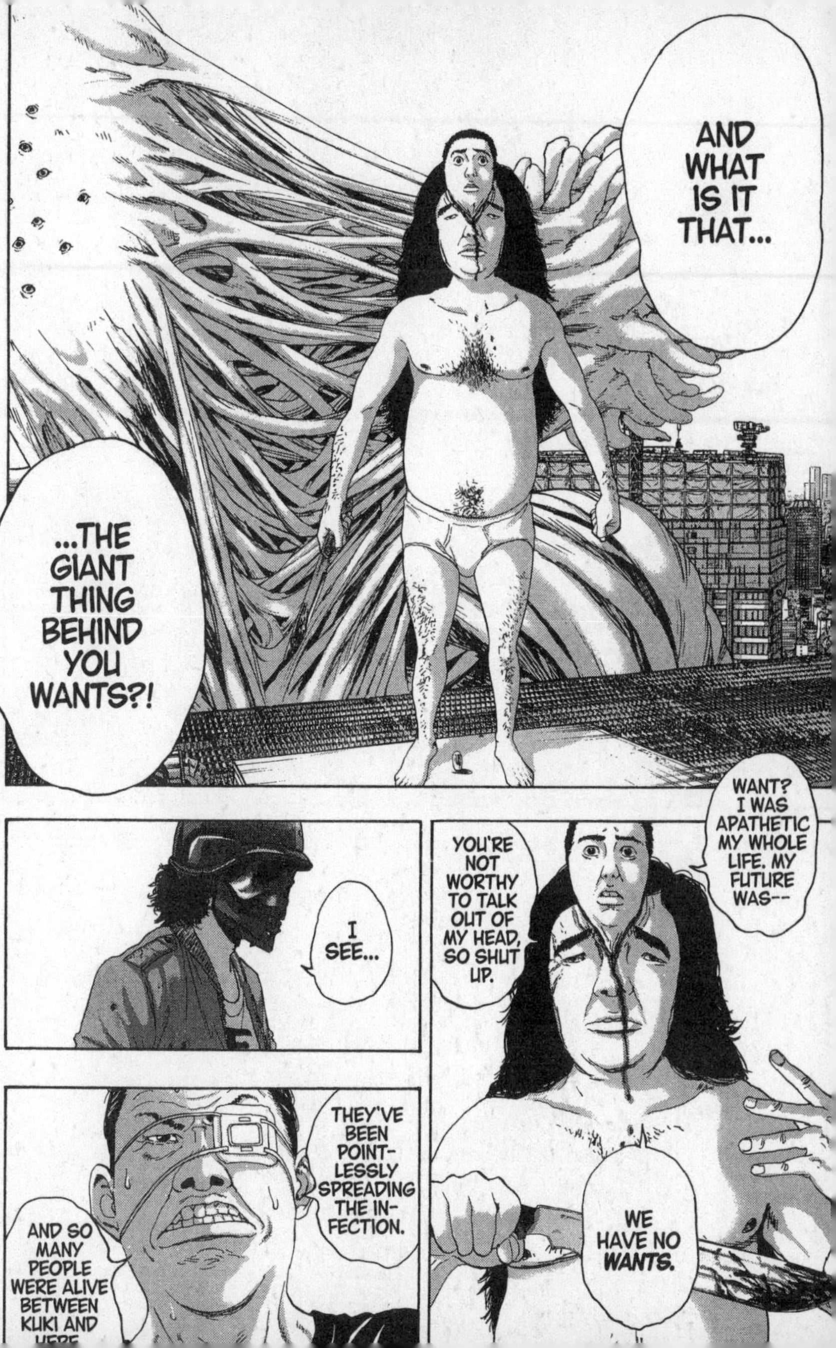
AND WHAT IS IT THAT...
...THE GIANT THING BEHIND YOU WANTS?!
WANT? I WAS APATHETIC MY WHOLE LIFE. MY FUTURE WAS--
YOU'RE NOT WORTHY TO TALK OUT OF MY HEAD, SO SHUT UP.
WE HAVE NO *WANTS.*
I SEE...
THEY'VE BEEN POINT-LESSLY SPREADING THE IN-FECTION.
AND SO MANY PEOPLE WERE ALIVE BETWEEN KUKI AND

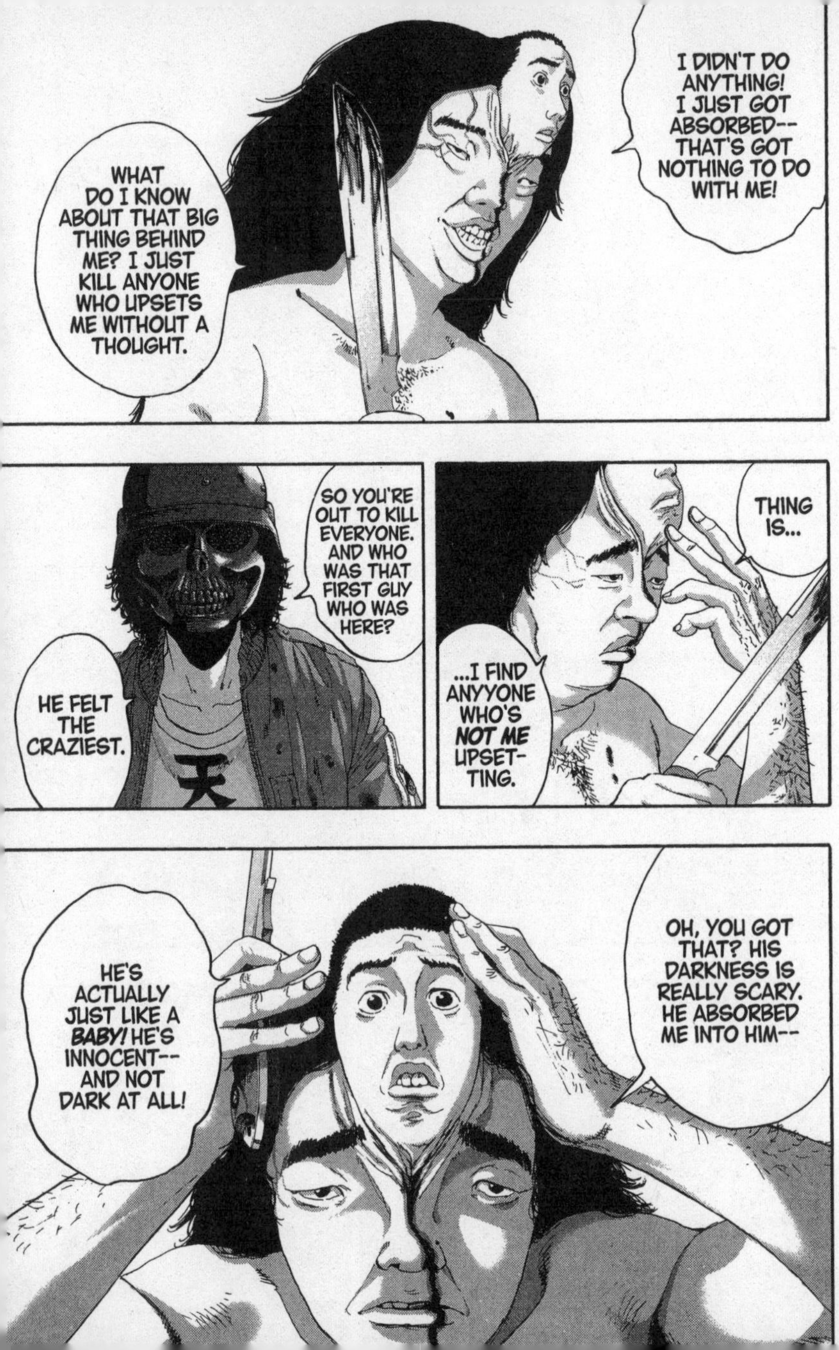
I DIDN'T DO ANYTHING! I JUST GOT ABSORBED-- THAT'S GOT NOTHING TO DO WITH ME!
WHAT DO I KNOW ABOUT THAT BIG THING BEHIND ME? I JUST KILL ANYONE WHO UPSETS ME WITHOUT A THOUGHT.
THING IS...
...I FIND ANYYONE WHO'S ***NOT ME*** UPSET-TING.
SO YOU'RE OUT TO KILL EVERYONE. AND WHO WAS THAT FIRST GUY WHO WAS HERE?
HE FELT THE CRAZIEST.
天
OH, YOU GOT THAT? HIS DARKNESS IS REALLY SCARY. HE ABSORBED ME INTO HIM--
HE'S ACTUALLY JUST LIKE A ***BABY!*** HE'S INNOCENT-- AND NOT DARK AT ALL!

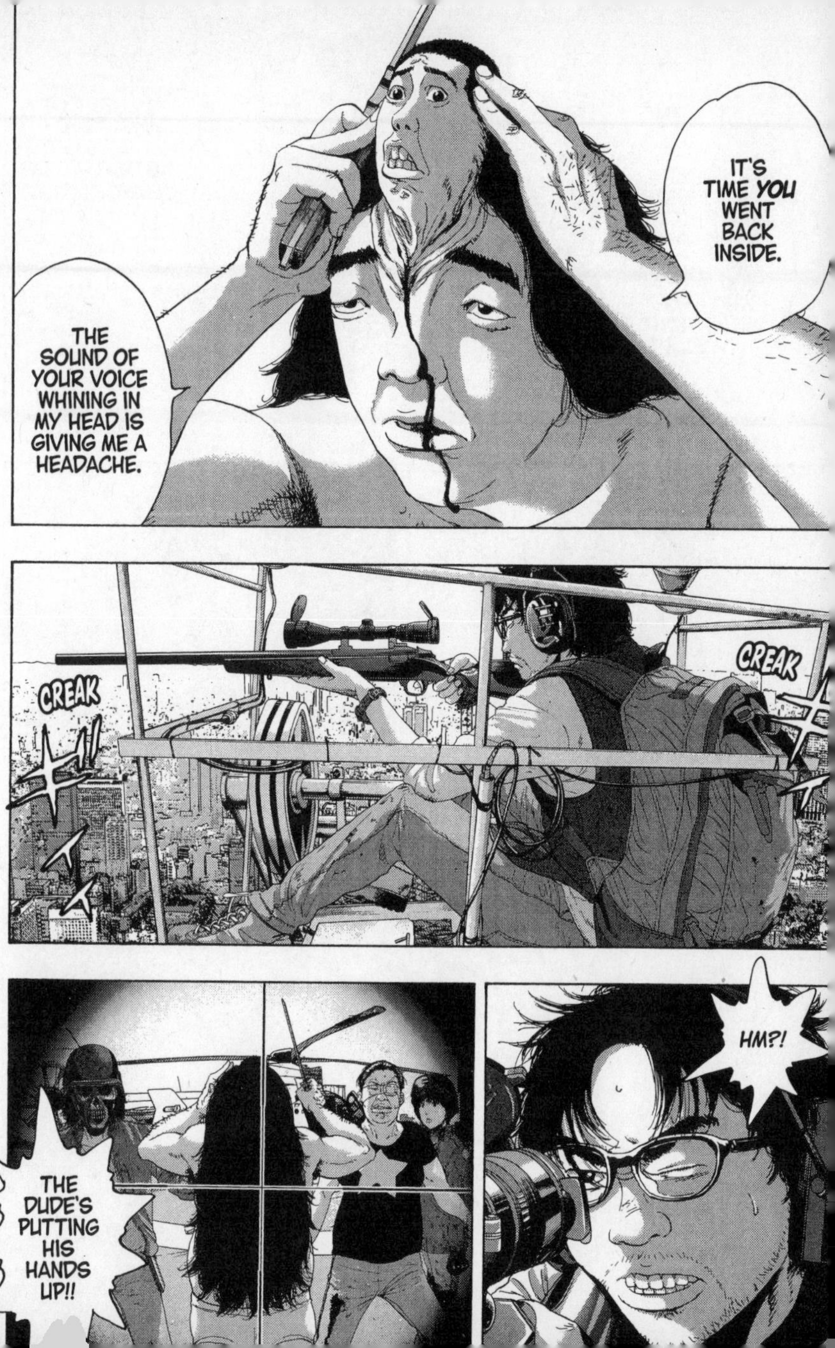
IT'S TIME YOU WENT BACK INSIDE.
THE SOUND OF YOUR VOICE WHINING IN MY HEAD IS GIVING ME A HEADACHE.
CREAK
CREAK
HM?!
THE DUDE'S PUTTING HIS HANDS UP!!

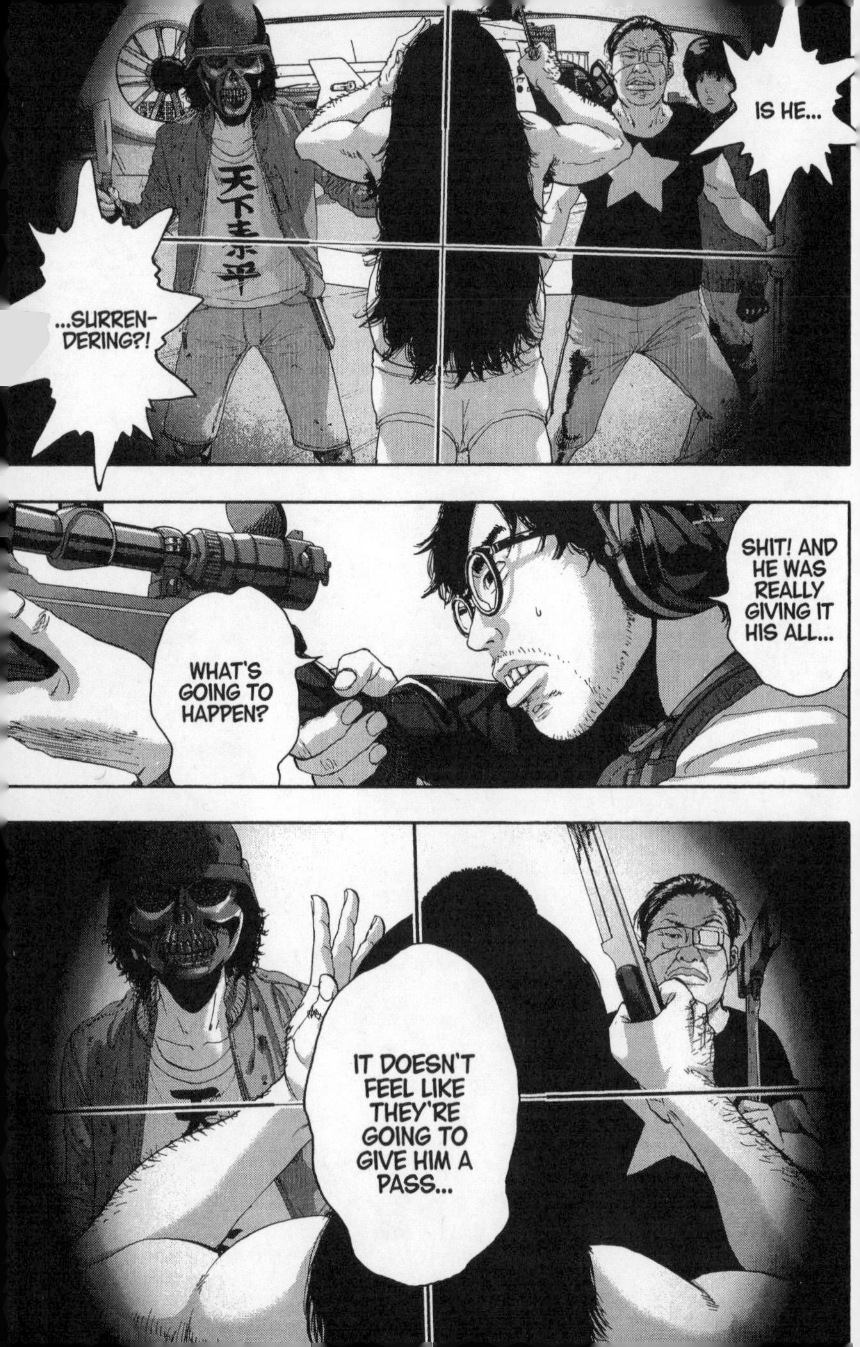
IS HE...
...SURREN-DERING?!
SHIT! AND HE WAS REALLY GIVING IT HIS ALL...
WHAT'S GOING TO HAPPEN?
IT DOESN'T FEEL LIKE THEY'RE GOING TO GIVE HIM A PASS...

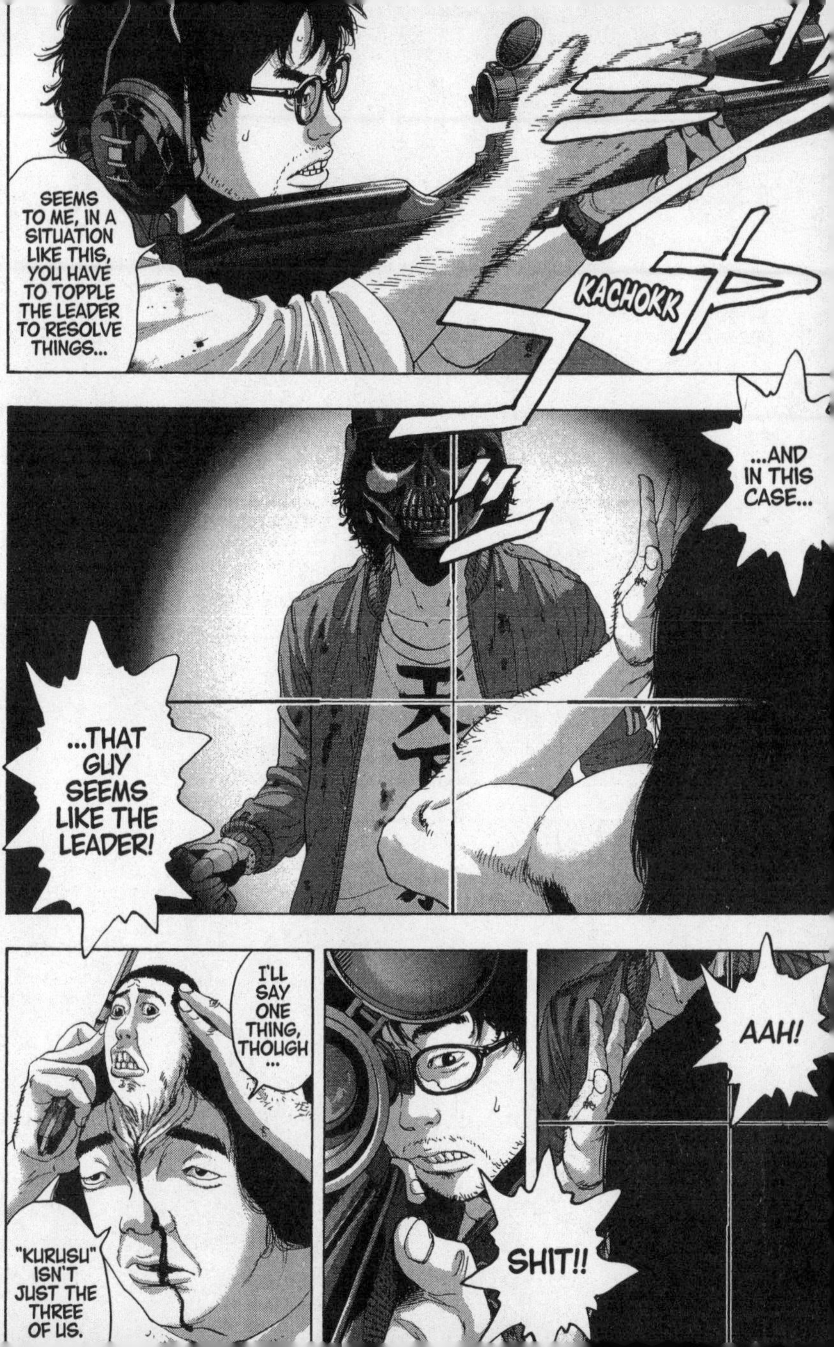
SEEMS TO ME, IN A SITUATION LIKE THIS, YOU HAVE TO TOPPLE THE LEADER TO RESOLVE THINGS...
KACHOKK
...AND IN THIS CASE...
...THAT GUY SEEMS LIKE THE LEADER!
AAH!
SHIT!!
I'LL SAY ONE THING, THOUGH...
"KURUSU" ISN'T JUST THE THREE OF US.

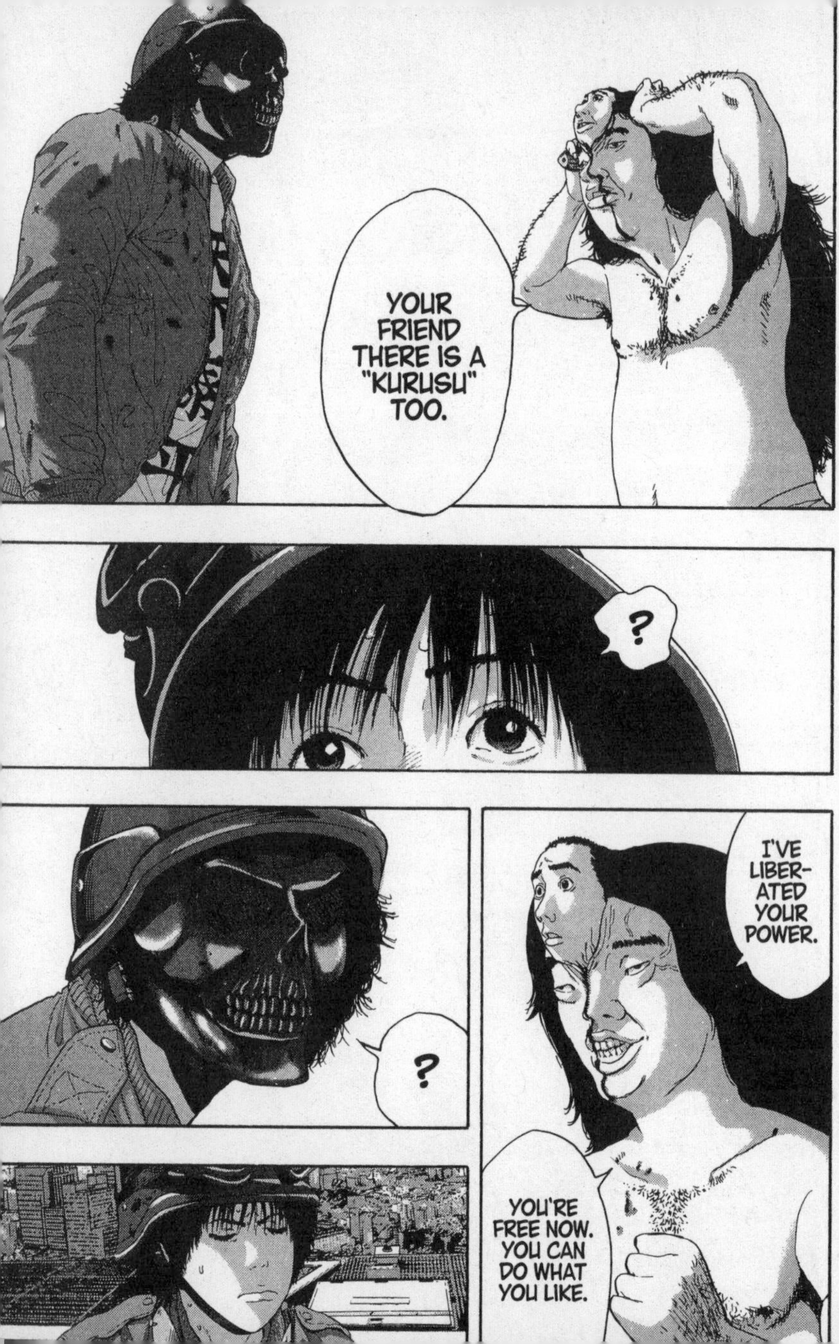
YOUR FRIEND THERE IS A "KURUSU" TOO.
?
I'VE LIBER-ATED YOUR POWER.
YOU'RE FREE NOW. YOU CAN DO WHAT YOU LIKE.
?

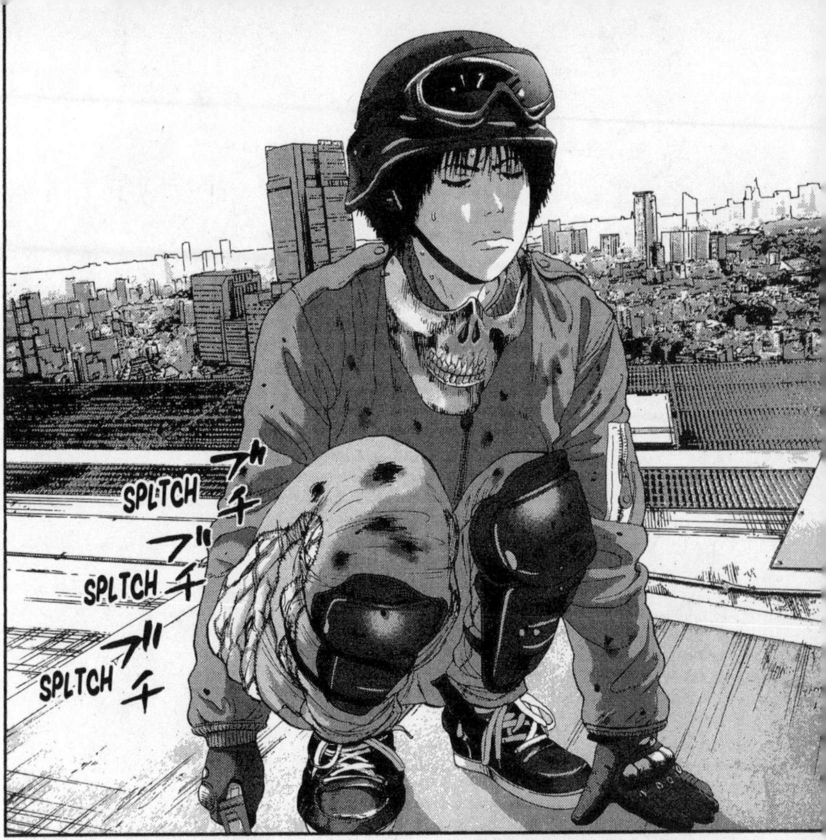
ブチ
SPLTCH
ブチ
SPLTCH
ブチ
SPLTCH

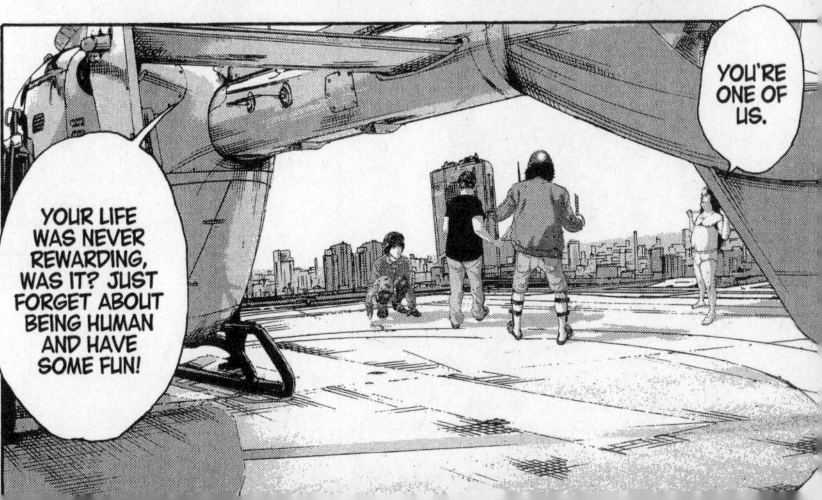
YOU'RE ONE OF US.
YOUR LIFE WAS NEVER REWARDING, WAS IT? JUST FORGET ABOUT BEING HUMAN AND HAVE SOME FUN!

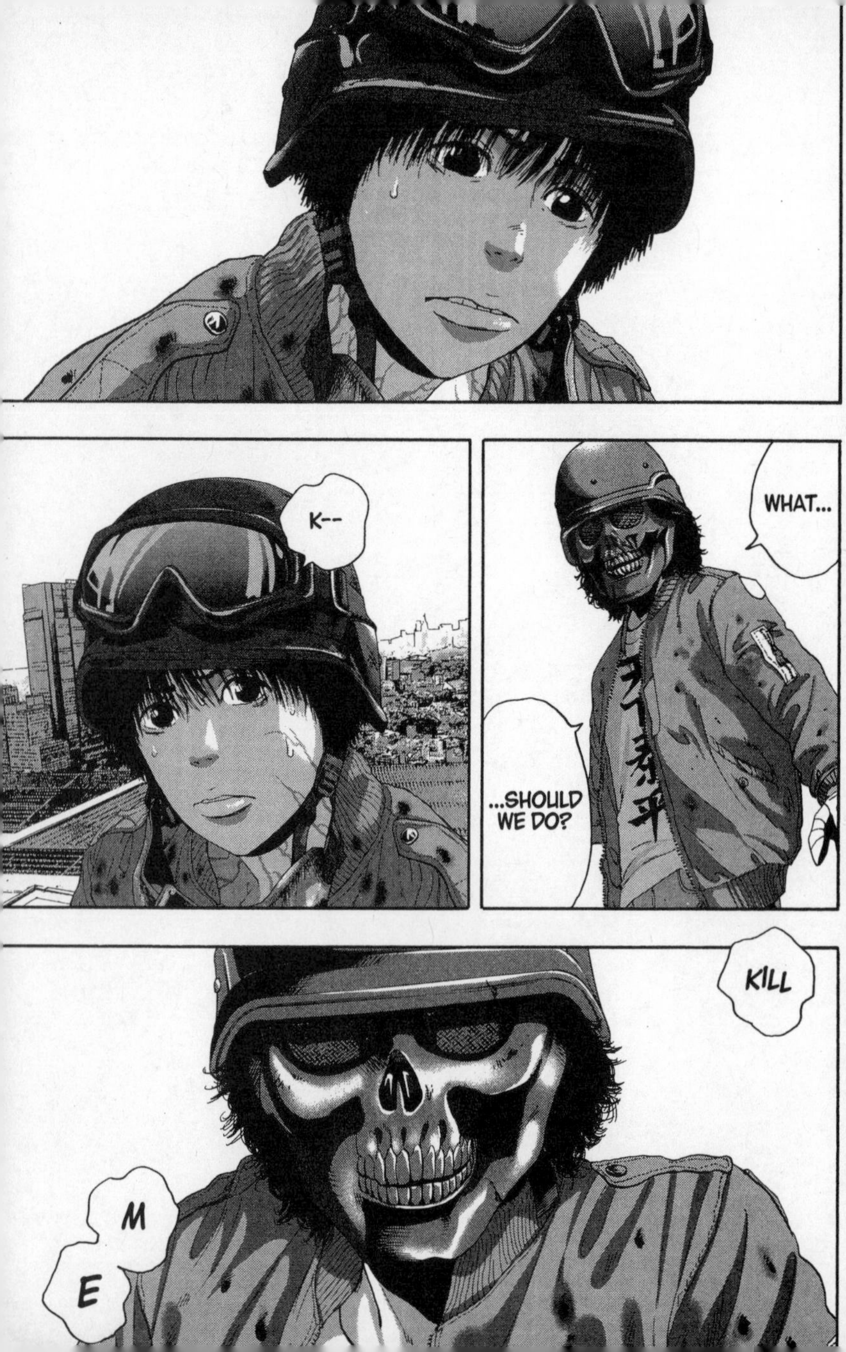
WHAT...
...SHOULD WE DO?
K--
KILL
M
E

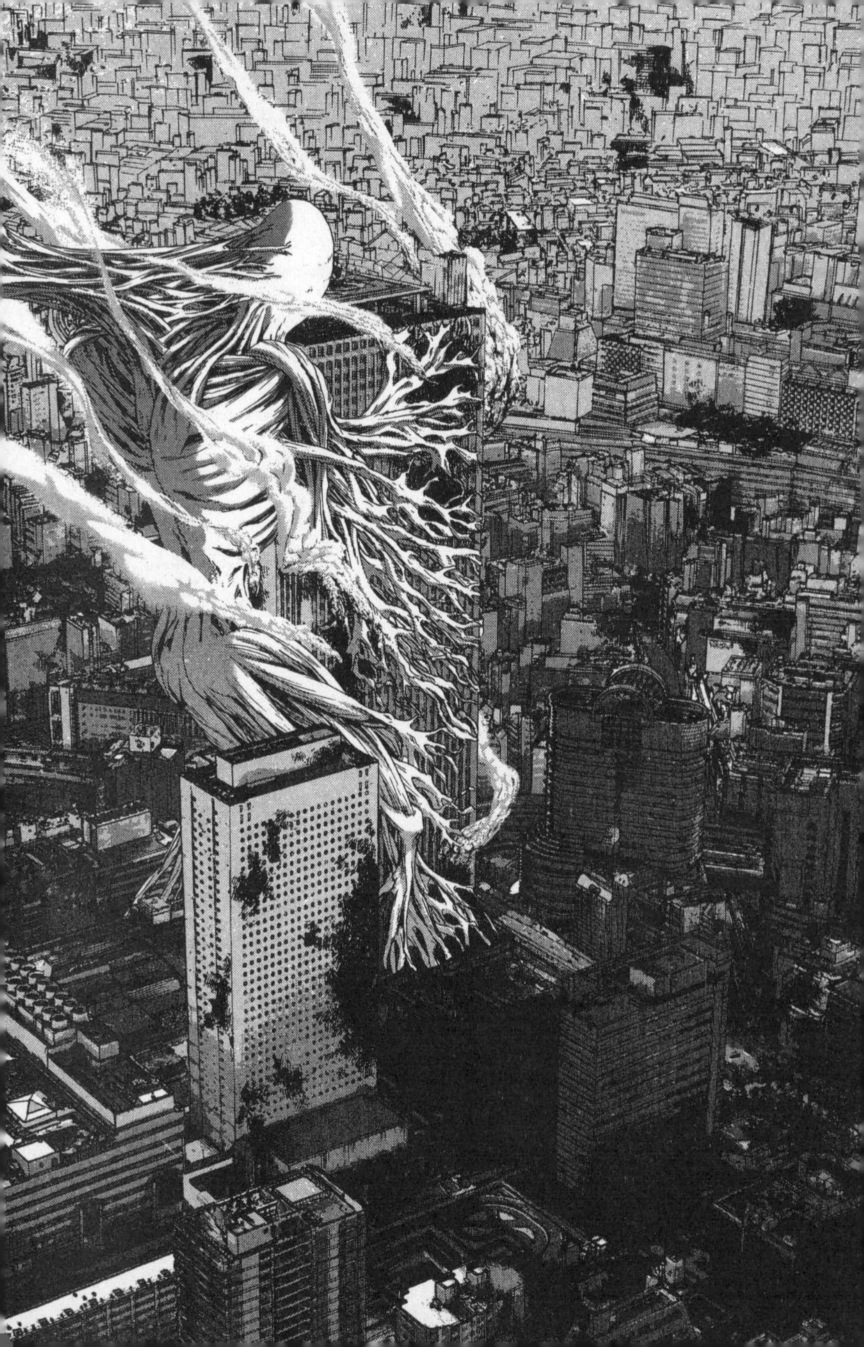

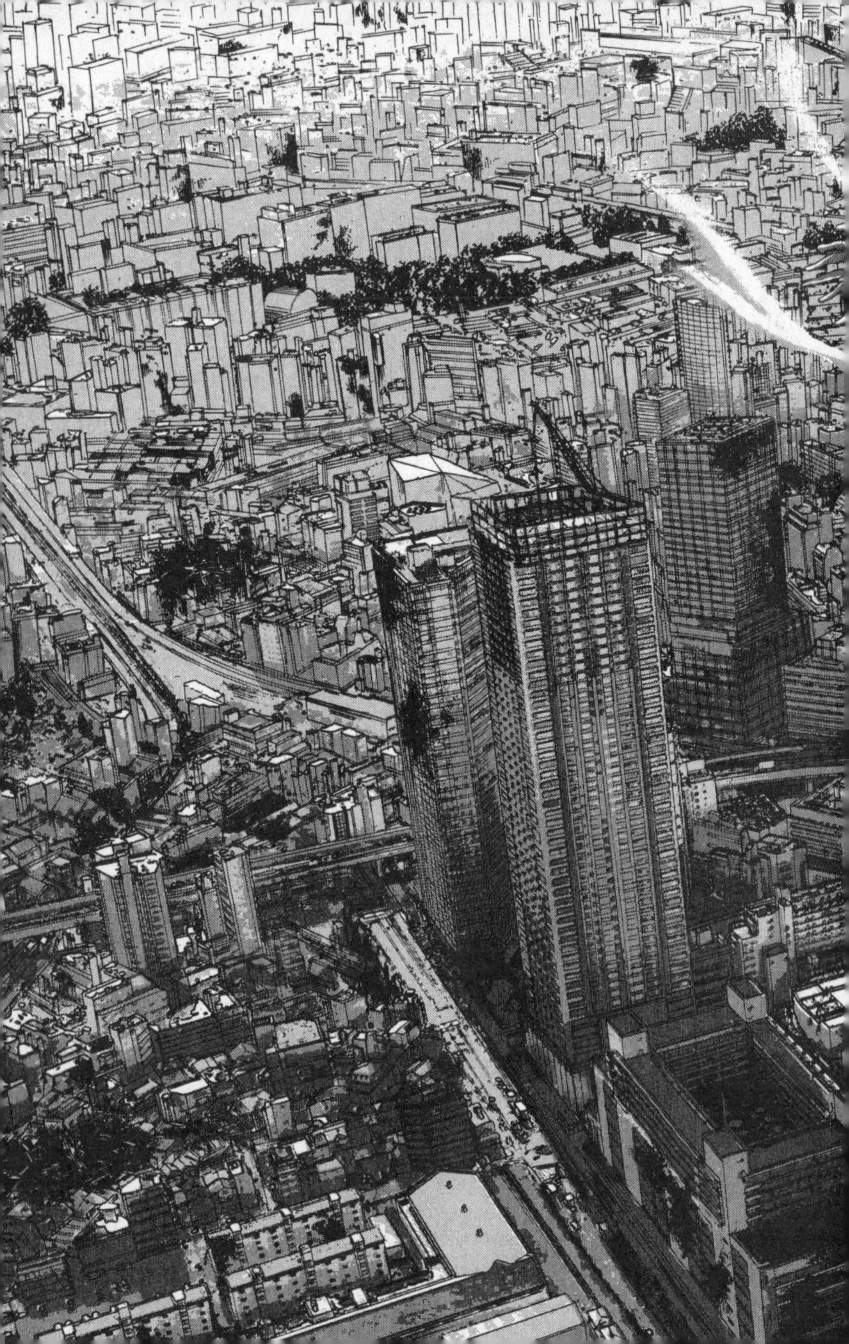

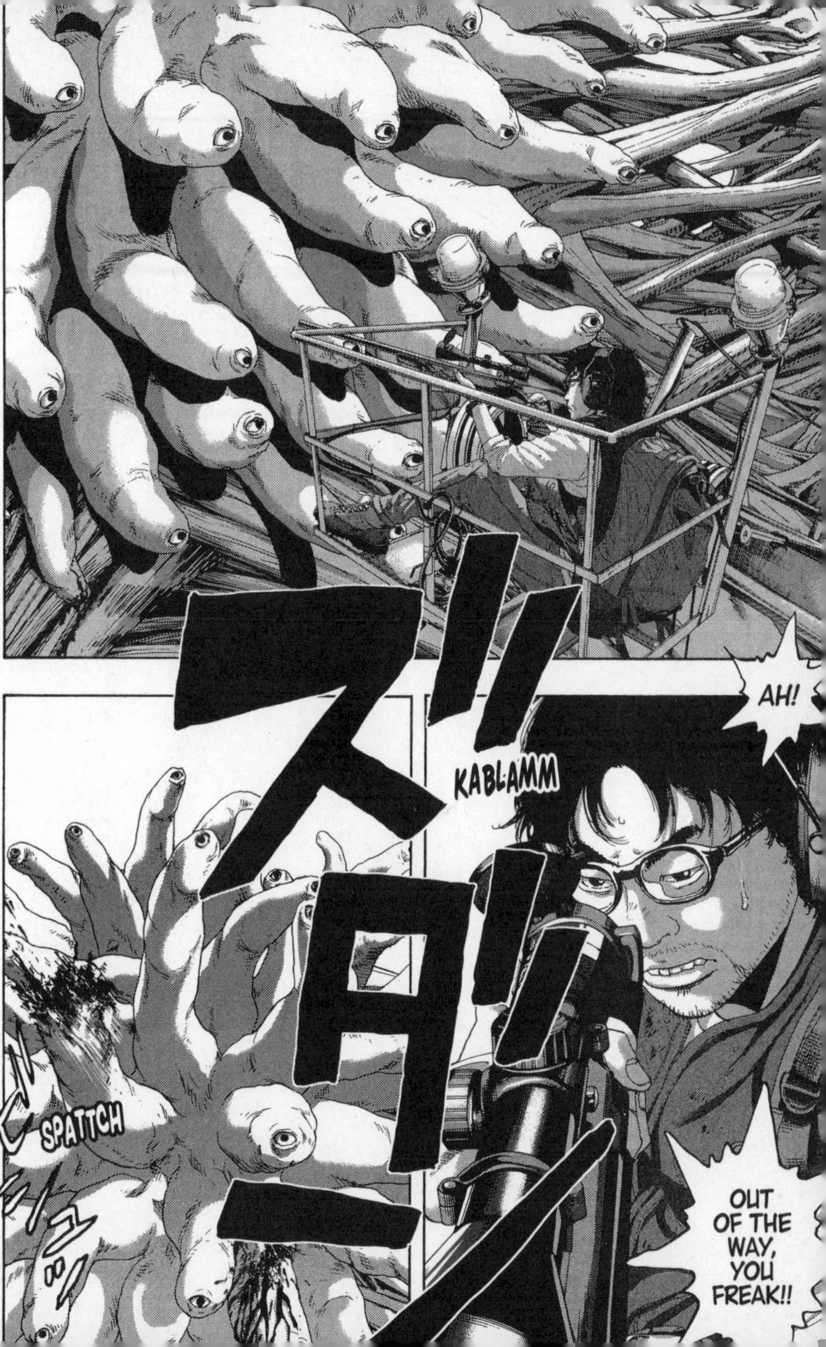
AH!
ズダーン
KABLAMM
OUT OF THE WAY, YOU FREAK!!
SPATTCH

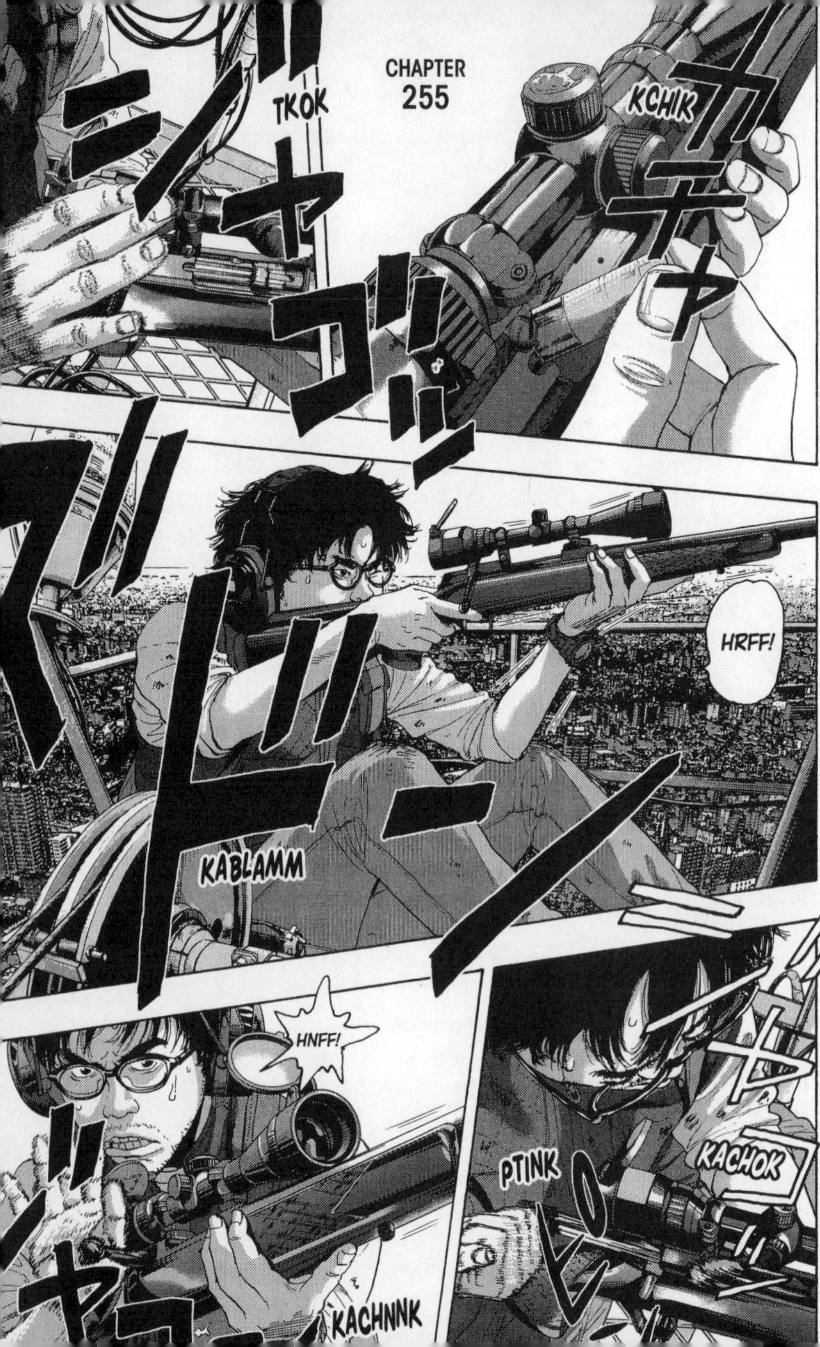
CHAPTER
255
KCHIK
TKOK
HRFF!
KABLAMM
KACHOK
PTINK
HNFF!
KACHNNK

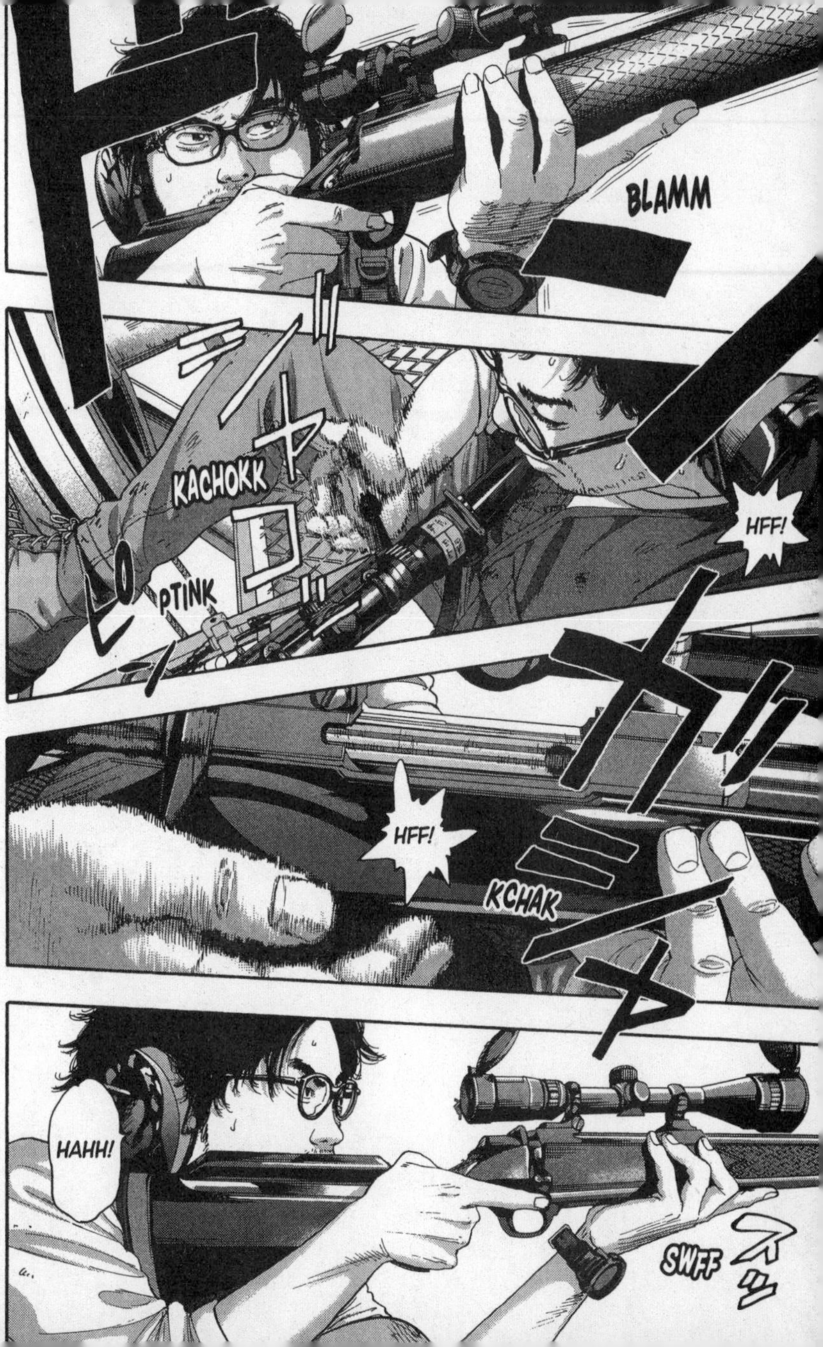
BLAMM
HFF!
KACHOKK
PTINK
HFF!
KCHAK
SWFF
HAHH!

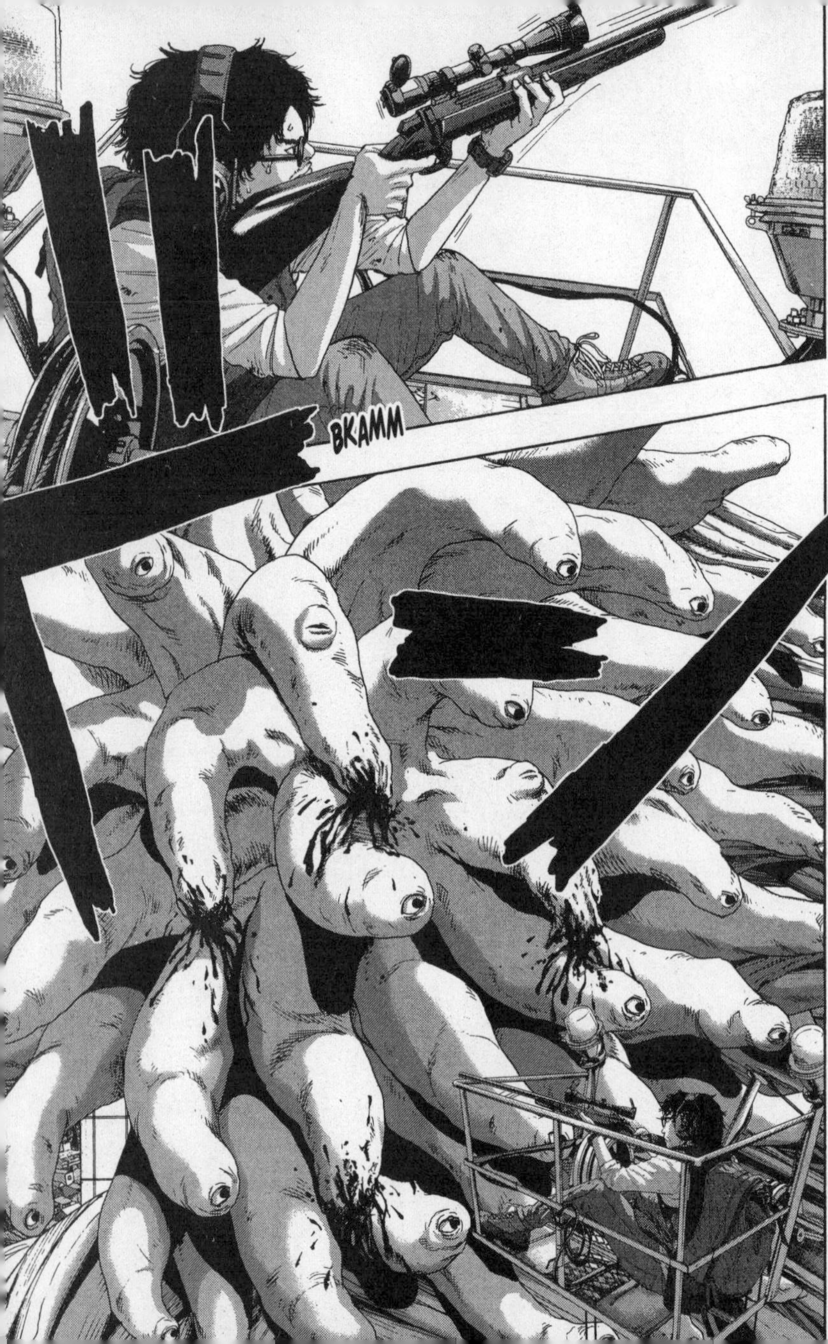
BKAMM

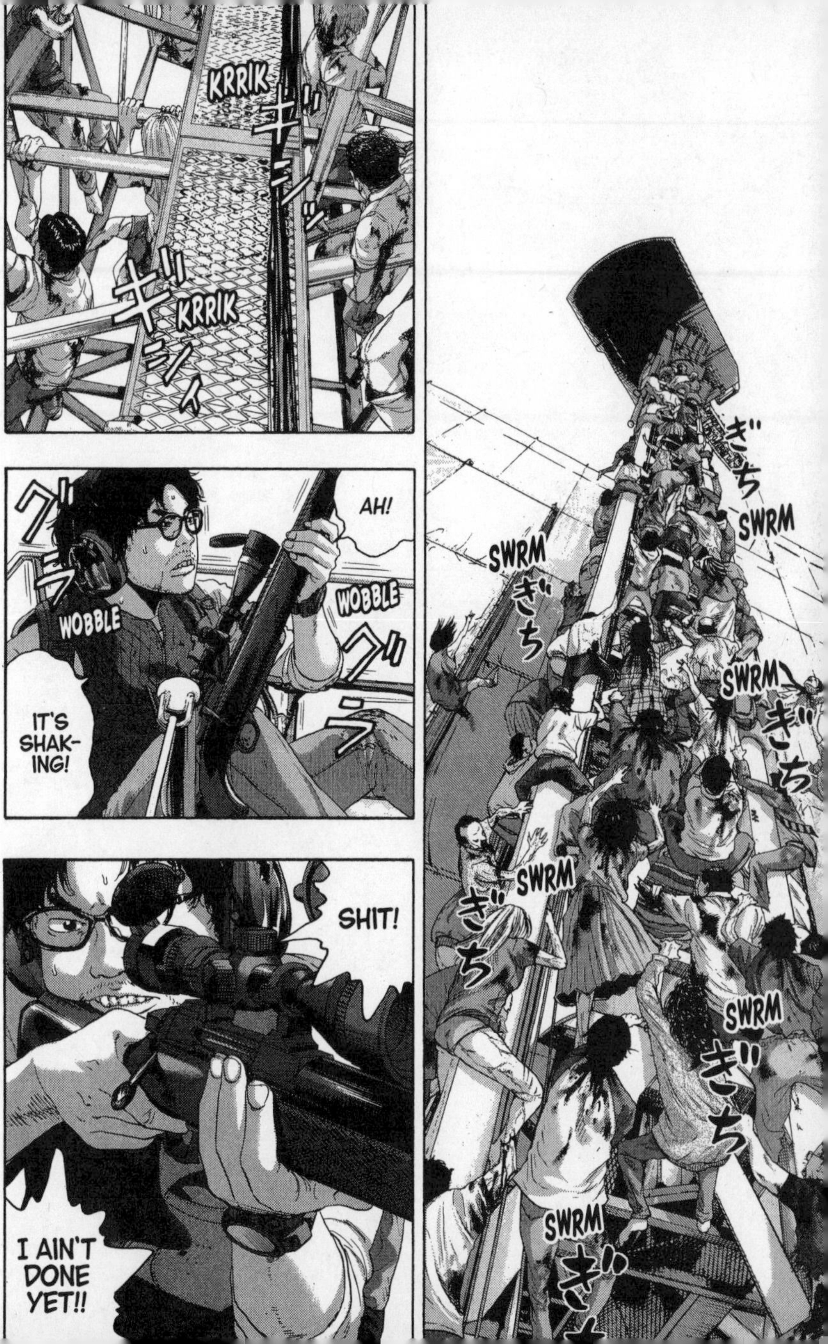
ぎち
SWRM
SWRM
ぎち
SWRM
ぎち
SWRM
ぎち
SWRM
ぎち
SWRM
ぎ
KRRIK
ギシッ
ギシィ
KRRIK
AH!
WOBBLE
グラ
グラ
WOBBLE
IT'S SHAK-ING!
SHIT!
I AIN'T DONE YET!!

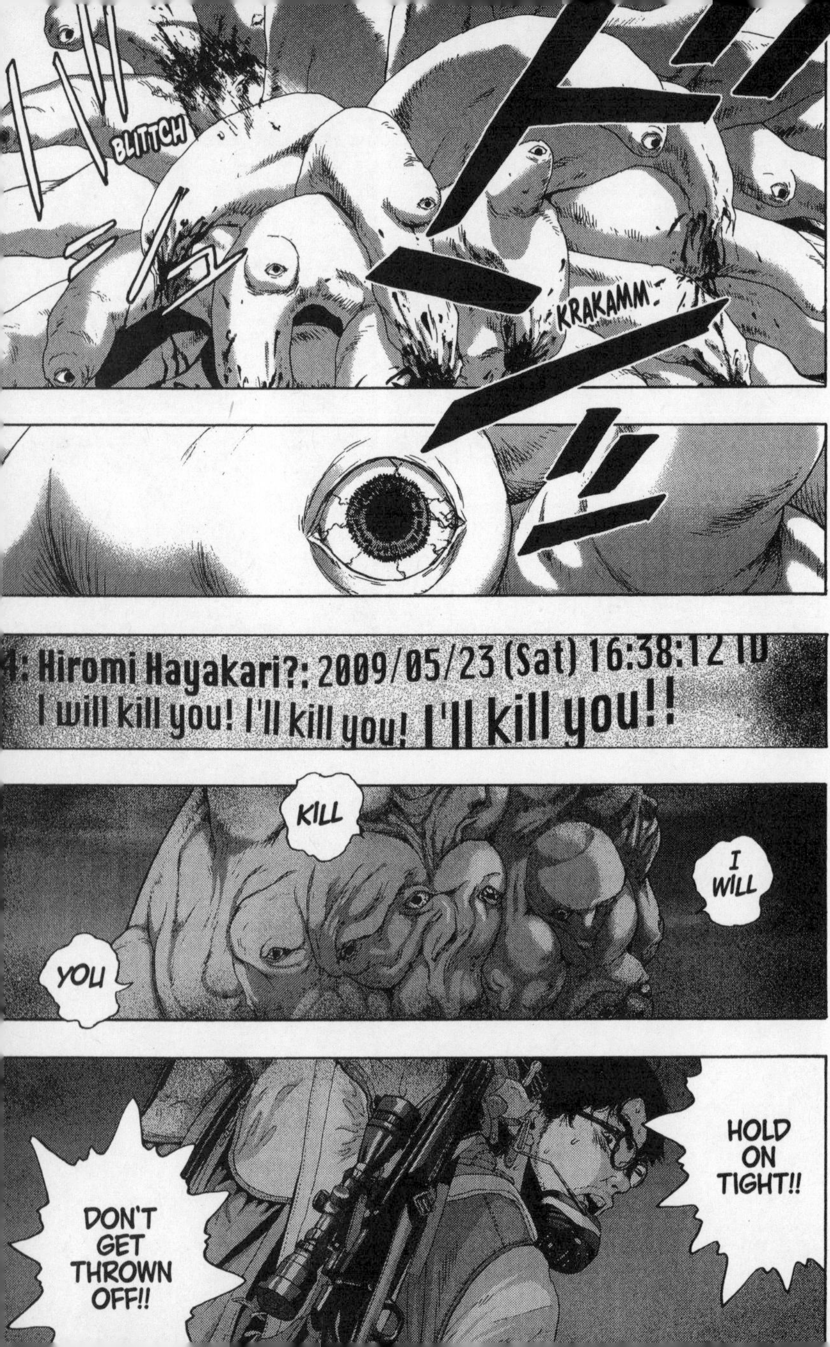
KRAKAMM
BLITTCH
4: Hiromi Hayakari?: 2009/05/23 (Sat) 16:38:12 ID
I will kill you! I'll kill you! I'll kill you!!
I WILL
KILL
YOU
HOLD ON TIGHT!!
DON'T GET THROWN OFF!!

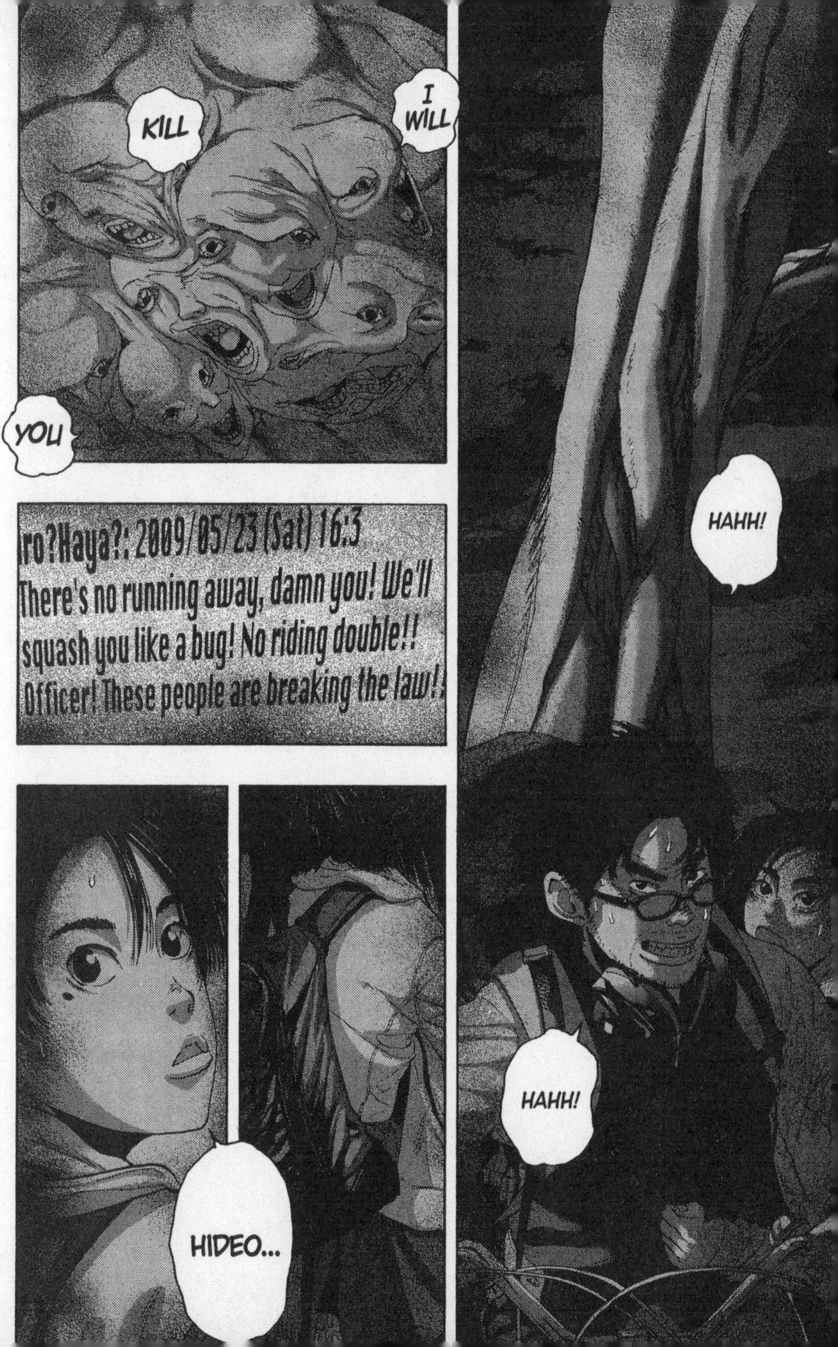
HAHH!
HAHH!
I WILL
KILL
YOU
ro?Haya?: 2009/05/23 (Sat) 16:3
There's no running away, damn you! We'll squash you like a bug! No riding double!!
Officer! These people are breaking the law!!
HIDEO...

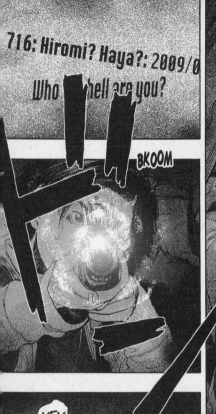

716: Hiromi? Haya?: 2009/0

Who **[the]** hell are you?

BKOOM

...WE WILL LIVE... TOGETHER.

HEY

THAT

HURTS

UGD

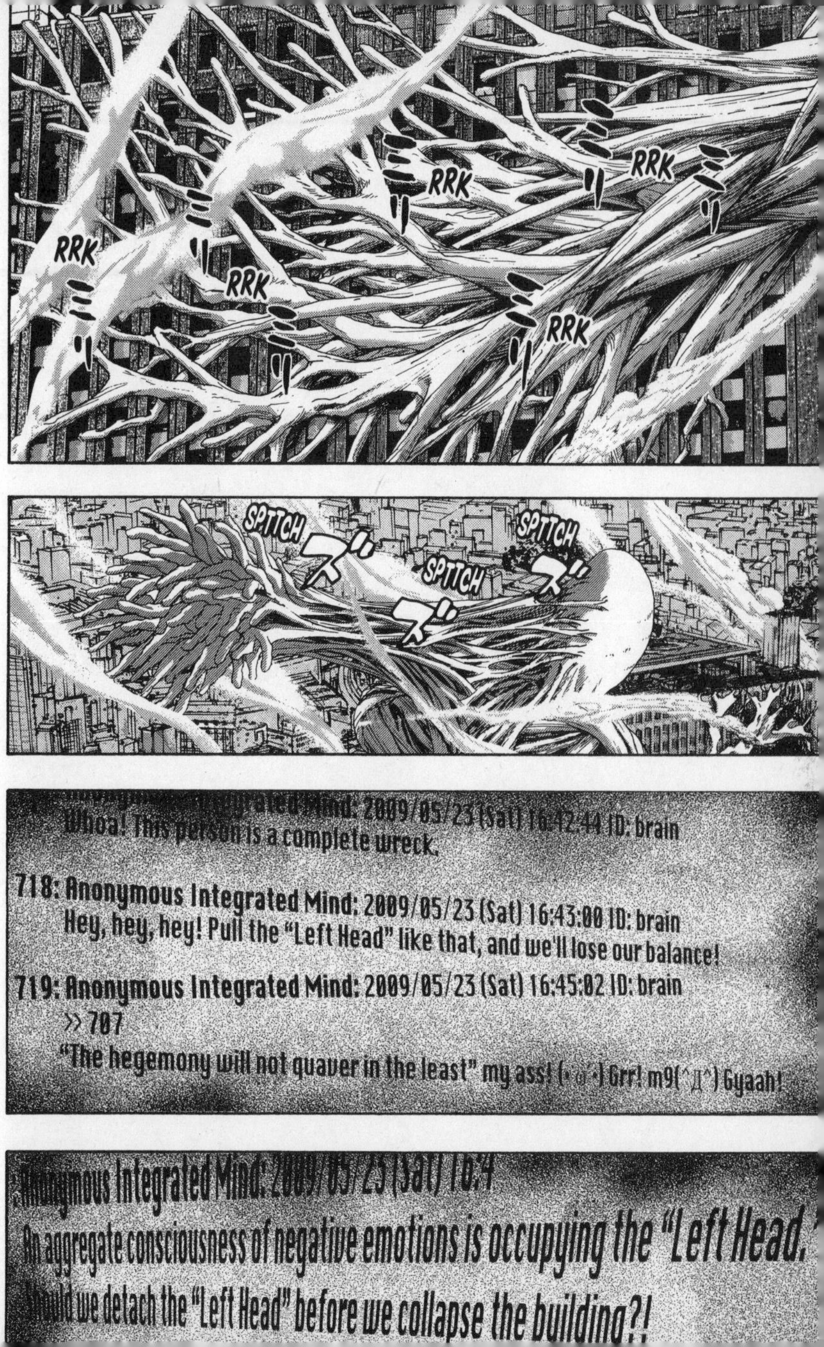
RRK
RRK
RRK
RRK
RRK
SPTTCH
SPTTCH
SPTTCH
Anonymous Integrated Mind: 2009/05/23 (Sat) 16:42:44 ID: brain
Whoa! This person is a complete wreck.
718: Anonymous Integrated Mind: 2009/05/23 (Sat) 16:43:00 ID: brain
Hey, hey, hey! Pull the "Left Head" like that, and we'll lose our balance!
719: Anonymous Integrated Mind: 2009/05/23 (Sat) 16:45:02 ID: brain
>> 707
"The hegemony will not quaver in the least" my ass! (･ω･) Grr! m9(^Д^) Gyaah!
Anonymous Integrated Mind: 2009/05/23 (Sat) 16:4
An aggregate consciousness of negative emotions is occupying the "Left Head."
Should we detach the "Left Head" before we collapse the building?!

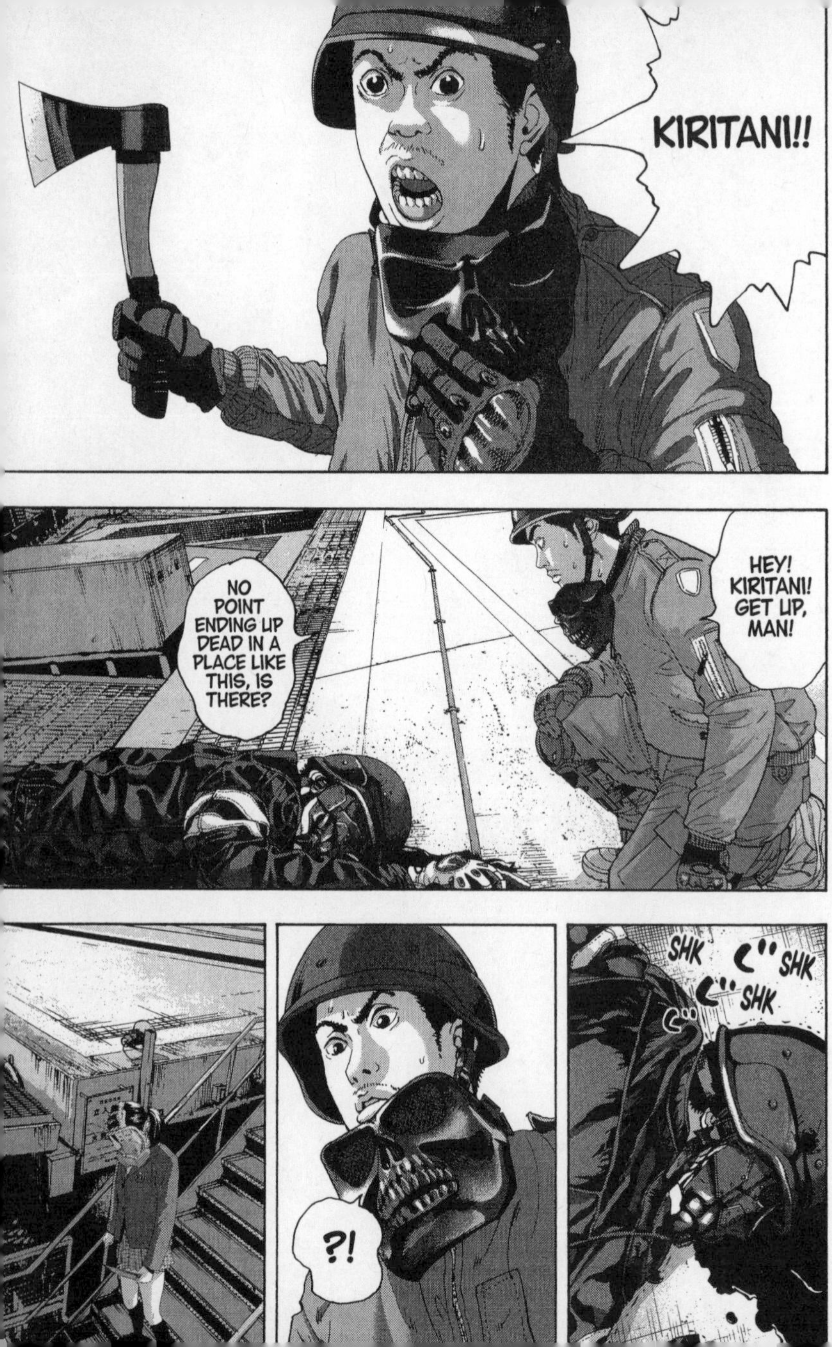
KIRITANI!!
HEY! KIRITANI! GET UP, MAN!
NO POINT ENDING UP DEAD IN A PLACE LIKE THIS, IS THERE?
SHK
SHK
SHK
?!

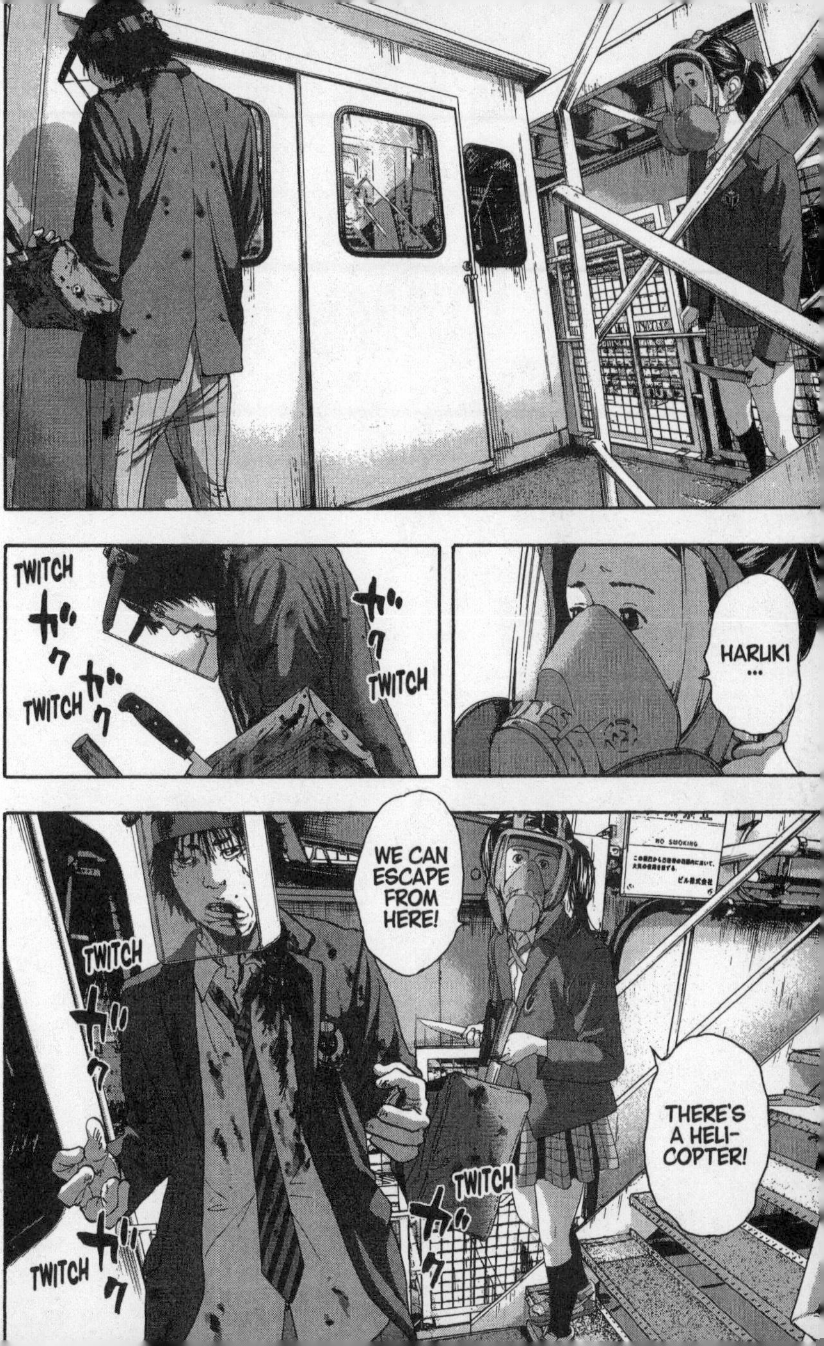
HARUKI ...
TWITCH
ガク
ガク
TWITCH
TWITCH
ガク
NO SMOKING
WE CAN ESCAPE FROM HERE!
THERE'S A HELI-COPTER!
TWITCH
ガク
TWITCH
ガク
TWITCH
ガク

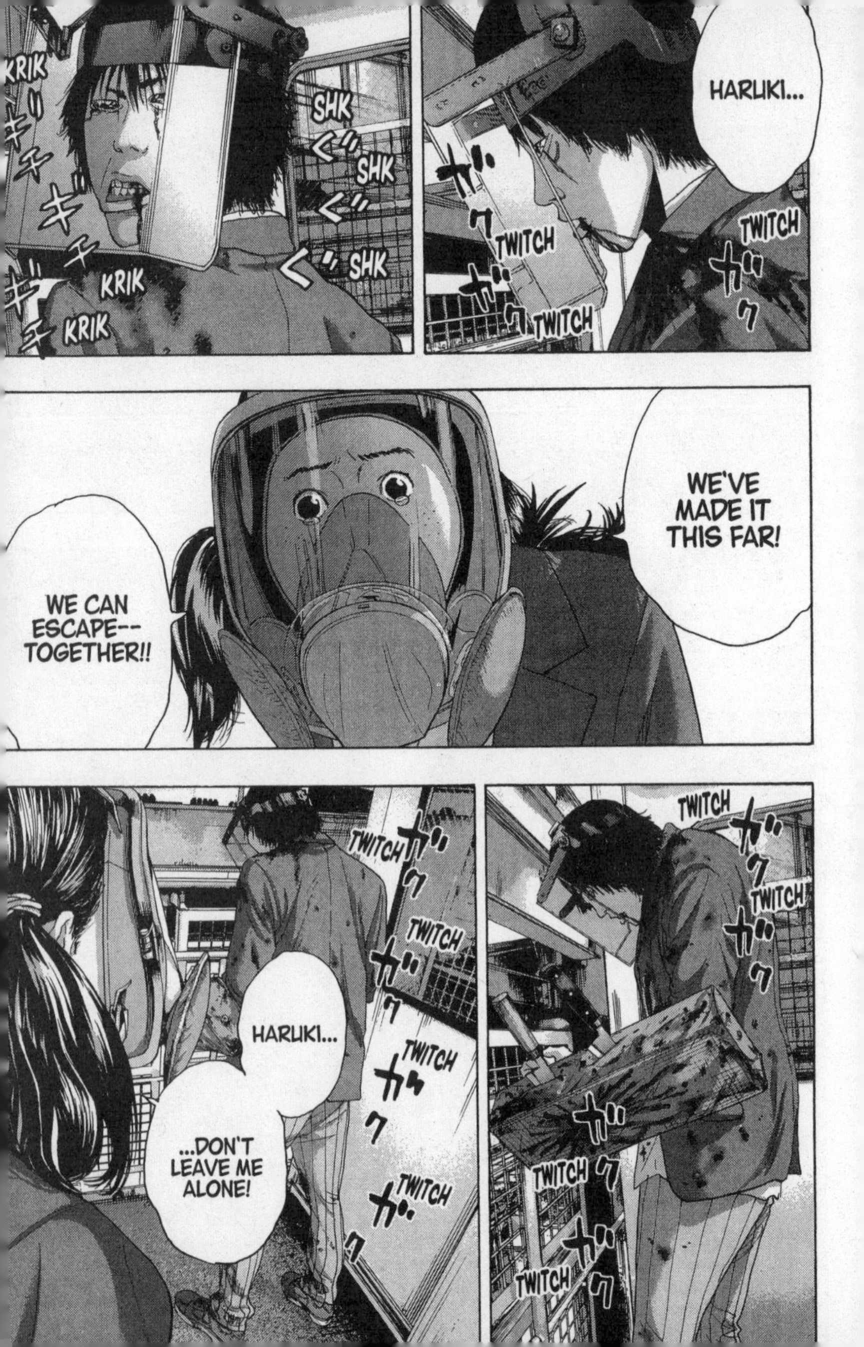
HARUKI...
TWITCH
TWITCH
TWITCH
KRIK
SHK
SHK
SHK
KRIK
KRIK
WE'VE MADE IT THIS FAR!
WE CAN ESCAPE-- TOGETHER!!
TWITCH
TWITCH
TWITCH
TWITCH
TWITCH
TWITCH
TWITCH
TWITCH
HARUKI...
...DON'T LEAVE ME ALONE!

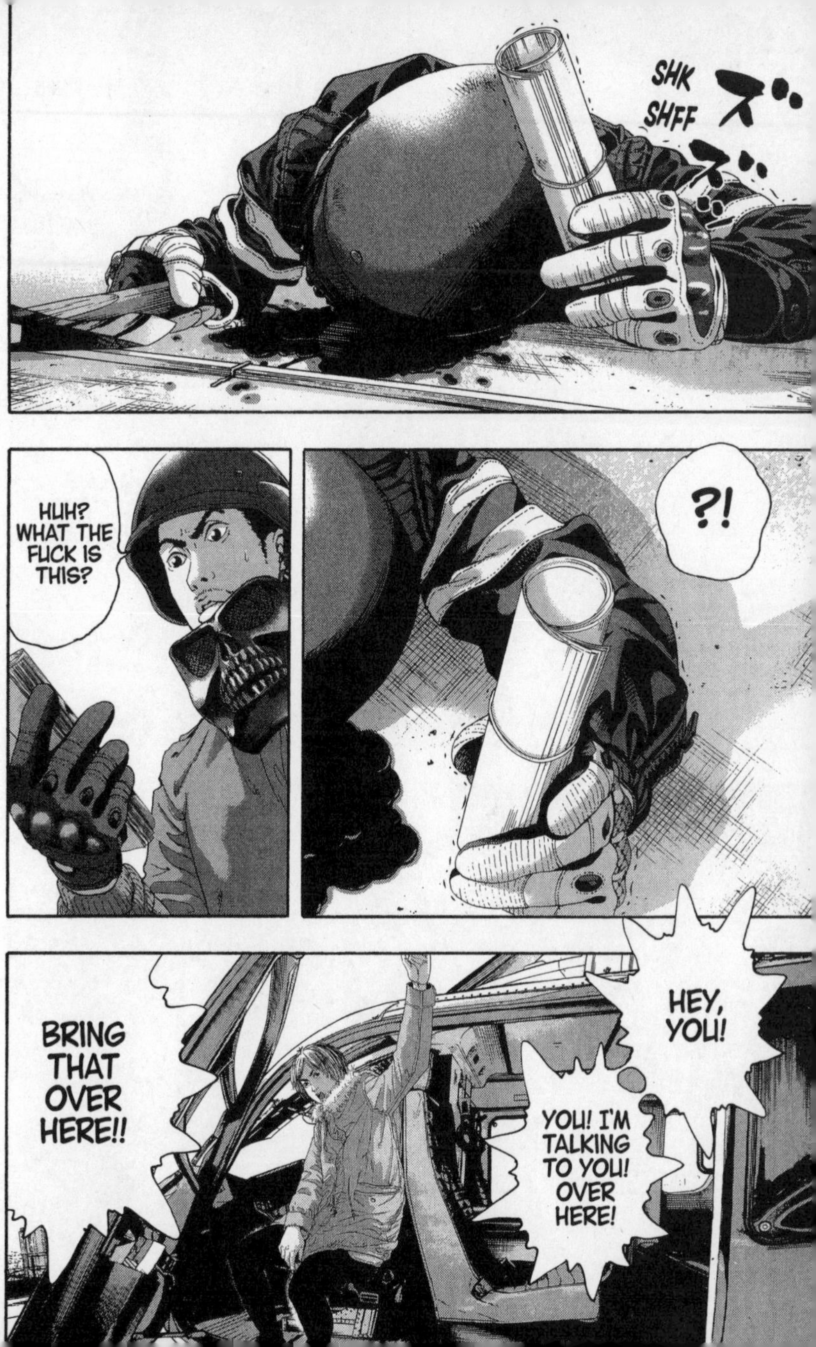
SHK
SHFF
?!
HUH? WHAT THE FUCK IS THIS?
HEY, YOU!
YOU! I'M TALKING TO YOU! OVER HERE!
BRING THAT OVER HERE!!

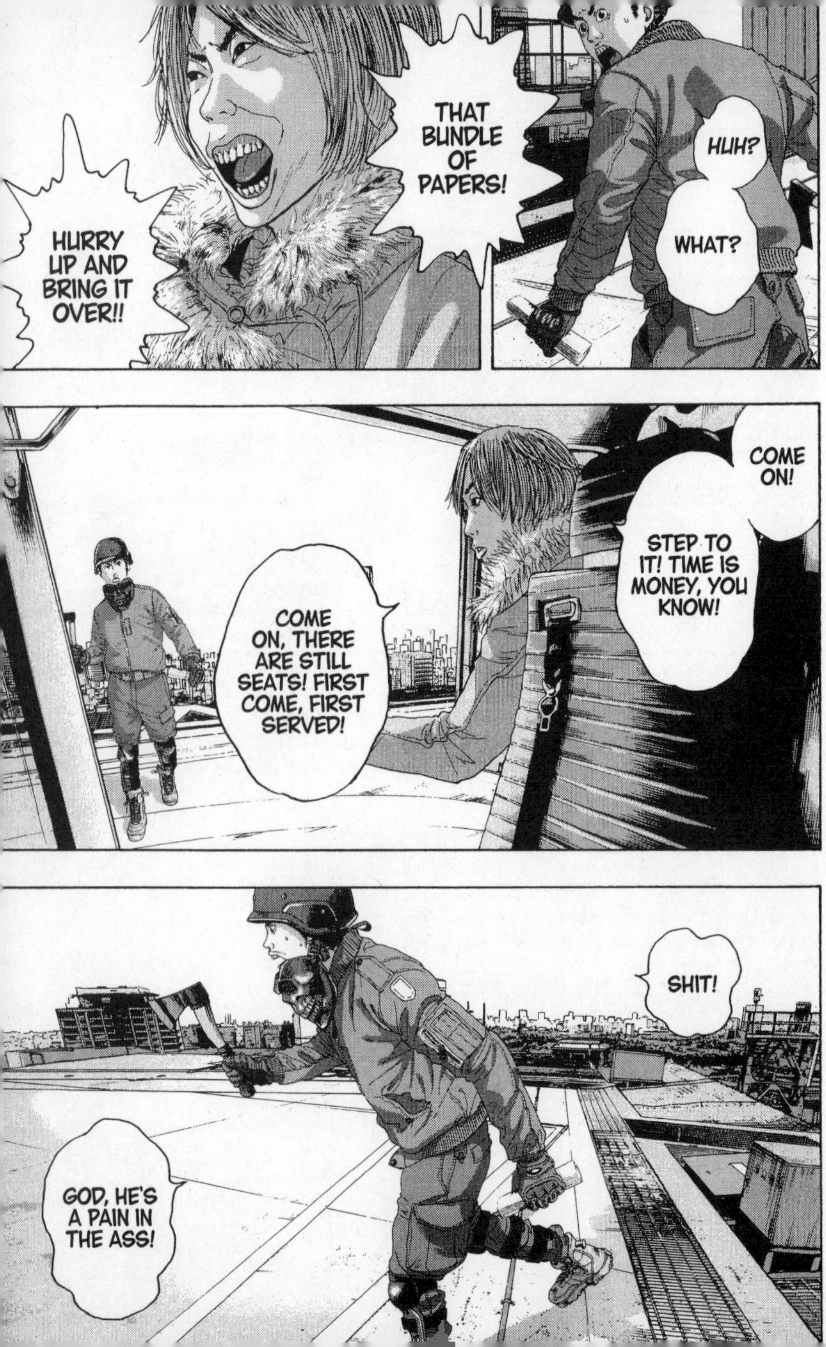
HUH?
WHAT?
THAT BUNDLE OF PAPERS!
HURRY UP AND BRING IT OVER!!
COME ON!
STEP TO IT! TIME IS MONEY, YOU KNOW!
COME ON, THERE ARE STILL SEATS! FIRST COME, FIRST SERVED!
SHIT!
GOD, HE'S A PAIN IN THE ASS!

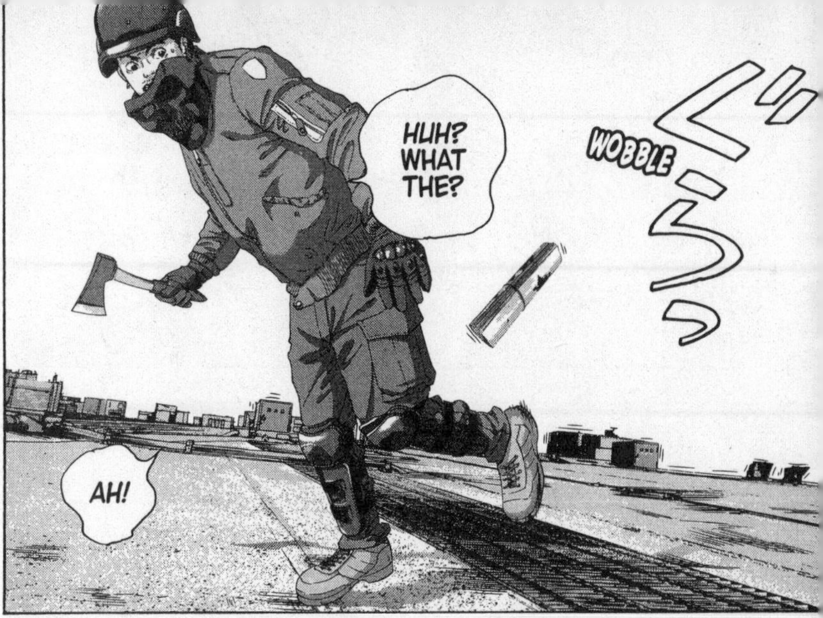
ぐらっ
WOBBLE
HUH? WHAT THE?
AH!
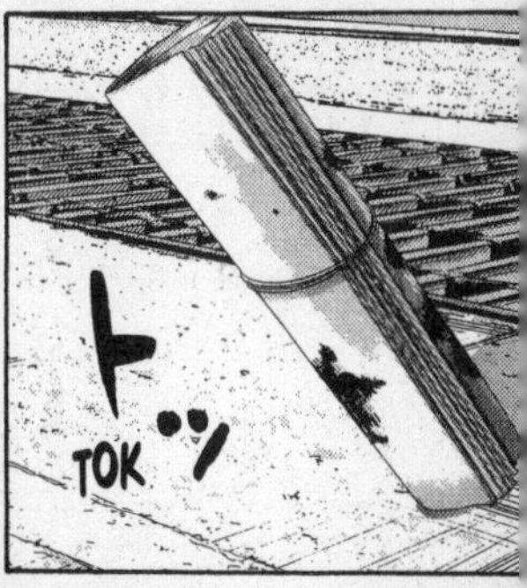
トッ
TOK
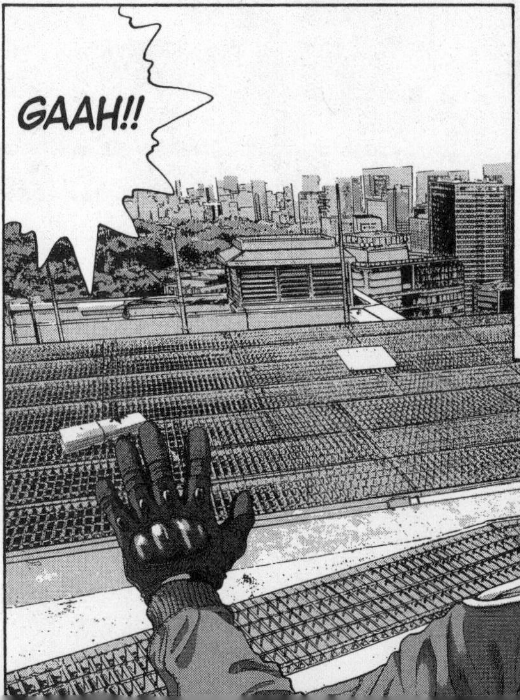
GAAH!!

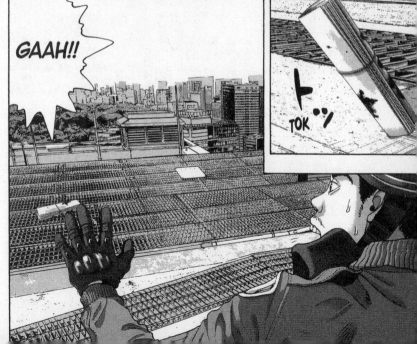

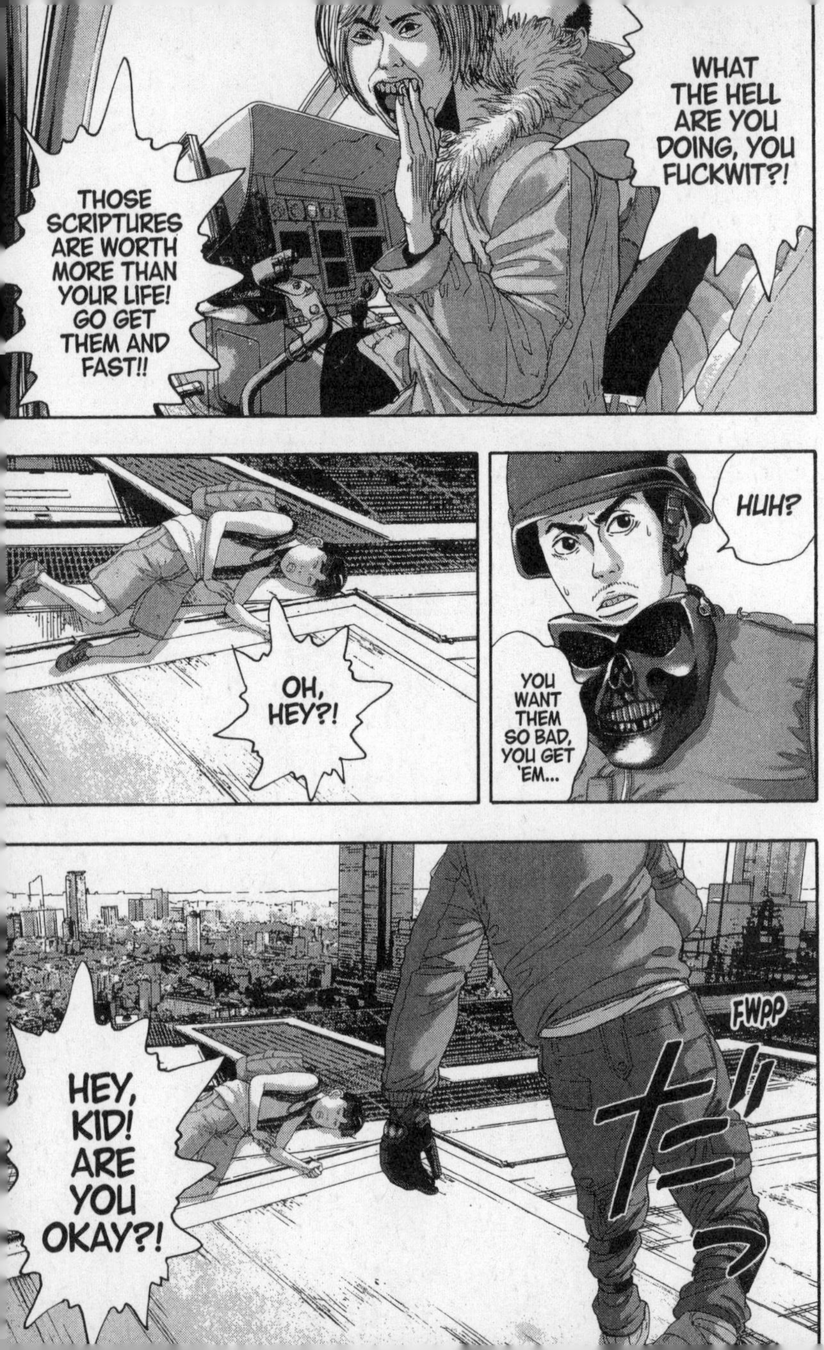
WHAT THE HELL ARE YOU DOING, YOU FUCKWIT?!
THOSE SCRIPTURES ARE WORTH MORE THAN YOUR LIFE! GO GET THEM AND FAST!!
HUH?
YOU WANT THEM SO BAD, YOU GET 'EM...
OH, HEY?!
FWPP
HEY, KID! ARE YOU OKAY?!

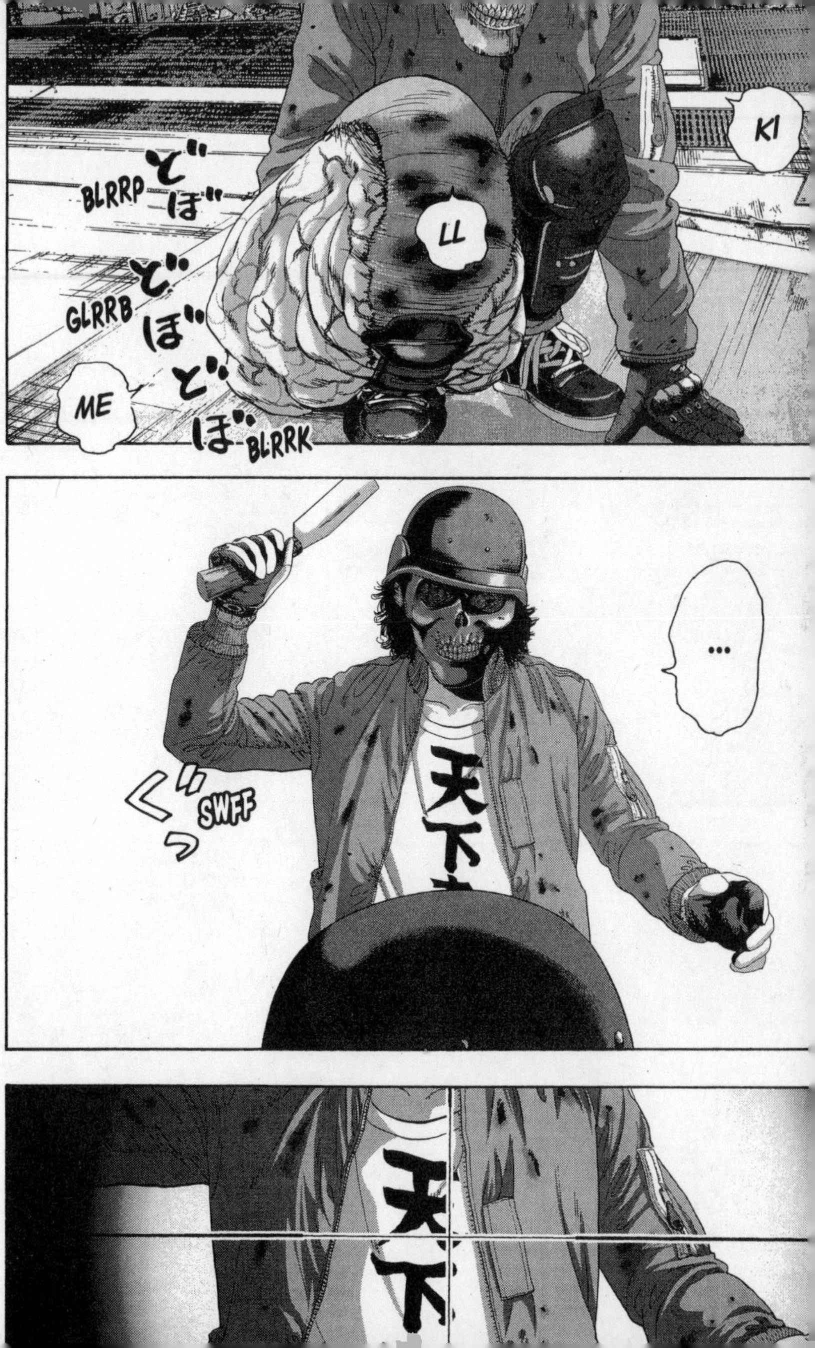
KI
LL
BLRRP
どぼ
GLRRB
どぼ
どぼ
BLRRK
ME
...
くっ
SWFF
天下
天下

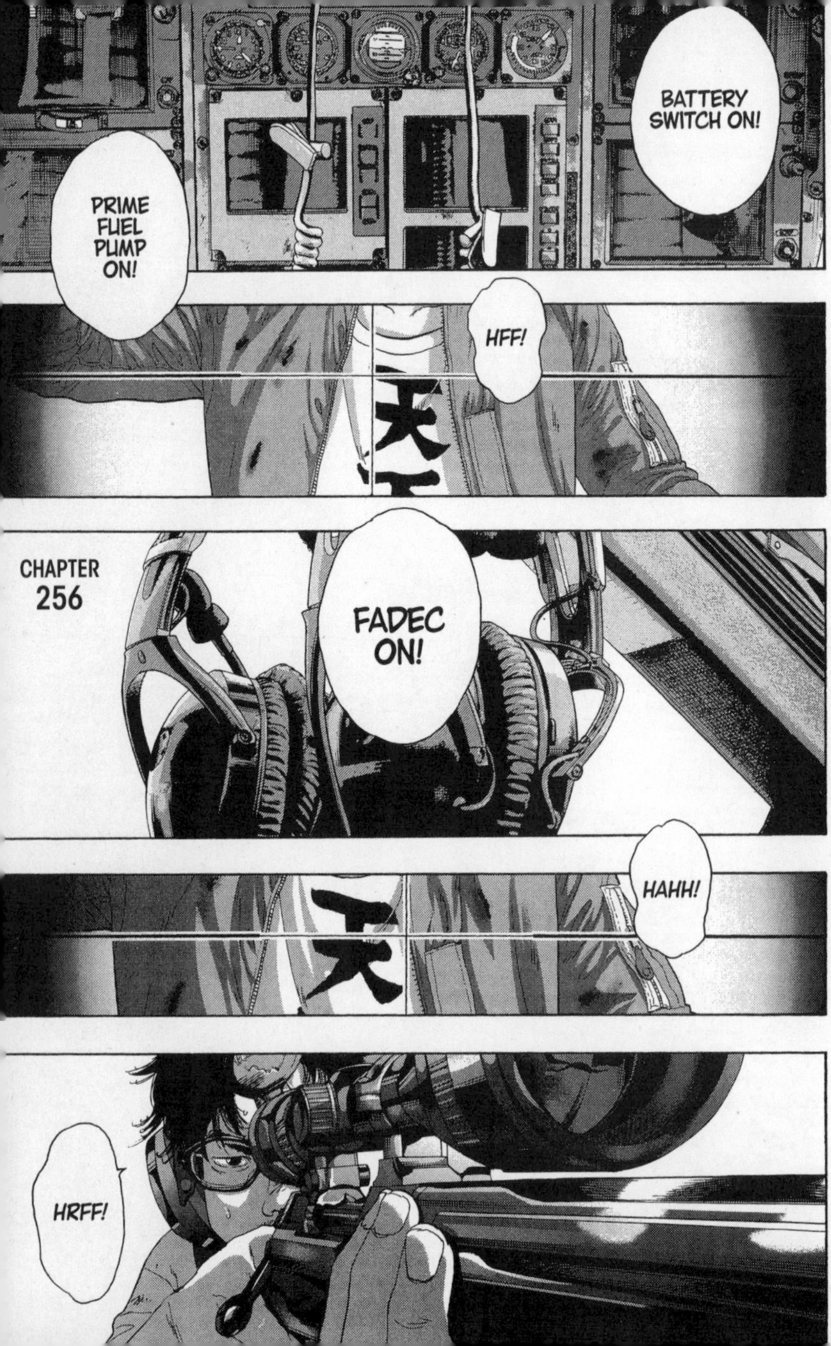
BATTERY SWITCH ON!
PRIME FUEL PUMP ON!
HFF!
FADEC ON!
CHAPTER 256
HAHH!
HRFF!

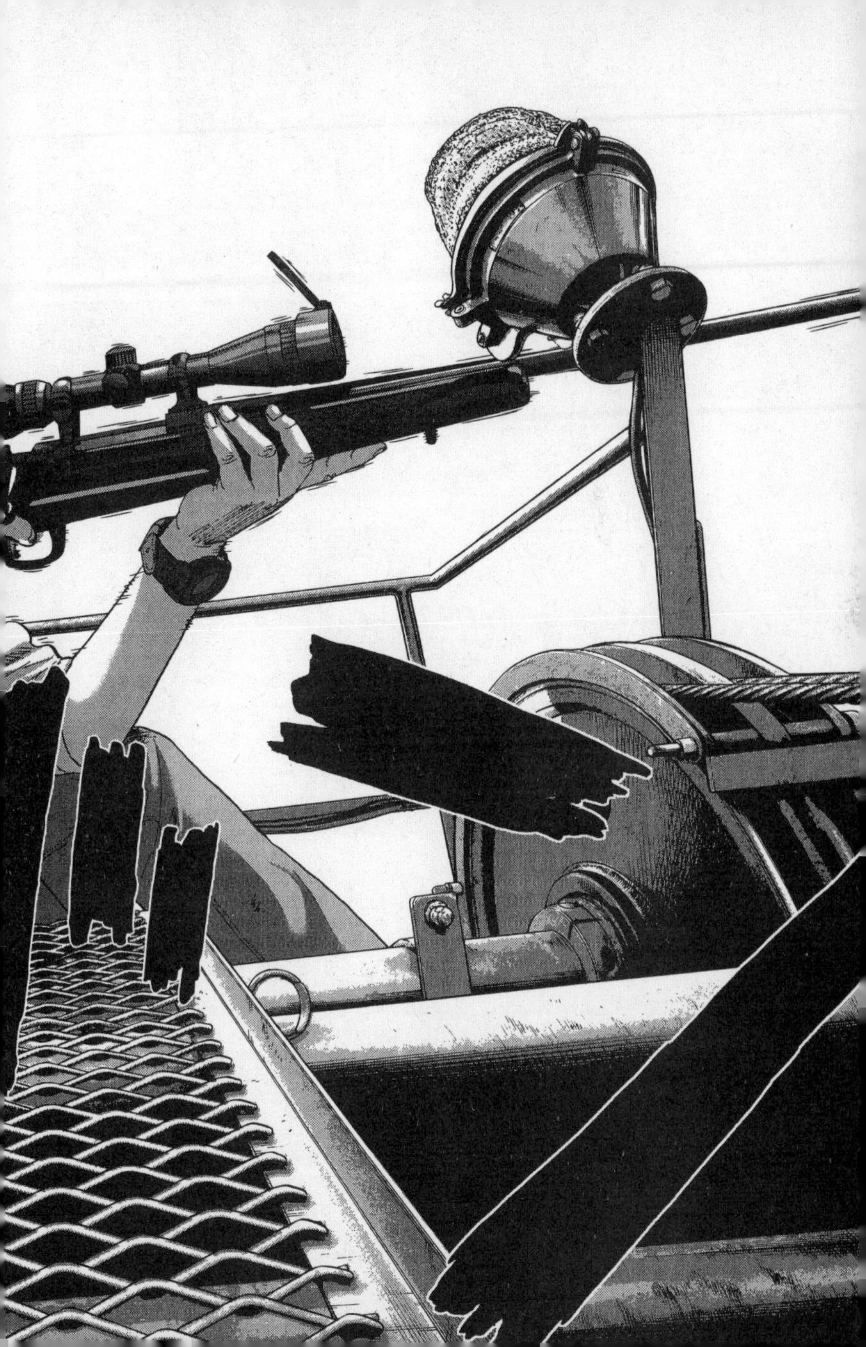

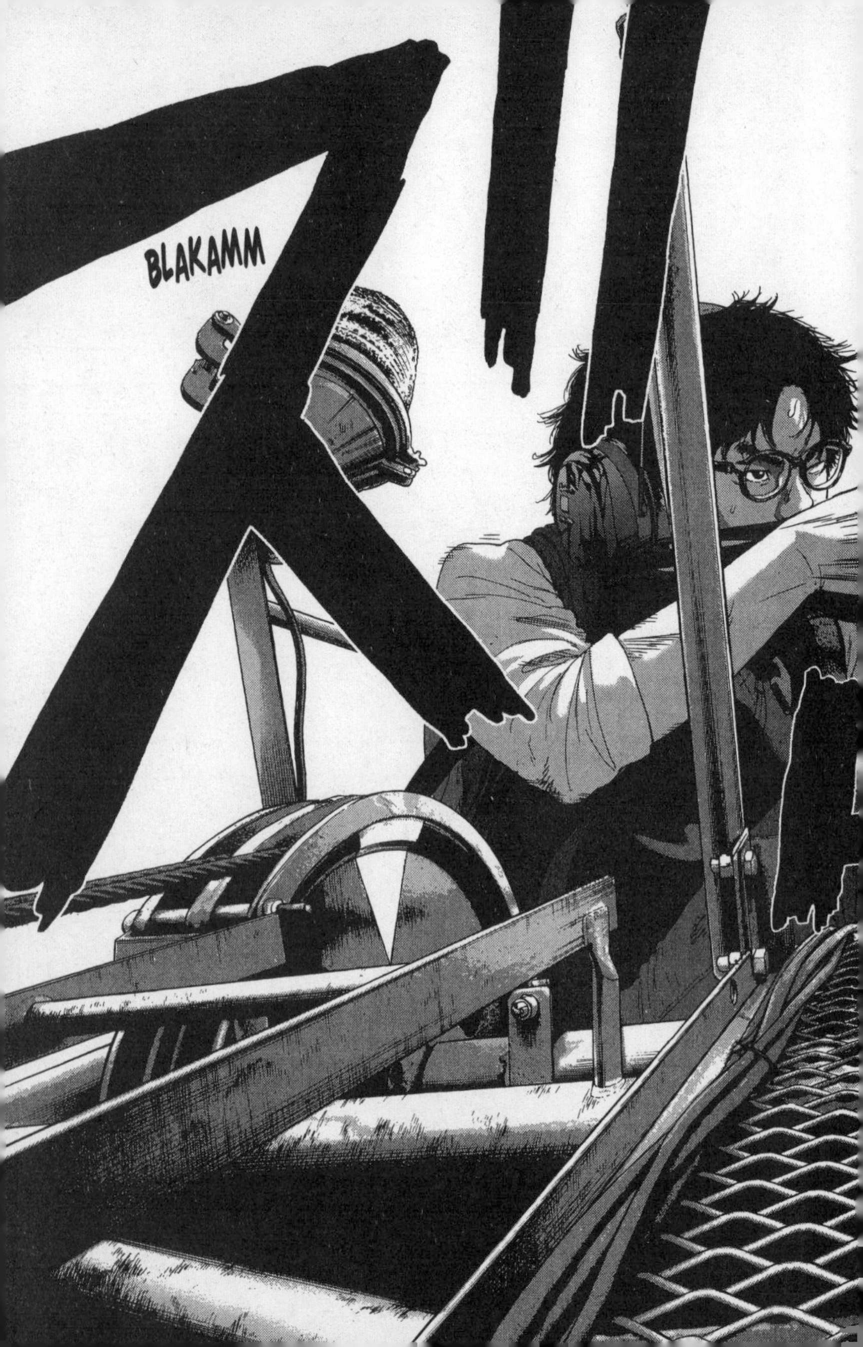
BLAKAMM

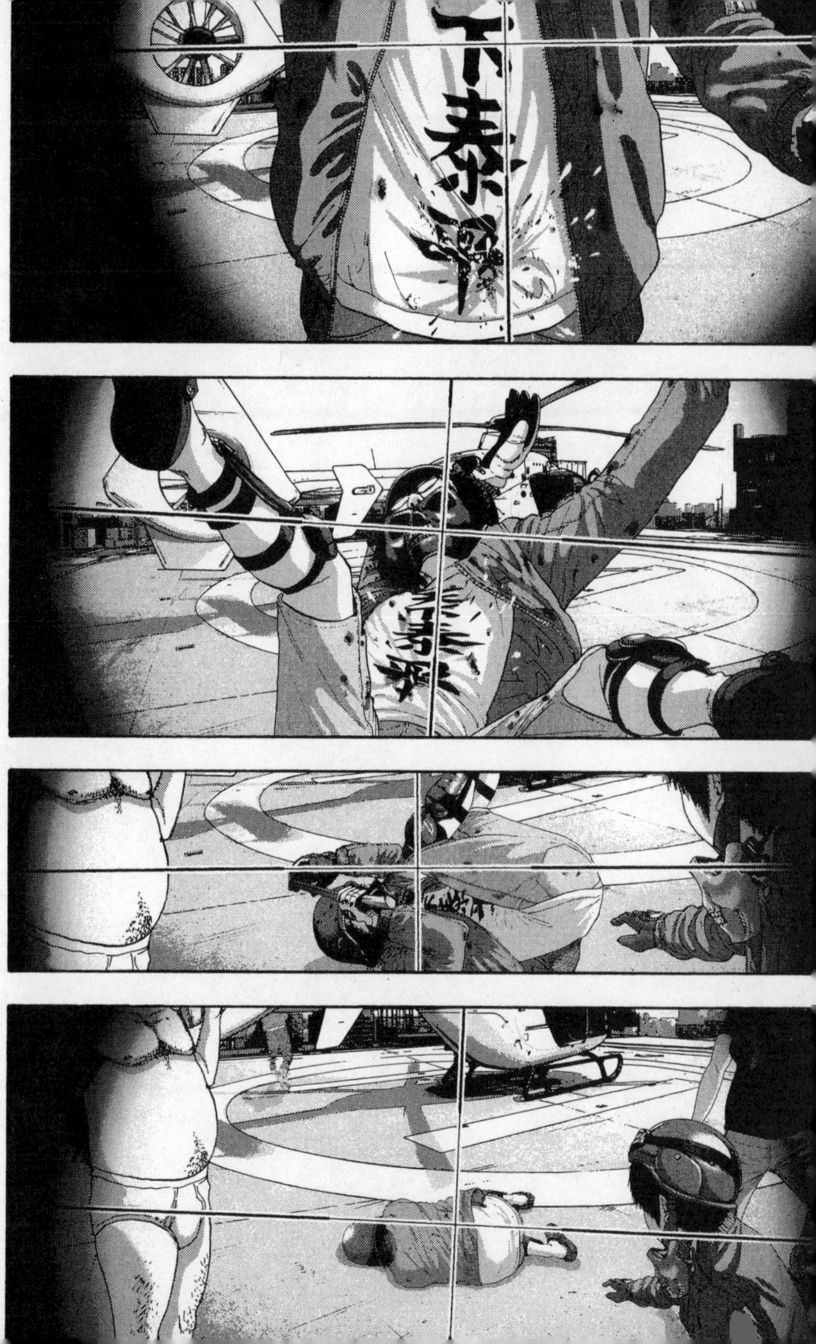

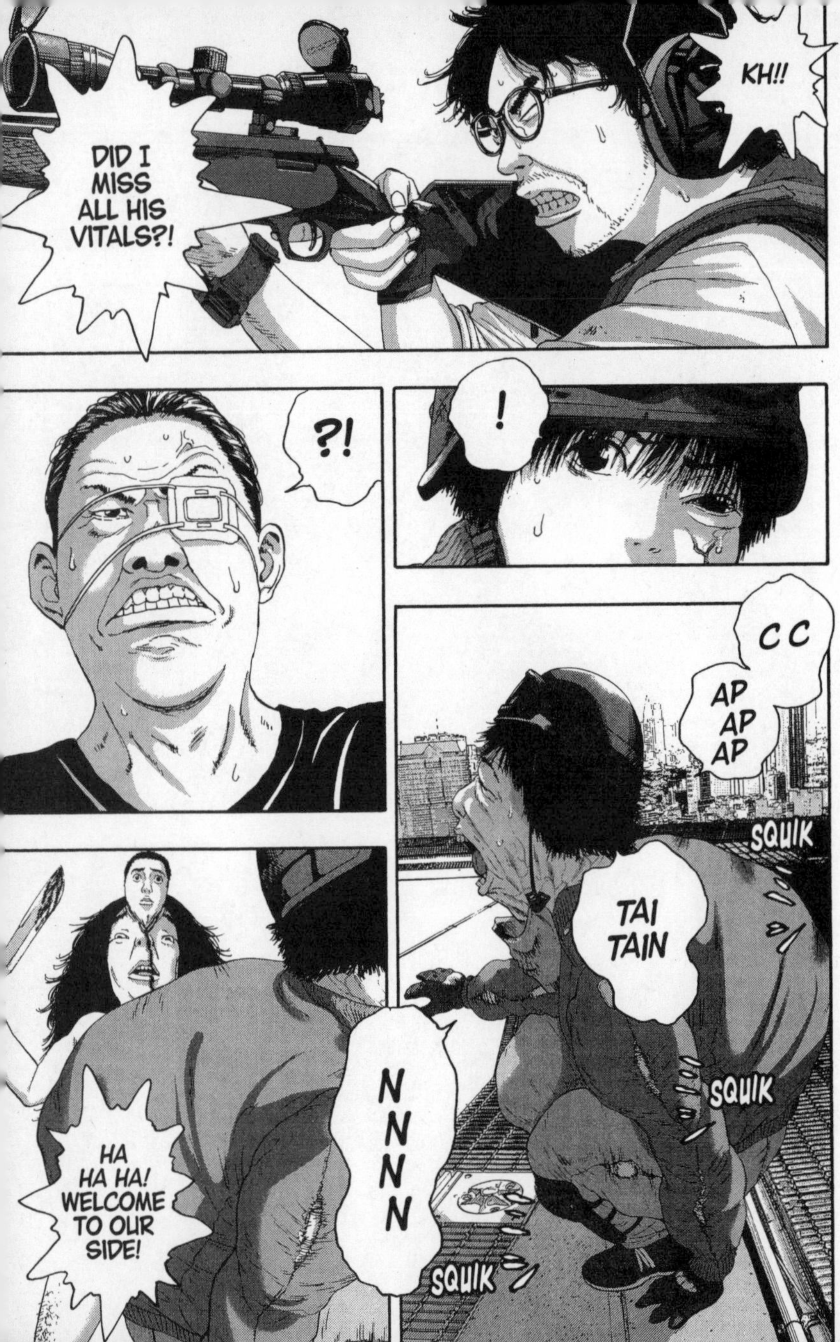
KH!!
DID I MISS ALL HIS VITALS?!
!
?!
CC
AP AP AP
SQUIK
TAI TAIN
SQUIK
SQUIK
NNNN
HA HA HA! WELCOME TO OUR SIDE!

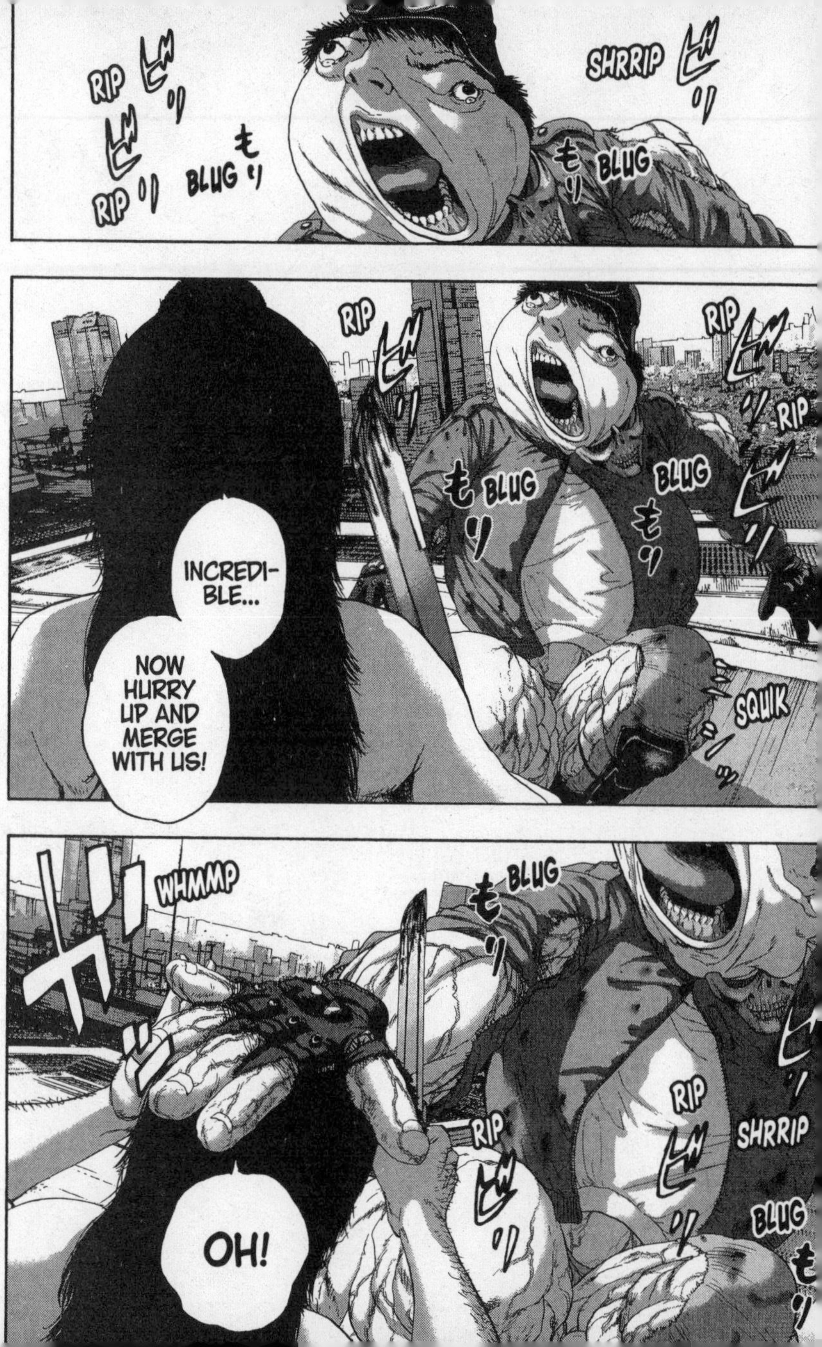
SHRRIP
ビリ
もり
BLUG
RIP
ビリ
ビリ
RIP
BLUG
もり
RIP
ビリ
RIP
ビリ
BLUG
もり
もり
BLUG
INCREDI-BLE...
NOW HURRY UP AND MERGE WITH US!
SQUIK
ビリ
SHRRIP
RIP
ビリ
RIP
ビリ
BLUG
もり
BLUG
もり
WHMMP
OH!

SQUITTCH

EEAAH!

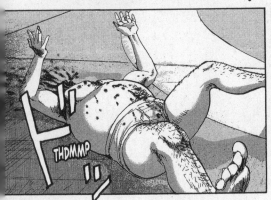

THDMMP

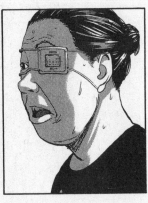

THIS...

...REALLY SUCKS...

AH! AM I...

...GOING TO GET EATEN AGAIN?

DRIP

PLIPIP

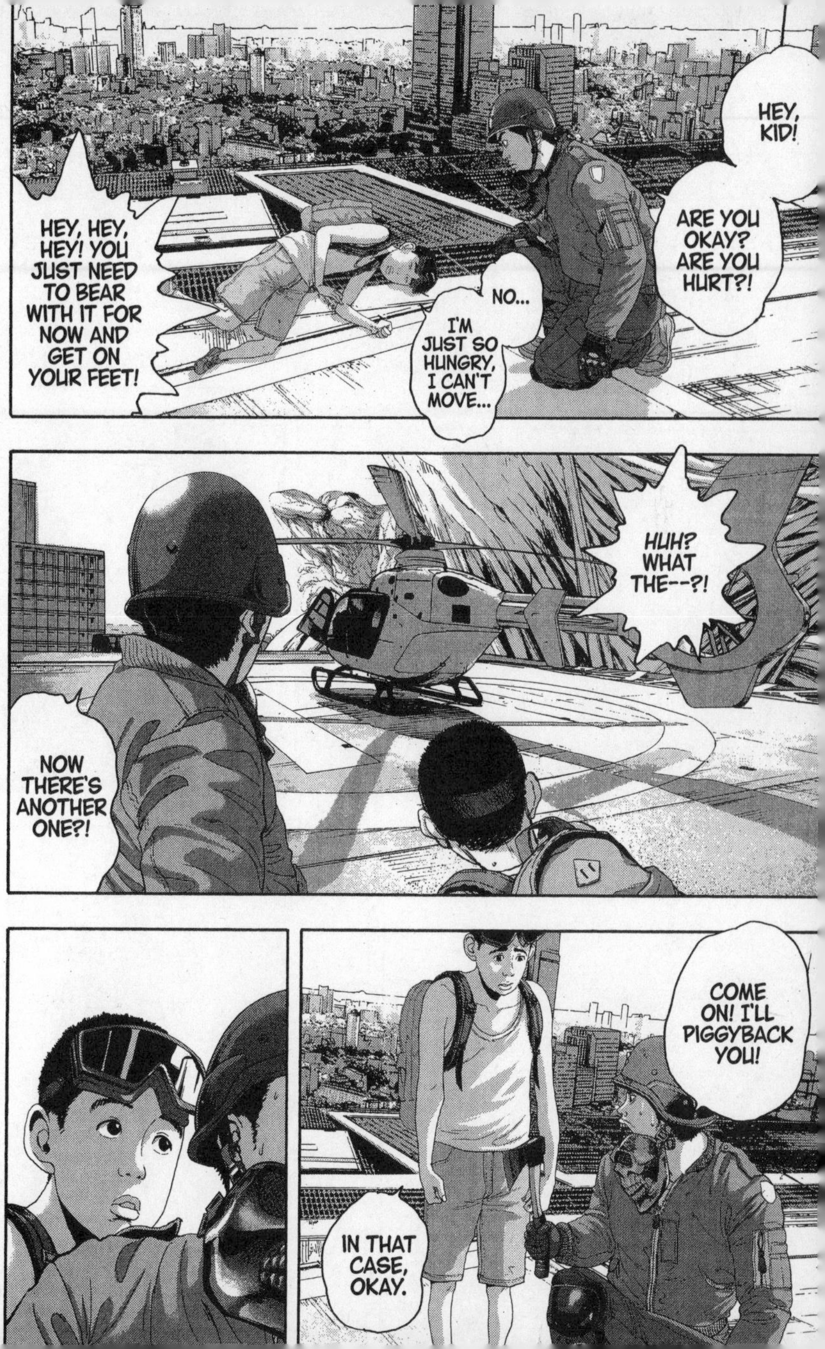
HEY, KID!
ARE YOU OKAY? ARE YOU HURT?!
NO...
I'M JUST SO HUNGRY, I CAN'T MOVE...
HEY, HEY, HEY! YOU JUST NEED TO BEAR WITH IT FOR NOW AND GET ON YOUR FEET!
HUH? WHAT THE--?!
NOW THERE'S ANOTHER ONE?!
COME ON! I'LL PIGGYBACK YOU!
IN THAT CASE, OKAY.

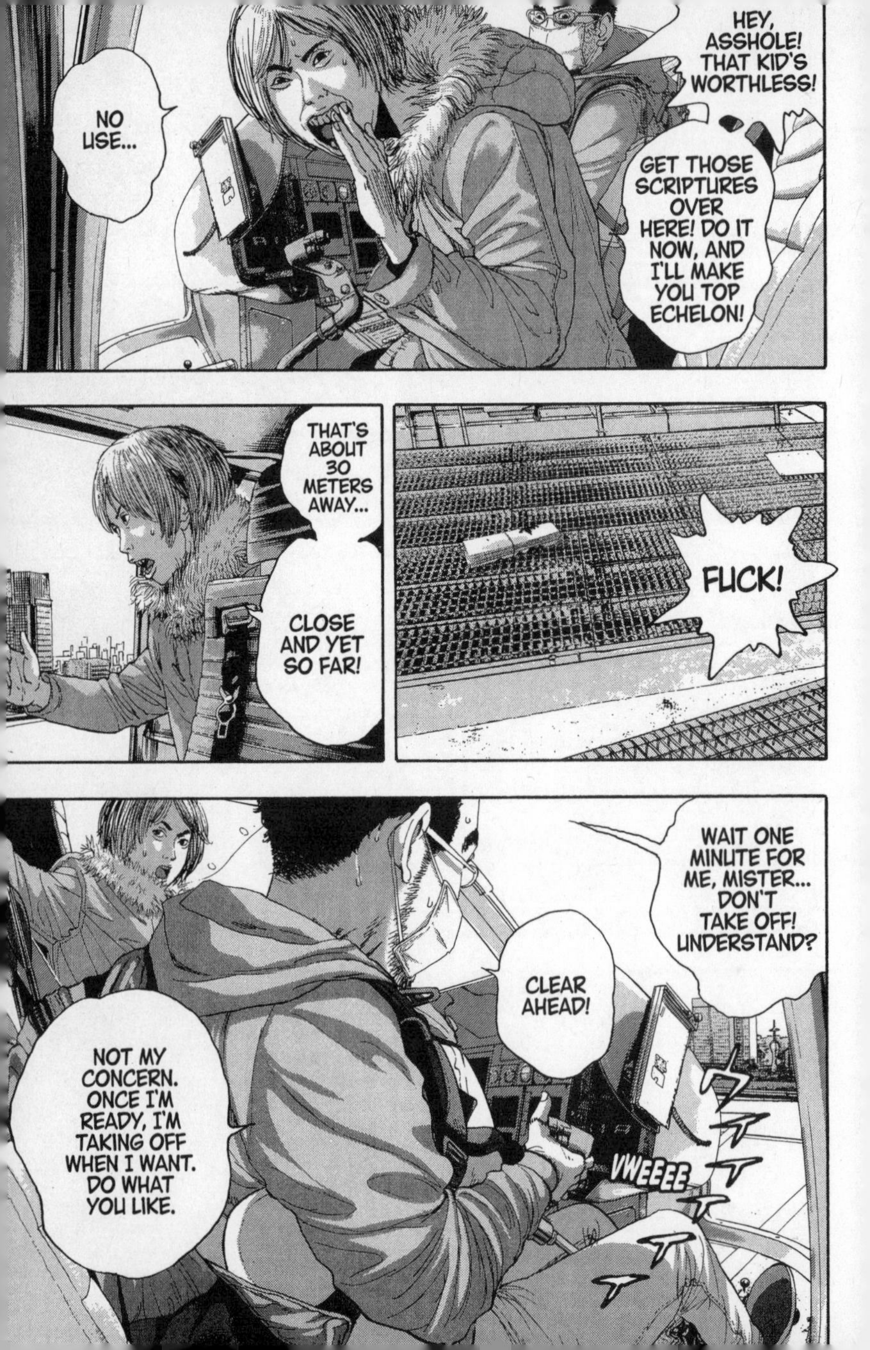
HEY, ASSHOLE! THAT KID'S WORTHLESS!
GET THOSE SCRIPTURES OVER HERE! DO IT NOW, AND I'LL MAKE YOU TOP ECHELON!
NO USE...
FUCK!
THAT'S ABOUT 30 METERS AWAY...
CLOSE AND YET SO FAR!
WAIT ONE MINUTE FOR ME, MISTER... DON'T TAKE OFF! UNDERSTAND?
CLEAR AHEAD!
NOT MY CONCERN. ONCE I'M READY, I'M TAKING OFF WHEN I WANT. DO WHAT YOU LIKE.
VWEEEE

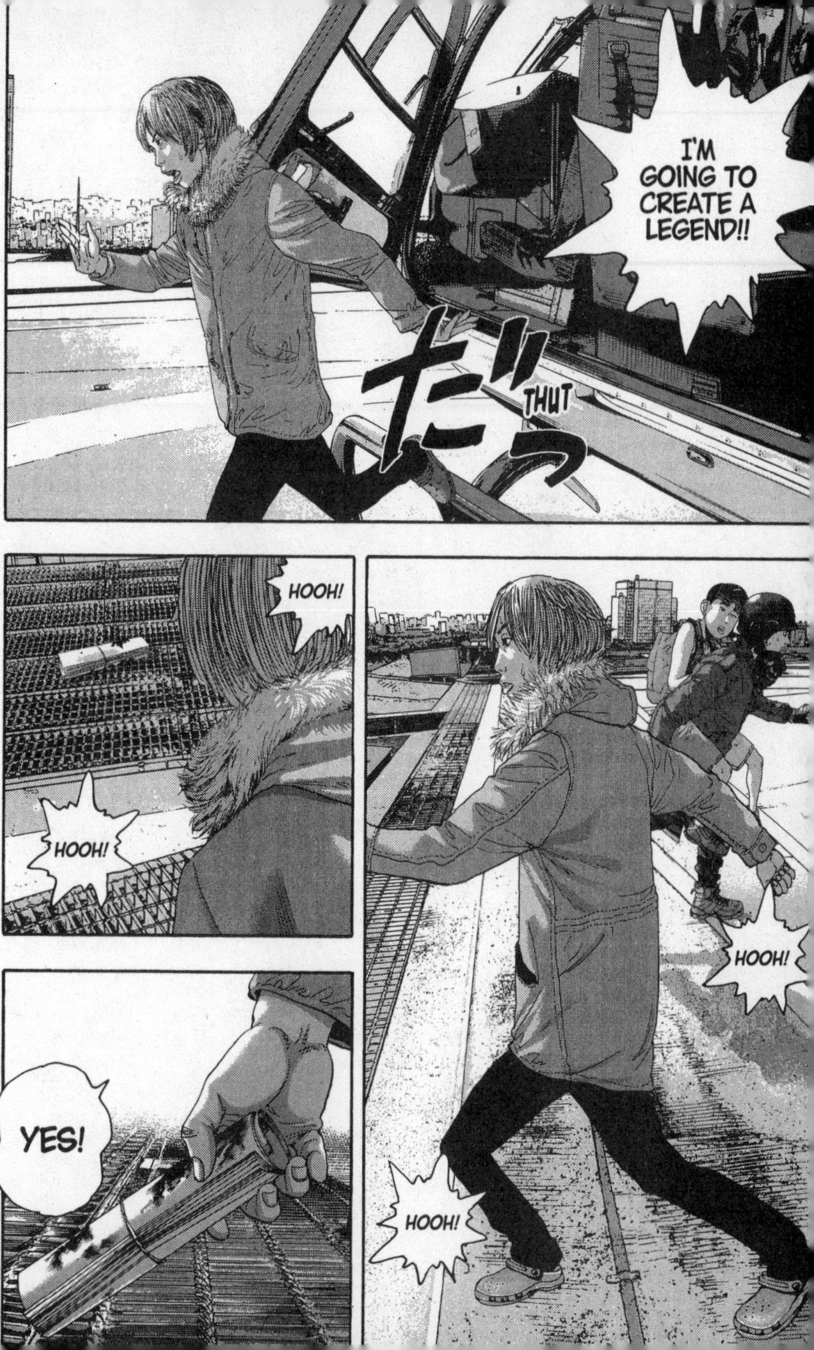
I'M GOING TO CREATE A LEGEND!!
だっ
THUT
HOOH!
HOOH!
HOOH!
HOOH!
YES!

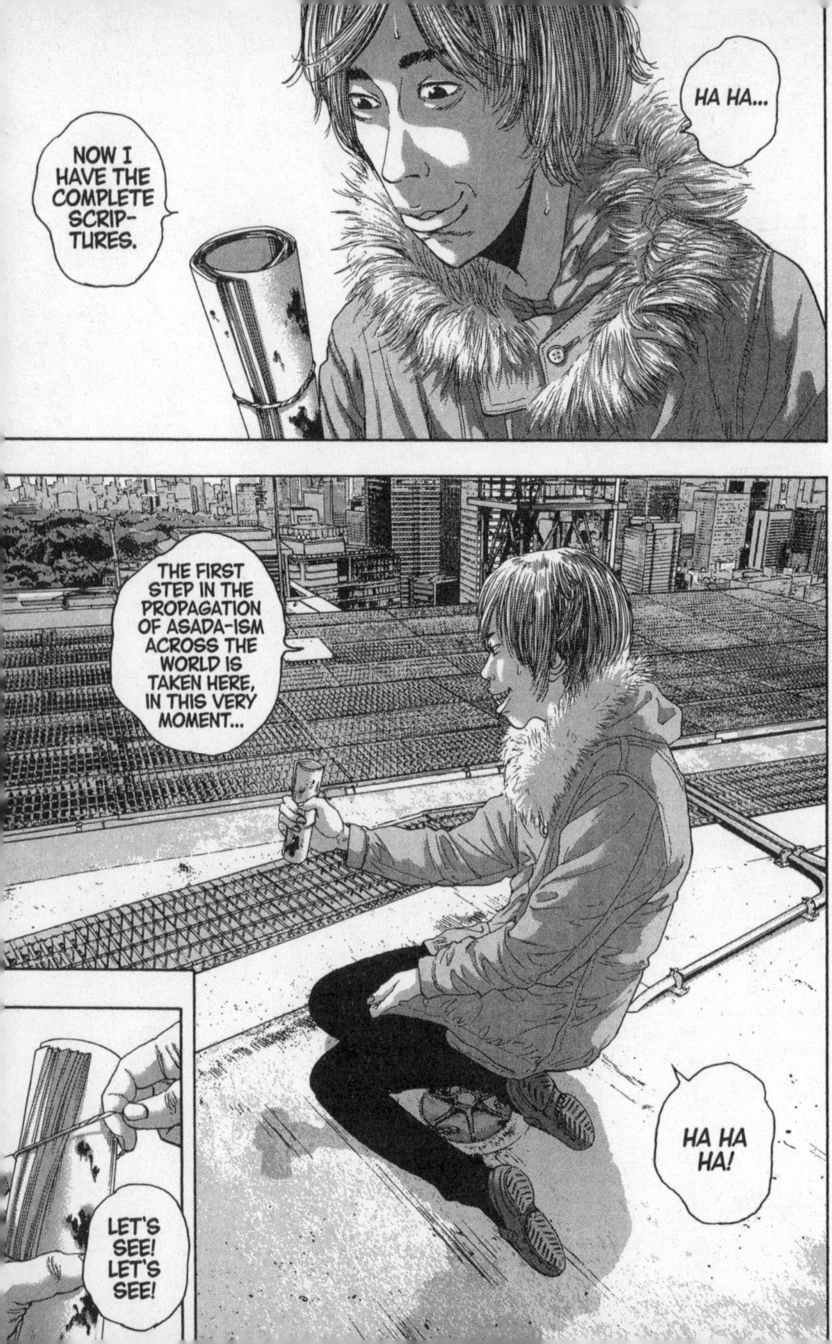
HA HA...
NOW I HAVE THE COMPLETE SCRIP-TURES.
THE FIRST STEP IN THE PROPAGATION OF ASADA-ISM ACROSS THE WORLD IS TAKEN HERE, IN THIS VERY MOMENT...
HA HA HA!
LET'S SEE! LET'S SEE!

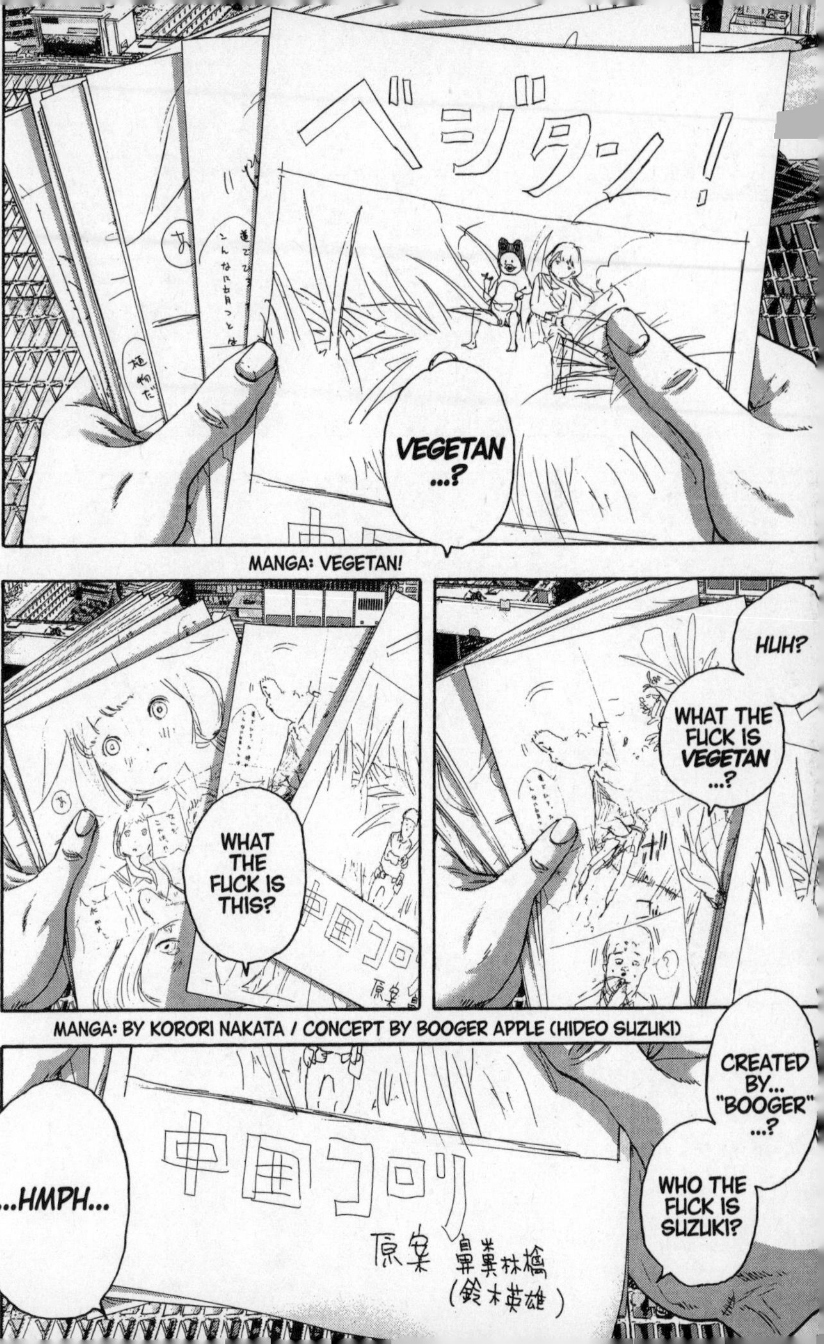
ベジタ〜ン!
VEGETAN ...?
MANGA: VEGETAN!
HUH?
WHAT THE FUCK IS VEGETAN ...?
WHAT THE FUCK IS THIS?
MANGA: BY KORORI NAKATA / CONCEPT BY BOOGER APPLE (HIDEO SUZUKI)
CREATED BY... "BOOGER" ...?
WHO THE FUCK IS SUZUKI?
中田コロリ
原案 鼻糞林檎 (鈴木英雄)
...HMPH...

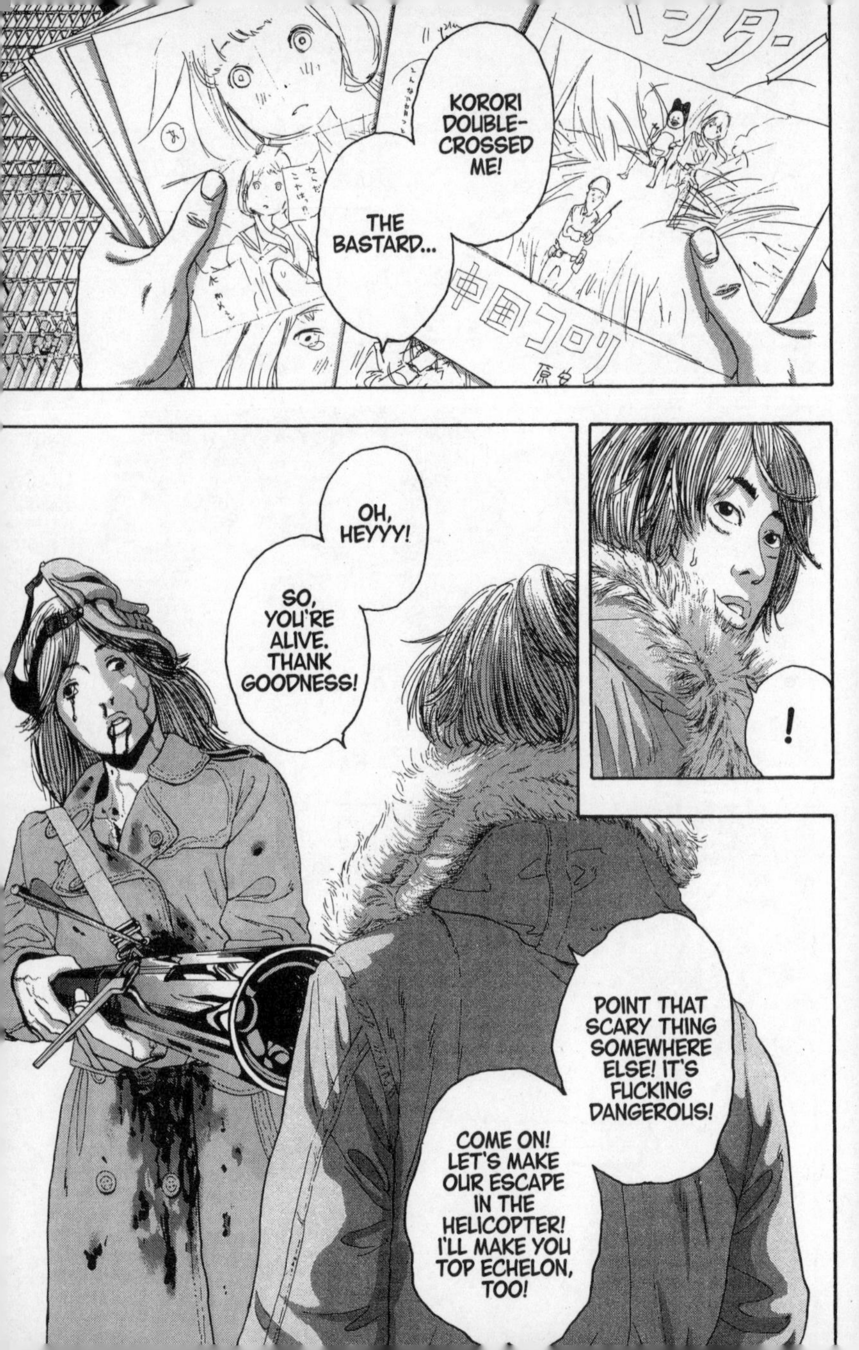
KORORI DOUBLE-CROSSED ME!
THE BASTARD...
!
POINT THAT SCARY THING SOMEWHERE ELSE! IT'S FUCKING DANGEROUS!
COME ON! LET'S MAKE OUR ESCAPE IN THE HELICOPTER! I'LL MAKE YOU TOP ECHELON, TOO!
OH, HEYYY!
SO, YOU'RE ALIVE. THANK GOODNESS!

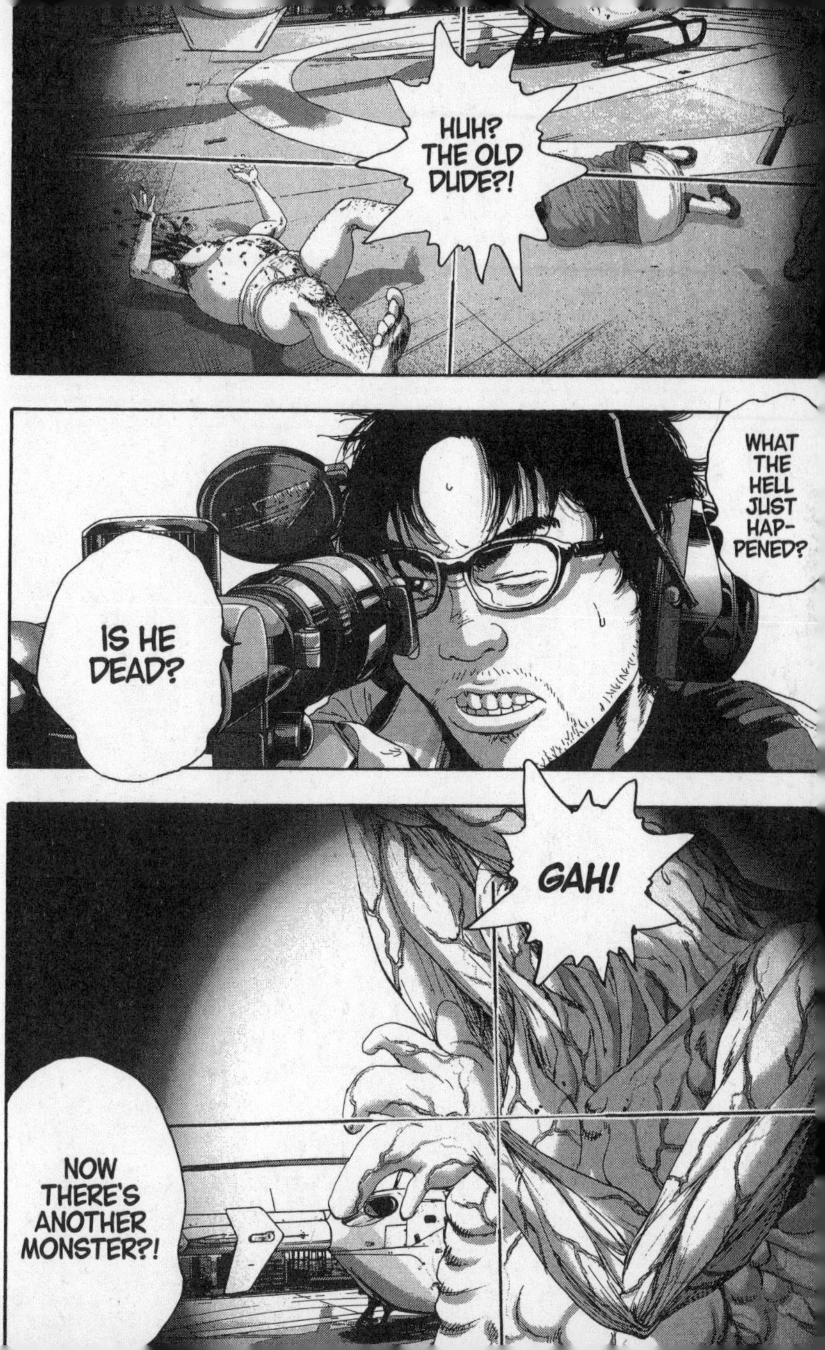
HUH? THE OLD DUDE?!
WHAT THE HELL JUST HAP- PENED?
IS HE DEAD?
GAH!
NOW THERE'S ANOTHER MONSTER?!

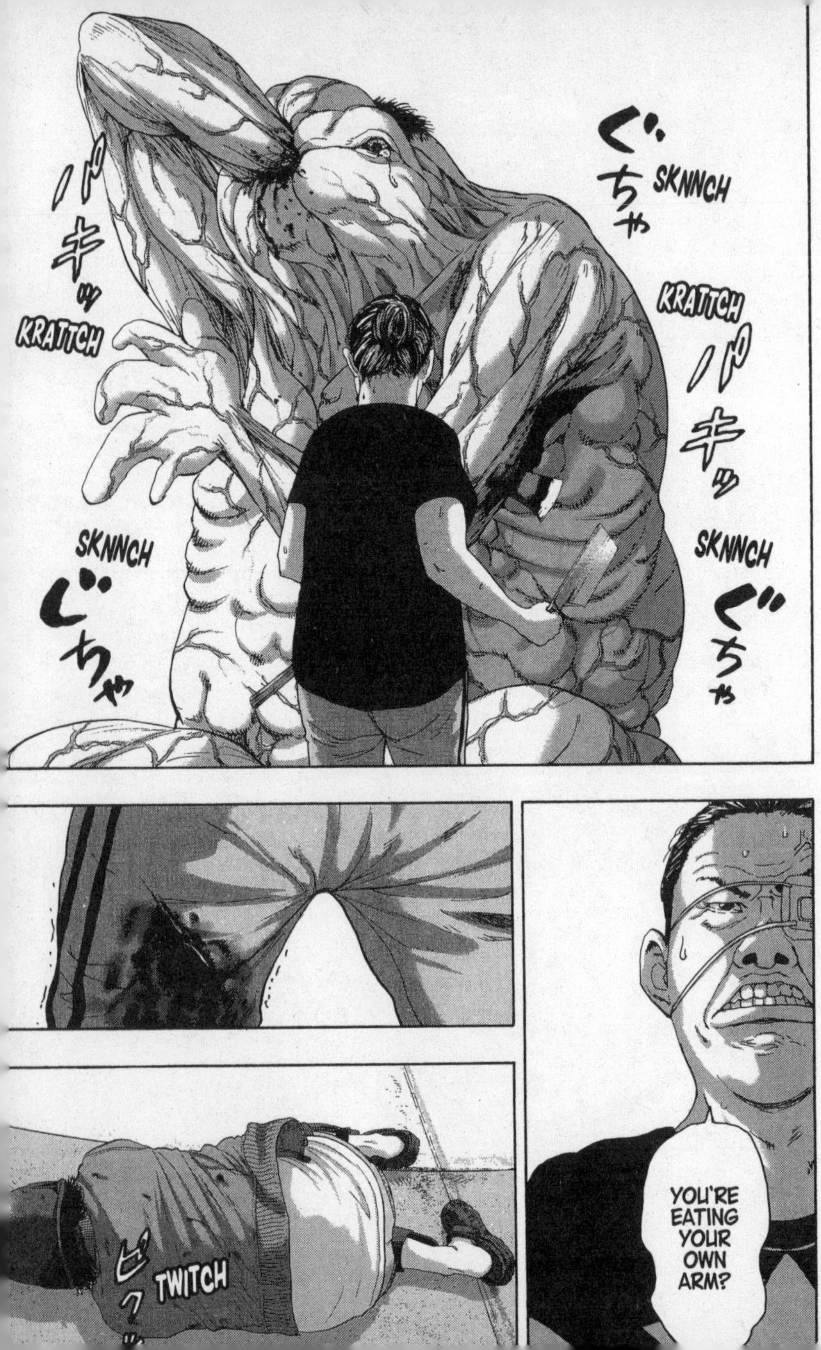
ぐちゃ
SKNNCH
KRATTCH
パキッ
SKNNCH
ぐちゃ
パキッ
KRATTCH
SKNNCH
ぐちゃ
YOU'RE EATING YOUR OWN ARM?
ピクッ
TWITCH

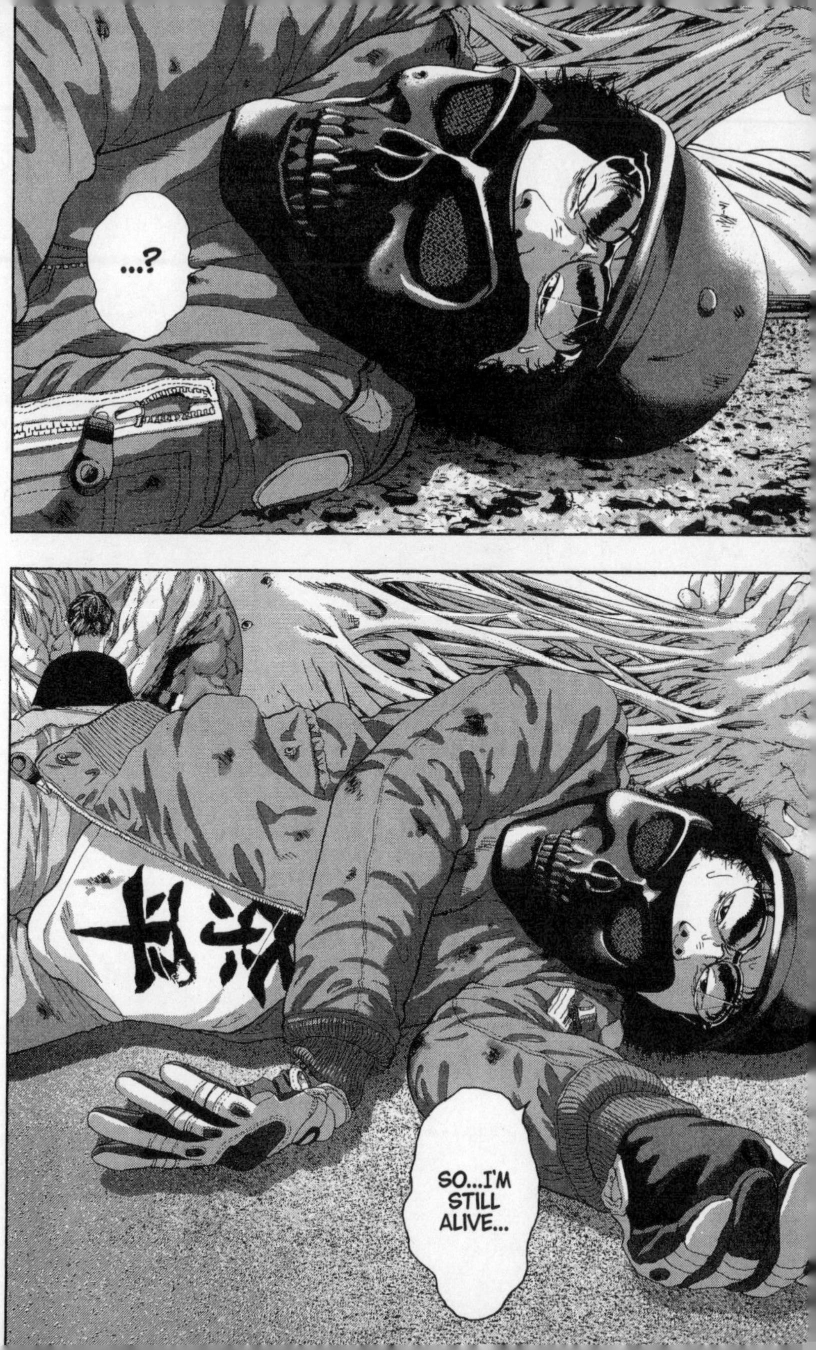
...?
SO...I'M STILL ALIVE...

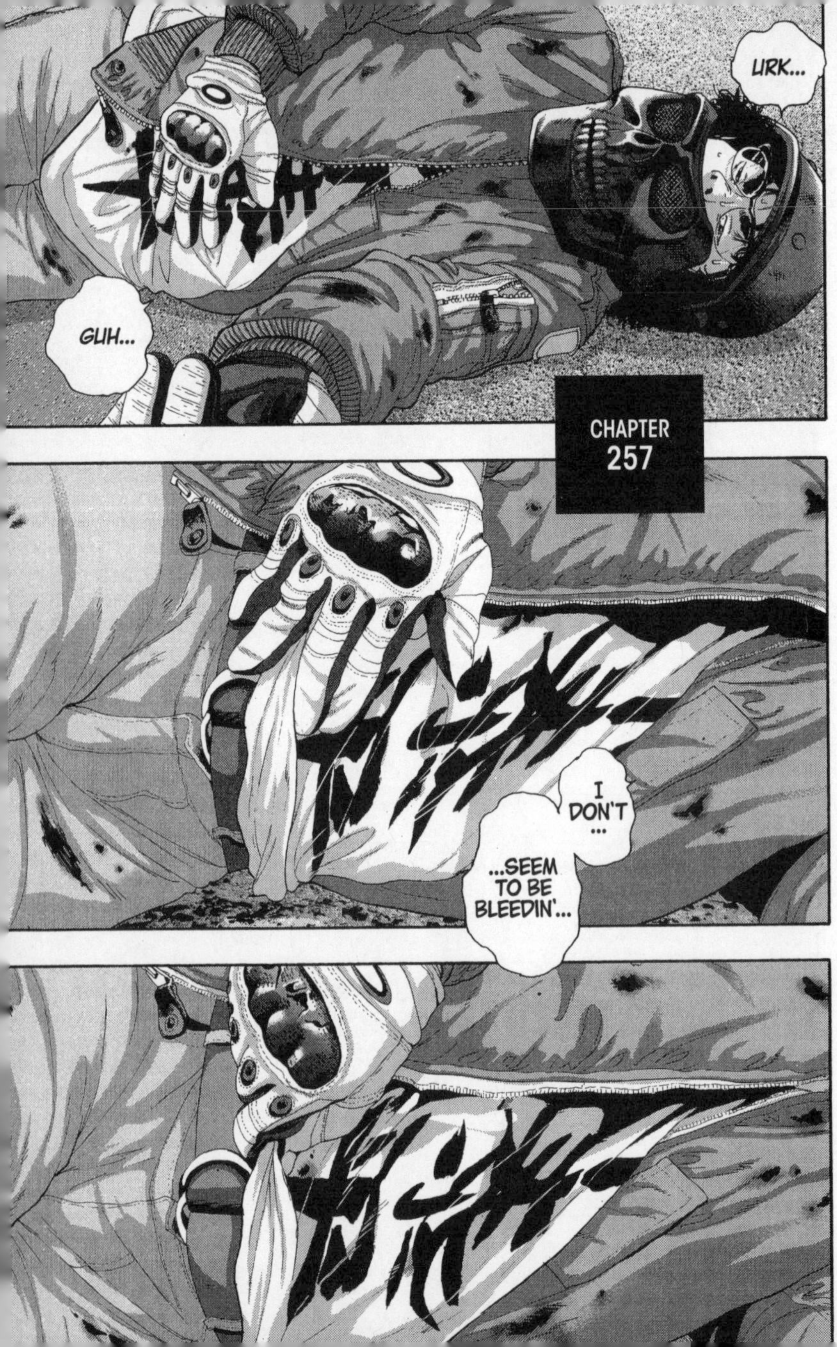
URK...
GUH...
CHAPTER 257
I DON'T ...
...SEEM TO BE BLEEDIN'...

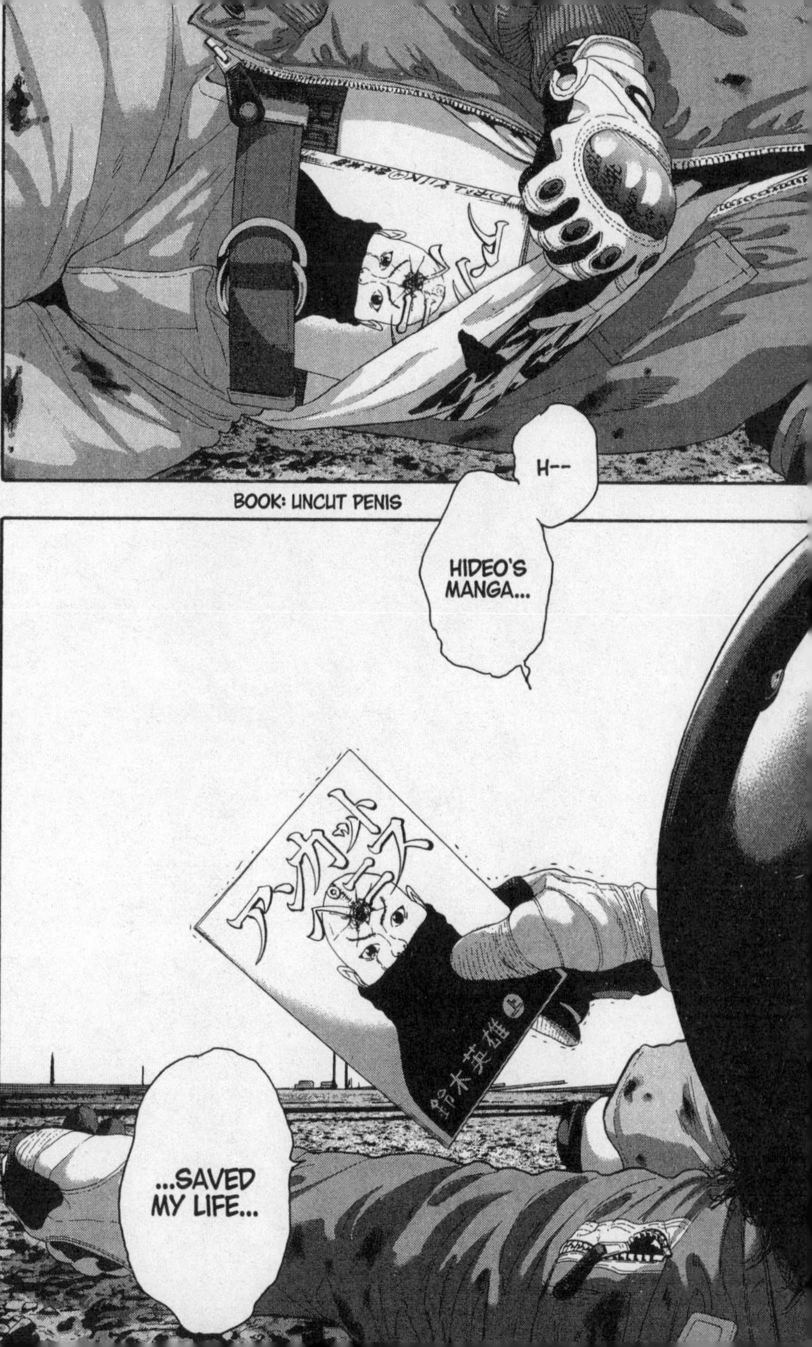

BOOK: UNCUT PENIS
H--
HIDEO'S MANGA...
...SAVED MY LIFE...

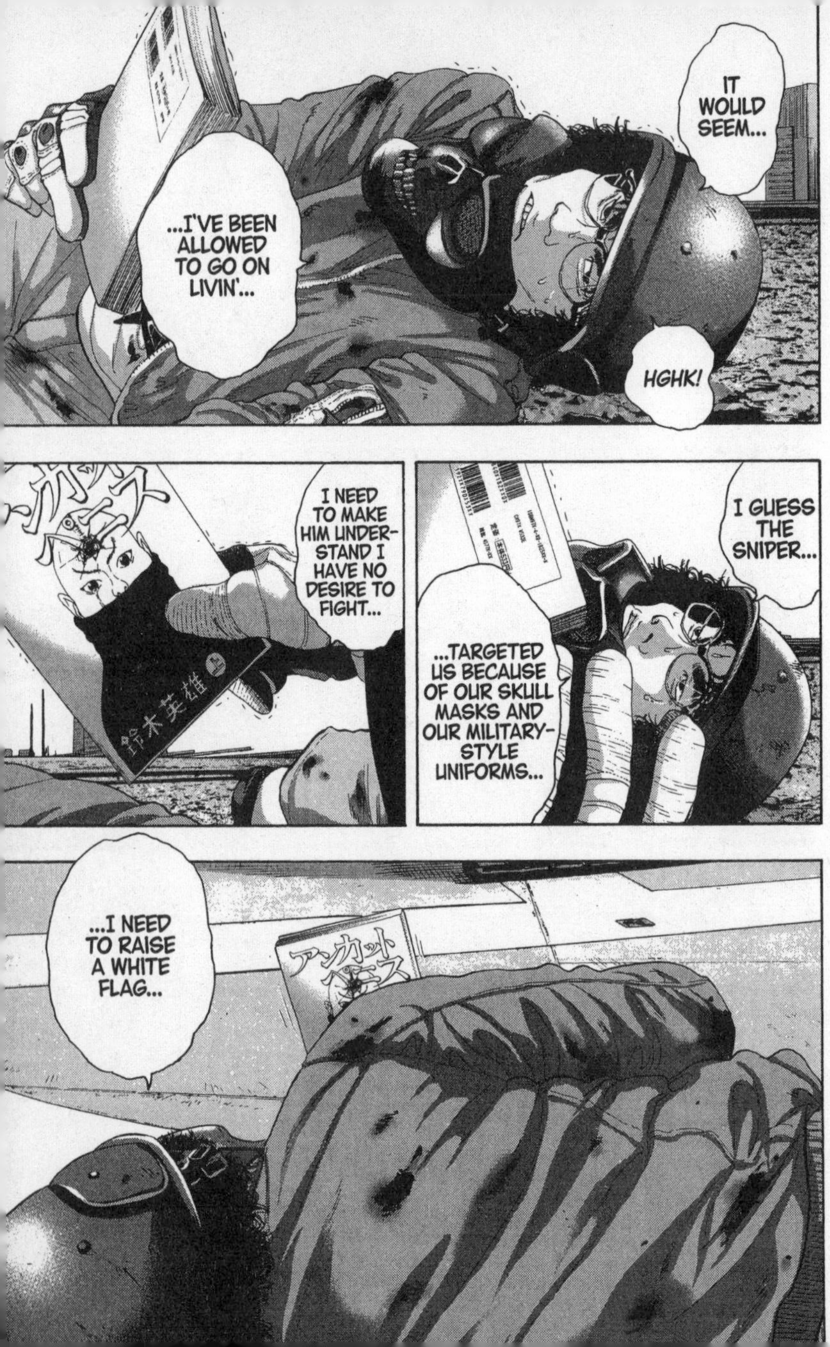
IT WOULD SEEM...
...I'VE BEEN ALLOWED TO GO ON LIVIN'...
HGHK!
I GUESS THE SNIPER...
...TARGETED US BECAUSE OF OUR SKULL MASKS AND OUR MILITARY-STYLE UNIFORMS...
I NEED TO MAKE HIM UNDER-STAND I HAVE NO DESIRE TO FIGHT...
...I NEED TO RAISE A WHITE FLAG...

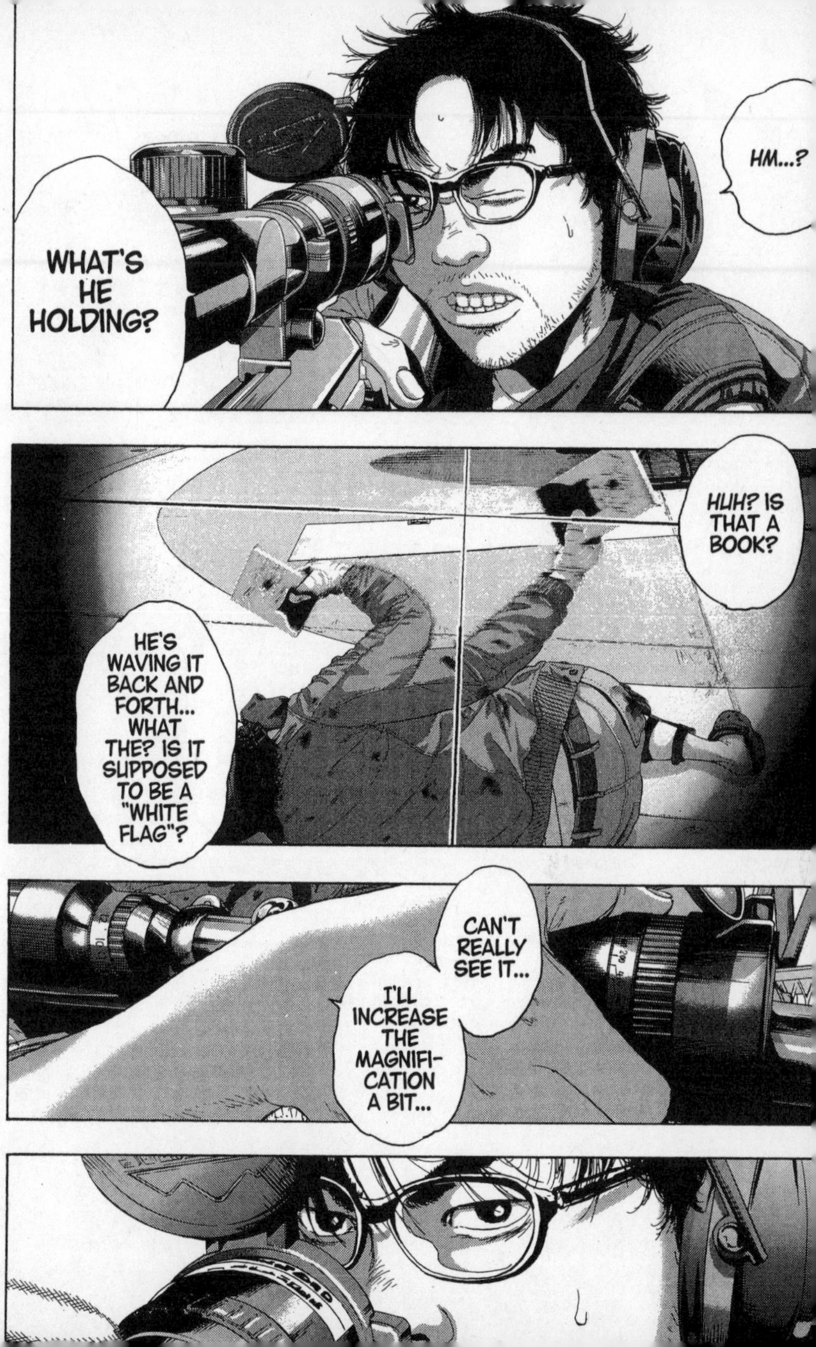
HM...?
WHAT'S HE HOLDING?
HUH? IS THAT A BOOK?
HE'S WAVING IT BACK AND FORTH... WHAT THE? IS IT SUPPOSED TO BE A "WHITE FLAG"?
CAN'T REALLY SEE IT...
I'LL INCREASE THE MAGNIFI-CATION A BIT...

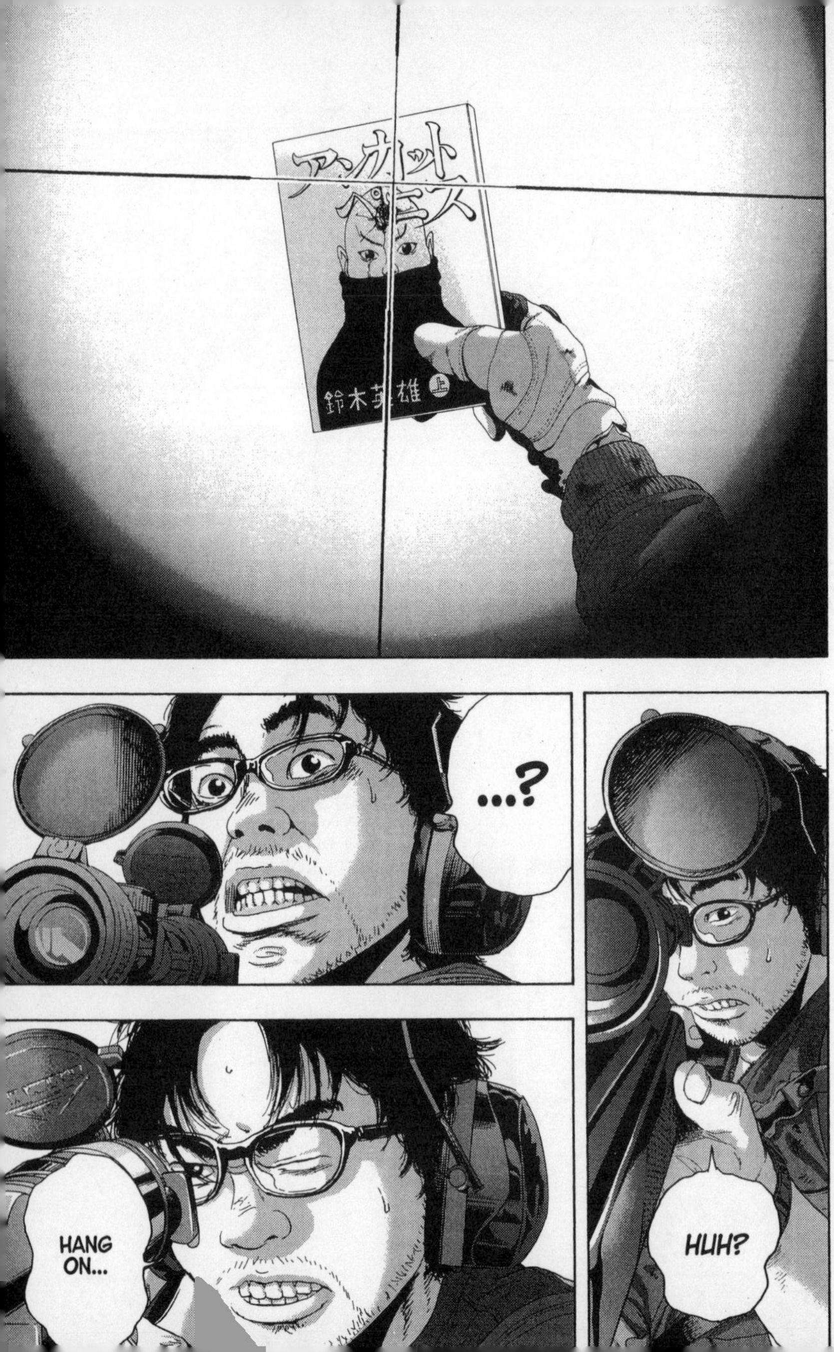
鈴木英雄
上
HUH?
...?
HANG ON...

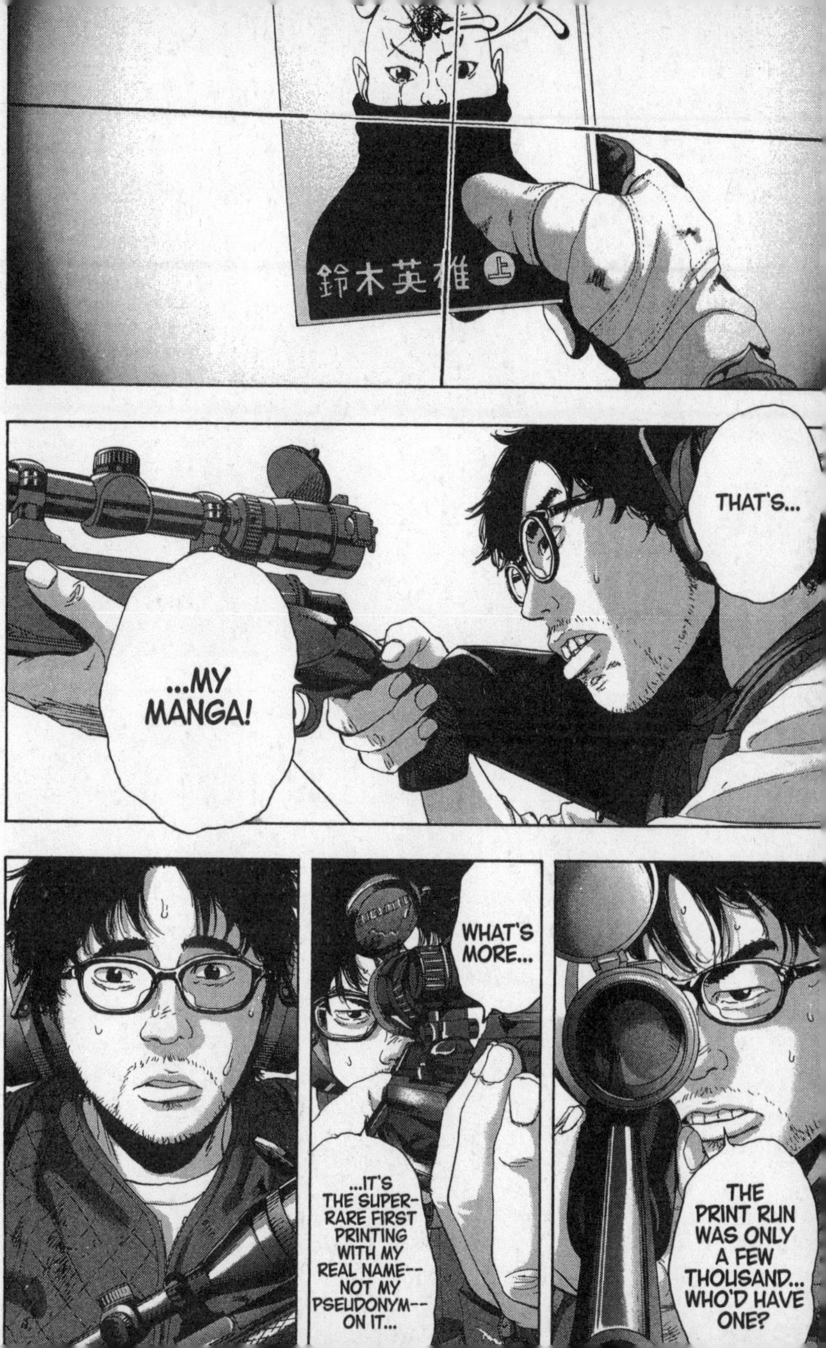
鈴木英雄 上
THAT'S...
...MY MANGA!
THE PRINT RUN WAS ONLY A FEW THOUSAND... WHO'D HAVE ONE?
WHAT'S MORE...
...IT'S THE SUPER-RARE FIRST PRINTING WITH MY REAL NAME--NOT MY PSEUDONYM--ON IT...

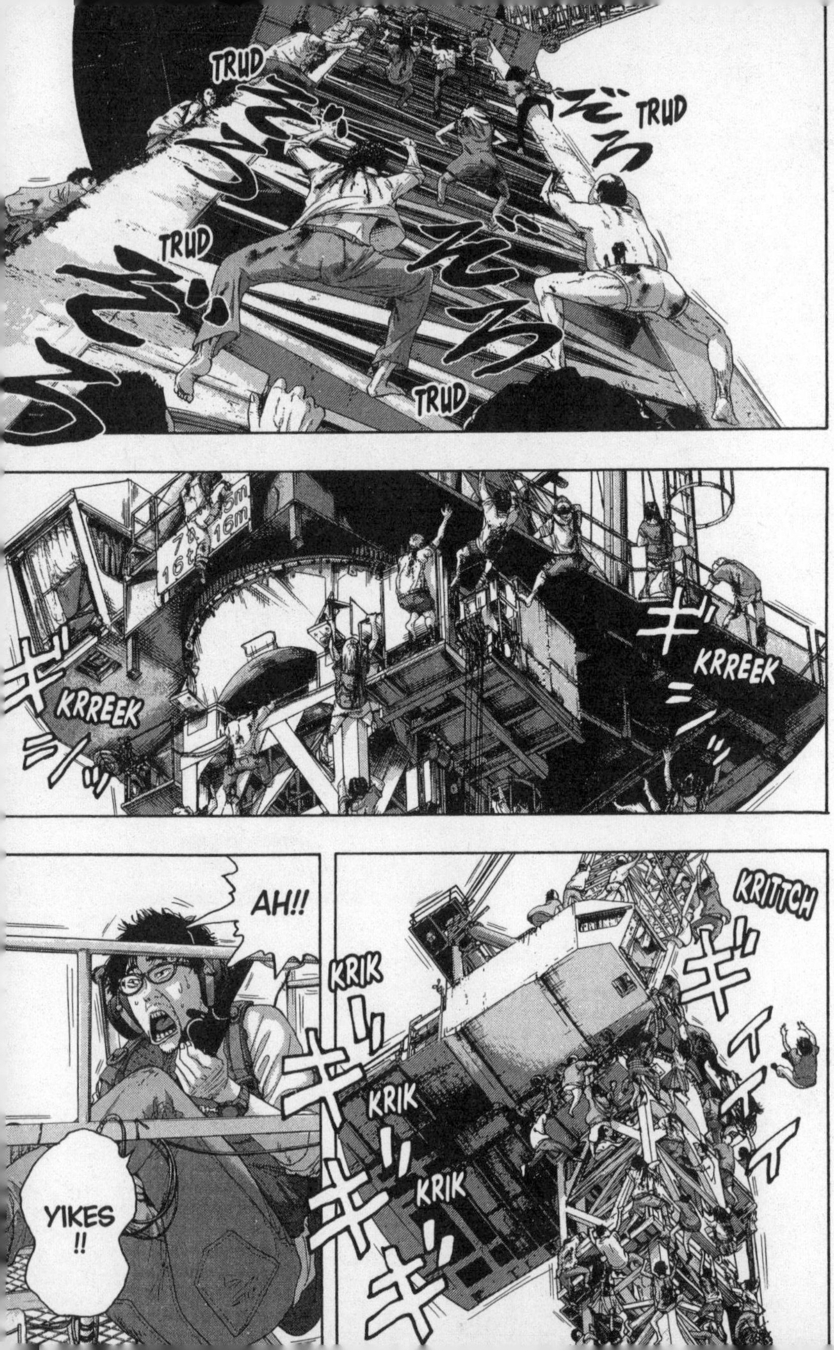
TRUD
TRUD
TRUD
TRUD
KRREEK
KRREEK
KRITTCH
KRIK
KRIK
KRIK
AH!!
YIKES !!

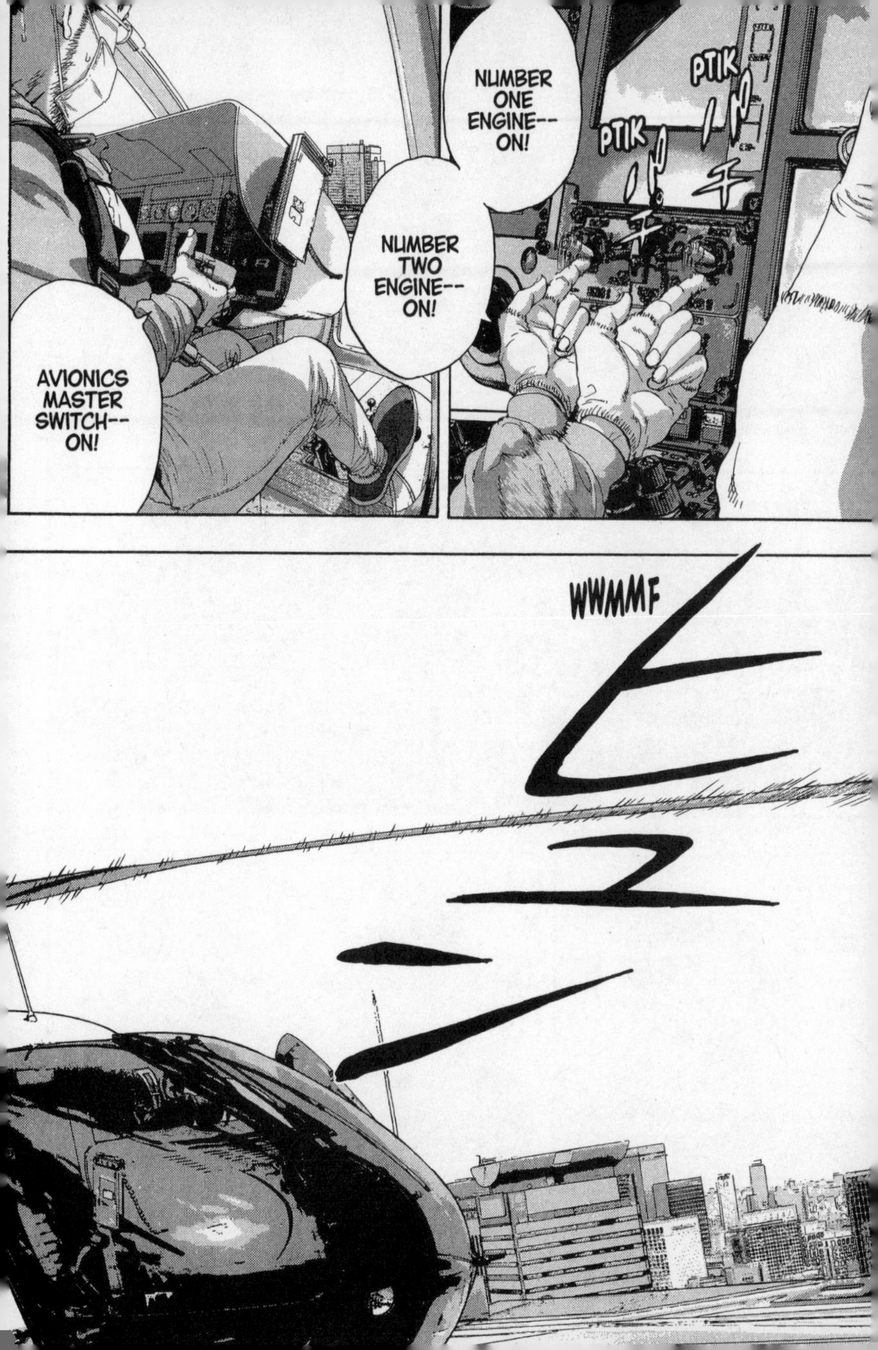
NUMBER ONE ENGINE-- ON!
NUMBER TWO ENGINE-- ON!
PTIK
PTIK
AVIONICS MASTER SWITCH-- ON!
WWMMF

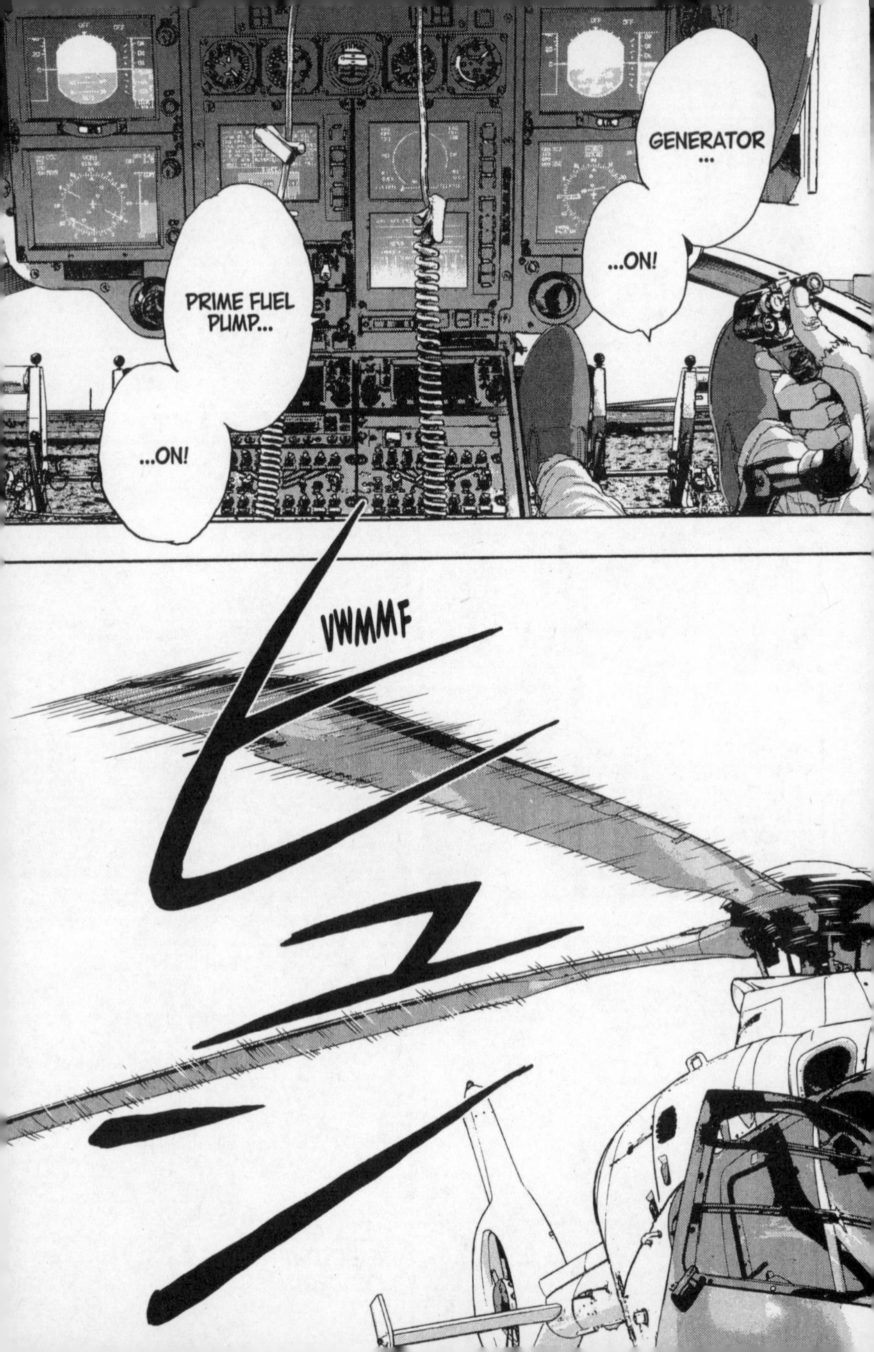
GENERATOR ...
...ON!
PRIME FUEL PUMP...
...ON!
VWMMF

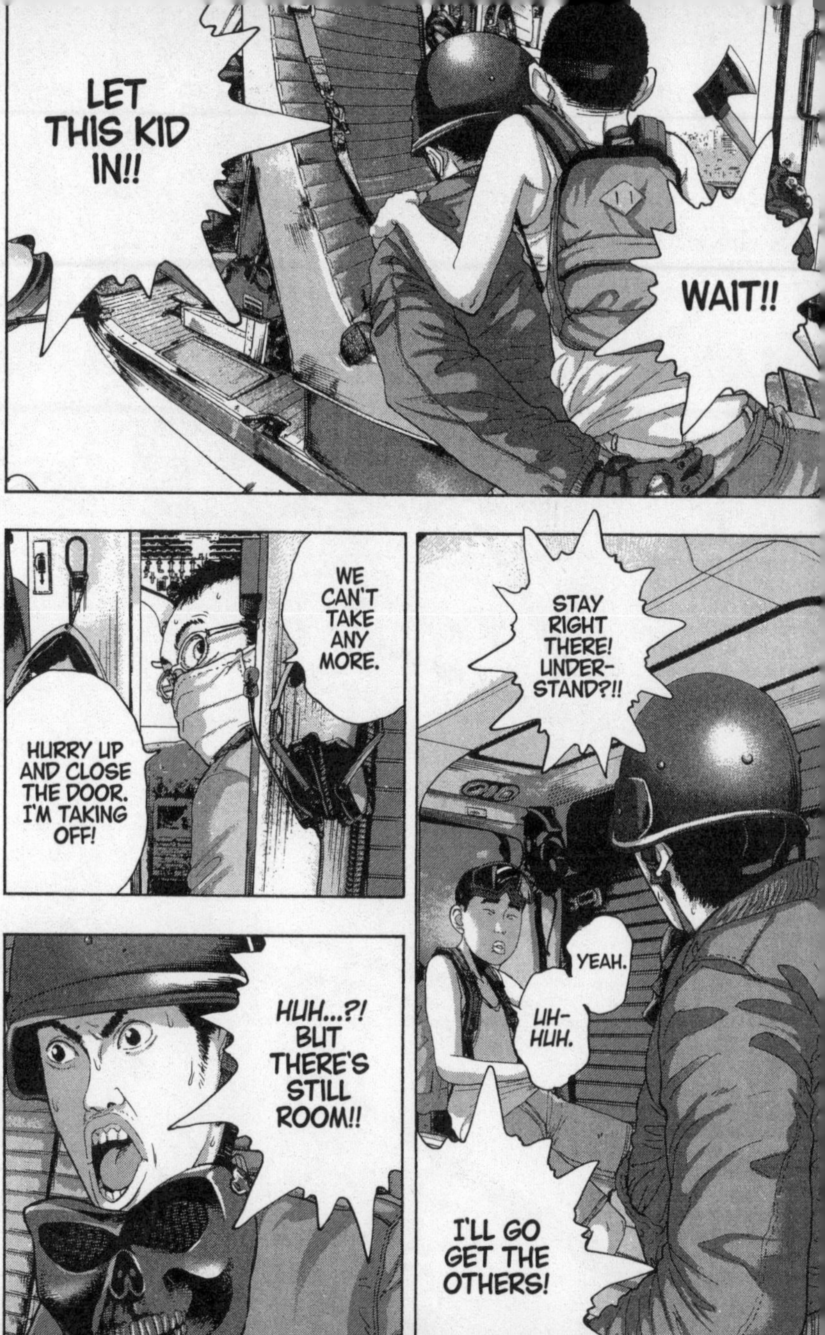
WAIT!!
LET THIS KID IN!!
STAY RIGHT THERE! UNDER-STAND?!!
YEAH.
UH-HUH.
I'LL GO GET THE OTHERS!
WE CAN'T TAKE ANY MORE.
HURRY UP AND CLOSE THE DOOR. I'M TAKING OFF!
HUH...?! BUT THERE'S STILL ROOM!!

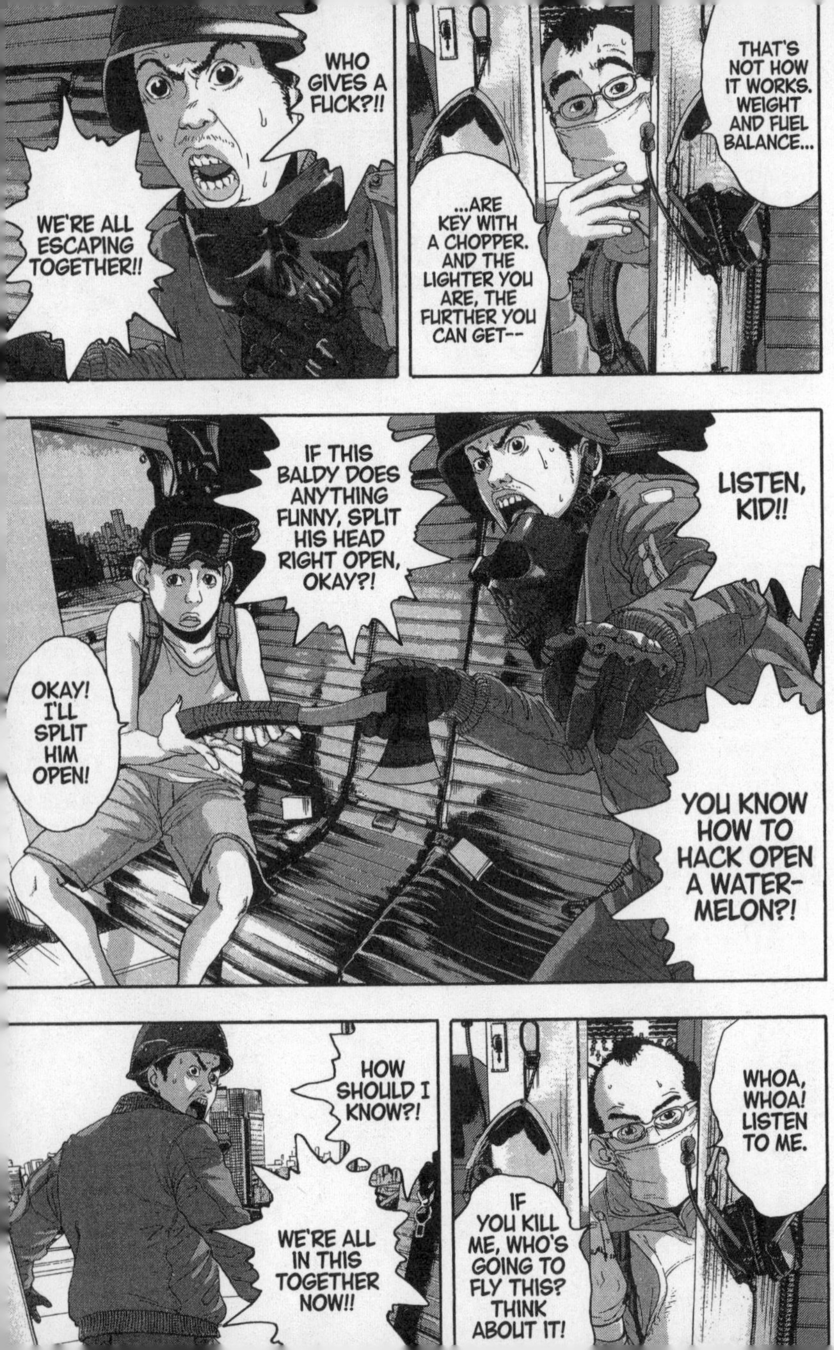
THAT'S NOT HOW IT WORKS. WEIGHT AND FUEL BALANCE...
...ARE KEY WITH A CHOPPER. AND THE LIGHTER YOU ARE, THE FURTHER YOU CAN GET--
WHO GIVES A FUCK?!!
WE'RE ALL ESCAPING TOGETHER!!
LISTEN, KID!!
YOU KNOW HOW TO HACK OPEN A WATER-MELON?!
IF THIS BALDY DOES ANYTHING FUNNY, SPLIT HIS HEAD RIGHT OPEN, OKAY?!
OKAY! I'LL SPLIT HIM OPEN!
WHOA, WHOA! LISTEN TO ME.
IF YOU KILL ME, WHO'S GOING TO FLY THIS? THINK ABOUT IT!
HOW SHOULD I KNOW?!
WE'RE ALL IN THIS TOGETHER NOW!!

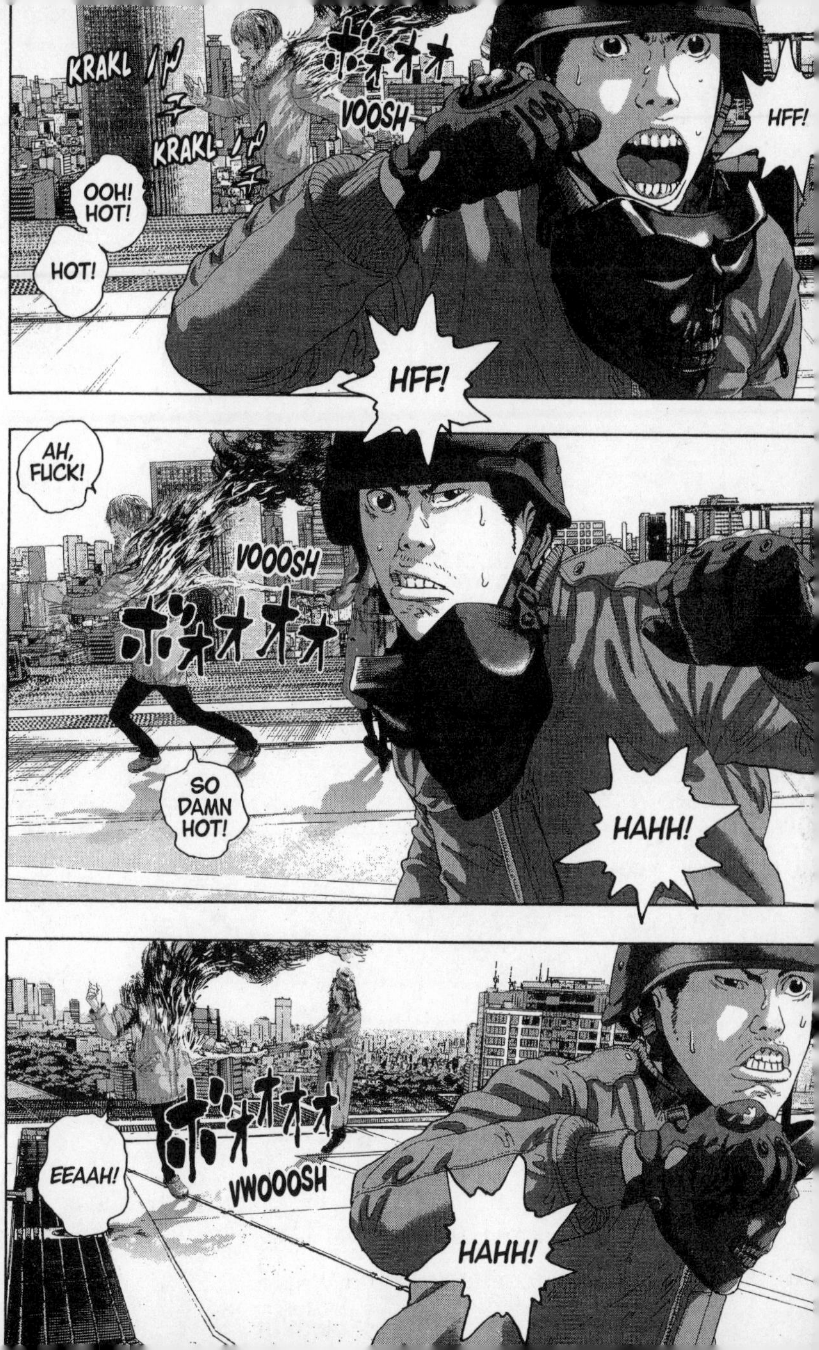
HFF!
ボオオオ
VOOSH
KRAKL パチ
KRAKL パチ
OOH! HOT!
HOT!
HFF!
HAHH!
VOOOSH
ボオオオオ
AH, FUCK!
SO DAMN HOT!
HAHH!
ボオオオオ
VWOOOSH
EEAAH!

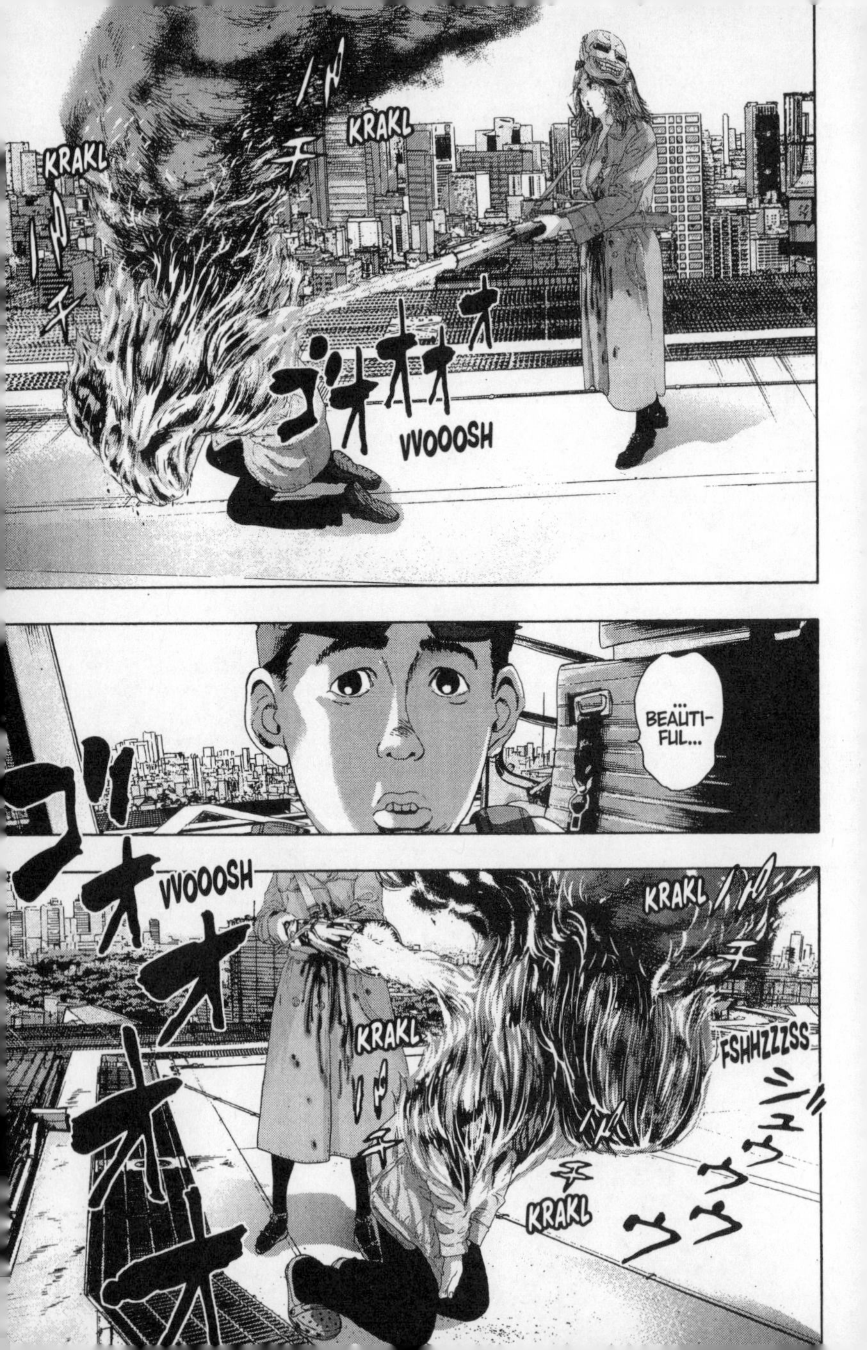
KRAKL
KRAKL
VVOOOSH
... BEAUTI-FUL...
KRAKL
VVOOOSH
FSHHZZZSS
KRAKL
KRAKL

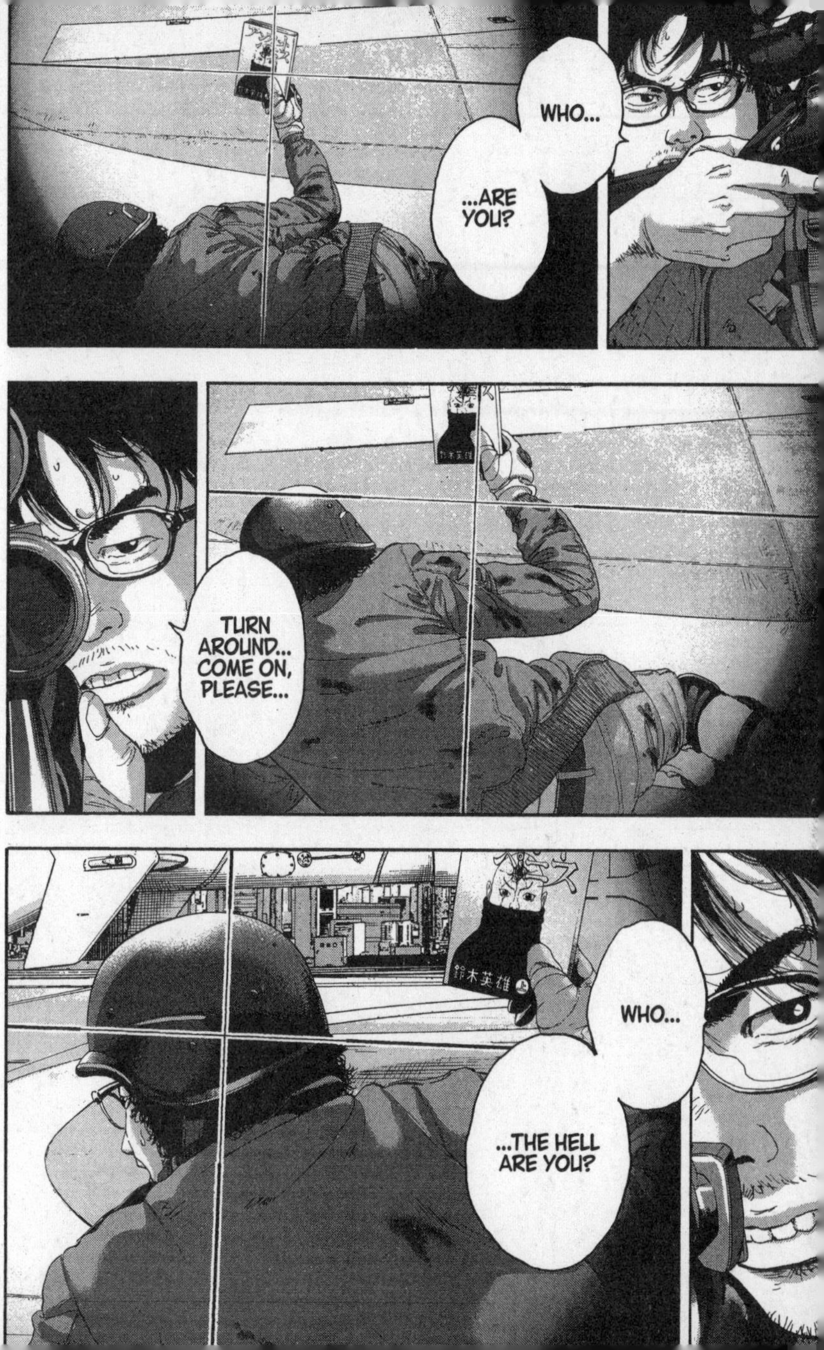
WHO...
...ARE YOU?
TURN AROUND... COME ON, PLEASE...
鈴木英雄
WHO...
...THE HELL ARE YOU?

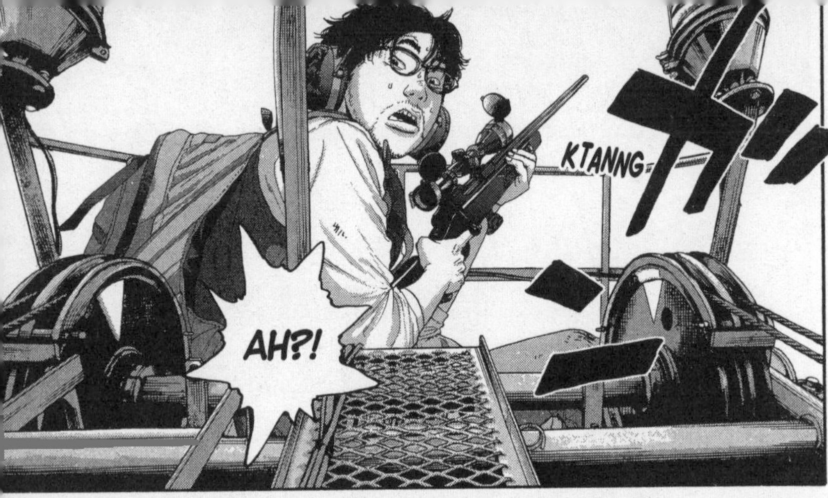
KTANNG
AH?!

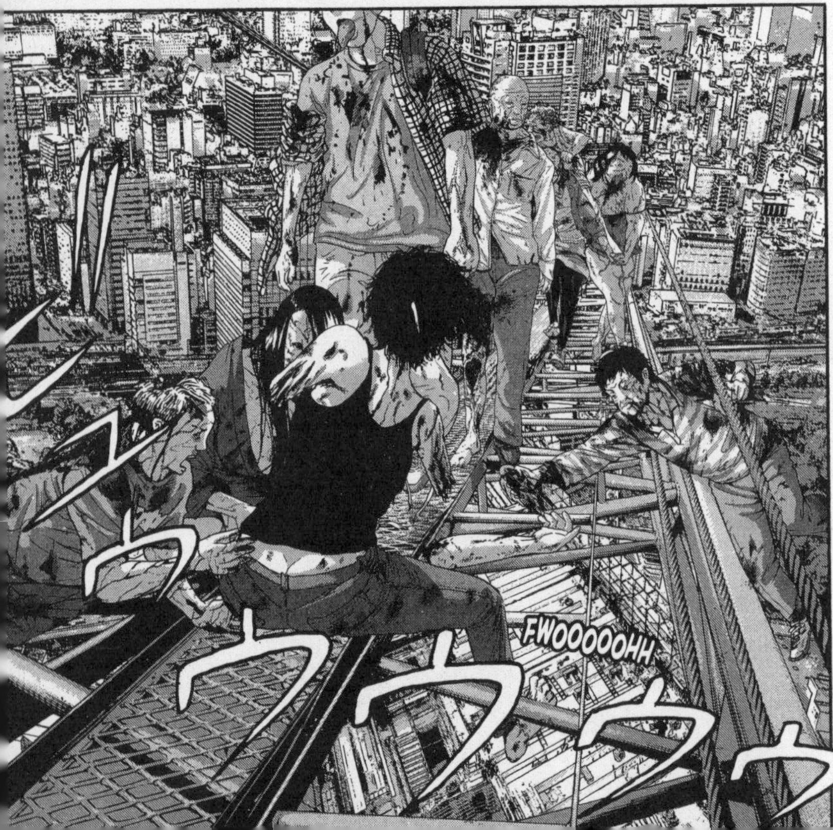
FWOOOOOHH
ウウウウ

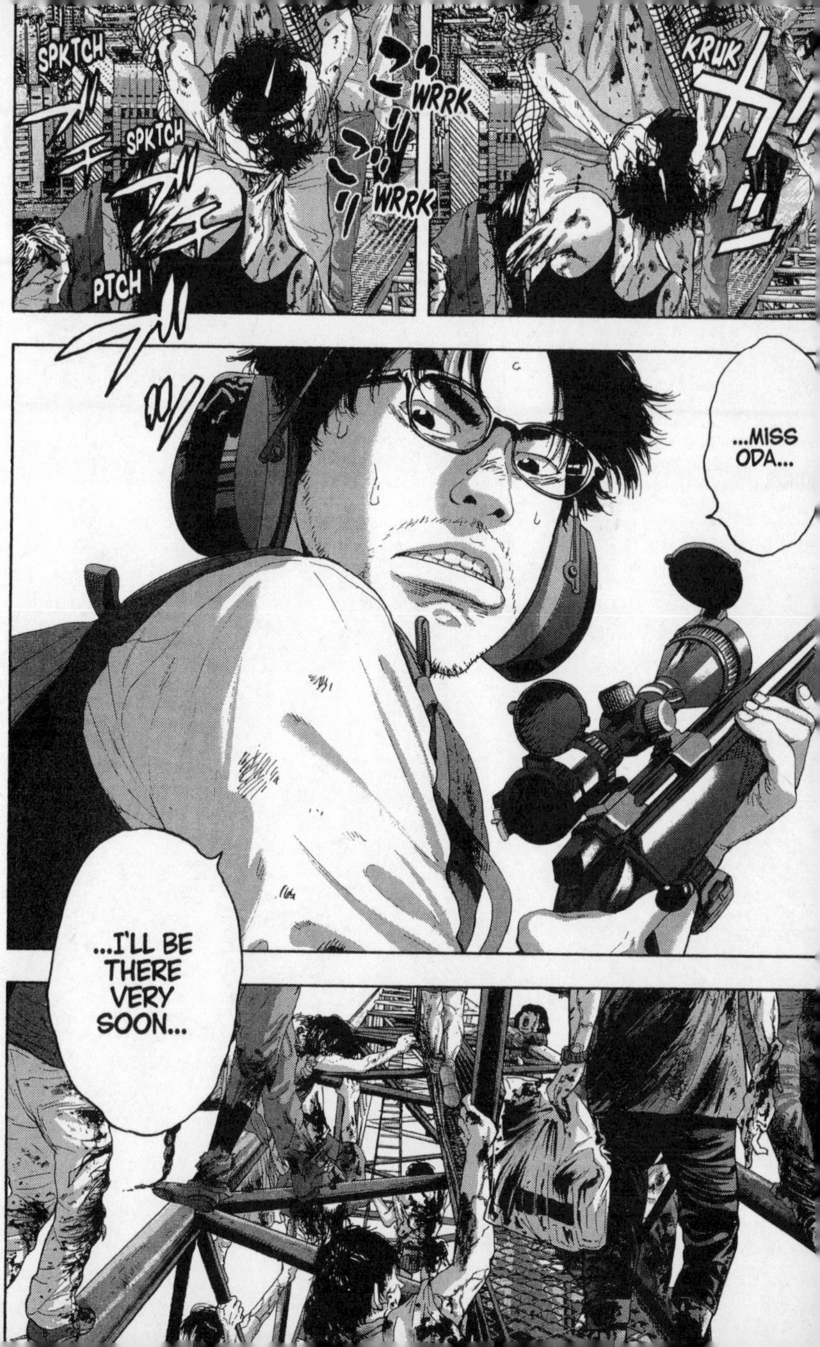
KRUK
SPKTCH
WRRK
SPKTCH
WRRK
PTCH
...MISS ODA...
...I'LL BE THERE VERY SOON...

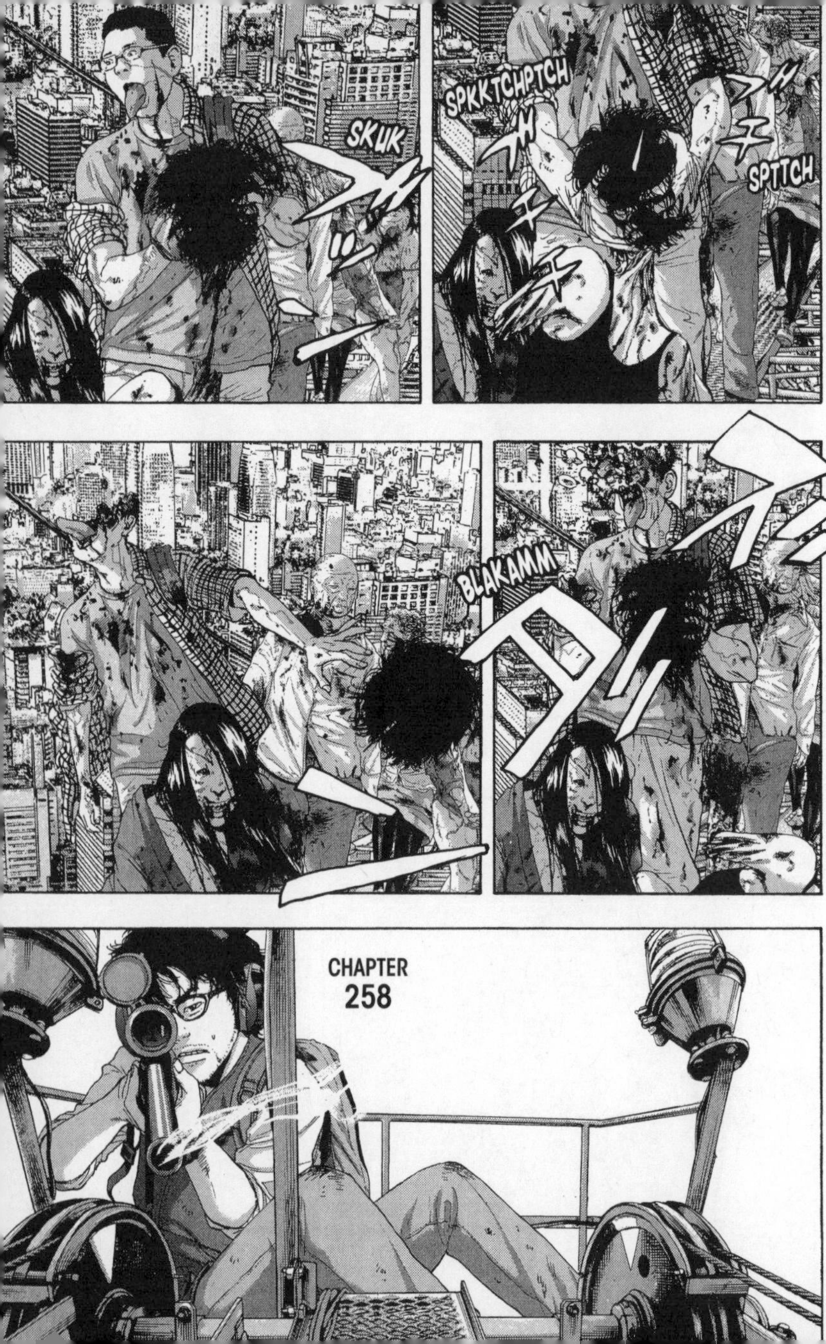
SPKKTCHPTCH
SPTTCH
SKUK
BLAKAMM
CHAPTER
258

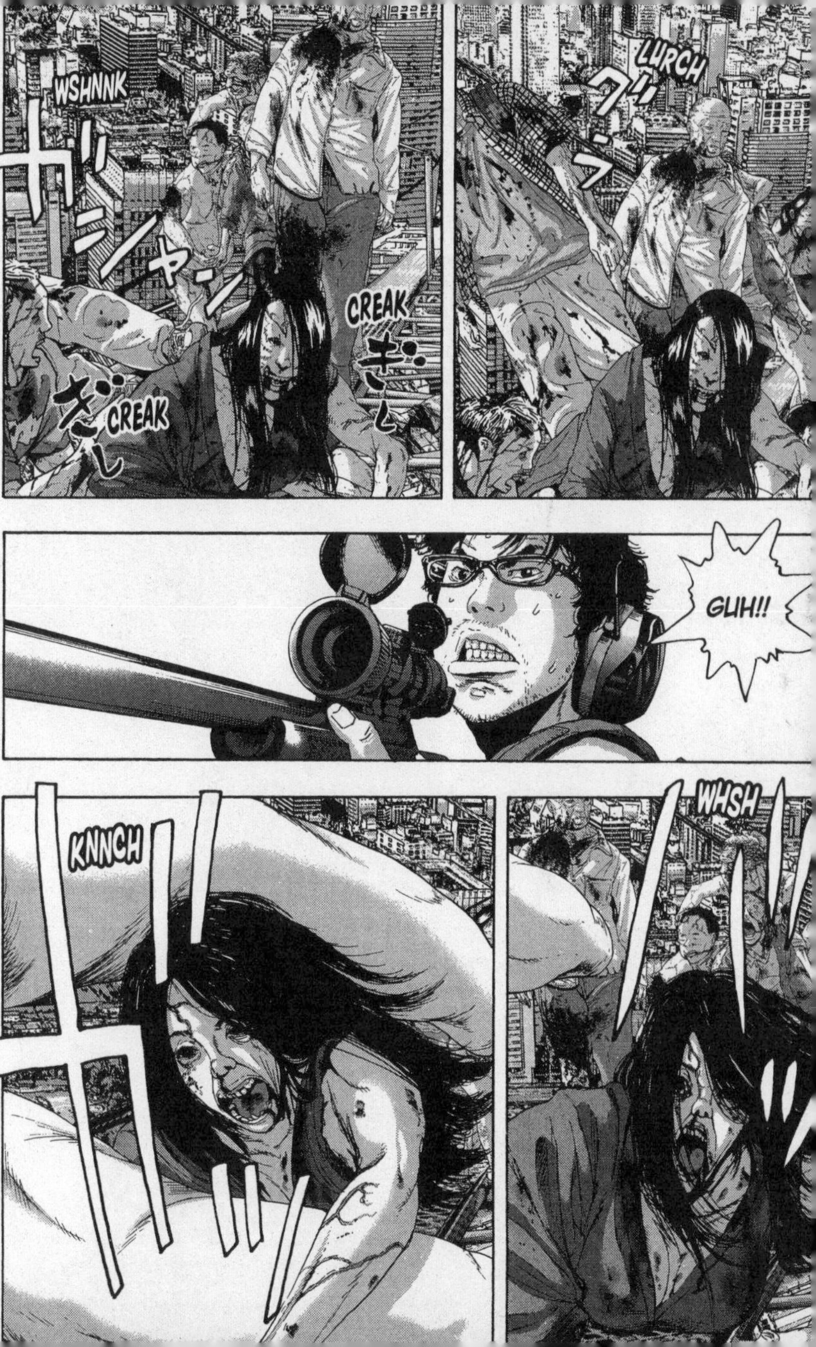
LURCH
WSHNNK
CREAK
ぎし
CREAK
ぎし
GUH!!
WHSH
KNNCH

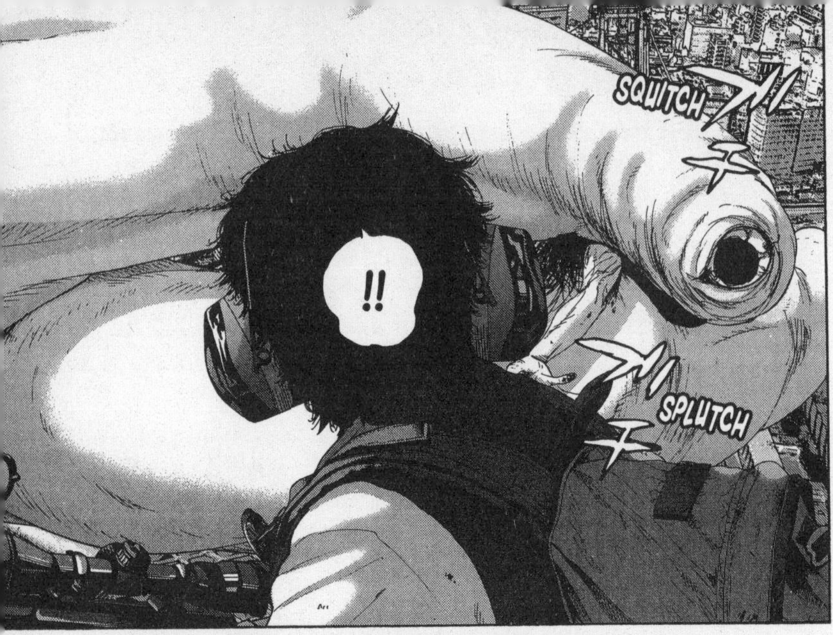
SQUITCH
!!
SPLUTCH

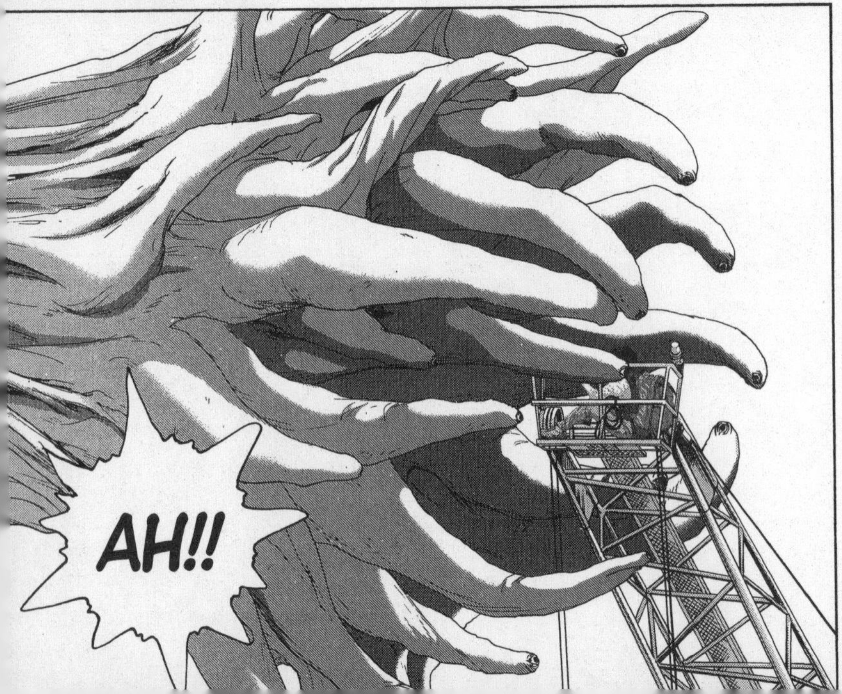
AH!!

HA HA...
WHSH
ズッ
WHSH
ズッ
WHSH
ズッ
KSHANNG
ズズッ
WHSH
WHSH
KRIKREE
KRIKREE

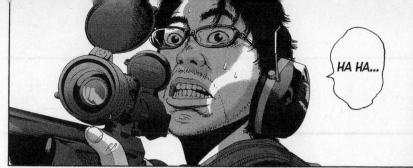

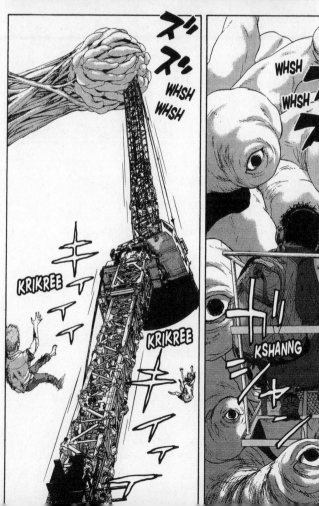

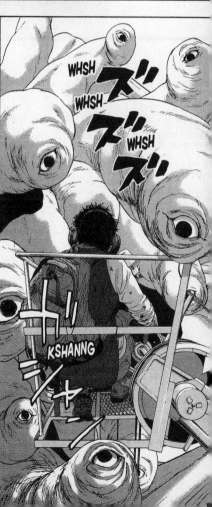

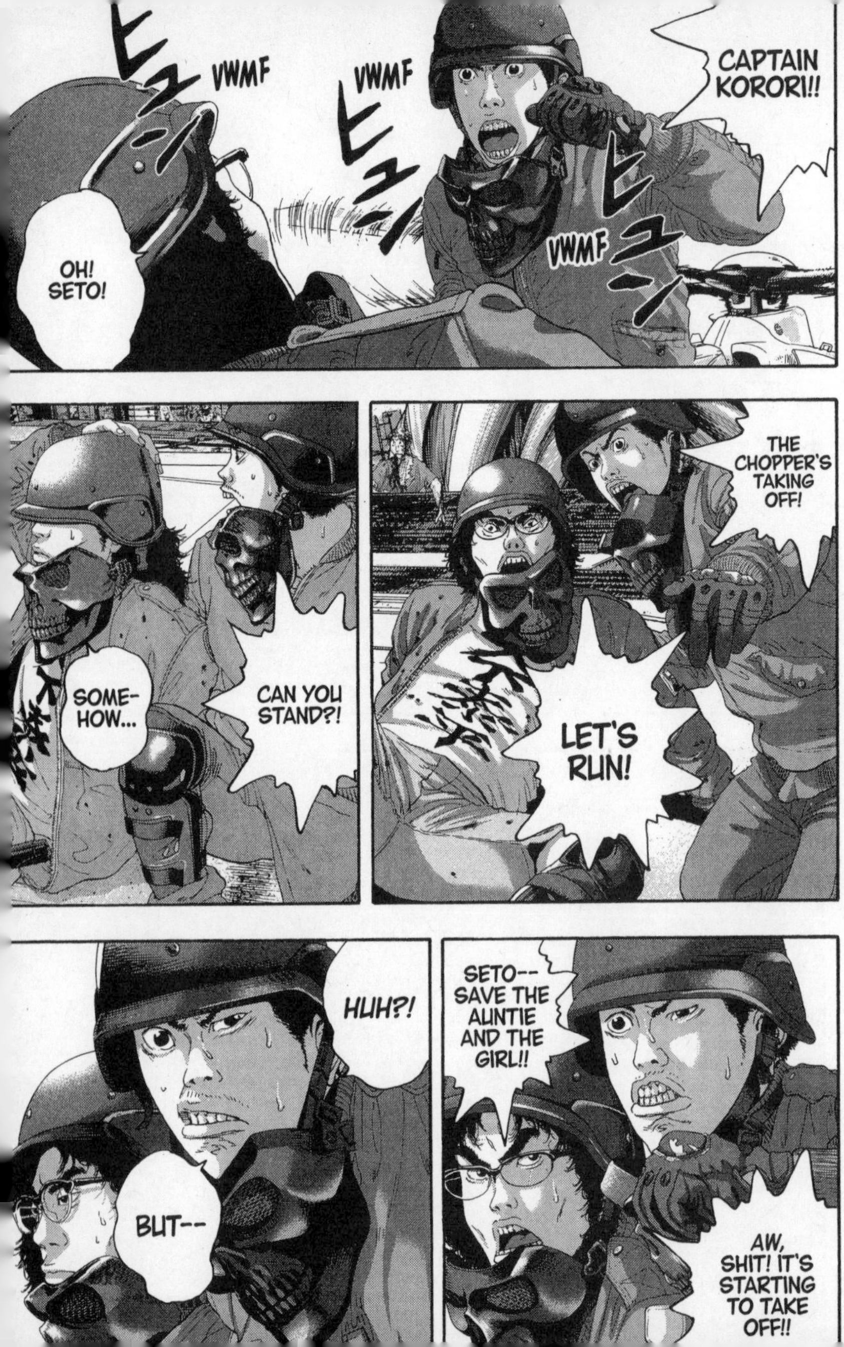
CAPTAIN KORORI!!
VWMF
VWMF
VWMF
OH! SETO!
THE CHOPPER'S TAKING OFF!
LET'S RUN!
CAN YOU STAND?!
SOME-HOW...
SETO-- SAVE THE AUNTIE AND THE GIRL!!
AW, SHIT! IT'S STARTING TO TAKE OFF!!
HUH?!
BUT--

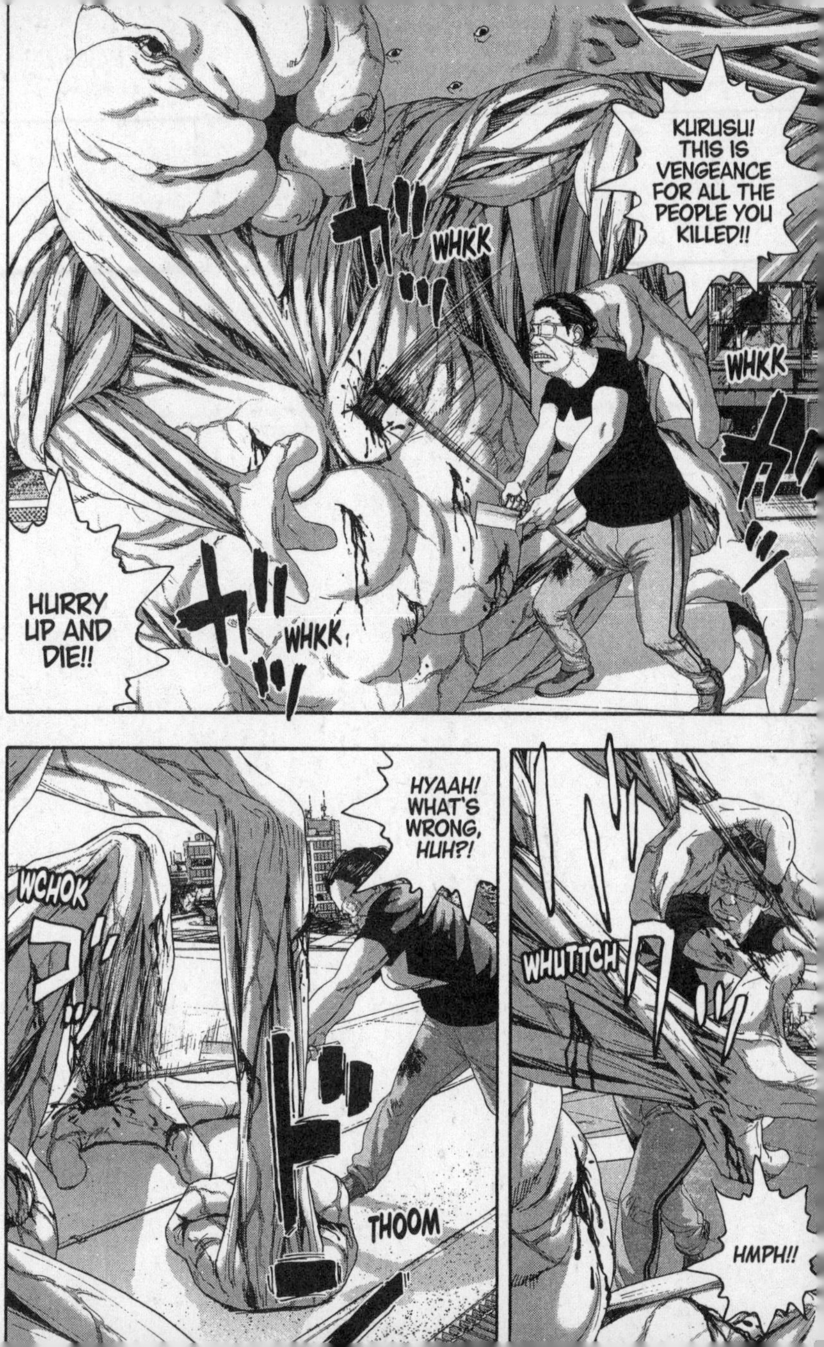
KURUSU! THIS IS VENGEANCE FOR ALL THE PEOPLE YOU KILLED!!
WHKK
WHKK
HURRY UP AND DIE!!
WHKK
WHUTTCH
HMPH!!
HYAAH! WHAT'S WRONG, HUH?!
WCHOK
THOOM

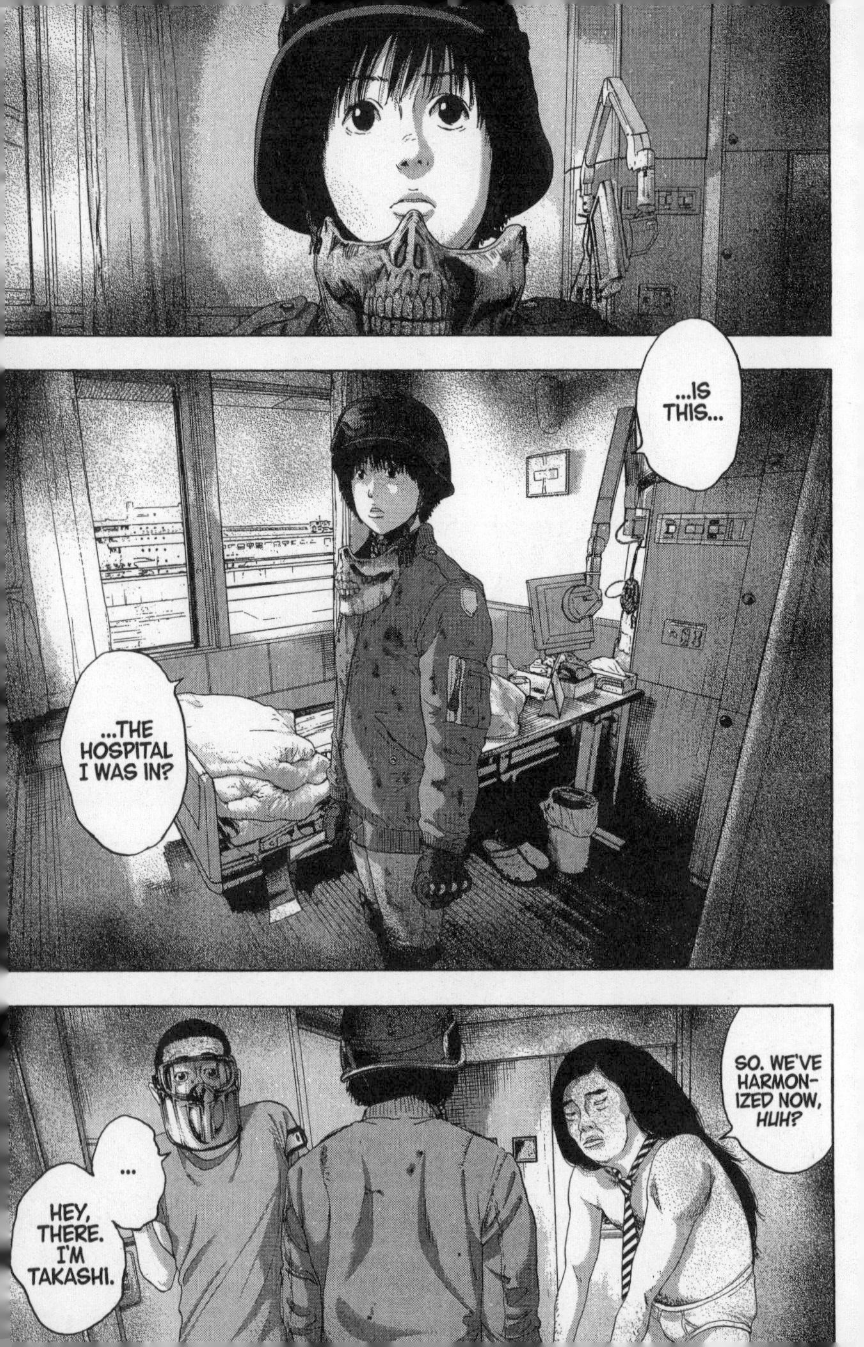
...IS THIS...
...THE HOSPITAL I WAS IN?
SO. WE'VE HARMON-IZED NOW, HUH?
...
HEY, THERE. I'M TAKASHI.

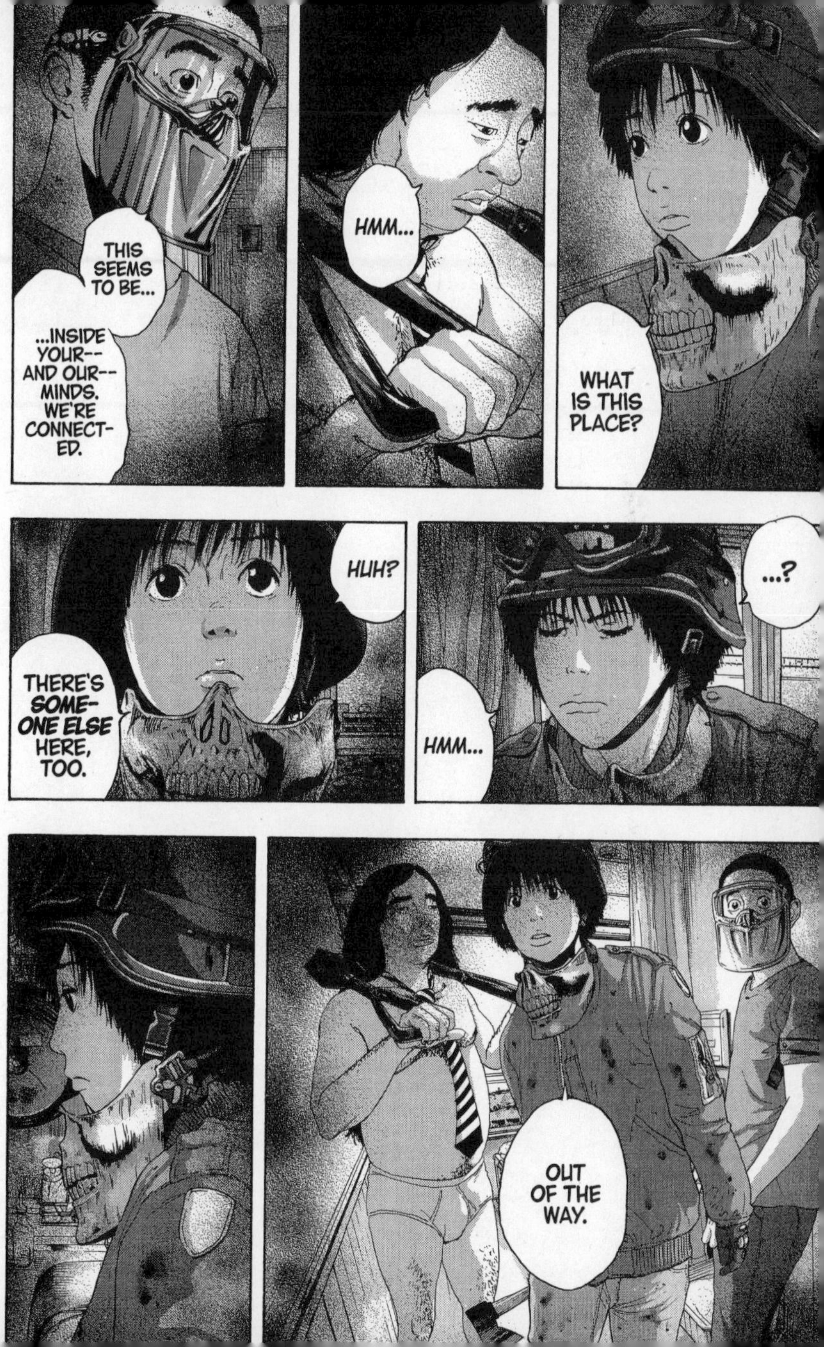
WHAT IS THIS PLACE?
HMM...
THIS SEEMS TO BE...
...INSIDE YOUR-- AND OUR-- MINDS. WE'RE CONNECT-ED.
...?
HMM...
HUH?
THERE'S SOME-ONE ELSE HERE, TOO.
OUT OF THE WAY.

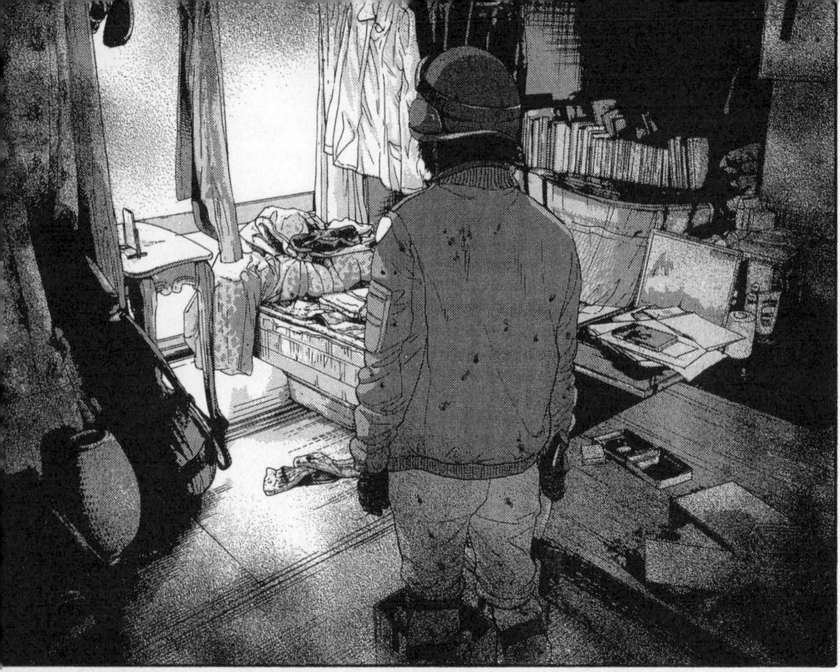

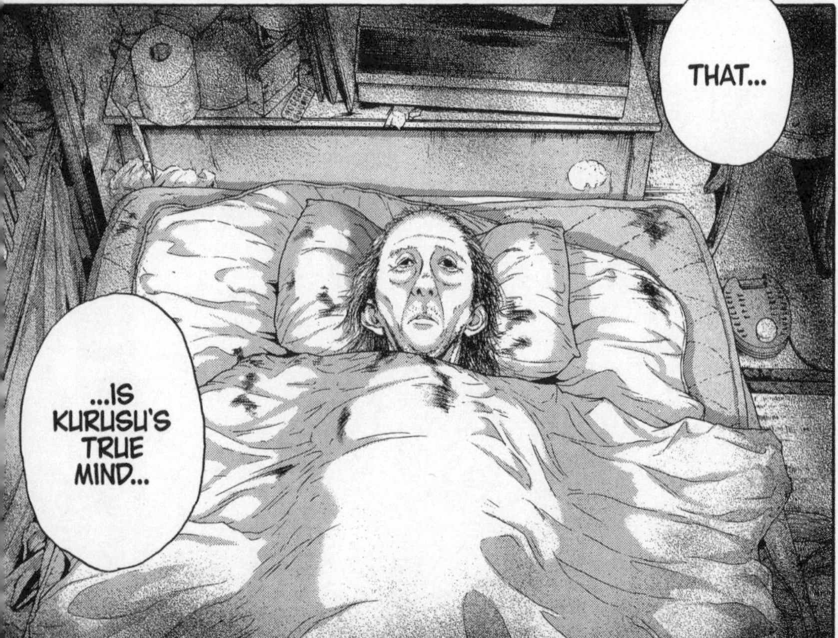
THAT...
...IS KURUSU'S TRUE MIND...

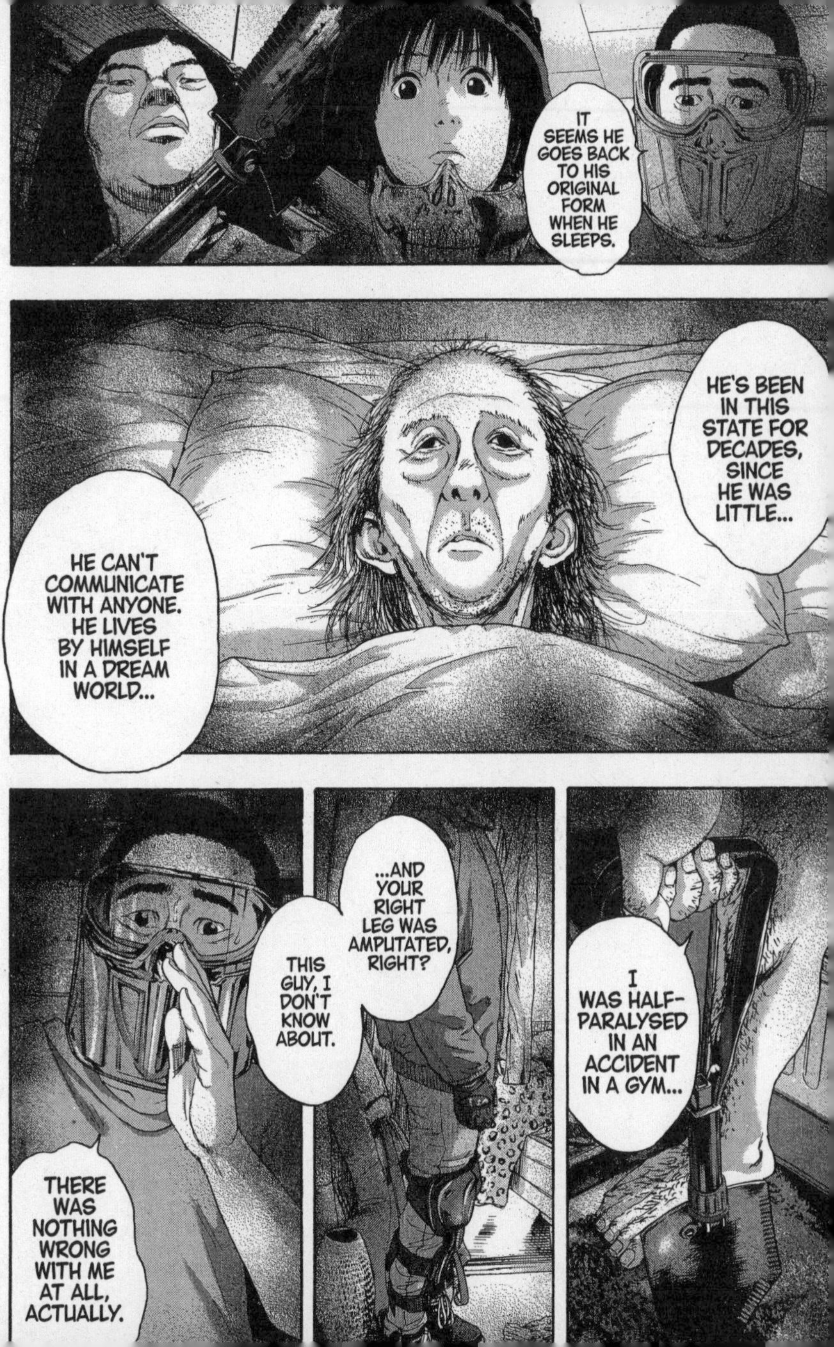
IT SEEMS HE GOES BACK TO HIS ORIGINAL FORM WHEN HE SLEEPS.
HE'S BEEN IN THIS STATE FOR DECADES, SINCE HE WAS LITTLE...
HE CAN'T COMMUNICATE WITH ANYONE. HE LIVES BY HIMSELF IN A DREAM WORLD...
I WAS HALF-PARALYSED IN AN ACCIDENT IN A GYM...
...AND YOUR RIGHT LEG WAS AMPUTATED, RIGHT?
THIS GUY, I DON'T KNOW ABOUT.
THERE WAS NOTHING WRONG WITH ME AT ALL, ACTUALLY.

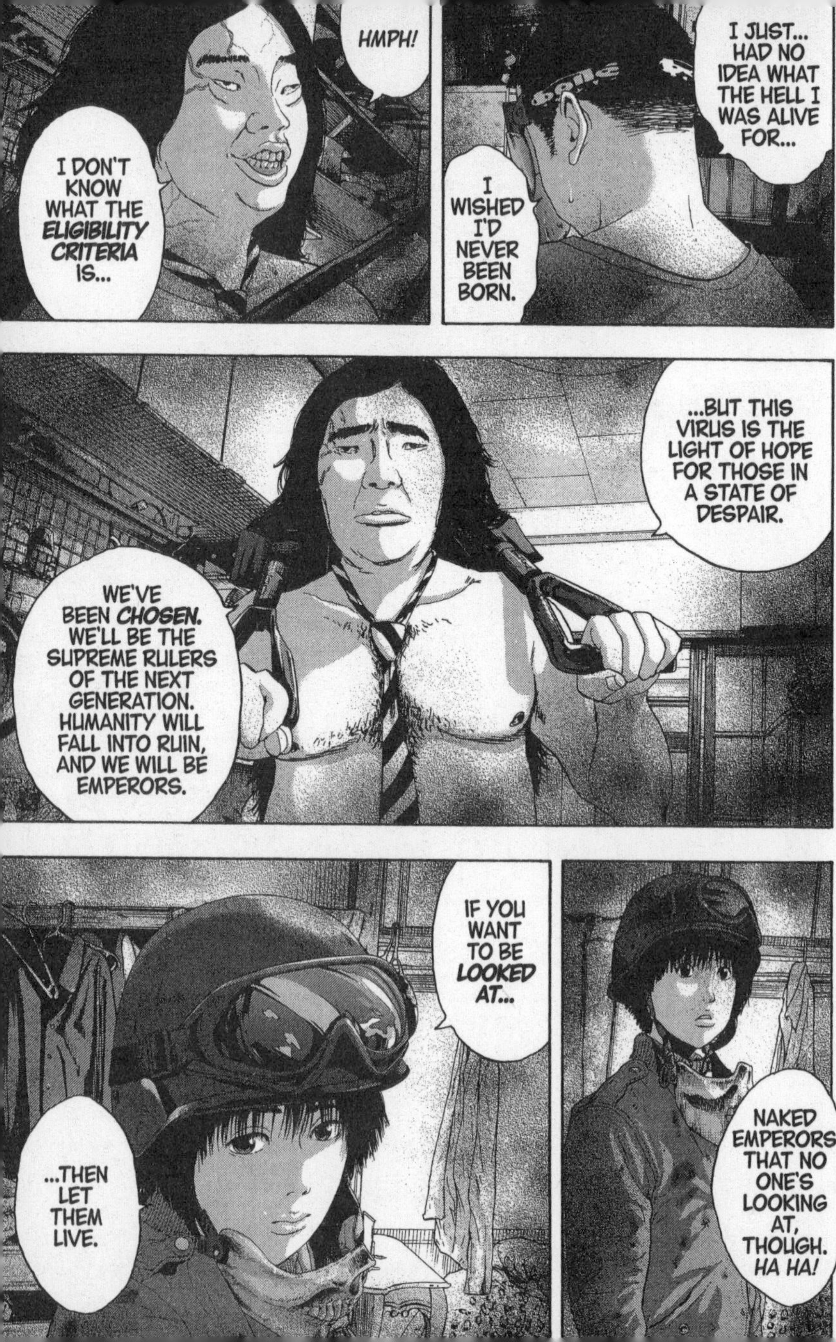
I JUST... HAD NO IDEA WHAT THE HELL I WAS ALIVE FOR...
I WISHED I'D NEVER BEEN BORN.
HMPH!
I DON'T KNOW WHAT THE ELIGIBILITY CRITERIA IS...
...BUT THIS VIRUS IS THE LIGHT OF HOPE FOR THOSE IN A STATE OF DESPAIR.
WE'VE BEEN CHOSEN. WE'LL BE THE SUPREME RULERS OF THE NEXT GENERATION. HUMANITY WILL FALL INTO RUIN, AND WE WILL BE EMPERORS.
NAKED EMPERORS THAT NO ONE'S LOOKING AT, THOUGH. HA HA!
IF YOU WANT TO BE LOOKED AT...
...THEN LET THEM LIVE.

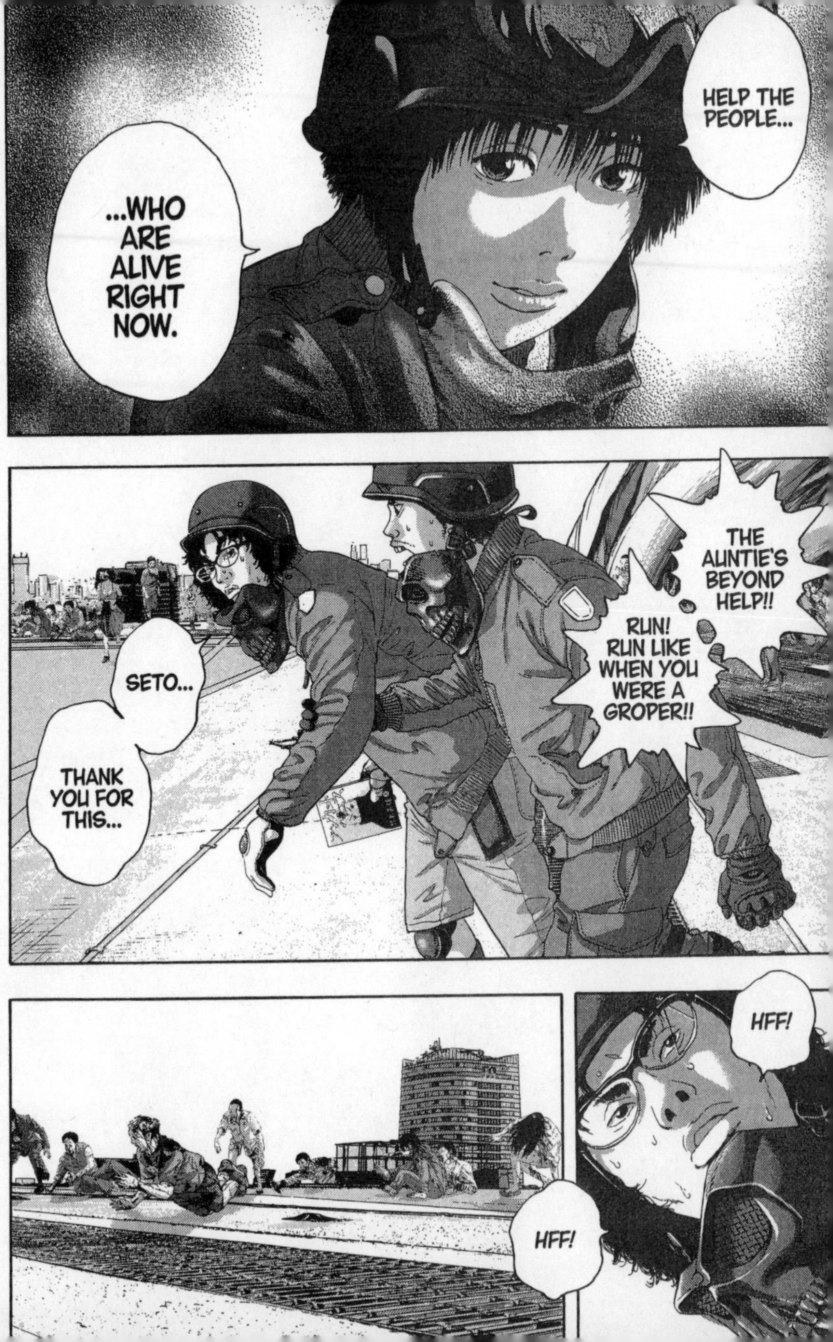
HELP THE PEOPLE...
...WHO ARE ALIVE RIGHT NOW.
THE AUNTIE'S BEYOND HELP!!
RUN! RUN LIKE WHEN YOU WERE A GROPER!!
SETO...
THANK YOU FOR THIS...
HFF!
HFF!

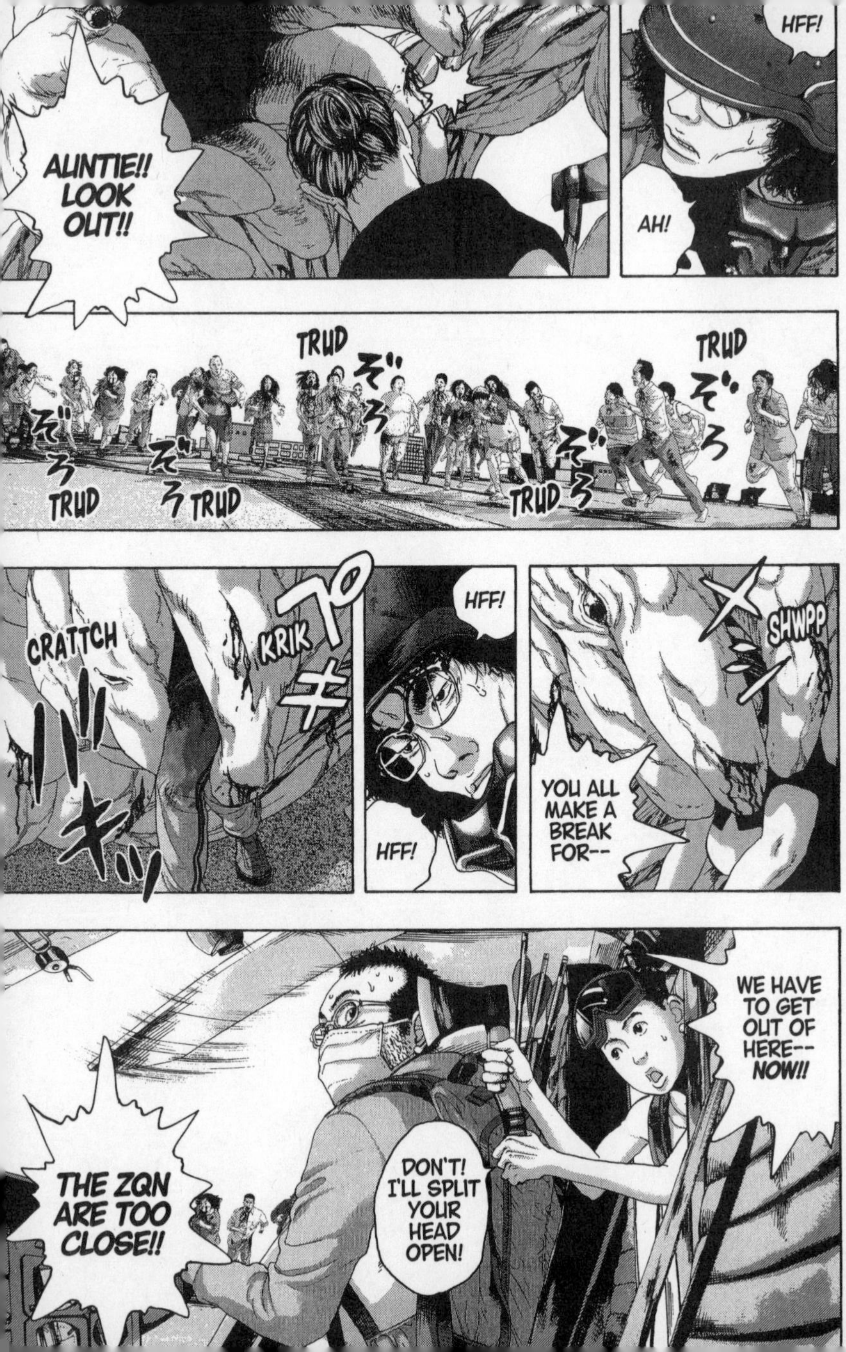
HFF!
AH!
AUNTIE!! LOOK OUT!!
TRUD
ぞろ
ぞろ
TRUD
TRUD
ぞろ
TRUD
ぞろ
TRUD
ぞろ
TRUD
SHWPP
YOU ALL MAKE A BREAK FOR--
HFF!
HFF!
KRIK
CRATTCH
WE HAVE TO GET OUT OF HERE-- NOW!!
DON'T! I'LL SPLIT YOUR HEAD OPEN!
THE ZQN ARE TOO CLOSE!!

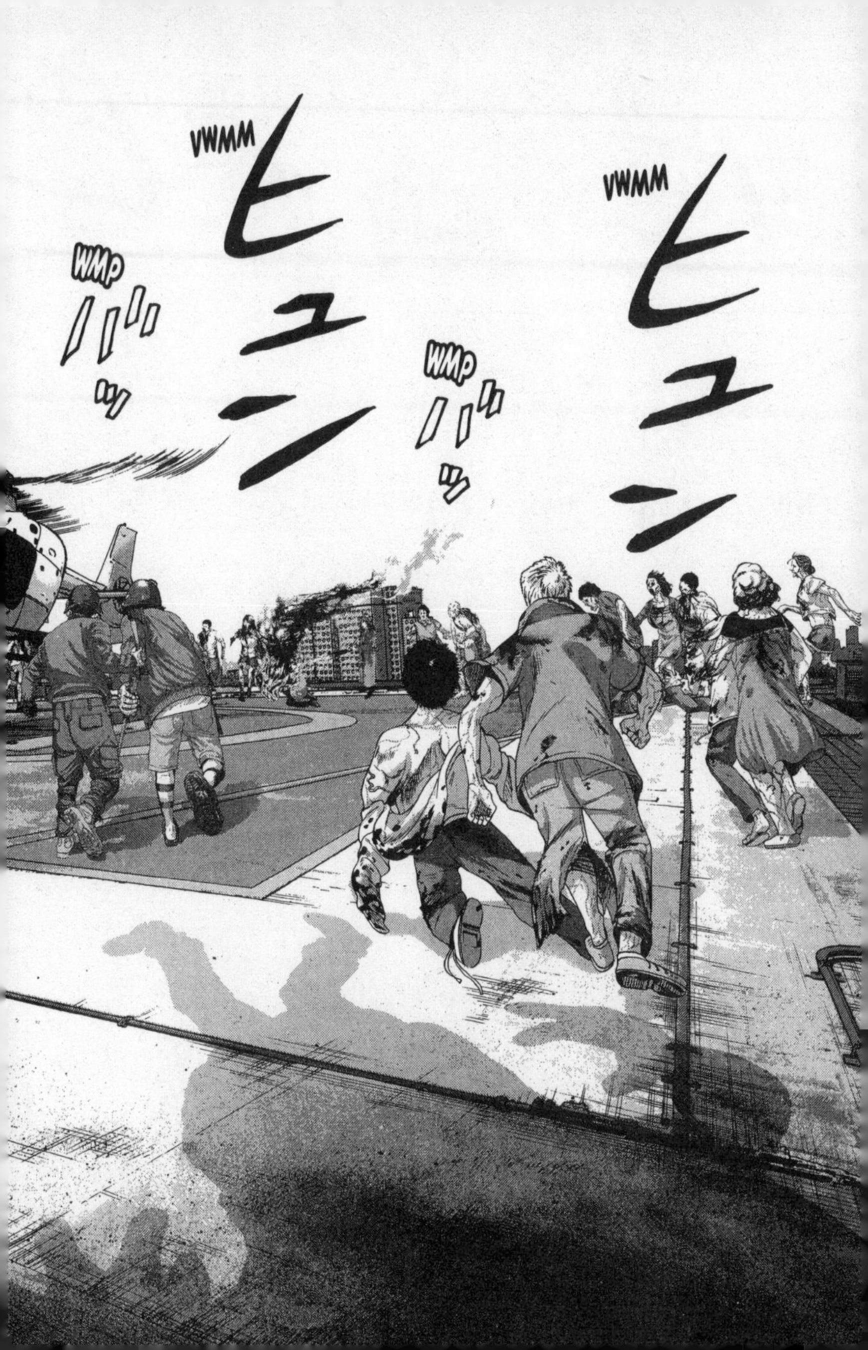
VWMM
ヒュン
WMP
バッ
VWMM
ヒュン
WMP
バッ

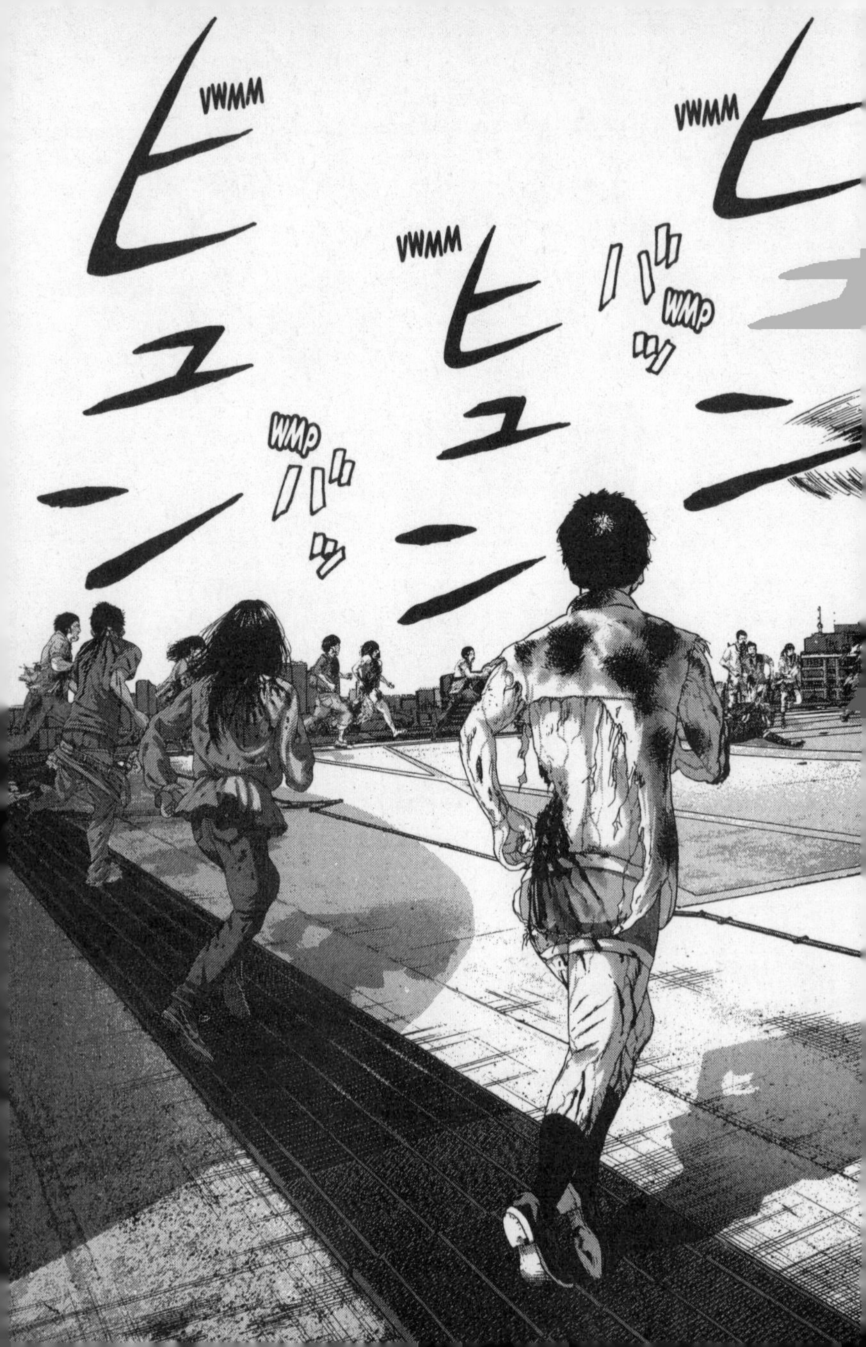

VWMM
ヒューン
VWMM
ヒューン
バッ
WMP
VWMM
ヒューン
WMP
バッ

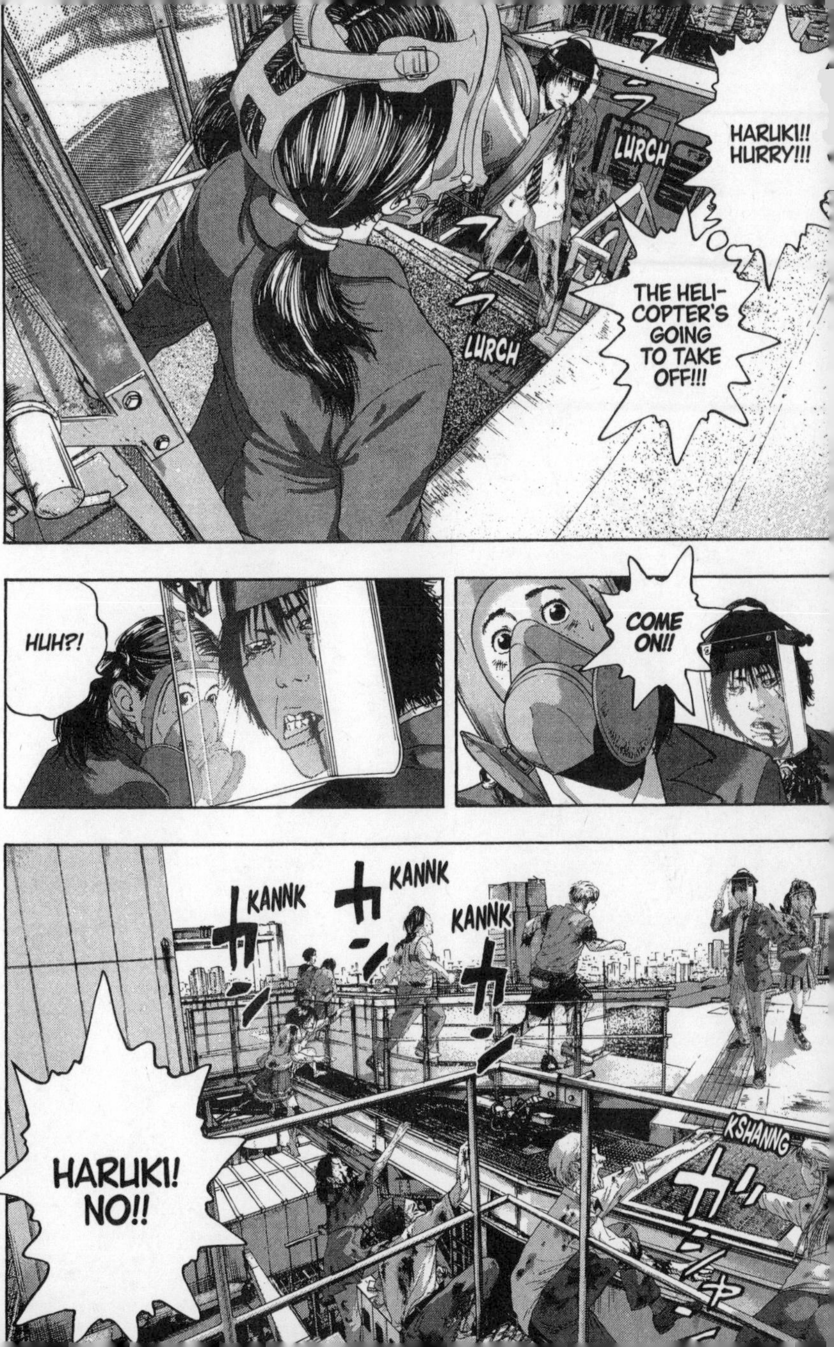
HARUKI!! HURRY!!!
THE HELI-COPTER'S GOING TO TAKE OFF!!!
LURCH
LURCH
COME ON!!
HUH?!
KANNK
KANNK
KANNK
KSHANNG
HARUKI! NO!!

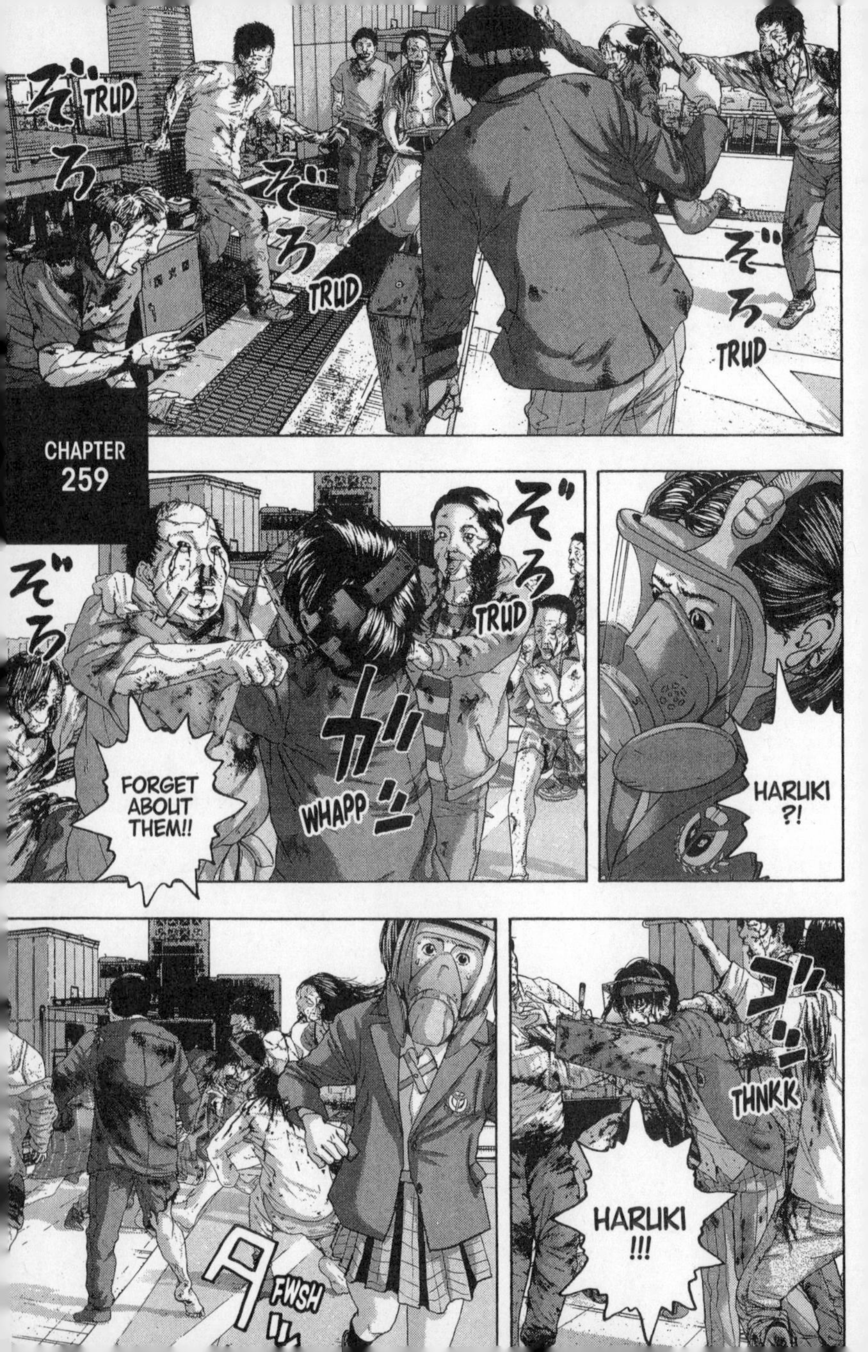
ぞろ
TRUD
ぞろ
TRUD
ぞろ
TRUD
CHAPTER 259
HARUKI ?!
ぞろ
TRUD
ガッ
WHAPP
ぞろ
FORGET ABOUT THEM!!
ゴッ
THNKK
HARUKI !!!
タ
FWSH

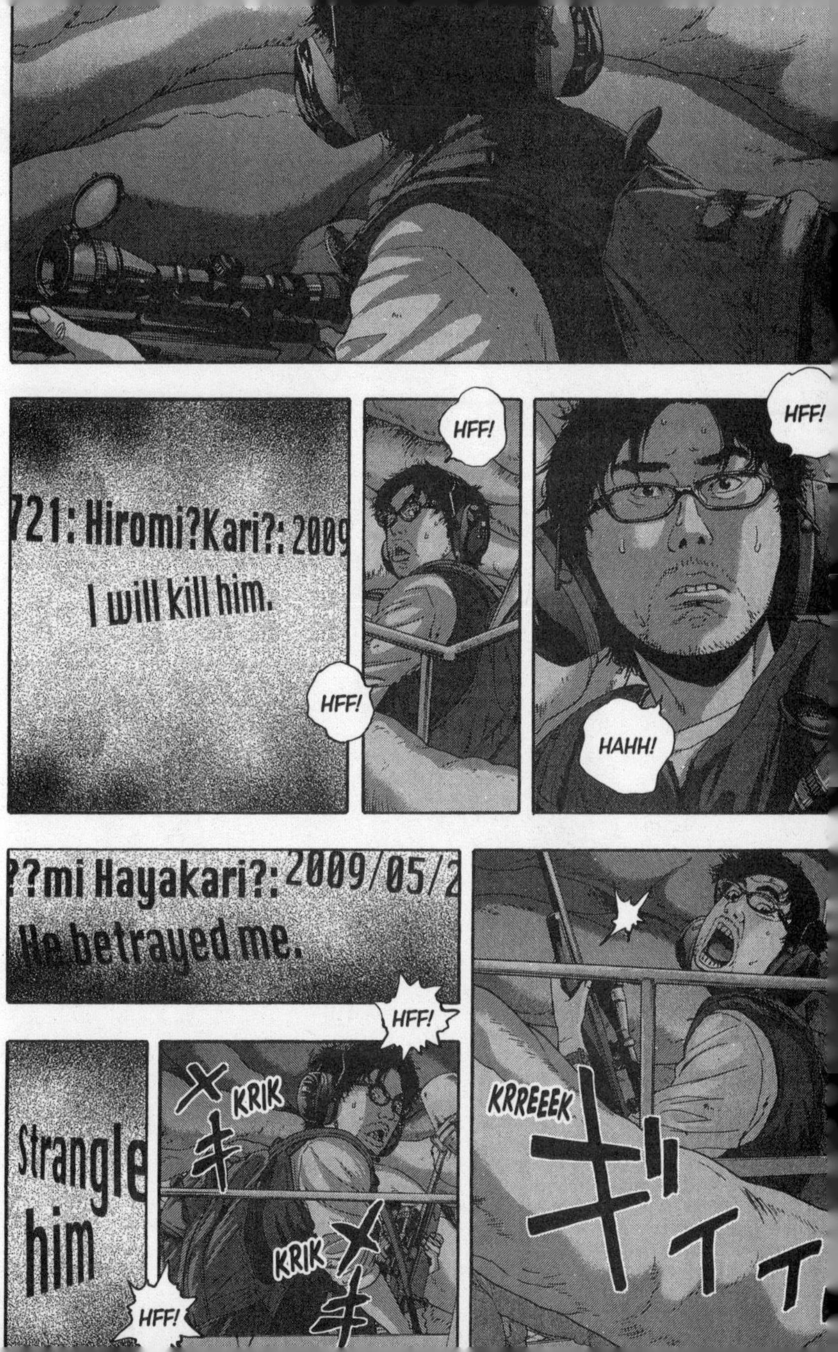

HFF!
HAHH!
HFF!
HFF!
721: Hiromi?Kari?: 2009
I will kill him.
KRREEEK
ギリィィ
??mi Hayakari?: 2009/05/2
He betrayed me.
HFF!
KRIK
キ
KRIK
キ
Strangle him
HFF!

kill kill kill kill kill kill
kill kill kill kill kill kill

KRREEE

KRREEEK

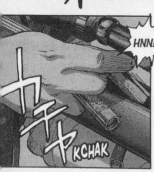
KCHAK

HNN!

SHWFF

HNN!

GUH!

725: Hiromi Hayakari: 2009/05/23 (Sat) 11:06:2
Don't kill him.

WRRKK

?!

SHIIIT!!

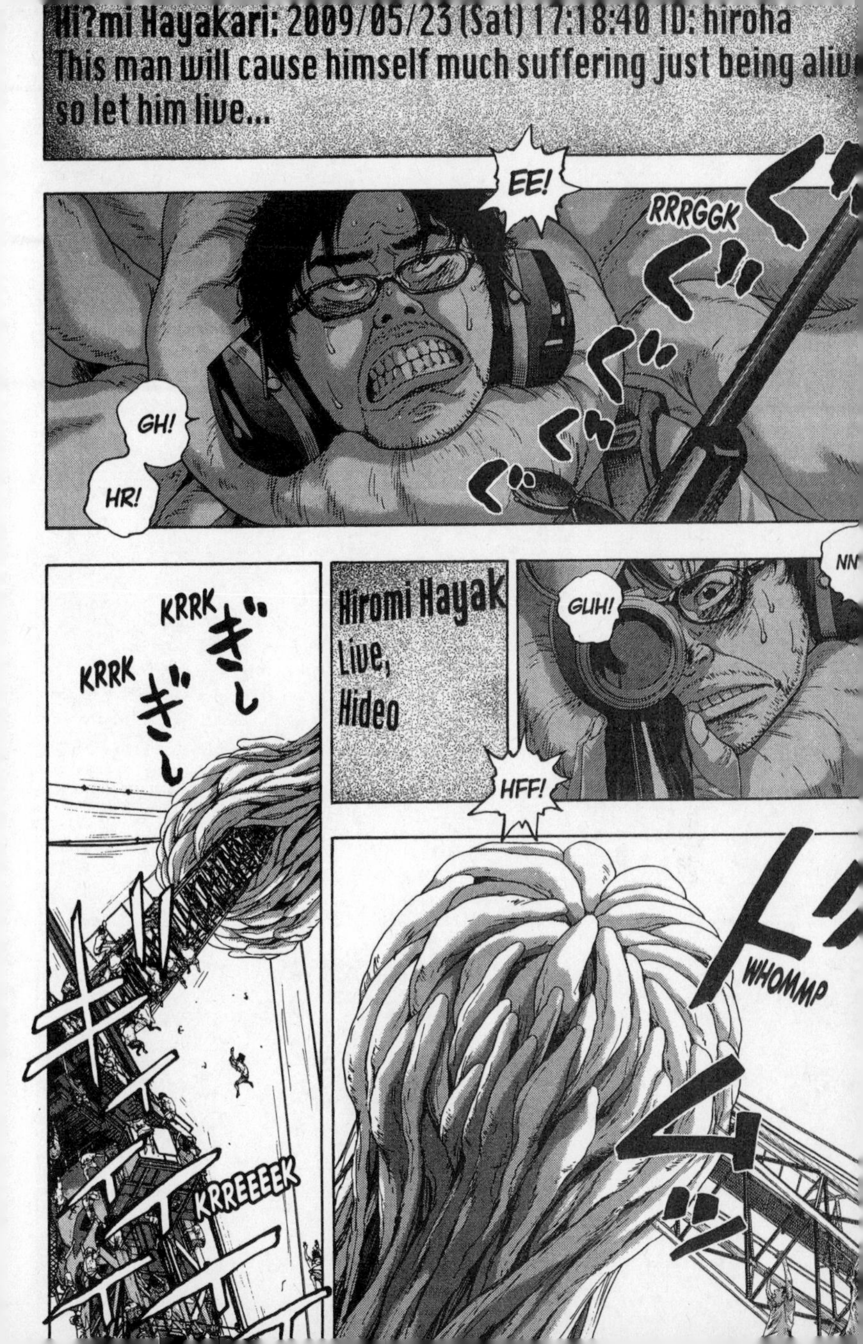
Hi?mi Hayakari: 2009/05/23 (Sat) 17:18:40 ID: hiroha
This man will cause himself much suffering just being aliv
so let him live...
EE!
RRRGGK
GH!
HR!
NN
GUH!
HFF!
Hiromi Hayak
Live,
Hideo
WHOMMP
KRRK
ぎし
KRRK
ぎし
KRREEEEK

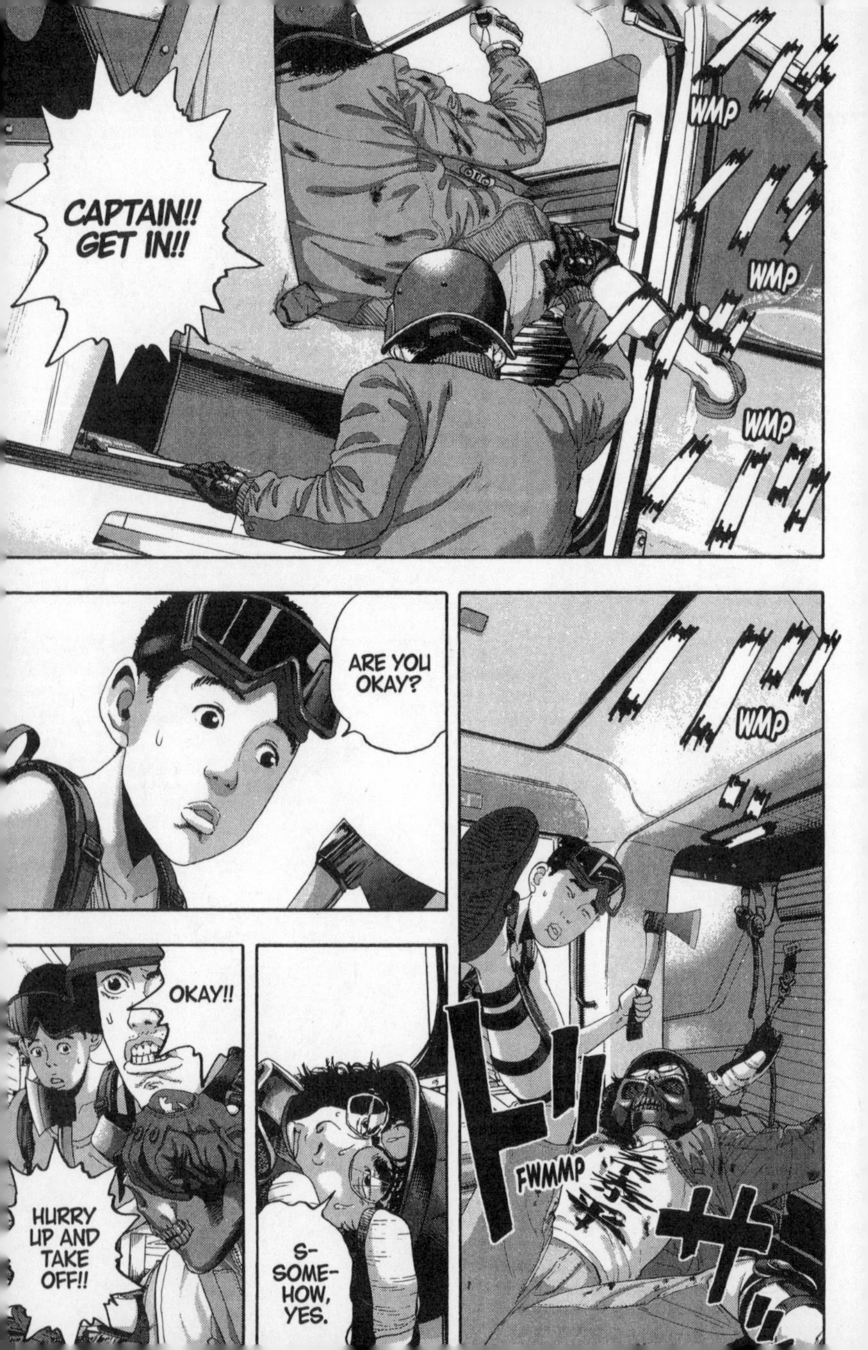
CAPTAIN!! GET IN!!
WMP
WMP
WMP
WMP
FWMMP
ARE YOU OKAY?
S-SOME-HOW, YES.
OKAY!!
HURRY UP AND TAKE OFF!!

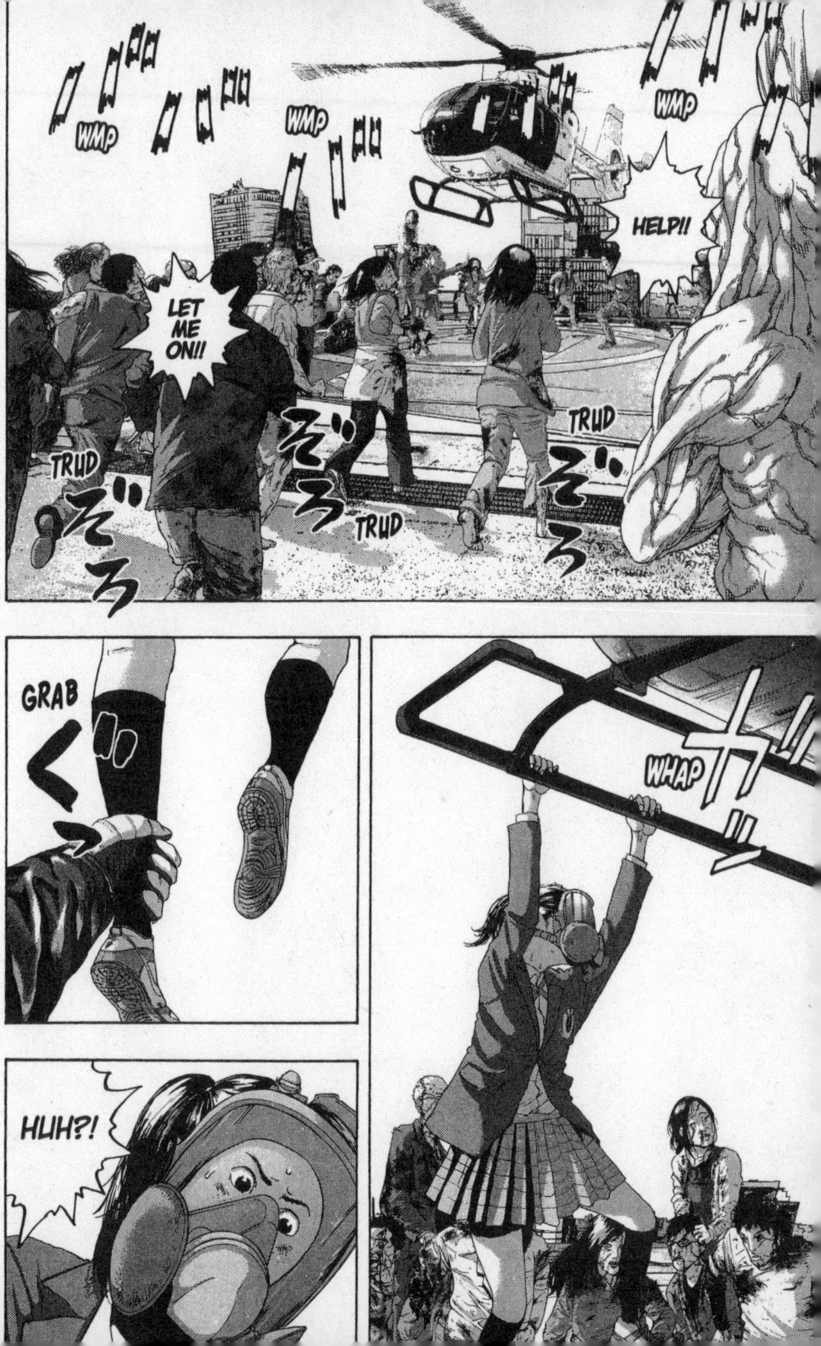
WMP
HELP!!
WMP
WMP
LET ME ON!!
TRUD
ぞろ
TRUD
ぞろ
TRUD
ぞろ
WHAP
GRAB
HUH?!

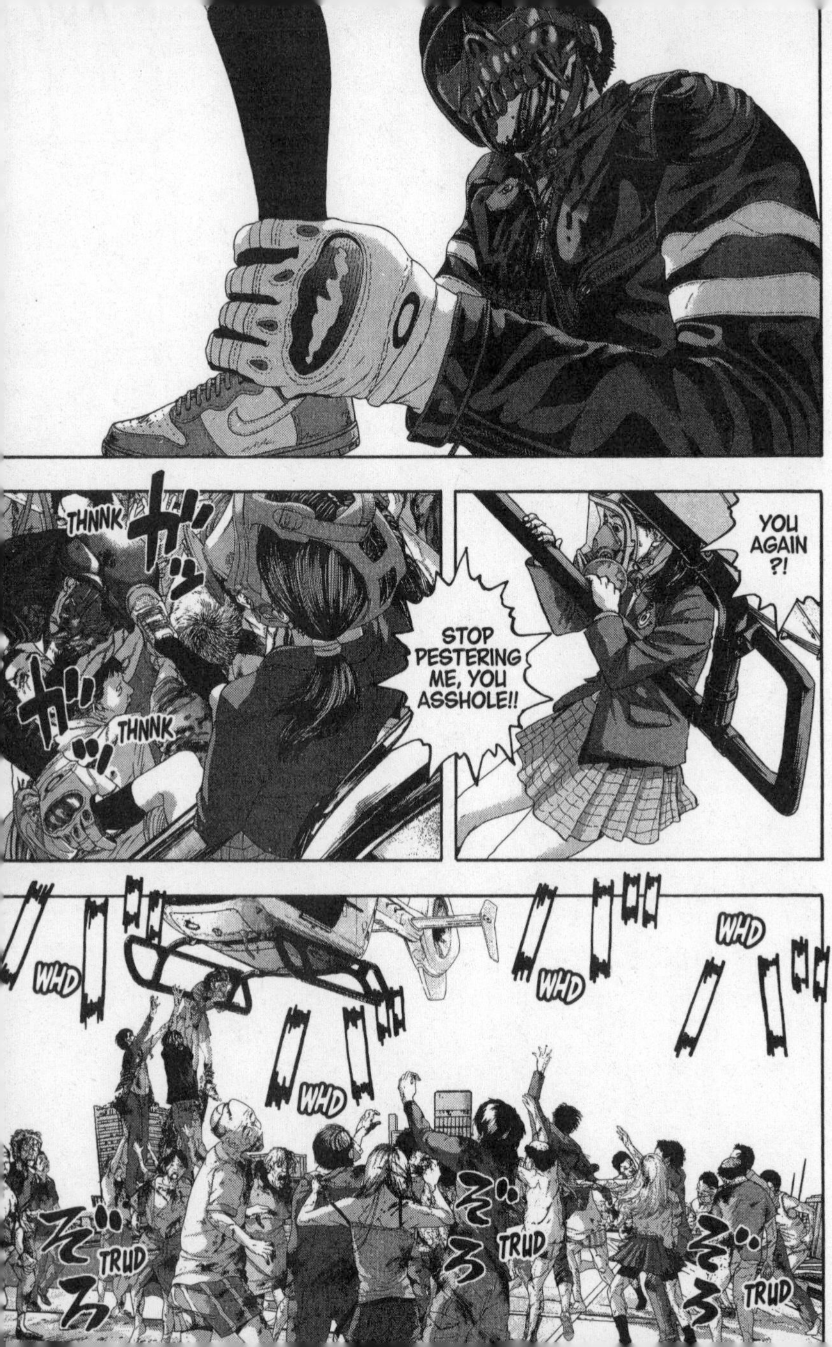
YOU AGAIN ?!
STOP PESTERING ME, YOU ASSHOLE!!
ガッ
THNNK
ガッ
THNNK
WHD
WHD
WHD
WHD
ぞろ
TRUD
ぞろ
TRUD
ぞろ
TRUD

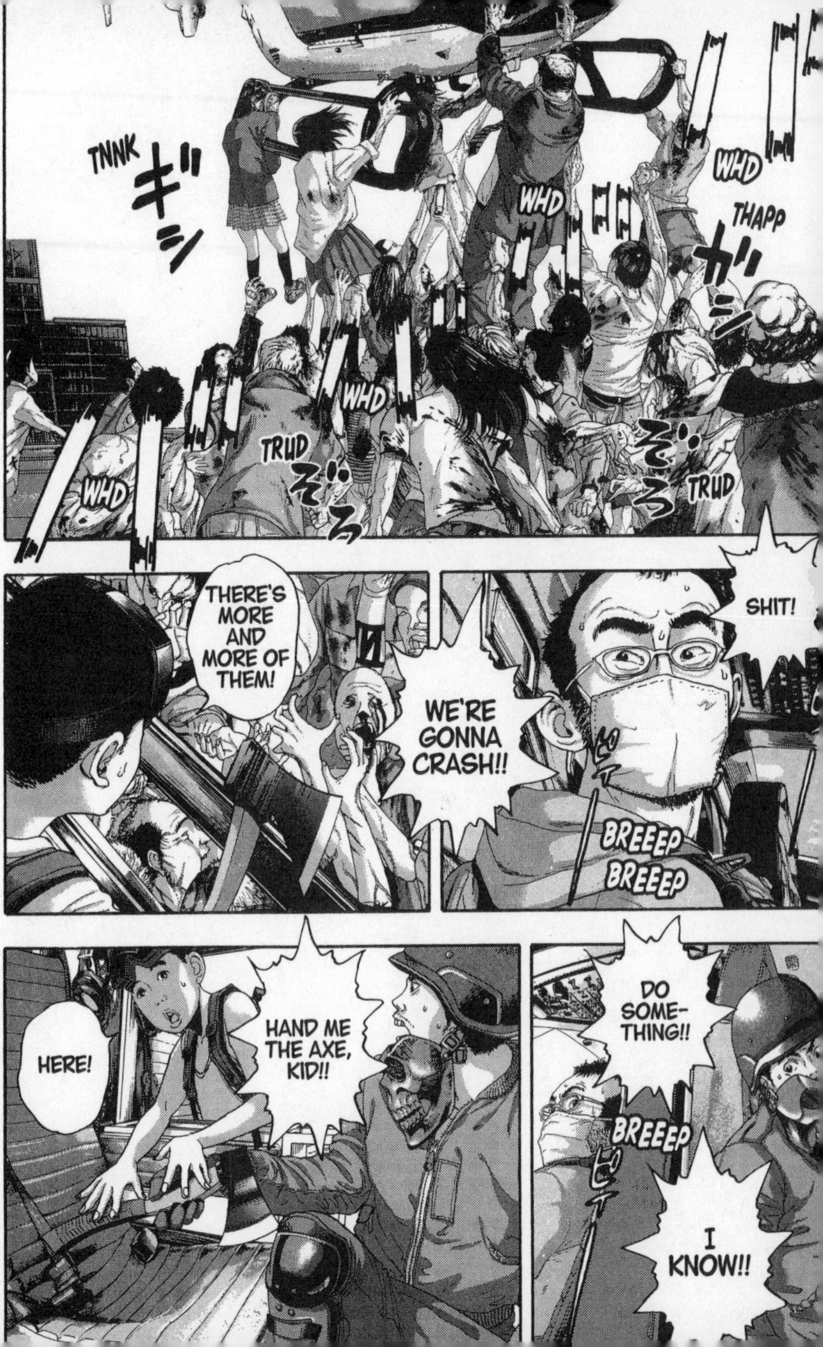
WHD
THAPP
ガシ
WHD
TNNK
ギシ
WHD
TRUD
ぞろ
TRUD
ぞろ
WHD
SHIT!
WE'RE GONNA CRASH!!
BREEEP
BREEEP
THERE'S MORE AND MORE OF THEM!
DO SOME-THING!!
BREEEP
I KNOW!!
HAND ME THE AXE, KID!!
HERE!

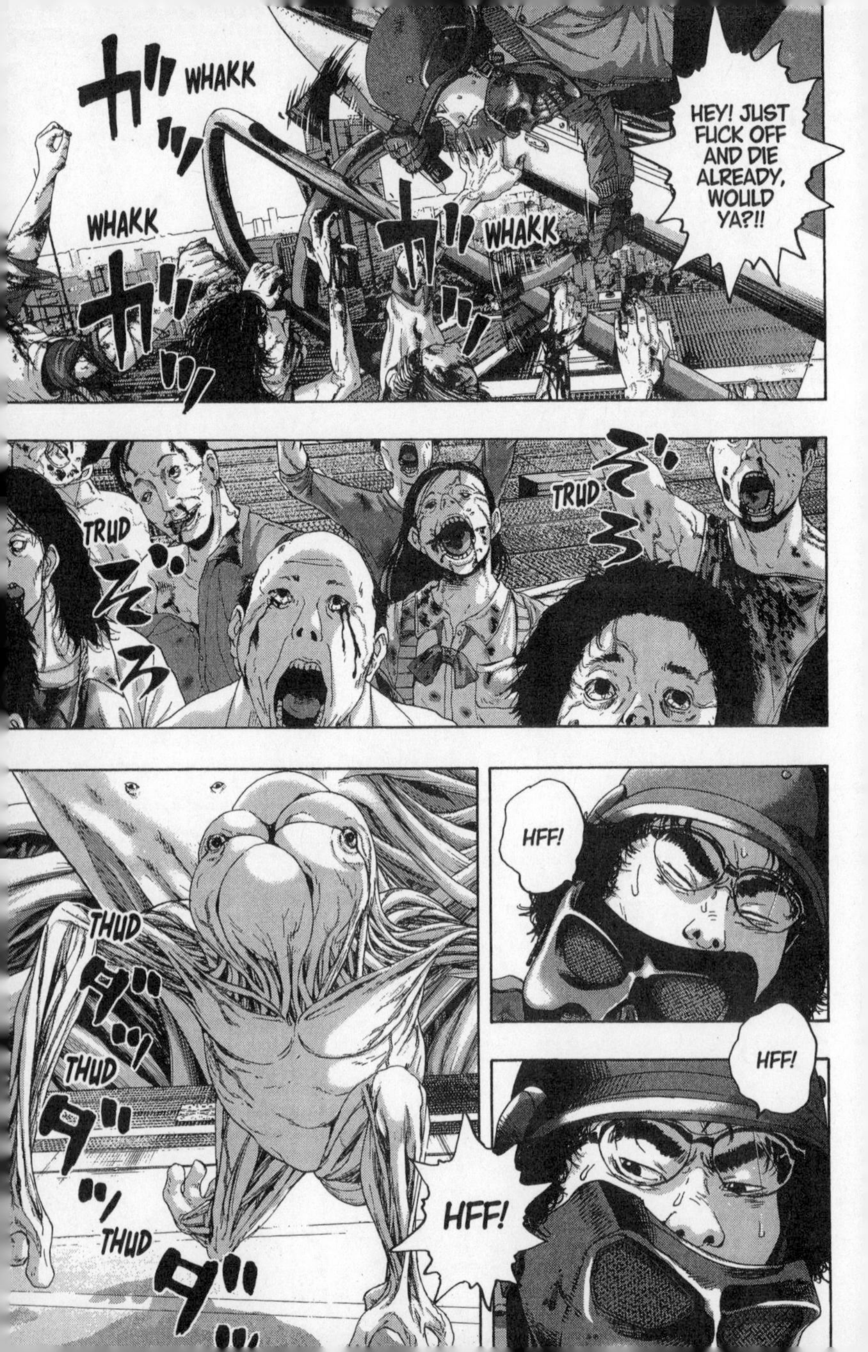
HEY! JUST FUCK OFF AND DIE ALREADY, WOULD YA?!!
ガッ
WHAKK
ガッ
WHAKK
WHAKK
ガッ
ぞろ
TRUD
TRUD
ぞろ
HFF!
HFF!
HFF!
THUD
ダッ
THUD
ダッ
THUD
ダッ

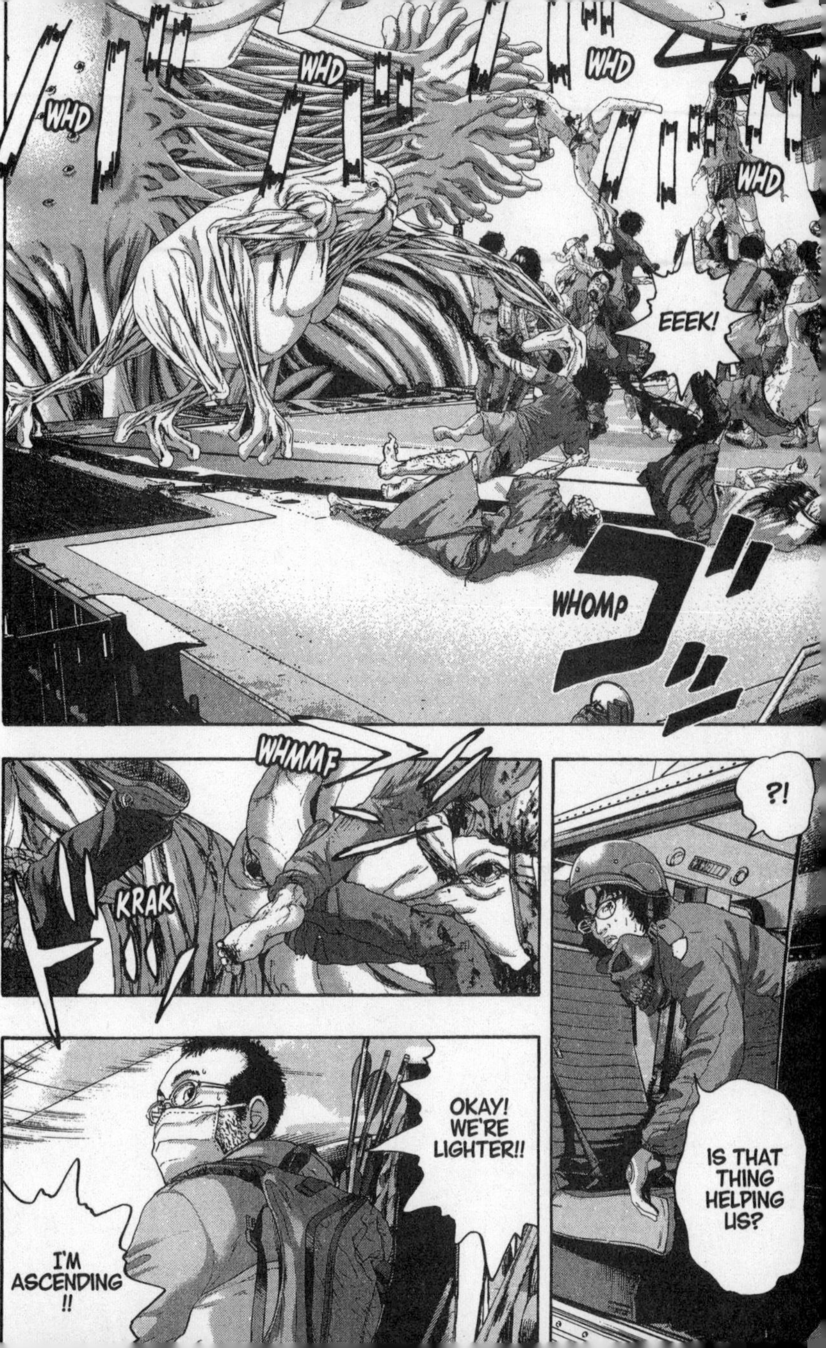
WHD
WHD
WHD
WHD
EEEK!
WHOMP
?!
IS THAT THING HELPING US?
WHMMF
KRAK
OKAY! WE'RE LIGHTER!!
I'M ASCENDING !!

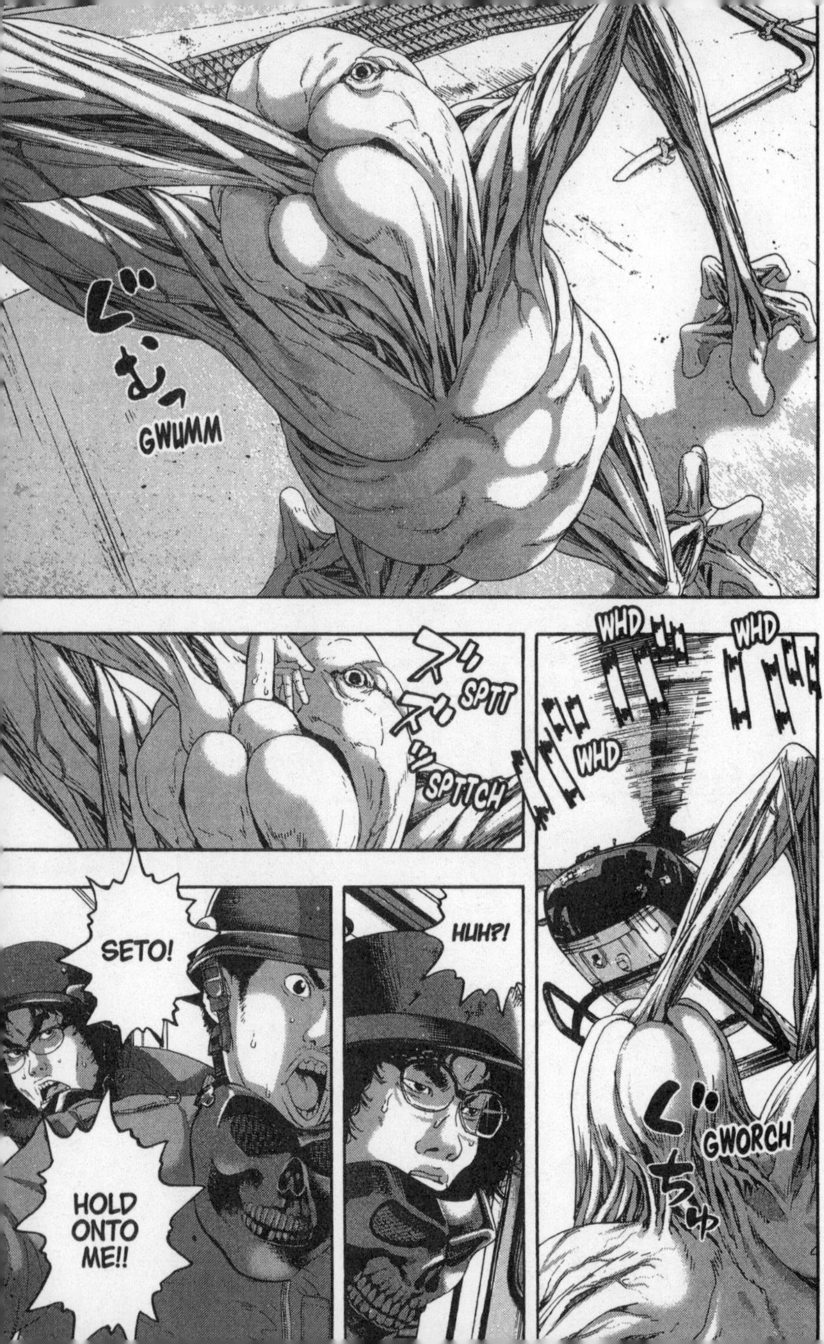
ぐむっ
GWUMM
WHD
WHD
WHD
ぐちゅ
GWORCH
ズズッ
SPTT
SPTTCH
HUH?!
SETO!
HOLD ONTO ME!!

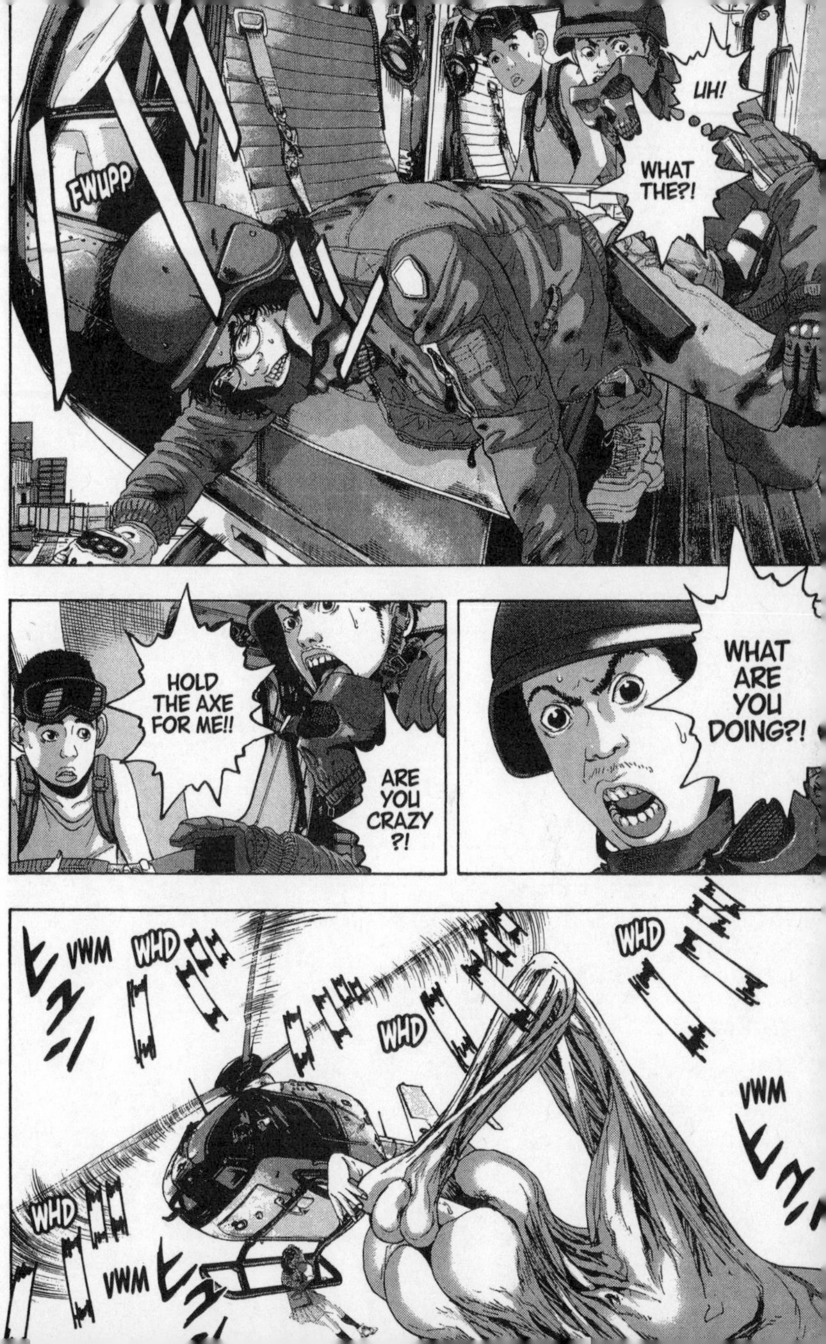
UH!
WHAT THE?!
FWUPP
WHAT ARE YOU DOING?!
HOLD THE AXE FOR ME!!
ARE YOU CRAZY ?!
WHD
VWM
WHD
WHD
VWM
WHD
VWM

SPTT

SPTT

SPTTCH

ARE YOU CRAZY?!

I'M SAVING AUNTIE!!

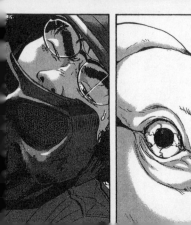

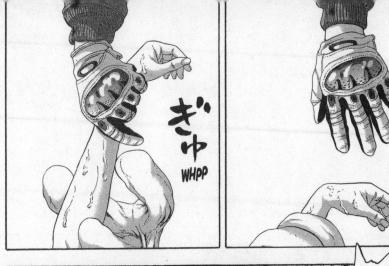

ぎゅ
WHPP
I'VE GOT HER!!
PULL ME IN!!
GRAAH! FUCK, YOU'RE HEAVY!!
GIMME A HAND HERE!!
WHAT ABOUT THE AXE?
PUT IT DOWN!
OKAY!
TOKK
ゴッ

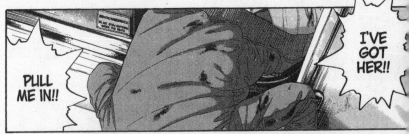

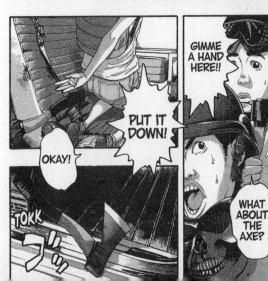

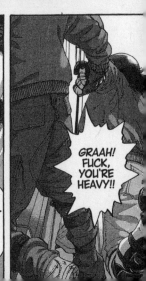

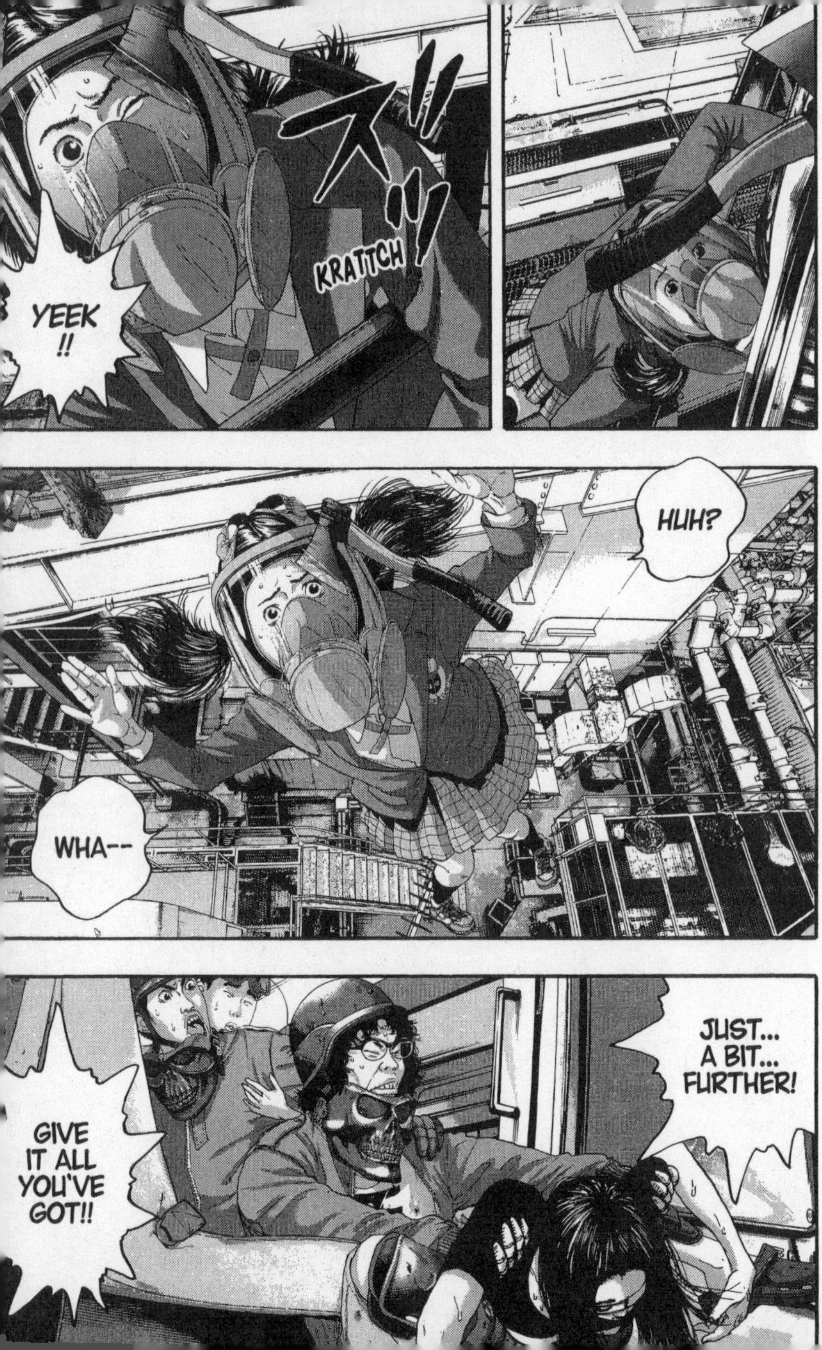
KRATTCH
YEEK !!
HUH?
WHA--
JUST... A BIT... FURTHER!
GIVE IT ALL YOU'VE GOT!!

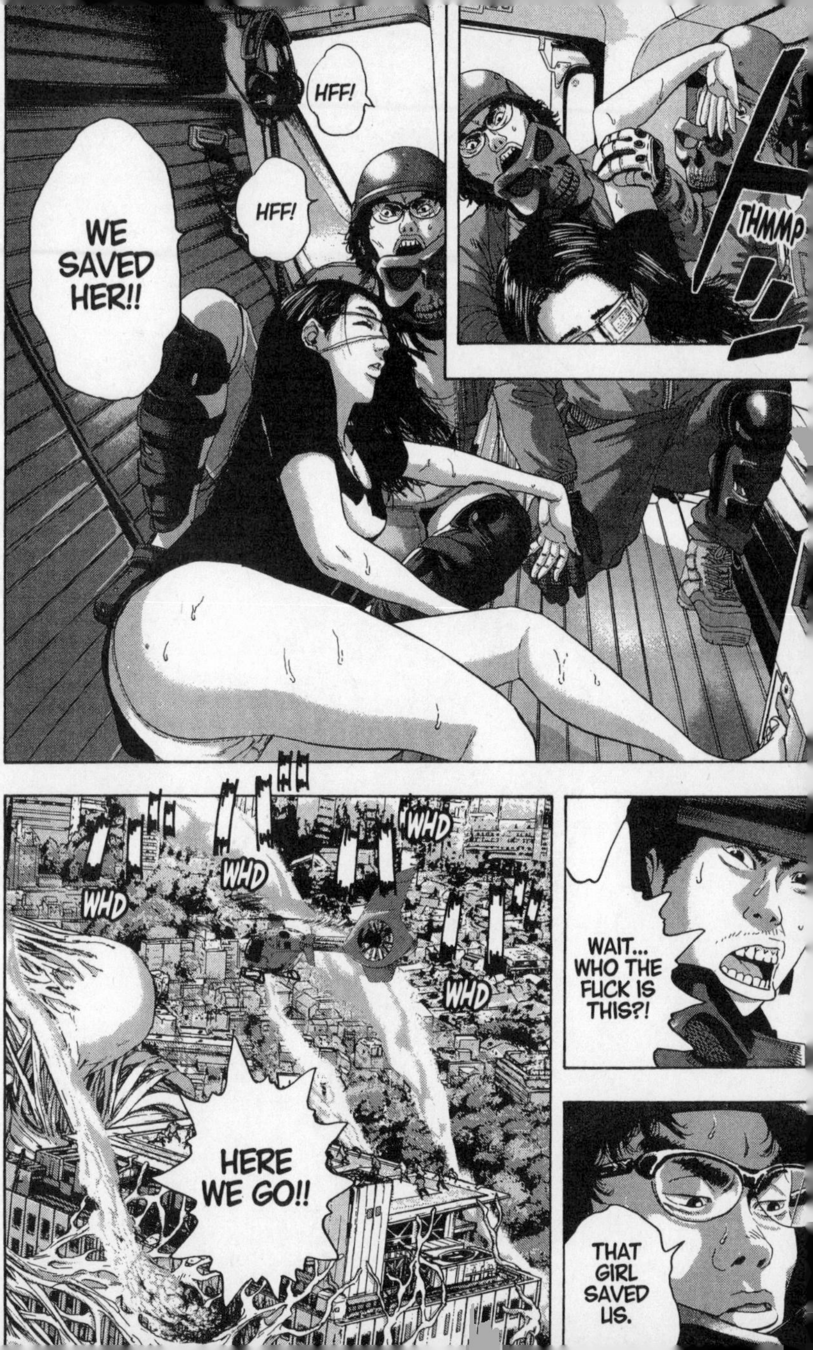
THMMP
HFF!
HFF!
WE SAVED HER!!
WAIT... WHO THE FUCK IS THIS?!
THAT GIRL SAVED US.
WHD
WHD
WHD
WHD
HERE WE GO!!

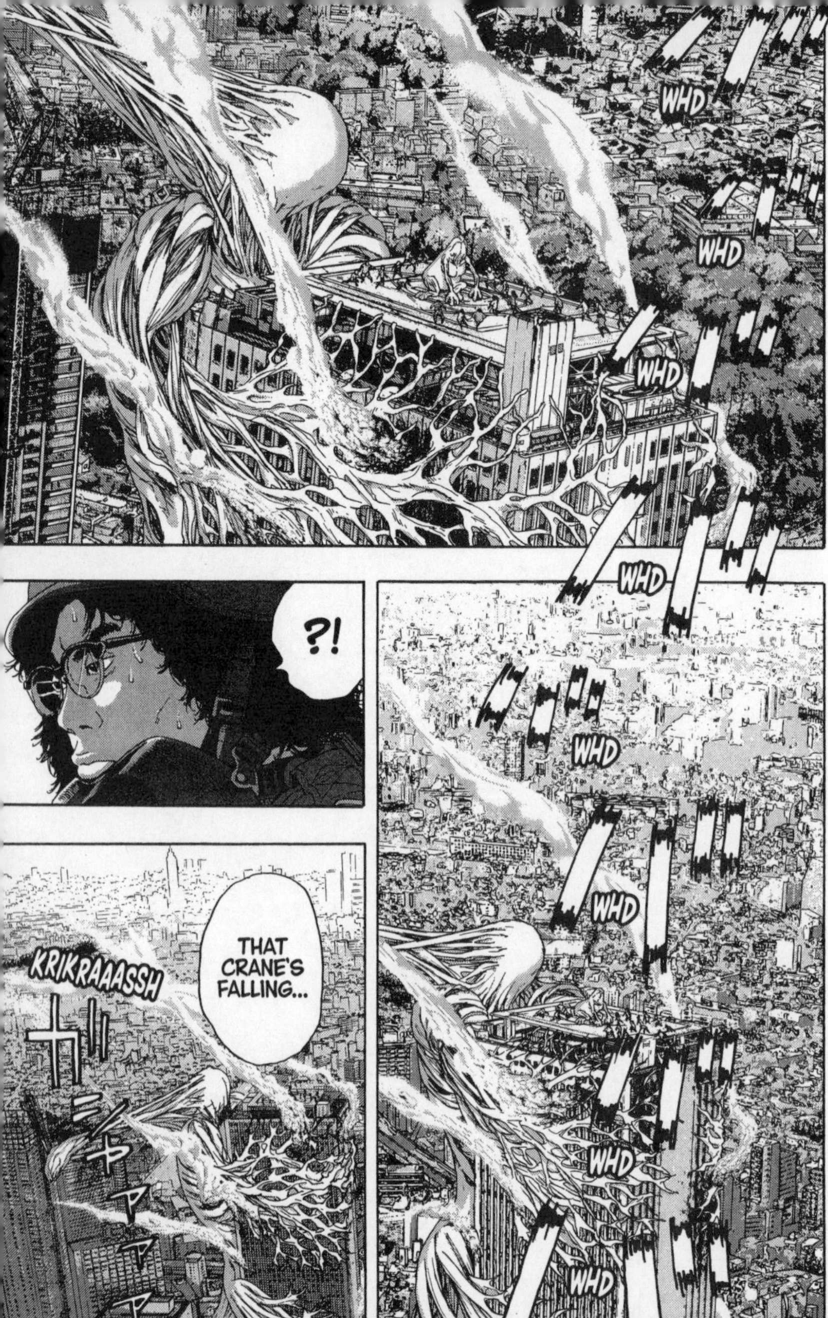
WHD
WHD
WHD
WHD
WHD
WHD
WHD
WHD
?!
THAT CRANE'S FALLING...
KRIKRAAASSH

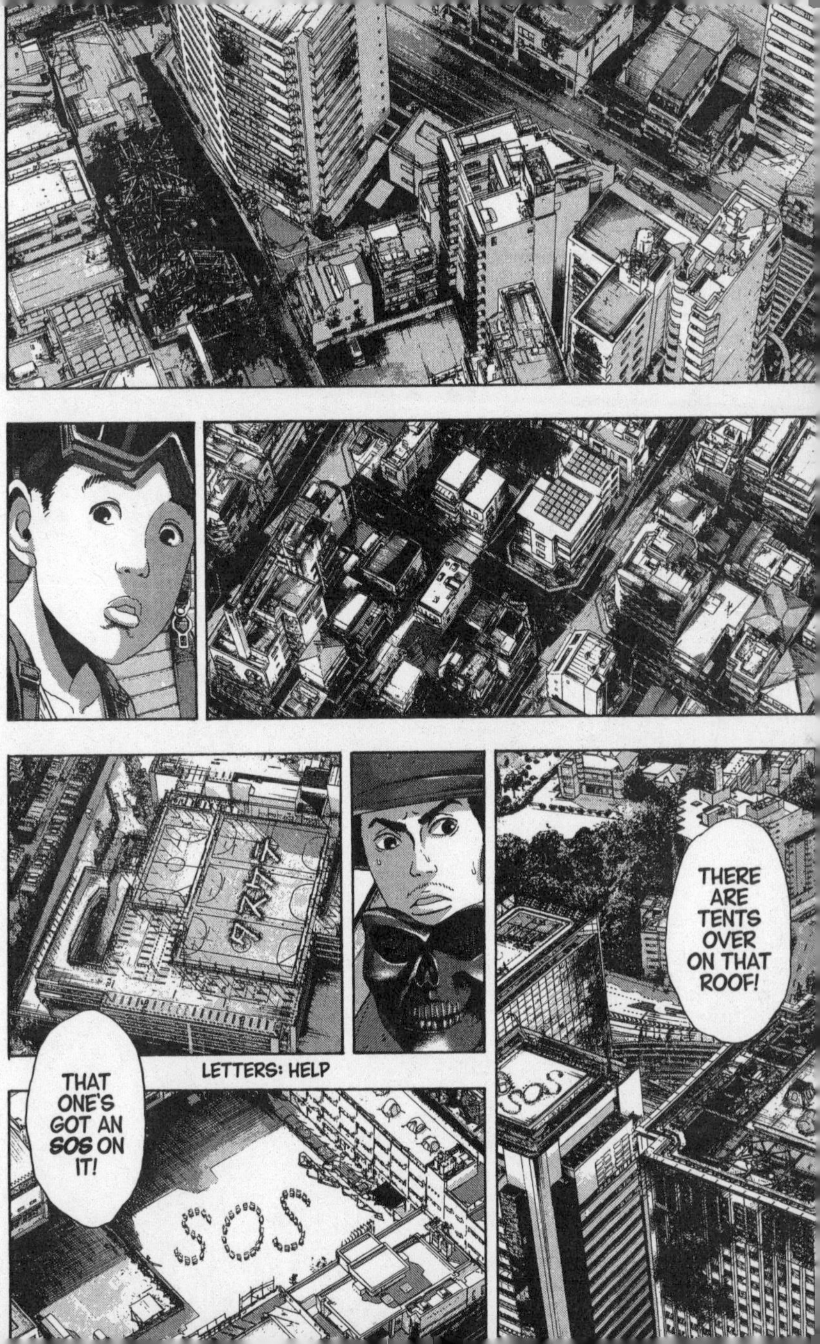
THERE ARE TENTS OVER ON THAT ROOF!
LETTERS: HELP
THAT ONE'S GOT AN SOS ON IT!

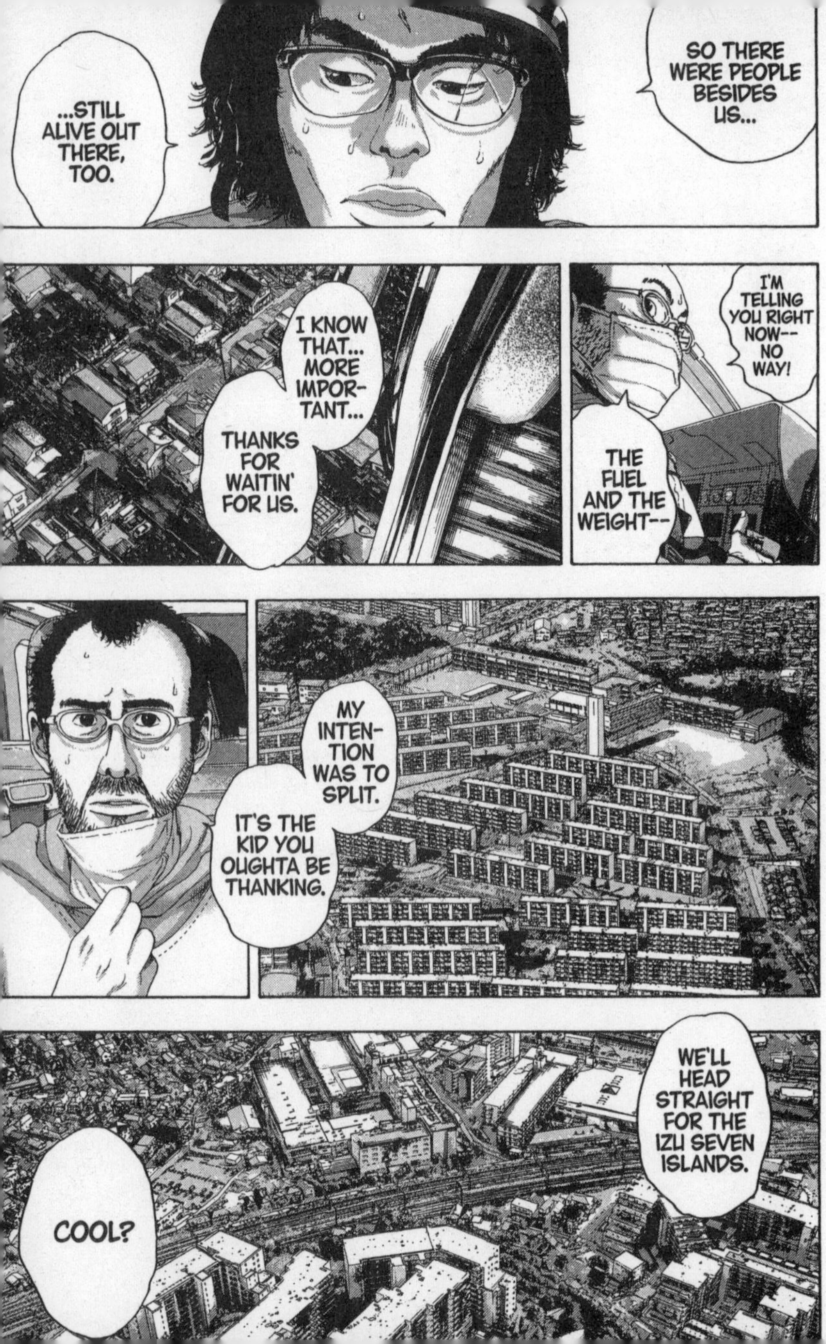
SO THERE WERE PEOPLE BESIDES US...
...STILL ALIVE OUT THERE, TOO.
I'M TELLING YOU RIGHT NOW-- NO WAY!
THE FUEL AND THE WEIGHT--
I KNOW THAT... MORE IMPOR-TANT...
THANKS FOR WAITIN' FOR US.
MY INTEN-TION WAS TO SPLIT.
IT'S THE KID YOU OUGHTA BE THANKING.
WE'LL HEAD STRAIGHT FOR THE IZU SEVEN ISLANDS.
COOL?

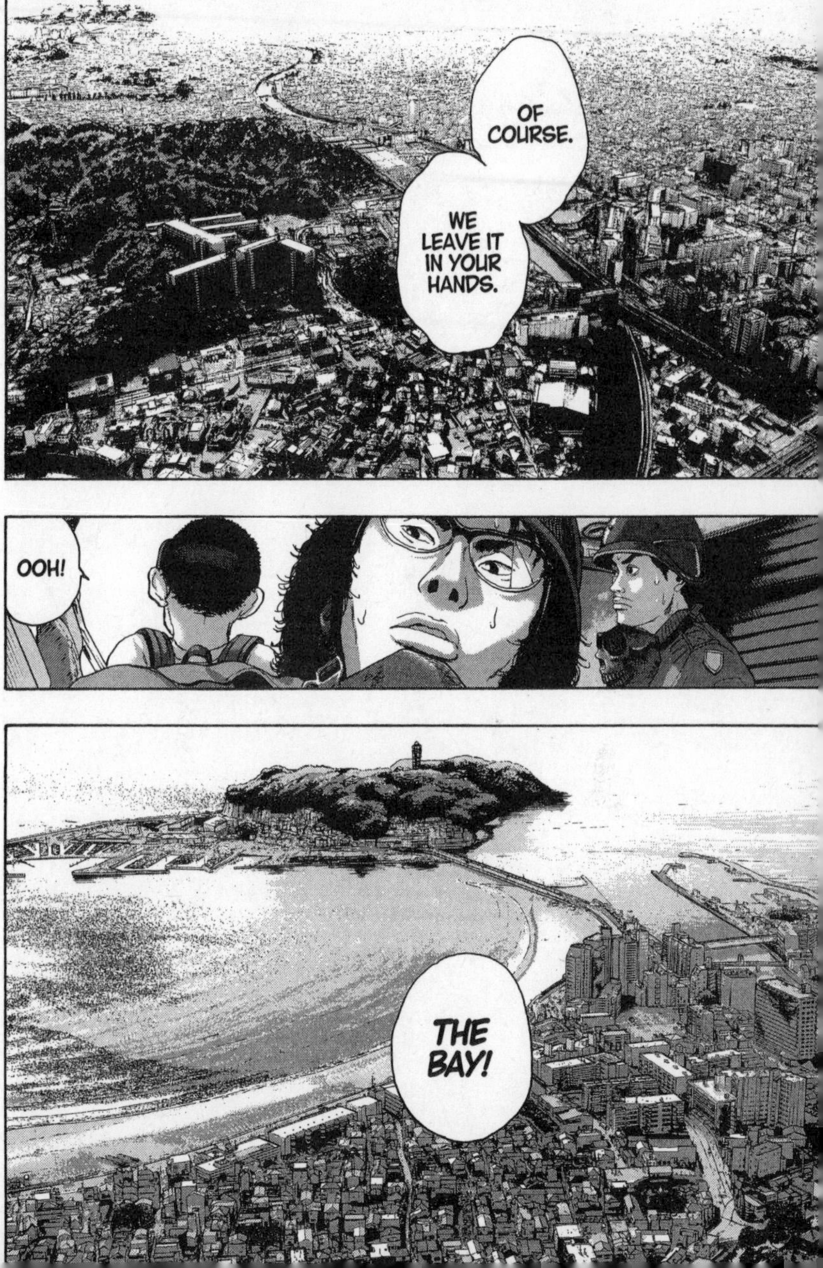
OF COURSE.
WE LEAVE IT IN YOUR HANDS.
OOH!
THE BAY!

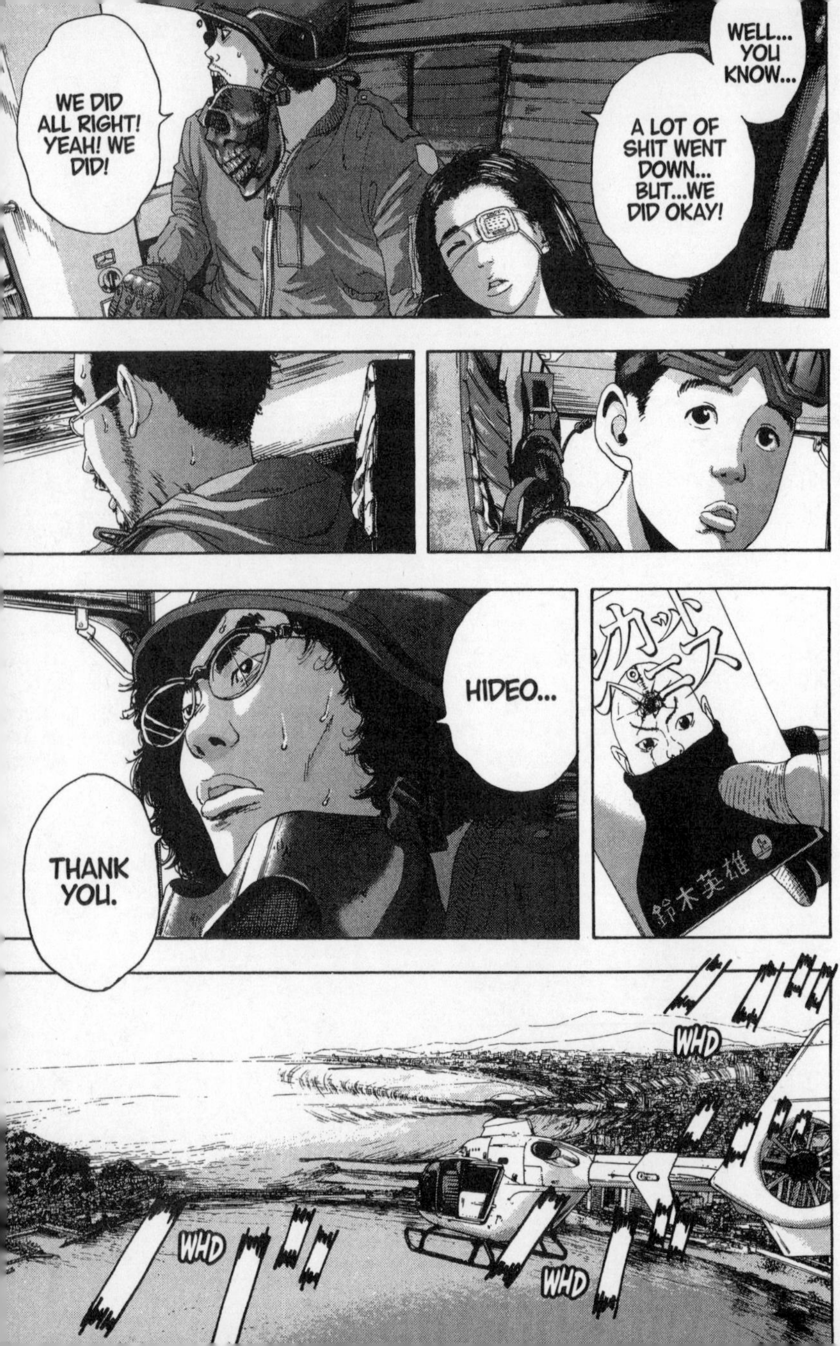
WELL... YOU KNOW...
A LOT OF SHIT WENT DOWN... BUT...WE DID OKAY!
WE DID ALL RIGHT! YEAH! WE DID!
鈴木英雄
HIDEO...
THANK YOU.
WHD
WHD
WHD

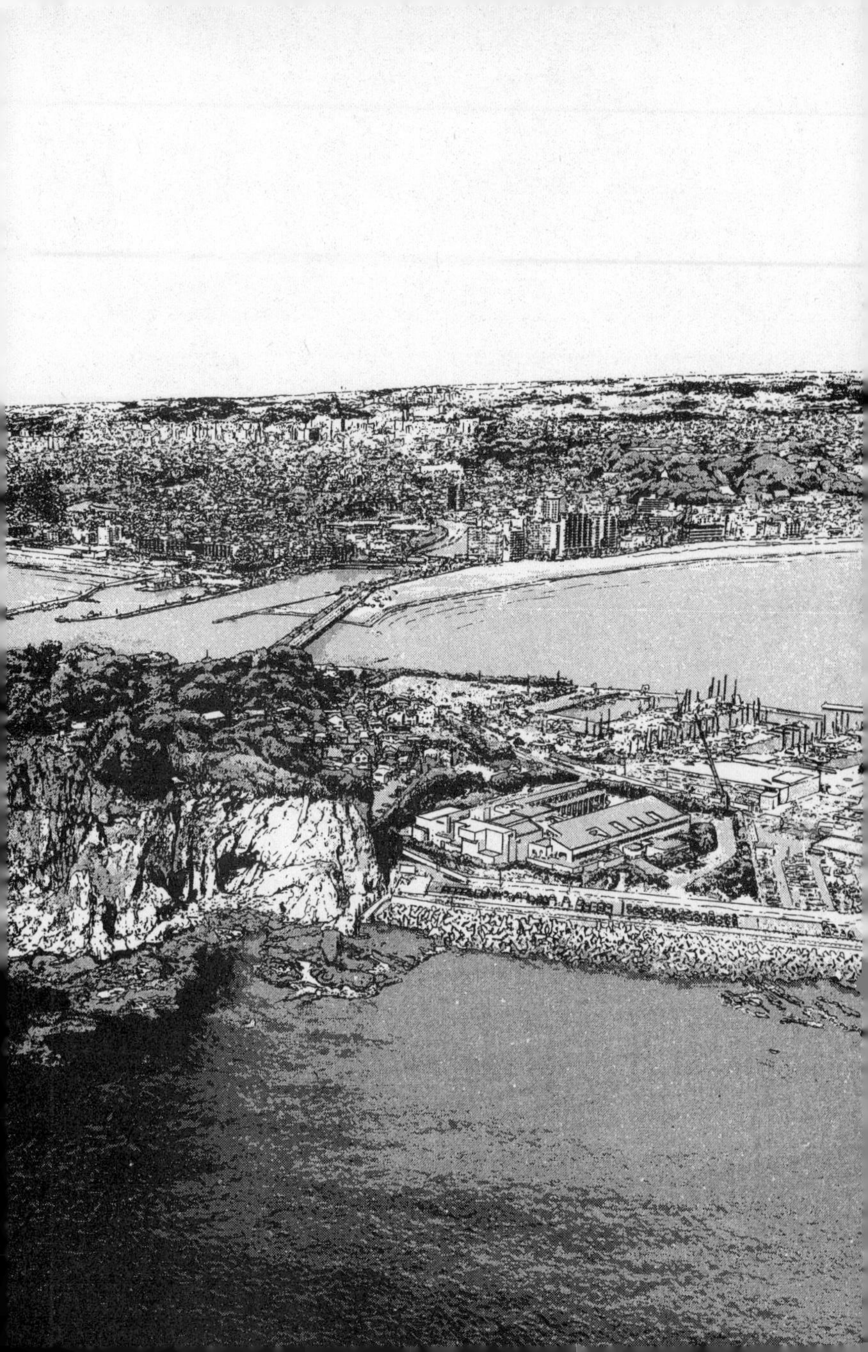

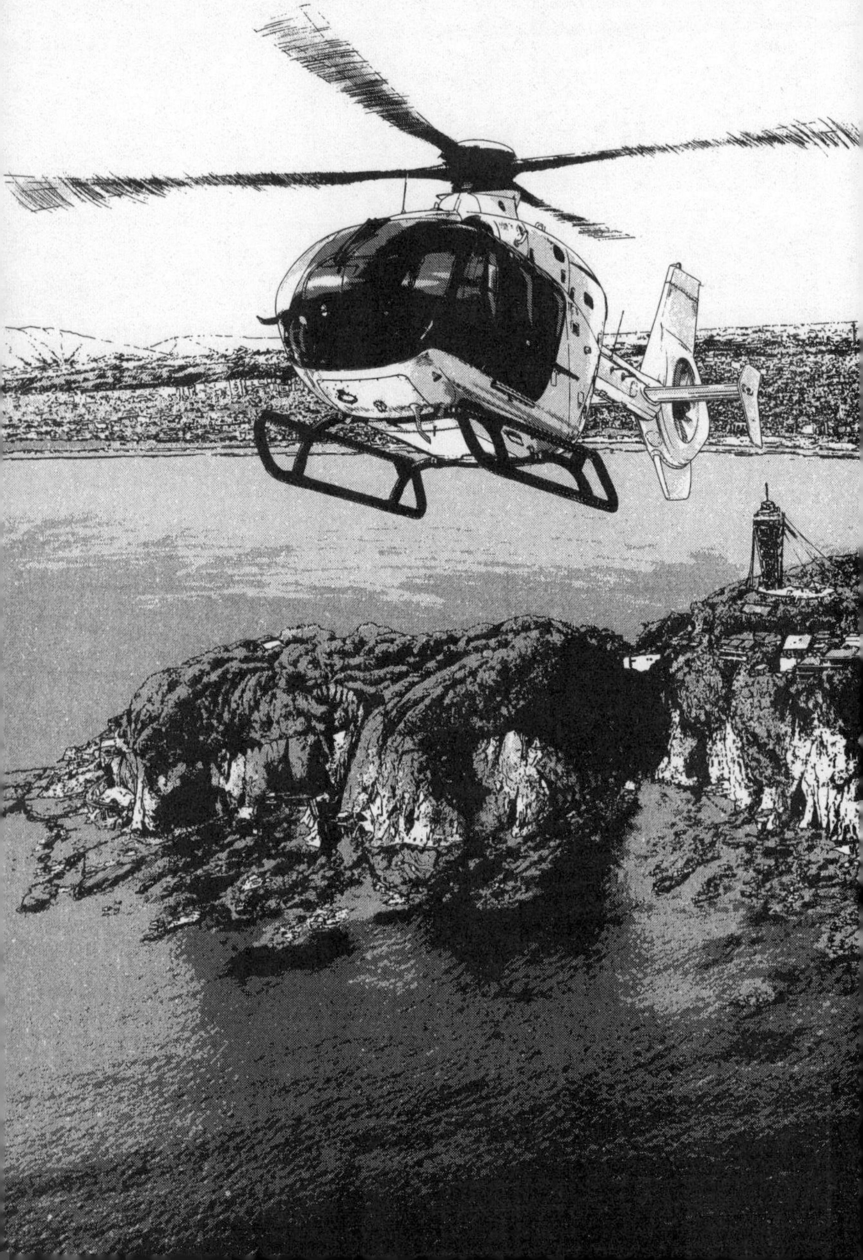

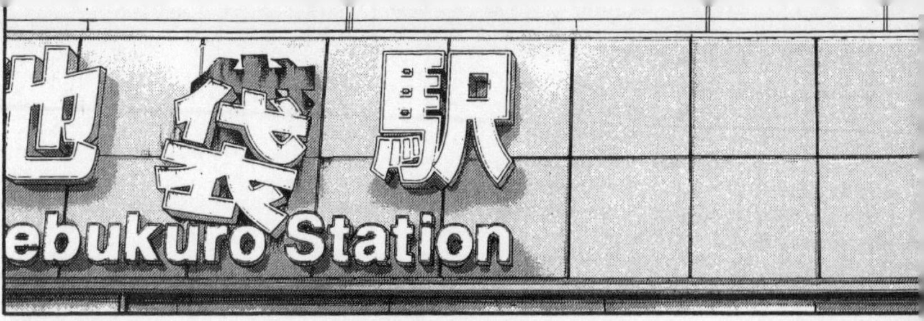
袋駅
ebukuro Station

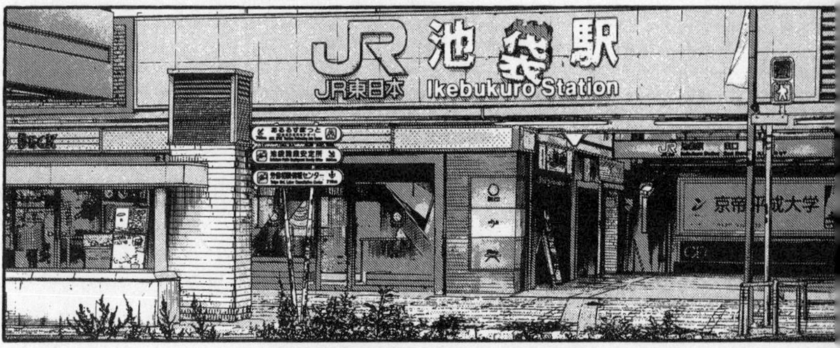
JR 池袋駅
JR東日本
Ikebukuro Station

SIGN: IKEBUKURO STATION / JR EAST

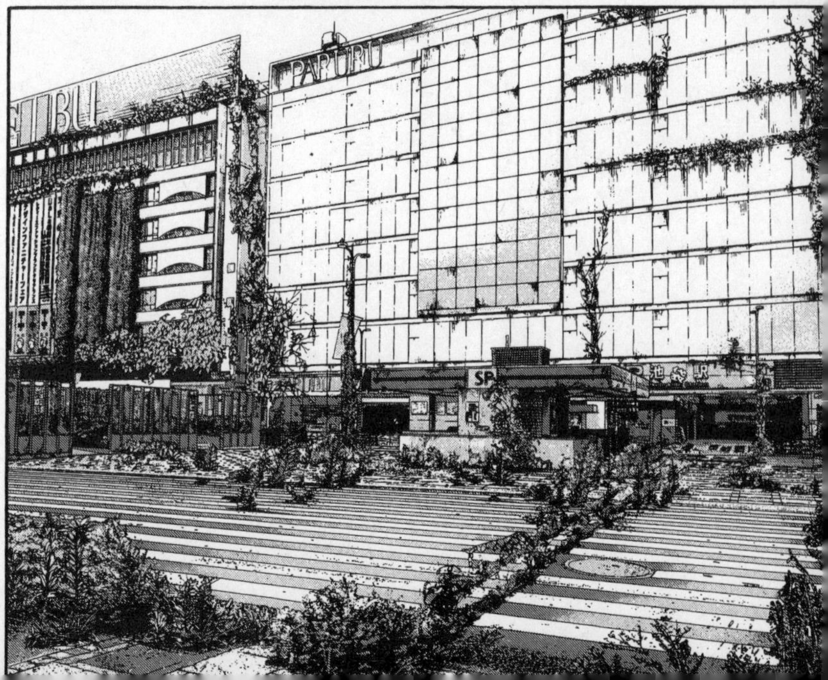
PARURU
池袋駅

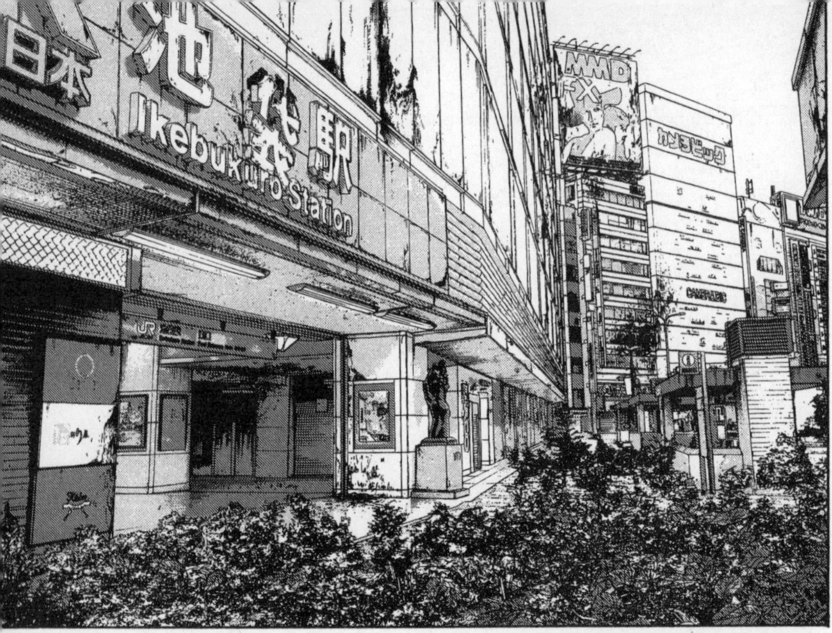
池袋駅
Ikebukuro Station

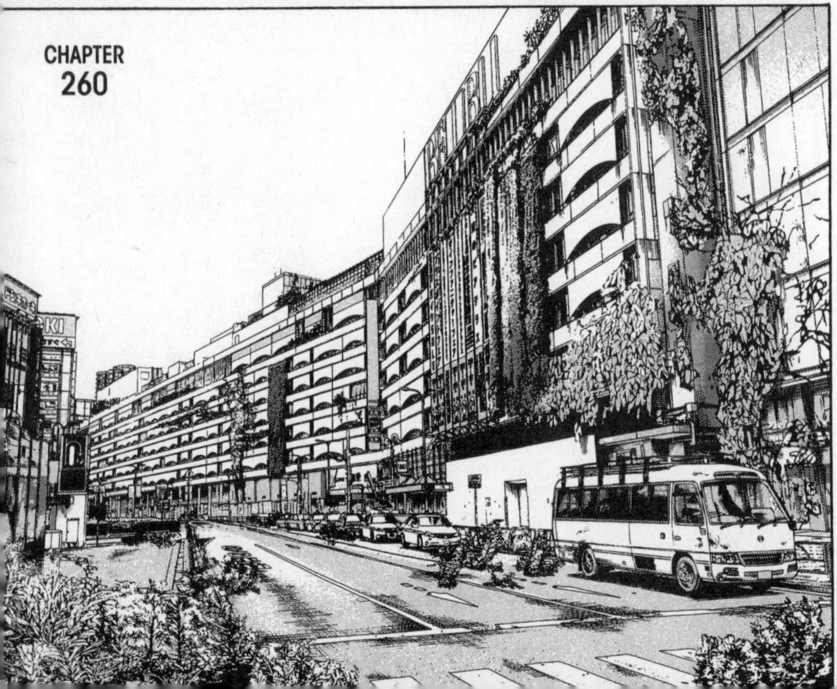
CHAPTER
260

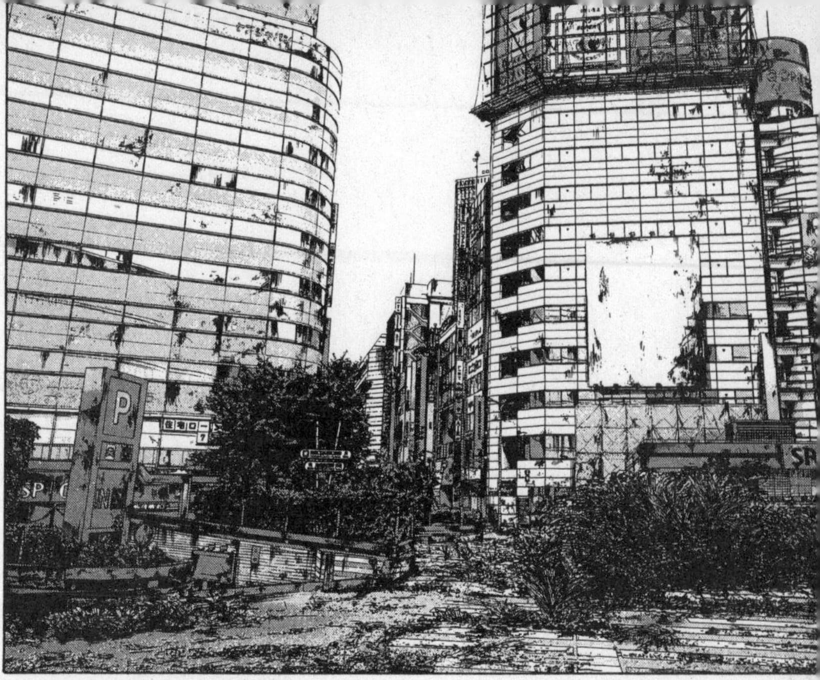
P

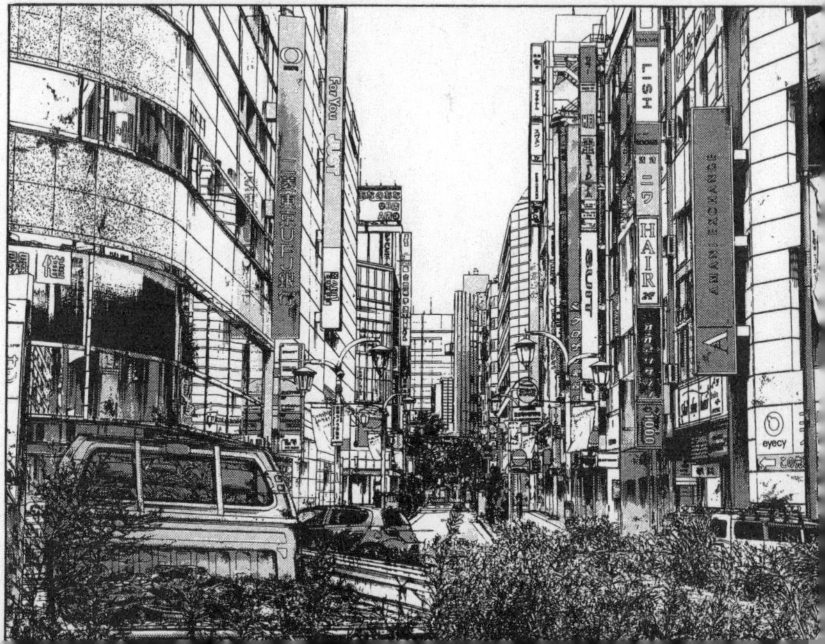
For You
三菱東京UFJ銀行
LISH
HAIR
eyecy

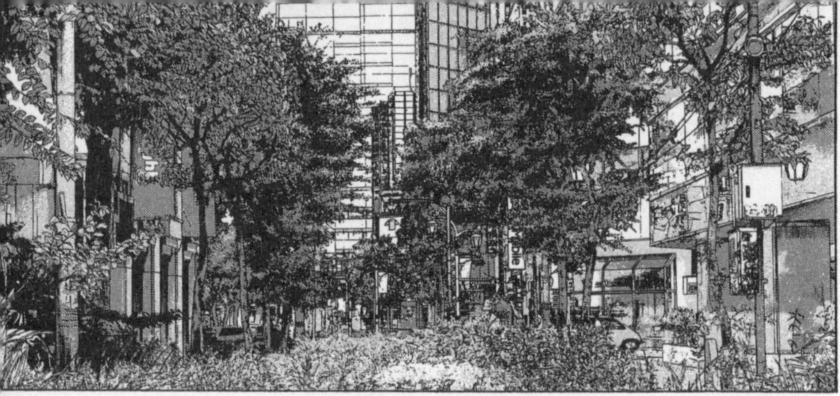
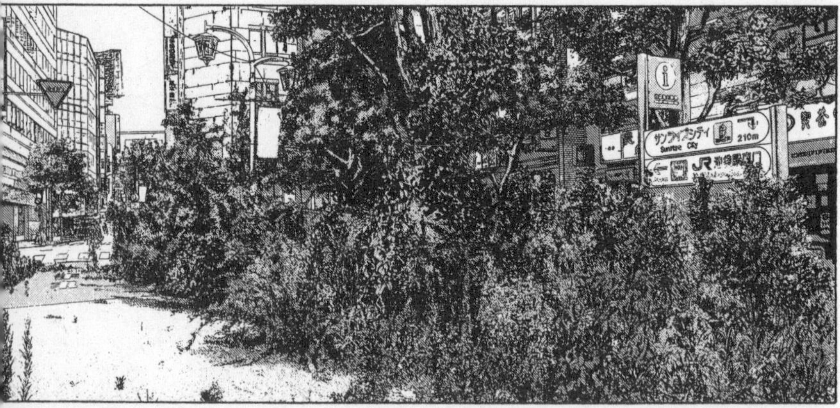
210m
JR
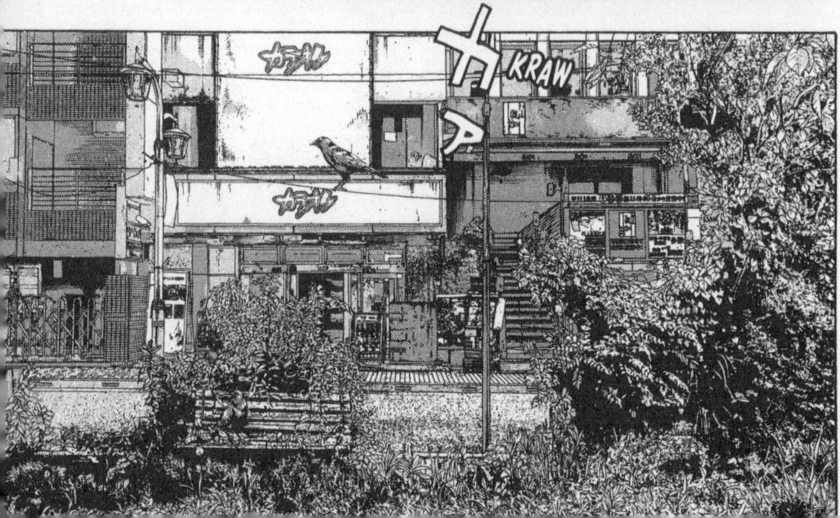
カラオケ
カァ
KRAW
カラオケ

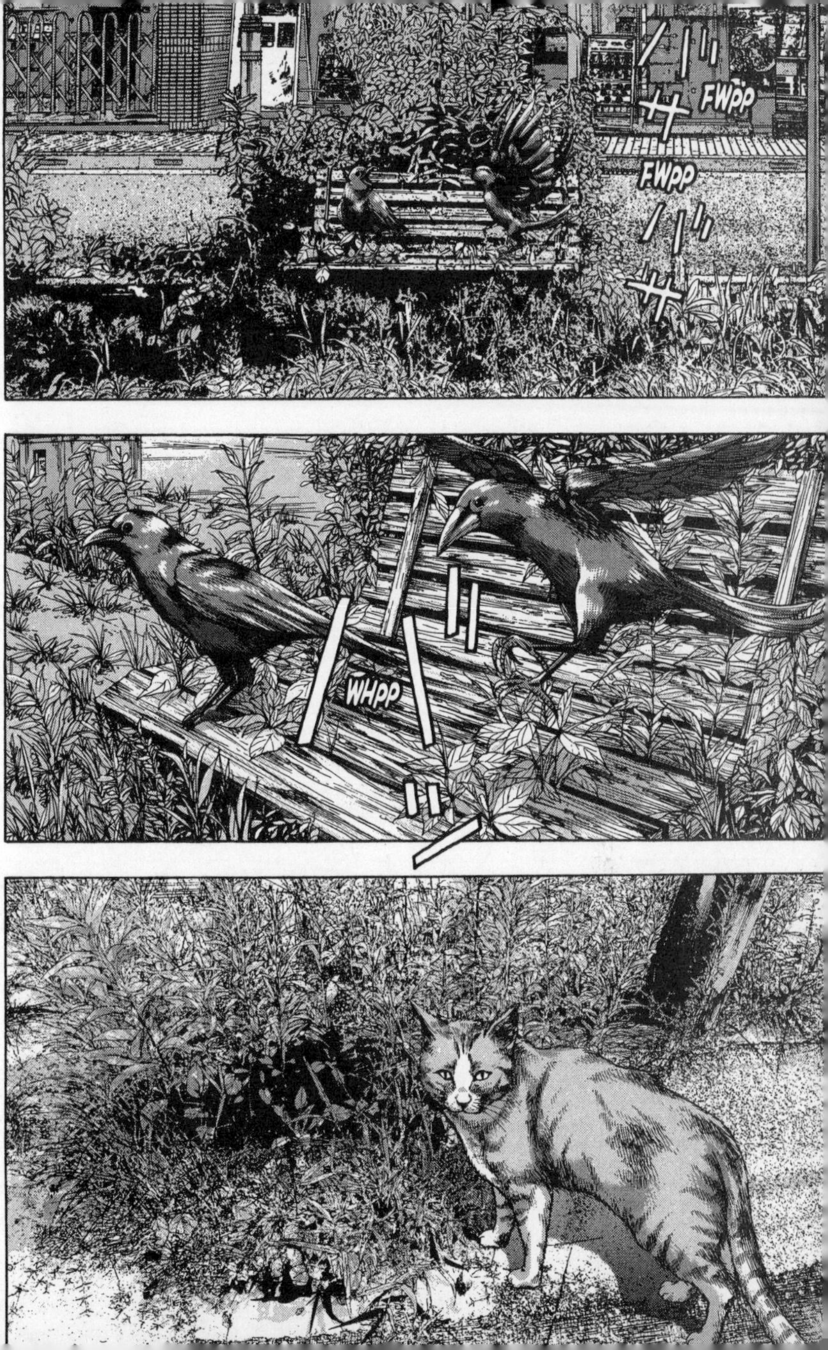
FWPP
FWPP
WHPP

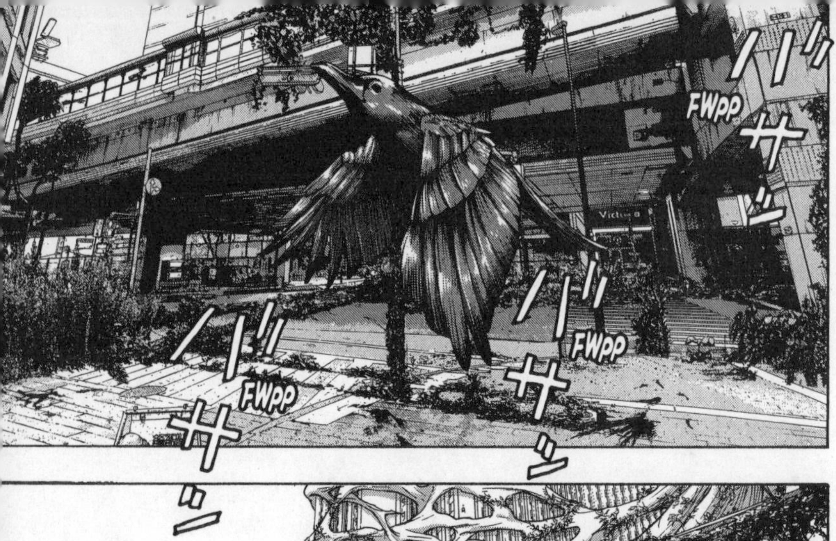
バサッ
FWPP
バサッ
FWPP
バサッ
FWPP
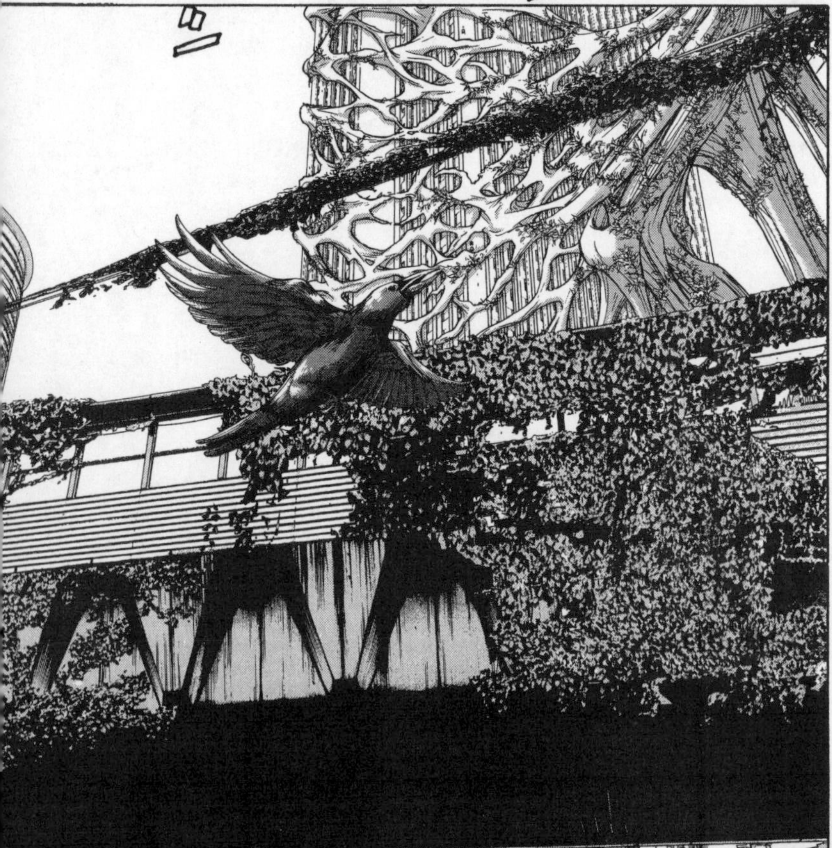

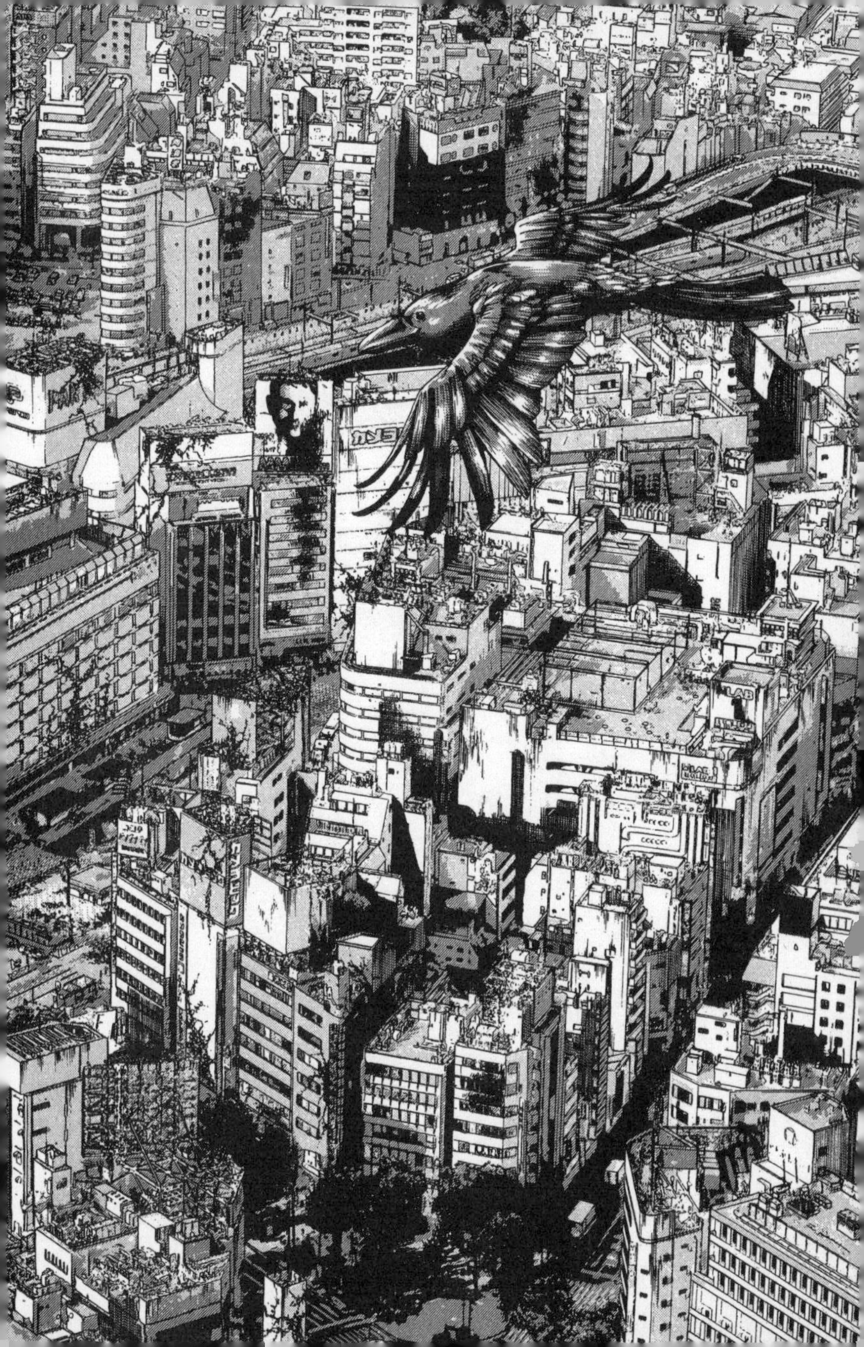

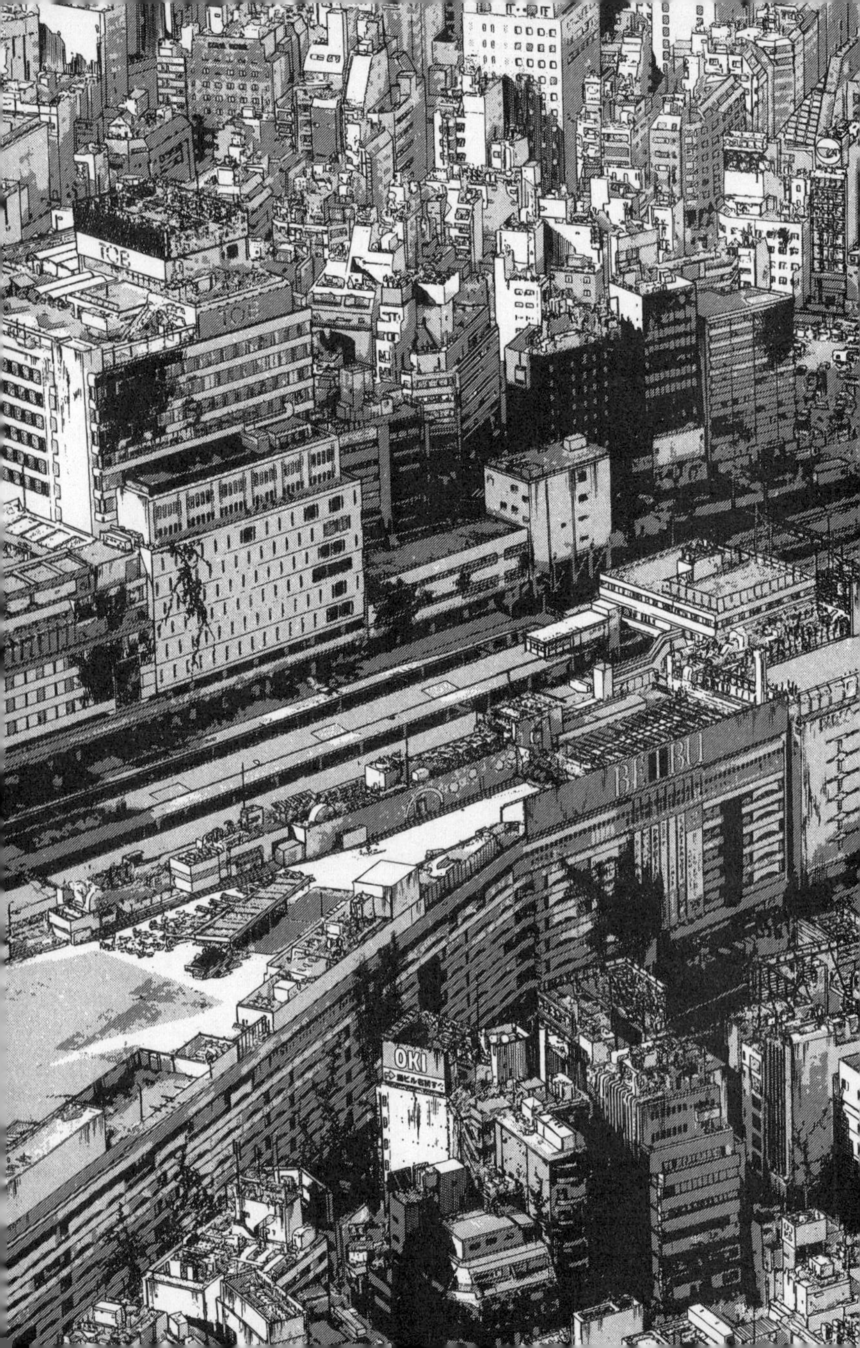
OKI

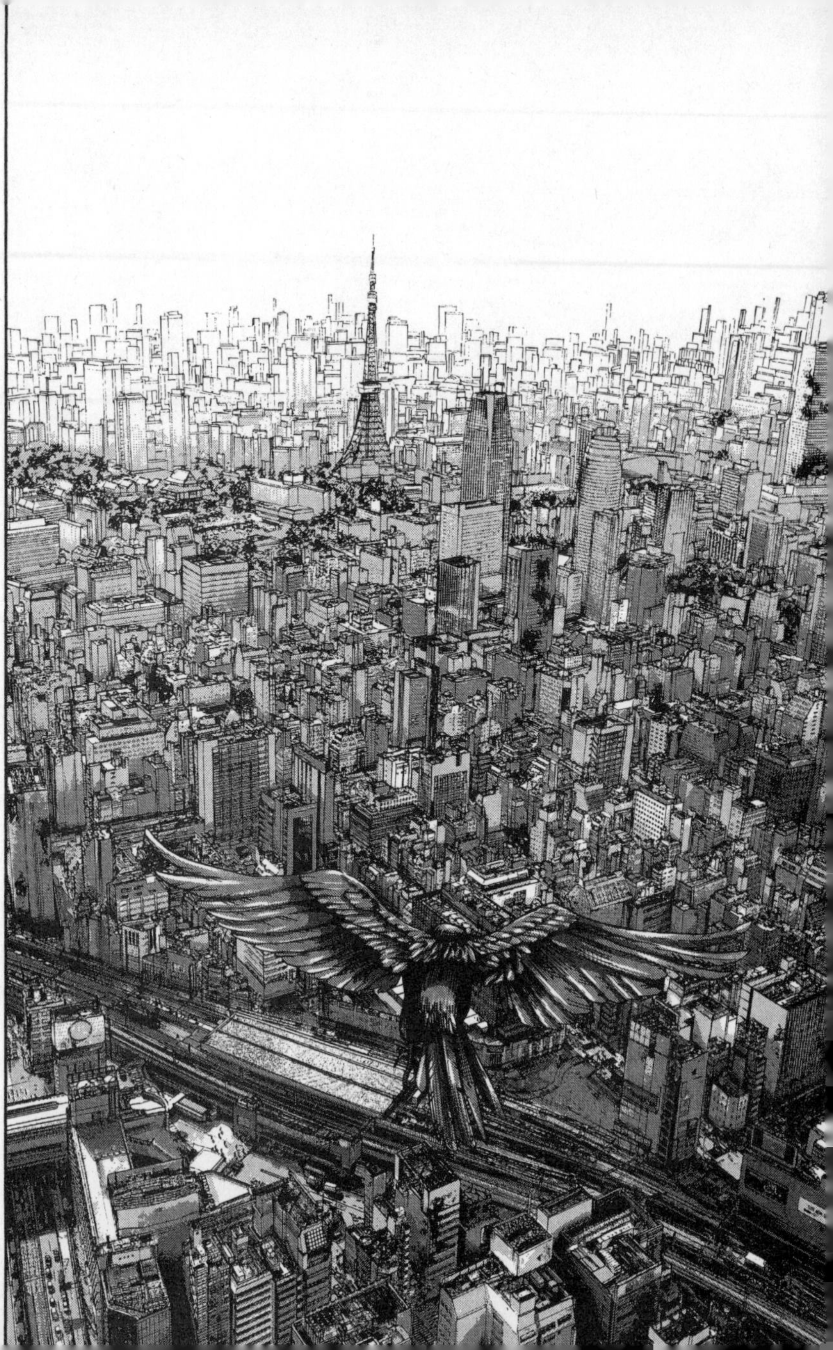

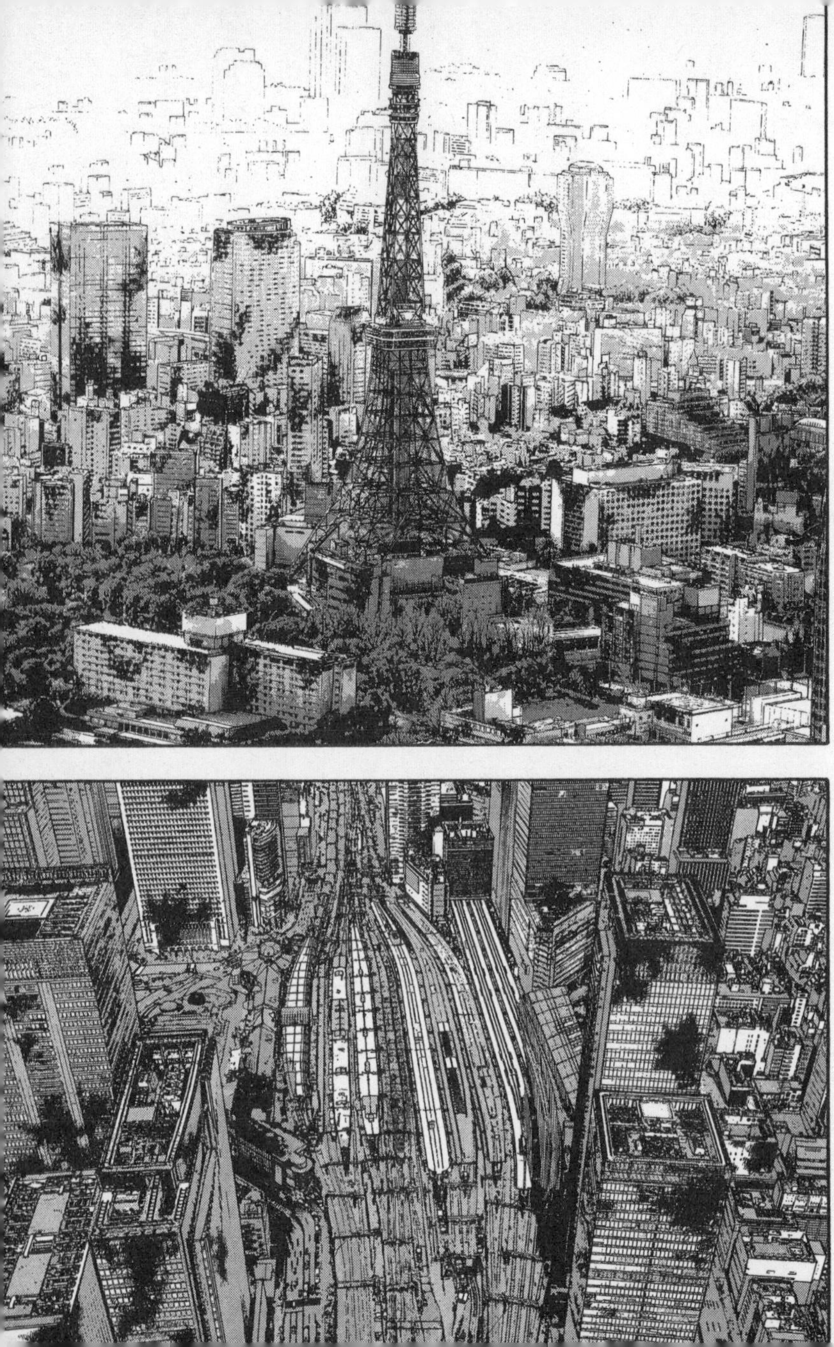

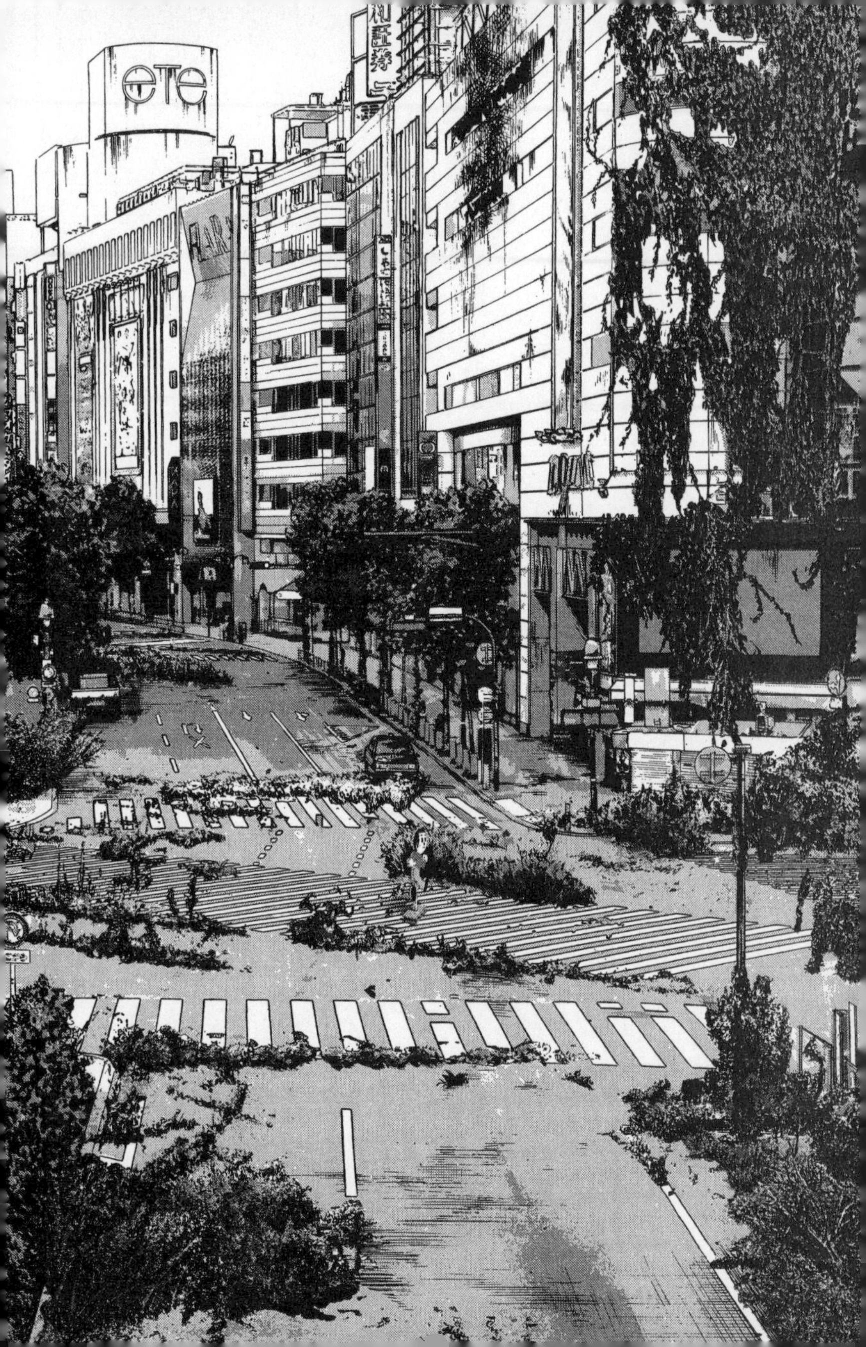
ete

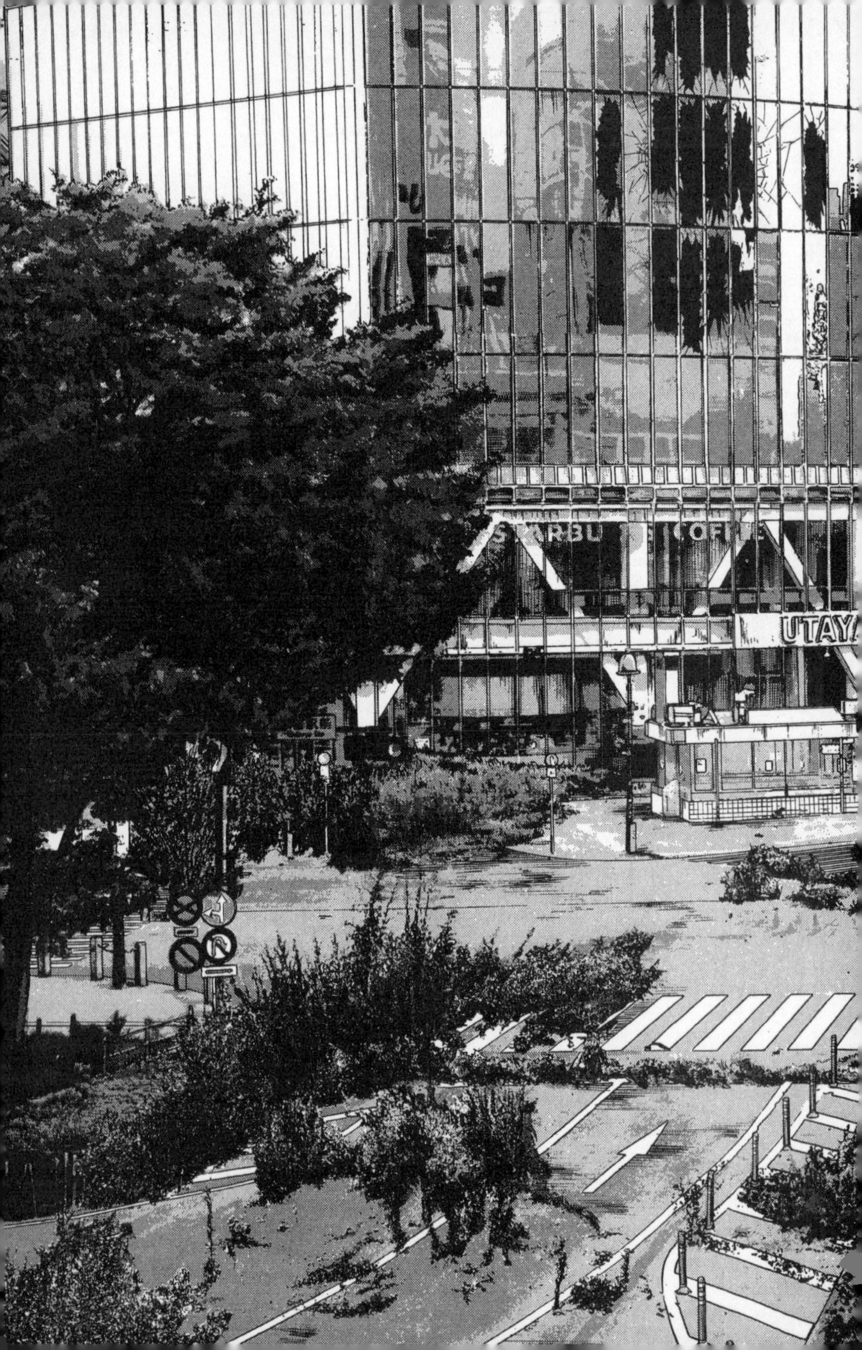

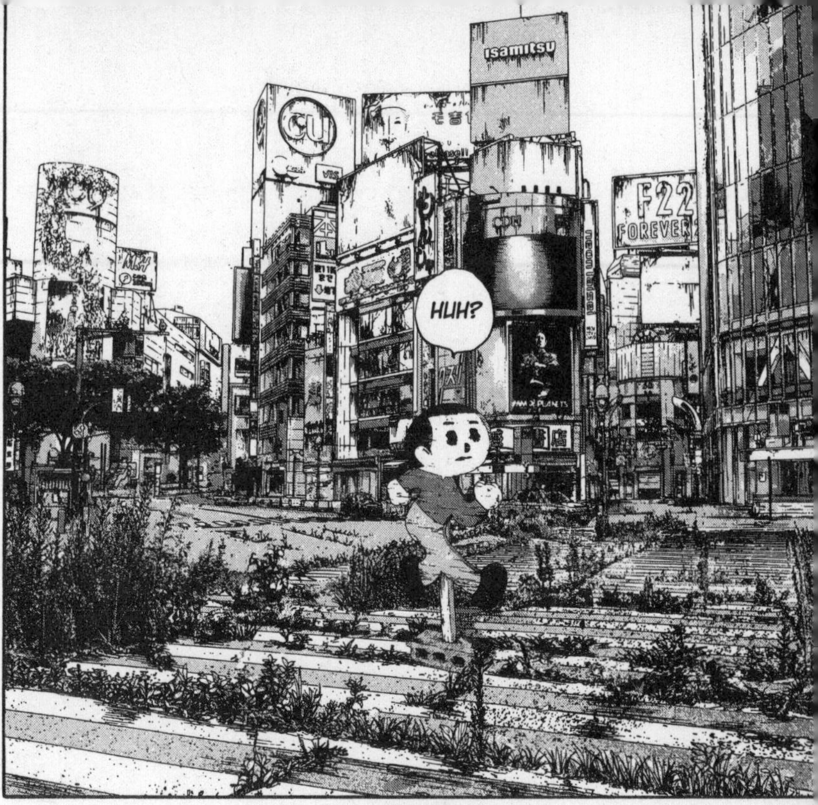
isamitsu
CU
F22
FOREVER
HUH?

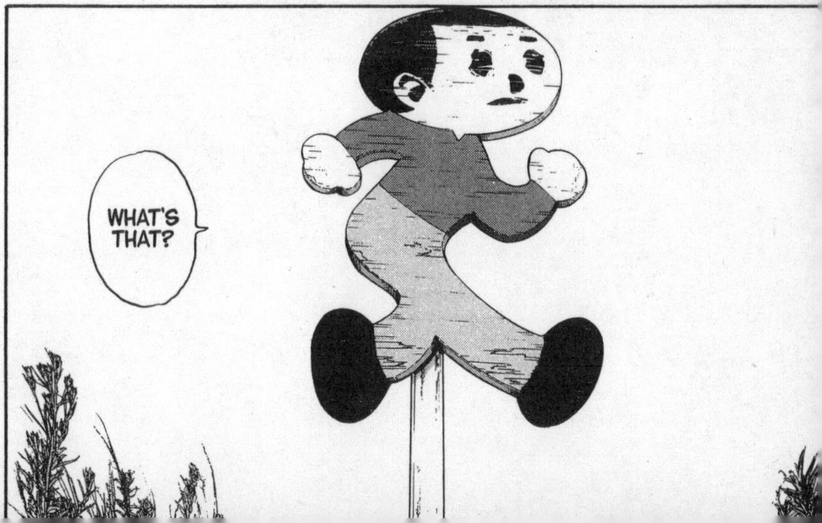
WHAT'S THAT?

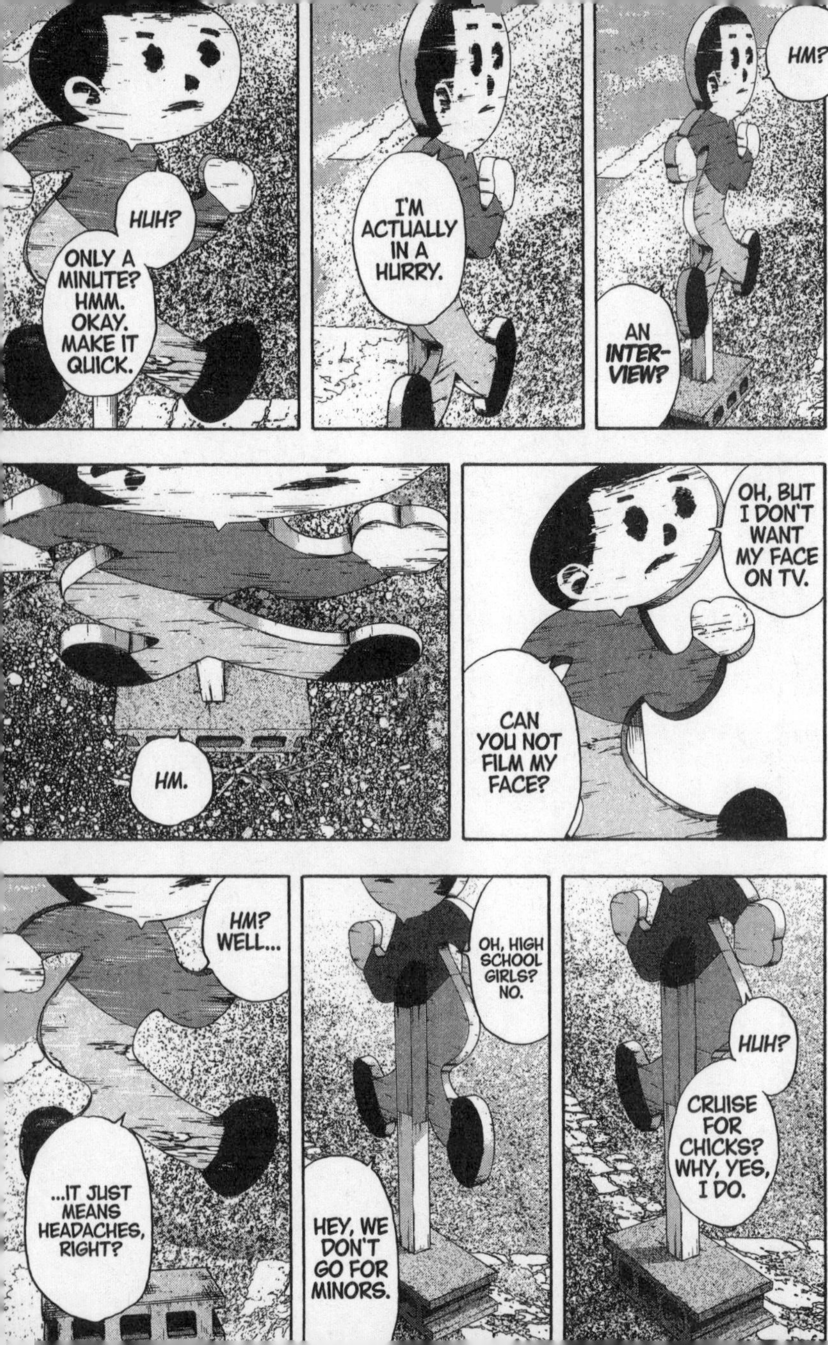
HM?
AN INTER-VIEW?
I'M ACTUALLY IN A HURRY.
HUH?
ONLY A MINUTE? HMM. OKAY. MAKE IT QUICK.
OH, BUT I DON'T WANT MY FACE ON TV.
CAN YOU NOT FILM MY FACE?
HM.
HUH?
CRUISE FOR CHICKS? WHY, YES, I DO.
OH, HIGH SCHOOL GIRLS? NO.
HEY, WE DON'T GO FOR MINORS.
HM? WELL...
...IT JUST MEANS HEADACHES, RIGHT?

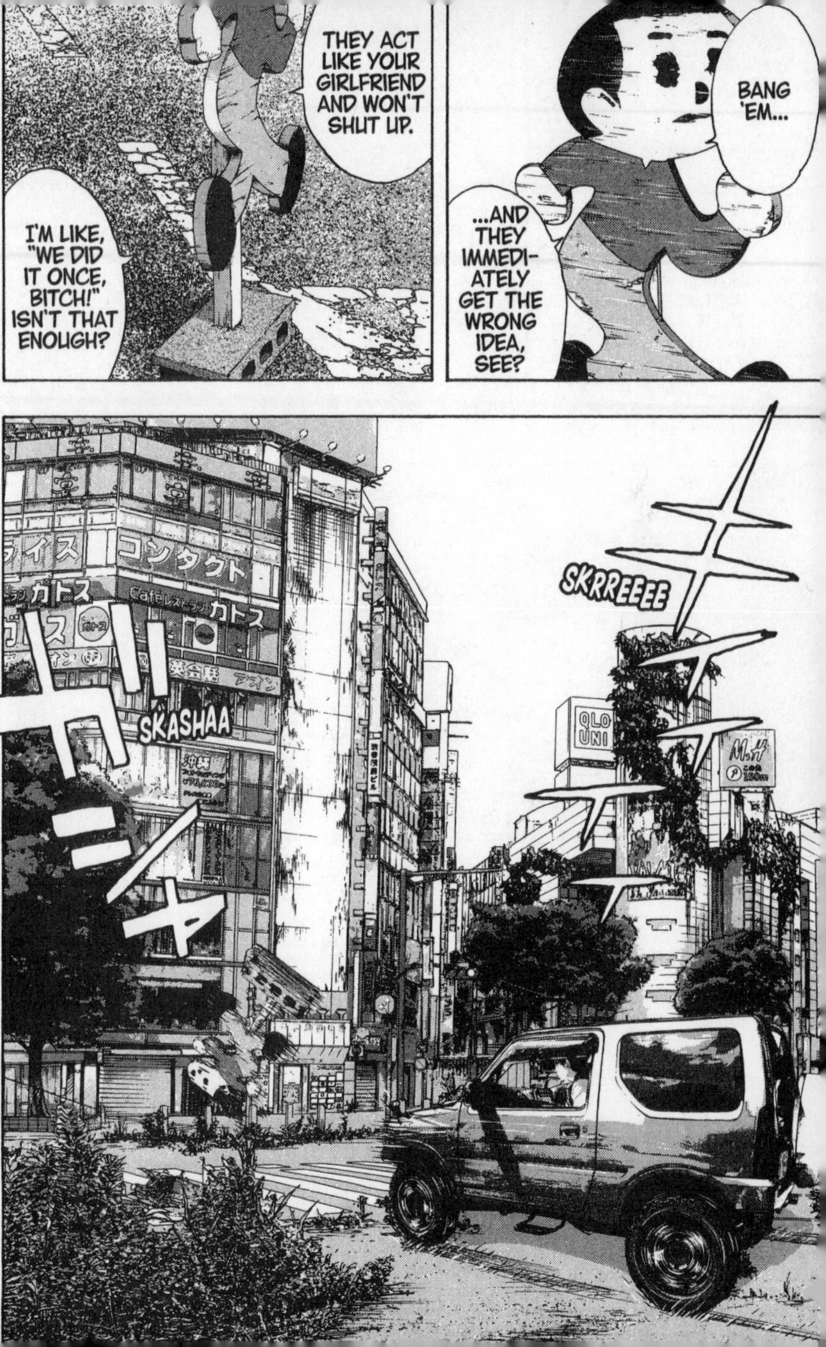
BANG 'EM...
...AND THEY IMMEDI-ATELY GET THE WRONG IDEA, SEE?
THEY ACT LIKE YOUR GIRLFRIEND AND WON'T SHUT UP.
I'M LIKE, "WE DID IT ONCE, BITCH!" ISN'T THAT ENOUGH?
SKRREEEE
QLO UNI
コンタクト
Cafeレストラン カトス
英会話
SKASHAA

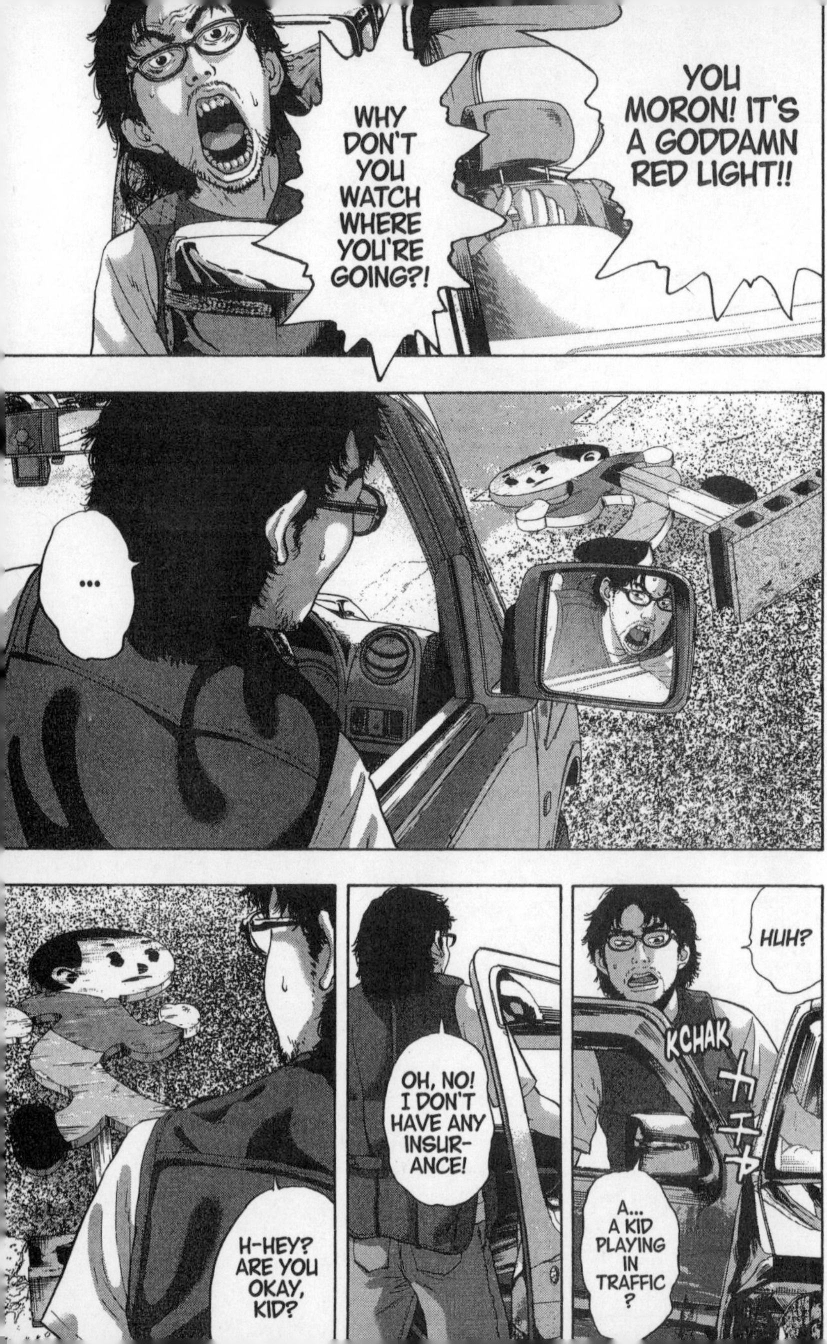
YOU MORON! IT'S A GODDAMN RED LIGHT!!
WHY DON'T YOU WATCH WHERE YOU'RE GOING?!
...
HUH?
KCHAK
A... A KID PLAYING IN TRAFFIC?
OH, NO! I DON'T HAVE ANY INSUR-ANCE!
H-HEY? ARE YOU OKAY, KID?

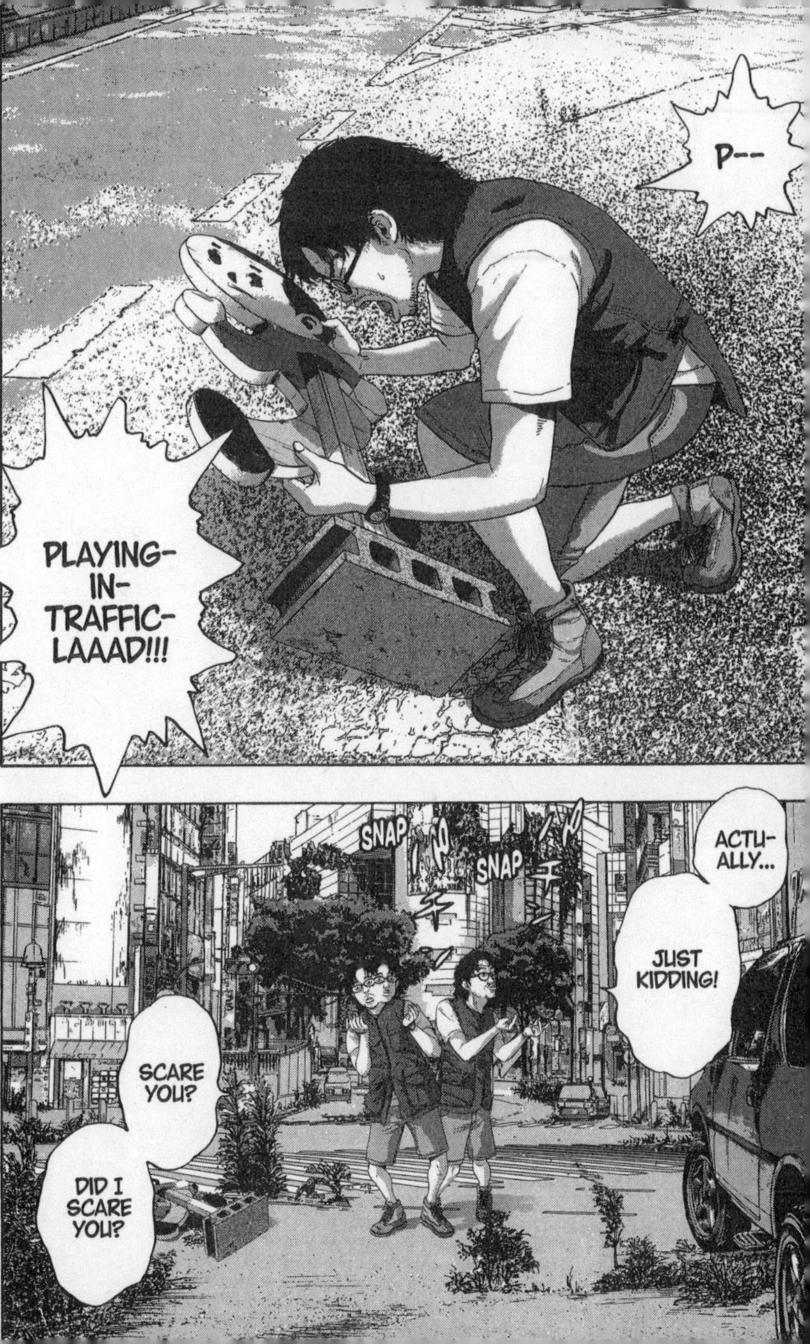
P--
PLAYING-IN-TRAFFIC-LAAAD!!!
ACTU-ALLY...
JUST KIDDING!
SNAP
SNAP
SCARE YOU?
DID I SCARE YOU?

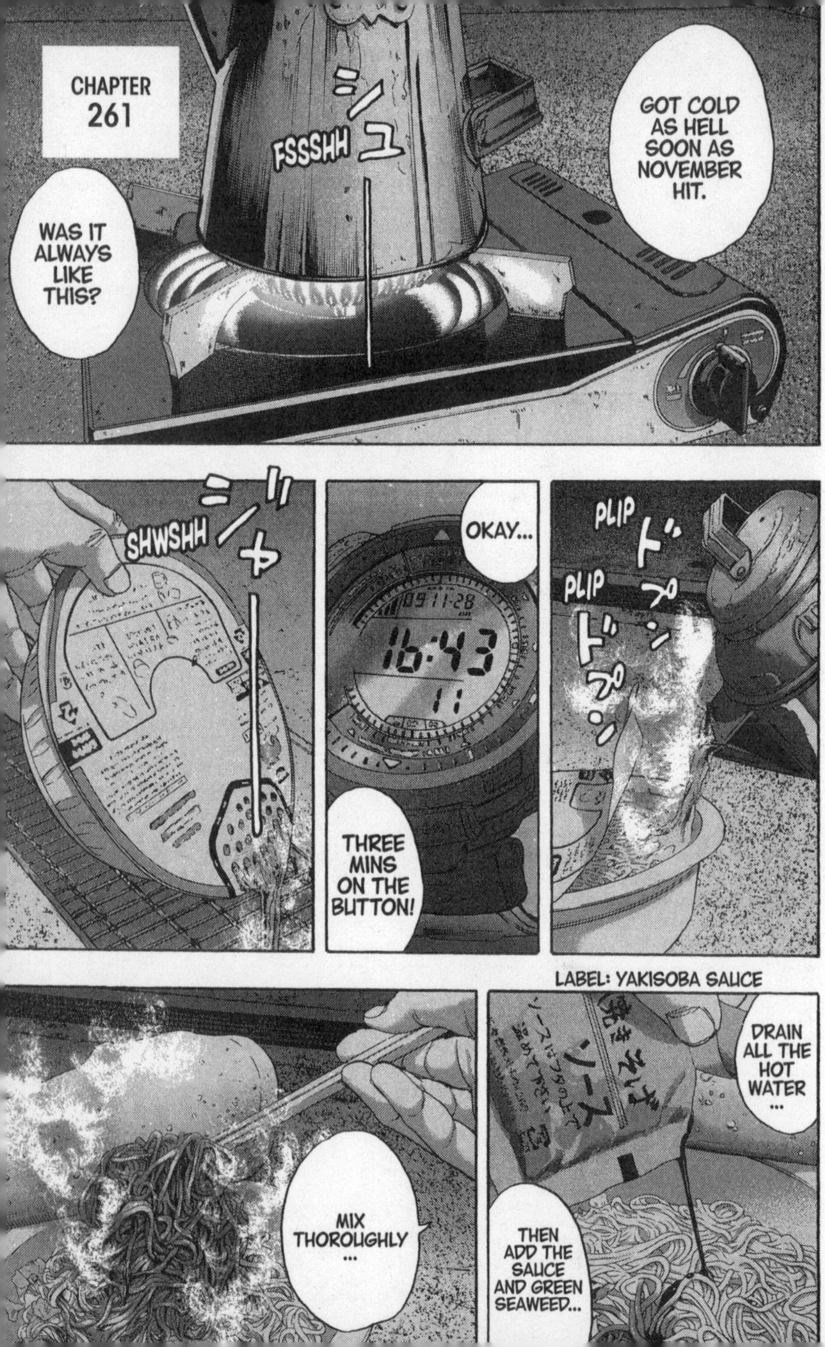
CHAPTER 261
GOT COLD AS HELL SOON AS NOVEMBER HIT.
FSSSHH
WAS IT ALWAYS LIKE THIS?
PLIP
PLIP
OKAY...
16:43
THREE MINS ON THE BUTTON!
SHWSHH
LABEL: YAKISOBA SAUCE
DRAIN ALL THE HOT WATER...
THEN ADD THE SAUCE AND GREEN SEAWEED...
MIX THOROUGHLY...

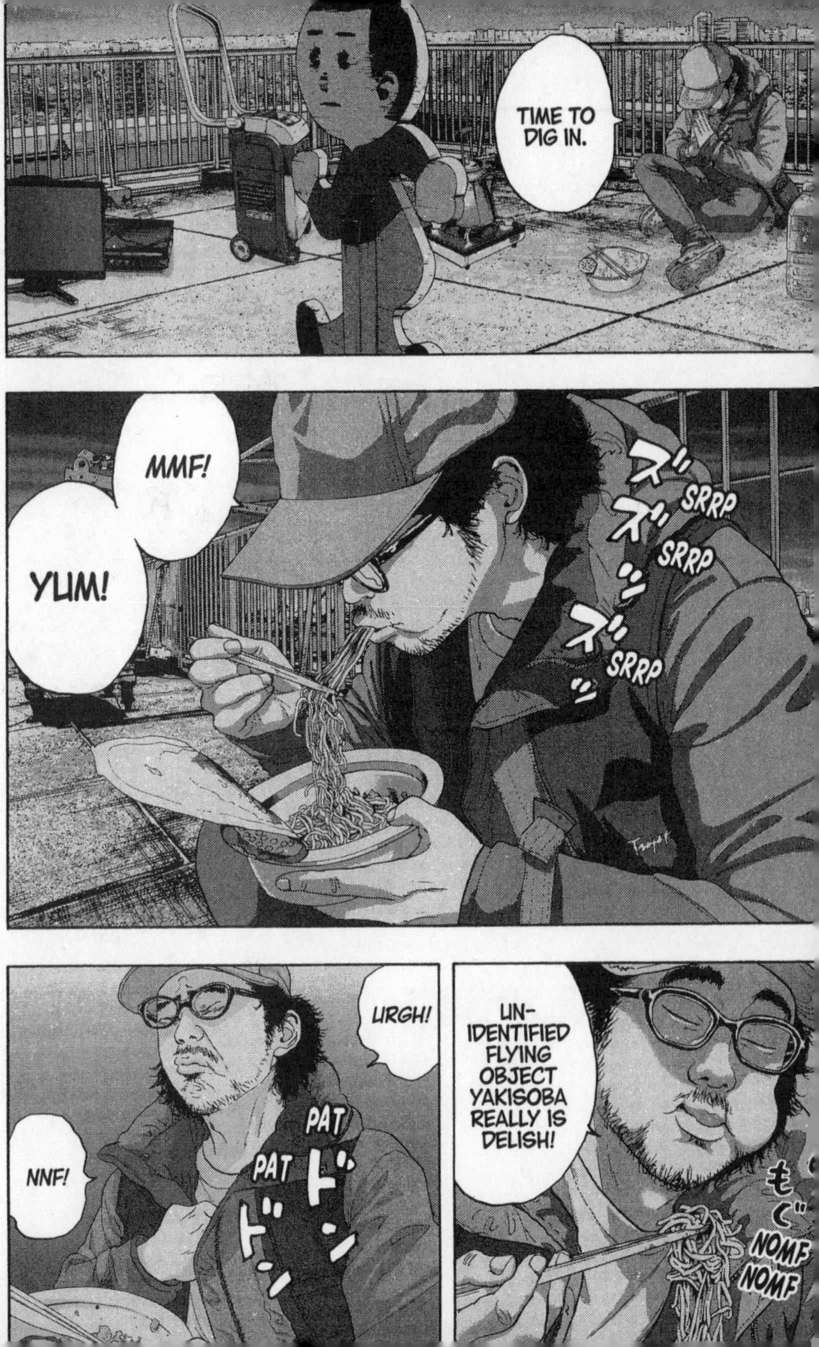
TIME TO DIG IN.
MMF!
YUM!
ズズ
SRRP
ズズ
SRRP
ッ
ズズ
SRRP
ッ
UN-IDENTIFIED FLYING OBJECT YAKISOBA REALLY IS DELISH!
もぐ
NOMF
NOMF
URGH!
PAT
ドン
PAT
ドン
NNF!

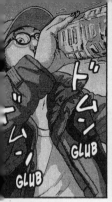

シャラ
KTAK
AND FOR DESSERT... VITAMIN PILLS.
カポッ
WHPP
ドムン
GLUB
GLUB
HHFFF...
THAT'S IT FOR DINNER.
THANK YOU FOR THE FEAST.
BOTTLE LABEL: 12 VITAMINS
STILL TWO YEARS UNTIL THE BEST BEFORE DATE.
IF THERE'S AN EXPIRY DATE, IT LASTS EVEN LONGER.
THE CUP NOODLES ARE PROBABLY GOOD FOR ANOTHER YEAR, AND I'VE GOT PLENTY.
ANYWAY... IT'S ALL FOR ME... ALONE IN TOKYO, THIS GIANT CITY.
IT'S AN EASY WIN.

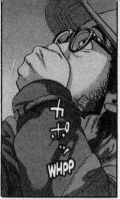

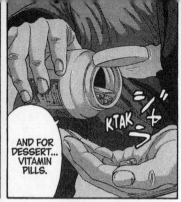

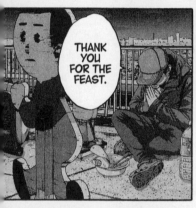

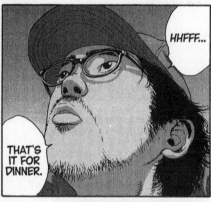

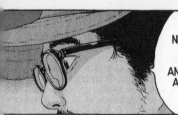

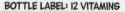

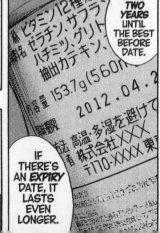

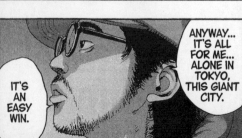

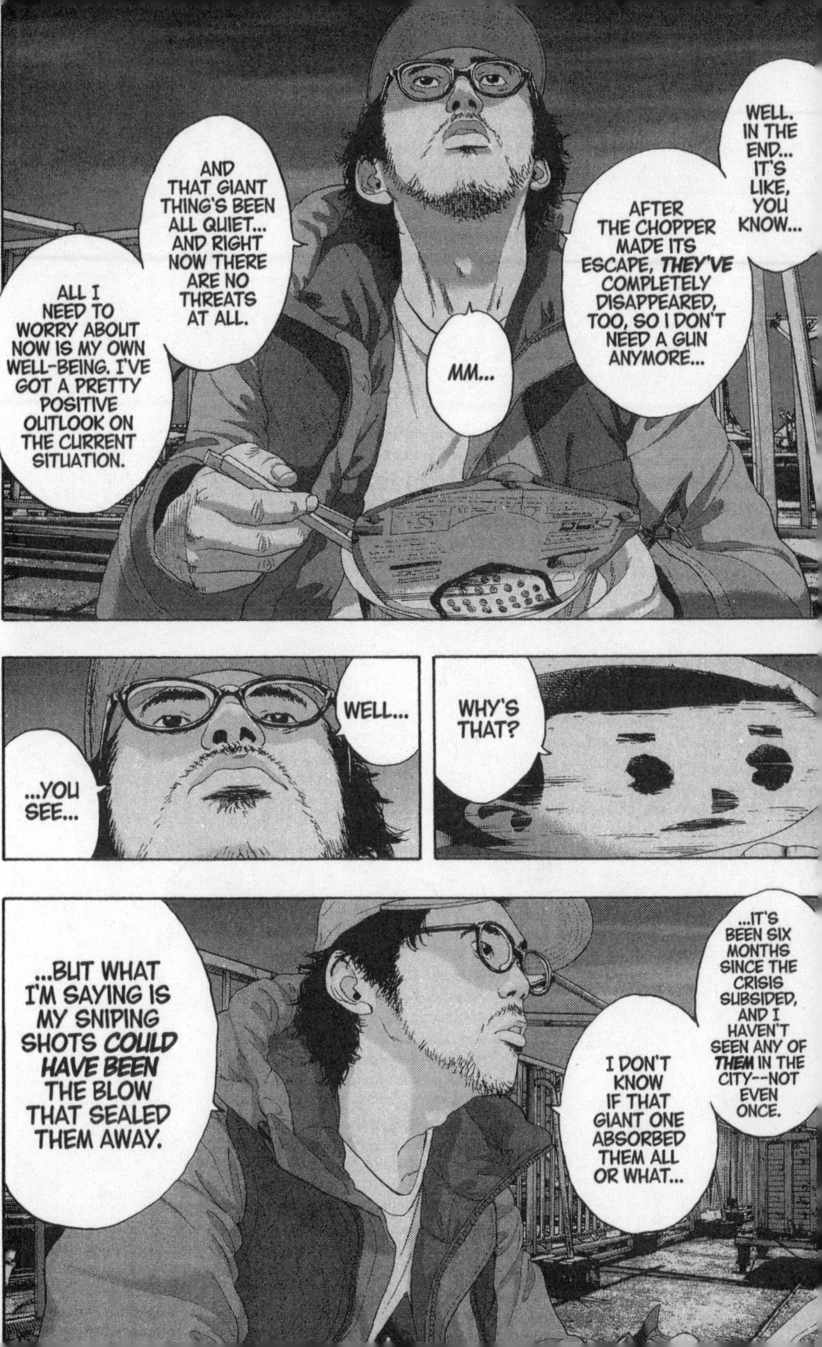
WELL. IN THE END... IT'S LIKE, YOU KNOW...
AFTER THE CHOPPER MADE ITS ESCAPE, *THEY'VE* COMPLETELY DISAPPEARED, TOO, SO I DON'T NEED A GUN ANYMORE...
MM...
AND THAT GIANT THING'S BEEN ALL QUIET... AND RIGHT NOW THERE ARE NO THREATS AT ALL.
ALL I NEED TO WORRY ABOUT NOW IS MY OWN WELL-BEING. I'VE GOT A PRETTY POSITIVE OUTLOOK ON THE CURRENT SITUATION.
WHY'S THAT?
WELL...
...YOU SEE...
...IT'S BEEN SIX MONTHS SINCE THE CRISIS SUBSIDED, AND I HAVEN'T SEEN ANY OF *THEM* IN THE CITY--NOT EVEN ONCE.
I DON'T KNOW IF THAT GIANT ONE ABSORBED THEM ALL OR WHAT...
...BUT WHAT I'M SAYING IS MY SNIPING SHOTS *COULD HAVE BEEN* THE BLOW THAT SEALED THEM AWAY.

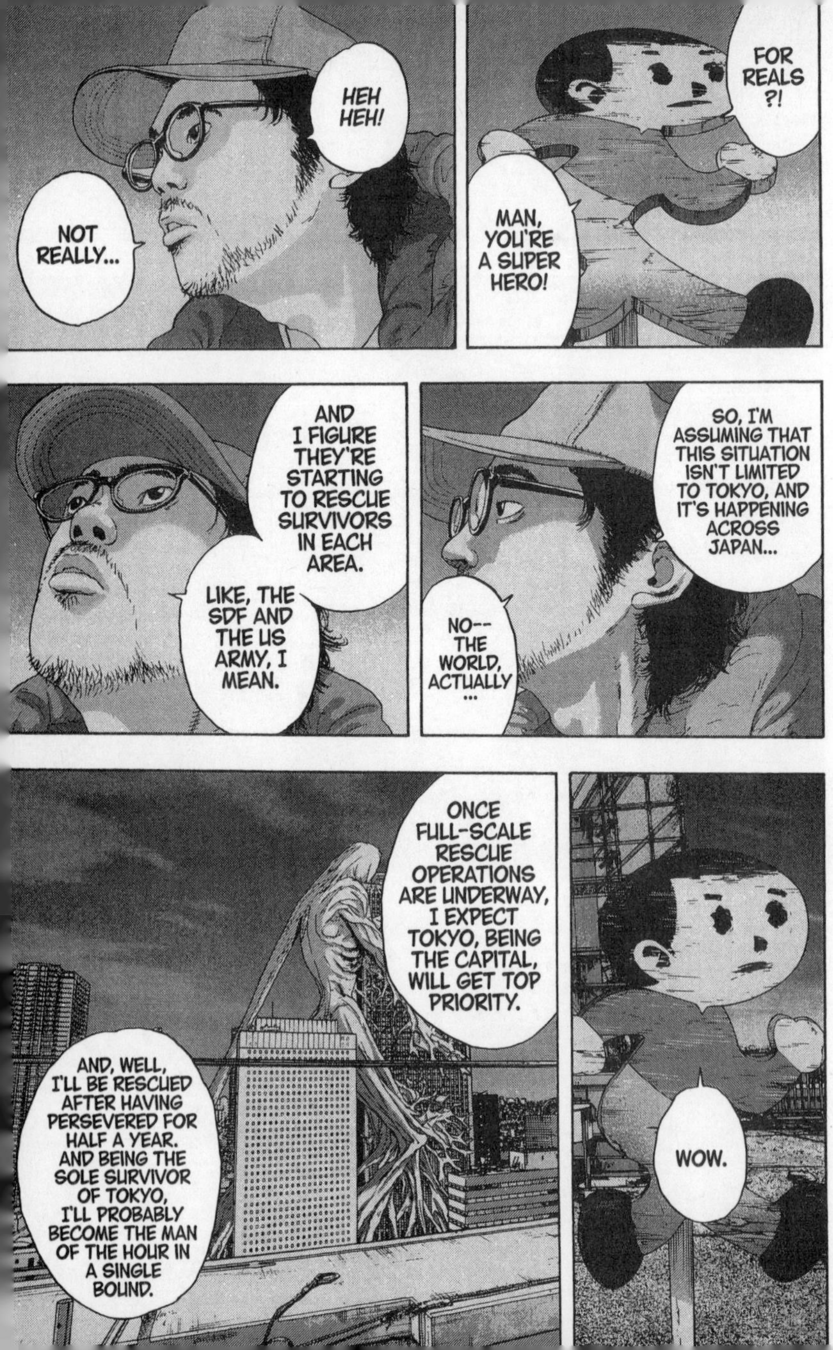
FOR REALS ?!
MAN, YOU'RE A SUPER HERO!
HEH HEH!
NOT REALLY...
SO, I'M ASSUMING THAT THIS SITUATION ISN'T LIMITED TO TOKYO, AND IT'S HAPPENING ACROSS JAPAN...
NO-- THE WORLD, ACTUALLY ...
AND I FIGURE THEY'RE STARTING TO RESCUE SURVIVORS IN EACH AREA.
LIKE, THE SDF AND THE US ARMY, I MEAN.
WOW.
ONCE FULL-SCALE RESCUE OPERATIONS ARE UNDERWAY, I EXPECT TOKYO, BEING THE CAPITAL, WILL GET TOP PRIORITY.
AND, WELL, I'LL BE RESCUED AFTER HAVING PERSEVERED FOR HALF A YEAR. AND BEING THE SOLE SURVIVOR OF TOKYO, I'LL PROBABLY BECOME THE MAN OF THE HOUR IN A SINGLE BOUND.

FOR REAL!!

YES!

FOR REALS?!

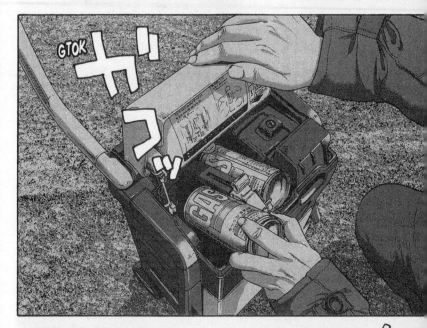

GTOK

9A (合計)

VRRMM

PUTT

PUTT

PUTT

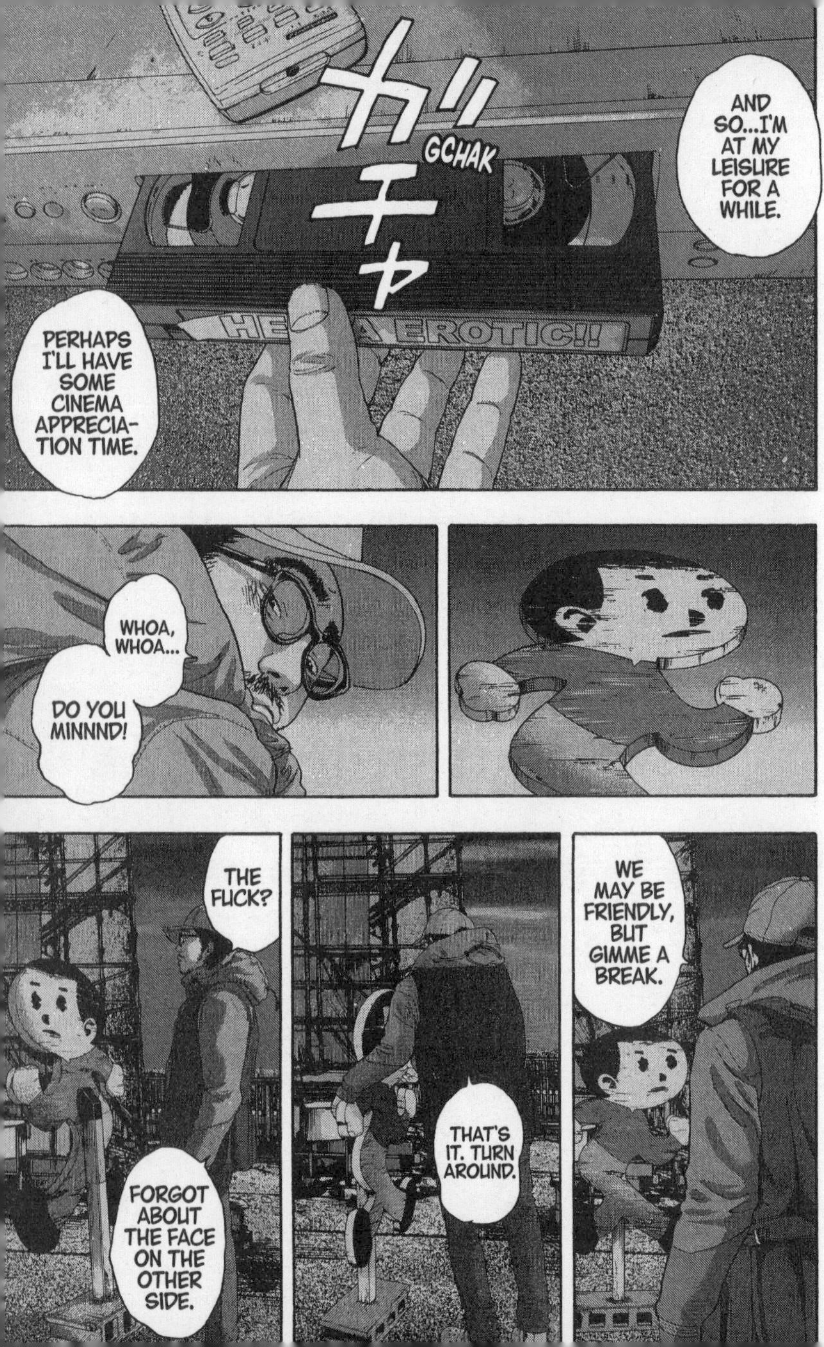
AND SO...I'M AT MY LEISURE FOR A WHILE.
カッチャ
GCHAK
PERHAPS I'LL HAVE SOME CINEMA APPRECIATION TIME.
WHOA, WHOA...
DO YOU MINNND!
WE MAY BE FRIENDLY, BUT GIMME A BREAK.
THAT'S IT. TURN AROUND.
THE FUCK?
FORGOT ABOUT THE FACE ON THE OTHER SIDE.

IT'S OKAY.
IT'LL BE OKAY.

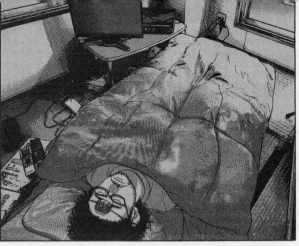

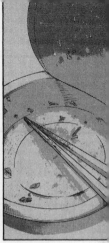

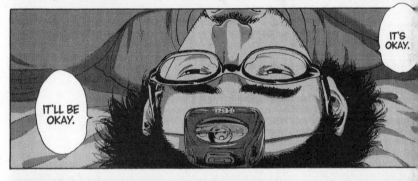

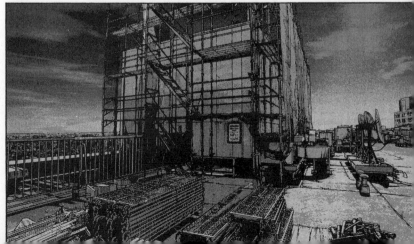

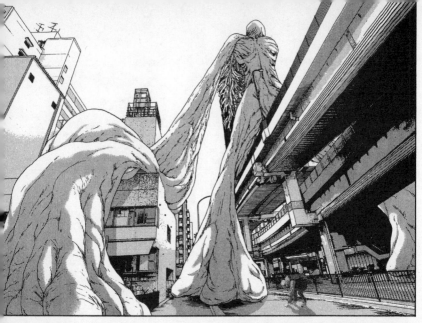

A SLUG CASING.

EMPTY.

OOH!

I HAVEN'T USED UP ALL MY AMMO, BUT...

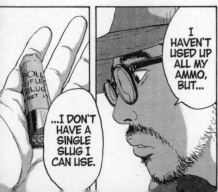

...I DON'T HAVE A SINGLE SLUG I CAN USE.

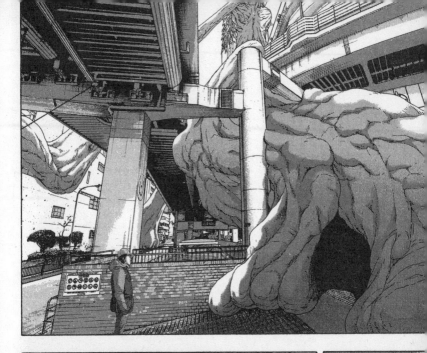

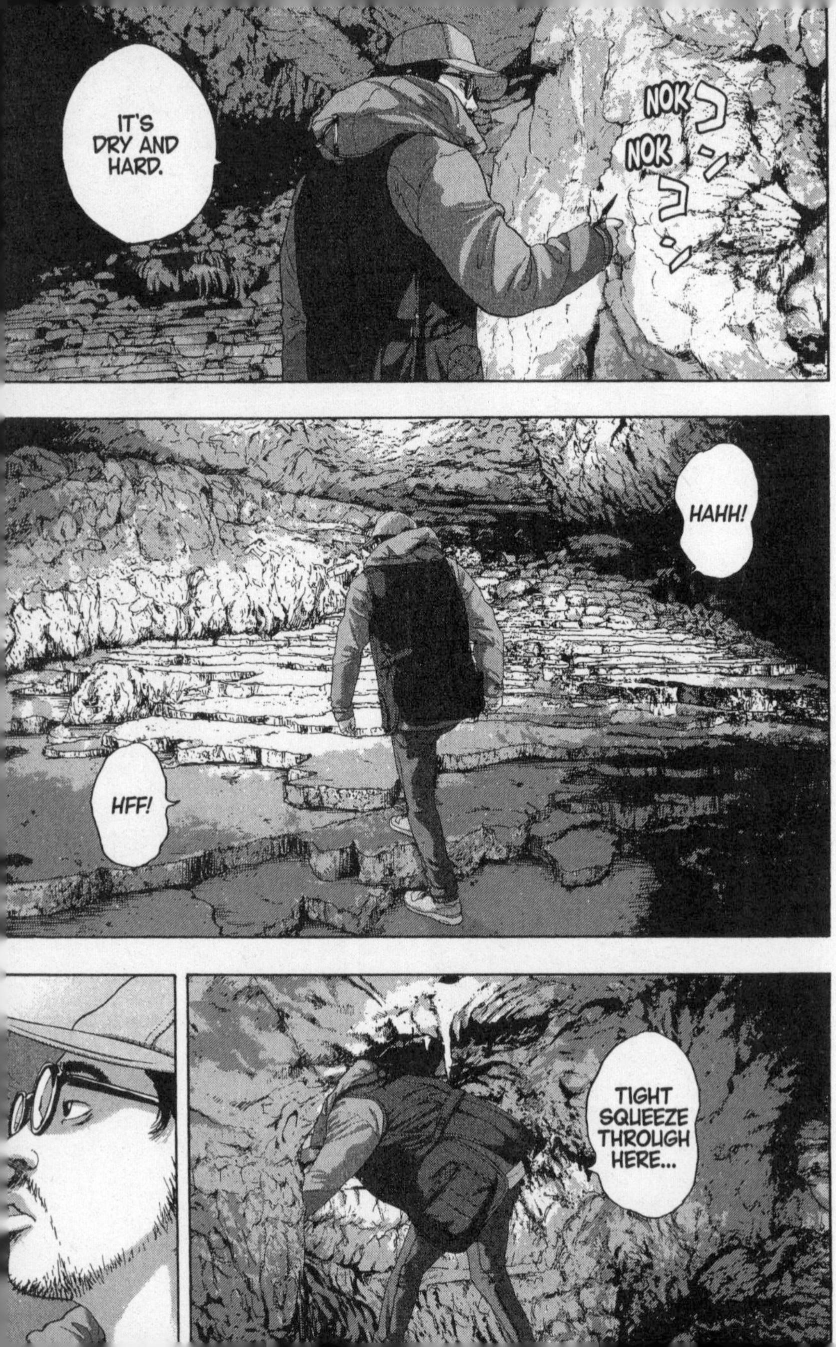
NOK
NOK
IT'S DRY AND HARD.
HAHH!
HFF!
TIGHT SQUEEZE THROUGH HERE...

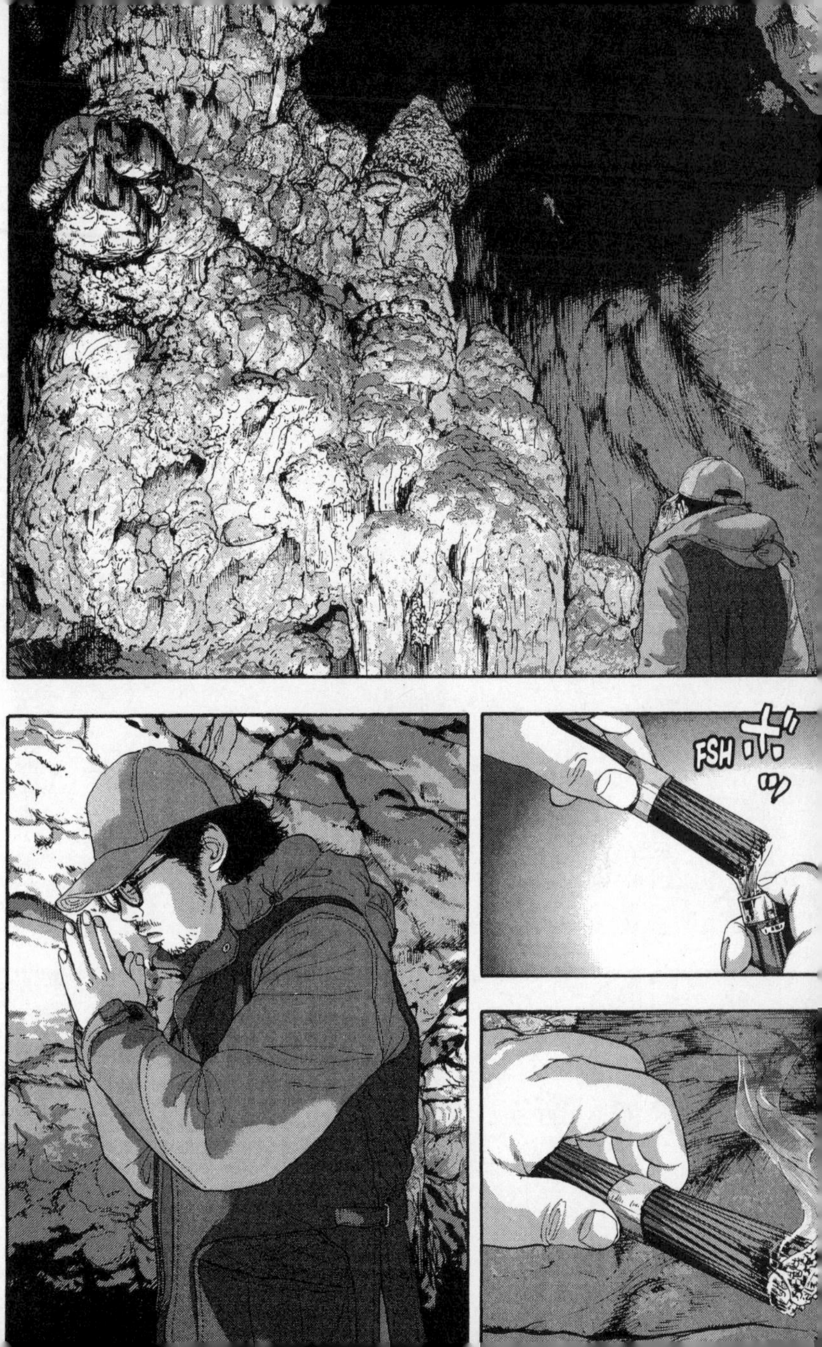
FSH
ボッ

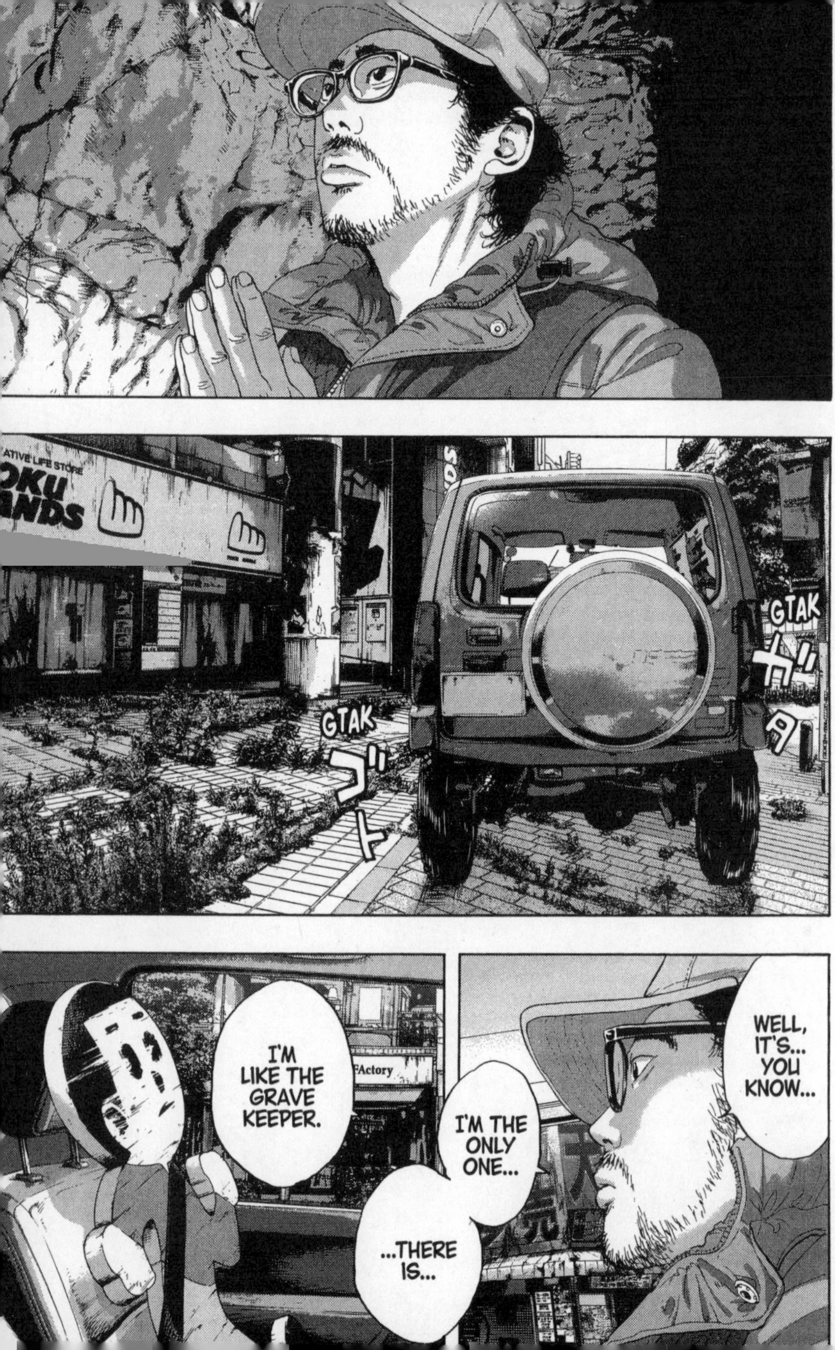
GTAK
ガタ
GTAK
ゴト
WELL, IT'S... YOU KNOW...
I'M THE ONLY ONE...
...THERE IS...
I'M LIKE THE GRAVE KEEPER.

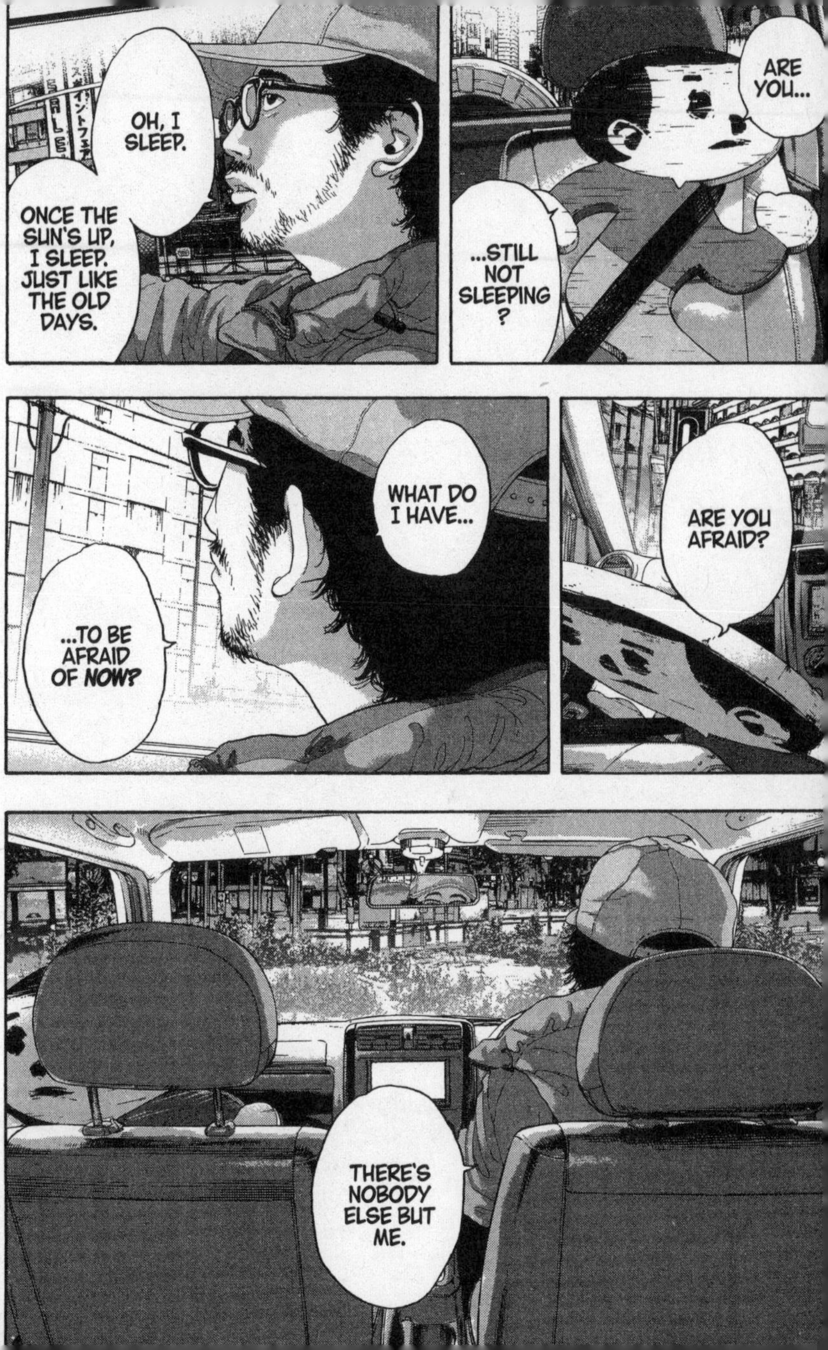
ARE YOU...
...STILL NOT SLEEPING?
OH, I SLEEP.
ONCE THE SUN'S UP, I SLEEP. JUST LIKE THE OLD DAYS.
ARE YOU AFRAID?
WHAT DO I HAVE...
...TO BE AFRAID OF NOW?
THERE'S NOBODY ELSE BUT ME.

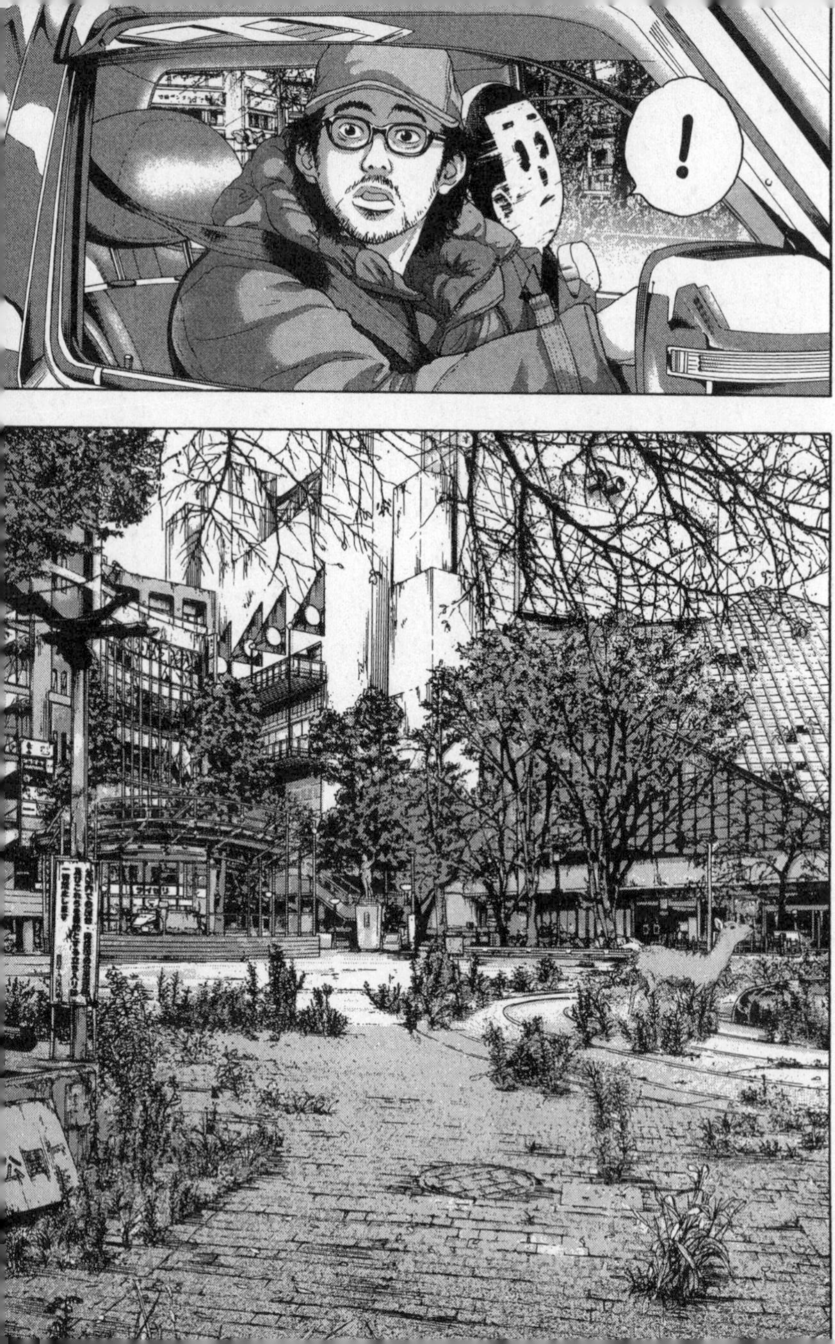
!
公園

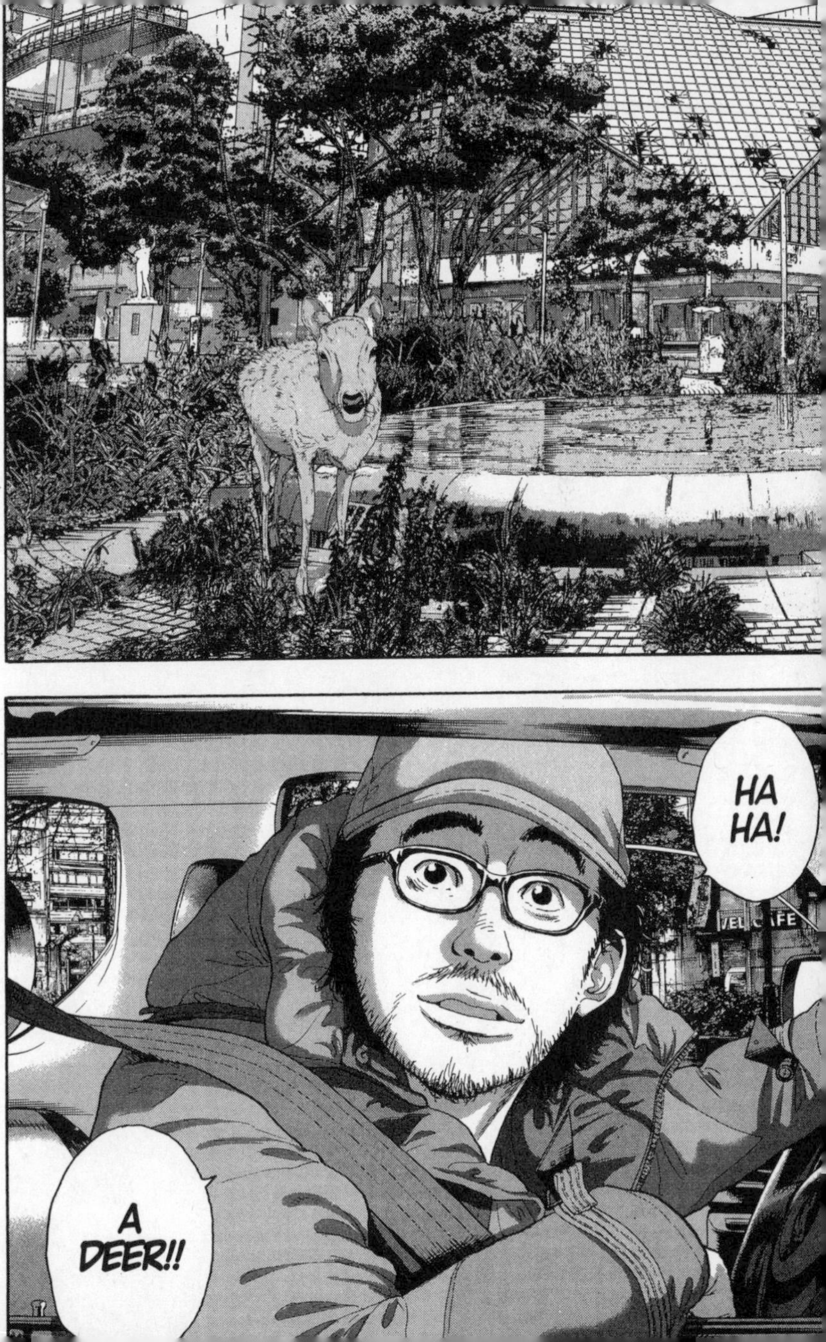
HA HA!
A DEER!!

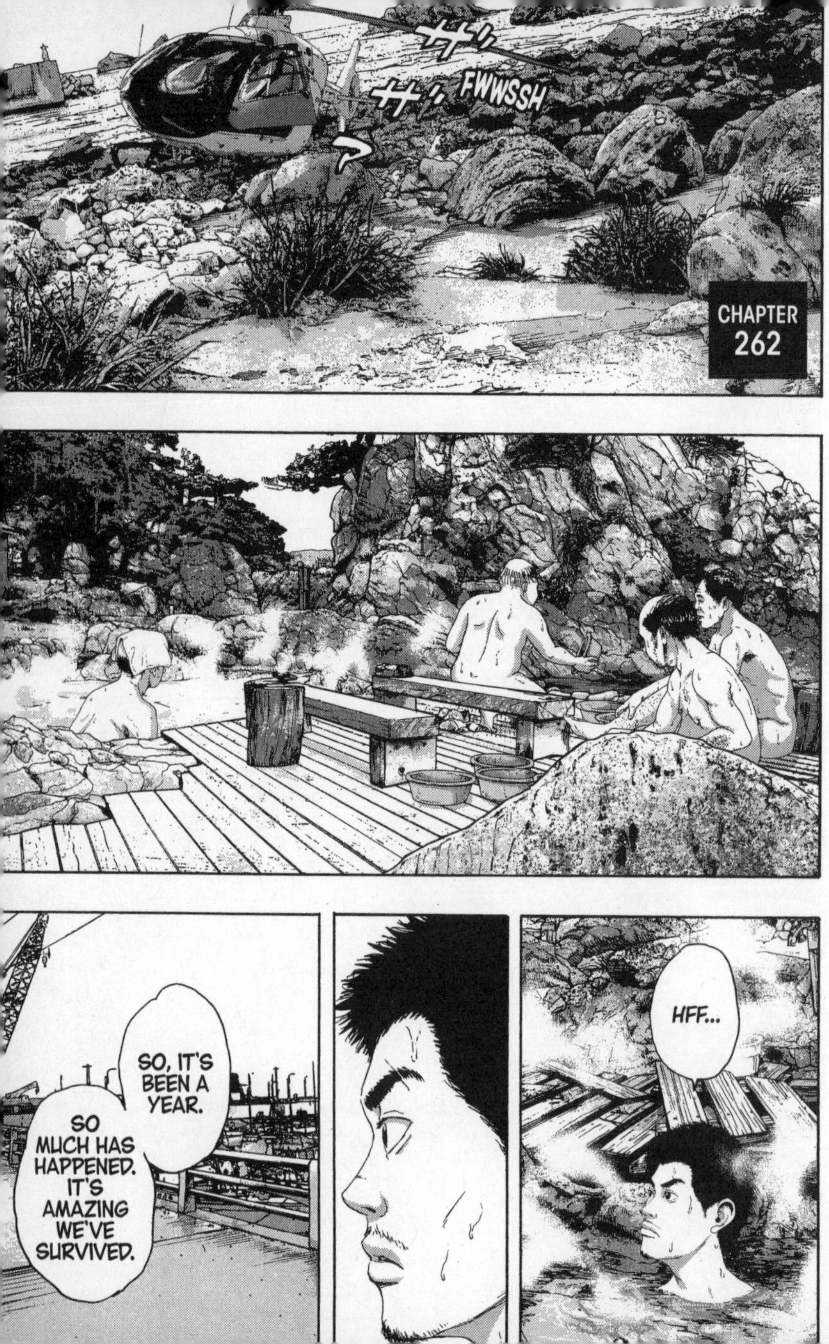
FWWSSH
CHAPTER 262
HFF...
SO, IT'S BEEN A YEAR.
SO MUCH HAS HAPPENED. IT'S AMAZING WE'VE SURVIVED.

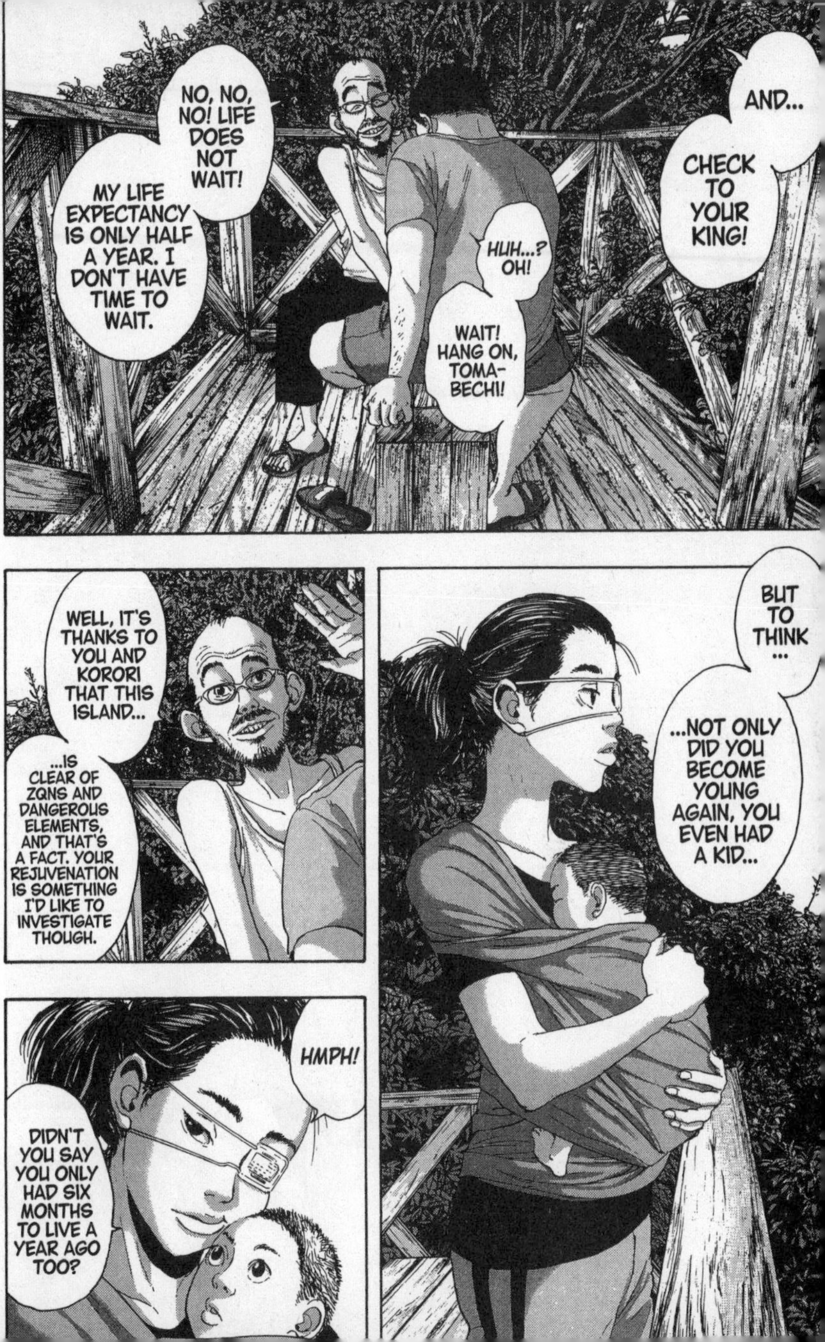
AND...
CHECK TO YOUR KING!
HUH...? OH!
WAIT! HANG ON, TOMA-BECHI!
NO, NO, NO! LIFE DOES NOT WAIT!
MY LIFE EXPECTANCY IS ONLY HALF A YEAR. I DON'T HAVE TIME TO WAIT.
BUT TO THINK...
...NOT ONLY DID YOU BECOME YOUNG AGAIN, YOU EVEN HAD A KID...
WELL, IT'S THANKS TO YOU AND KORORI THAT THIS ISLAND...
...IS CLEAR OF ZQNS AND DANGEROUS ELEMENTS, AND THAT'S A FACT. YOUR REJUVENATION IS SOMETHING I'D LIKE TO INVESTIGATE THOUGH.
HMPH!
DIDN'T YOU SAY YOU ONLY HAD SIX MONTHS TO LIVE A YEAR AGO TOO?

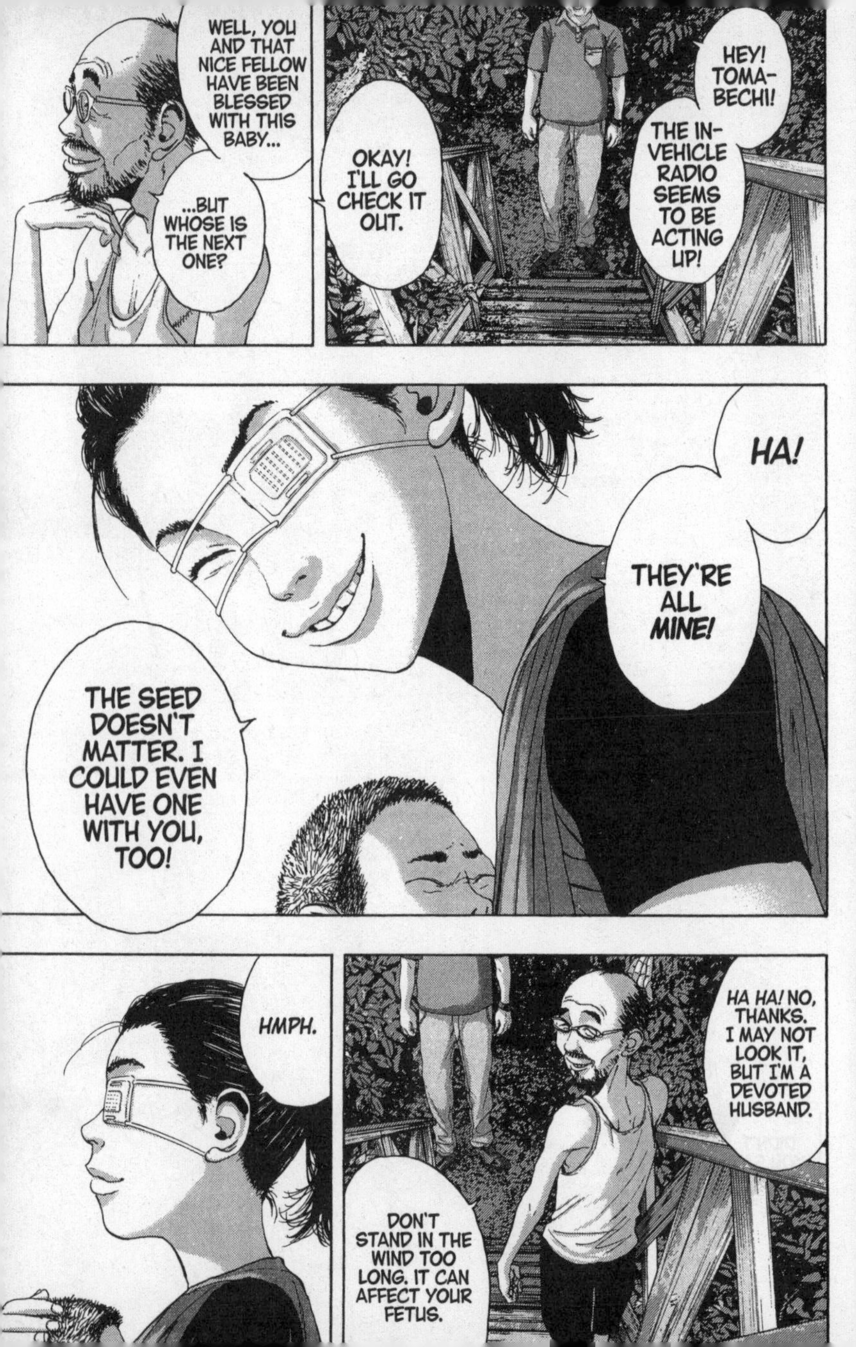
HEY! TOMA-BECHI!
THE IN-VEHICLE RADIO SEEMS TO BE ACTING UP!
OKAY! I'LL GO CHECK IT OUT.
WELL, YOU AND THAT NICE FELLOW HAVE BEEN BLESSED WITH THIS BABY...
...BUT WHOSE IS THE NEXT ONE?
HA!
THEY'RE ALL MINE!
THE SEED DOESN'T MATTER. I COULD EVEN HAVE ONE WITH YOU, TOO!
HA HA! NO, THANKS. I MAY NOT LOOK IT, BUT I'M A DEVOTED HUSBAND.
DON'T STAND IN THE WIND TOO LONG. IT CAN AFFECT YOUR FETUS.
HMPH.

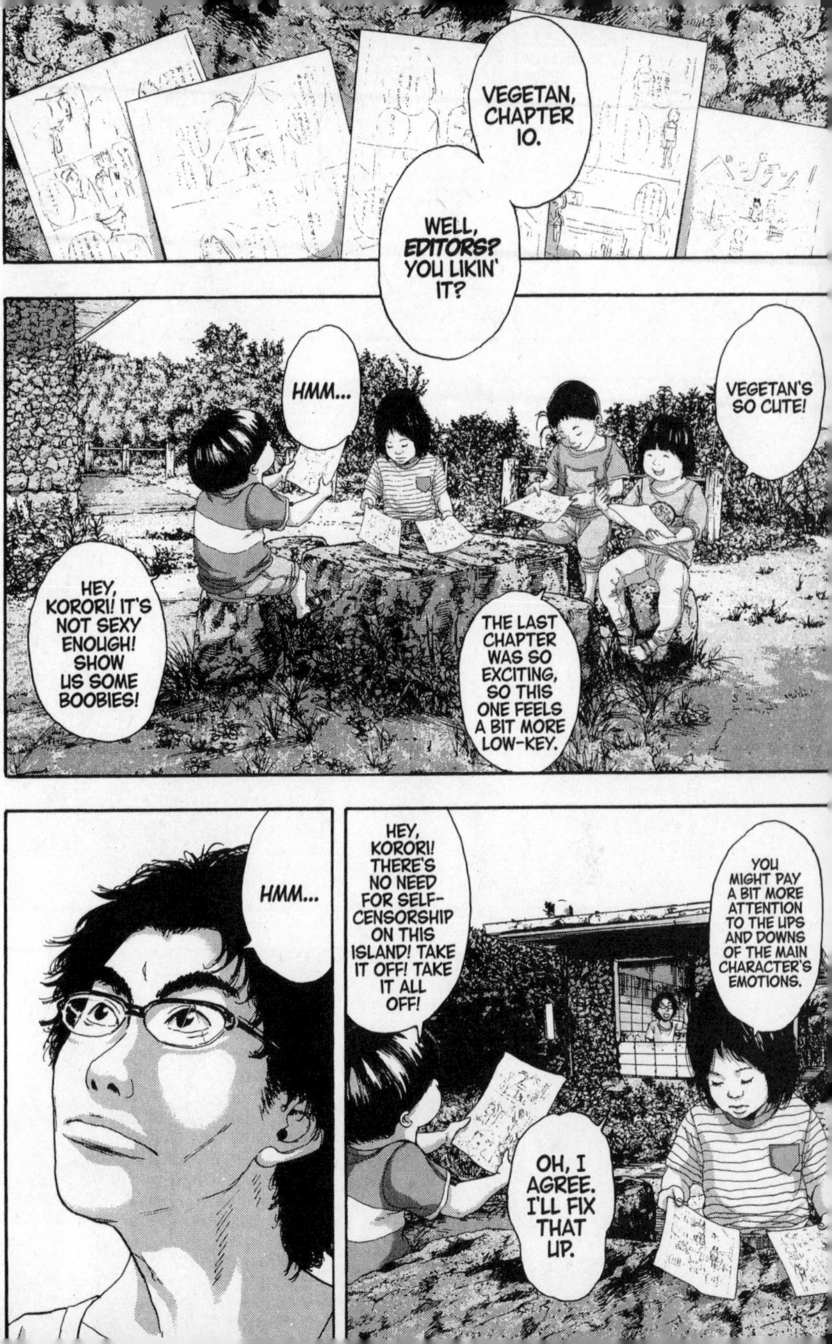
VEGETAN, CHAPTER 10.
WELL, EDITORS? YOU LIKIN' IT?
VEGETAN'S SO CUTE!
THE LAST CHAPTER WAS SO EXCITING, SO THIS ONE FEELS A BIT MORE LOW-KEY.
HMM...
HEY, KORORI! IT'S NOT SEXY ENOUGH! SHOW US SOME BOOBIES!
YOU MIGHT PAY A BIT MORE ATTENTION TO THE UPS AND DOWNS OF THE MAIN CHARACTER'S EMOTIONS.
HEY, KORORI! THERE'S NO NEED FOR SELF-CENSORSHIP ON THIS ISLAND! TAKE IT OFF! TAKE IT ALL OFF!
OH, I AGREE. I'LL FIX THAT UP.
HMM...

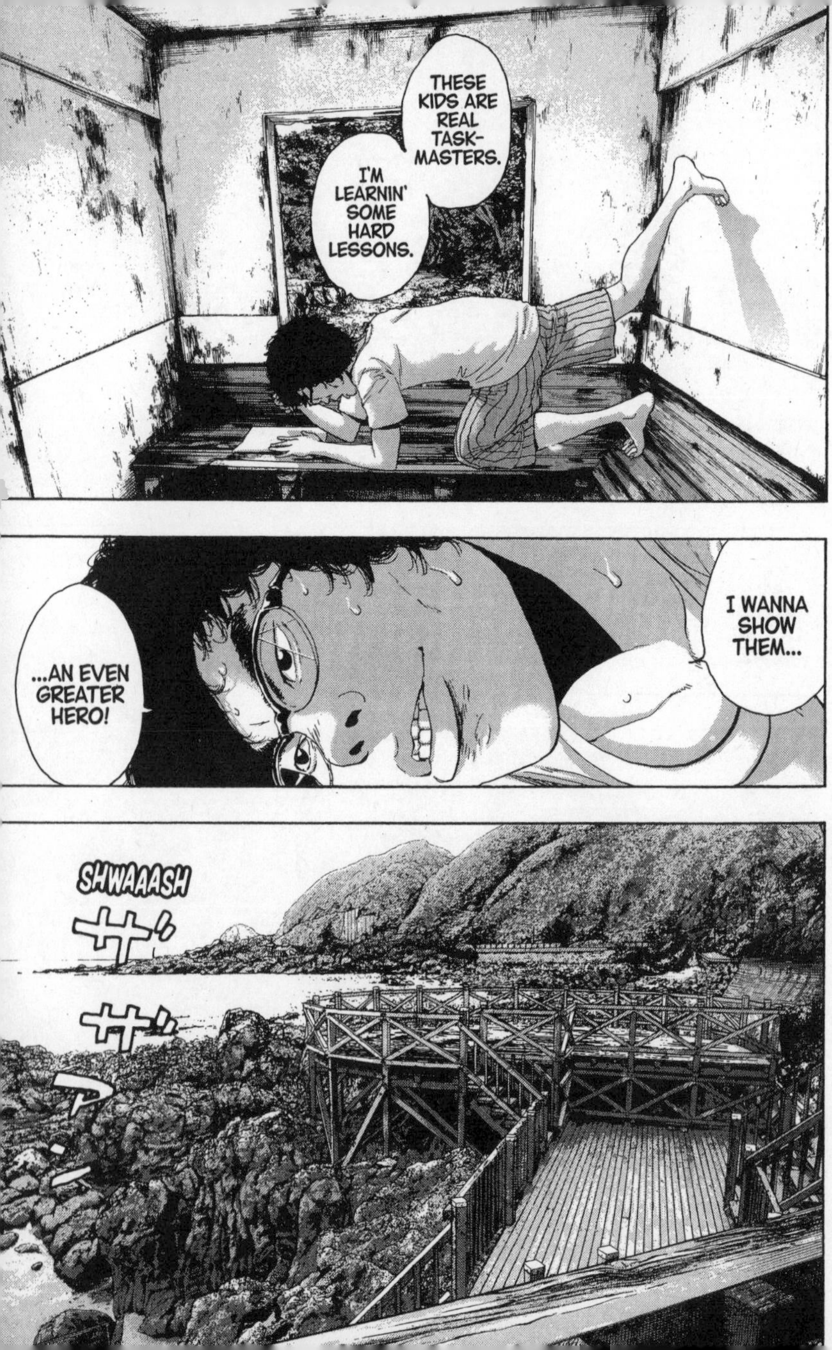
THESE KIDS ARE REAL TASK-MASTERS.
I'M LEARNIN' SOME HARD LESSONS.
I WANNA SHOW THEM...
...AN EVEN GREATER HERO!
SHWAAASH

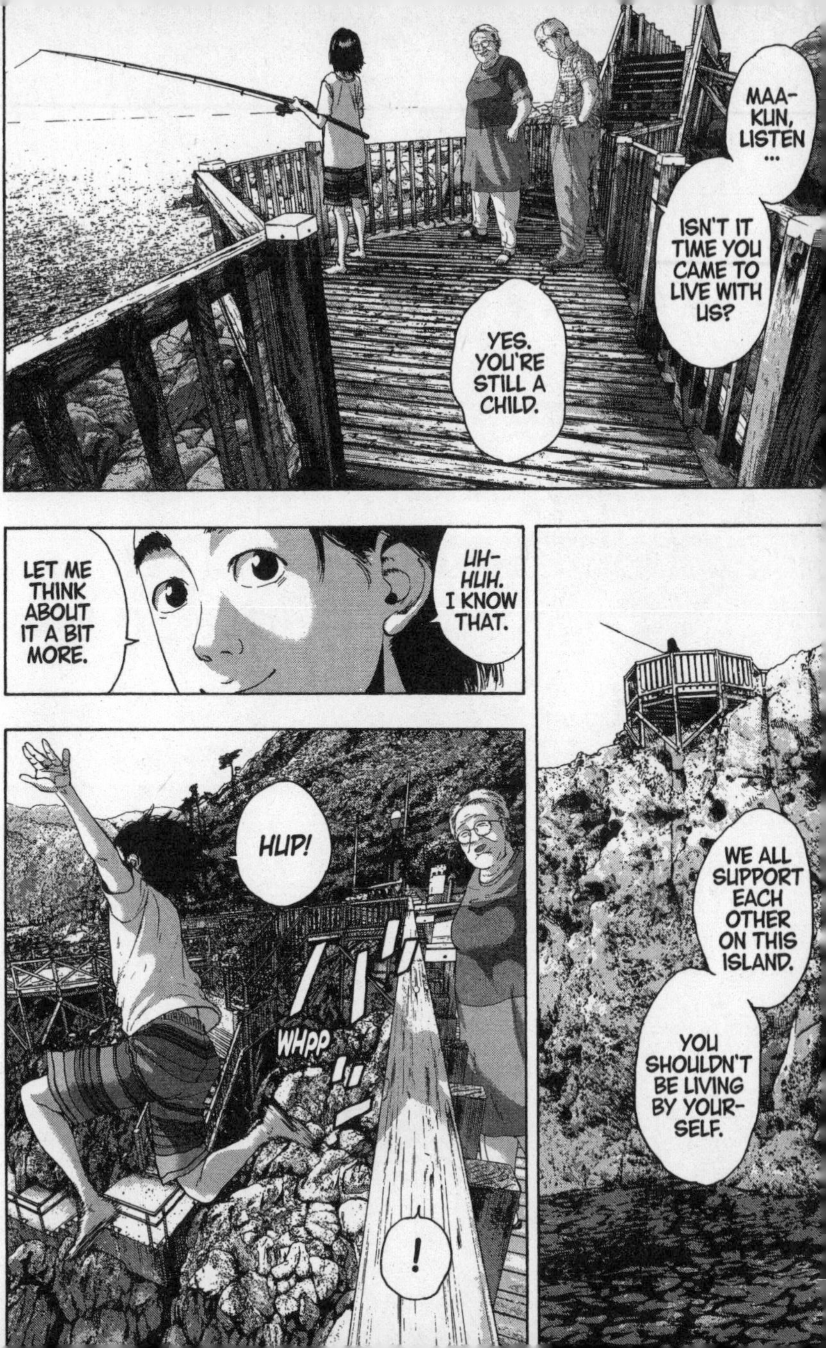
MAA-KUN, LISTEN...
ISN'T IT TIME YOU CAME TO LIVE WITH US?
YES. YOU'RE STILL A CHILD.
WE ALL SUPPORT EACH OTHER ON THIS ISLAND.
YOU SHOULDN'T BE LIVING BY YOUR-SELF.
UH-HUH. I KNOW THAT.
LET ME THINK ABOUT IT A BIT MORE.
HUP!
WHPP
!

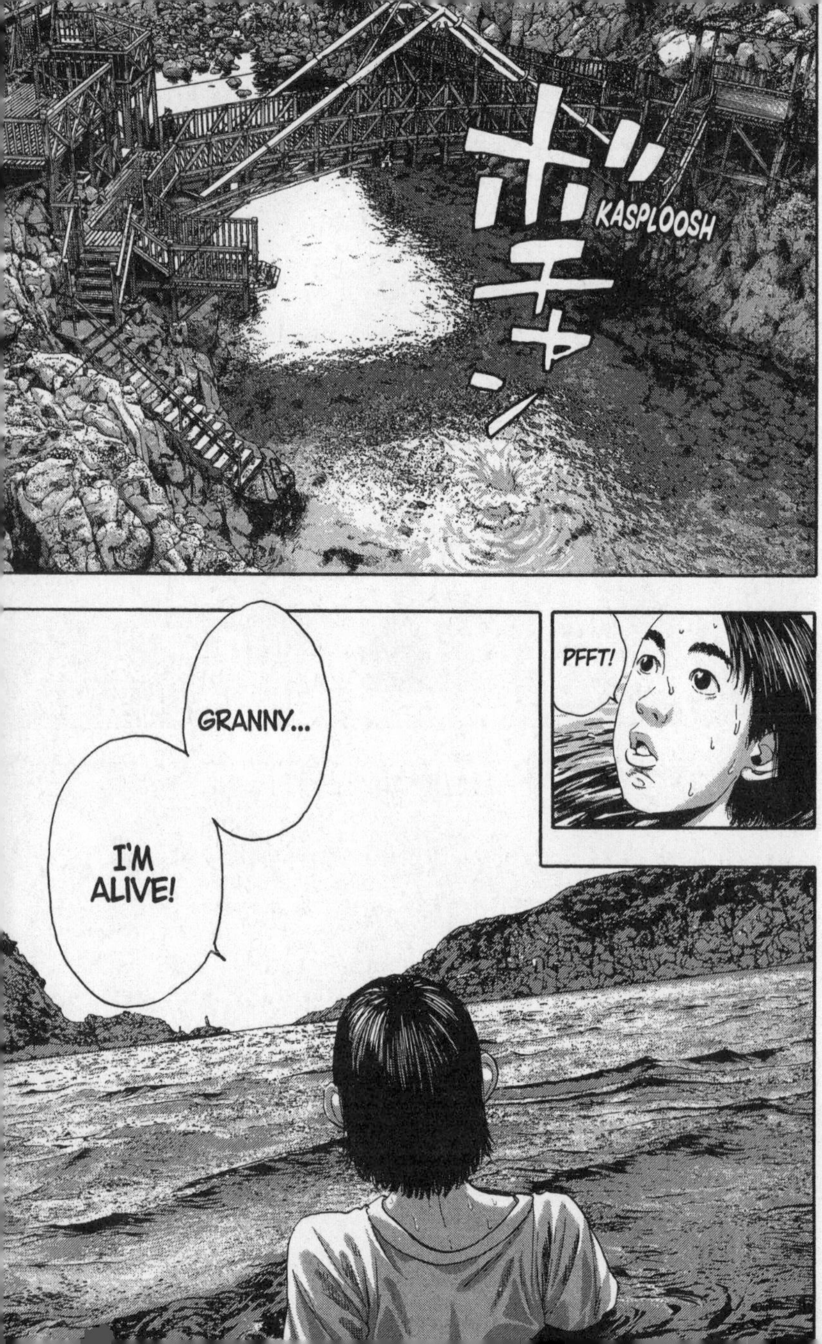
KASPLOOSH
PFFT!
GRANNY...
I'M ALIVE!

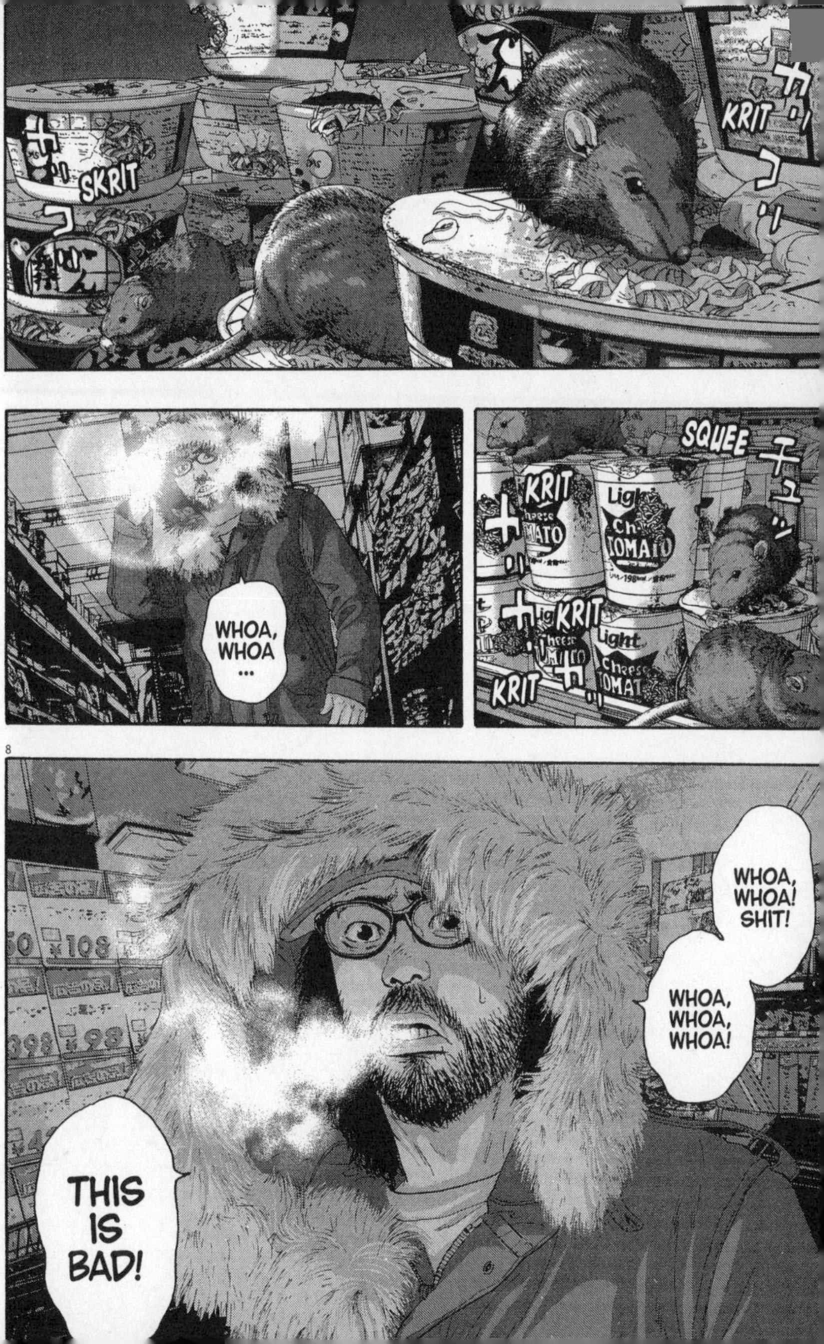
KRIT
SKRIT
SQUEE
KRIT
KRIT
KRIT
WHOA, WHOA ...
WHOA, WHOA! SHIT!
WHOA, WHOA, WHOA!
THIS IS BAD!

8

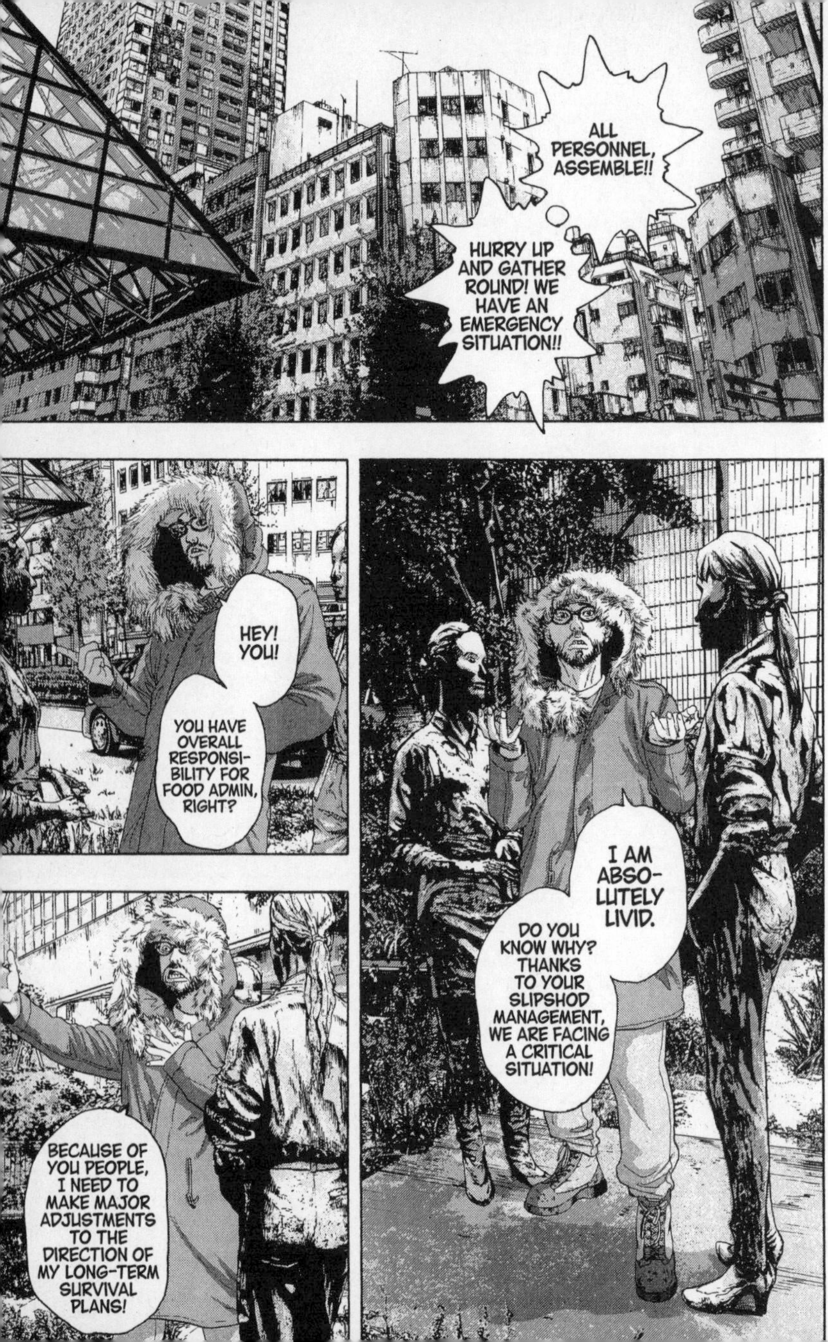
ALL PERSONNEL, ASSEMBLE!!
HURRY UP AND GATHER ROUND! WE HAVE AN EMERGENCY SITUATION!!
I AM ABSOLUTELY LIVID.
DO YOU KNOW WHY? THANKS TO YOUR SLIPSHOD MANAGEMENT, WE ARE FACING A CRITICAL SITUATION!
HEY! YOU!
YOU HAVE OVERALL RESPONSIBILITY FOR FOOD ADMIN, RIGHT?
BECAUSE OF YOU PEOPLE, I NEED TO MAKE MAJOR ADJUSTMENTS TO THE DIRECTION OF MY LONG-TERM SURVIVAL PLANS!

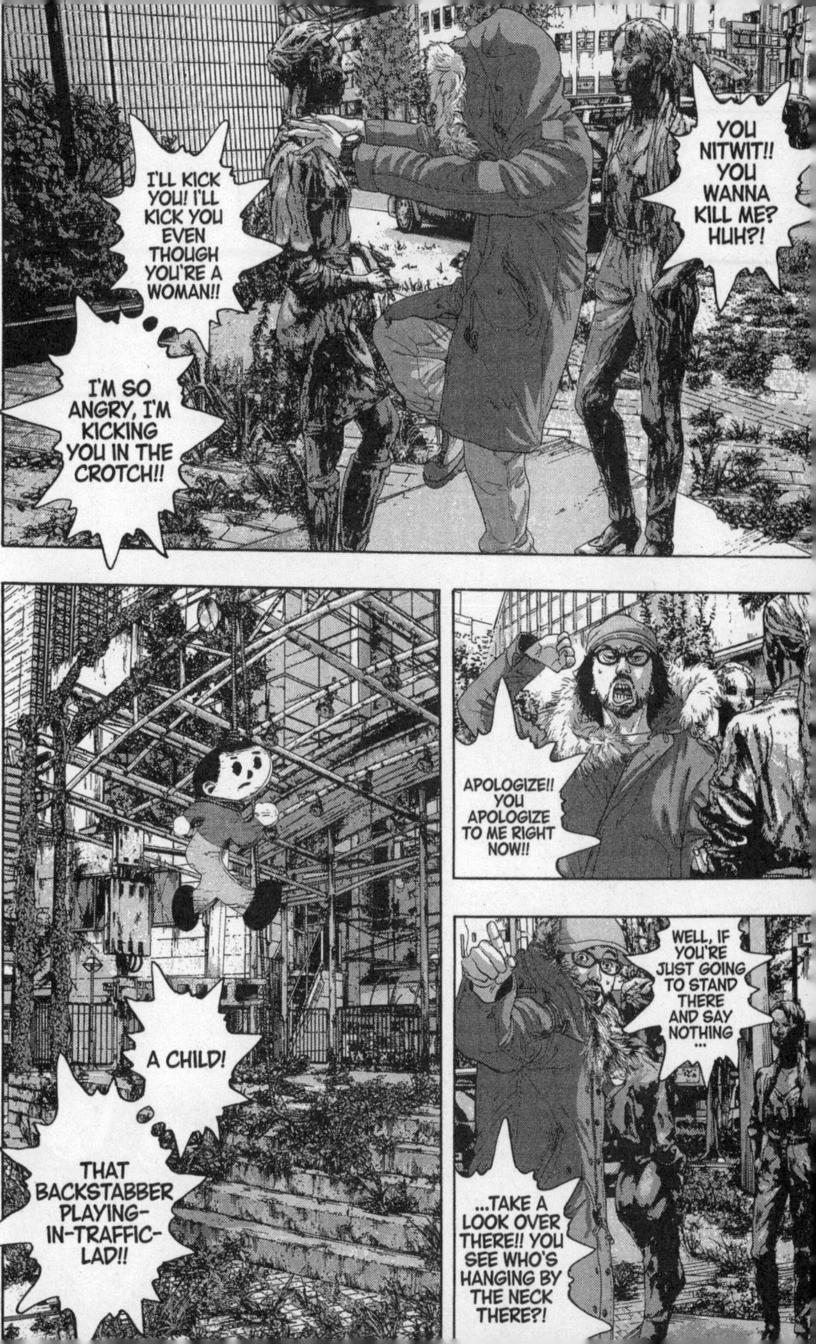
YOU NITWIT!! YOU WANNA KILL ME? HUH?!
I'LL KICK YOU! I'LL KICK YOU EVEN THOUGH YOU'RE A WOMAN!!
I'M SO ANGRY, I'M KICKING YOU IN THE CROTCH!!
APOLOGIZE!! YOU APOLOGIZE TO ME RIGHT NOW!!
WELL, IF YOU'RE JUST GOING TO STAND THERE AND SAY NOTHING ...
...TAKE A LOOK OVER THERE!! YOU SEE WHO'S HANGING BY THE NECK THERE?!
A CHILD!
THAT BACKSTABBER PLAYING-IN-TRAFFIC-LAD!!

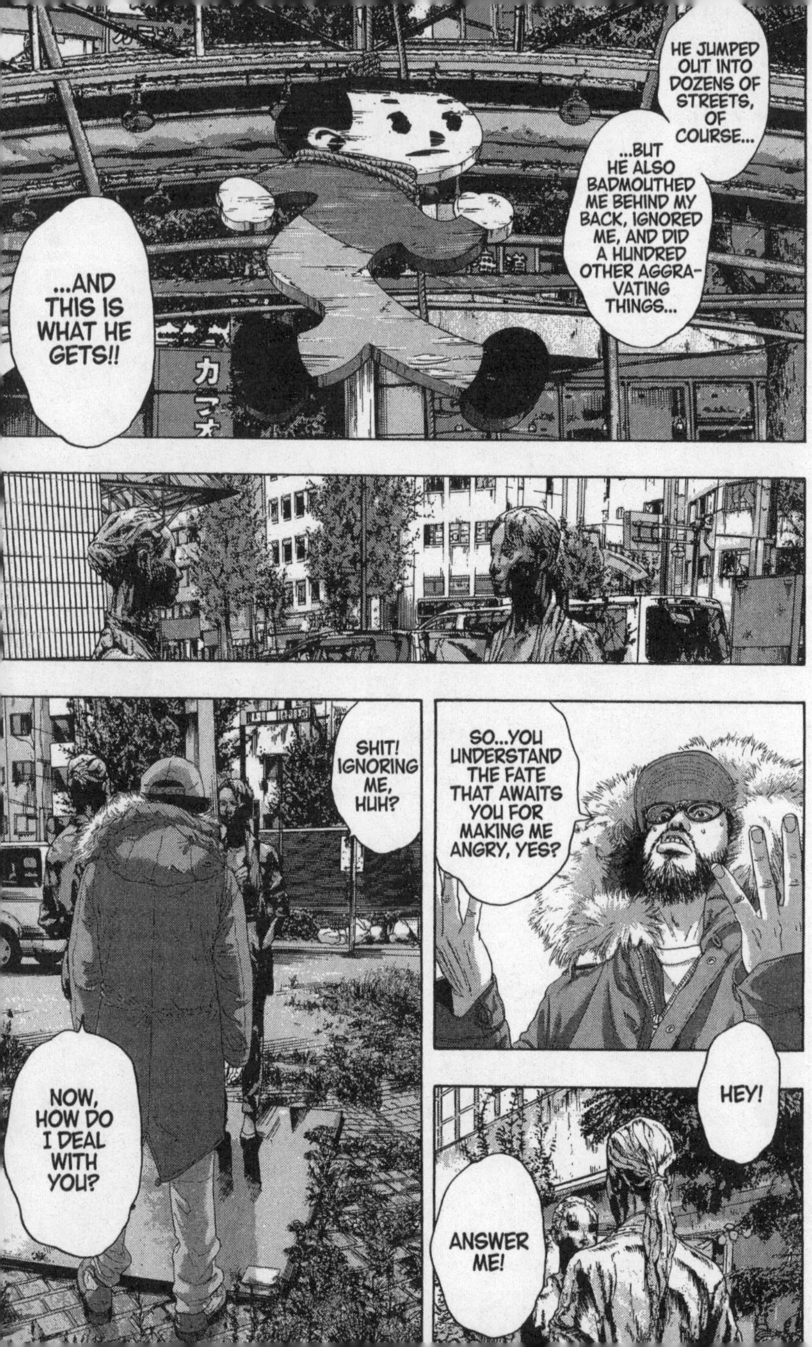
HE JUMPED OUT INTO DOZENS OF STREETS, OF COURSE...
...BUT HE ALSO BADMOUTHED ME BEHIND MY BACK, IGNORED ME, AND DID A HUNDRED OTHER AGGRA-VATING THINGS...
...AND THIS IS WHAT HE GETS!!
SO...YOU UNDERSTAND THE FATE THAT AWAITS YOU FOR MAKING ME ANGRY, YES?
HEY!
ANSWER ME!
SHIT! IGNORING ME, HUH?
NOW, HOW DO I DEAL WITH YOU?

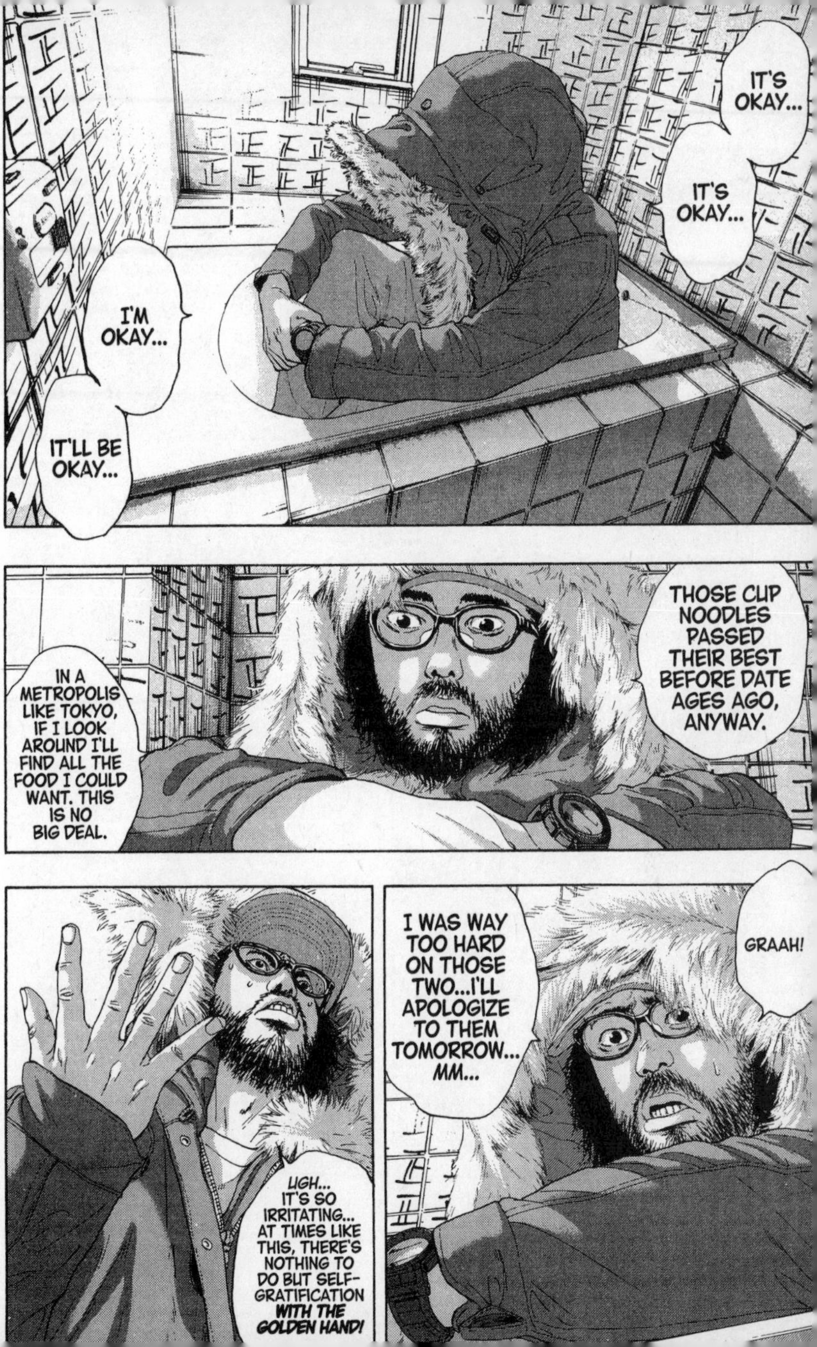
IT'S OKAY...
IT'S OKAY...
I'M OKAY...
IT'LL BE OKAY...
THOSE CUP NOODLES PASSED THEIR BEST BEFORE DATE AGES AGO, ANYWAY.
IN A METROPOLIS LIKE TOKYO, IF I LOOK AROUND I'LL FIND ALL THE FOOD I COULD WANT. THIS IS NO BIG DEAL.
GRAAH!
I WAS WAY TOO HARD ON THOSE TWO...I'LL APOLOGIZE TO THEM TOMORROW... MM...
UGH... IT'S SO IRRITATING... AT TIMES LIKE THIS, THERE'S NOTHING TO DO BUT SELF-GRATIFICATION ***WITH THE GOLDEN HAND!***

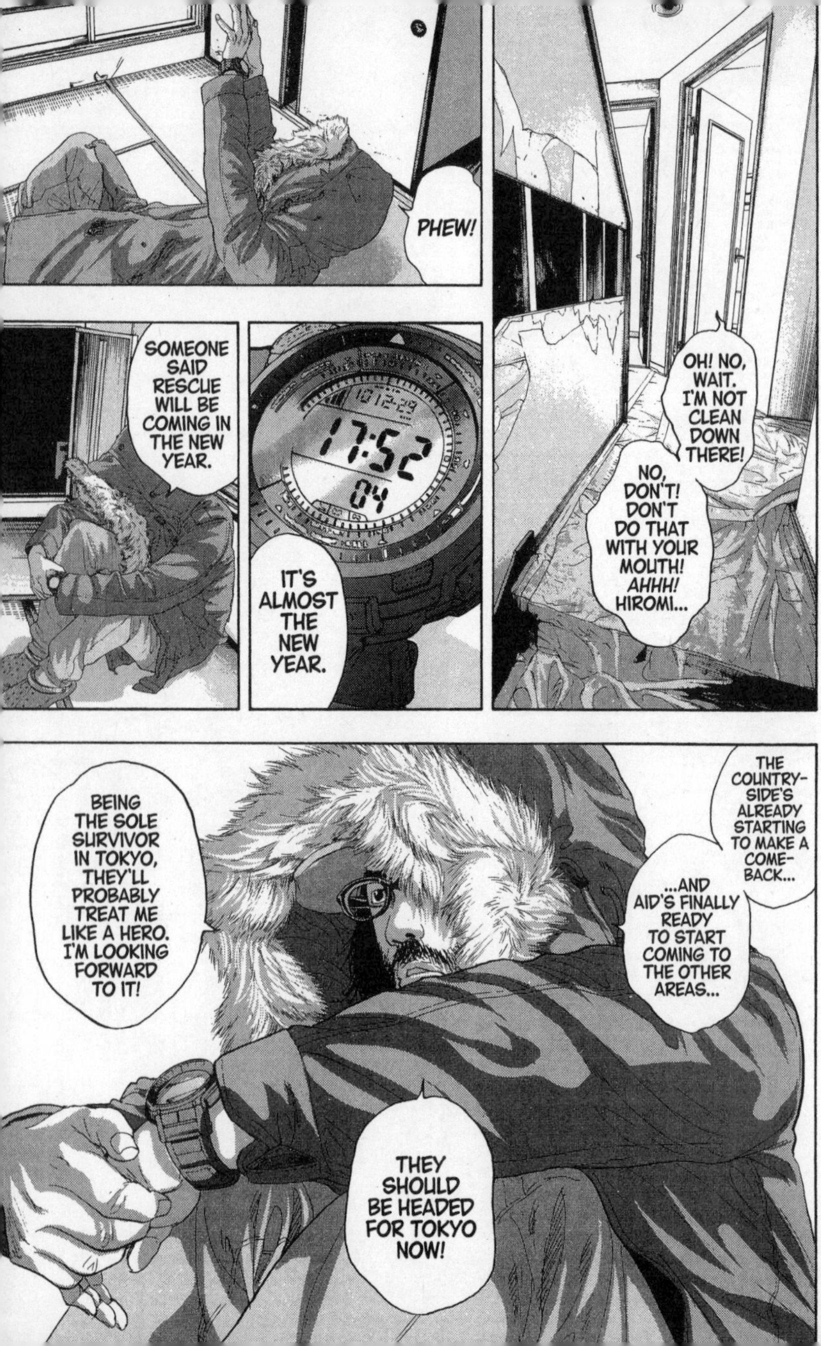
OH! NO, WAIT. I'M NOT CLEAN DOWN THERE!
NO, DON'T! DON'T DO THAT WITH YOUR MOUTH! AHHH! HIROMI...
PHEW!
17:52
IT'S ALMOST THE NEW YEAR.
SOMEONE SAID RESCUE WILL BE COMING IN THE NEW YEAR.
THE COUNTRY-SIDE'S ALREADY STARTING TO MAKE A COME-BACK...
...AND AID'S FINALLY READY TO START COMING TO THE OTHER AREAS...
BEING THE SOLE SURVIVOR IN TOKYO, THEY'LL PROBABLY TREAT ME LIKE A HERO. I'M LOOKING FORWARD TO IT!
THEY SHOULD BE HEADED FOR TOKYO NOW!

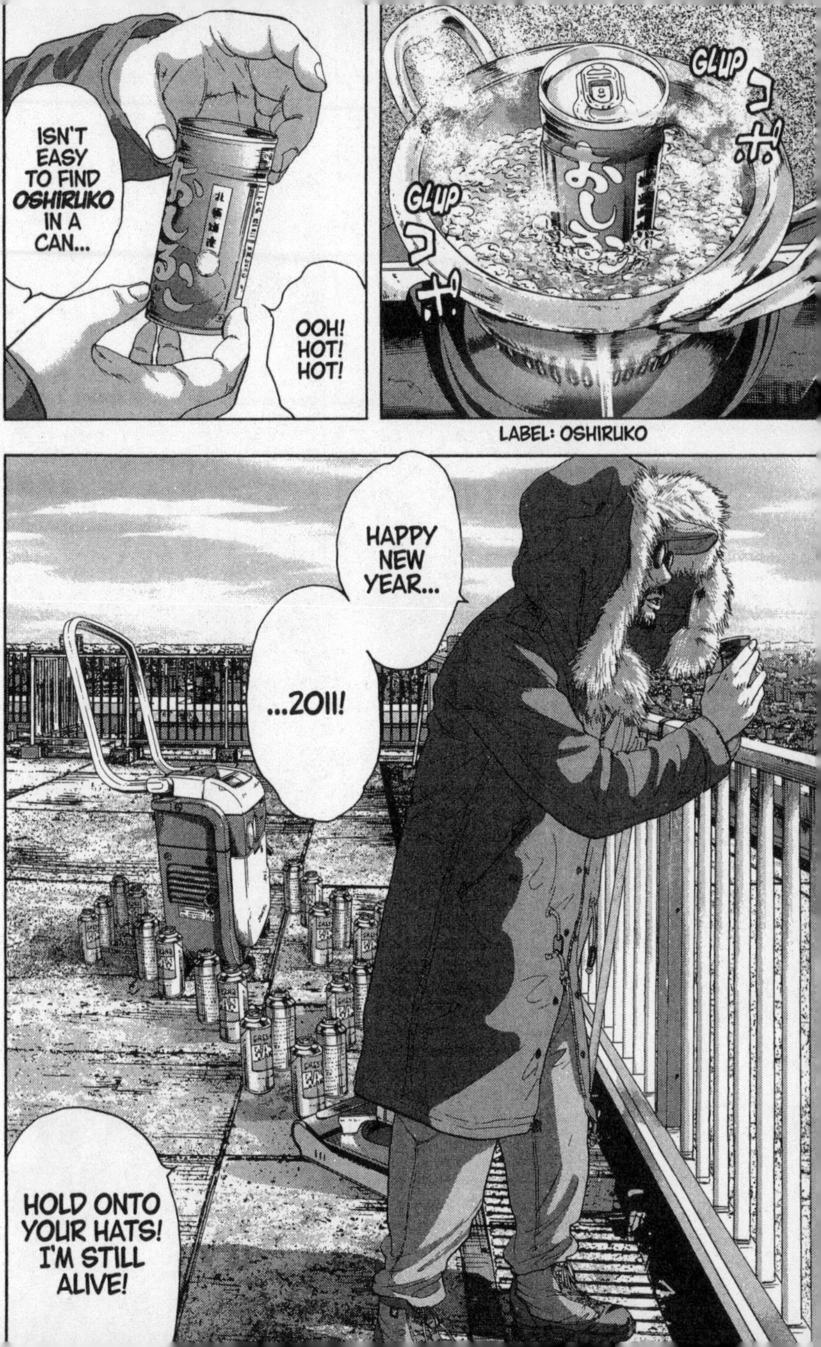

GLUP
コポ
GLUP
コポ
LABEL: OSHIRUKO
ISN'T EASY TO FIND OSHIRUKO IN A CAN...
OOH! HOT! HOT!
HAPPY NEW YEAR...
...2011!
HOLD ONTO YOUR HATS! I'M STILL ALIVE!

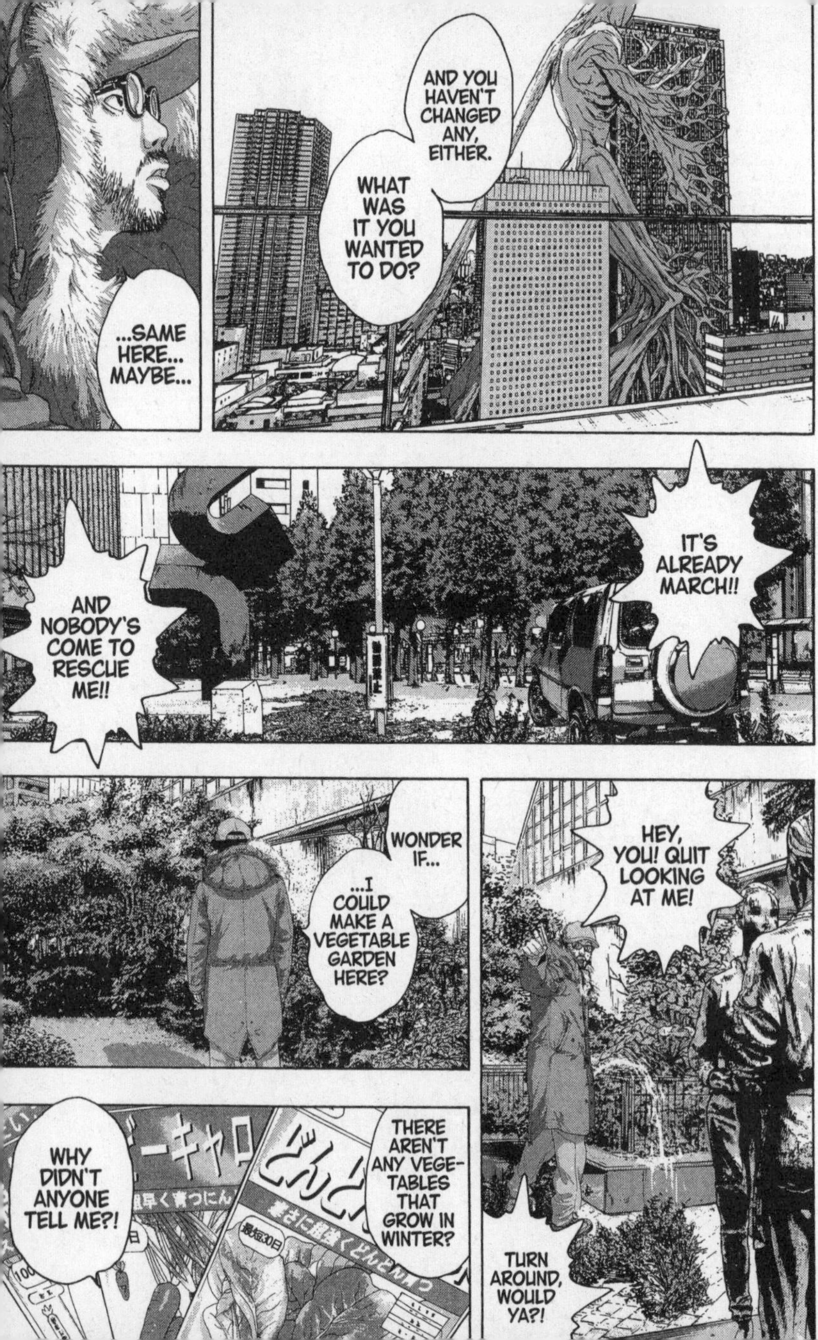
AND YOU HAVEN'T CHANGED ANY, EITHER.
WHAT WAS IT YOU WANTED TO DO?
...SAME HERE... MAYBE...
IT'S ALREADY MARCH!!
AND NOBODY'S COME TO RESCUE ME!!
HEY, YOU! QUIT LOOKING AT ME!
TURN AROUND, WOULD YA?!
WONDER IF...
...I COULD MAKE A VEGETABLE GARDEN HERE?
THERE AREN'T ANY VEGE-TABLES THAT GROW IN WINTER?
WHY DIDN'T ANYONE TELL ME?!

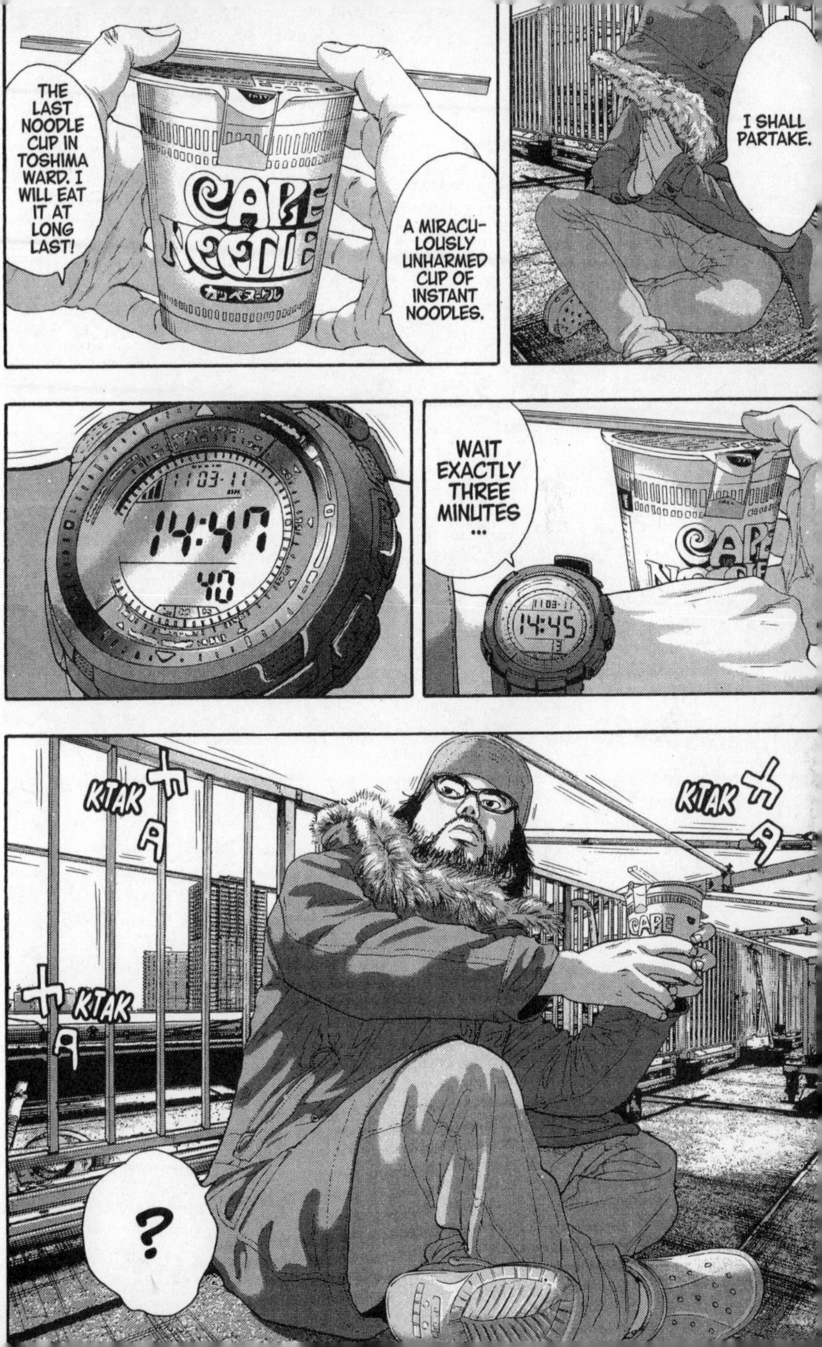
I SHALL PARTAKE.
A MIRACULOUSLY UNHARMED CUP OF INSTANT NOODLES.
THE LAST NOODLE CUP IN TOSHIMA WARD. I WILL EAT IT AT LONG LAST!
WAIT EXACTLY THREE MINUTES ...
KTAK カタ
KTAK カタ
KTAK カタ
?

KTAK

KTAK

HUH?!

KTAK

KLATTA

SHAK-ING?

KLATTA

KLATTA

KLATTA

NOOO!!!

KLATTA

GAH! OW!

HOT!! HOT!!

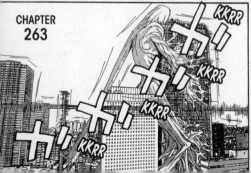

CHAPTER 263

KKRR

KKRR

KKRR

IS IT THAT MONSTER?!

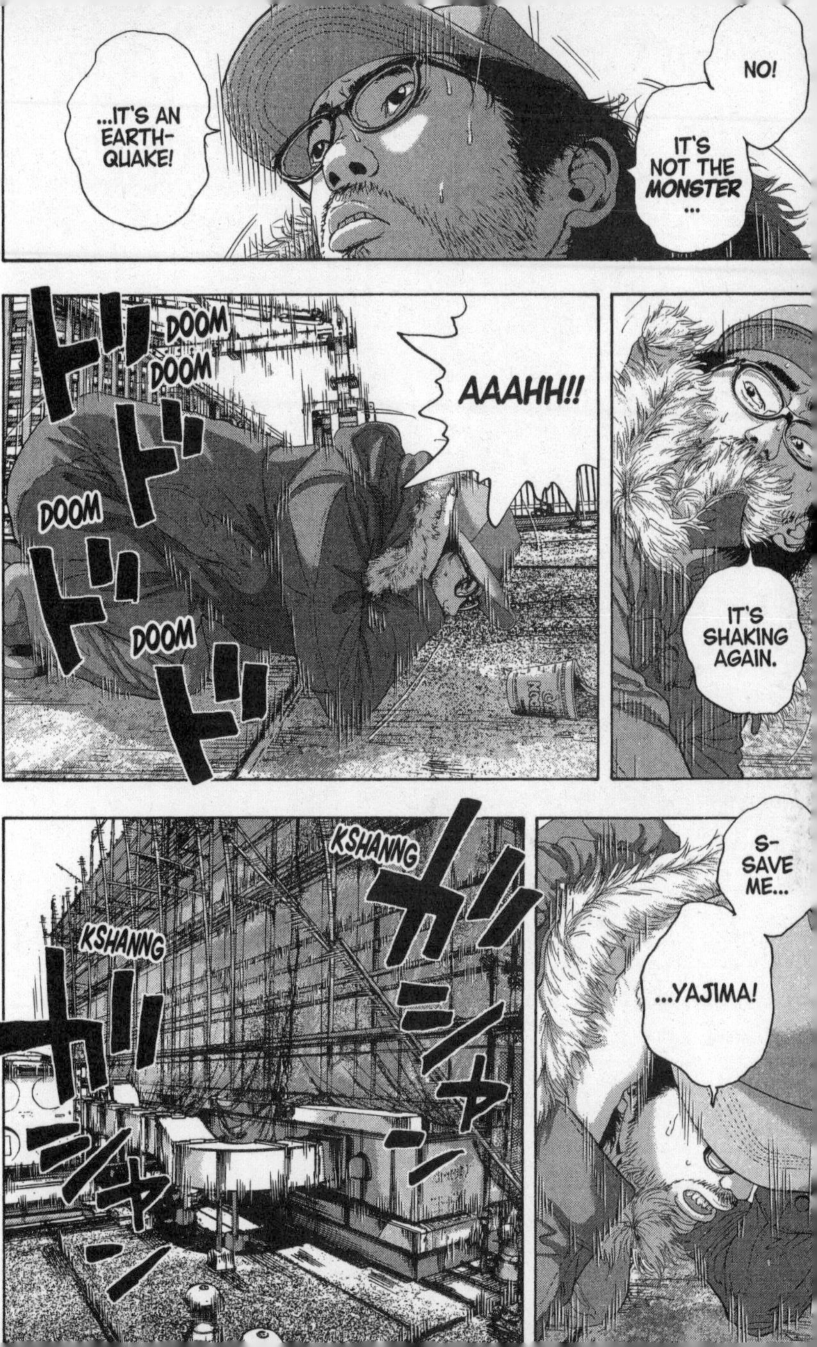
NO!
IT'S NOT THE MONSTER ...
...IT'S AN EARTH-QUAKE!
IT'S SHAKING AGAIN.
AAAHH!!
DOOM
DOOM
DOOM
DOOM
S-SAVE ME...
...YAJIMA!
KSHANNG
KSHANNG

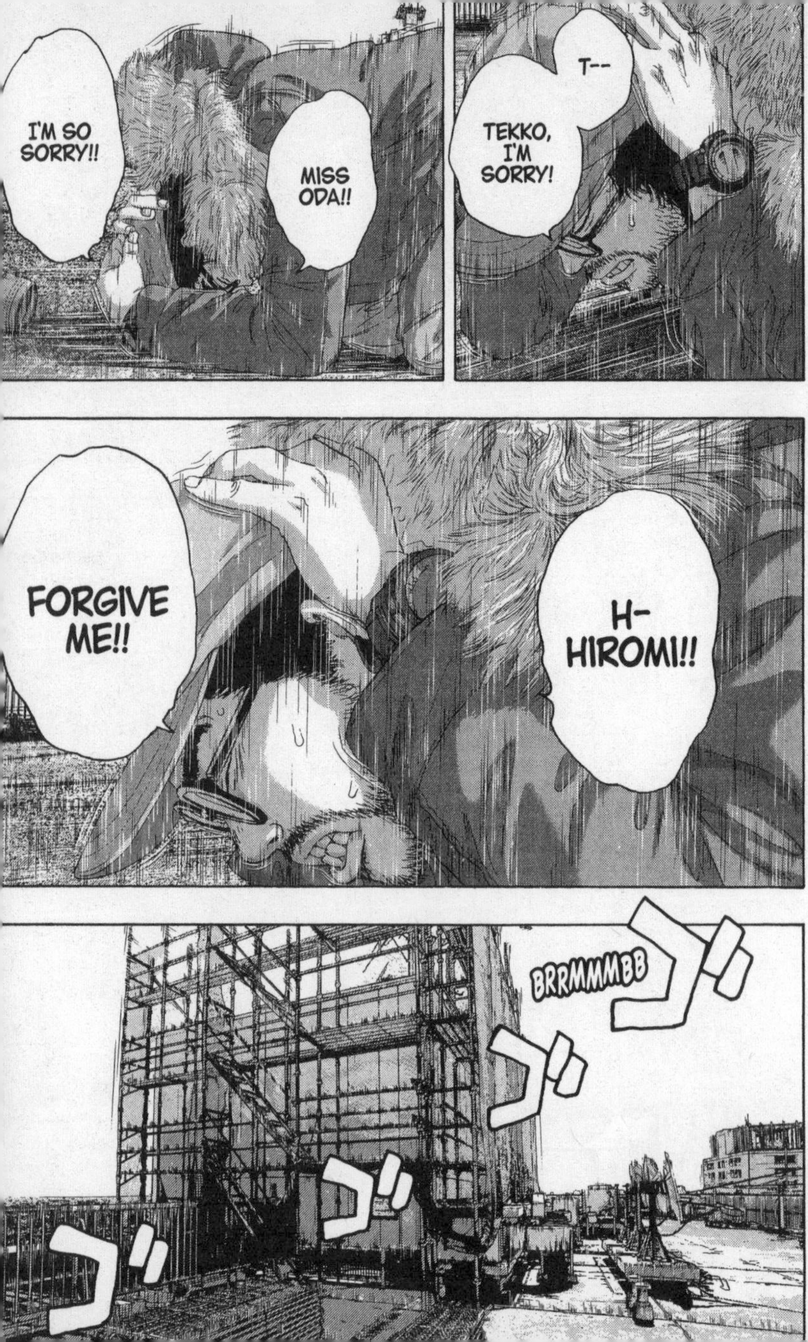
T--
TEKKO, I'M SORRY!
MISS ODA!!
I'M SO SORRY!!
H- HIROMI!!
FORGIVE ME!!
BRRMMMBB

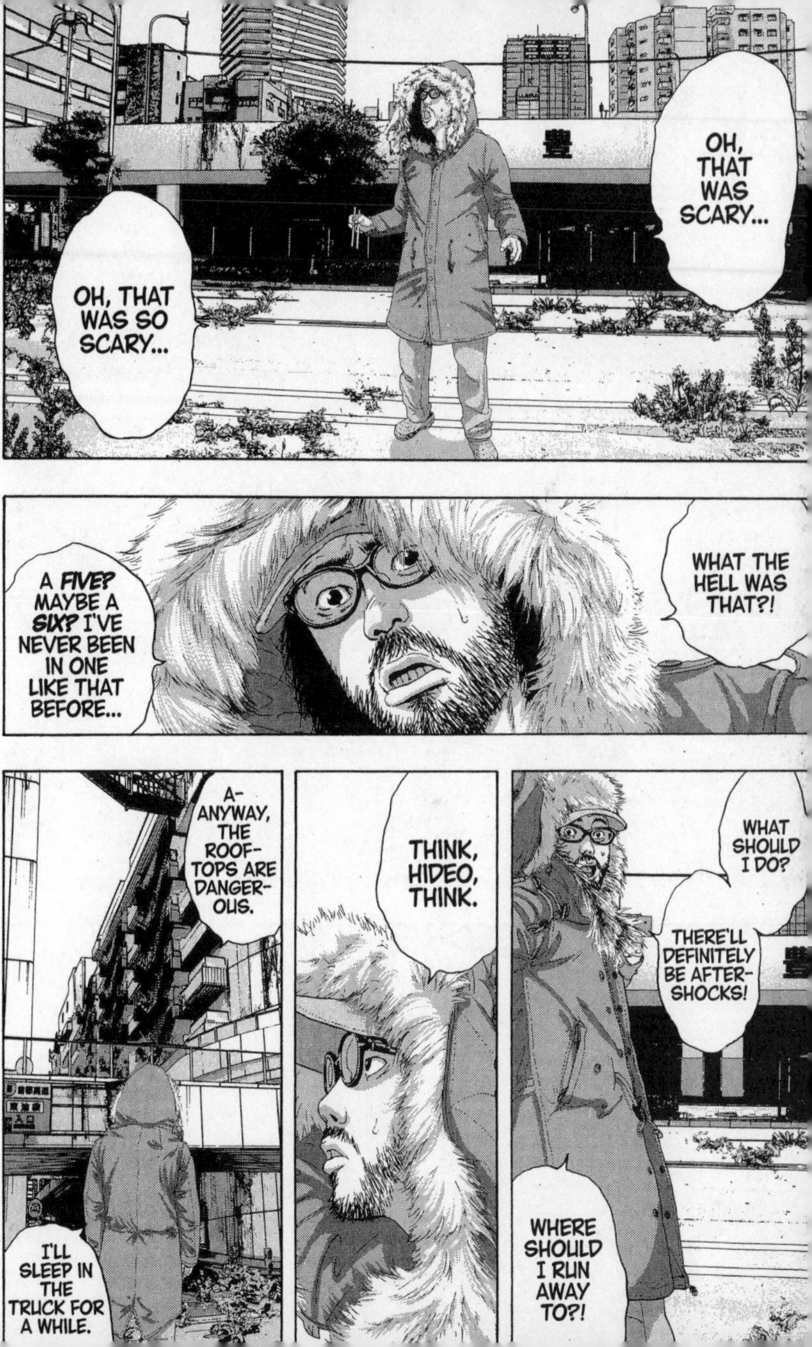
OH, THAT WAS SCARY...
OH, THAT WAS SO SCARY...
WHAT THE HELL WAS THAT?!
A FIVE? MAYBE A SIX? I'VE NEVER BEEN IN ONE LIKE THAT BEFORE...
WHAT SHOULD I DO?
THERE'LL DEFINITELY BE AFTER-SHOCKS!
WHERE SHOULD I RUN AWAY TO?!
THINK, HIDEO, THINK.
A- ANYWAY, THE ROOF-TOPS ARE DANGER-OUS.
I'LL SLEEP IN THE TRUCK FOR A WHILE.

Toshima Ward
kebukuro East
Entrance Park
MMF! RMMF! TEKKO...
SHUKK
SHUKK

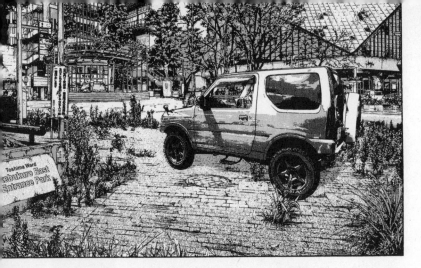

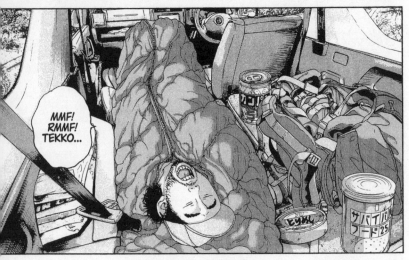

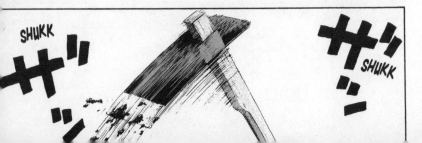

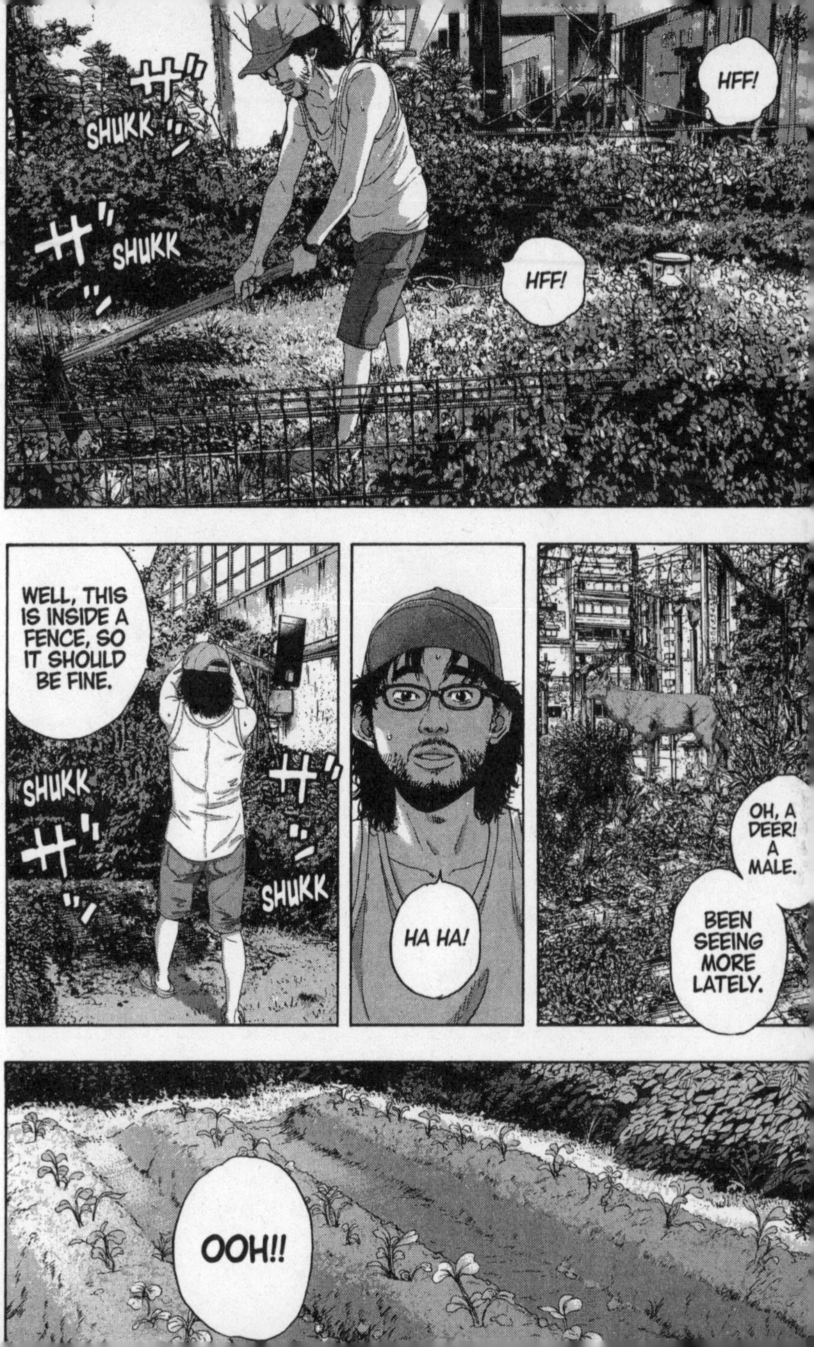
HFF!
HFF!
SHUKK
SHUKK
OH, A DEER! A MALE.
BEEN SEEING MORE LATELY.
HA HA!
WELL, THIS IS INSIDE A FENCE, SO IT SHOULD BE FINE.
SHUKK
SHUKK
OOH!!

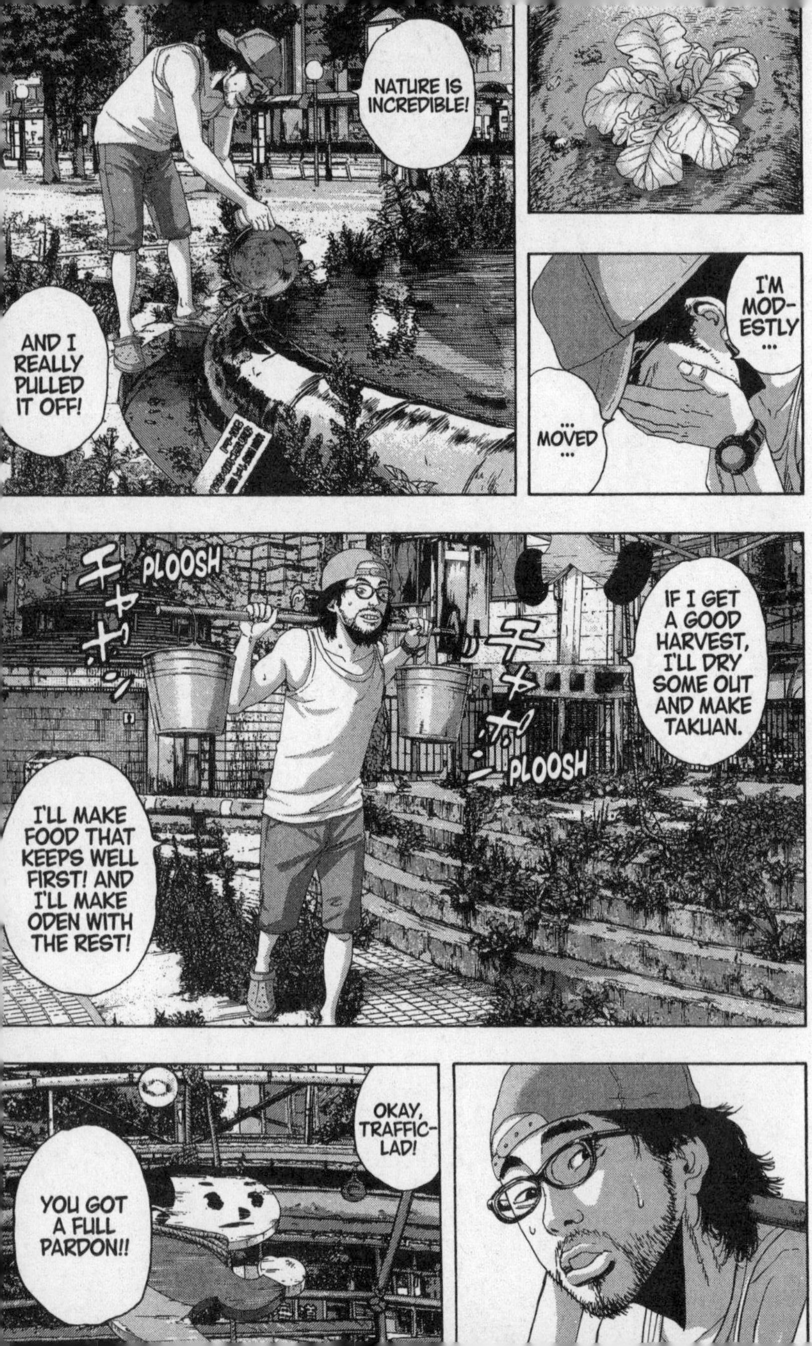
I'M MODESTLY ...
... MOVED ...
NATURE IS INCREDIBLE!
AND I REALLY PULLED IT OFF!
IF I GET A GOOD HARVEST, I'LL DRY SOME OUT AND MAKE TAKUAN.
PLOOSH
PLOOSH
I'LL MAKE FOOD THAT KEEPS WELL FIRST! AND I'LL MAKE ODEN WITH THE REST!
OKAY, TRAFFIC-LAD!
YOU GOT A FULL PARDON!!

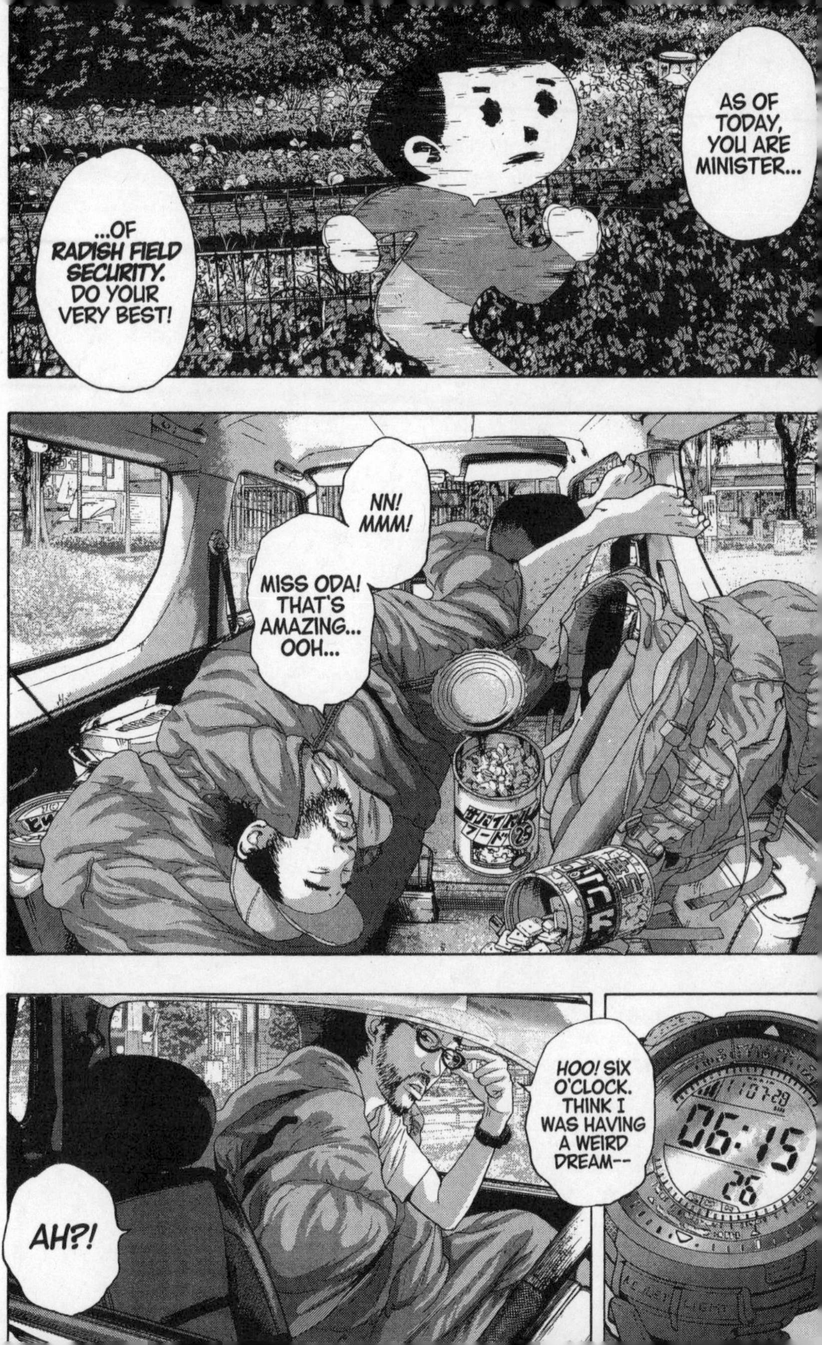
AS OF TODAY, YOU ARE MINISTER...
...OF RADISH FIELD SECURITY. DO YOUR VERY BEST!
NN! MMM!
MISS ODA! THAT'S AMAZING... OOH...
HOO! SIX O'CLOCK. THINK I WAS HAVING A WEIRD DREAM--
06:15
26
AH?!

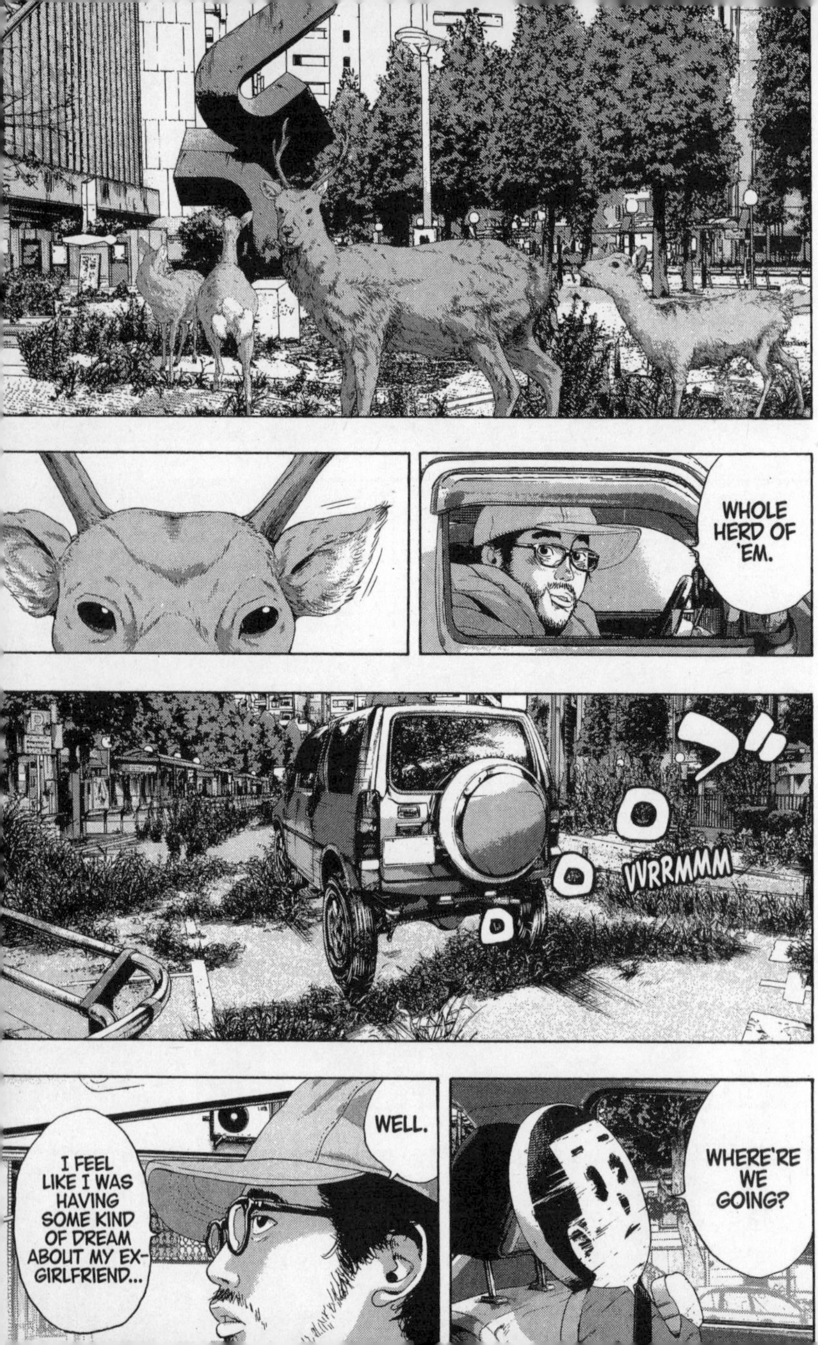
WHOLE HERD OF 'EM.
VVRRMMM
WHERE'RE WE GOING?
WELL.
I FEEL LIKE I WAS HAVING SOME KIND OF DREAM ABOUT MY EX-GIRLFRIEND...

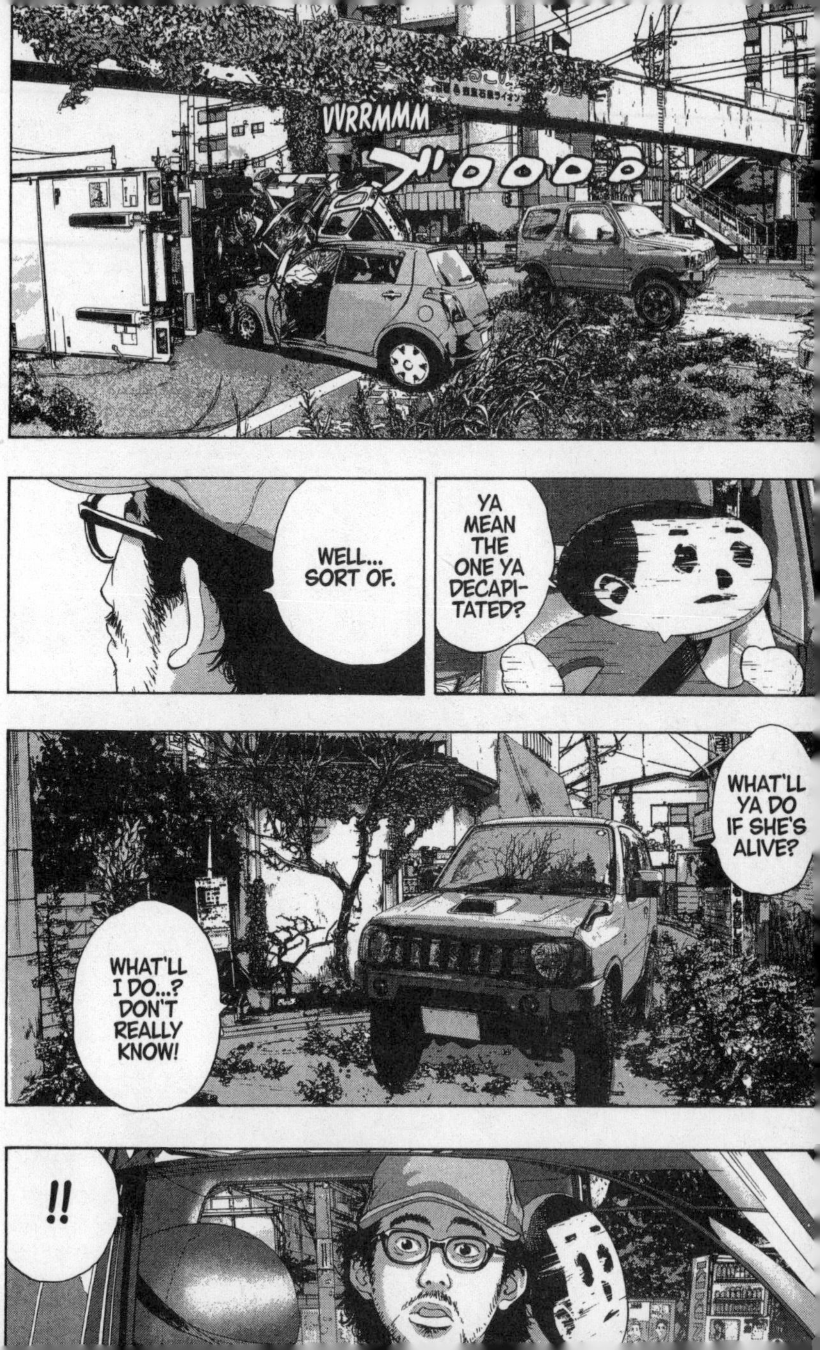
VVRRMMM
ブロロロロ
YA MEAN THE ONE YA DECAPITATED?
WELL... SORT OF.
WHAT'LL YA DO IF SHE'S ALIVE?
WHAT'LL I DO...? DON'T REALLY KNOW!
!!

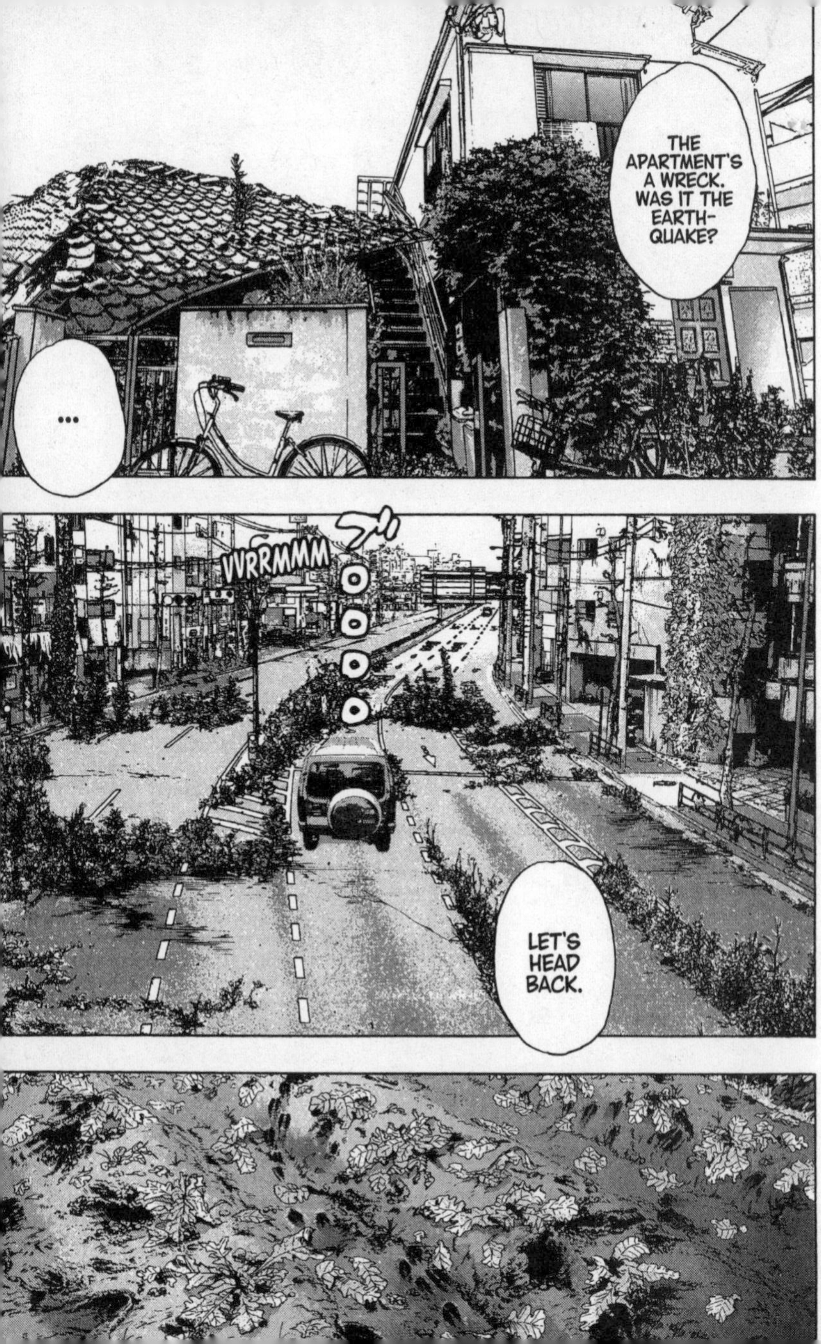
THE APARTMENT'S A WRECK. WAS IT THE EARTH-QUAKE?
...
VVRRMMM
LET'S HEAD BACK.

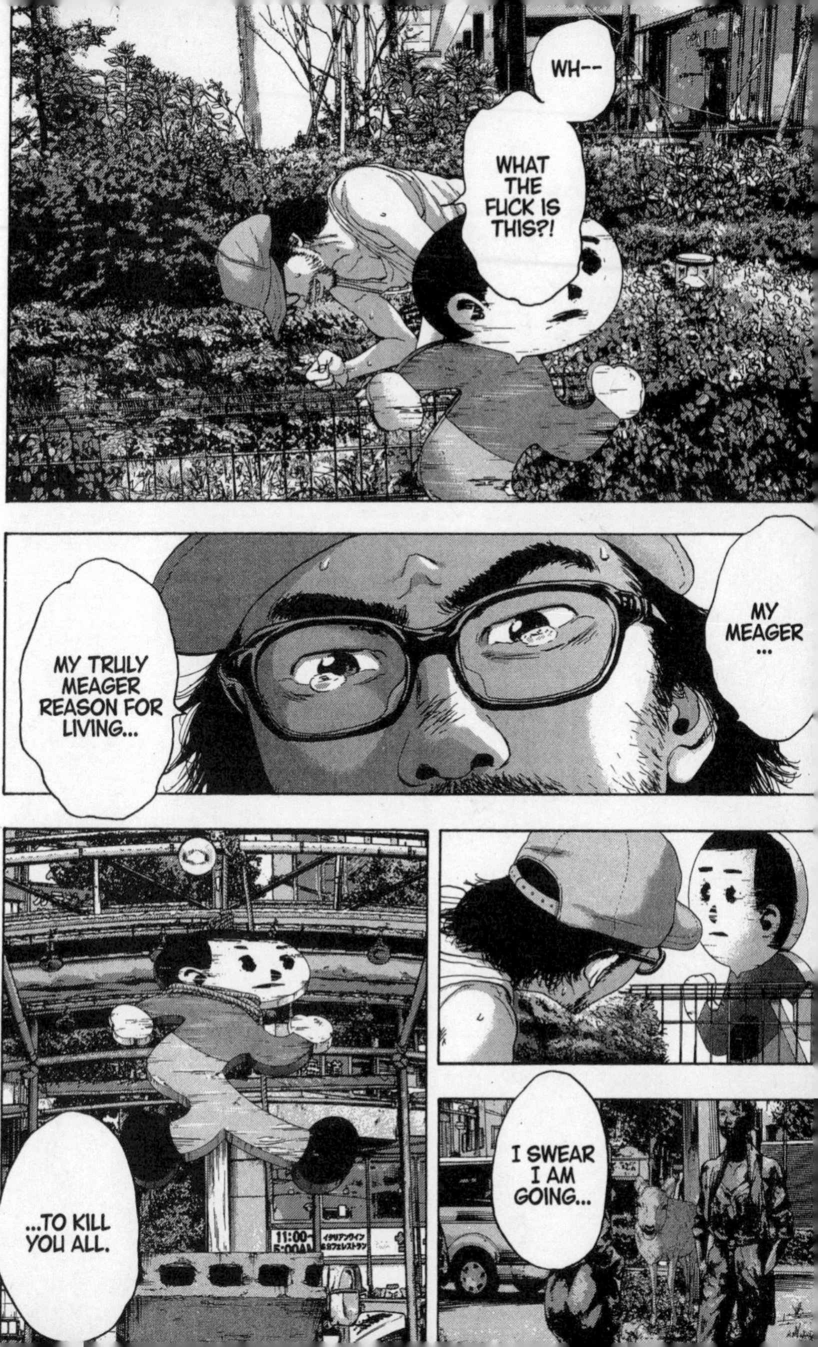
WH--
WHAT THE FUCK IS THIS?!
MY MEAGER ...
MY TRULY MEAGER REASON FOR LIVING...
I SWEAR I AM GOING...
...TO KILL YOU ALL.

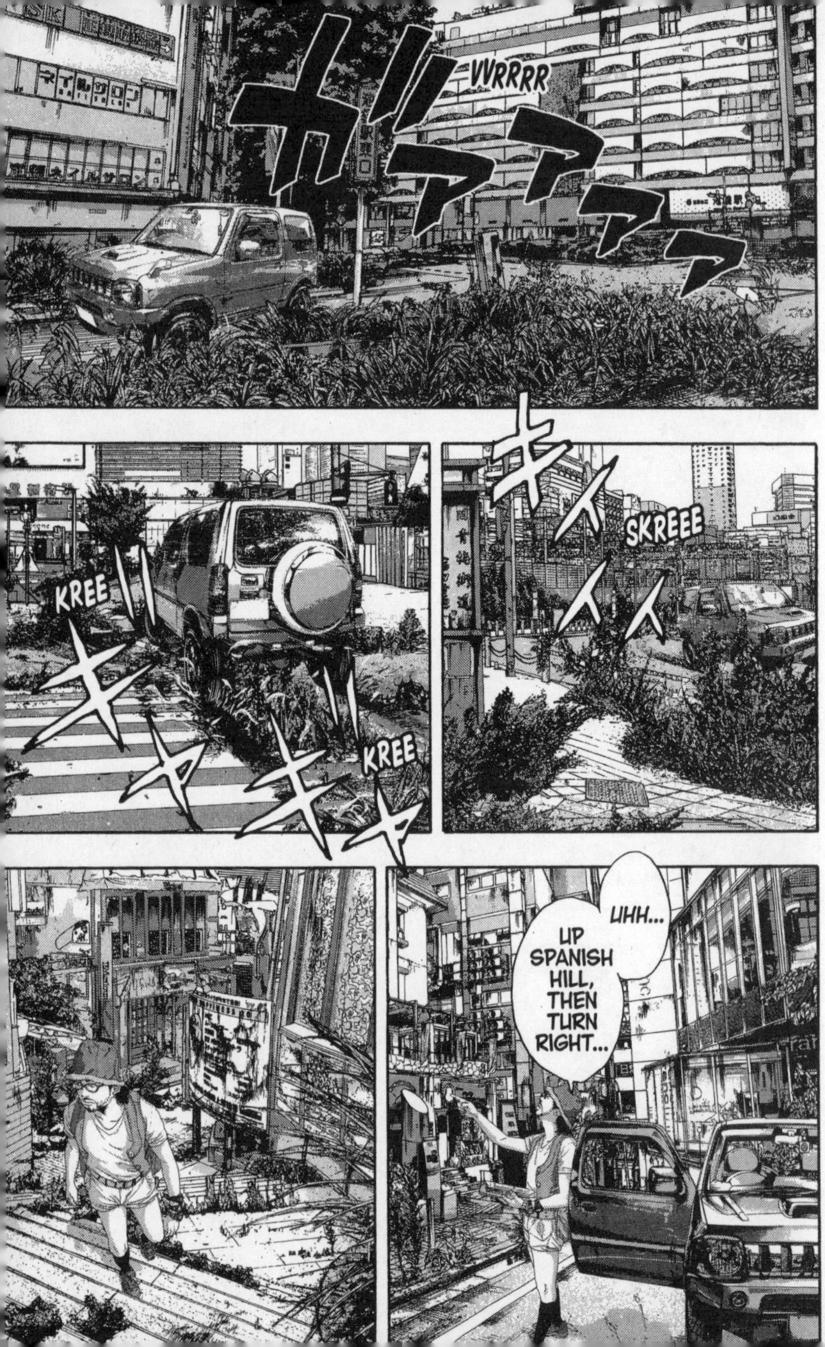
VVRRRR
SKREEE
KREE
KREE
UHH...
UP SPANISH HILL, THEN TURN RIGHT...

EXCUSE ME...

AS MESSED UP AS YOU'D EXPECT A GUN STORE TO BE.

TPLINK

?

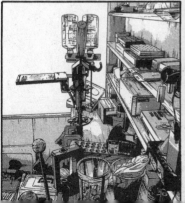

EVEN IF I CAN'T GET A GUN, I WAS HOPING FOR SOME BULLETS...

...BUT THERE'S NOT A SINGLE ONE LEFT...

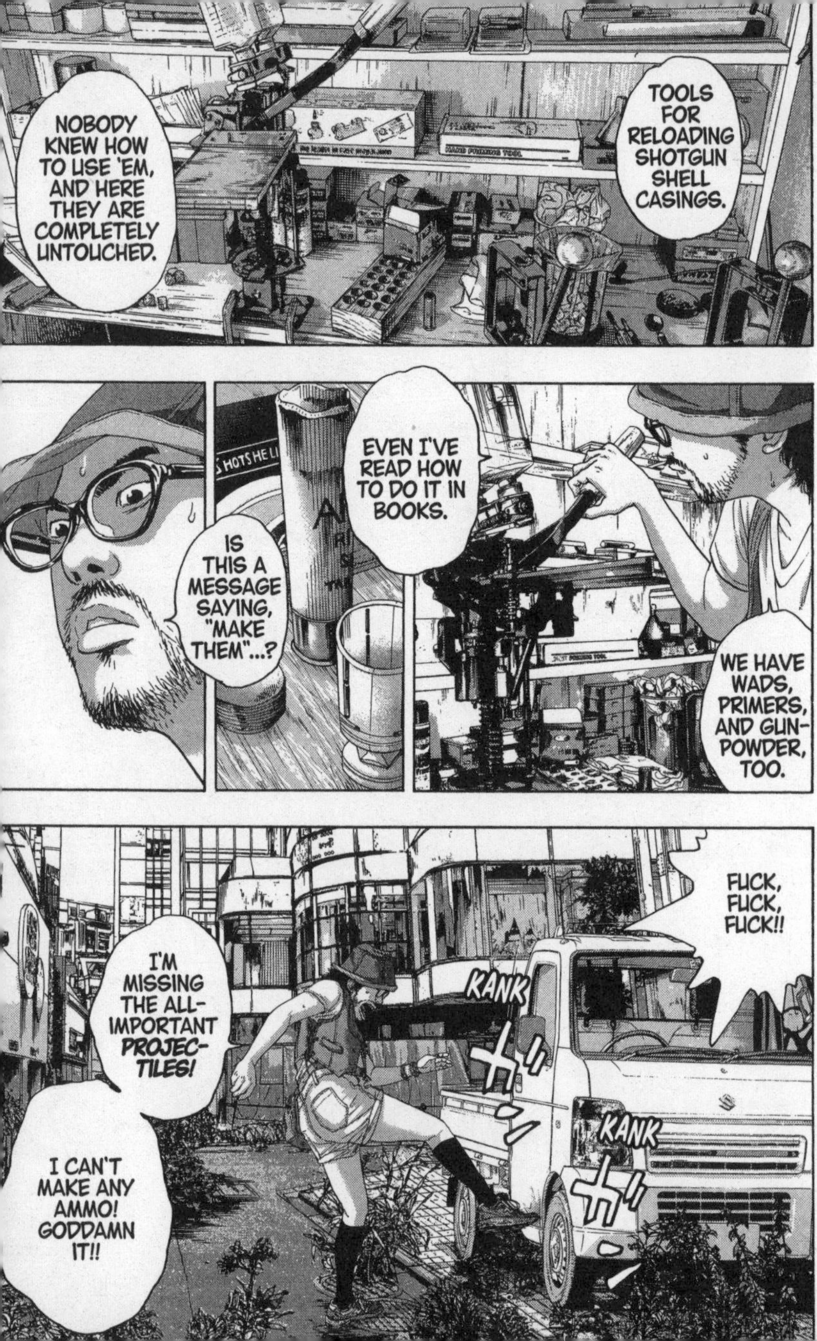
TOOLS FOR RELOADING SHOTGUN SHELL CASINGS.
NOBODY KNEW HOW TO USE 'EM, AND HERE THEY ARE COMPLETELY UNTOUCHED.
EVEN I'VE READ HOW TO DO IT IN BOOKS.
WE HAVE WADS, PRIMERS, AND GUN-POWDER, TOO.
IS THIS A MESSAGE SAYING, "MAKE THEM"...?
FUCK, FUCK, FUCK!!
KANK
KANK
I'M MISSING THE ALL-IMPORTANT PROJEC-TILES!
I CAN'T MAKE ANY AMMO! GODDAMN IT!!

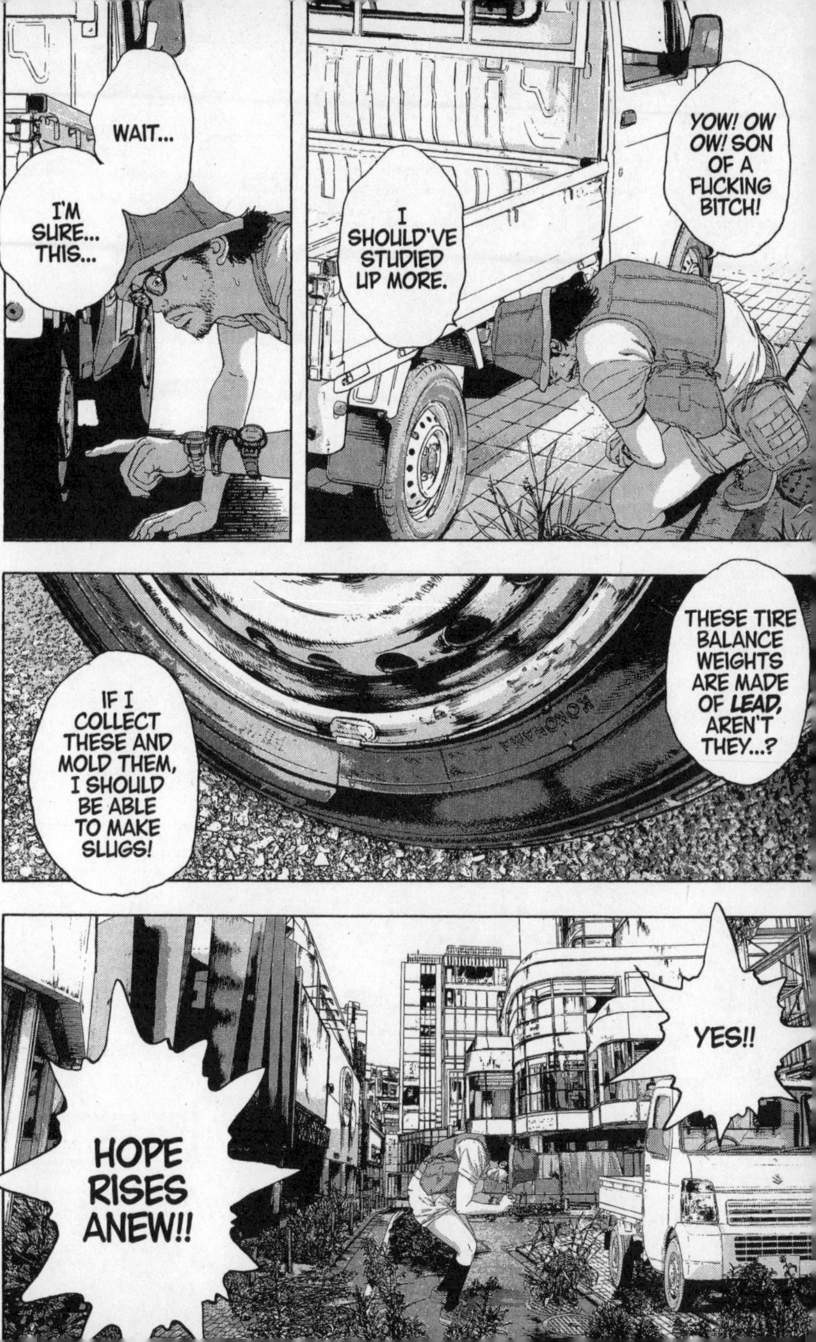
YOW! OW OW! SON OF A FUCKING BITCH!
I SHOULD'VE STUDIED UP MORE.
WAIT...
I'M SURE... THIS...
THESE TIRE BALANCE WEIGHTS ARE MADE OF *LEAD*, AREN'T THEY...?
IF I COLLECT THESE AND MOLD THEM, I SHOULD BE ABLE TO MAKE SLUGS!
YES!!
HOPE RISES ANEW!!

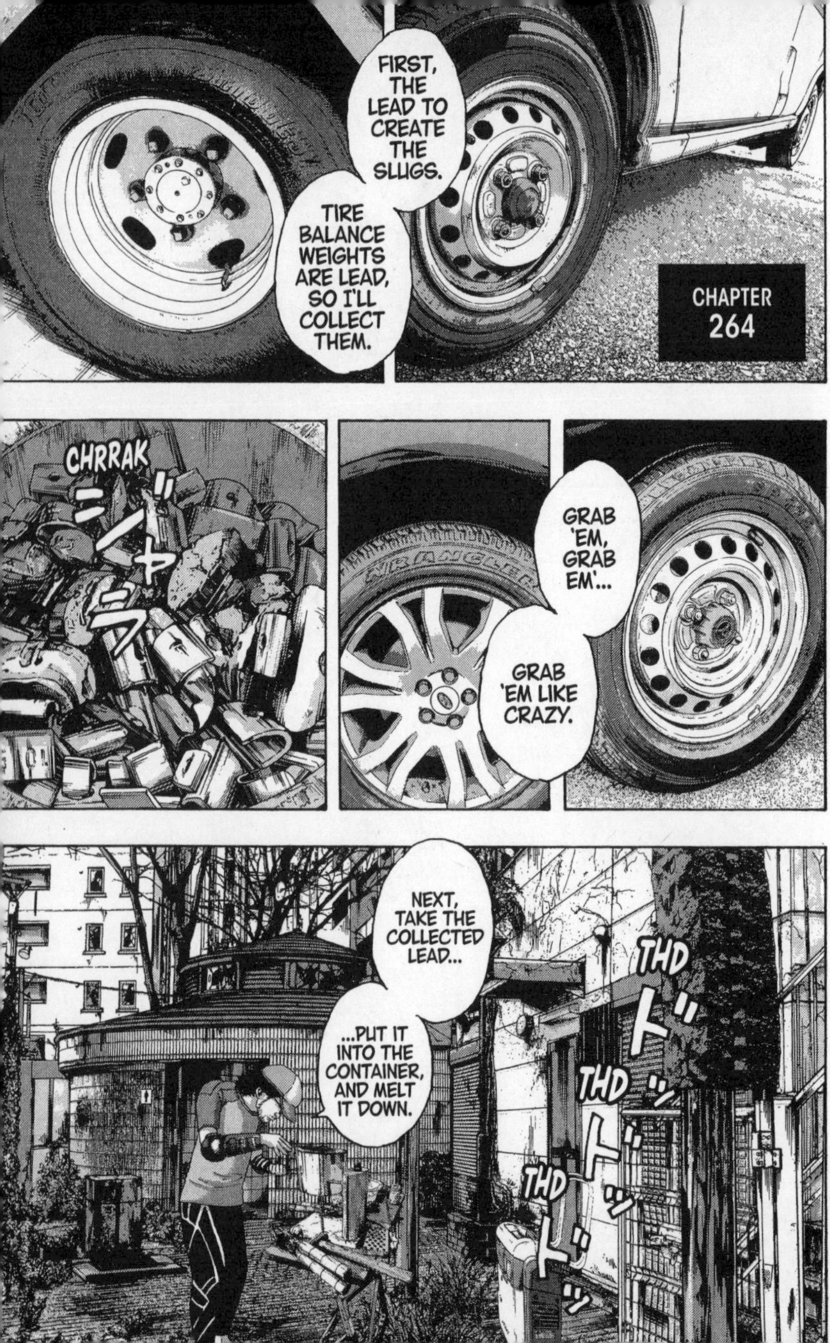
CHAPTER 264
FIRST, THE LEAD TO CREATE THE SLUGS.
TIRE BALANCE WEIGHTS ARE LEAD, SO I'LL COLLECT THEM.
GRAB 'EM, GRAB EM'...
GRAB 'EM LIKE CRAZY.
CHRRAK
ジャラ
NEXT, TAKE THE COLLECTED LEAD...
...PUT IT INTO THE CONTAINER, AND MELT IT DOWN.
THD
ドッ
THD
ドッ
THD
ドッ

NEXT, CARRREFULLY POUR THE MELTED LEAD INTO THE SLUG MOLD! AND WATCH OUT NOT TO BURN YOURSELF.

PLIP

PLIP

PLIP

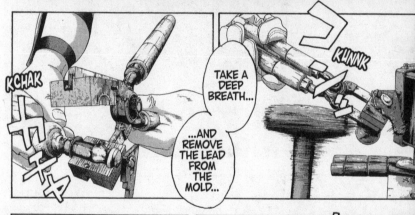

TAKE A DEEP BREATH...

...AND REMOVE THE LEAD FROM THE MOLD...

KCHAK

KUNNK

...THEN PUT IT IN WATER AND COOL IT DOWN FULLY.

PLOOP

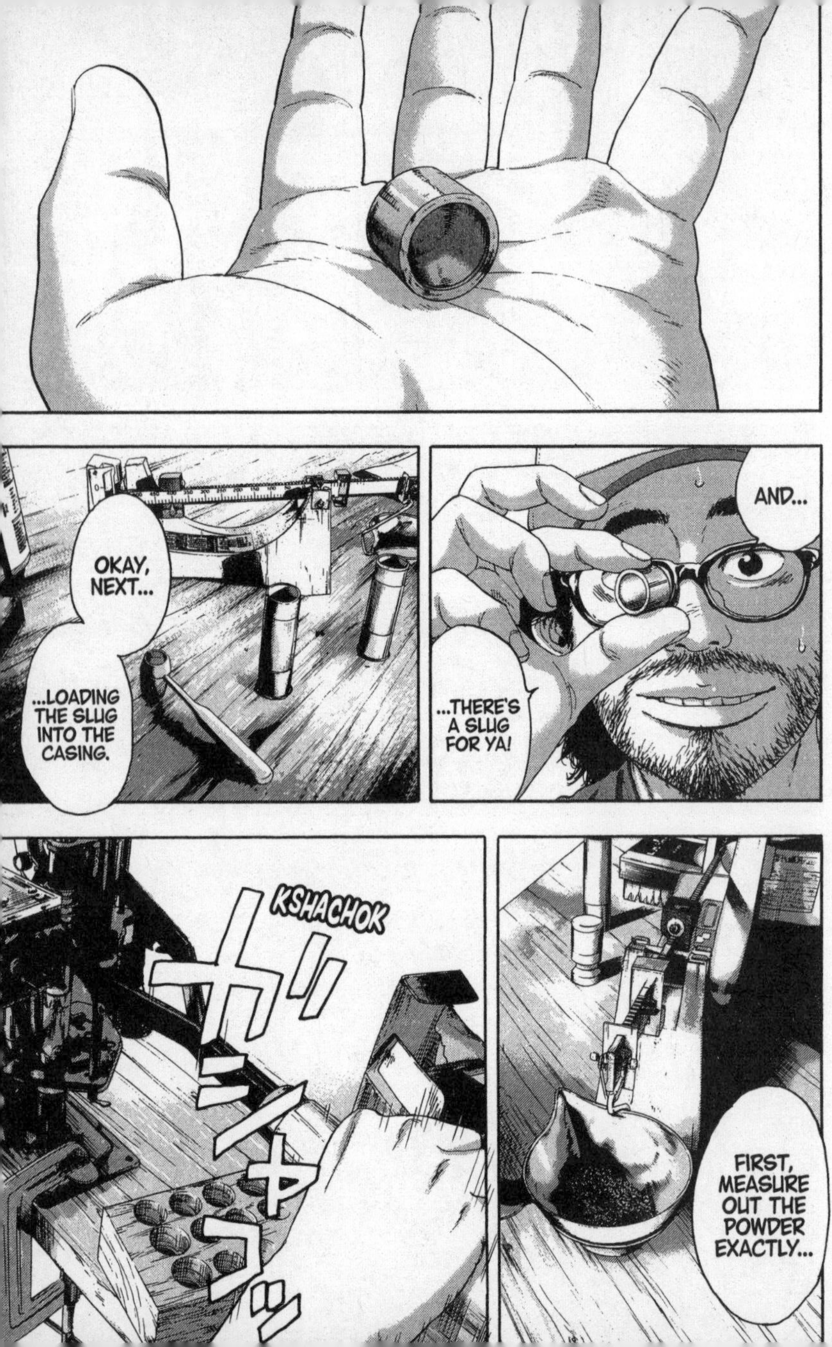
AND...
...THERE'S A SLUG FOR YA!
OKAY, NEXT...
...LOADING THE SLUG INTO THE CASING.
FIRST, MEASURE OUT THE POWDER EXACTLY...
KSHACHOK

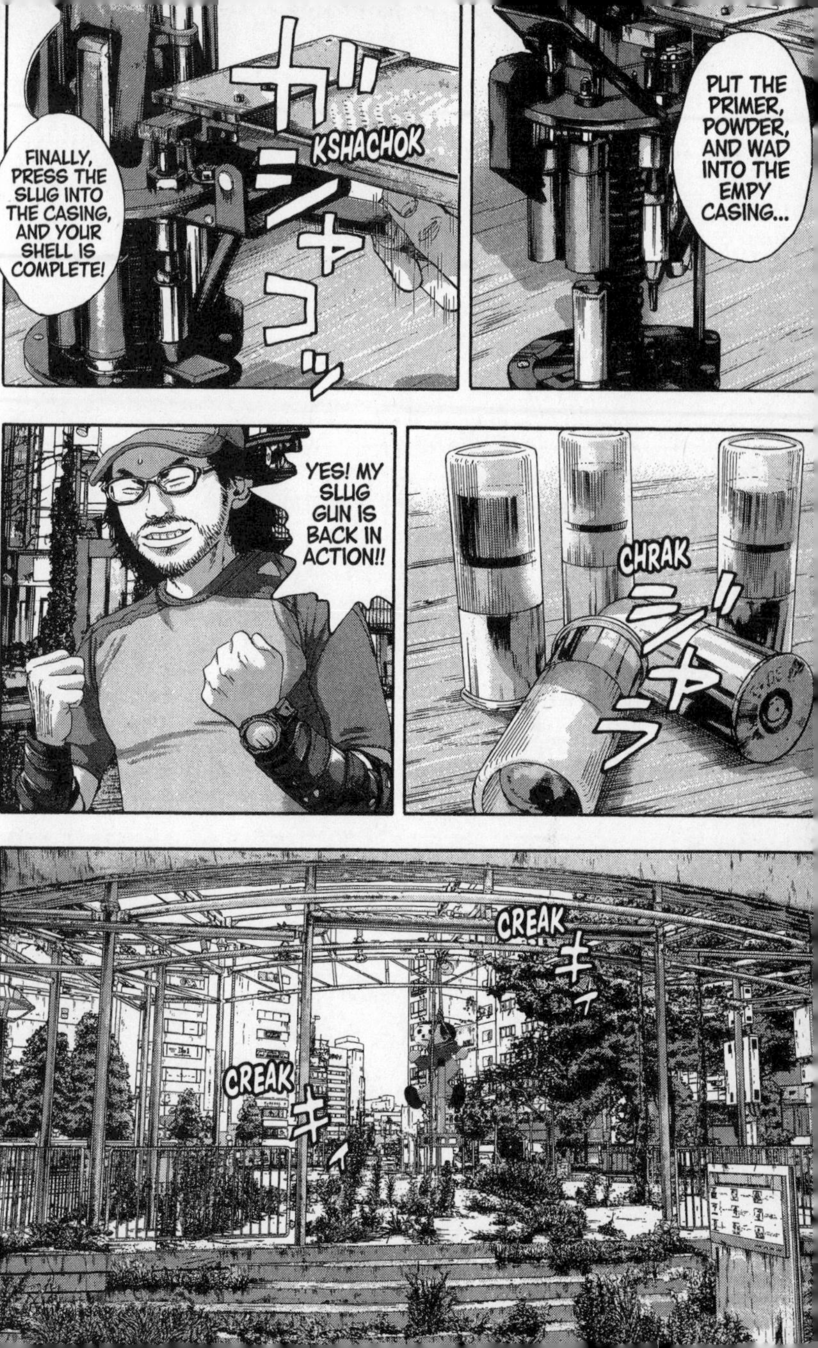
PUT THE PRIMER, POWDER, AND WAD INTO THE EMPY CASING...
ガシャコッ
KSHACHOK
FINALLY, PRESS THE SLUG INTO THE CASING, AND YOUR SHELL IS COMPLETE!
CHRAK
ジャラ
YES! MY SLUG GUN IS BACK IN ACTION!!
CREAK
キィ
CREAK
キィ

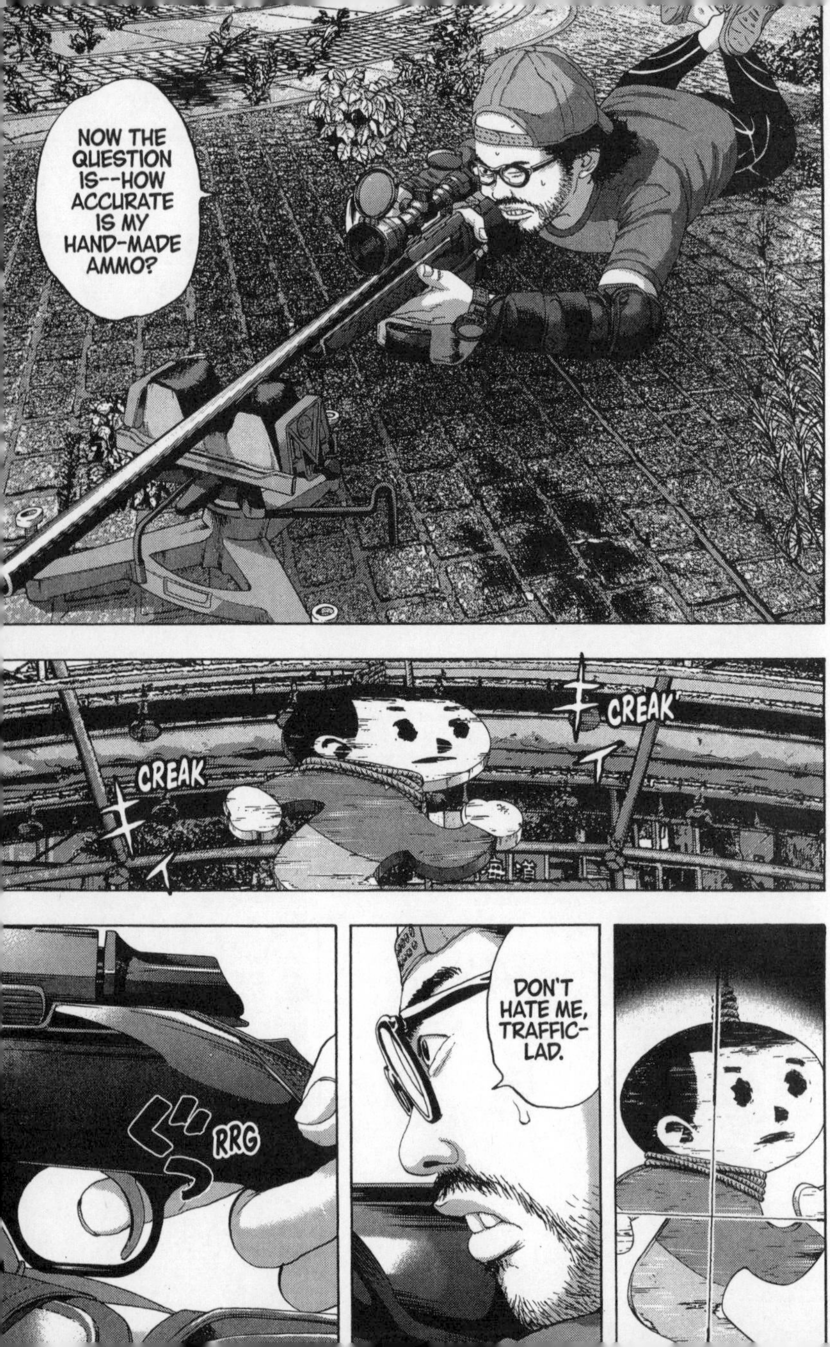
NOW THE QUESTION IS--HOW ACCURATE IS MY HAND-MADE AMMO?
CREAK
CREAK
DON'T HATE ME, TRAFFIC-LAD.
RRG

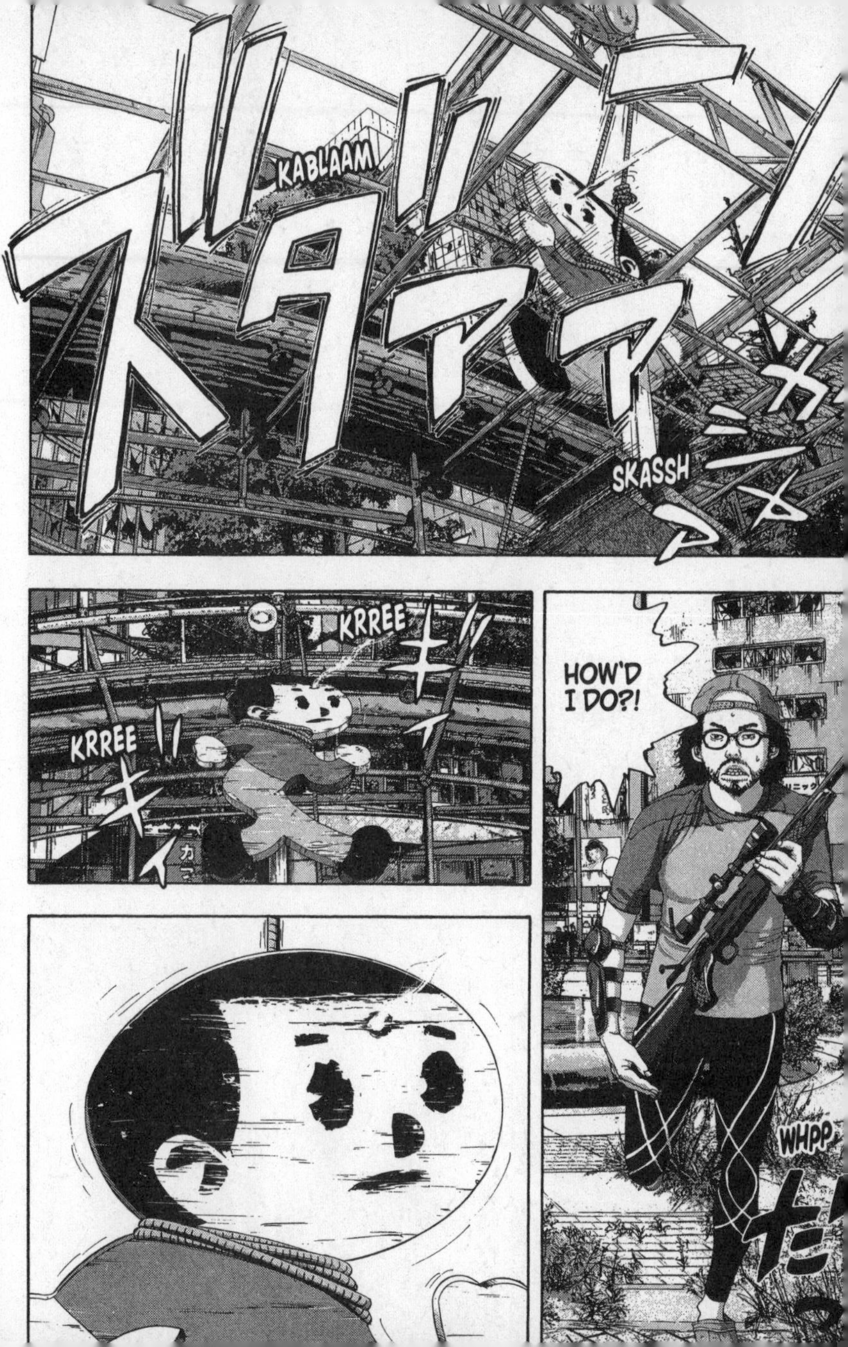
KABLAAM
SKASSH
HOW'D I DO?!
WHPP
KRREE
KRREE

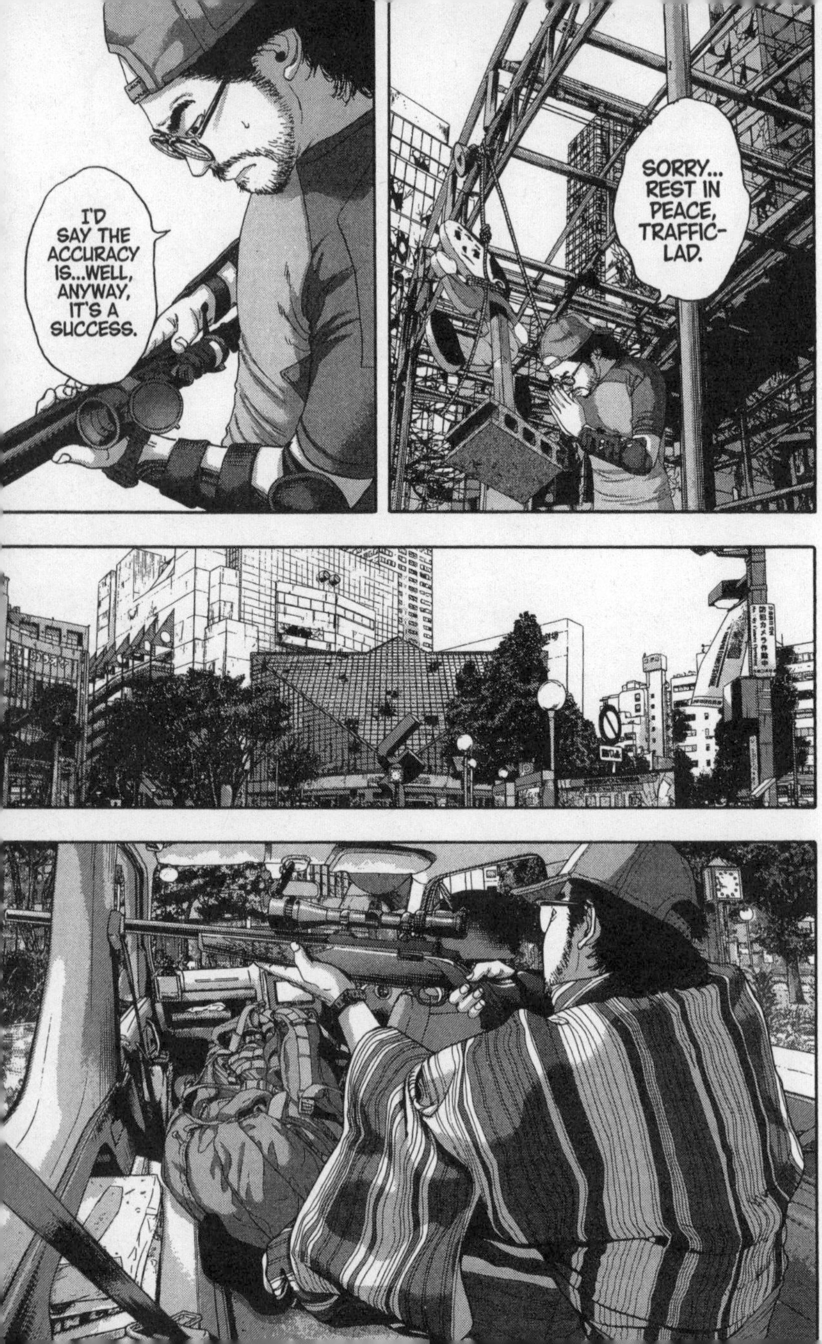
SORRY... REST IN PEACE, TRAFFIC-LAD.
I'D SAY THE ACCURACY IS...WELL, ANYWAY, IT'S A SUCCESS.

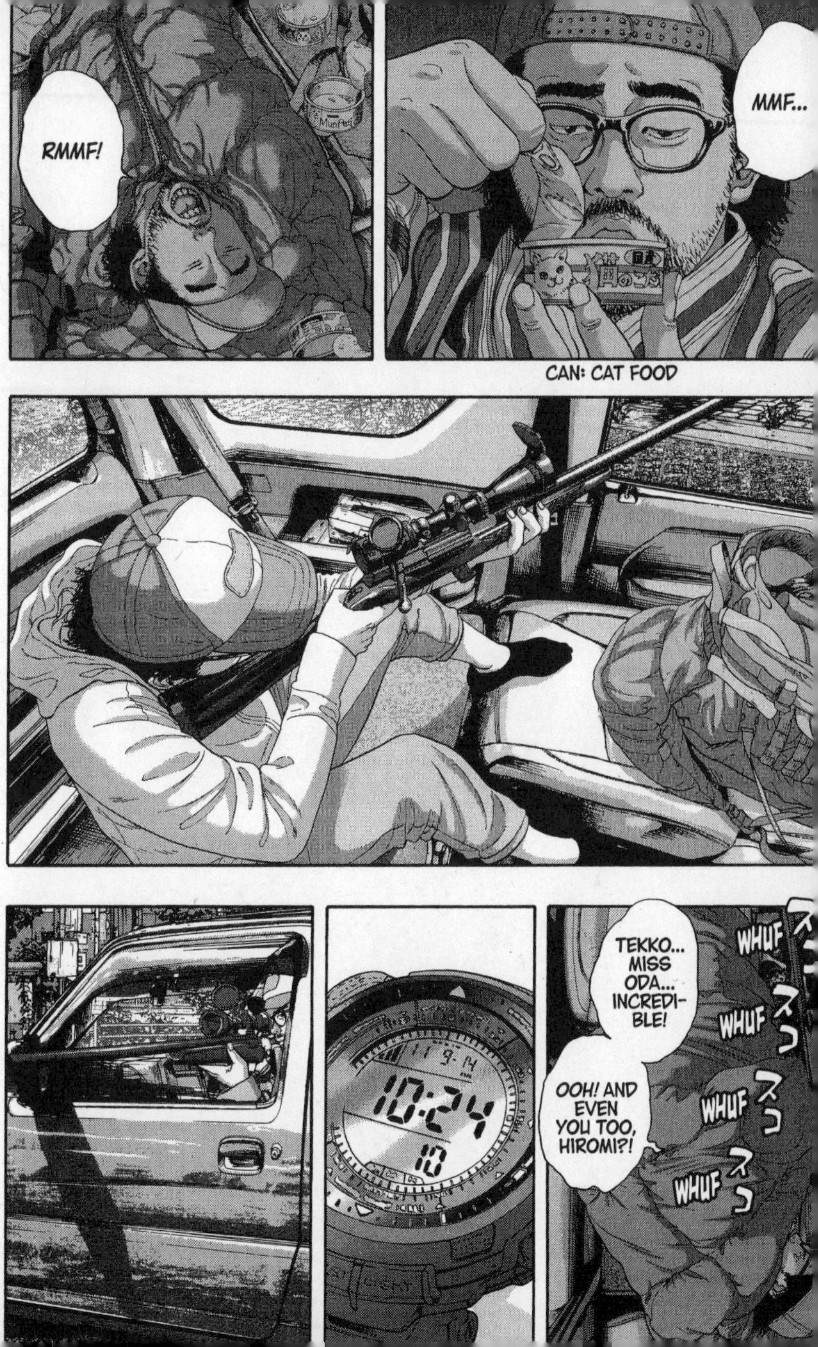
MMF...
CAN: CAT FOOD
RMMF!
WHUF
スコ
WHUF
スコ
WHUF
スコ
WHUF
スコ
TEKKO... MISS ODA... INCREDI-BLE!
OOH! AND EVEN YOU TOO, HIROMI?!
9-14
10:24
10

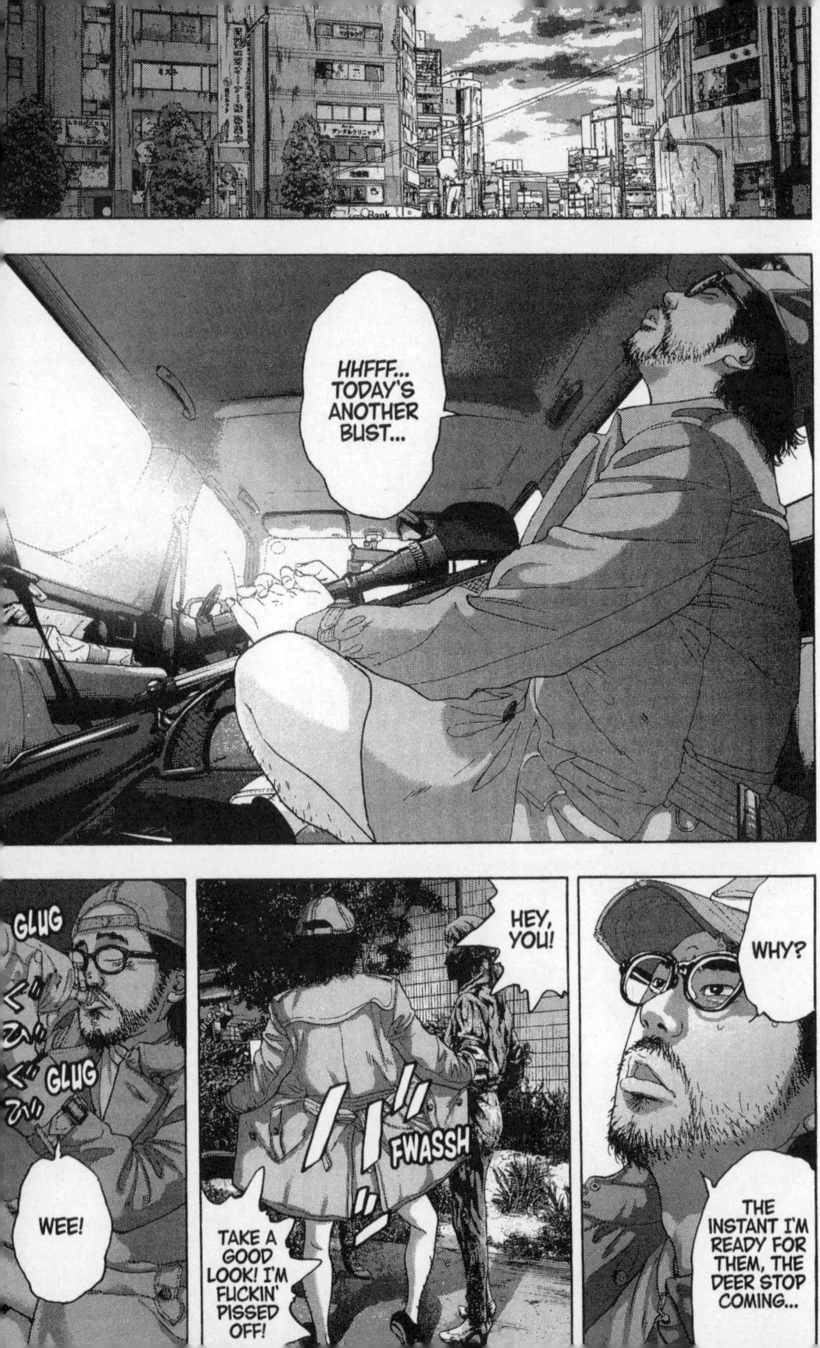
HHFFF... TODAY'S ANOTHER BUST...
WHY?
THE INSTANT I'M READY FOR THEM, THE DEER STOP COMING...
HEY, YOU!
FWASSH
TAKE A GOOD LOOK! I'M FUCKIN' PISSED OFF!
GLUG
GLUG
WEE!

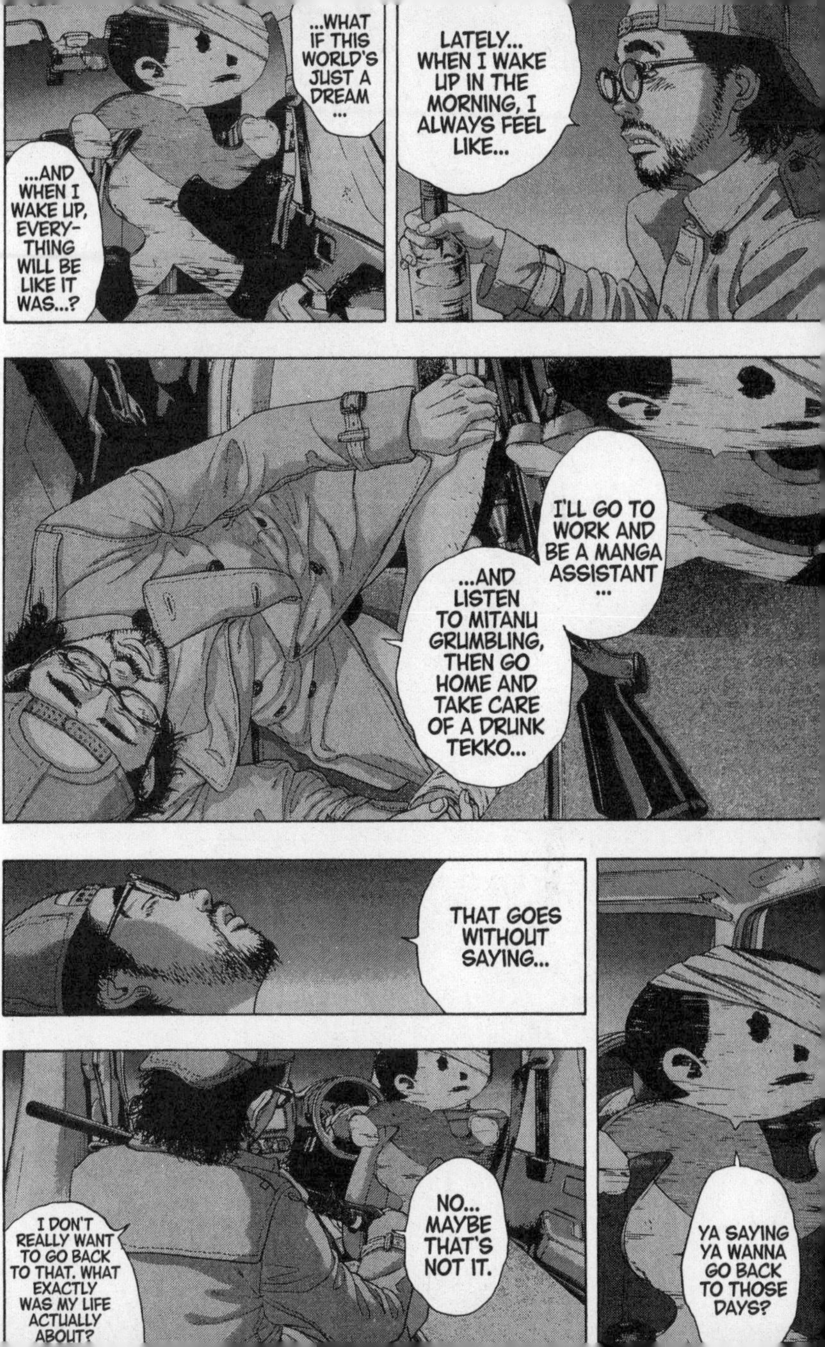
LATELY... WHEN I WAKE UP IN THE MORNING, I ALWAYS FEEL LIKE...
...WHAT IF THIS WORLD'S JUST A DREAM ...
...AND WHEN I WAKE UP, EVERY-THING WILL BE LIKE IT WAS...?
I'LL GO TO WORK AND BE A MANGA ASSISTANT ...
...AND LISTEN TO MITANU GRUMBLING, THEN GO HOME AND TAKE CARE OF A DRUNK TEKKO...
YA SAYING YA WANNA GO BACK TO THOSE DAYS?
THAT GOES WITHOUT SAYING...
NO... MAYBE THAT'S NOT IT.
I DON'T REALLY WANT TO GO BACK TO THAT. WHAT EXACTLY WAS MY LIFE ACTUALLY ABOUT?

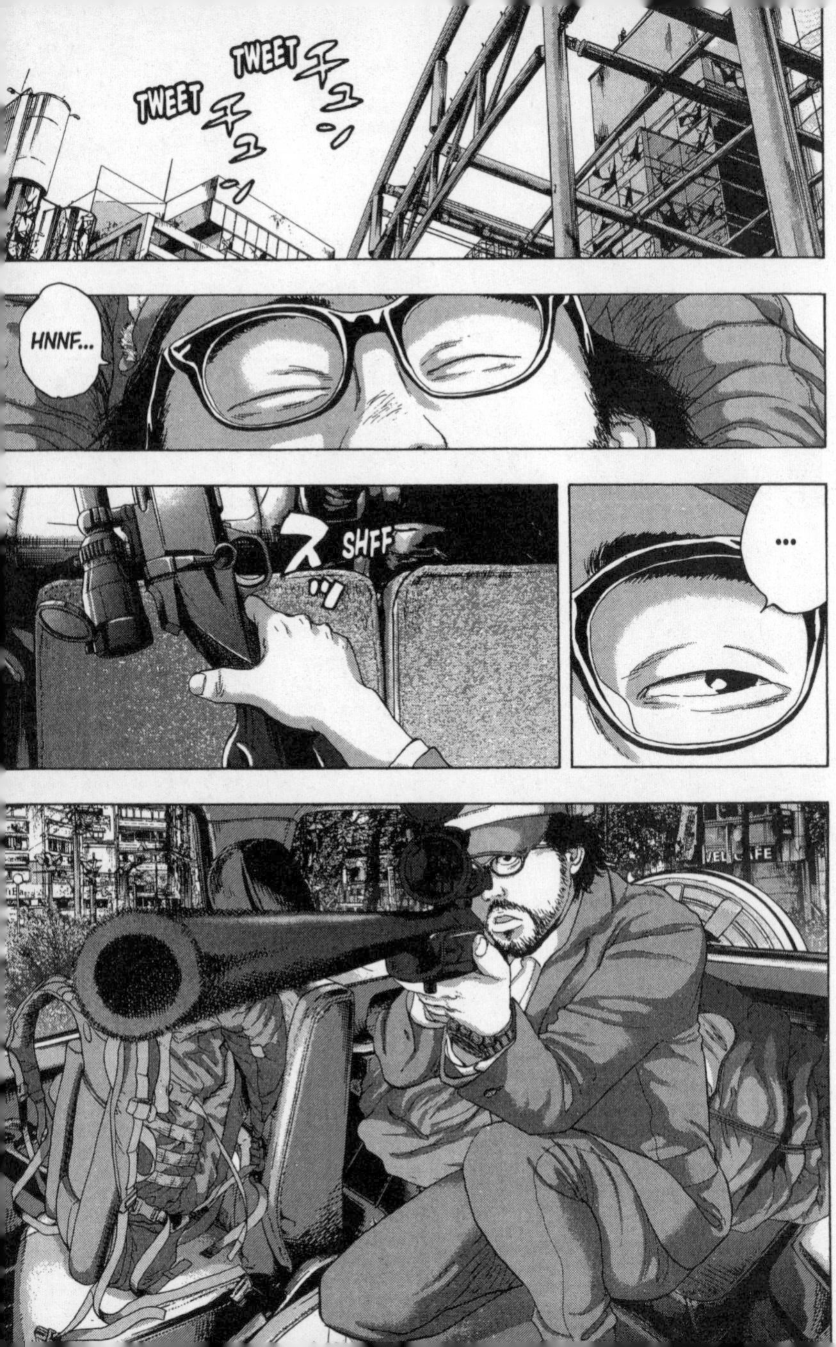
TWEET
チュン
TWEET
チュン
HNNF...
...
スッ
SHFF

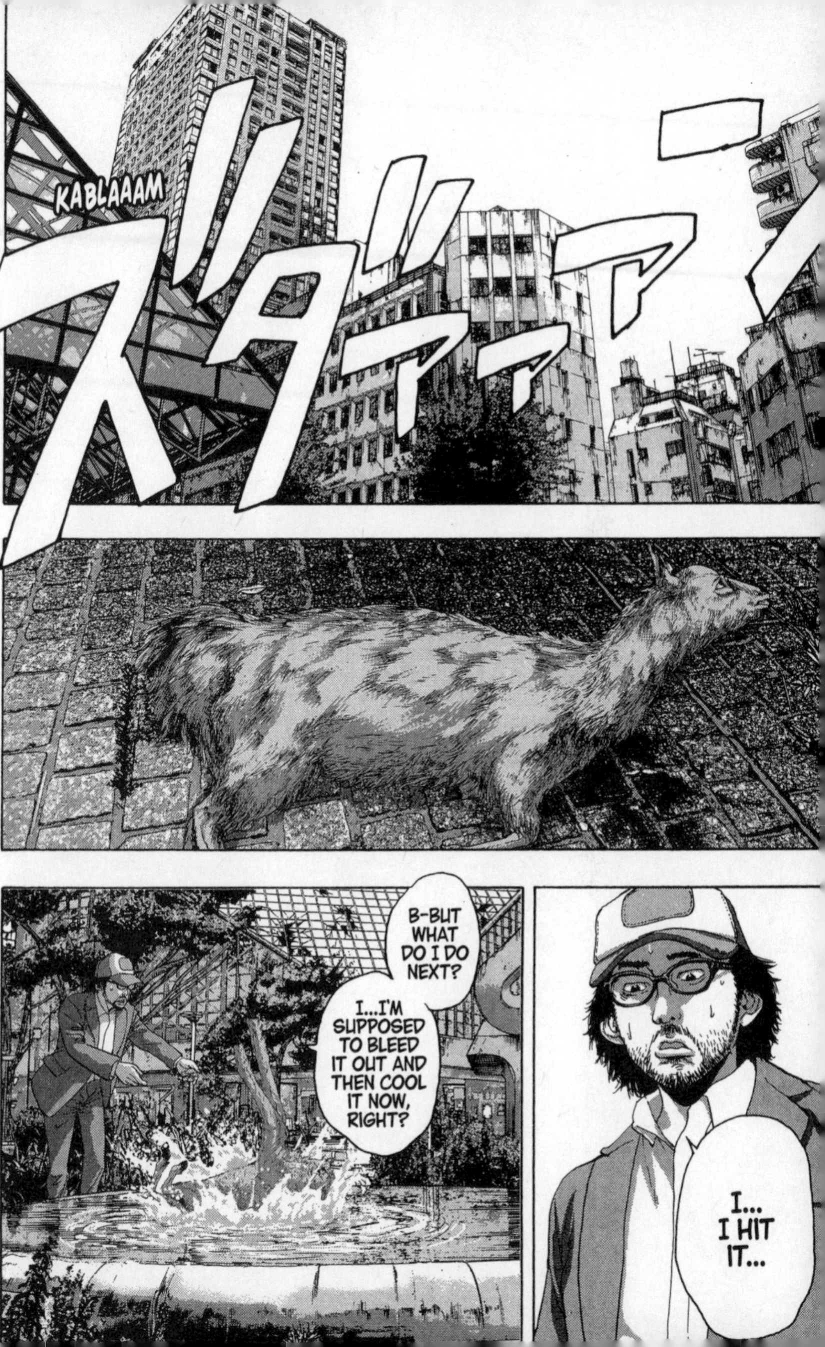
KABLAAM
I...
I HIT IT...
B-BUT WHAT DO I DO NEXT?
I...I'M SUPPOSED TO BLEED IT OUT AND THEN COOL IT NOW, RIGHT?

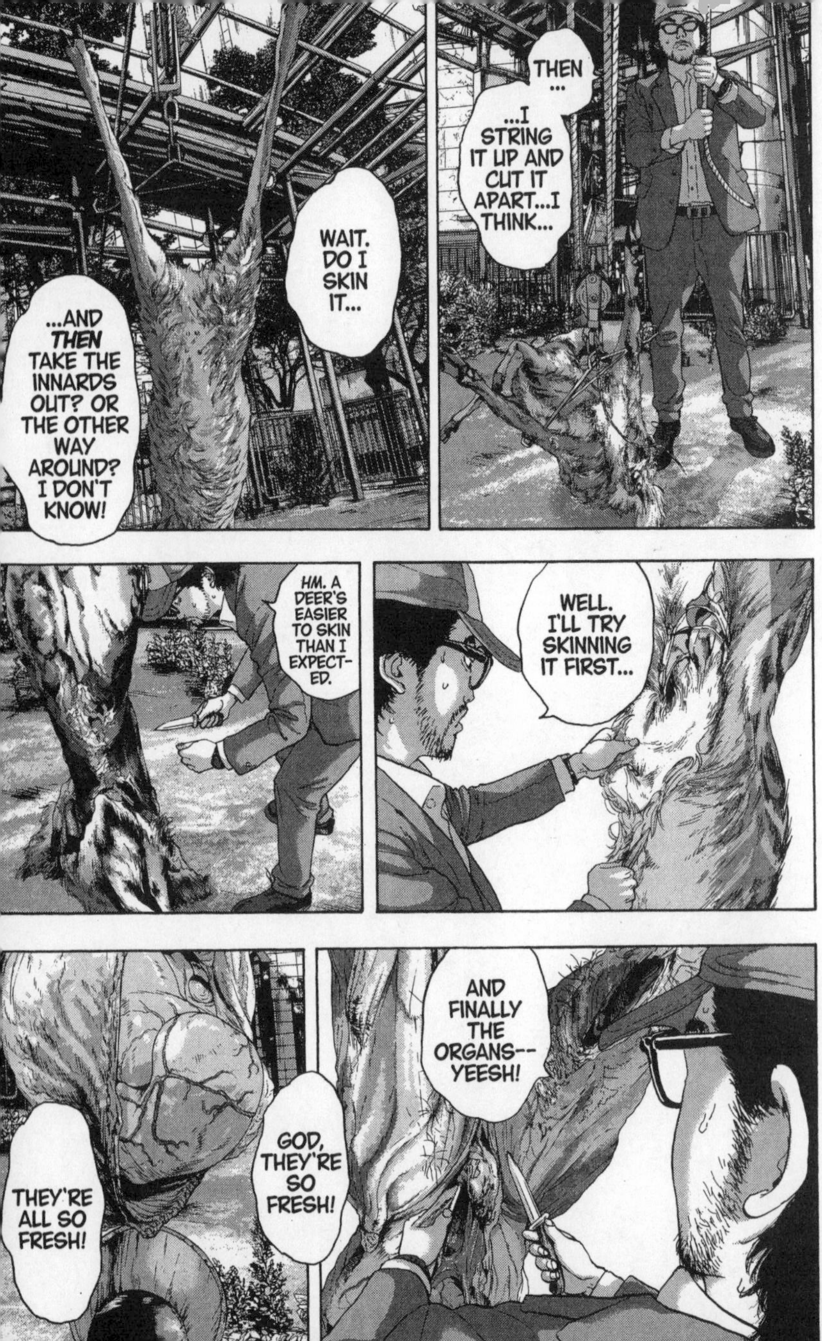
THEN ...
...I STRING IT UP AND CUT IT APART...I THINK...
WAIT. DO I SKIN IT...
...AND *THEN* TAKE THE INNARDS OUT? OR THE OTHER WAY AROUND? I DON'T KNOW!
WELL. I'LL TRY SKINNING IT FIRST...
HM. A DEER'S EASIER TO SKIN THAN I EXPECTED.
AND FINALLY THE ORGANS-- YEESH!
GOD, THEY'RE SO FRESH!
THEY'RE ALL SO FRESH!

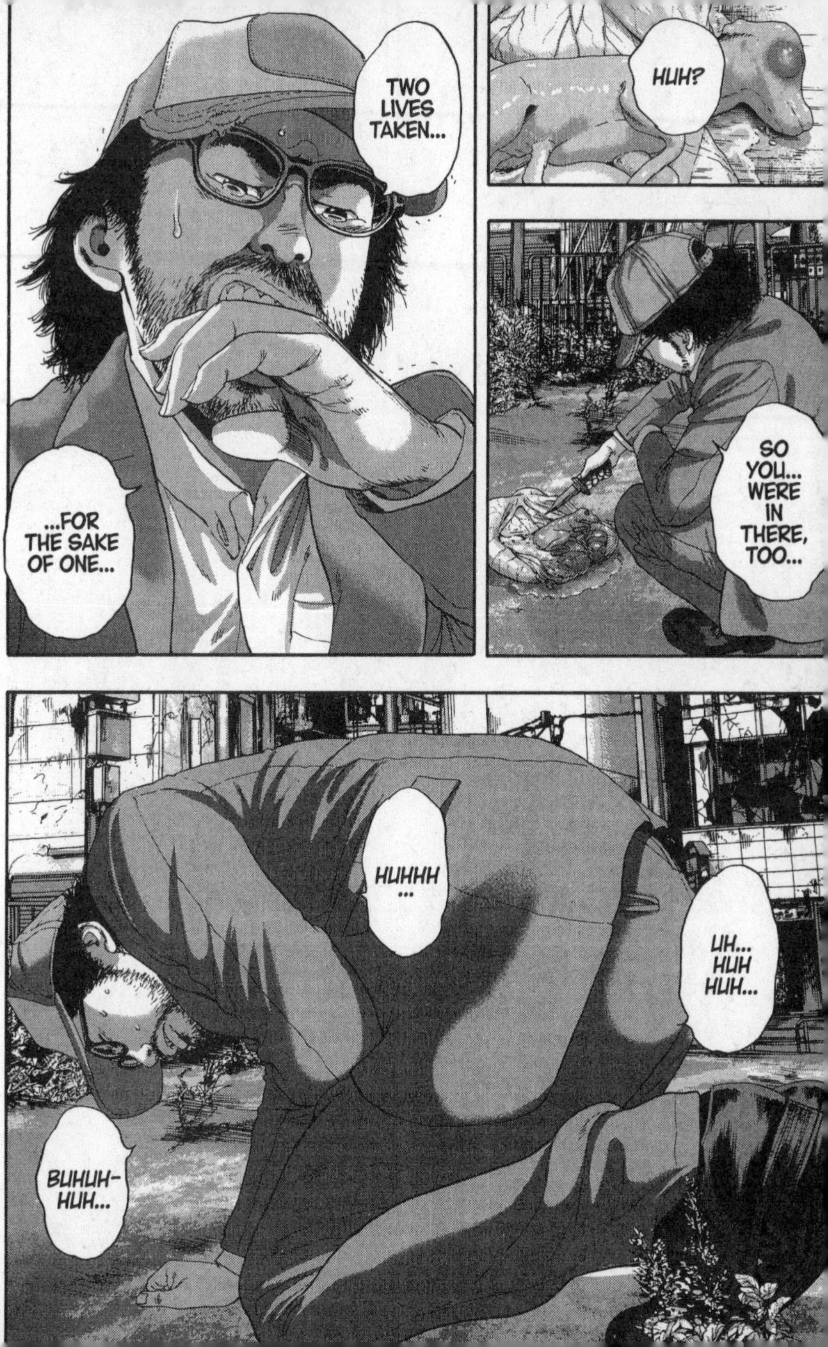
HUH?
SO YOU... WERE IN THERE, TOO...
TWO LIVES TAKEN...
...FOR THE SAKE OF ONE...
UH... HUH HUH...
HUHHH...
BUHUH-HUH...

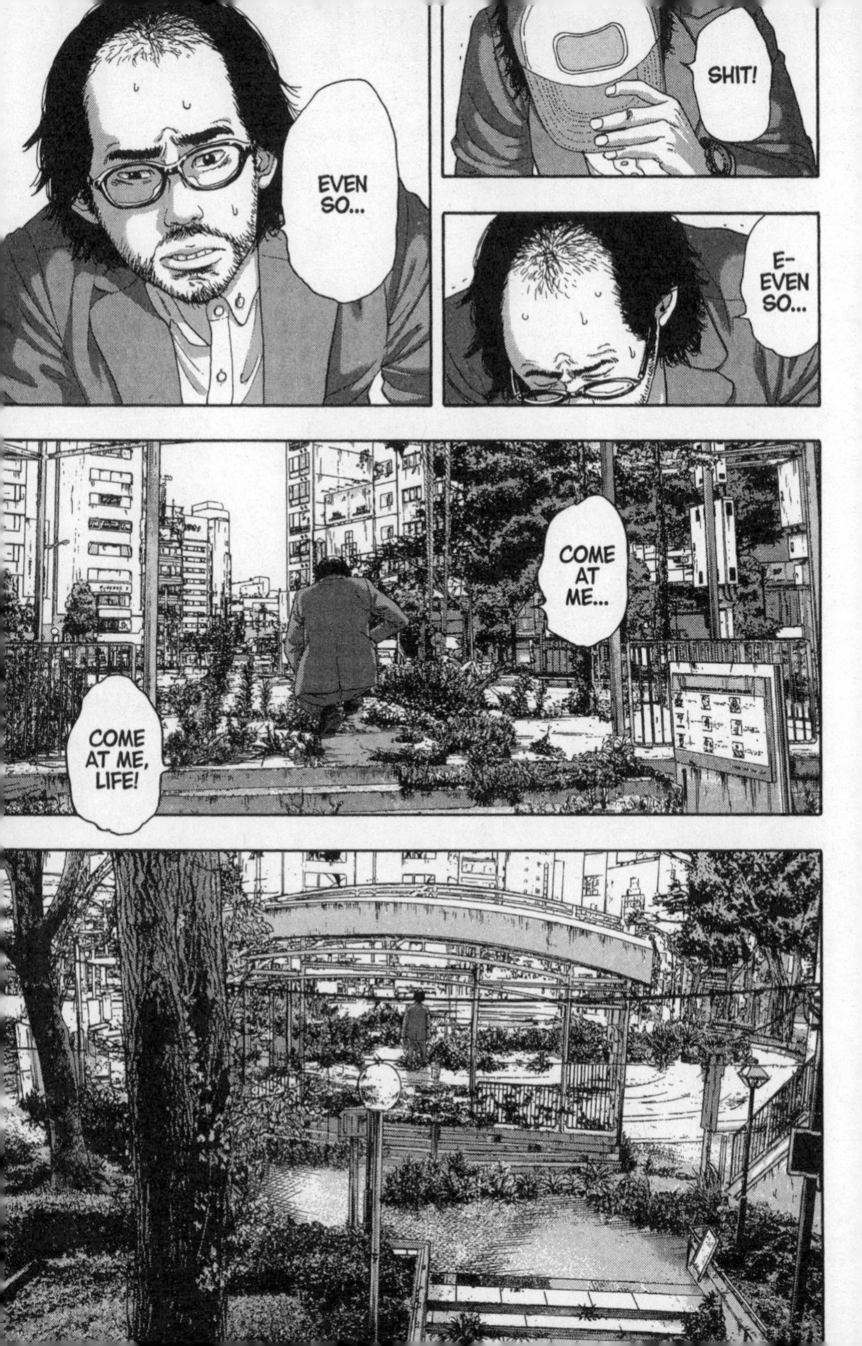
SHIT!
E-EVEN SO...
EVEN SO...
COME AT ME...
COME AT ME, LIFE!

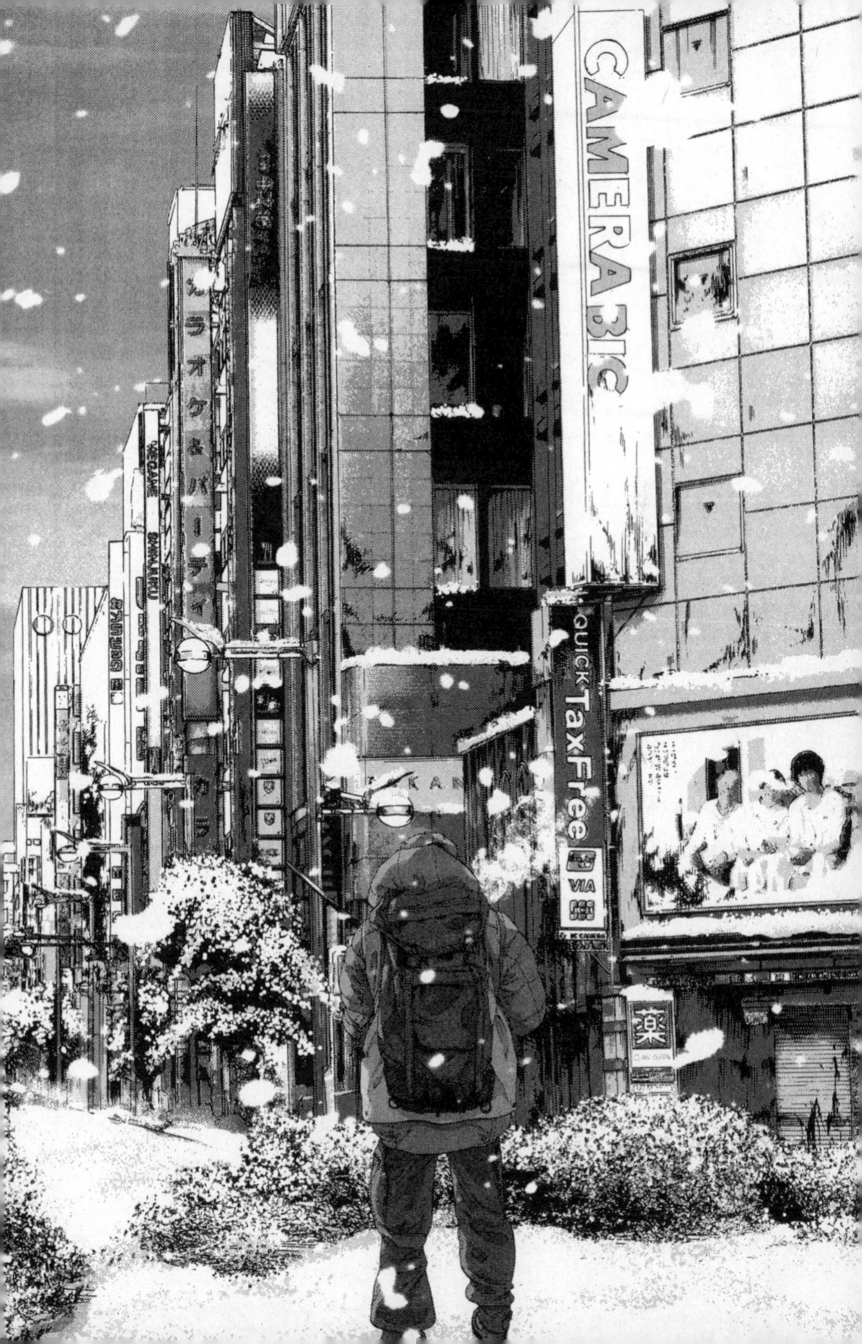
CAMERA BIC
QUICK TaxFree
VIA
薬

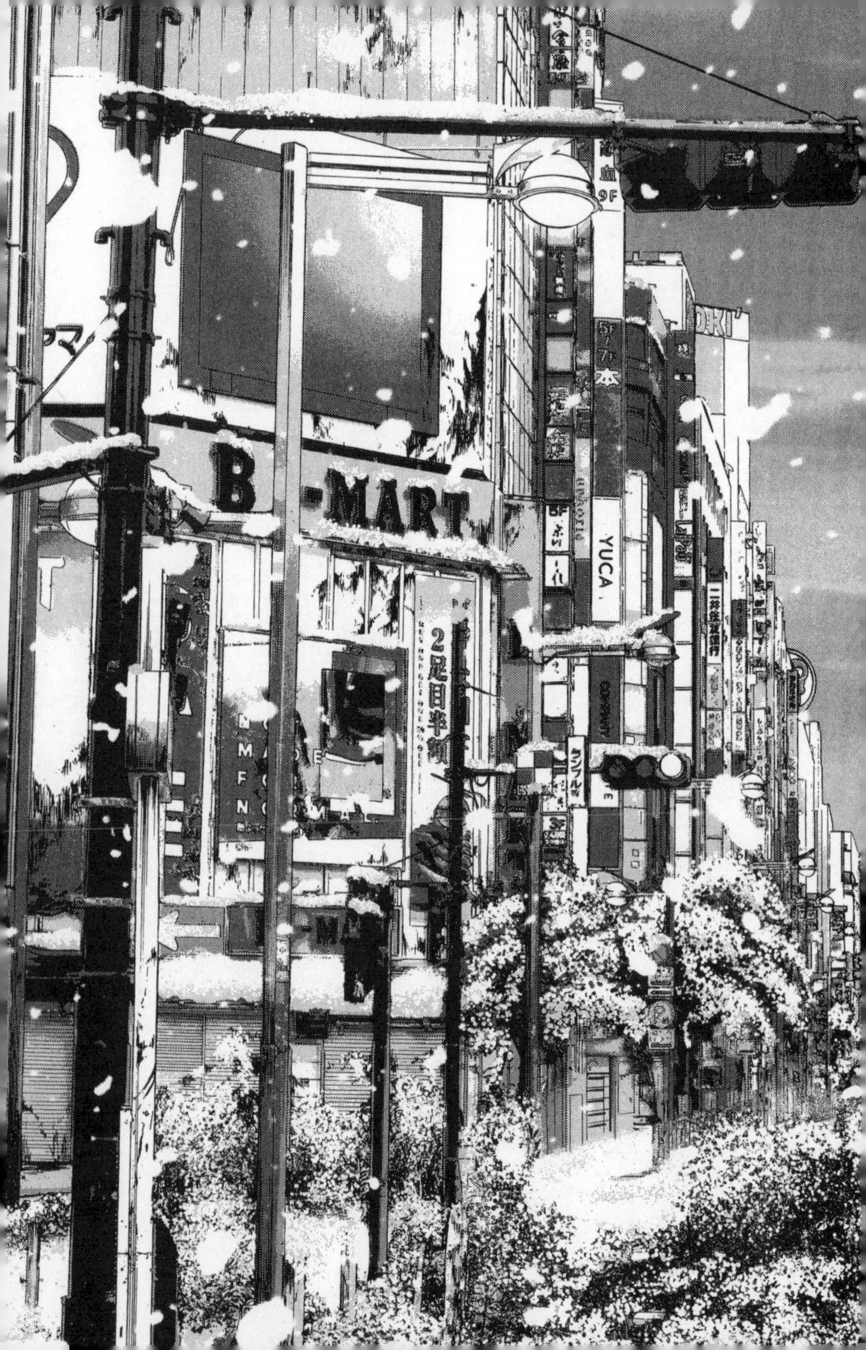
YUCA
2足目半額
B-MART

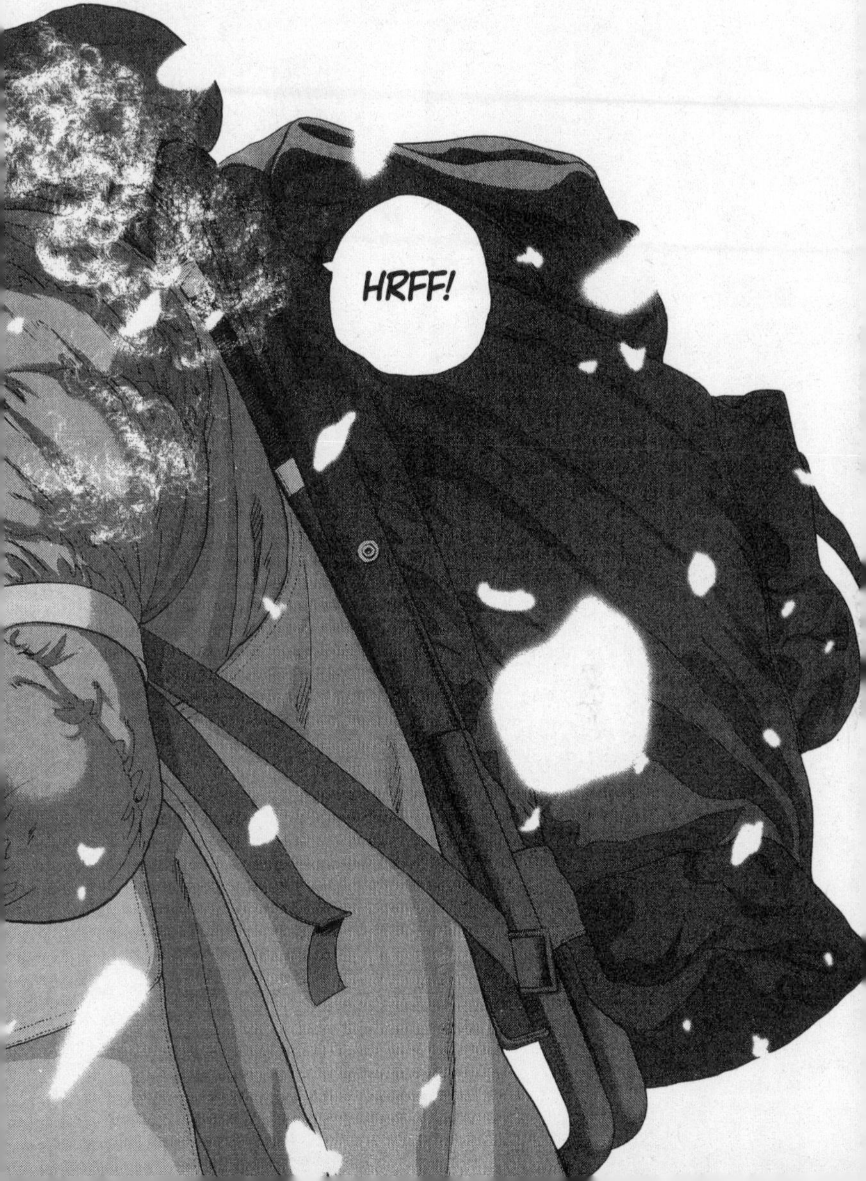
HRFF!

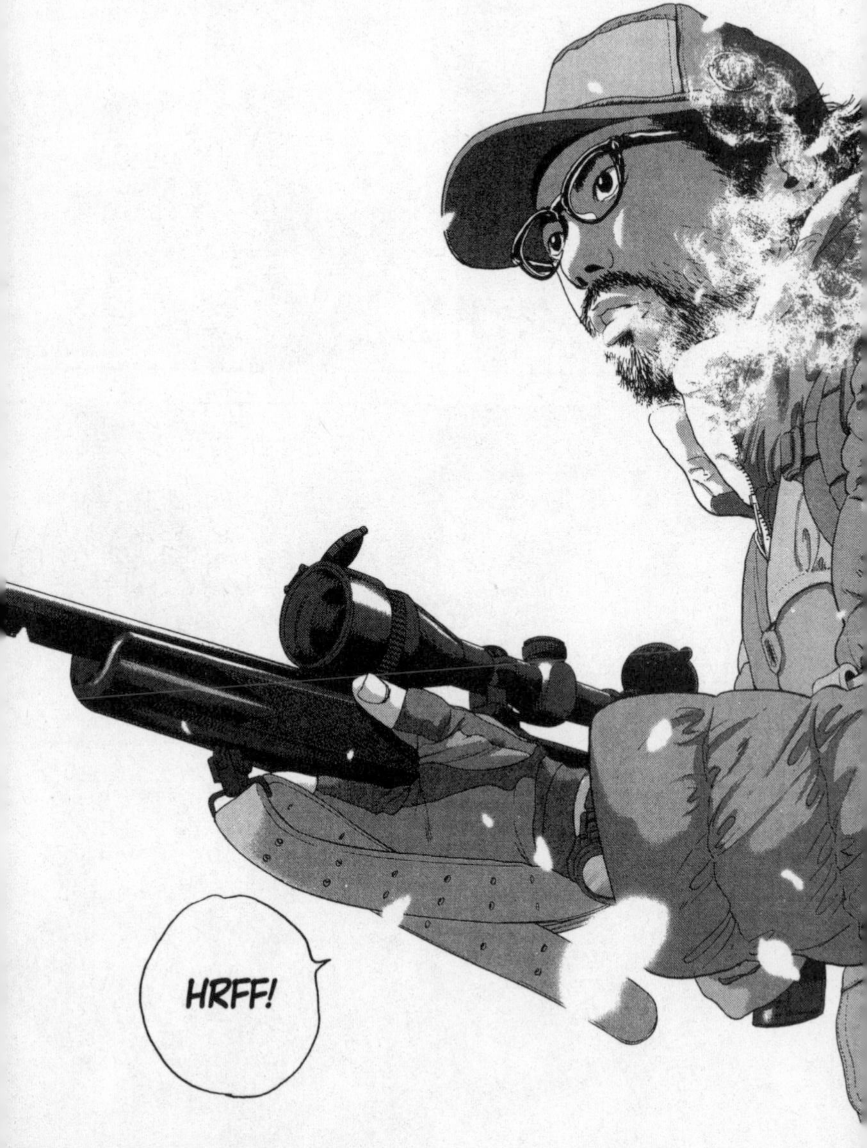
HRFF!

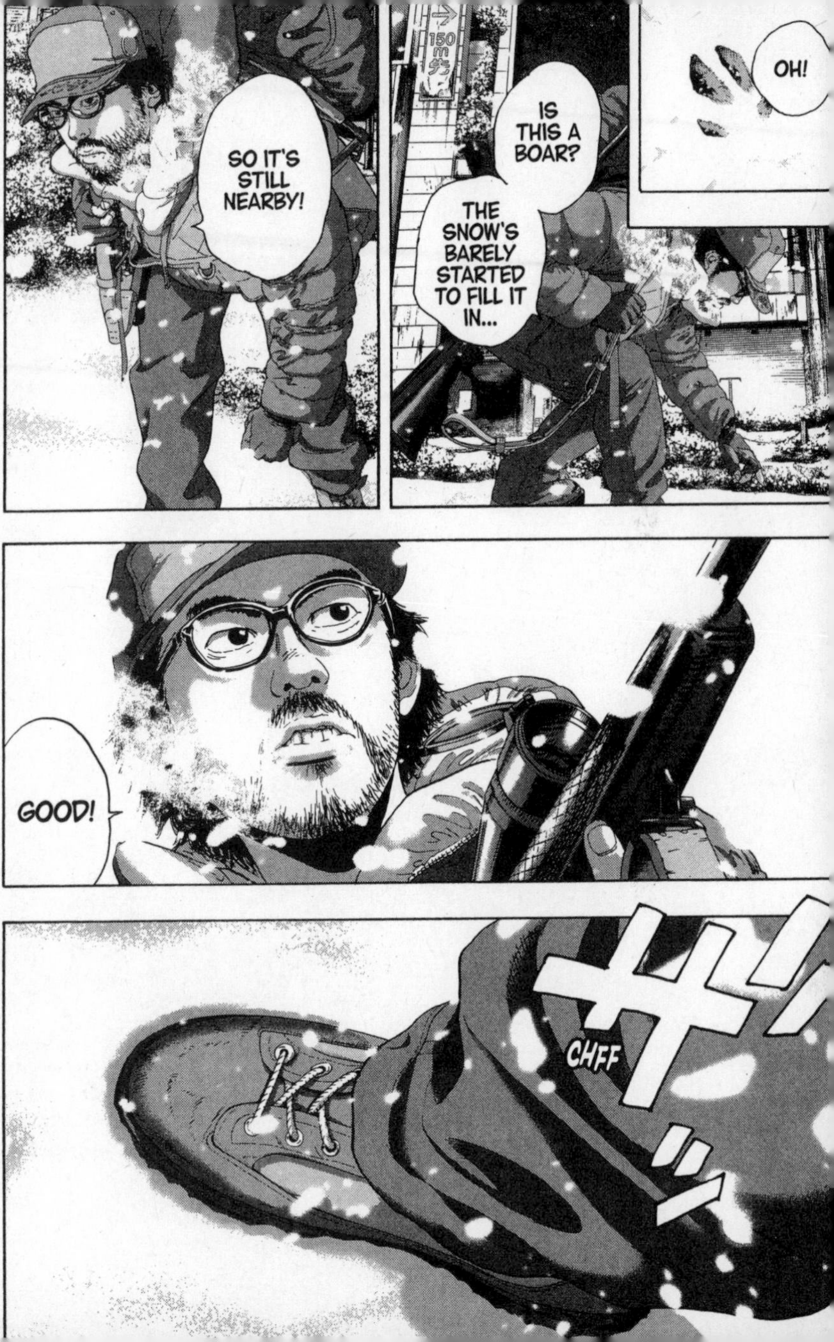
OH!
IS THIS A BOAR?
THE SNOW'S BARELY STARTED TO FILL IT IN...
SO IT'S STILL NEARBY!
GOOD!
ザッ
CHFF

This is dedicated to my father.
May he forever rest in peace.

—Kengo Hanazawa

I AM A HERO

TRANSLATION NOTES

APTER 251

the flashback scene in the gym, a cruel bully yells, "A pig that doesn't climb is just a pig!" He is referring the animated Ghibli film *Porco Rosso* and the line "A pig that doesn't fly is just a pig" or "A pig that doesn't is an ordinary pig."

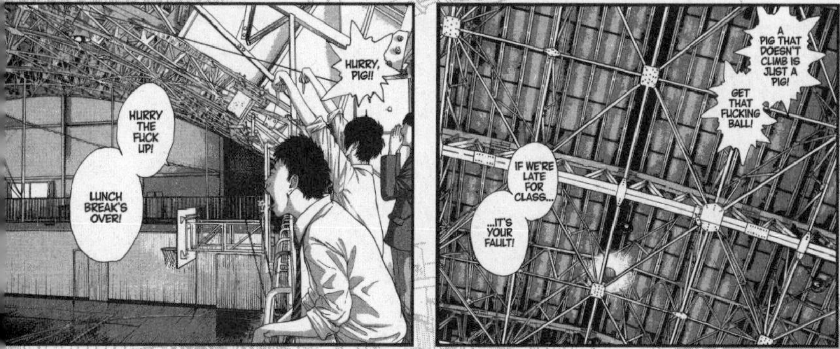
A PIG THAT DOESN'T CLIMB IS JUST A PIG!
GET THAT FUCKING BALL!
IF WE'RE LATE FOR CLASS...
...IT'S YOUR FAULT!
HURRY, PIG!!
HURRY THE FUCK UP!
LUNCH BREAK'S OVER!

APTER 256

leo Suzuki pitched the *Vegetan* manga series to his editor in *I Am a Hero Omnibus* Volume 1, chapter Fellow manga creator and zombie apocalypse survivor Nakata Korori overheard Hideo's pitch—and it an impression.

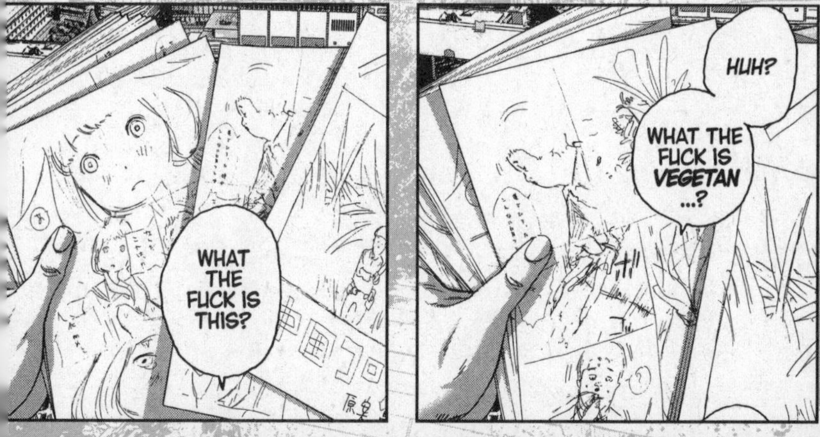
HUH?
WHAT THE FUCK IS VEGETAN ...?
WHAT THE FUCK IS THIS?

HOW SHOULD I KNOW?!

WE'RE ALL IN THIS TOGETHER NOW!!

CHAPTER 257

When Seto exclaims, "We're all in [this] together now!!" he's actually using [the] Japanese expression *Ichirentakus[ho]* here, which means "to share the sa[me] fate" or "be in the same boat." [The] expression translates literally to the low[...] "being born on the same lotus lea[f in] Buddhist heaven."

CHAPTER 259

The young boy sees and shouts, "[...] bay!" in this chapter. He's proba[bly] excited about seeing Sagami B[ay.] Enoshima Island is also seen as [this] happens, indicating that the survivors [are] already a good distance from Tokyo.

CHAPTER 261

Hideo discovers that, "Unidentified Flying Object yakisoba really is delish!" Nissin Foods has a yakisoba noodle product called Nissin Yakisoba UFO. The "UFO" is an acronym for the English romanizations of the Japanese words for "tasty" (*umai*), "thick" (*futoi*), and "big" (*ookii*). However, the word UFO is also used as-is in Japan with the same meaning, and this noodle's packaging also includes the English words "Unidentified Flying Object" in very small print. The packaging and advertisements are often space themed. However, Hideo uses the actual Japanese translation of "UFO" here with kanji—rather than the English "UFO."

UNIDENTIFIED FLYING OBJECT YAKISOBA REALLY IS DELISH!

NOMP NOMP

ISN'T EASY TO FIND *OSHIRUKO* IN A CAN...

CHAPTER 262

Oshiruko is a sweet porridge of adzuki beans boiled and crushed [then] eaten with rice-flour dumplings.

CHAPTER 263

Takuan is a Japanese pickled daikon radish dish. *Oden* is a kin[d of] Japanese hot pot meal. Later in this chapter, when Hideo ment[ions] "Spanish Hill," he is referring to "Spain-zaka," the nickname f[or a] particular street in Shibuya also known as the "Spain Slope[" or] "Spanish Hill."

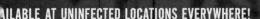

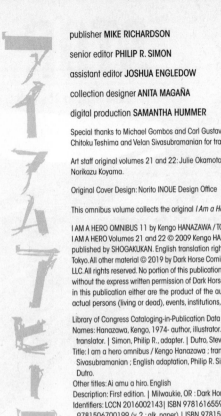

publisher **MIKE RICHARDSON**

senior editor **PHILIP R. SIMON**

assistant editor **JOSHUA ENGLEDOW**

collection designer **ANITA MAGAÑA**

digital production **SAMANTHA HUMMER**

Special thanks to Michael Gombos and Carl Gustav Horn for editorial assistance and advice. Special thanks to Chitoku Teshima and Velan Sivasubramanian for translation assistance.

Art staff original volumes 21 and 22: Julie Okamoto, Yukihiro Kamiya, Kurao Nabe, Miki Imai, Satomi Hayashi, Norikazu Koyama.

Original Cover Design: Norito INOUE Design Office

This omnibus volume collects the original *I Am a Hero* volumes 21 and 22, published in Japan.

I AM A HERO OMNIBUS 11 by Kengo HANAZAWA / TOCHKA

Library of Congress Cataloging-in-Publication Data
Names: Hanazawa, Kengo, 1974- author, illustrator. | Sivasubramanian, Kumar,
  translator. | Simon, Philip R., adapter. | Dutro, Steve, letterer.
Title: I am a hero omnibus / Kengo Hanazawa ; translation, Kumar
  Sivasubramanian ; English adaptation, Philip R. Simon ; lettering, Steve
  Dutro.
Other titles: Ai amu a hiro. English
Description: First edition. | Milwaukie, OR : Dark Horse Manga, 2016-
Identifiers: LCCN 2016002143| ISBN 9781616559205 (v. 1 : alk. paper) | ISBN
  9781506700199 (v. 2 : alk. paper) | ISBN 9781506701455 (v. 3 : alk. paper)
  | ISBN 9781506703497 (v. 4 : alk. paper) | ISBN 9781506703503 (v. 5 : alk.
  paper) | ISBN 9781506703961 (v. 6 : alk. paper) | ISBN 9781506707020 (v. 7
  : alk. paper) | ISBN 9781506707501 (v. 8 : alk. paper) | ISBN
  9781506708300 (v. 9 : alk. paper) | ISBN 9781506708317 (v. 10 : alk.
  paper) | ISBN 9781506708324 (v. 11 : alk. paper)
Subjects: LCSH: Zombies--Comic books, strips, etc. | Graphic novels.
Classification: LCC PN6790.J34 A4313 2016 | DDC 741.5/952--dc23
LC record available at https://lccn.loc.gov/2016002143

Dark Horse Manga | A division of Dark Horse Comics LLC
10956 SE Main Street, Milwaukie, OR 97222

DarkHorse.com

To find a comics shop in your area, visit the Comic Shop Locator Service at comicshoplocator.com

First edition: October 2019
ISBN 978-1-50670-832-4

10 9 8 7 6 5 4 3 2 1

Printed in the United States of America

STOP

This is the back of the book!

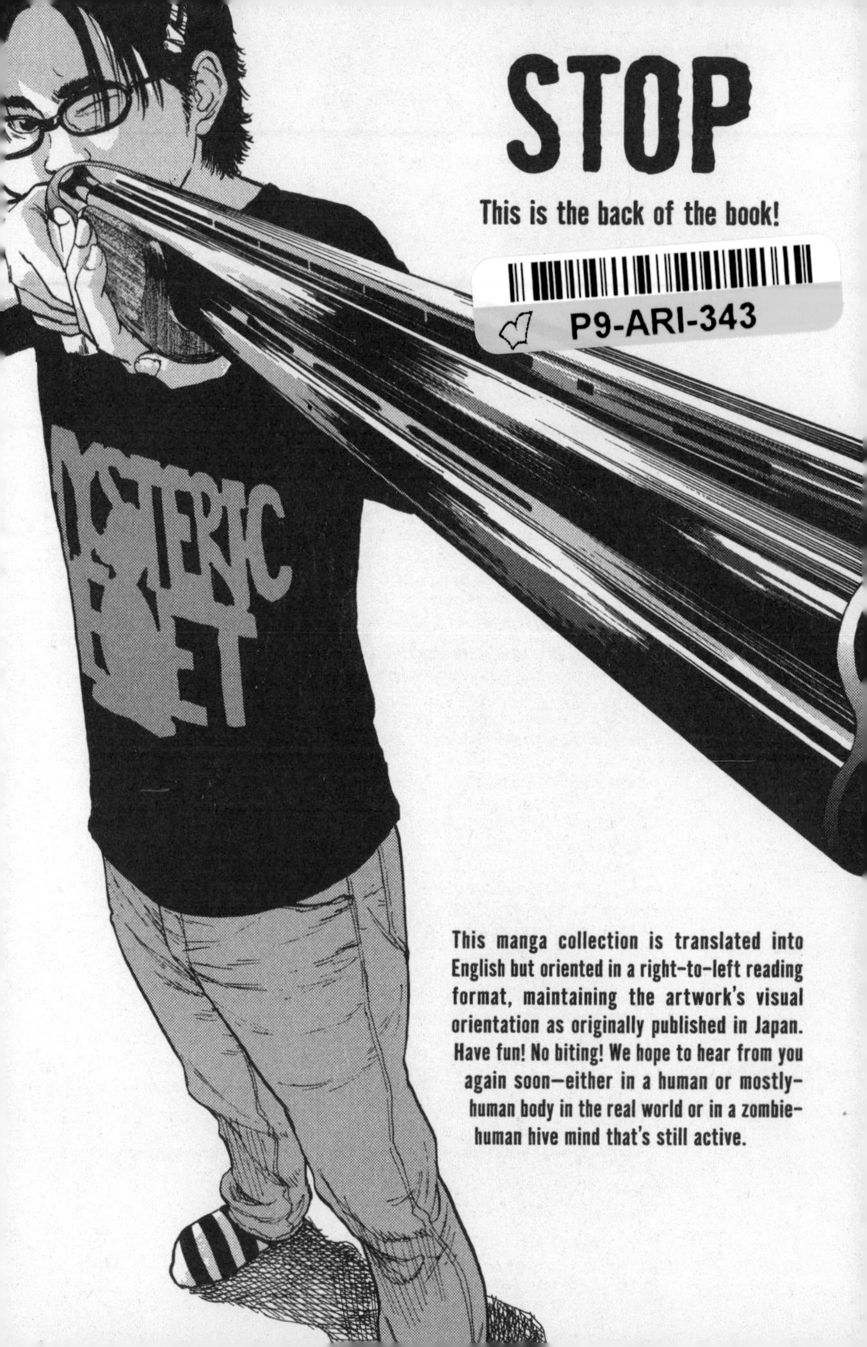

This manga collection is translated into English but oriented in a right-to-left reading format, maintaining the artwork's visual orientation as originally published in Japan. Have fun! No biting! We hope to hear from you again soon—either in a human or mostly-human body in the real world or in a zombie-human hive mind that's still active.